Cyberspace Crime

The International Library of Criminology, Criminal Justice and Penology
Series Editors: Gerald Mars and David Nelken

Titles in the Series:

Cyberspace Crime

Edited by

David S. Wall

University of Leeds, UK

Published by
Dartmouth Publishing Company
Ashgate Publishing Limited
Gower House
Croft Road
Aldershot
Hants GU11 3HR
England

Ashgate Publishing Company
Suite 420
101 Cherry Street
Burlington, VT 05401-4405
USA

Ashgate website: http://www.ashgate.com

British Library Cataloguing in Publication Data
Cyberspace crime. – (The international library of
    criminology, criminal justice and penology)
    1. Computer crimes
    I. Wall, David, 1956–
    364.1'68

Library of Congress Cataloging-in-Publication Data
Cyberspace crime / edited by D.S. Wall.
            p. cm. — (The international library of criminology, criminal justice, and penology)
        Includes bibliographical references.
        ISBN 0-7546-2190-1 (alk. paper)
            1. Computer crimes. I. Wall, David, 1956– II. International library of criminology,
    criminal justice & penology.

HV6773 .C93 2003
364.16'8—dc21

                                                                                        2002066593

ISBN 0 7546 2190 1

Printed in Great Britain by The Cromwell Press, Trowbridge, Wiltshire

Contents

PART III   CRIMINAL JUSTICE PROCESSES

Acknowledgements

The editor and publishers wish to thank the following for permission to use copyright material.

Blackwell Publishing Ltd for the essays: Tim Jordan and Paul Taylor (1998), 'A Sociology of Hackers', *Sociological Review*, November, pp. 757–80. Copyright © 1998 Editorial Board of The Sociological Review; Jon Spencer (1999), 'Crime on the Internet: Its Presentation and Representation', *Howard Journal*, **38**, pp. 241–51. Copyright © 1999 Blackwell Publishers; Clive Walker (1996), 'Fundamental Rights, Fair Trials and the New Audio-Visual Sector', *Modern Law Review*, **59**, pp. 517–39. Copyright © 1996 Modern Law Review Ltd.

Centre for World Dialogue for the essay: Dorothy E. Denning (2000), 'Cyberterrorism: The Logic Bomb versus the Truck Bomb', *Global Dialogue*, Autumn, pp. 29–37.

Elsevier Science for the essays: Liz Duff and Simon Gardiner (1996), 'Computer Crime in the Global Village: Strategies for Control and Regulation – in Defence of the Hacker', *International Journal of the Sociology of Law*, **24**, pp. 211–28. Copyright © 1996 Academic Press; Amanda Chandler (1996), 'The Changing Definition and Image of Hackers in Popular Discourse', *International Journal of the Sociology of Law*, **24**, pp. 229–51. Copyright © 1996 Academic Press.

Georgetown University Law Center for the essay: Marty Rimm (1995), 'Marketing Pornography on the Information Superhighway: A Survey of 917,410 Images, Descriptions, Short Stories, and Animations Downloaded 8.5 Million Times by Consumers in Over 2000 Cities in Forty Countries, Provinces, and Territories', *Georgetown Law Journal*, **83**, pp. 1849–915. Copyright © 1995 Georgetown Law Review.

Harvard Journal of Law & Technology for the essay: Marc D. Goodman (1997), 'Why the Police Don't Care about Computer Crime', *Harvard Journal of Law and Technology*, **10**, pp. 465–94.

Donna L. Hoffman and Thomas P. Novak (1995), 'A Detailed Analysis of the Conceptual, Logical, and Methodological Flaws in the Article: "Marketing Pornography on the Information Superhighway"', Owen Graduate School of Management, Vanderbilt University, pp. 1–21. Copyright © 1995 Donna Hoffman and Thomas Novak.

Issues in Science and Technology for the essay: George Smith (1998), 'An Electronic Pearl Harbor? Not Likely', *Issues in Science and Technology*, **15**, pp. 68–73. Copyright © 1998 University of Texas at Dallas, Richardson, TX.

Series Preface

The International Library of Criminology, Criminal Justice and Penology, represents an important publishing initiative to bring together the most significant journal essays in contemporary criminology, criminal justice and penology. The series makes available to researchers, teachers and students an extensive range of essays which are indispensable for obtaining an overview of the latest theories and findings in this fast changing subject.

This series consists of volumes dealing with criminological schools and theories as well as with approaches to particular areas of crime, criminal justice and penology. Each volume is edited by a recognised authority who has selected twenty or so of the best journal articles in the field of their special competence and provided an informative introduction giving a summary of the field and the relevance of the articles chosen. The original pagination is retained for ease of reference.

The difficulties of keeping on top of the steadily growing literature in criminology are complicated by the many disciplines from which its theories and findings are drawn (sociology, law, sociology of law, psychology, psychiatry, philosophy and economics are the most obvious). The development of new specialisms with their own journals (policing, victimology, mediation) as well as the debates between rival schools of thought (feminist criminology, left realism, critical criminology, abolitionism etc.) make necessary overviews that offer syntheses of the state of the art. These problems are addressed by the INTERNATIONAL LIBRARY in making available for research and teaching the key essays from specialist journals.

GERALD MARS
Professor in Applied Anthropology, Universities of North London
and Northumbria Business Schools

DAVID NELKEN
Distinguished Research Professor, Cardiff Law Schoool,
University of Wales, Cardiff

Introduction

It is now more than a decade since the Internet metamorphosed from a 'prosaic set of wires' (Walker *et al.*, 2000, p. 3) into an ever-increasing part of our social, commercial and educational lives. The Internet has developed far beyond our initial expectations, and this trend will continue as communications and information technologies converge during the forthcoming decades. But its impacts, both good and bad, will further diverge and it is the 'bad', or what has come to be termed 'cybercrime', that this volume is concerned with. As for the term 'cybercrime', it actually means little more than signifying the occurrence of a harmful behaviour that is somehow related to a networked computer (NCIS, 1999): it has no specific reference point in law and it is a concept that has been largely invented by the mass media. Indeed, there is a line of legal debate which questions whether or not 'there are indeed such things as cybercrimes' (Brenner, 2001, para. 1). In fact, the term 'cyberspace crime', the title of this collection, would be a more precise and accurate descriptor, although it is the term 'cybercrime' that has become absorbed into the popular parlance and which regularly invokes knee-jerk responses from media, policy-makers, politicians, academics and the public alike. Consequently, because of its considerable linguistic agency, it is therefore a term that cannot easily be dismissed.

This volume has three Parts. Part I contains a number of viewpoints that have been expressed in order to facilitate our understanding of cyberspace crime/cybercrimes. The essays in Part II each address one of the following types of cybercrime: trespass/hacking, thefts/deceptions, obscenities/pornography, violence and their associated problems of definition and resolution. Part III contains a selection of essays that each deal with the impact of cyberspace crime on specific criminal justice processes: the police and the trial process.

Theoretical Perspectives and Viewpoints

Grabosky and Smith (1998, p. 1) remind us that when Willie Sutton, the notorious American 1950s bank robber, was asked why he robbed banks, it is alleged that he replied: '[b]ecause that's where the money is'. Since crime tends to follow opportunity and the Internet provides many new opportunities, then new crimes will certainly emerge. But, as many of the following chapters attest, values in cyberspace are mostly attached to ideas and to the ways in which those ideas are expressed, rather than to tangible objects, thus causing us to put into perspective the ways in which we think about crimes on the Internet. This path of criminological discovery finds a resonance in a number of other volumes in the Ashgate/Dartmouth International Library of Criminology, Criminal Justice and Penology; see, for example, the contributions to Richard Hollinger's (1997) volume on computer crimes, but also the pioneering studies of fraud, work-based crime and white-collar crime that are included in the volumes edited, respectively, by Mike Levi (1999, vols 1 and 2), Gerald Mars (2001a, 2001b) and David Nelken (1994).

In our quest for knowledge and understanding about this relatively new subject area it is vital that we seek to disaggregate the rhetoric from the reality – not least because public opinion is rapidly shaped by the various media outlets which have become sensitized to the fact that public anxiety about the impacts of new technology makes stories about it newsworthy, often regardless of whether or not there is a specific victim or victim group. When we begin to review the media coverage of cybercrimes over the past decade, two observations become plainly apparent. First, we have yet to experience either the much anticipated 'Electronic Pearl Harbor' (Chapter 14; also see Taylor, 2001, p. 69) or the all enveloping 'cyber-Tsunami' (Wall, 2001, p. 3) which can destroy infrastructures and bring nation-states to their knees. Although such possibilities are of great concern, criminal/ harmful impacts have tended to follow the overall increase in the number and breadth of commercial, educational, moral and political opportunities that the Internet has generated. So, while major infrastructure protection is needed, the day-to-day experience of netizens is likely to be less dramatic than anticipated because the majority of cybercrimes tend to be small-impact, though multiple, victimizations.

The second observation is that online society – and there is some justification in using the term 'society' – will expand further. But, rather than go on a moral holiday, as is frequently implied by media coverage, the greater majority of netizens tend to bring with them to cyberspace their existing normative values (Wall, 2000, 2001). Not only is it emerging that public attitudes towards the Internet are characterized more by reflexivity than resistance, but online behaviour is more likely to be responsible than wrongful.

The year 2002 is an opportune time to take stock of the substantive literature on cybercrimes because it marks, more or less, the end of the first decade of life with the World Wide Web. This volume of essays contains, under one cover, a collection of some of the most influential and/or useful, short academic publications on the subject of cyberspace crime/cybercrime that were available in English at the point of compilation during April 2002. The writings in this volume not only represent a cross-section of the existing literature, they also span Internet developments during the previous decade and, in many ways, pick up where Richard Hollinger's (1997) *Crime, Deviance and the Computer* left off.

A quick look through the sources of this literature will reveal their eclectic nature; they are drawn from quite a broad range of disciplines, although most are from socio-legal studies, whose scholars have been engaged in debates about Internet policy for many years. In fact, one could argue that it is mainly the criminologists who have been slow to explore cyberspace crime and to engage in debate about them in order to develop useful bodies of knowledge that could enlighten the public and provide the basis for informed policy. In the criminologists' defence, however, it could simply be argued that comparatively little research funding has been made available for the study of cyberspace crime, thus reducing the number of opportunities for substantive empirical research. Or perhaps this simply amounts to further evidence of the fact that criminology is now 'only one of many settings in which crime is discussed' (Garland and Sparks, 2000, p. 201).

While the above points may explain the differentials in disciplinary engagement, academic work is further delayed by the lengthy time-frame for the production of refereed academic journals. It takes much longer to produce an academic output than it does, say, a more journalistic treatment. It takes time to conceive the essay, conduct the research, write the text, have it sent it out for referees' comments, revise on the basis of those comments, copy-edit, proofread, and wait for a vacant publication slot in the journal. Consequently, academic essays can regularly take between two and three years from conception to publication, and thus the selection of work here might not necessarily match current concerns.

The first chapter is one of my own publications, which I include in order to establish some of the parameters. In this piece, I begin to explore the meaning of cybercrimes and argue that, whilst most commentators would agree that cybercrimes exist, few actually agree on what they are. This overall lack of consensus is compounded by my assertion that the Internet has different levels of impact. First, it *facilitates existing crimes* by providing new forms of communications – for example, drug-dealers can conclude their deals by e-mail. Second, it *provides new opportunities for existing crimes* – fraudsters can now, for example, simultaneously reach many potential victims over a wide range of jurisdictions in order to gain their trust, prior to deceiving them. Third, it *creates entirely new opportunities for new types of 'criminal' behaviour* – for example, the appropriation of intellectual properties in the form of brand names, Internet domain names, copyrighted music in the form of MP3 files, celebrity images and so on (see also further Wall, 2001, p. 3).

Each level of impact generates quite different methodological implications for developing further our understanding of cybercrimes. We can, for example, draw upon some of the existing criminological literature, especially that on white-collar crimes, to illuminate the first and second levels of impact. For the third level, however, we must start looking elsewhere to assist our understanding – for example, towards some of the debates in American intellectual property law over the political economy of information capital (Boyle, 1996; Madow, 1993) – or in extreme cases, arrive at entirely new forms of understanding. My main argument, however, is that a meaningful understanding of cybercrimes is unlikely to be facilitated by grouping together diverse activities such as trespass (hacking and cracking), theft/deception, obscenities/ pornography and violence under one heading. Instead, each different type of harmful behaviour results from individual motivations and invokes quite different types of public response, different bodies of law, different methods of law enforcement and different types of resolution and therefore must be explored differently.

In Chapter 2, Peter Grabosky and Russell Smith review ten frequently experienced forms of digital crime/cybercrime in order to identify the most appropriate means of developing countermeasures. They conclude that a strict crime control response is not usually feasible because of the limited capacity of law enforcement and the absence of frontiers in cyberspace. But, they also observe that overregulation can stifle commercial and technological development and that, therefore, a balance has to be sought which allows a tolerable degree of illegality in return for the creative exploitation of the technology. Most importantly, the locus of controlling the extent of digital crime is to be found in the marketplace, which has the ability to provide appropriate responses that governments are often unwilling or unable to achieve. Grabosky and Smith believe that a combination of traditional crime control measures and technological countermeasures can keep digital crime within manageable limits.

Following Grabosky and Smith is a useful short dialogue about virtual criminality (Chapters 3 to 6 inclusive) from *Social and Legal Studies* in 2001. In this dialogue, a range of opinions are expressed over the nature of virtual criminality (Capeller, Chapter 4; Grabosky, Chapter 5) and also over its governance (Snyder, Chapter 6). To augment the latter discussion over the governance of cyberspace crime, I have, at this point in the collection (Chapter 7), included Graham Greenleaf's discussion of some of the contemporary theories of Internet regulation. Although it is not specifically about crime, this essay will be of interest to 'regulatory scholars' (Braithwaite, 2000, p. 228) who are considering the analysis of online deviance and also the means by which to exercise control over it. Greenleaf draws usefully upon the work of Lawrence

Lessig (1999) and others to explore the relationship between the law, the architecture of the Internet, social norms and the opportunities created by the market. Greenleaf, like Lessig, adopts a 'digital realist' approach in which he argues that the law itself has a limited direct impact upon behaviour, but does shape the environment in which the behaviour takes place, thus shaping the behaviour itself. The broader themes expressed within this perspective are not so far removed from existing criminological theories which emphasize the impact of environment on opportunities and behaviour. Where it departs from these theories is that it considers the specific nature and implications of the architecture of the Internet, as 'codes' rather than, say, buildings or bounded spaces.

Cybercrimes

For the reasons outlined earlier, the contributions to Part II are grouped into what I view as four key generic groups of cybercrime.

Trespass

Following the rise in public concern about cyber-trespass during the 1990s, the literature on cybercrimes has differentiated increasingly between hackers and crackers. Simply put, hacking is perceived as an ethical act, whereas cracking is considered to be unethical. The chapters covering cyber-trespass, although with some overlap, can be divided into those which discuss hacking and those which discuss the implications of cracking.

Following the demise of the Cold War and the explosion in the growth of communications and information technologies, there developed a marked shift in public opinion about hackers. After long being revered as the genius of youth, they came to be reviled as the newly configured enemy within, replacing communism as 'a kind of catch-all bogeyman' (Barlow, 1990). In Chapter 8, Amanda Chandler analyses this shift in public sympathies away from the hackers. This theme also emerges in Chapter 9 where Liz Duff and Simon Gardiner review the case for hacking. Duff and Gardiner conclude that the odds are now stacked highly against hacking because of fundamental shifts in the power balance within cyberspace. The reality is such that the 'trespass of cyberspace has been moved from the traditional civil law to the criminal law in the same way as trespass to land is increasingly being criminalized'. Consequently, the hackers' credo, which states that open access to knowledge and information in cyberspace will empower individuals, has been reduced to little more than optimistic utopian rhetoric. However, although hacking has become marginalized, Tim Jordan and Paul Taylor, in Chapter 10, found that whilst the active core of the hacking community is not as large as it is often made out to be, there nevertheless exists an identifiable community which is not only externally defined, but which is internally constructed through shared values and, importantly, culturally reproduces itself.

Crackers, as opposed to hackers, are mainly driven by new criminal opportunities, as Dave Mann and Mike Sutton illustrate in their award-winning work on 'net crime' (Chapter 11). Mann and Sutton set the findings of their empirical research against the literature on conventional criminal behaviour to demonstrate the various ways in which cracking represents a 'change in the organization of thieving'. They clearly demonstrate that high-technology devices, like smart cards, are very susceptible to crackers who have the ingenuity to crack the codes then disseminate the information about the process through newsgroups, thus rendering obsolete previously crimeproof systems.

At the far reaches of (cyber)trespass is cyber-terrorism, discussed by Dorothy Denning in Chapter 12. Denning acknowledges that none of the cyber-terror scenarios that she identifies, nor indeed any similar ones, have ever been played out, but she does report that central to the cyber-terror debate is the presumption that it is not a case of 'if', but 'when'. So, on the one hand, risk assessments, such as wargames, prepare us for the worst-case scenarios and enable the relevant authorities to develop responses yet, on the other hand, as indicated earlier, once the rhetoric of risk assessments, such as likening cybercrime to a terrestrial military scenario, is adopted, it is easy to succumb to the view that risk assessments actually represent reality and therefore require extreme measures to combat them. David Speer's essay (Chapter 13), for example, is a practical example of this danger. Whilst he usefully outlines the challenges of cybercrime, Speer falls into the trap of allowing risk assessments to shape the framework of his analysis, which narrows its scope. Consequently, the only perceivable way to combat cybercrime is to use hard law and stringent technological countermeasures, further shifting the debate towards the interests of the state and corporate interests and away from important principles such as liberty and freedom of expression.

Perhaps the classic exposition of the confusion between risk and reality is to be found in George Smith's 'Electronic Pearl Harbor' (Chapter 14). Smith uses the example of Information Warfare to demonstrate that our understanding of the 'crime' is riddled with hoaxes and myths which 'contaminate everything from official reports to newspaper stories' (p. 243). He questions whether the predicted 'Electronic Pearl Harbor' could ever happen, and yet he qualifies his critical position with the observation that 'even the small number of examples of malicious behavior . . . demonstrate that computer security issues in our increasingly technological world will be of primary concern well into the foreseeable future' (p. 248). But Smith stipulates that the two positions are not mutually exclusive and concludes by warning policy-makers to ignore the: 'Chicken Littles' with their unsupported claims, those pushing security products, hoaxes, myths and other 'electronic ghost stories' (p. 248).

Theft/Deceptions

In contrast to hacking and cracking, which can have considerable (public) impacts, the consequences of economic espionage and other cyber-thefts tend to be less immediately visible. In Chapter 15, Hedieh Nasheri and Tim O'Hearn illustrate the measures that the US government has taken to protect US trade secrets through substantive law and empowering existing bodies to enforce it. They then consider the core issues of economic espionage before reviewing the legal instruments and procedures which are utilized to protect victims. These instruments and procedures operate within the rather contradictory framework of international competition versus international cooperation. Nasheri and O'Hearn observe that businesses have to strike a crucial balance between their need to share sensitive information with appropriate parties in order to be able to compete on a worldwide basis and their (simultaneous) need to protect the same information from competitors, vandals, suppliers, customers and foreign governments.

The initiatives that Nasheri and O'Hearn describe are fairly unique to the USA, as the theft of trade secrets is not a crime in the UK. In Chapter 16, David Freedman discusses the arguments for and against the extension of UK criminal law to include confidential commercial information. He follows through the arguments made by the Law Commission in its 1997 report which recommended that trade secrets be protected by the criminal law. His main concern is that the scope for any new UK trade secret law needs to be carefully circumscribed, because to make it too broad could mean that it might endanger legitimate interests by acting outside of the existing rationale for criminal liability. Yet, to make the law too narrow might well jeopardize its effectiveness.

The debate over the strategic advantages of invoking either the civil or criminal law echoes the debates which feature in my two chapters (Chapters 1 and 26) within this volume and also in Grabosky and Smith (Chapter 2) on the preferences of corporate victims for private justice solutions instead of invoking the (public) criminal justice processes. It is clearly the case that large corporate victims do not always want the public model of criminal justice that the police and state criminal justice systems provide – this has been a longstanding preference with regard to credit-card fraud (see Levi and Handley, 1998). The general issue of cyber-fraud and theft is underrepresented within the existing body of published academic literature, largely because of the delays that were outlined earlier (also see Levi, 2001, pp. 44–58).

Violence

In common with cyber-theft and deceptions, public concern about cyber-violence is increasing. Hate-speech – dealt with at length elsewhere (see, for example, Becker *et al.*, 2000) – has long been an unpleasant feature of the Internet and its regulation is often frustrated by the protections afforded to it by various constitutional protections of freedom of expression. In recent years, other less visible and increasingly personal forms of cyber-violence, such as cyber-stalking and online harassment, have generated further concern. In Chapter 17, Louise Ellison and Yaman Akdeniz observe that, whilst bodies of law exist in many different jurisdictions to protect individuals against online harassment, there are a number of serious impediments to the apprehension of online stalkers, especially where they have anonymized themselves or they are crossing jurisdictional boundaries. Nevertheless, Ellison and Akdeniz conclude that the law provides little effective protection for online users from harassment and that there are a number of alternative solutions which allow users to both empower and protect themselves, such as by adopting neutral online identities or by participating in online self-help groups.

Ellison and Akdeniz's (legal) policy discussion is complemented by Matt Williams' interesting and useful research note (Chapter 18) about his ongoing work on violent language on the Internet. He maintains that, in contrast to similar types of crimes in the terrestrial world which are the subject of intensive investigation, new forms of sociopathic behaviour present themselves in abundance on the Internet and are being disregarded because of their 'virtual status'. By using a multimethod approach, including ethnographic methods, linguistic, case source and discourse analysis, Williams seeks to unravel the link between the aetiology of online deviance and the discourses of surveillance, regulation and mediation. He identifies the various forms of 'virtual deviance' that manifest themselves within online communities – for example, the practice of derision and its effects. Williams' analysis seeks to further understand speech-related cybercrimes by disaggregating illocutionary speech where 'the speech is the act of doing', from perlocutionary speech which has a delayed effect: 'what is said at one point in time may have a consequence that is temporarily distant' (p. 299).

Obscenity/Pornography

The relationship between pornography and the internet is both curious and contradictory (see further Wall, 2001, p. 6). It was the fear of unrestrained access to sexually-explicit or pornographic materials that fuelled public concern about the Internet and no doubt discouraged some people, particularly concerned parents, from using it. Yet, ironically, it was the very presence of pornographic materials on the Internet that encouraged people – mostly men – to use it, thus creating a market for sexually explicit materials and subsequently driving the development of the technology that was designed to deliver pornography in the form of an electronic service.

Perhaps more controversially, the virtual sex trade not only pioneered the virtual transaction, but also demonstrated the commercial potential of the Internet to the normally conservative business community. Finally, this trade has played an important role in the governance of the Internet. By seeking increased public legitimacy, and thus freedom from restraint, so that they can ply their trade, the 'adult' sites which peddle consensual adult pornography have not only joined forces to create economies of scale and to share common trust relationships with the customers, but they have also sought to expose and expel child pornographers from the Internet (Wall, 2001, p. 173). The organization called Adult Sites Against Child Pornography (ASACP), for example, is one such arrangement. Through its www site <http://www.asacp.org/reportsite.html> it provides its members and ordinary netizens with a facility to report offensive www pages.

The following sources cover a range of debates about sexually explicit materials and the Internet. Taking a cyber-libertarian stance, Nadine Strossen observes, in Chapter 19, that many law enforcement officials believe that trade-offs constantly have to be made between individual rights and public safety. She argues that this dichotomy is not only oversimplified but very misleading, because the alleged dangers of online expression frequently become exaggerated. Furthermore, she believes that the types of criminal law and policing strategy that have operated effectively in other media are equally effective within cyberspace. Strossen concludes that:

> . . . everyone who values human life – and human rights – must of course be vigilant against the fear, insecurity, and manipulation caused by terrorists and other criminals. But we must also be vigilant against the fear, insecurity, and manipulation caused by those who seek to fight against criminals. (p. 315)

In Chapter 20, Clive Walker and Yaman Akdeniz discuss the regulation of pornography within both the United Kingdom and the European Union. Their conclusions are very much in line with those of Strossen, namely that the Internet is truly a 'mass medium' and that most jurisdictions already have in place effective, existing bodies of law. However, Walker and Akdeniz's analysis further concludes that the people who are most concerned about the Internet are typically those who do not use it, yet it is their concerns which are frequently exploited by politicians and the mass media. This observation brings us to a most interesting episode when precisely this form of exploitation, whether intentional or not, took place and culminated in the US Communications Decency Act 1996 (CDA).

Underlying the passage of the Communications Decency Act was a series of high-profile, contemporary feminist debates about the impact of pornography upon women. The increasing prevalence of pornography on the Internet during the early 1990s, combined with the publicity generated by a 1995 study by Marty Rimm (Chapter 21) in which he purported to demonstrate that the majority of Internet traffic was related to pornography, fanned the flames of broader public concern and further raised the profile of the pornography debate, with the result that the CDA was passed. Rimm's findings were published in a special issue of the prestigious *Georgetown Law Journal* alongside a response by Catharine MacKinnon, entitled 'Vindication and Resistance . . .' (Chapter 22). However, Rimm's methodology was subsequently discredited by authors such as Donna Hoffman and Thomas Novak (Chapter 23) (see also Wallace and Mangan, 1996) and became the subject of a fierce critique. This critique helped to turn the debate over responses to pornography on the Internet and part of the Communications Decency Act was subsequently overturned following a legal action by a team from the American Civil Liberties Union, which included Nadine Strossen (see also Heins, 2001, p. 100).

In the final contribution to this section (Chapter 24), Jon Spencer considers the presentation and representation of crime on the Internet with special reference to sexually explicit materials. Spencer believes that the Internet signifies the divergence of traditional alliances between governments and media, resulting in the reshaping of the relationship between media interests, government and the state. He concludes that, whilst media conglomerates have Internet interests, they are not able to exercise the same degree of control as they do, for example, over newsprint. Furthermore, the Internet blurs the boundaries between fact and fiction. Only certain types of crime are deemed newsworthy and therefore become represented in the media with the result that untypical crimes 'are rendered an everyday occurrence' (p. 441).

Criminal Justice Processes

Not only has the Internet transformed aspects of criminal behaviour, thus presenting the various criminal justice processes with a new set of substantive challenges, but communications and information technologies which increasingly use the Internet have had, and continue to have, a marked impact on those same processes. Part III considers some of the issues relating to policing the Internet and also to the impact of the Internet and C & IT on police work and the trial process.

In his analysis of police force responses to the demands upon the organization created by new forms of technology, Marc Goodman (Chapter 25) makes the very poignant observation that cybercrimes are simply not seen as a priority by police departments around the world because greater and greater political emphasis is being placed on issues such as violent crime reduction and community-based policing. He observes that when police forces are challenged as to their lack of engagement with computer crime, police managers frequently claim not to have the resources. But he also contends that the true reasons are much more complex and enigmatic as they are more likely to be related to a combination of social, cultural, and political factors. Goodman believes that mass police training programmes, combined with the provision of new equipment are the only way of enabling the public police to engage with computer crimes.

In my chapter on the policing and the regulation of cyberspace (Chapter 26) I echo Goodman's conclusions about the internal organization of policing and their response to 'hard policing issues', but I also argue that the public police are only a small part of the overall process of policing the Internet, as in the terrestrial world: 'not all policing lies in the police'

(Reiner, 2000, p. xi). Therefore, in addressing the bigger picture we must not just ask why cybercrimes occur but, more importantly, we must ask why cybercrimes do not occur more often. The answer to the latter question is that a multitiered system of policing is already operating in cyberspace to regulate Internet behaviour. This multitiered system is mainly based on self-regulation by Internet users, user groups and also Internet service providers. However, where the seriousness of the crime warrants, cases might be passed to the various state funded non-police and public police organizations. This pluralistic model combines elements of both public and private models of policing. So we do not need new forms of regulation or policing; rather, we need to adapt, develop and build upon those which exist already. But the principle of self-policing is inherently limited in scope and has a fairly low ceiling of efficacy and, as this system operates upon a self-appointed mandate, it lacks formal mechanisms of accountability. In order to gain legitimacy and become effective, thus preventing minor miscarriages of justice, a system(s) of accountability needs to be incorporated.

Moving from the policing of the Internet to the impact of C & IT on policing, Peter Manning (Chapter 27) looks at the effect of information technology on police practices and argues that IT-driven crime analysis and crime mapping is potentially one of the greatest innovations in policing in recent times. This is because it, uniquely, provides the police with an opportunity to resolve some of the basic contradictions in its mandate – namely that the police 'can control crime, reduce the fear of crime, and yet be an almost entirely responsive, demand-driven, situational force dispensing just in time and just enough, order maintenance' (p. 509). However, Manning's research found that crime mapping has little or no impact on operational policing because of the lack of an infrastructure of 'support and interpretation; the distribution of the information, isolated and unintegrated databases, and lack of on-line access by patrol officers, renders the extant software and analytic capacity ineffectual' (p. 491).

Interestingly, Manning's findings initially appear to contradict those of Janet Chan, who studied the impact of information technology in an Australian police force (Chapter 28). Chan, like Manning, found that, following the introduction of C & IT into police practice, there still remained the cultural dominance of law-enforcement policing and its accompanying resentments towards the demands of management and external agencies. However, she also found that technological change was redefining 'the value of communicative and technical resources, institutionalized accountability through built-in formats and procedures of reporting, and restructured the daily routines of operational policing' (p. 530). So the outcome of this redefinition was that information technology was slowly changing the deeply embedded assumptions behind police practice.

Whereas Goodman (Chapter 25) and Wall (Chapter 26) focus on who should police the Internet, Peter Sommer gets to grips with the practical problems of making computer evidence admissible in court once that decision has been made (Chapter 29). The intangible nature of 'digital footprints', that comprise evidence, combined with the conditions laid down by s.69 of the UK Police and Criminal Evidence Act 1984 and equivalents in other jurisdictions regarding the admissibility of evidence, can create a series of problems for the police and the other organizations involved in computer forensics. Currently there are many complications with the procedures for 'freezing the scene' in order to ensure that evidence is admissible, and also in interrogating a frozen system to establish which are relevant files and which are not. A further set of complicating issues arise when investigators seek to obtain and analyse a suspect's Internet-based activities, such as obtaining traffic data from an Internet Service Provider (ISP) or eavesdropping on communications in progress. Sommer proposes that a new code of practice be introduced to cover specifically the issue of computer-based evidence.

The final chapter (Chapter 30) in Part III is Clive Walker's study of the impact of the Internet on the trial process. Walker observes that the Internet has provided a public portal into the workings of the criminal justice process which allows the public instant access to information, developments and decisions, particularly with regard to celebrity trials and the trial of celebrities where the public demand for information is the greatest. Furthermore, the Internet provides a forum, through its many newsgroups, for discussion about the substantive issues within the trial. However, the instantaneous dissemination of information and the increased public involvement in discussion can create cyber-contempt, breaking the laws of *sub judice* and questioning the fairness of the judicial process.

Conclusion

This volume has been constructed from the sources available at the time of compilation in April 2002 and it has been structured in a way that will allow readers to map their way through some of the key issues and topics in cyberspace crime. In one sense, this collection demonstrates the amount of work that has already been done in this area; in another sense, the apparent lack of empirical and theoretical coherence between much of the work demonstrates the shortfalls in existing work. Particularly telling from the references, for example, is the observation that many of the authors appear to have been unaware of the work of the others at the time of writing.

Yet, on balance, the essays show many encouraging signs, particularly the emergence of a critical stance against broad unsubstantiated claims about all engrossing cyber-tsunamis. In fact, a fairly common view is emerging that the reality of cybercrime is turning out to be far less dramatic than anticipated. Indeed, it would appear – though we need the empirical research to firmly establish this point – that many 'cyberspace crimes' fall within our current bodies of criminological understanding. Nevertheless, some clearly do not and these require criminological attention because they fall outside the paradigm of current criminology (Wall, 2002, p. 187). The future would appear to have in store a permanent revolution for criminology because not only, as stated earlier, is criminology only one of the many forums for the discussion of crime (Garland and Sparks, 2000, p. 201), but it is also likely that, as we begin to come to grips with cybercrime, new converging technologies will continue to throw up novel sets of issues and new forms of harmful behaviour. One thing is certain: whilst the solutions may often turn out to be quite simple, the significant challenge will be to identify the problems in the first place.

References

Barlow, J.P. (1990), 'Crime and Puzzlement: In Advance of the Law on the Electronic Frontier', *Whole Earth Review*, Fall 1990, pp. 45–57, also at <http://www.eff.org/pub/Publications/John_Perry_Barlow/HTML/crime_and_puzzlement_1.html>.

Barlow, J.P. (1994), 'The Economy of Ideas: A Framework for Rethinking Patents and Copyrights in the Digital Age (Everything You Know About Intellectual Property is Wrong)', *Wired*, **2** (3), p. 84.

Becker, P., Byers, B. and Jipson, A. (2000), 'The Contentious American Debate: The First Amendment and Internet-based Hate Speech', *International Review of Law, Computers and Technology*, **14** (1).

Boyle, J. (1996), *Shamans, Software and Spleens: Law and the Construction of the Information Society*, Cambridge, MA: Harvard University Press.

Braithwaite, J. (2000), 'The New Regulatory State And The Transformation of Criminology', *British Journal of Criminology*, **40** (2), pp. 222–38.

Brenner, S. (2001), 'Is There Such a Thing as "Virtual Crime"?', *California Criminal Law Review*, **4** (1), p. 11. Also at <http://www.boalt.org/CCLR/v4/v4brenner.htm>.

Garland, D. and Sparks, R. (2000), 'Criminology, Social Theory and the Challenge of our Times', *British Journal of Criminology*, **40** (2), pp. 189–204.

Grabosky, P.N. and Smith, R.G. (1998), *Crime in the Digital Age: Controlling Communications and Cyberspace Illegalities*, Somerset, NJ: Transaction Publishers.

Heins, M. (2001), 'Criminalizing Online Speech to "Protect" the Young: What are the Benefits and Costs?', in D.S. Wall (ed.), *Crime and the Internet*, London: Routledge, pp. 100–12.

Hollinger, R. (ed.) (1997), *Crime, Deviance and the Computer*, International Library of Criminology, Criminal Justice and Penology, Aldershot: Ashgate.

Law Commission (1997), *Legislating the Criminal Code: Misuse of Trade Secrets*, Consultation Paper 150, London: Law Commission for England and Wales.

Lessig, L. (1999), 'The Law Of The Horse: What Cyberlaw Might Teach', *Harvard Law Review*, **113**, p. 501.

Levi, M. (ed.) (1999), *Fraud: Organization, Motivation and Control*, Vols I and II, International Library of Criminology, Criminal Justice and Penology, Aldershot: Ashgate.

Levi, M. (2001), 'Between the Risk and the Reality Falls the Shadow: Evidence and Urban Legends in Computer Fraud (With Apologies to TS Eliot)', in D.S. Wall (ed.), *Crime and the Internet*, London: Routledge, pp. 44–58.

Levi, M. and Handley, J. (1998), *The Prevention of Plastic and Cheque Fraud Revisited*, HORS 182, London: Home Office.

Madow, M. (1993), 'Private Ownership of Public Image: Popular Culture and Publicity Rights', *California Law Review*, **81**, pp. 125–240.

Mars, G. (ed.) (2001a), *Occupational Crime*, International Library of Criminology, Criminal Justice and Penology, Aldershot: Ashgate.

Mars, G. (ed.) (2001b), *Work Place Sabotage*, International Library of Criminology, Criminal Justice and Penology, Aldershot: Ashgate.

NCIS (1999), *Project Trawler: Crime On The Information Highways*, London: NCIS.

Nelken, D. (ed.) (1994), *White-Collar Crime*, International Library of Criminology, Criminal Justice and Penology, Aldershot: Ashgate.

Reiner, R. (2000), *The Politics of the Police*, 3rd edn, Oxford: Oxford University Press.

Taylor, P.A. (2001), 'Hacktivism: In Search of Lost Ethics?', in D.S. Wall (ed.), *Crime and the Internet*, London: Routledge, pp. 59–73.

Walker, C.P., Wall, D.S. and Akdeniz, Y. (2000), 'The Internet, Law and Society', in Y. Akdeniz, C.P. Walker and D.S. Wall (eds), *The Internet, Law and Society*, London: Longman, pp. 3–24.

Wall, D.S. (2000), 'Policing the Internet: Maintaining Order and Law on the Cyber-beat', in Y. Akdeniz, C.P. Walker and D.S. Wall (eds), *The Internet, Law and Society*, London: Longman, pp. 154–74.

Wall, D.S. (2001), 'CyberCrimes and the Internet', in D.S. Wall (ed.), *Crime and the Internet*, London: Routledge, pp. 1–17.

Wall, D.S. (2002), 'Insecurity and the Policing of Cyberspace', in A. Crawford (ed.), *Crime and Insecurity*, Cullompton: Willan, pp. 186–209.

Wallace, J. and Mangan, M. (1996), *Sex, Laws, and Cyberspace: Freedom and Censorship on the Frontiers of the Online Revolution*, New York: Henry Holt.

Recommended Further Reading

I have included below some edited collections and monographs which cover the issues of cyberspace crime, either in part or in whole, which readers might find useful to consult.

Akdeniz, Y., Walker, C.P. and Wall, D.S. (eds) (2000), *The Internet, Law and Society*, London: Longman.

Barrett, N. (1998), *Digital Crime: Policing the Cybernation*, London: Kogan Page.

Grabosky, P.N. and Smith, R.G. (1998), *Crime in the Digital Age: Controlling Communications and Cyberspace Illegalities*, Somerset, NJ: Transaction Publishers.

Grabosky, P.N., Smith, R.G. and Dempsey, G. (2001), *Electronic Theft: Crimes of Acquisition in the Digital Age*, Cambridge: Cambridge University Press.

Thomas, D. and Loader, B. (eds) (2000), *Cybercrime: Law Enforcement, Security and Surveillance in the Information Age*, New York and London: Routledge.

Walker, C. (ed.) (1998), 'Crime, Criminal Justice and the Internet', Special edition, *Criminal Law Review*, London: Sweet and Maxwell.

Wall, D.S. (ed.) (2000), 'Cybercrimes and Cyberliberties', Special Issue of *International Review of Law Computers and Technology*, **14** (1) (with editorial).

Wall, D.S. (ed.) (2001), *Crime and the Internet*, London: Routledge.

Wallace, J. and Mangan, M. (1996), *Sex, Laws, and Cyberspace: Freedom and Censorship on the Frontiers of the Online Revolution*, New York: Henry Holt.

Part I
Theoretical Perspectives
and Viewpoints

[1]

Cybercrimes: New Wine, No Bottles?[1]

David Wall

INTRODUCTION

Over the past two decades, the concept of cyberspace has developed from science fiction into a socially constructed reality (Benedikt, 1991; Gibson, 1984). It is now: 'a place without physical walls or even physical dimensions', where 'interaction occurs as if it happened in the real world and in real-time, but constitutes only a "virtual reality"'(Byassee, 1995: 199; Tribe, 1991: 15). The inhabitants of cyberspace are a virtual community of 'social aggregations that emerge from the Net[2] when enough people carry on public discussions long enough, with sufficient human feeling, to form webs of personal relationships in cyberspace' (Rheingold, 1994: 5). Only time will tell whether or not this virtual community will become Saradar and Ravetz's 'new civilisation which emerges through our human-computer interface and mediation' (1996: 1). What is certain is that the Internet creates considerably more opportunities for individuals to come into contact and to interact with others socially, economically and politically. Furthermore, as the 'intellectual land grab' (Boyle, 1996: 125) takes place for cyberspace, the emerging political economy of information capital will cause interests to become established and new distinctions to emerge between acceptable and deviant behaviour. Not only do new risk communities now accompany the old, but many previously acceptable activities have become relabelled as undesirable and now sit next to those behaviours which have been traditionally accepted as undesirable.

This chapter will explore the deviant behaviour that is becoming known as 'cybercrime'. The term cybercrime is mainly used here as a heuristic device and signifies the point(s) at which conventional understandings of crime are challenged. It is distinguished from 'high-tech' crimes, which relate to the theft of computer parts (Grundy and Wood, 1996), but is not so easily distinguished from computer crimes, of which hacking (pre-Internet, see later) was one. The first part of this chapter will consider the social impact of cyberspace, which is the site where cybercrimes can take place. The second part will outline the contours of cybercrimes by focusing upon four particular areas of undesirable behaviour which are causing concern: cyber-trespass, cyber-theft, cyber-obscenity and cyber-violence. The third part will look at who the victims of cybercrimes are and the fourth part will consider the issues which relate to the governance of this behaviour.

THE SOCIAL[3] IMPACT OF CYBERSPACE

Love it or loathe it, the Internet is here to stay. Not since the commercialisation of the radio in the 1920s has there been such a rapid growth in the usage of information technology (Walker, 1997: 9). At its current rate of growth it is estimated that there will probably be more than 500 million global netizens by the turn of the century (Mandel, 1993). In the United Kingdom, the numbers are much less, but the increase in usage is nevertheless striking. The House of Lords Select Committee on Science and Technology report estimated that in 1995/6, over a quarter of all households in the United Kingdom had personal computers and that the Internet Service Providers had in the region of 300 000 customers (1995–6: paras 1.1, 1.6). Today, the numbers are about double that figure.

Developed from a United States Department of Defence initiative to create a communications system that would survive a thermonuclear attack, the Internet has developed far beyond its original military and academic goals. During the past decade the Internet has developed into an exciting new public domain, which, by virtue of its ability to bypass geo-political, economic and social boundaries, is potentially free of conventional politics, social order and regulation. It has created a quantum leap in communications that is surpassing the introduction of the telephone, radio and television. What is significantly different this time is that the communications are two-way and can reach a potentially infinite number of people across a wide range of jurisdictions almost without restriction. So, the Internet, and particularly the cyberspace it creates, is not just a case of 'old wine in new bottles', or even 'new wine in new bottles'; for the most part it is more an example of 'new wine in no bottles'![4] Thus, cyberspace is reformulating the debate over modernity 'in ways that are not so mediated by literary and epistemological considerations, as was the case during the 1980s' (Escobar, 1996: 113).

One of the most obvious impacts of the colonisation of cyberspace has been the way that it has accelerated some of the qualities that have come to characterise high modernity, particularly the 'discontinuities' highlighted by Giddens (1990: 6) which separate modern and traditional social orders. According to Giddens, the social orders which bind time and space have become *disembedded* and *distanciated*; 'lifted out of local contexts of interaction and restructured across indefinite spans of time-space' (Giddens, 1990: 14; Bottoms and Wiles, 1996). The social impact of cyberspace upon the individual is only starting to be recognised. For the first time in history, individuals are free to develop social relations that are commensurate with their own interests or lifestyles and are potentially more meaningful than they could otherwise be. Individuals can now work in three dimensions instead of two, meaning that it is possible, for example, to do office work without office politics, and to work where abilities can be maximised, rather than where they are physically situated. However, whilst this form of social relationship has the advantage of avoiding the pitfalls of destructive *gemeinschaft*, it does, nevertheless, have a dark side in that it encourages the social deskilling[5] of the individual. A major concern is that over time, our terrestrial social life will tend to become both specialised and compartmentalised. As access to the Internet becomes more widely available through falling prices and public access policies, major divisions in society will come to be based upon access to information as much as upon socio-economic grounds. Those who do not engage with the technology will become excluded and the knowledge gap, or information

exclusion, will put a new spin on our understanding of
social exclusion.

In addition to engendering social and behavioural change,
cyberspace has reconfigured many socially understood
meanings which help to shape our behaviour. Unlike the
terrestrial world, cyberspace is a virtual environment in which
economic value is attached to ideas rather than physical
property (Barlow, 1994). Consequently, as the numbers of
intellectual property laws increase to establish ownership
over these ideas, they are not only becoming commodified,
but the process is, in effect, creating a new political economy
of information capital (see Boyle, 1996). Because of this
characteristic, these ideas or properties, and their value,
are constantly faced with the threat of being appropriated,
damaged or distorted.

So, perhaps the most important change from the point
of view of this discussion is that cyberspace has now become an important quasi-industrial environment for capitalist
production and it is also the site where intellectual, as
opposed to physical, products are manufactured, traded,
purchased and consumed. We have now an emphasis upon
intellectual properties in the form of images and likenesses,
copyrightable, trademarkable and patentable materials. These
intellectual properties have immense value, due to the fact
that the costs of reproduction are minimal. But these qualities
also make them more vulnerable to appropriation.[6] As the
nature of more familiar forms of property is changing, then
so are the legitimate means by which goods are obtained.
Money is rapidly becoming an electronic medium, cyber-
cash can now be withdrawn from the many cyber-banks
that are springing up, to be spent in any one of a number
of cyber-shopping malls. In these ways, and others, cyberspace lays bare our conventional understanding of ownership
and control. It also blurs the traditional boundaries between criminal and civil activities and also public and private
law. Perhaps more importantly, it challenges many of the
principles upon which our conventional understandings of
crime and policing are based. Consequently, a number of
important questions emerge as to what exactly are cybercrimes
and to what extent do they differ from other activities that
we currently recognise as crime?

THE CONTOURS OF CYBERCRIME

Traditional criminal activities, broadly speaking, display some fairly characteristic and commonly understood features (Gottfredson and Hirschi, 1990; Braithwaite, 1992). First, they tend to take place in real time as their time frame is determined by physical circumstances, such as speed and mode of transport. Second, they also tend to take place within defined geographical and social boundaries within which the actions they describe are governed by a body of substantive law that is germane to the area enclosed by the boundary (see Johnson and Post, 1996). Furthermore, the place where the criminal behaviour takes place is usually the same as where its impact is felt. Third, serious frauds and many white-collar crimes notwithstanding, the debate over traditional crimes is mainly located within working-class subcultures. Fourth, there are a set of consensual or core values about what does, or what does not, constitute a crime. Finally, traditional criminology has tended to be offender- rather than victim- or offence-based.

In contrast, cybercrimes differ from our understanding of traditional criminal activity in a number of distinctive ways. First, they do not respect time, space or place in that they have no easily definable boundaries, can span jurisdictions and they are instantaneous (Johnson and Post, 1996; Betts and Anthes, 1995: 16). Second, they are contentious in so far as there does not yet exist a core set of values about them which informs general opinion. At one level the culture of law enforcement is still informed by terrestrial conceptions of law; at another level few test cases have yet to go through the criminal courts to change legal cultures (Wall, 1997).[7] Third, they require considerable technical knowledge to be enacted, knowledge which is typically gained from further or higher education: although this is rapidly changing. Fourth, as the following arguments will demonstrate, there is no one set of consensual or core values about what does or what does not constitute a cybercrime. Furthermore, there is often some confusion as to whether what are regarded by some as cybercrimes, are in fact criminal activities (see later discussion). Finally, dis-

cussion of cybercrimes tends to be largely offence-, and to
a lesser extent victim-based. Any discussion of the offenders
tends to be in individual terms.

In short, cybercrimes possess qualities which turn many
existing conceptions of traditional crime on their head;
however, it will be demonstrated later that these descriptions of criminal activity serve to outline the respective polar
positions. In practice, most of the (cyber) criminal activities discussed later in this chapter fall somewhere between
the two. Some types of cybercrime resemble traditional crimes
more than others, others resemble white-collar crimes whilst
the remainder represent completely new forms of deviant
behaviour.

There have been a number of attempts to classify
cybercrimes. Some (Young, 1995: 1; Wasik, 1991) have
focused upon the offender and have typologised them. Others
have concentrated upon specific behaviours: the cybercrimes
themselves (Schlozberg, 1983; Duff and Gardiner, 1996:
213). The main problem with these classifications is that
they tend to have been established before the full commercial
exploitation of the Internet and some even before the sophisticated development of the graphics user-interface, which
has facilitated the commercialisation of the Internet. In the
USA the FBI's National Computer Crime Squad identified
a number of crime categories which it currently investigates.[8]
They are: intrusions of the Public Switched Network (the
telephone company); major computer network intrusions;
network integrity violations; privacy violations; industrial
espionage; pirated computer software; and other crimes
where the computer is a major factor in committing the
criminal offence. Although the National Computer Crime
Squad's charter limits its investigations to violations of the
Federal Computer Fraud and Abuse Act (1986)[9] the coverage,
according to Fraser (1996), is still rather broad and im-
precise, referring to location rather than activities.

One of the more useful attempts to understand cybercrimes
was undertaken by the United Nations, which concluded
in its *Manual on the Prevention and Control of Computer-Related
Crime* (United Nations, 1995) that whilst there is a consensus amongst experts that cybercrime exists because 'the
computer has also created a host of potentially new mis-

uses or abuses that may, or should, be criminal as well' (United Nations, 1995: para 22), it nevertheless accepts that authors cannot agree as to what cybercrime actually is, arguing that definitions have tended to be functional, relating to the study for which they were written (United Nations, 1995: para 21).[10] The United Nations were not alone in reaching this conclusion as the Council of Europe's Committee on Crime Problems also avoided a formal definition of cybercrime, choosing instead to discuss the functional characteristics of specific activities. The committee wisely left individual countries to adapt the functional classification to their particular legal systems and historical traditions (United Nations, 1995: para 23). The United Nations manual did, however, discuss the role of criminal law, arguing that since it recognises the concepts of unlawful or fraudulent intent and also of claim of right, then any criminal laws relating to cybercrime would need to distinguish between accidental misuse of a computer system, negligent misuse of a computer system and intended, unauthorised access to or misuse of a computer system, amounting to computer abuse. It also argued that annoying behaviour must be distinguished from criminal behaviour in law (United Nations, 1995: para 24): points that were reflected in the European Commission Select Committee's recent Green Paper on the protection of minors (1996) (see later).

Beyond the problem of the specifics of definition, is the added difficulty of locating cybercrimes within an appropriate body of literature. Attempts to liken cybercrimes to white-collar crimes, state Duff and Gardiner (1996: 213), can be misleading as most forms of hacking cannot be seen as white-collar crime although the literature on white-collar crimes does inform the debate over cybercrimes. Much of the problem here is that the main body of literature on white-collar crime pre-dates the recent and rapid expansion of the Internet, and the term 'white-collar crime' has, to some extent, also become a residual category into which many non-traditional crimes have been placed. However, whilst it is clearly wrong to attempt to define cybercrimes as white-collar crimes, it is nevertheless possible to draw upon the literature on white-collar crimes to inform the debate over the nature of cybercrimes.

A transposition of Nelken's (1997: 896) analysis of the problematic nature of white-collar crimes is particularly useful to our understanding of the nature of cybercrimes. Firstly, cybercrime is a contested concept. Not only is the nature of the subject matter in discussions of cybercrimes frequently unclear, but there is often doubt as to whether or not the behaviours actually count as crime in a formal-legal sense. This confusion arises from the fact that the definition of the severity of the offence has often been evaluated by the victims (see next section). Secondly, there is a problem of causality in that normal frameworks of criminological explanation don't really fit. There is often confusion between the 'how' and the 'why' (Levi, 1985). Furthermore, the search for causality is confused by the problem of what it is that actually needs to be explained, especially as it is often hard to distinguish between criminal behaviour and that which is deemed as normal business practice. On the one hand lies the problem of explaining cybercrime in terms used for traditional crimes, whilst on the other hand is the problem of either over-explaining or rationalising accounts so that they resemble normal business behaviour (Nelken, 1997: 907). Like white-collar crimes, the behaviour which constitutes cybercrimes is often indistinguishable from normal legal behaviour. Thirdly, there is the ambivalence of responses to cybercrimes, and these responses are important in the subsequent shaping of this behaviour. A good example of this ambivalence can be seen in the cases of the hackers Matthew Bevan, Richard Pryce and also Ehud Tannenbaum. Operating as 'Kuji' and 'Datastream Cowboy', Bevan and Pryce achieved what Campbell has described as 'a notoriety out of all proportion to their actions', when they haphazardly penetrated US Air Force and defence contractors' computers (Campbell, 1997: 2). Since 1994 this penetration had been portrayed as the work of foreign agents and was claimed to be 'the greatest electronic danger yet to hit the US Air Force on its home turf' (ibid.). At one point in the investigation, Bevan and Pryce were allegedly accused by US military sources as being 'a greater threat to world peace than Adolf Hitler' (Gunner, 1998: 5). In 1996, the Senate Armed Services Committee were told that 'Datastream Cowboy' had caused more harm than the KGB and was the 'No 1 threat to US security' (Ungoed-Thomas, 1998: 1). The truth was subsequently found to be less dramatic, as the public portrayal of the two Britons as major threats to US national security was largely hype. Pryce's version of events is somewhat different to that depicted by the US military. 'We embarrassed them by showing how lax their security was and that's why they made out we had been a huge security threat' (Ungoed-Thomas, 1998: 1).[11] Campbell believes that the inside story of the Bevan and Pryce cases shows that the forensic work was too poor to have stood up in court (ibid.).[12] In a similar case, the hacking abilities of Ehud Tannenbaum, also known as 'The Analyser', were reviled by the US, but applauded by many Israelis (Sharrock, 1998: 2).

Such ambiguity encourages the redefinition of legal behaviour as illegal and helps to obscure the dissonance between social and legal definitions of crime, especially regarding the location of the boundary between cybercrimes and the risk-taking that characterises normal business practice. So, instead of making hard and fast classifications that will become quickly outdated with techno-social change, the following discussion will identify and focus upon generic groups of offences which are raising concerns as we enter the twenty-first century. The purpose of this exercise is, therefore, to outline the contours of cybercrimes and illustrate the range of activities, rather than define hard and fast categories. The four groups are cyber-trespass, cyber-theft, cyber-obscenity and cyber-violence.

Cyber-trespass

Cyber-trespass includes acts which involve the crossing of established boundaries into space which has already been claimed. Crucial to the development of the Internet[13] was the computer hacker, who possessed a high level of specialised knowledge, along with a belief in freedom of access to all information. Initially the hackers were applauded as a celebration of the genius of youth and the pioneering spirit of America (Chandler, 1996: 229), but they have subsequently become demonised (Chandler, 1996; Duff and Gardiner, 1996; Ross, 1990: para 4; Sterling, 1994). Their

skills and beliefs are now widely regarded as a major threat
to the interests of those who are attempting to effect
monopoly control over cyberspace: namely commerce and
the state (see above). It is because of this ideological bag-
gage that the term 'cyber-trespasser' is preferred to the
term 'hacker'. Furthermore, when the range of behaviours
within this group is examined it is found that they clearly
represent a spectrum of qualitatively different types of trespass; with intellectually motivated acts of trespass at one
end and politically or criminally motivated trespass at the
other. In its mildest form, cyber-trespass is little more than
an intellectual challenge resulting in a harmless trespass,
at its worst it is full-blown information warfare (see later)
(Szafranski, 1995: 56).[14] The latter has been taken so seriously
by the United States Air Force that in late 1996 it created
the 609th Information Warfare Squadron (Cook, 1998) (but
see later discussion). In the UK, the Computer Misuse Act
1990 made hacking a criminal offence regardless of whether
or not damage was done (Akdeniz, 1996b).

Four basic types of cyber-trespasser can be identified from
the literature, Young (1995: 10), distinguishes between *uto-*
pians who naively believe that they are contributing to society
by demonstrating its vulnerabilities, and *cyberpunks* who are
aggressively anti-establishment, and who intentionally cause
harm to targets which offend them. In addition, we can
also identify two further types of cyber-trespassers, the *cyber-*
spy and the *cyber-terrorist*. The latter two are characterised
by their motivation, typically for politics, morality or money,
to disrupt a prevailing order. The former two (*utopians* and
cyberpunks) on the other hand, tend to create disruption as
the result of being at a particular site. In practice, however,
the practical distinction between the two groups is hard to
delineate because, as stated earlier, cyber-spies and terrorists
must by definition be expert hackers to be able to gain
access to sites. For the most part, any significant acts of
cyber-trespass will tend to lie between these extreme
positions.

The differences between the different types of cyber-trespass are illustrated by the following examples. The first
example is entry to a site followed by the manipulation of
presentational data, such as WWW pages, so that they mis-

represent the organisation that they are supposed to represent. Two poignant cases occurred in 1997 when the
websites of both the Conservative and Labour parties were
entered and defaced. Images were transformed and replaced
and texts were changed so as to misrepresent the sites. A
similar intrusion occurred the previous year at the site of
the University of York's Conservative Club (Wall, 1997).
More recently a number of very popular sites have fallen
victim to the hacker (McCormack, 1997), of which the defacing
of the Spice Girls WWW site was probably the most well
known.[15] In most cases, it is hard to ascertain whether or
not these actions are merely pranks, or were intended to
destabilise, either commercially or politically, the organisations running the sites. Furthermore, the University of York
case, in particular, revealed the evidential problem of establishing the actual identity of the perpetrator. Whilst it was
possible to trace the time and place of the hacking/trespass,
the account used to gain access to the computing system
and even the particular machine, it was impossible to
establish conclusively who had committed the act. Significantly, the manipulated data could easily have been
important research findings, or important statements of
policy, national party manifestos, business portfolios and
so on; the list is endless. Moreover, it is probable that such
acts would not necessarily be detected quickly.

The second example is entry to a site, followed by the
deliberate planting of viruses, worms, Trojan horses or logic
bombs to disrupt or disable a particular function. Although
the outcomes are usually similar, mainly disruption, there
are some subtle differences between the four. Viruses are
usually created with malicious intent to erase data or damage hard drives. They are programs which can reproduce
themselves within a computer by attaching themselves to
software. They can be passed from computer to computer
within the software they attach themselves to, either through
the Internet or by disk. Worms, unlike viruses, are transmitted in much the same way, but reproduce themselves
like worms. They are not designed to erase data so much
as to create chaos by using up machine or network space
and causing systems to crash. Trojan horses and logic bombs
are mainly methods of delivering viruses or worms. Trojan

horses are programs that are hidden inside apparently
normal software which can, once introduced into a host
system, be triggered to distort information, cause damage
or even system failure. Logic bombs, once inserted in a
host computer system, are designed either to go off on a
specific date or after access to the system has been gained
a certain number of times (Akdeniz, 1996b).[16] Perhaps the
best known of these logic bombs is the Michelangelo virus
which only activates on Michelangelo's birthday. Alternatively
there are blackmail viruses which are designed to be
neutralised by a code once a ransom has been paid. An
example of this occurred during the late 1980s, when a
number of organisations, all over the world, received sets
of free floppy disks which purported to be AIDS training
packages. In fact, the disks contained sleeping viruses which
the targets themselves inadvertently activated by loading
the disk. Once loaded, the viruses could only be disabled
by a code that was released once the victims had sent a
sum of money to a specified address in the USA (Chandler,
1996: 241).

The third and fourth examples of cyber-trespass are cyber-
spying and cyber-terrorism. Cyber-spying is where entry
and exit to secret sources of information is effected as discreetly as possible in order to avoid detection.[17] Cyberterrorism, by comparison, is the wilful destruction of
material following entry to a site. In its extreme form it
becomes information warfare, which is defined as intruders
entering state computer systems with the intention of causing
damage to their contents and thus causing considerable
damage to a target society (Szafranski, 1995: 56). Such is
the concern about information warfare within military circles
that military strategists are preparing counter-information
warfare strategies. Although the term warfare is frequently
used, the targets are more likely to be non-military than
military institutions. Also, and often confusingly, the term
is mainly used in relation to the activities of cyber-terrorists
rather than struggles between different nation-states.

As is often the case with new domains, imaginative rhetoric
can exaggerate their impacts: however, this observation does
not understate the potential impact of attack by cyber-
terrorists. Sterling has warned that: 'hackers in Amtrak

computers or in air-traffic controller computers, will kill somebody someday' (Sterling 1994: 185). It is not inconceivable, for example, that cyber-terrorists might break into a nation-state's central computer system and steal national secrets. In February 1998, the vulnerability of the US military computers was further highlighted when it was discovered that hackers had entered the Pentagon's system via a way-station computer in the United Arab Emirates. The implications of the attack were played down by the Pentagon, who suggested, in contrast to previous occurrences of hacking (see earlier), that the break-ins were the result of a contest perpetrated by a small group of amateurs (Dolinar, 1998: A03). In this case what is not known is whether the hackers left themselves trap doors: 'the digital equivalent of the key under the welcome mat to use next time' (Dolinar, 1998: A03).

As vulnerable as military computers are, the potential impact of an attack to computer systems which deal with the economic fabric of the state, such as tax codes, social security payments, national insurance codes or pension details, could be possibly more serious in the long term than an attack upon military systems. The wrongful calculation of income tax, national insurance payments or alteration of criminal records could, for example, cause irreparable damage to relations between the public and a nation-state; creating a loss of public confidence in government and ultimately destabilising the society. At the time of writing, these scenarios still remain possibilities and it is perhaps of greater significance that they have not yet taken place.

Cyber-Theft

Cyber-theft refers to a range of different types of appropriation that can take place within cyberspace. At one extreme are more traditional patterns of theft, whilst at the other are those acts which will cause us to reconsider our understanding of property and therefore the act of theft. Three types or groups of cyber-theft are identified here, theft of cyber-credit, cyber-cash and cyber-piracy (the appropriation of intellectual properties).

118   *David Wall*

Cyber-credit relates to the fraudulent use of appropriated credit cards to buy goods over the Internet from a
cyber-shopping mall. This is to be distinguished from the
general issue of the fraudulent use of credit cards on two
grounds. Firstly, the offender does not actually need to
have a physical credit card to shop over the Internet: only
the card number, name on the card and expiry date are
required. All are details that can be obtained from a discarded credit card receipt.[18] So, the thief is effectively stealing
a large part of the victim's identity in cyberspace. Secondly,
the policing of the offence is complicated by the fact that
the act can be initiated in one jurisdiction and committed
in another.

The cyber-cash concept is developing rapidly and while
the developers envisage the eventual establishment of a
self-contained monetary system within cyberspace, current
concepts of cyber-cash are related to the use of smart cards
which are loaded with electronic cash equivalents at specific
banking points. Such points of access will eventually be
available through the Internet. At the time of writing, six
major UK banks were all represented in two trials of cyber-
cash facilities (AAP Newsfeed, 1998).[19] In Leeds a pilot
scheme for smart Visa cash cards was in operation during
1997 and 1998 and another by Mondex at Nottingham
University. Under these schemes the user would load cash
credits onto their smart card at various convenient locations.
These credits, with the smart card, could then be used to
buy goods in shops, in lieu of cash. Likely to be brought
into operation throughout the UK, this same cyber-cash
system will eventually be used to purchase goods and services
over the Internet with appropriate readers. Whilst the security
potential of cyber-cash is considerably greater than
conventional cash, especially when transactions are
accompanied by a personal identification number, it is highly
likely that the illegal reproduction of cyber-cash credits will
quickly become a challenge for offenders.

Cyber-piracy is the appropriation of the new forms of
intellectual property that have been created within, and
given value by, the inhabitants of cyberspace. It is becoming an increasingly challenging type of cyber-theft. It will
be remembered from earlier that one of the distinguishing

characteristics of cyberspace was the fact that monetary values are attached to ideas rather than objects. In parallel to the growth in the Internet has been an increase in the number and complexity of intellectual property laws relating to trademarks, copyright, patents and in the USA privacy and publicity (Boyle, 1996; Madow, 1993; Wall, 1996; Vagg, 1995). Thus the intersection of the medium of cyberspace and more restrictive intellectual property laws has become quite a potent combination, especially during a time when, as Baudrillard observes, economic activity has come to be the outcome rather than the cause of cultural values and norms (Vagg, 1995: 87; Baudrillard, 1988). Importantly, the fact that productive ideas can now be effected without the need for expensive physical production, means that the monetary value of those ideas is further increased. Therefore, these various forms of intellectual property, especially trademarks, domain names and character merchandising, are becoming its real estate, or so to speak. So the terrain of cyberspace becomes marked by the struggle for control over this 'intellectual' real estate. This development also raises concerns about the proliferation of intellectual property laws, particularly with regard to the increase in monopoly control, but also, for example, unjust enrichment (Boyle, 1996; Wall, forthcoming). More specifically, the establishment of monopoly control in law, even if not in practice, means the ability to determine where the boundaries lie between desirable and undesirable behaviours.

There are two emerging, but related, strands of this type of piracy. The first exists at the peripheries of cyberspace. It is the counterfeiting of products such as toiletries, designer labels and character merchandising, which is becoming a rapidly expanding business. Perhaps the most common example of the act of appropriation of intellectual properties is the (physical) production of counterfeit products which are, typically, direct copies of the original being made and sold through the cyber-shopping malls. There is some confusion here between intellectual and physical property, but other examples of counterfeiting are emerging which are purely within the confines of cyberspace. For example, where pictures of a famous pop star are appropriated from Internet images or scanned from physical sources. They are then repackaged in a glossy and professional format with some explanatory text and sold, via a cyber-shopping mall, to customers who purchase them in good faith. To frustrate detection, the mall may be on a server in the USA and the proceeds paid into an Australian bank account. The whole operation would take little more than a couple of weeks, by which time the deception is detected, the proceeds have been removed from the bank account and the perpetrators gone.

In many ways, the above examples of cyber-theft are fairly predictable in that, although the medium is quite different and detection of the offence is thwarted by the nature of cyberspace, they nevertheless follow the *actus reus* and *mens rea* of many traditional thefts. The second variant of cyber-piracy/theft (of intellectual properties) is quite different and finds the boundaries between criminal and civil extremely blurred. It is where owners' interests in their properties, for example, in images, trademarks, texts or general character merchandising, are threatened by theft or release into the public domain of the Internet. This threat takes the form of 'dilution', a term used in intellectual property law to describe the reduction in value through unrestricted use and also to justify the continuation of legal control,[20] even though the appropriation may not necessarily be motivated by the prospect of financial gain, such as for artistic or moral reasons.[21] Of the many possible examples that could be given, three culturally different, yet significant, examples of the appropriation of popular iconography through the WWW spring to mind which illustrate the point: they are Elvis Presley, the Tellytubbies and the pop-group, Oasis.

The posthumous ownership of Elvis Presley's intellectual properties (trademarks, image and likeness etc.) was established during the 1980s under US law by five landmark cases and, in some states, legislation, for example, the Tennessee Celebrity Rights Act 1984 (see Wall, 1996). Elvis Presley Enterprises, who are charged by Elvis' descendants to vigorously and aggressively police the Elvis image, have been described as the 'Darth Vader of merchandising' (Gwynne, 1997: 48). They see the appropriation of the intellectual property known as Elvis as an offence which is against the law. An interesting point here is that although these acts fall under US civil law, the transporting of counterfeit goods across state boundaries is a federal matter. In 1987 (on the tenth anniversary of the death of Elvis) the FBI in Memphis arrested a number of Elvis merchandisers. During the late 1980s and early 1990s the estate of Elvis Presley established fairly secure legal controls over his intellectual properties. However, this control was tested by the fact that as the WWW developed, the image of Elvis Presley became the focus of a number of websites and the Elvis image became further developed away from its original form – to the point that if he suddenly came back from the dead, it is possible that he would have some difficulty in laying claim to it all (Wall, 1996). In fear of diluting the image and the subsequent fall in its intellectual property value, lawyers working on behalf of Elvis Presley Enterprises have identified risk groups, which could threaten the intellectual property value. Within the context of this discussion these are the WWW site owners, who have been perceived as infringing the rights of Elvis Presley Enterprises and who have been sent sternly phrased cease and desist letters (Wall, 1996). One such offender was identified as Andrea Berman, owner of the Unofficial Elvis home page,[22] who had created a 'Cyber tour' of Graceland, which as the name suggests, contained copyrighted pictures, audio clips and information about Elvis and the Graceland mansion. She was sent a cease and desist letter which stated that 'EPE will have no choice but to exercise its rights under the law to their fullest extent'[23] and in fear of punitive action she immediately signed an affidavit, subsequently regretting that she had not sought legal advice beforehand.[24]

A similar situation developed in 1997, when a set of four technicolour aliens and their friendly vacuum cleaner became very popular with infant TV viewers; the Tellytubbies also became popular with students. Furthermore, and much to the consternation of the programme's producers, Tinky-Winky became a gay icon due to the fact that he sported a large purple plastic shopping bag. This growing interest subsequently led to many Tellytubby related sites appearing on the WWW which contained a variety of materials that were mainly taken from promotional materials. The

122   *David Wall*

BBC, who owned the rights to the Tellytubbies, felt that
these sites were misrepresenting the original aims of the
children's television programme. The BBC's lawyers responded by sending stern cease and desist letters to the
site owners. When word of these actions got around the
various WWW sites, most were discontinued. A policing
function was achieved without recourse to the formal legal
process.

Also in 1997, the pop group Oasis and its management,
Ignition, sent an e-mail message to hundreds of unofficial
fan WWW sites asking them to remove photographs, sound
clips and text containing lyrics from their sites. The message
accused WWW site owners of 'stealing from the band they
claim to support' and warned them that failure to remove
any pictures, lyrics or sound clips by a specified date would
lead to legal action. Whilst most of the unofficial sites are
run by dedicated fans and make no money, Ignition argued
that bootleggers can use them as a source of pictures and
music and sell them, as posters, CDs or in other forms.
Uhlig observes that this may be one of the first examples
of a pop group to try to censor its fans' 'out-pourings'
over the Internet. In response, the fans apparently see the
Ignition's statement more as an attempt by the record
company to suppress information that it does not want made
public; however, the irony of Oasis' own record of flouting
conventions was not lost on them (Uhlig, 1997).

The point of these examples is that they demonstrate
the extent to which owners of the intellectual properties
feel that appropriation threatens their interests, threats which
they took very seriously indeed. In many ways these defensive actions are quite normal and common business
practices, but are notable for two reasons. Firstly, as described earlier, the Internet has complicated the issue by
providing a new medium for the transmission of intellectual products. Secondly, as also stated earlier, in a new
environment such as cyberspace, these policing activities
are serving to define, or redefine, the boundaries between
the legal and the illegal, rather than vice versa, especially
where corporate interests intersect with those of the state,
for example, the Customs and Excise through the VAT
and tax evasion in the UK, which counterfeiting and piracy

involve. So they are not only identifying risks to their product, but are also labelling the main risk groups. In this way, the outcome is little different to the actions of the state police against those they perceive as criminals. This risk assessment function becomes very important as the pluralisation of policing continues to increase. Interestingly, the legality of some of these policing actions against the so-called appropriators is contestable, as the use of the intellectual properties may possibly be covered by the provision of various defences in the intellectual property laws of most jurisdictions. Such defences may be based upon educational, transformative or fair use. Rarely, for example, are the appropriated properties used on the Internet in a commercial sense; rather they tend to be the centre of a parody, or as a news item which is accompanied by discussion.[25] Furthermore, in some cases there may be a public interest in the public availability of the property. In the extreme, there is the irony that the cease and desist actions themselves could amount to acts of harassment or even stalking.

Cyber-obscenity

In 1995 research published as 'The Carnegie Mellon Survey' (Rimm, 1995) suggested that as much as half of all Internet use may be related to the consumption of pornography, mostly in relation to the usenet discussion groups. It purported to identify '917,410 images, descriptions, short stories, and animations downloaded 8.5 million times by consumers in over 2000 cities in forty countries, provinces, and territories' (Rimm, 1995: 1849). The debate which followed this publication was a major contributor to the development of a panic over the use of the Internet. However, the methodology by which this estimate was calculated was subsequently found to be flawed, as it concentrated upon newsgroups and bulletin boards (see Wallace and Mangan, 1996). The true figure was subsequently estimated to be in the region of less than 1 per cent. However, whilst the panic has subsequently subsided, it nevertheless made a lasting impact upon the direction of the debate over Internet regulation. It was, for example, instrumental in

the debate leading up to the initial passage of the Communications Decency Act 1996 (47 USC s.223) in the US
(see later) which, although partially overturned in 1997,[26]
laid the precedent for legislative intervention.

Overall, the debate over the regulation of obscene materials on the WWW has tended to lack focus and has been
characterised by emotive rhetoric. This was largely because
of the fact that pornography is defined by the obscenity
laws of individual legal jurisdictions, which can vary. In
Britain, for example, individuals regularly consume images
that might be classed as obscene in many middle-Eastern
countries. And yet, what individuals class as obscene in the
United Kingdom may be acceptable to the citizens of many
Scandinavian countries. In seeking to clarify this issue in
relation to pornography, the European Commission's *Green
Paper on the Protection of Minors and Human Dignity in Audio-
Visual and Information Services* made the important distinction
between situations where children might gain access to sites
with pornographic content and illegal, obscene, acts which
are subject to penal sanctions.[27] Of course, whilst the former
are not necessary illegal, they may nevertheless still be
deemed as harmful for children's development (European
Commission Select Committee, 1996: ch. 1). The usefulness
of such a distinction is that it identifies the point at which
self-regulation may cease and state intervention might start,
particularly where specific moral and political agendas drive
public opinions.

The discussion over cyber-pornography is dealt with more
fully elsewhere (see Akdeniz, 1996a; 1997a), but for the
purposes of this discussion, the moral panic over pornography which arose then subsided during the early to
mid-1990s was an important driving factor in the wider
debate which has called for a policing policy for the virtual
community. Moreover, the pornography issue highlights the
fact that future criminologies of cyberspace will have to
reflect its unbounded nature and will have to accommodate
a set of dynamics which both undermine conventional understandings of causality and cut across the traditional
treatment of crime.

Cyber-violence

Cyber-violence refers to the violent impact of the cyber activities of another upon an individual or social grouping. Whilst such activities do not have to have a direct physical manifestation, the victim nevertheless feels the violence of the act and can bear long-term psychological scars as a consequence. The activities referred to here range from cyber-stalking to hate-speech and bomb-talk.

Cyber-stalking can take a number of different forms. It can range from the persistent tracking and harassment of an individual by another, for example by the persistent sending of e-mails, through to the sending of obscene messages or even death threats. The problem lies in deciding where to draw the line between the genuine threat and the nuisance. The flexibility of this borderline was apparent in the renowned Jake Baker case.[28] During the mid-1990s, Baker was prosecuted after publishing fantasy rape-torture and snuff stories on the 'alt.sex.stories' newsgroup. In one story called 'Doe', Baker named the victim as one of his fellow students (Wallace and Mangan, 1996: 63). Baker had not stalked the girl in the real sense of surreptitiously following the victim; in fact he had not even contacted her. Moreover, it was later suggested that the girl's real name was only used because one of the syllables in it rhymed with the popular name for the male phallus. Yet, he had caused her and the others who had read the story considerable worry. Although it was about violence, the Baker case eventually became one in which the central issue became his right of freedom of speech.

A second form of cyber-violence is cyber-hate, or hate-speech. If cyber-stalking violates the individual, then cyber-hate violates social or ethnic groupings. The Internet is the site of some very disturbing hate-speech. Perhaps one of the most dramatic examples of hate-speech on the WWW is Holocaust denial, which, as the name implies, attempts to rewrite history by denying that the persecution of the Jewish people by the Nazis ever took place.[29] A number of WWW sites are devoted to the issue of holocaust denial (see Greenberg, 1997: 673).

126　　　　　　　　　　*David Wall*

Bomb-talk is another, worrying, form of cyber-violence in so far as it provides the technologies by which to carry out the ideas circulated by hate-speech. It exists at the extreme of a spectrum of 'Tech-Talk' whereby subversive technological ideas are circulated over the Internet via bulletin boards, user groups and IRC. At one end of the spectrum is the free circulation of sophisticated technologies which are designed to circumnavigate existing infrastructural frameworks.[30] For example, Pryce, the hacker mentioned earlier, stated that he used bulletin boards to get software and also access to hardware.

> 'I used to get software off the bulletin boards and from one of them I got a "bluebox", which could recreate the various frequencies to get free phone calls,' he said. 'I would phone South America and this software would make noises which would make the operator think I had hung up. I could then make calls anywhere in the world for free.' (Ungoed-Thomas, 1998: 1)

At the other end of the spectrum is bomb-talk which ranges from circulation of instructions as to how to make a bomb or other weaponry to the deliberate targeting of groups with a view to committing an act (see Wallace and Mangan, 1996: 153). Perhaps the most vivid example of the latter was the alleged use of the Internet by members of various militias in the planning of the Oklahoma bombing.

The policing of both of these latter examples of cyber-violence is frustrated by the fact that in some jurisdictions, for example the United States and Canada, whilst the intent behind hate-speech might contravene criminal codes, the fact that they are speech gives them protection under the United States Constitution and Canadian Charter of Rights[31] which guarantee freedoms of expression.

The four generic areas of cybercrimes illustrated above provide a useful categorisation of offences whilst also creating space to include the broad range of activities that can occur within them. Such categorisation is arguably more useful than lumping activities, such as fraud, hacking, espionage and theft of intellectual property, under the banner of economic crimes as is the case in the recent European Union report on legal aspects of computer-related crime

(Seiber, 1998).[32] Especially problematic with this approach is the observation that some of the acts mentioned do not necessarily involve a financial motive. Furthermore, the examples cited earlier demonstrate the contested nature of the acts, the problems of identifying causality and also the ambivalent responses that are made towards the 'offences'. The examples also demonstrate the inadvisability of attempting tight definitions of cybercrimes, particularly as the focus has been upon the offence rather than the offender or the offended (victim). The following section will draw upon the previous discussion to make some observations about the victims of cybercrimes.

VICTIMS OF CYBERCRIMES

Other than the fact that the great majority of the victims are members of the virtual community, experience of victimisation varies and is hard to collectivise. It will be some time before a comprehensive sociology of cyber-victimisation can develop, especially as most of the discussion of cybercrimes has tended to focus upon the deviant act rather than either the deviant group or the victims. Furthermore, it is also too early to attempt an assessment of the extent of cyber-victimisation; indeed there are some very good reasons as to why this might never be possible. Each of the above categories denotes a particular victim group; however, this group does not necessarily contain an internal coherence. The literature on white-collar victimisation (Zedner, 1997: 593; Box, 1983: 17) illuminates our understanding of cyber-victimisation and suggests that it is likely that cyber-victims will vary considerably in terms of their status, level of victimisation and group collectivity. They will range from individuals to corporate bodies to whole societies and the (cyber) harms done to them will traverse from the actual to the felt. In some cases there is no primary victim, as many victims of cybercrimes are secondary, or indirect, for example, as with cyber-piracy or cyber-spying/terrorism. In other cases, such as cyber-stalking or the theft of cyber-cash, the victimisation is felt directly by the individual. Furthermore, as is the case with reporting

128   *David Wall*

behaviour for white-collar crimes, it is likely that many victims
of cybercrimes may be unwilling to acknowledge that they
have been a victim, especially those in the business sector
who may fear adverse publicity and negative economic
consequences (Steele, 1997: 500). Or it may simply take
victims some time to realise that they have been victimised.
Alternatively, where the victimisation has been imputed by
a third party upon the basis of an ideological, political,
moral, or commercial assessment of risk, the victim or victim
group may simply be unaware that they have been victimised,
or even believe that they have not, as can be the case with
the various forms of pornography and hate-speech.

THE GOVERNANCE OF CYBERCRIMES

Two important and very practical concerns exist with regard to the debate over the criminalisation of cybercrimes.
Firstly, much of the rhetoric regarding the extent of
cybercrimes has not only been 'overblown', but has subsequently led to considerable funding for state security and
policing organisations. The two may not in fact be mutually
exclusive as this increased funding, in turn, raises the concern that those organisations will then seek to justify that
increased expenditure by creating new 'security markets'
for their services. But Campbell believes that the 'oversold
threats' regarding the threat of breaches of security that
were made during the investigation of the hackers Bevan
and Pryce (see earlier), helped win funding from Congress
for the cyber-investigators, funding which led to the development of new military and intelligence 'infowar' units (see
earlier), which have subsequently sold their security services
to private corporations (Campbell, 1997: 2). Secondly, another
problem arising from overblown rhetoric is the great danger
that deviant cyber-behaviours become the subject of formal
regulation before they are fully understood. A graphic
example of this process emerged following the previously
mentioned panic over obscenity during the mid-1990s. A
solution, in the form of the now partly repealed (US)
Communications Decency Act 1996, was sought before the
problem had been properly identified (Wallace and Mangan,
1996: 174, Akdeniz; 1997c: 1003).

The panic over pornography also gripped the debate over Internet regulation in the United Kingdom. In August 1996, for example, the Club and Vice Unit of the Metropolitan Police issued a stern letter to Internet Service Providers to demand that they ban 133 newsgroups (Walker, 1997: 28).[33] At this time it was not unknown for senior police officers to make dramatic pronouncements to the effect that the Internet was little more than a library of pornography (Uhlig, 1996). Interestingly, such views were in contrast to the views of Chief Constable David Blakey who emphasised that 'it is not necessarily for the police to patrol the super-highway looking for violations' (Blakey, 1996: 18). Like many previously new situations, most of the issues highlighted above will resolve themselves in practice, especially forms of regulation and remedy. However, the point made earlier remains very pertinent, namely that the unique properties of cyberspace challenge many of our conventional understandings of crime and control. Moreover, the traditional referents – class, ethnicity, gender – are not necessarily relevant anymore. And where formal procedures are undertaken, there has to be a respect for due process in the pursuit of justice.

At the time of writing, there remain three distinct characteristics of cyberspace that we are continually going to have to come to terms with. The first is the aforementioned fact that the robustness of the Internet is going to frustrate attempts at direct governance by removing the possibility of the ultimate sanction: disconnection. The second characteristic is the problem of deciding in which particular jurisdiction cyberspace lies. Can it, for example, exist independently of the real world which is organised into its geographical jurisdictions? In practice, the conflict (of laws) is not so much a problem for law as a practical problem for the administration of law, as the following two examples demonstrate. Within the USA, the few legal cases, mostly prosecutions involving child pornography, that have reached the courts have been the subject of forum shopping, which not only provides a way around the problem, but, as recent practice in the USA has demonstrated, can also work to the advantage rather than disadvantage of the prosecution. In *United States of America v. Robert A. Thomas and Carleen Thomas*,[34] a case involving the misuse of bulletin boards, the prosecutors not only had a choice of forum but they also chose for the trial, the Sixth Circuit which covers an area of the USA, mostly Tennessee, where they felt the population would feel most offended by the subject matter of the prosecution. However, such advantage would not be found as easily in inter-jurisdictional offences such as when, in the mid-1990s, a police lieutenant from Jefferson County, Kentucky, USA broke a major child-pornography ring in the United Kingdom, without leaving his state. Lieutenant Baker received an 'e-mailed' pointer from a source in Switzerland which led him to an Internet site based at Birmingham University in the United Kingdom. After three months of investigation, Baker contacted Interpol, the Metropolitan Police and the West Midlands Police, who arrested the distributors (Sussman, 1995).[35] Whilst it is arguable that one could see this as an example of cross-border police co-operation, it is as likely that the decision to pass the case to the British was also prompted by the complexities of obtaining extradition orders.

The third characteristic is the shift of power that cyberspace creates. The traditional exercise of power has been to restrict physical, economic or mental access to an environment whether it be by coercive means, mobilising the agenda or through the use of ideological apparatus (Lukes, 1974). In cyberspace, information is not only the source of power, but also facilitates access.

Of particular interest to observers will be whether or not these characteristics effect a check upon the general encroachment of the nanny state and the control culture that has developed within it. Inherent to this control culture is the rather pessimistic, Hobbesian, view of human nature which asserts that anarchy will prevail in the absence of regulation by the nation-state. Therefore, it is widely assumed that without regulation, netizens cannot be trusted to behave in an orderly manner. This lack of trust became quite clear during the 'libraries of porn' debates that followed the publication of the Carnegie–Mellon findings (see earlier). And yet, with the exception of very extreme behaviours, the experience of cyberspace does not bear out the pessimists' predictions. Steele, for example, puts forward the commonly held view that 'The lack of a legal barrier has led to a rapidly growing sub-culture which preys upon the inhabitants of cyberspace' (1997: 500). However, two points emerge in response to such views. Firstly, why then are there not more cybercrimes and why, for the most part, does the system clearly seem to police itself? Second, we must be somewhat wary, but not be too dismissive, of reports which show that the number of incidents of cybercrimes have proliferated (see above), especially when those reports originate from people who are currently engaged in the growing cybercrime industry.

Views upon the regulation of cybercrimes are therefore split between the pessimists, who wish to impose stringent regulations, and the optimists who believe that individuals can regulate themselves effectively: part of the long-standing liberal tradition. In 1919 (US) Judge Oliver Wendell Holmes argued in the case of *Abrams v United States* that 'the ultimate good desired is better reached by free trade in ideas' on the basis that 'the best test of truth is the power of the thought to get itself accepted in the competition of the market'.[36] Simply put, Wallace and Mangan hope that 'truth and beauty [will] drown out violence and smut' (Wallace and Mangan, 1996: 81; Walker and Akdeniz, 1998). Interestingly, in order to demonstrate the futility of over-regulation, Wallace and Mangan cite the example of the failure of sixteenth-century French censorship policy and observe that even the sanction of death failed to staunch the distribution of books (1996).

There is considerable evidence to favour a more liberal and optimistic approach. Indeed, a system of multi-tiered governance is rapidly developing within cyberspace which is largely based upon self-regulation by netizens of cyberspace, but which also has various higher tiers of governance to accommodate situations to which self-regulation does not apply or is not applied (Akdeniz, 1997a; Walker, 1997: 28; Wall, 1997: 222; Wall, 1998). Where self-regulation either fails or is inappropriate, then the regulating functions are split between three further groups. First are the Internet Service Providers who have created regulatory organisations such as the Internet Watch Foundation to overview the use of the Internet and to bring to the attention of ISPs illegal materials (Akdeniz, 1997a). Second are the

132   *David Wall*

state-funded non-police organisations such as Customs and
Excise in the United Kingdom who seek to investigate VAT
or tax frauds or the Postal Service Investigators in the USA
who investigate misuse of the postal service. Third are the
state-funded police organisations such as the regular (Home
Office) funded police in the United Kingdom and any
specialised units which they may have created to deal with
specific problems. In the USA the FBI has created a
computer crimes unit for the simple purpose of dealing
with a wide range of Internet and computer-related crimes
(Wall, 1997: 224).

Not only is wholesale external regulation virtually impossible to effect, but it is also highly impracticable as a
form of general governance. It is more appropriate to control
or remedy the more extreme and specific forms of behaviour,
such as child pornography. In any form of regulation, there
is always a dilemma between the need to punish past
behaviour and the need to protect individuals from the
future behaviour of others. Over the past two centuries,
these legally based models have arguably failed with regard to traditional crimes; it is therefore likely that they
will continue to fail as models for dealing with new types
of offending behaviour. The application of the laws of the
Internet is clearly more problematic than the more terrestrial laws. Self-regulation is a far more feasible basis for a
system of governance and it is also a more preferable way
of protecting the future than external regulation which for
the most part is driven by an agenda which seeks to punish
the past. Interestingly, the recent EC report on legal aspects
of computer-related crime (Seiber, 1998) takes this approach,
but it also argues that for self-regulation to be effective
there also needs to be in place an infrastructure of international agreements over the boundaries of acceptable and
non-acceptable activities. Yet, any framework of non-legal
remedies, such as the regulation in technology, education
and industry and also in procedural law should preserve,
and not interfere with, fundamental civil liberties. Consequently, a criminology of cyberspace will have to explore
normative perceptions of deviance in addition to their
impacts.

CONCLUSIONS: TO BOLDLY GO . . .

It is no coincidence that the debate over the control of cyberspace, the aforementioned intellectual land grab, has corresponded with the increased potential for the commercial and political exploitation of the Internet. Consequently, it is of little surprise that initiatives to introduce control have come from two directions: sovereign states, whose interests have become threatened; and commerce, who wish to gain monopoly over areas currently in the public domain of cyberspace. Thus, groups with access to cyberspace have increasingly come to be evaluated in terms of either their potential threat to established commercial or political interests, or in terms of their potential opposition to those new interests. Consequently, we see the labelling of specific groups, for example the hackers, according to their perceived level of risk. It is against this backdrop that the behaviours of these groups are increasingly becoming defined, or redefined as cybercrimes. Such definitions are largely normative and at this early stage there is the very real problem of evaluating their true impact. We need to be able to distinguish between real and the virtually real behaviours: we need to be able to identify those which are actually a threat to society and those which, for various reasons, we are told are a threat.

It is fairly early on in the life and times of cyberspace to start predicting its impacts with any degree of certainty, especially as the power-play has only just started to develop. It is very likely that some behaviours will work themselves out and will either cease to be popular or it may be the case that developments in technology will simply eradicate them: much in the same way that British Telecom's 1471 last-caller service almost eliminated the obscene phone call.[37] However, at the end of the day we shall be left with a series of new types of 'criminal' behaviour, which in some cases will cause us to rethink and augment our existing understandings of crimes and deviant behaviours. Understandings, which are largely based upon our social experiences of traditionally bounded space. This shall be one of the challenges for criminology during the twenty-first century.

134   *David Wall*

NOTES

1. This chapter builds upon and develops themes that were first raised in Wall (1997). My thanks go to the editors and also Yaman Akdeniz and Clive Walker at the University of Leeds.
2. The term Internet is also frequently referred to as the information super-highway. It is the medium which facilitates the World Wide Web, newsgroups, file transfer protocol (FTP), gophers, Internet Relay Chat (IRC), e-mail and other methods of communication.
3. The term 'social' is being used quite broadly, given the recent debates over the death of the social (Rose, 1996: 327).
4. Paraphrasing John Perry Barlow's 'Selling Wine Without Bottles: the Economy of Mind on the Global Net' <http://www.eff.org/pub/ Publications/John Perry Barlow/HTML/idea economy article.html>
5. Extending Braverman's (1976) hypothesis to the construction of social life.
6. For a discussion of the policing and maintenance of intellectual property see Wall (1996).
7. Although a number of cases involving child pornography are currently in the process of going through the courts.
8. See the FBI pages at <http://www.fbi.gov>, more specifically see <http://www.fbi.gov/congress/compcrm/compcrm.htm>
9. Pub. L. No. 99-474, 100 Stat. 1213 (1986) with the amending 18 U.S.C. § 1030.
10. Rather confusingly, the UN have tended to use the term 'computer crime' to include many of the activities referred to in this chapter as cybercrimes.
11. In March 1997 Pryce admitted 12 offences under the Computer Misuse Act 1990 which makes hacking/trespass a criminal act; however, conspiracy charges against both Bevan and Pryce were dropped in November 1997 (Ungoed-Thomas, 1998: 2).
12. Perhaps the greatest irony of Bevan's case is that he is now employed as a security consultant by the types of institutions into whose systems he once used to hack, in order to test their online security systems.
13. For further discussion of the 'demonisation' of the hacker see Chandler (1996); Duff and Gardiner (1996); Ross (1990: para 4); Sterling (1994).
14. For further details of Information Warfare see United States Air Force Fact Sheet 95-20; also see Szafranski, (1995). Also see the executive summary of the Information Warfare Tutorial at <http:/ /144.99.192.240/usacs/iw/tutorial/exesum.htm>.
15. At the time of writing (April 1998) a number of examples of hacked web sites could be found at <http://www.2600.com>.
16. Sometimes referred to as sleeping viruses or time-bombs.
17. An example of computer spying was illustrated in the case of the Hanover Group (Hafner and Markoff, 1991; Young, 1995: 11).
18. See 'Credit Card Fraud Technique' at <http://www.echotech.com/ ccfraud.htm>.

19. The concept of cyber-cash is differentiated here from the company called CyberCash which offers web and electronic credit card, cheque, and cash products (Electronic Commerce Briefing, 1998).
20. The dilution argument is highly contested (Madow, 1993).
21. For example, in the UK the authors of the Jet report, in direct contrast to those who had commissioned it, felt that its publication was in the public interest, which puts a slightly different spin on this argument. See Akdeniz (1997a).
22. <http://sunsite.unc.edu/elvis/elvishom.html>.
23. Letter to Berman dated 10/11/94.
24. Interview with Berman (see Wall, 1996).
25. See, for example, the decision in the Scientology case cited in Wallace and Mangan (1996).
26. *ACLU et al. v. Reno* (1997), 117 S. Ct. 2329.
27. In November 1997 this resulted in an EU action plan, *Communication from the Commission to the European Parliament, the Council, the Economic and Social Committee and the Committee of the Regions Action Plan on promoting safe use of the Internet*, November 1997.
28. *United States v Alkhabaz* (1997); U.S. App. LEXIS 9060; (1996) 104 F.3d 1492; (1995) 48 F.3d 1220 and U.S. App. Lexis 11244.
29. See *R. v. Zundel* 95 D.L.R. (4th) 202 (1992) and (Can.Sup. Ct. Aug. 27, 1992, unreported).
30. See Mann and Sutton (1998) for a very useful description of the use of news groups for the distribution of information about the technologies used for committing offences.
31. In the USA by the First Amendment to the US Constitution and in Canada the Canadian Charter of Rights s. 2.
32. This chapter was written after the EC report was published and it therefore does not fully engage with it.
33. Also reported at <http://www.ukvbc.net/censorship>.
34. 74 F.3d 701; 1996 U.S. App. Lexis 1069; 1996 Fed App. 0032P (6th Cir.).
35. See *R v Fellows* and *R v Arnold*, ibid.
36. *Abrams v. United States* (1919), 250 U.S. 616, 63 L. Ed. 1173, 40 S. Ct. 17 (Holmes, J., dissenting).
37. Although there are an increasing number of ways to prevent the transmission of the sender's number, especially with mobile phones.

REFERENCES

AAP Newsfeed (1998) 'Nationwide General News; Finance Wire', *AAP Newsfeed*, 18 March.
Akdeniz, Y. (1996a) 'Computer Pornography: a Comparative Study of US and UK Obscenity Laws and Child Pornography Laws in Relation to the Internet', *International Review of Law, Computers and Technology*, 10(2), 235–61.

136   *David Wall*

Akdeniz, Y. (1996b) 'Section 3 of the Computer Misuse Act 1990: an Antidote for Computer Viruses', *Web Journal of Contemporary Legal Issues*, 3.

Akdeniz, Y. (1997a) 'Governance of Pornography and Child Pornography on the Global Internet: a Multi-Layered Approach', in L. Edwards and C. Wealde (eds.), *Law and the Internet: Regulating Cyberspace* (Oxford: Hart Publishing), 222–41.

Akdeniz, Y. (1997b) 'Copyright and the Internet', *New Law Journal*, 147, 965–6.

Akdeniz, Y. (1997c) 'The Battle for the Communications Decency Act 1996 is Over', *New Law Journal*, 147, 1003.

Barlow, J. P. (1994) 'The Economy of Ideas: a Framework for Rethinking Patents and Copyrights in the Digital Age (Everything you Know about Intellectual Property is Wrong)', *Wired*, 2(3), 84.

Baudrillard, J. (1988) 'Consumer Society', in M. Poster, *Jean Baudrillard: Selected Writings* (Oxford: Blackwell), 29–56.

Benedikt, M. (ed.) (1991) *Cyberspace: the First Steps* (Cambridge, Mass.: MIT Press).

Betts, M. and Anthes, G. H. (1995) 'On-line Boundaries Unclear: Internet Tramples Legal Jurisdictions', *Computerworld*, 5 June, 16.

Blakey, D. (1996) 'Policing Cyberspace', *Policing Today*, 2(1), 19–21.

Bottoms, A. and Wiles, P. (1996) 'Understanding Crime Prevention in Late Modern Societies', in T. Bennett (ed.), *Preventing Crime and Disorder: Targeting Strategies and Responsibilities* (Cambridge: University of Cambridge, Institute of Criminology).

Box, S. (1983) *Power, Crime and Mystification* (London: Routledge).

Boyle, J. (1996) *Shamans, Software and Spleens: Law and the Construction of the Information Society* (Cambridge, Mass.: Harvard University Press).

Braithwaite, J. (1992) *Crime, Shame and Reintegration* (Cambridge: Cambridge University Press).

Braverman, H. (1976) *Labour and Monopoly Capital* (New York: Monthly Review Press).

Byassee, W. S. (1995) 'Jurisdiction of Cyberspace: Applying Real World Precedent to the Virtual Community', *Wake Forest Law Review*, 30, 197–220.

Campbell, D. (1997) 'More Naked Gun than Top Gun', *The Guardian* (OnLine), 27 November, 2.

Chandler, A. (1996) 'The Changing Definition and Image of Hackers in Popular Discourse', *International Journal of the Sociology of Law*, 24, 229–51.

Cohen, S. (1980) *Folk Devils and Moral Panics* (Oxford: Basil Blackwell).

Cook, N. (1998) 'The Big Question: Can Saddam be Beaten by Bombing Alone?', *Jane's Defence Weekly*, 29(8), 19.

Dolinar, L. (1998) 'Hackers hit Pentagon System/Organised Attack Highlights Flaws', *Newsday*, 26 February, A03.

Duff, L. and Gardiner, S. (1996) 'Computer Crime in the Global Village: Strategies for Control and Regulation – in Defence of the Hacker', *International Journal of the Sociology of Law*, 24, 211–28.

Electronic Commerce Briefing (1998) 'CyberCash still Chasing the Money', *Electronic Commerce Briefing*, no. 506, 1 March.

Escobar, A. (1996) 'Welcome to Cyberia: Notes on the Anthropology of Cyberculture', in Z. Saradar and J. R. Ravetz (eds.), *Cyberfutures: Culture and Politics on the Information Superhighway* (London: Pluto Press).

European Commission Select Committee (1996) *Green Paper on the Protection of Minors and Human Dignity in Audio-Visual and Information Services* (Brussels-Luxembourg).

Fraser, B. T. (1996) 'Computer Crime Research Resources', School of Library and Information Studies, Florida State University, <http://mailer.fsu.edu/~btf1553/ccrr/search1.htm>.

Gibson, W. (1984) *Neuromancer* (London: HarperCollins).

Giddens, A. (1990) *The Consequences of Modernity* (London: Polity Press).

Gottfredson, G. and Hirschi, T. (1990) *A General Theory of Crime* (Stanford: Stanford University Press).

Greenberg, S. (1997) 'Threats, Harassment and Hate On-line: Recent Developments', *The Boston Public Interest Law Journal*, 6, 673.

Grundy, M. and Wood, B. (eds.) (1996) *A Growth Industry: the Theft of Computer Hardware and Component Parts* (Manchester: Henry Fielding Centre, University of Manchester, Association of Chief Police Officers).

Gunner, E. (1998) 'Rogue Hacker Turned Legit Code-Cracker', *Computer Weekly*, 7 May, 5.

Gwynne, S. C. (1997) 'Love Me Legal Tender', *Time Magazine*, 11 August, 46–9.

Hafner, K. and Markoff, J. (1991) *Cyberpunk: Outlaws and Hackers on the Computer Frontier* (New York: Simon & Schuster).

The Herald (1996) 'Inquiry into Pornography on Tory Students' Internet Page', *The (Glasgow) Herald*, 19 August, 6.

House of Lords Select Committee on Science and Technology (1995–6) *Information Society*, HL 77 (London: HMSO).

Johnson, D. and Post, D. G. (1996) 'Law and Borders: the Rise of Law in Cyberspace', <http://www.law.syr.edu/Course.Materials/Chon/borders.html>.

Kumar, K. (1978) *Prophecy and Progress: the Sociology of Post-Industrial Society* (Harmondsworth: Penguin).

Levi, A. (1985) 'A Criminological and Sociological Approach to Theories of and Research into Economic Crime', in D. Magnuson (ed.), *Economic Crime-Programs for Future Research Report No. 18* (Stockholm: National Council for Crime Prevention, Sweden), 32–72.

Lukes, S. (1974) *Power: A Radical View* (London: Macmillan).

Madow, M. (1993) 'Private Ownership of Public Image: Popular Culture and Publicity Rights', *California Law Review*, 81, 125–240.

Mandel, T. F. (1993) *Surfing the Wild Internet* (SCAN: Business Intelligence Program, SRI International, Menlo Park, No. 2109, March.

Mann, D. and Sutton, M. (1998) '>>Netcrime: More Change in the Organisation of Thieving', *British Journal of Criminology*, 38, 210–29.

McCormack, M. (1997) 'Net Closing on High Profile Hackers', *Electronic Telegraph*, 23 September, Issue 851.

Nelken, D. (1997) 'White-Collar Crime', in M. Maguire, R. Morgan and R. Reiner (eds.), (1997) *The Oxford Handbook of Criminology*, 2nd edn (Oxford: Oxford University Press), 891–925.

Rheingold, H. (1994) *The Virtual Community: Homesteading the Electronic Frontier* (New York: Harper Perennial).

Rimm, M. (1995) 'Marketing Pornography on the Information Super-highway: a Survey of 917,410 Images, Descriptions, Short Stories, and Animations Downloaded 8.5 Million Times by Consumers in over 2000 Cities in Forty Countries, Provinces, and Territories', *Georgetown Law Journal*, 83(5), 1849–1934.

Rose, N. (1996) 'The Death of the Social: Re-figuring the Territory of Government', *Economy and Society*, 25, 327–56.

Ross, A. (1990), 'Hacking Away at the Counter-culture', *Postmodern Culture*, 1/1: <http://jefferson.village.virginia.edu/pmc/issue.990/contents.990.html>.

Saradar, Z. and Ravetz, J. R. (1996) 'Reaping the Technological Whirl-wind', in Z. Saradar and J. R. Ravetz (eds.), *Cyberfutures: Culture and Politics on the Information Super-highway* (London: Pluto Press).

Schlozberg, S. (1983) *Computers and Penal Legislation* (Oslo: Norwegian Research Centre for Computers and Law).

Seiber, U. (1998) *Legal Aspects of Computer Related Crime in the Information Society*, Legal Advisory Board for the Information Market, <http://www2.echo.lu/legal/en/comcrime/sieber.html>.

Sharrock, D. (1998) 'The Hacker Who Turned Himself In', *The Guardian*, 26 March, Online, 2–3.

Steele, H. L. (1997) 'The Web that Binds Us All: the Future Legal Environment of the Internet', *Houston Journal of International Law*, 19, 495–517.

Sterling, B. (1994) *The Hacker Crackdown* (London: Penguin Books).

Sussman, V. (1995) 'Policing Cyberspace', US News 38; World Rep., 23 Jan. 1995, at 54, Lexis, News Library, Usnews file, 1995 WL 3113171.

Szafranski, Col. R. (1995) 'A Theory of Information Warfare: Preparing for 2020', *Air Chronicles*, 1, 56–65. <http://www.cdsar.af.mil/apj/szfran.html>.

Tribe, L. H. (1991) 'The Constitution in Cyberspace: Law and Liberty Beyond the Electronic Frontier', *The Humanist*, 26 March, 15.

Uhlig, R. (1996) '"Safety Net" on Internet will Catch Child Porn', *Electronic Telegraph*, 23 September, no. 488.

Uhlig, R. (1997) 'Oasis Threatens Fans over Internet Piracy', *Electronic Telegraph*, Friday, 16 May, Issue 721.

Ungoed-Thomas, J. (1998) 'The Schoolboy Spy', *Sunday Times*, 29 March, 5, 1–2.

United Nations (1995), *International Review of Criminal Policy No. 43 and 44 – United Nations Manual on the Prevention and Control of Computer-Related Crime*, <http://www.ifs.univie.ac.at/~pr2gq1/rev4344.html#crime>.

Vagg, J. (1995) 'The Policing of Signs: Trademark Infringement and Law Enforcement', *European Journal on Criminal Policy and Research*, 3(2), 75–92.

Walker, C. P. (1997) 'Cyber-Contempt: Fair Trials and the Internet', in E. Barendt (ed.), *The Year Book of Media and Entertainment Law* (Oxford: Clarendon Press), 3–29.

Walker, C. P. and Akdeniz, Y. (1998) 'Virtual(e-) Democracy', *Public Law*, Autumn.

Wall, D. S. (1996), 'Reconstructing the Soul of Elvis: the Social Development and Legal Maintenance of Elvis Presley as Intellectual Property', *International Journal of the Sociology of Law*, 24, 117–43.

Wall, D. S. (1997) 'Policing the Virtual Community: the Internet, Cyber-Crimes and the Policing of Cyberspace', in P. Francis, P. Davies and V. Jupp (eds.), *Policing Futures, the Police, Law Enforcement and the Twenty-First Century* (London: Macmillan), 208–36.

Wall, D. S. (1998) 'Catching Cyber-Criminals: Policing the Internet', *International Review of Law Computers and Technology*, 12(2).

Wall, D. S. (forthcoming) *Policing the Soul of Elvis* (London: Pluto Press).

Wallace, J. and Mangan, M. (1996) *Sex, Laws and Cyberspace* (New York: Henry Holt).

Wasik, M. (1991), *Crime and the Computer* (Oxford: Clarendon Press).

Young, L. F. (1995), 'United States Computer Crime Laws, Criminals and Deterrence', *International Yearbook of Law, Computers and Technology*, 9, 1–16.

Zedner, L. (1997) 'Victims', in M. Maguire, R. Morgan and R. Reiner (eds.), *The Oxford Handbook of Criminology*, 2nd edn (Oxford: Oxford University Press), 577–611.

[2]

Digital Crime in the Twenty-First Century[1]

P. N. Grabosky and Russell G. Smith

At the beginning of the twenty-first century, the convergence of computing and communications technologies has altered considerably the way in which industrialized communities function. It has created untold benefits for education, delivery of health services, recreation, and commerce, and changed considerably the nature of modern workplaces and patterns of employment. Unfortunately, it has also created unprecedented opportunities for crime (see Grabosky and Smith, 1998). Identifying these vulnerabilities, and mobilizing appropriate countermeasures, will be one of the great challenges facing us as the new millennium unfolds.

This article will suggest that much computer-related illegality lies beyond the capacity of contemporary law enforcement and regulatory agencies alone to control, and that security in cyberspace will depend on the efforts of a wide range of institutions, as well as on a degree of self-help by potential victims of digital crime. The ideal configuration may be expected to differ, depending upon the activity in question, but is likely to entail a mix of law enforcement, technological, and market solutions. Given the fact that cyberspace knows no boundaries, and that computer crime often transcends national frontiers, effective countermeasures will also require a substantial degree of international cooperation.

P.N. Grabosky, Director of Research, and Russell G. Smith, Senior Research Analyst, Australian Institute of Criminology, GPO Box 2944, Canberra, ACT, 2601, Australia (Email: Peter.Grabosky@aic.gov.au)

We begin by discussing ten of the latest forms of digital crime — that is, crime that involves information systems as instruments or as targets of illegality. By digital, we refer to the fact that information systems simply operate by reducing data to streams of "1s" and "0s." Almost every type of information is thus able to be transmitted across telecommunications networks connected either by wires or by means of radio communications.

Varieties of Digital Crime

The variety of criminal activity that can be committed with or against information systems is surprisingly diverse. Some of these are not really new in substance — only the medium is new. Others represent entirely new forms of illegality altogether. These forms of crime are not necessarily mutually exclusive, nor is the following list exhaustive.

Theft of Telecommunications Services

The "phone phreakers" of three decades ago set a precedent for what has become a major criminal industry. The market for stolen communications services is now large. There are those who simply seek to avoid or to obtain a discount on the cost of a telephone call while there are others, such as illegal immigrants, who are unable to acquire legitimate information services without disclosing their identity and their status. There are others still who appropriate information services to conduct illicit business with less risk of detection. All pose a significant challenge to carriers, service providers, and to the general public — who often bear the financial burden of fraud.

The means of stealing telecommunications services are diverse, and include the "cloning" of cellular phones, and the counterfeiting of telephone cards. It may also entail gaining unauthorized access to an organization's telephone switchboard (PBX). By gaining access to a PBX, individuals or criminal organizations can obtain access to dial-in / dial-out circuits and then make their own calls or sell call time to third parties (Gold, 1999). Offenders may gain access to the switchboard by impersonating a technician, by fraudulently obtaining an employee's access code, or by using software available on the Internet. Some sophisticated offenders loop between PBX systems to evade detection. Additional forms of service theft include capturing "calling card" details and on-selling calls charged to the calling card account, and counterfeiting or illicit reprogramming of stored value telephone cards.

It has been suggested that as long ago as 1990, security failures at one major telecommunications carrier cost approximately £290 million, and that more recently, up to five per cent of total industry turnover has been lost to fraud (Schieck, 1995, 2–5; Newman, 1998). Costs to individual subscribers can also be significant. In one case, computer hackers in the United States illegally obtained access to Scotland Yard's telephone network and made £620,000 worth of international calls for which Scotland Yard was responsible (Tendler and Nuttall, 1996).

Communications in Furtherance of Criminal Conspiracies

Just as legitimate organizations in the private and public sectors rely upon information systems for communications and record keeping, so too are the activities of criminal organizations enhanced by technology. There is evidence of telecommunications equipment being used to facilitate organized drug trafficking, gambling, prostitution, money laundering, child pornography, and trade in weapons (in those jurisdictions where such activities are illegal). The use of encryption technology may also place criminal communications beyond the reach of law enforcement.

The use of computer networks to produce and distribute child pornography has become the subject of increasing attention. Today, these materials can be imported across national borders at the speed of light (Grant, David, and Grabosky, 1997). The more overt manifestations of Internet child pornography entail a modest degree of organization, as required by the infrastructure of IRC and WWW, but the activity appears largely confined to individuals.

By contrast, some of the less publicly visible traffic in child pornography activity appears to entail a greater degree of organization. Although knowledge is confined to that conduct that has been the target of successful police investigation, there appear to have been a number of networks established that have extended across national borders, use sophisticated technologies of concealment, and entail a significant degree of coordination.

Illustrative of such activity was the Wonderland Club, an international network with members in at least fourteen nations ranging from Europe, through North America, to Australia. Access to the group was password protected, and content was encrypted. Police investigation of the activity, code-named "Operation Cathedral" resulted in approximately 100 arrests around the world, and the seizure of over 100,000 images in September, 1998.

Information Piracy/Counterfeiting/Forgery

Digital technology permits perfect reproduction and easy dissemination of print, graphics, sound, and multimedia combinations. It is now possible, for example, to download music from the latest compact disks and feature films from the Internet. The temptation to reproduce copyright material for personal use, for sale at a lower price, or indeed, for free distribution, has proven irresistible to many. According to the *Straits Times* (8 November 1999), a copy of the most recent James Bond Film *The World Is Not Enough*, was available free on the Internet before its official release. This, and similar incidents, have caused considerable concern to owners of copyright material. When creators of a work, in whatever medium, are unable to profit from their creations, there can be a chilling effect on creative effort generally, in addition to financial loss.

Each year, it has been estimated that losses of between US$15 and US$17 billion are sustained by industry by reason of copyright infringement (United States, Information Infrastructure Task Force, 1995, 131). The Software Publishers Association has estimated that $7.4 billion worth of software was lost to piracy in 1993 with $2 billion of that being stolen from the Internet (Meyer and Underwood, 1994). Ryan (1998) puts the cost of foreign piracy to American industry at more than $10 billion in 1996, including $1.8 billion in the film industry, $1.2 billion in music, $3.8 billion in business application software, and $690 million in book publishing.

As broadband services continue to become available with text, graphics, sound, and video information being freely accessible via cable modems, the potential for copyright infringement involving such works will be enhanced enormously.

Dissemination of Offensive Materials

Content considered by some to be objectionable exists in abundance in cyberspace. This includes, among much else, sexually explicit materials (including child pornography, as we have seen above), racist propaganda, and instructions for the fabrication of incendiary and explosive devices. Telecommunications systems can also be used for harassing, threatening or intrusive communications, from the traditional obscene telephone call to its contemporary manifestation in "cyber-stalking," in which persistent messages are sent to an unwilling recipient.

One man allegedly stole nude photographs of his former girlfriend and her new boyfriend and posted them on the Internet, along with her name, address, and telephone number. The unfortunate couple, residents of Kenosha, Wisconsin, received phone calls and e-mails from strangers as far away as Denmark who said they had seen the photos on the Internet. Investigations also revealed that the suspect was maintaining records about the woman's movements and compiling information about her family (Spice and Sink, 1999).

In another case a rejected suitor posted invitations on the Internet under the name of a 28-year-old woman, the would-be object of his affections, that said that she had fantasies of rape and gang rape. He then communicated via email with men who replied to the solicitations and gave out personal information about the woman, including her address, phone number, details of her physical appearance and how to bypass her home security system. Strange men turned up at her home on six different occasions and she received many obscene phone calls. Although the woman was not physically assaulted, she would not answer the phone, was afraid to leave her home, and lost her job (Miller, 1999; Miller and Maharaj, 1999).

One former university student in California used email to harass five female students in 1998. He bought information on the Internet about the women using a professor's credit card and then sent 100 messages including death threats, graphic sexual descriptions, and references to their daily activities. He apparently made the threats in response to perceived teasing about his appearance.

Digital Extortion

Computer networks may also be used in carrying out criminal extortion. *The Sunday Times* (London) reported in 1996, that over forty financial institutions in the United Kingdom and the United States had been attacked electronically during the previous three years. In England, financial institutions were reported to have paid significant amounts to sophisticated computer criminals who threatened to wipe out computer systems (*The Sunday Times*, 2 June 1996). The article cited four incidents between 1993 and 1995 in which a total of £42.5 million were paid by senior executives of the organizations concerned, who were convinced of the extortionists' capacity to crash their computer systems (Denning, 1999, 233–4).

One case, which illustrates the transnational reach of extortionists, involved a number of German hackers who compromised the system of an Internet Service Provider (ISP) in South Florida, disabling eight of the ISPs ten servers. The offenders obtained personal information and credit card details of 10,000 subscribers, and, communicating via electronic mail through one of the compromised accounts, demanded that US$30,000 be delivered to a mail drop in Germany. Cooperation between United States and German authorities resulted in the arrest of the extortionists (Bauer, 1998).

More recently, an extortionist in Eastern Europe obtained the credit card details of customers of a North American–based on-line music retailer, and published some on the Internet when the retailer refused to comply with his demands (Markoff, 2000).

Electronic Money Laundering and Tax Evasion

For some time now, electronic funds transfers have assisted in concealing and in moving the proceeds of crime. Emerging technologies will greatly assist in concealing the origin of ill-gotten gains. Legitimately derived income may also be more easily concealed from taxation authorities. Large financial institutions will no longer be the only ones with the ability to achieve electronic funds transfers transiting numerous jurisdictions at the speed of light. The development of informal banking institutions and parallel banking systems may permit central bank supervision to be bypassed, but can also facilitate the evasion of cash transaction reporting requirements in those nations which have them. Traditional underground banks, that have flourished in Asian countries for centuries, will enjoy even greater capacity through the use of telecommunications.

With the emergence and proliferation of various technologies of electronic commerce, one can easily envisage how traditional countermeasures against money laundering and tax evasion may soon be of limited value. I may soon be able to sell you a quantity of heroin, in return for an untraceable transfer of stored value to my "smart-card," which I then download anonymously to my account in a financial institution situated in an overseas jurisdiction that protects the privacy of banking clients. I can discreetly draw upon these funds as and when I may require, downloading them back to my stored value card (Wahlert, 1996).

Electronic Vandalism and Terrorism

As never before, western industrial society is dependent upon complex data processing and telecommunications systems. Damage to, or interference with, any of these systems can lead to catastrophic consequences. Whether motivated by curiosity or vindictiveness, electronic intruders cause inconvenience at best, and have the potential for inflicting massive harm (Hundley and Anderson, 1995; Schwartau, 1994).

Although this potential has yet to be realized, a number of individuals and protest groups have hacked the official web pages of various governmental and commercial organizations (Rathmell, 1997).[2] This may also operate in reverse. Early in 1999, an organized hacking incident was apparently directed at a server that hosted the Internet domain for East Timor, which at the time was seeking its independence from Indonesia (Creed, 1999).

Defense planners around the world are investing substantially in information warfare means of disrupting the information technology infrastructure of defense systems (Stix, 1995).[3] Attempts were made to disrupt the computer systems of the Sri Lankan Government (Associated Press, 1998), and of the North Atlantic Treaty Organization during the 1999 bombing of Belgrade (British Broadcasting Corporation, 1999).

Electronic Sales and Investment Fraud

As electronic commerce becomes more prevalent, the application of digital technology to fraudulent business endeavors will be that much greater. The use of the telephone for fraudulent sales pitches, deceptive charitable solicitations, or bogus investment overtures is increasingly common. Cyberspace now abounds with a wide variety of investment opportunities, from traditional securities such as stocks and bonds, to more exotic possibilities such as coconut farming, the sale and leaseback of automatic teller machines, and worldwide telephone lotteries (Cella and Stark, 1997, 837–44). Indeed, the digital age has been accompanied by unprecedented opportunities for misinformation. Fraudsters now enjoy direct access to millions of prospective victims around the world, instantaneously and at minimal cost.

Classic pyramid schemes and "Exciting, Low-Risk Investment Opportunities" are not uncommon. The technology of the World Wide Web is ideally suited to investment solicitations. In the words of two SEC staff: "At very little cost, and from the privacy of a basement office or living room, the fraudster can produce a home page that looks better and more sophisticated than that of a Fortune 500 company" (Cella and Stark, 1997, 822).

Illegal Interception of Digital Information

Developments also provide new opportunities for electronic eavesdropping. From activities as time-honored as surveillance of an unfaithful spouse, to the newest forms of political and industrial espionage, information interception has increasing applications. Here again, technological developments create new vulnerabilities. In New York, for example, two individuals recently used a sophisticated scanning device to pick up some 80,000 cellular telephone numbers from motorists who drove past their Brooklyn apartment. Had the two not been arrested, they could have used the information to create cloned mobile telephones which could have resulted in up to $100 million in illegal calls being made (*West Australian*, 9 July 1996, 47). Organized criminals in Amsterdam have obtained unauthorized access to information systems of the Dutch police.

The electromagnetic signals emitted by a computer may themselves be intercepted. Cables may act as broadcast antennas. In many jurisdictions, existing law does not prevent the remote monitoring of computer radiation. It has been reported that the notorious American hacker Kevin Poulsen was able to gain access to law enforcement and national security wiretap data prior to his arrest in 1991 (Littman, 1997). In 1995, hackers employed by a criminal organization attacked the communications system of the Amsterdam Police. The hackers succeeded in gaining police operational intelligence, and in disrupting police communications (Rathmell, 1997).

Electronic Funds Transfer Crime

The proliferation of electronic funds transfer systems will enhance the risk that such transactions may be intercepted and diverted. Existing systems such as Automated Teller Machines, and Electronic Funds Transfer at Point of Sale technologies have already been the targets of fraudulent activity and the development of stored value cards or smart cards, super smart cards and optical memory cards will no doubt invite some individuals to apply their talents to the challenge of electronic counterfeiting and overcoming security access systems. Just as the simple telephone card can be reprogrammed, smart cards are vulnerable to re-engineering. Credit card details can be captured and used by unauthorized persons. The transfer of funds from home between accounts and in payment of transactions will also create vulnerabilities in terms of theft and fraud and the widescale development of electronic money for use on the Internet will lead to further opportunities for crime. What for the past quarter century has been loosely described as "computer fraud" will have numerous new manifestations.

In 1994, a Russian hacker, Vladimir Levin, operating from St. Petersburg, accessed the computers of Citibank's central wire transfer department, and transferred funds from large corporate accounts to other accounts, which had been opened by his accomplices in the United States, the Netherlands, Finland, Germany, and Israel. Officials from one of the corporate victims, located in Argentina, notified the bank, and the suspect accounts, located in San Francisco, were frozen. The accomplice was arrested. Another accomplice was caught attempting to withdraw funds from an account in Rotterdam. Although Russian law precluded Levin's extradition, he was arrested during a visit to the United States and subsequently imprisoned (Denning, 1999, 55).

Common Themes and Issues

Secrecy and Anonymity

A number of common themes and issues are present in each of the forms of digital crime described above. The first concerns the way in which technologies can conceal the content of communications and disguise the identity of users. Technologies of encryption, for example, can limit access by law enforcement personnel to communications carried out in furtherance of a conspiracy, or to the dissemination of objectionable materials between consenting parties (Denning, 1999). Also important are technologies for concealing a communicator's identity. Electronic impersonation, colloquially termed "spoofing," can be used in furtherance of a variety of criminal activities, including fraud, criminal conspiracy, harassment, and vandalism. Technologies of anonymity further complicate the task of identifying a suspect (Froomkin, 1995).

In addition to victims of digital crime being reluctant to report their victimization to the authorities, the technologies of secrecy and anonymity noted above often make detection of the offender extremely difficult. Those who seek to mask their identity on computer networks are often able to do so, by means of "looping," or "weaving" through multiple sites in a variety of nations. Anonymous remailers and encryption devices can shield one from the scrutiny of all but the most determined and technologically sophisticated regulatory and enforcement agencies. Some crimes do not result in detection or loss until some time after the event. Considerable time may elapse before the activation of a computer virus, or between the insertion of a "logic bomb" and its detonation. Finally, technology has greatly facilitated so-called identity-related economic crime in which offenders fabricate documents through the use of desktop publishing equipment to misrepresent their own identity or make use of another's identity for illegitimate purposes (Smith, 1999).

Motivations

Given the diversity of digital crime, it is not surprising that the various types of behavior discussed above flow from a wide range of motives. Some of these are as old as human society, including greed, lust, revenge, and curiosity. Revenge in the modern era can also entail an ideological dimension. Of considerable significance, if not unique to computer related crime, is the intellectual challenge of defeating a complex system. Motivations, whether on the part of individuals or in the aggregate, are very difficult to change. For this reason, the most strategically advantageous approaches to digital crime will be concerned with the reduction of opportunities, and with the enhancement of guardianship.

Opportunities

While motives tend not to change, the variety and number of opportunities for the commission of digital crime have proliferated. The exponential growth in connectivity of computing and communications creates parallel opportunities for prospective offenders, and parallel risks for prospective victims. As the Internet becomes increasingly a medium of commerce, it will become increasingly a medium of fraud.

The most effective way of eliminating opportunities for digital crime is simply to pull the plug. This is of course unrealistic — the affluent nations of the world are now highly dependent on information technology. For the poorer nations, information technology is probably a necessary, if not sufficient, path to economic development. Thus, the challenge lies in managing risk so as to achieve the maximum benefits that flow from new technologies, while minimizing the downside. A merchant could scrutinize every credit card transaction to drastically reduce the risk of fraud, but in the process drive away legitimate customers. At a higher level, nations around the world are in the process of forging policies on where to draw the line on such fundamental questions as the balance between the citizen's privacy and the imperatives of law enforcement, and freedom of expression versus the protection of certain cultural values.

There are many technologies that reduce the opportunity to commit digital crime. Given that so much digital crime depends upon unauthorized access to information systems, access control and authentication technologies have become essential. Sophisticated advice and products for computer crime prevention are provided by one of the world's growth industries today, namely computer security.

Denning (1999) offers a comprehensive inventory of technologies for reducing opportunities for computer crime. She describes technologies of encryption and anonymity, which permit concealment of the content of communications (such as a consumer's credit card details, or the identity of the communicator (not all participants in discussion groups on reproductive health wish to disclose their identities). Denning also outlines technologies of authentication, from basic passwords to various biometric devices such as fingerprint or voice recognition technology and retinal imaging, which greatly enhance the difficulty of obtaining unauthorized access to information systems. Virus detectors can identify and block malicious computer code, while blocking and filtering programs can screen out unwanted content. A rich variety of commercial software now exists with which to block access to certain sites (Venditto, 1996).

Guardians

Much digital crime takes place simply because of the absence of a capable guardian. Capable guardianship has evolved over human history, from feudalism to the rise of the state and the proliferation of public institutions of social control, as well as to the post-modern era in which employees of private security services vastly outnumber sworn police officers in many industrial democracies. Here again, it may be instructive to compare digital crime with more conventional types of crime.

Guardianship against conventional crime involves preventive efforts on the part of prospective victims, contributions by members of the general public or commercial third parties, as well as the activities of law enforcement agencies. Indeed, it is often only when private efforts at crime prevention fail that the criminal process is mobilized. So it is that owners of motor vehicles are encouraged to lock their vehicles at all times, that insurance contracts may offer premium discounts for crime prevention measures such as theft alarms, and that some car parks have video surveillance or private security guards in attendance. Often, it is only when these systems fail that the assistance of law enforcement is sought.

Technology can also enhance guardianship. Denning (1999) describes various technologies for detecting attempted intrusions into information systems. Alarms can indicate when repeated login attempts fail because of incorrect passwords or when access is sought outside of normal working hours. Other anomaly detection devices will identify unusual patterns of system use, including atypical destination and duration of telephone calls, or unusual spending patterns using credit cards.

Guardianship can also be enhanced by market forces. A market is currently emerging for ISPs specializing in content suitable for family consumption, guaranteed to be free of sex, violence, and vilification. Market forces may also generate second-order controlling influences. As large organizations begin to appreciate their vulnerability to electronic theft or vandalism, they may be expected to insure against potential losses. It is very much in the interests of insurance companies to require appropriate security precautions on the part of their policyholders. Indeed, decisions to set and to price insurance may well depend upon security practices of prospective policy holders. Sub-contractors may also be required to have strict IT integrity programs in place as a condition of doing business.

Citizen concern about the availability of undesirable content has given rise to the private monitoring and surveillance of cyberspace. Among the more prominent organizations involved in such surveillance is the Simon Wiesenthal Center, whose "CyberWatch Hotline"[4] invites notification of anti–Semitic and racist material.

Citizen co-production can also complement activities undertaken by agencies of the state. An example of collaborative public-private effort in furtherance of controlling objectionable content is the Netherlands Hotline for Child Pornography on Internet, an initiative of the Foundation for Dutch Internet

Providers (NLIP), the Dutch National Criminal Intelligence Service (CRI), Internet users, and the National Bureau against Racism (LBR). Users who encounter child pornography originating in the Netherlands, identifiable by a domain name address ending in "nl" are encouraged to report the site to meld-punt@xs4all.nl. The originator is warned about the posting, and asked to desist from further such activity. If the warning is ignored, then the hotline will forward any available information to the vice-squad of the local police.[5]

The policing of terrestrial space is now very much a pluralistic endeavor, and so too is the policing of cyberspace. Responsibilities for the control of digital crime will be similarly shared between agents of the state, information security specialists in the private sector, and the individual user. In cyberspace today, as in terrestrial space two millennia ago, the first line of defense will be self-defense — in other words, minding one's own store.

Extra-Territorial Issues

One of the more significant aspects of digital crime is its global reach. Although international offending is by no means a uniquely modern phenomenon, the global nature of cyberspace significantly enhances the ability of offenders to commit crimes in one country that will affect individuals in a variety of other countries. This poses great challenges for the detection, investigation, and prosecution of offenders.

Two problems arise in relation to the prosecution of telecommunications offenses that have an inter-jurisdictional aspect: first, determining where the offense occurred in order to decide which law to apply and, secondly, obtaining evidence and ensuring that the offender can be located and tried before a court. Both these questions raise complex legal problems of jurisdiction and extradition (see Lanham, Weinberg, Brown, and Ryan, 1987).

Even if one is able to decide which law is applicable, further difficulties may arise in applying that law. In a unitary jurisdiction, such as New Zealand, where there is one law and one law enforcement agency, determining and applying the applicable law is difficult enough. Criminal activities committed from across the globe, however, pose even greater problems. Sovereign governments are finding it difficult to exercise control over online behavior at home, not to mention abroad. A resident of Chicago who falls victim to a telemarketing scam originating in Albania, for example, can expect little assistance from law enforcement agencies in either jurisdiction. As a result, regulation by territorially-based rules may prove to be inappropriate for these types of offenses (Post, 1995).

Extraterritorial law enforcement costs are also often prohibitive. The time, money, and uncertainty required by international investigations, and if successful, extradition proceedings, can be so high as to preclude attention to all but the most serious offending. Moreover, the cooperation across international boundaries in furtherance of such enforcement usually requires a congruence of values and priorities that, despite prevailing trends towards globalization, exists only infrequently.

Other issues that may complicate investigation entail the logistics of search and seizure during real time, the sheer volume of material within which incriminating evidence may be contained, and the encryption of information, which may render it entirely inaccessible, or accessible only after a massive application of decryption technology. If an online financial newsletter originating in the Bahamas contains fraudulent speculation about the prospects of a company whose shares are traded on the Australian Stock Exchange, where has the offense occurred?

Traditionally, the jurisdiction of courts was local. That is, courts could only entertain prosecutions in respect to offenses committed against local laws where there existed a sufficient link between the offense and the jurisdiction in question. There is, however, always the possibility that legislatures will confer extraterritorial jurisdiction for some crimes. Some common examples include offenses committed on the high seas, counterfeiting offenses, crimes committed by members of the defense forces, and, recently in Australia, sexual relations between Australians and children overseas who are under sixteen years of age.

In rare circumstances, a nation's laws may apply to acts committed overseas by foreign nationals. Recent war crimes prosecutions in Australia involved defendants resident elsewhere at the times the alleged offenses were committed. These circumstances are, to say the least, most unusual. But in a shrinking world where the financial burdens of extradition are unlikely to decline, they may become more common.

To the extent that international digital crime is amenable to international enforcement, it will require concerted international co-operation. Past performance in the context of other forms of criminality would suggest that this cooperation is unlikely to be forthcoming except in the relatively infrequent types of illegality where there is widespread international consensus about the activity in question (such as child pornography or fraud on a scale likely to destabilize financial markets), and about the desirability of suppressing it. In many instances, extradition is likely to be more cumbersome, the greater the cultural and ideological distance between the two parties.

Even so, this would assume a seamless world system of stable sovereign states—such a system does not exist today, nor is it likely to exist in our lifetime. Law enforcement and regulatory vacuums exist in some parts of the world, certainly in those settings where the state has effectively collapsed. Even where state power does exist in full force, the corruption of individual regimes can impede international cooperation.

Countermeasures

It has long been recognized that the criminal justice system is a very imperfect means of social control, and that effective crime prevention requires the contribution of families, schools, and many other institutions of civil society. This is no less the case with digital crime than it is with traditional forms. It will be immediately apparent that the detection, investigation, and prosecution of all of the above forms of digital crime pose formidable challenges. Crime in the digital age can be committed by an individual in one jurisdiction against a victim or victims on the other side of the globe. The control of cybercrime lies beyond the capacity of any one agency. What principles can we articulate to assist us in controlling computer crime?

The Importance of Prevention

It is a great deal more difficult to pursue an online offender to the ends of the earth than to prevent the offense in the first place. The trite homily that prevention is better than cure is nowhere more appropriate than in cyberspace. It applies no less to high-technology crime than it does to residential burglary. Just as one would be most unwise to leave one's house unlocked when heading off to work in the morning, so too is it foolish to leave one's information systems accessible to unauthorized persons.

Effective digital crime prevention entails carrying out risk analyses of information systems and the creation of effective policies and procedures to protect them from damage or misuse. In the workplace, for example, policies should be created on the use of office telecommunications and computing facilities for personal purposes and whether staff should be able to encrypt communications in order to prevent them from being read by others. Efforts are also needed to ensure that software and disks are regularly checked for viruses and malicious code that could damage systems and the information that they contain.

The prevention of digital crime may also entail the use of electronic monitoring of usage. For two decades now, call accounting systems, which produce call-logs for each telephone extension, systematically compile data on the length, cost, and destination of each call. Now, new "Internet Manager" software can create custom reports on Internet usage by individual employees. Similarly, the use of sophisticated neural networks are able to analyze computer usage to ensure that unusual transactions or usage that might involve criminality are able to be promptly detected and dealt with. In making use of such electronic crime prevention technologies, however, considerations of privacy and confidentiality need to be considered and respected.

The Role of Self Help

Another key principle in the prevention of digital crime is the need to raise awareness on the part of prospective victims to the risks that they face. Individuals and institutions should be made aware of the potential consequences of an attack on their information assets, and of the basic precautionary measures that they should take. Those agencies that stand to gain the most from electronic commerce have the greatest interest in developing secure payments systems. Technologies of computer security can provide significant protection against various forms of computer crime. But there are other, "low-technology" measures that should not be overlooked. Perhaps foremost among these is staff selection. Surveys of businesses reveal that one's own staff often pose a greater threat to one's information assets than do so called "outsiders." Disgruntled employees and former employees constitute a significant risk. Suffice it to say that great care should be taken when engaging and disengaging staff, or in outsourcing IT activities to the private sector. Similarly, systems and the information contained therein should be backed up regularly. This will not prevent an attack, but it will reduce the risk of irretrievable loss of or damage to data in the event of an attack or system failure.

The Use of Non-governmental Resources

More generally, given the resource constraints that most governments face, it is desirable to enlist the assistance of private sector and community interests in the prevention and detection of digital crime.

Market forces will generate powerful influences in furtherance of electronic crime control. Given the immense fortunes that stand to be made by those who develop secure processes for electronic commerce, they hardly need any prompting from government. In some sectors, there are ample commercial incentives that can operate in furtherance of digital crime prevention. Information security promises to become one of the growth industries of this century. Some of the new developments in information security that have begun to emerge include technologies of authentication. The simple password for access to a computer system, vulnerable to theft or determination by other means, is being complemented or succeeded altogether by biometric authentication methods such as retinal imaging and voice or finger printing. Detection of unauthorized access to or use of computer systems can be facilitated by such technologies as artificial intelligence, which can identify anomalous patterns of use according to time of day and keystroke patterns.

Issues of objectionable content can be addressed at the individual level by blocking and filtering software, by which systems administrators can prevent employees' access to certain types of sites. Simple software can track web sites visited and the amount of time spent at each site. Internet Manager software enables a systems administrator to develop a custom blocking list that could deny access to pages containing certain specified keywords. Other software called Surfwatch can develop customized access categories. When an employee clicks for a page, the software matches the user ID with the content allowable for the assigned category, then either loads the requested page, or advises the user that her request has been denied. The software logs denied requests for later inspection by management. Some software packages can also measure and record the bandwith consumed by Internet applications.

In extreme cases, some would take the law into their own hands. The metaphor of cyberspace as a frontier is not entirely inappropriate. There are vigilantes in cyberspace. In some instances, self-help by victims of digital crime may itself entail illegality. "Counter-hacking" by private citizens or by government agencies, has been suggested as one way of responding to illegal intrusions. A group calling itself Ethical Hackers Against Pedophilia have threatened to disable the computers of those whom they find dealing in digital child pornography. Public sector managers would be well advised to avoid becoming the initiator or the target of counter hacking.

A radical response to the problem of software piracy is to make use of so-called Logic Bombs which are installed into programs. When activated through an act of unauthorized copying, the malicious code would destroy the copied data and even damage other software or hardware belonging to the offender.

Enhancing the Capacity of Law Enforcement

The continuing uptake of digital technology around the world means that law enforcement agencies will be required to keep abreast of rapidly developing technologies. This will entail training in new investigative techniques. As new technologies are exploited by criminals, it becomes even more important for law enforcement not to be left behind. This is a significant challenge, given the emerging trend for skilled investigators to be "poached" by the private sector. The collaboration of law enforcement with specialized expertise residing in the private sector will be a common feature in years to come.

And it will be important for public sector managers to develop close ties with law enforcement, to report suspected illegality to them, as well to provide them with assistance when required. The police and the institutions that they serve in both public and private sectors should be familiar with each others' needs.

The Importance of International Cooperation

As already mentioned, the global nature of cyberspace necessitates the development of new strategies to combat criminal activity that can originate from the other side of the world. The basic approach to overcoming the transnational issues of digital crime lies in developing cooperation between nations. This is more easily said than done, given the significant differences in legal systems, values, and priorities around the world.

Enlisting the assistance of overseas authorities is not an automatic process, and often requires pre-existing agreements relating to formal mutual assistance in criminal matters.[6] Nevertheless, there are numerous examples of successful measures, and the web of mutual assistance is being woven ever more tightly.

Conclusion

It has become trite to suggest that the world is a shrinking place. On the one hand, this shrinking is highly beneficial. People around the world now enjoy economic, cultural, and recreational opportunities that were previously not accessible. On the other hand, the rapid mobility of people, money, information, ideas, and commodities generally, has provided new opportunities for crime. Linkages between events and institutions at home and abroad are inevitable, and will inevitably proliferate. This will require unprecedented cooperation between nations, and will inevitably generate tensions arising from differences in national values. Even within nations, tensions between such values as privacy and the imperatives of law enforcement will be high on the public agenda. New organizational forms will emerge to combat new manifestations of criminality.

There is a significant danger that premature regulatory interventions may not only fail to achieve their desired effect, but may also have a negative impact on the development of technology for the benefit of all. Over-regulation, or premature regulatory intervention may run the risk of chilling investment and innovation. Given the increasingly competitive nature of the global marketplace, governments may be forced to choose between paternalistic imperatives and those of commercial development and economic growth.

The challenge facing those who would minimize digital crime is to seek a balance that would allow a tolerable degree of illegality in return for creative exploitation of the technology. Even at this early stage of the technological revolution, it may be useful for individuals, interest groups, and governments to articulate their preferences and let these serve as signals to the market. Markets may then be able to provide appropriate responses that governments are unwilling or unable to achieve. Digital crime is bound to increase as the new century unfolds. By making effective use of traditional crime control measures coupled with some sophisticated technological solutions, it may, however, be able to be kept within manageable limits.

Notes

1. This article updates and expands some material previously published as Grabosky, P. N., and Smith, R.G., 1997, "Telecommunications and Crime: Regulatory Dilemmas," *Law and Policy*, 19, 3, 317–41. Opinions expressed in this article are those of the authors and not necessarily those of the Australian Institute of Criminology or the Australian Government.

2. See also <http://www.2600.com/hacked–pages/> (visited 4 January 2000).

3. See also the website of the Institute for the Advanced Study of Information Warfare (IASIW) <http://www.psycom.net/iwar.1.html> (visited 4 May 2000).

4. See <http://www.wiesenthal.com/watch/index.html> (visited 4 May 2000).

5. More information about the Netherlands hotline against child pornography on Internet can be found at <http://www.meldpunt.org/meldpunt-eng.htm> (visited 4 May 2000).

6. Following recent amendments to the Mutual Assistance in Criminal Matters Act 1987, Australia may now grant assistance in criminal matters to any country. Bilateral mutual assistance treaties are currently in force with 18 nations. A further four treaties have been signed, but are not yet in force.

References

Associated Press. (1998). First Cyber Terrorist Action Reported. <*http://www.tech-server.com/newsroom/ntn/info/050698/info9_25501_noframes.html*> (visited 4 January 2000).

British Broadcasting Corporation. (1999). Nato Under "Cyber Attack," <*http://www.flora.org/flora.mai-not/10498*> (visited 4 January 1999).

Creed, A. (1999). Indonesian Govt. Suspected in Irish ISP Hack. *Newsbytes*, 21 February. <*http://www.ccurrents.com/newstoday/99/02/21/news8.html*> (visited 10 January 2000).

Denning, D. (1999). *Information Warfare and Security*. Boston: Addison Wesley.

Edwards, O. (1995). Hackers from Hell. *Forbes*, 9 October, p. 182.

Gold, S. (1999). BT Starts Switchboard Anti-Hacking Investigation. *Newsbytes*, 11 January. <http://www.infowar.com/> (visited 23 December 1999).

Grabosky, P. N., and Smith, R. G. (1998). *Crime in the Digital Age: Controlling Telecommunications and Cyberspace Illegalities*, Leichhardt: Federation Press/New Brunswick: Transaction Publishers.

Grant, A., David, F., and Grabosky, P. (1997). Child Pornography in the Digital Age. *Transnational Organized Crime*, 3 (4), 171–88.

Hundley, R., and Anderson, R. (1995). Emerging Challenge: Security and Safety in Cyberspace. *IEEE Technology and Society Magazine*, 14 (4), 19–28.

Lanham, D., Weinberg, M., Brown, K. E., and Ryan, G. (1987). *Criminal Fraud*. Sydney: Law Book Co.

Littman, J. (1997). *The Watchman: The Twisted Life and Crimes of Serial Hacker Kevin Poulsen*. Boston: Little Brown.

Meyer, M., and Underwood, A. (1994). Crimes of the Net. *Bulletin/Newsweek*, 15 November, pp. 68–9.

Miller, G., and Maharaj, D. (1999). N. Hollywood man charged in 1st cyber-stalking case. *Los Angeles Times*, 22 January. <http://www.cs.csubak.edu/~donna/news/crime.html#stalking> (visited 12 June 1999).

Newman, K. (1998). Phone Call Scams Skim Off Millions. *New Zealand Herald*, 20 August. <*http://www.infowar.com/*> (visited 23 December 1999).

Post, D. G. (1995). Anarchy, State, and the Internet: An Essay on Law-Making in Cyberspace. *Journal of ONLINE Law*, art. 3.

Rathmell, A. (1997). Cyber-terrorism: The Shape of Future Conflict? *Royal United Service Institute Journal*, October, pp. 40–6 <*http://www.kcl.ac.uk/orgs/icsa/rusi.htm#who*> (visited 21 December 1999).

Ryan, M. (1998). *Knowledge Diplomacy: Global Competition and the Politics of Intellectual Property*. Washington, DC: Brookings.

Schieck, M. (1995). Combating Fraud in Cable and Telecommunications. *IIC Communications Topics*, No. 13. London: International Institute of Communications.

Schwartau, W. (1994). *Information Warfare: Chaos on the Electronic Superhighway*. New York: Thunder's Mouth Press.

Smith, R. G. (1999). Identity-Related Economic Crime: Risks and Countermeasures. In *Trends and Issues in Crime and Criminal Justice*, No. 129. Canberra: Australian Institute of Criminology.

Stoll, C. (1991). *The Cuckoo's Egg*. London: Pan Books.

Tendler, S., and Nuttall, N. (1996). Hackers Leave Red-Faced Yard with $1.29m Bill. *The Australian*, 6 August, p. 37.

Two on Phone Scam Counts. (1996).*West Australian*, 9 July, p. 47.

United States, Information Infrastructure Task Force 1995. *Intellectual Property and the National Information Infrastructure: Report of the Working Group on Intellectual Property Rights*. (Bruce A. Lehman: Chair). Washington, DC: United States Patent and Trademark Office.

Venditto, G. (1996). Safe Computing. *Internet World*, September, pp. 48–58.

Wahlert, G. (1996). Implications for Law Enforcement of the Move to a Cashless Society. In Graycar, A., and Grabosky, P. N. (eds.). *Money Laundering* (pp. 22–8). Canberra: Australian Institute of Criminology.

[3]

DIALOGUE AND DEBATE
THE NATURE OF VIRTUAL CRIMINALITY

Alan Norrie

The latest contribution to our *Dialogue and Debate* section is stimulated by Wanda Capeller's bold and wide-ranging attempt to grasp the nature of virtual criminality as a phenomenon of the internet age. Moving from a discussion of emergent characteristics of late modern society to forms of criminal deviance and modes of regulation, Capeller suggests that the internet has to be seen as giving rise to new forms of criminality and new problems of regulation. She suggests that these in turn invoke the need for a new criminological paradigm, one that emphasizes the abstract, systemic nature of criminality in the computer age. Her article is a sophisticated attempt to think about the nature of crime, criminality and its control in the context of a new social medium and changing social times.

Responding to Capeller, Peter Grabosky is sceptical about the absolute novelty of these phenomena, and he relates new forms of crime and problems of control to characteristics of criminality that predate the development of the internet. At the same time, he acknowledges that recognizable crimes can now be committed in completely different ways, and that problems of regulation are concomitantly enhanced. Francis Snyder takes up Capeller's arguments about the novelty of internet crime and its control. Drawing on his experience of transnational regulation in other areas, he argues that the field must be understood not only in terms of new sites of criminality, but also in terms of new sites of governance which draw on different modes of control. He concludes by encouraging Capeller to develop her conception of a new systemic paradigm for computer crime.

It is plain that the internet has opened up many new opportunities for communication and that many of these have positive social effects. It is also clear that it has introduced a whole series of new phenomena, issues and problems that are central to our understanding of modern crime, crime control and criminality. It is on the precise character of these phenomena that the present dialogue hinges. In considering something so novel as internet crime, it serves to initiate debate and to raise as many questions as it answers. We hope that

SOCIAL & LEGAL STUDIES 0964 6639 (200106) 10:2 Copyright © 2001
SAGE Publications, London, Thousand Oaks, CA and New Delhi,
Vol. 10(2), 227–228; 017403

it will provoke further thought and investigation into a set of problems that will surely not recede as technology advances.

As ever, we are reliant on our readers and writers to pursue the debates published in these pages. We would in this case particularly like to thank Andre-Jean Arnaud for his assistance in bringing this discussion to fruition. If you would like to contribute further thoughts on the arguments presented here, or suggest other issues for discussion, please write to Alan Norrie at *School of Law, King's College London, Strand, London WC2R 2LS*, UK [alan.norrie@kcl.ac.uk].

[4]

NOT SUCH A NEAT NET: SOME COMMENTS ON VIRTUAL CRIMINALITY

WANDA CAPELLER
Université des Sciences Sociales de Toulouse, France

At the level of the advanced technologies, we seem to be witnessing a change of perspective concerning our ability to control, and even to understand, events. (Paul Virilio, *Un paysage d'événements*, 1996)

INTRODUCTION

THE INTENSE development of communication technologies and the advent of virtual reality requires the scientific community to revise its philosophical, historical and sociological assumptions. New techno-social realities appear nowadays as a 'material context' in the form of electronic meeting points where the corporeal limits of communication are surpassed (Grass, 1989). Cyberspace, where these technological and cultural mutations occur, and where abstract worlds based on the simulation of the real world are possible, reflects above all a society of individuals (Virilio, 1996: 24). Traditional forms of social recognition and social integration are altered by changes in the means of communication and information. Consequently, cyberspace requires a rethink of the most tangible political and ethical problems of contemporary society (Holmes, 1997: 1).

While cyberspace is used in a purely instrumental way, to acquire things and to satisfy needs, it might also be seen as a world where new cultural forms are being created, which have an immediate and active effect on the lives of people (Holmes, 1997: 3). In this sense, David Holmes maintains that, more than a tool at the service of pre-established communities, virtual technologies and the authorities that are represented in them are contexts where new realities and new politics emerge, in 'world-spaces' and 'world-periods' which have never existed before (Holmes, 1997). A shift takes place from seeing virtual space as a service or support, to seeing it as a context where varied forms of interaction can take place.

SOCIAL & LEGAL STUDIES 0964 6639 (200106) 10:2 Copyright © 2001
SAGE Publications, London, Thousand Oaks, CA and New Delhi,
Vol. 10(2), 229–242; 017404

While techno-human interactions generally base their references on pre-virtual relationships, in this new context, there is a dematerialization of the body (Green, 1997: 59–78) and a sense of real virtual communities emerging from an apparent void. In this context, the idea of a virtual utopia where one could reappraise cultures and identities, and enjoy direct communication with others free of restriction, has given way to doubts and questions. These not only concern issues linked to identity and subjectivity, as in the new types of citizenship or 'cityzennet' (a term used in American literature; Green, 1997), but also concerns about the context in which commercial relations take place, in what is called the cybermarket. This is an open space, where unrestricted exchange takes place, and where the possibilities of state and legal regulation are still a matter of controversy. Here is precisely where one part of the illegal economy insinuates itself, just as it did in pre-virtual markets, beyond the limits allowed by different states (Capeller, 1997). The cybermarket also emerges as a criminal or deviant interactive site, forming a material context where new kinds of criminality appear, in other words, a *virtual criminality*.

Consequently, one wonders about the neutrality of virtual space and about its content. On this subject, some hold that the decline of politics, the social and the civic should be seen as constructive, as a sign of the independence of cyberspace, which should not become 'the toy of states' (Virilio, 1996: 24–5). Others maintain, however, that the digital era cannot be seen as a 'universal network without someone in charge' (Virilio, 1996: 24). In either case, one can perceive a change in behavioural patterns as deviant and criminal behaviour appear in virtual space. *Discontinuities* emerge in the criminal field, which does not mean, however, that there is a drop in the traditional forms of criminal activities. The latter continue to exist, thus also assuring *continuity*. Continuities also appear as soon as a traditional form of criminality enters the virtual world, such as organized crime. The possibility of transnational organized crime filtering into virtual contexts is unquestionable, reinforcing the possibility of new sites where interactive crime can develop.

As regards control of virtual space, it is still possible to find, under certain aspects, traces of control practices of a positivist nature, especially when dealing with computerized identification (Bourcier, 1998: 39–59). In fact, methods of identification are developed by creating 'virtual subjects' based on 'biometric systems which recognise an individual by his or her physical, morphological and even genetic characteristics' (Bourcier, 1988: 44). In general, however, a revision of criminological patterns is necessary, as the criminological universe is incapable of explaining the new forms of criminality and deviance which make up cybercrime. Perhaps these will become predominant in the 21st century, for though cyberculture is not universal, virtual criminality is expanding at an alarming rate.

In order to understand this problem better, I would like initially to explore some concepts that can be found at the centre of a study on late modern society (Giddens, 1994), in which traditional human relations are replaced by disembodied relations (Holmes, 1997). In order to understand the present analysis more clearly, these concepts can be explained as opposite pairs: *trust* and *risk*, and *anonymity* and *accountability*. After discussing these, I suggest that new forms of virtual criminality have adopted cyberspace not as a support system, but more as a way to use a framework and context that has already been created for the use of virtual communities. Consequently, it is worth analysing the way in which so-called *space traffickers'* function in cyberspace. They behave like members of a 'club' or of a community, in the more traditional sense, when really they are a virtual community. Finally I analyse the reasons for a precarious and inefficient control structure, which wrongly treats these problems in the virtual space as if it were merely a support system, and consider possible ways to develop these cybercontrol schemes. These observations suggest the need for a new criminological paradigm, which I will indicate briefly by way of conclusion.

CHANGING NOTIONS IN ADVANCED MODERNITY

TRUST AND RISK

Nowadays the notion of trust is linked to that of risk, as it presupposes, above all, an awareness of the latter. Nevertheless, according to Luhmann, trust is not the same as the feeling of security, in as far as the latter implies certainty and the stability of things that are familiar. Trust rather makes the individual return to things that are possible, and the individual who does not master the inherent implications of the available choices remains in a situation of *passive security*, exposed to dangerous situations (Giddens, 1994: 38–9). Based on these comments about advanced modernity, Anthony Giddens argues that trust is, as of now, 'connected to the absence of time and space' (Giddens, 1994: 40). According to Giddens, one does not have to trust either in someone whose activities were visible and whose ways of reasoning transparent, or in a system where the internal structures were well known and understood. Thus, as well as to risk, trust seems basically connected to uncertainty, the individual leaving his or her fate to chance.

Giddens also affirms that 'trust is not the faith in the reliability of a person or of a system', but derived from such a faith. In his own words, 'one can talk about trust towards symbolic guarantees or expert systems, but this rests on the faith in the validity of principles of which one is ignorant, and not the faith in "moral correctness" (the good intentions) of others'. Trust depends upon the *good* functioning of the system rather than how it functions as such (Giddens, 1994: 41). Relating this to the cyberworld, if the virtual space in which cybercriminality establishes itself is shaped by its context, it reflects the presence of uncertainty, chance and risk. If a *world society of risk* already exists, it is now possible to refer to a *virtual society of risk*.

We are aware how progress potentially creates important risks, and how the actions of human beings can escape their control (Lautman, 1996: 273–85). To talk about risks, and not only about harm and danger, is to talk

232 SOCIAL & LEGAL STUDIES 10(2)

about events that affect an activity shared by others within a social space. Indeed, to predict and to calculate risks presupposes first of all the creation of a 'social space of shared activities' (Worms, 1996: 287–307). In this respect, certain characteristics associated with risk have already been pointed out (Ewald, 1985), particularly its collective feature which has left its mark on certain groups or 'populations', and its capacity to acquire a 'capital', which allows for economic budgeting against risk (Worms, 1996: 291ff.). Furthermore, it has also been confirmed that risk presupposes social relations, that the constitution of risk is always social (Worms, 1996).

The move from the welfare state to 'the risk society' is well underway, the latter emerging as the basic foundations of industrial society were undermined during a modernisation process that also challenged its particular forms of rationality. Contemporary society achieves stability while operating beyond insurable limits, and aggravates danger by not taking risk into account or accepting its responsibility to do so (Worms, 1996: 342). The term 'risk society' identifies a period in which social, political and ecological (individual or collective) risks, generated by the drive for renewal, increasingly escape society's control and security agencies. Faced with the dynamism of risk society, contemporary societies still decide and react following the model of the old industrial society, with political and legal systems unable to cope with new realities (Beck, 1994: 333–44).

Furthermore, the transition from the industrial era to the state of risk of contemporary society has taken place in an unplanned way, in keeping with a dynamic modernization which has totally ignored possible repercussions and dangers (Beck, 1994: 334). This surpasses the limits of security, as had been conceived by western industrial society, and upsets the basic principles of the present social order. Difficulty in controlling these problems persists in particular within the framework of decision making, whether political or legal (Beck, 1994).

It can be claimed that trust and risk form the basis of virtual interaction. In the electronic environment, matters of trust and risk are evident in a new *context*. We shall, therefore, talk about *virtual risk*, not only when referring to electronic commerce, to contracts, to the income of the author of an audiovisual project or to the protection of an individual's rights, but also – and above all – when surfing in cyberdeviant spaces. If people were already abandoned in 'the turbulence of the world-wide society of risk' (Beck, 1994: 335), nowadays, they are equally exposed to virtual risk. Furthermore, anonymity in cyberspace increases the risk.

ANONYMITY AND ACCOUNTABILITY: TO SURF IN THE SHADOW OF THE LAW?

In virtual space, anonymity can mean both the simple protection of information sources and danger. Certain psychologists consider that anonymity is desirable when it allows the users of the Net – 'Netizens' (McClellan, 1995:

76; Rheingold, 1995: 22) – to take on different psychological identities. Some who use electronic communication like to conceal themselves by adopting the body of another, by being another person, by living in another world (Rheingold, 1993 quoted by Branscomb, 1995). Others maintain that, in cyberspace, one should protect anonymity, but that this should be limited by law, especially as regards accountability (Branscomb, 1995: 1642). The absence of accountability encourages offensive behaviour and a lack of civility.

Despite this, the last few years have witnessed a tendency towards an increase in anonymity in cyberspace. It is difficult to discover the origin of electronic messages. Some online servers do not allow users to be anonymous, in order to identify and control them if necessary. Others, however, allow anonymity, for example by 'immediately granting addresses, which permits the user to be sent messages to an address that has been assigned for the occasion while preserving his/her anonymity' (*Internet. Enjeux juridique*, 1997: 48). In any case, even if online servers may sometimes have to become censors (Branscomb, 1995: 1645), they are faced with a world of users navigating on different interconnected webs (*Internet. Enjeux juridique*, 1997: 8), which makes tracking them difficult.

The use of the internet has not always been anonymous (*Internet. Enjeux juridique*, 1997: 24), but even if an internet server knows the address of a user and the name of her site, she can always operate through an anonymous server or adopt other stratagems (*Internet. Enjeux juridique*, 1997: 26). Moreover, when a company is exposed to malicious schemes on the Net, two solutions are possible. First, it may seek to isolate the computer, which would prevent the user from continuing to navigate the web system; and second, it may resort to cryptography, that is, the encoding of messages. This last solution, which no doubt protects data, makes controls more difficult and favours anonymity and organized crime (Haas and Vassileff, 1996). The American cryptographic system, PGP (*Pretty Good Privacy*), offers anonymity to its users, as it is impossible to know their identity, their nationality or even from which continent they send their messages (Haas and Vassileff, 1996). This type of solution is adopted by businessmen and bankers, who worry about the progress of 'sniffers'. These are computer programmes that allow client data in transactions to be sniffed or absorbed, and the crimes that can derive from them, especially credit card fraud (cf. int. suppl. *Le Monde*, suppl. Multimedias, 25–6 October 1998: 34).

The possibility of remaining anonymous in cyberspace is endless because of its characteristics: because the internet is not centralized, is transnational, is fleeting and volatile in its content, is constantly changing technologically and has an ownerless operating procedure, and because of the strategies available to the user (*Internet. Enjeux juridiques*, 1997: 47). Even those who have no experience in using this system are able to cover up their tracks, by sending their messages to servers which simply operate as transmitters of everything they receive without ever indicating the origin (*Le Monde*, 19–20 May 1996). The impact of anonymity is significant on a system that is continuously expanding and which has now progressively developed into a space available to the general public. These changes in the nature of the internet have been the cause of certain unmanageable consequences, while the growing 'social-ization' of virtual space has given rise to conditions that are favourable for the establishment of illegal interactions, whether economic or not.

Trust and *risk*, *anonymity* and *accountability* are all entangled in the virtual community as the result of a complex interactive process that brings about the rise of an *abstract* and *systemic criminal field*. A certain amount of fantasy and anxiety are settling into this badly understood network, particularly regarding 'the capacity of states to ensure that delinquency and criminality, part of any society, can be confined to marginal limits in the virtual world, as elsewhere' (Brault, 1996). Recent literature about the Net shows increasing concern regarding new forms of virtual criminality, and urges specialists to renew their thoughts on the subject.

THE 'SPACE TRAFFICKERS'

The existence of 'Netcriminals' or 'Netdeviants' questions the supposed neu-trality of cyberspace. Most pronouncements are limited to declaring that 'the information highways can be used to carry out new types of crimes' (Haas and Vassileff, 1996), but we must go beyond this. Cyberspace is not only a *means* or a *support* for criminal action, it is a true *autonomous environment* in which systemic and abstract criminal actions are spreading. The distinc-tion between *support* and *environment* is essential in order to understand these new phenomena.

The concept of *support* reflects the idea of computers as tools through which illegal acts can be carried out. Thus it is said that 'the information high-ways can be used to carry out new types of crimes' (Haas and Vassileff, 1996), or 'Internet is a particularly effective medium for criminal recruitment and the dissemination of criminal techniques' (Mann and Sutton, 1998). McLuhan's assertion that 'the medium is the message' shows how technology and automatism shape our lives and become an extension of ourselves. The idea that the internet is not only a support for criminal activities emerges mainly because of the dynamism peculiar to the system and the intensity of the transformations within it. However, one must also bear in mind the role of virtual operators, who contribute to the idea that the internet is not just a means for committing offences. Indeed, virtual operators are co-constituents (Giddens, 1984) of these systems. They produce and reproduce *real material frameworks* in which unlawful relationships materialize. They create a real community of illegal, interactive, virtual action. And this community is based, as we have observed, on the complex interaction of elements that are found at the centre of this abstract system, above all *trust, risk, anonymity* and *accountability*.

This material framework accommodates disembodied interactive activities in various fields, including the field of criminality. It becomes, therefore, a privileged scene for the offer and demand of illicit services, creating a unique environment which is, at the same time, protected by anonymity. In this field, virtual criminal activities proliferate. The system consists of a radically different environment where those who want to embark on such activities are recruited, and new 'criminal techniques' (Mann and Sutton, 1998: 201) are spread. Admittedly, obtaining illegal profits through industrial innovations is not, in itself, a new practice. Yet the fact that these innovations are transmitted and diffused in real immediate time as unlawful techniques, identifies in a radically new way the *virtual criminal field*. This is without taking into account the flexibility of the system and the absence of a central control (Mann and Sutton, 1998: 203) which contribute to trouble jurists.

The scientific community has found it hard to grasp these phenomena, and one can distinguish four different historical phases of analysis. The first phase covers a period of 30 years, between 1946 and 1976, during which North American scientists tried to discover the *nature* of this rising criminality. The following phase, from 1977 to 1988, can be identified as one of *criminalization*, when attempts were made to determine corrective measures for electronic abuse. Following this phase, from 1988 to 1993, in a period of demonization, efforts at criminalization bring about the identification of 'hackers' and 'crackers', and a search is undertaken to find the most appropriate punishments. As of 1993, we enter a period of *censorship*, when an intensive development of electronic information and communication takes place, especially on the internet (Mann and Sutton, 1998: xviii).

The last few years have witnessed a shift from an occasionally provocative deviance, committed within the electronic computer system, towards a more and more sophisticated virtual criminality. Initially, deviant acts were introduced into computer systems by means of virus infections, questioning the security of computers. The main worries then centred on electronic piracy, for example the stealing of strategic information, violation of the confidentiality of state or company files, destruction of data or programmes, infiltration of dishonest hackers in servers and, through them, into the networks to which they give access (Mann and Sutton, 1998; see also Hollinger, 1997). At the end of the 1970s, 'computer criminality' had already become a genuine social problem, prompting the creation of new legal categories to cover this field, mainly in the United States but also in Europe (Hollinger, 1997: Introduction).

Nowadays, the 'old-fashioned' hackers have given way to a 'hi-tech' criminality mainly aimed at gaining financial profit. It is no longer a matter of *problematic behaviour* but *genuine criminal behaviour* (Brault, 1996). Some authors make an effort to try to understand the structure of the so-called *newsgroups*, which are open exchange groups where anyone can leave messages with total freedom. Usually, these newsgroups are created for scientific or other types of interchange, without any criminal implication. The large North American university servers manage millions of such worldwide 'forums'. They are grouped into wide subject categories, and the main ones (science, computer technology, society, entertainment, discussions, etc.) are quite well organized. On the other hand, it is possible to find forums in different languages on much more modest sites. Discussion is generally supervised by chairpersons, who try to maintain order while relying on self-control. In this type of interaction, a newsgroup is generally only formed after a complex process, usually endorsed by votes (*Le Monde*, 19–20 May 1996). However, newsgroups can also appear in the 'alt', an alternative, anarchic virtual space. It is in these spaces that religious sects, political extremists, racist and xenophobic groups, pornographic addicts, the 'hardest' groups that interact in fields of criminal activity, establish themselves (Mann and Sutton, 1998: 201). The members of these newsgroups interact like the members of an association, in the more traditional sense of the term (Mann and Sutton, 1998: 213). From a psychological point of view, some consider that *hackers* express a sense of adventure, almost heroic, anti-state and anti-bureaucratic – similar to the conquerors of the 'New World', in the past. The Netdeviants are the new 'techno-cowboys' of postmodern societies (Sterling, 1992 quoted by Mann and Sutton, 1998: 206).

Putting aside psychological considerations, however, it should be noted that virtual anarchy exists. A distinction between the *contents* of the messages circulating among the members of these newsgroups has been established, so that the degree of inconvenience caused by their actions can be determined. In this respect, some specific measures have been adopted in Europe. In 1997, two studies dealing with the circulation of illicit content on the Net were published in the European Parliament, the 'Green Book on the Protection of Minors and Human Dignity in Audio-visual and News Services', and the 'Report by the Commission on Illegal and Harmful Contents on the Internet' (European Parliament. *Journal Officiel* C 215, 16 July 1997: 0037). These two texts clearly distinguish between unlawful and harmful contents, affirming 'that they deal with distinct objectives posing different problems and calling for different solutions' (*Journal Officiel*, C 215, 1997). It must be noted that both these texts refer to the internet as a 'support' for the circulation of illegal and harmful contents. Thus, Europe deprives itself of a truly effective control system from the beginning, ignoring the specific nature of what it seeks to master.

The Green Book confirms that what is unlawful are 'the contents which could be the object of a general ban, whatever the age of those to whom they are potentially directed, as for example those related to child pornography' (*Journal Officiel*, C 215, 1997). Harmful contents are, according to these texts, 'those which are liable to damage the physical, mental or moral development of minors, and which should be available to adults' (*Journal Officiel*, C 215, 1997). In the European Parliament, the Commission for public freedom and internal affairs maintains that 'the Internet network is used increasingly to spread child pornography, because it constitutes a practically uncontrollable market, and it is also exploited for the most unimaginable perversions'. And, in addition, that 'audiovisual pornography and sexual tourism are practices that favour the movement towards paedophile acts, removing the taboos surrounding them' (European Parliament, Travaux préparatoires de la Commission des libertés publiques et des affaires intérieures. *Journal Officiel* C 358, 24 November 1997).

There has been a strong movement in both European countries and the United States to combat pornography and paedophilia. In these countries, which are keen supporters of freedom of expression, 'moral entrepreneurs' shocked by the transmission of unlawful images of children have appealed for extended laws (Hollinger, 1997: xxviii). The new virtual technologies are creating new frameworks of 'moral dilemma' around the subject of the sexual language used on the Net and virtual vices like cyberprostitution (Nahikian, 1996) or other cybercrimes (Wilson, 1997).

Various other newsgroups that are apparently less harmful have also entered the Net, for example those that organize themselves around the growing industry of interactive games ('Internet Gambling'), which have had significant repercussions. In 1997, the Australian Institute of Criminology and the Australian Institute for Gambling Research proposed a colloquium on the subject, given the expansion of such practices (McMillen and Grabosky, 1998). Other newsgroups, even more dangerous, can also be found on the Net, such as terrorist groups, drug dealers or members of transnational criminal organizations. Using the expression 'money laundering', anyone can find sites that openly propose profitable solutions!

Whether forbidden or not, such newsgroups can easily be consulted. Even if a newsgroup is not accessible via the server of one's own online service, it is sufficient to connect to a public server, some of which allow the user to not only read messages but also send them. The American server Zippo, for example, offers direct access to newsgroups via the World Wide Web, including those that are controversial and which are grouped together in the separate, 'alt.*restricted' category (Pinguet, 1996).

Virtual criminality has become a worrying matter both globally and nationally. In 1998, for example, the French cyberpolice detected 424 virtual criminal cases. Newspapers and television have recently become aware of these problems and have begun to inform the general public, the majority of whom do not yet navigate the Net. The European Union proposes restrictive measures to respond to these virtual criminal activities, and suggests setting up an international committee. A debate on cybercontrol is called for.

CYBERCONTROL, WHAT KIND OF REGULATION?

The debate over cybercontrol is becoming increasingly central to contemporary society. A *Lex Informatica* is being developed mainly concerning issues linked to evidence, procedure and to criminal accountability (Mefford, 1997). From this point of view, it is possible to say that cyberspace is no longer a lawless zone. It has been said, moreover, that 'the idea of a legal void with regard to the internet is not very realistic' (Brault, 1996). The enforcement of a national law would not be a major problem in various fields, for example, around artistic and literary copyright and patent rights, but 'real problems appear with an international network' and 'obvious questions would arise when trying to determine who is responsible' (Brault, 1996).

What type of control should there be? Some of the features of the internet that have been listed above, *transnationality, fleetingness,* the *volatile nature of its contents* and *operators' strategies* in the virtual community have a direct impact on criminal matters. *Transnationality,* in particular, makes it difficult to enforce criminal law (*Internet. Enjeux juridiques,* 1997: 47), starting with aspects linked to criminal responsibility (Branscomb, 1995: 1645) – especially the delicate issue of the responsibility for a crime committed on the internet. In France, for example, online servers have considered themselves the victims of the technological ignorance of the judicial authorities (Gras, 1996).

It is also necessary to mention the *fleetingness* and the *volatile nature of content.* Distributors confirm that it is materially impossible for an online server to control the entire content of the messages transmitted by the new groups that are appearing in the virtual community (Gras, 1996). On this subject, in France, a report presented by the Interministerial Committee for the Internet demonstrated that these problems cause difficulties for criminal research and for the enforcement of certain rules (*Internet. Enjeux juridiques,* 1997: 50–52). *Virtual operators' strategies* are also difficult to grasp in an abstract world that is rapidly changing, where the status and role of the operators are extremely mutable. A user can be simultaneously a server, an editor or a consumer, witnessing a great confusion of the different roles in the virtual community. This makes it very difficult not only to understand the virtual offence but also the meaning of the categories on which the legal approach is based. Furthermore, the confusion of roles makes it sometimes impossible to determine which legal norm to apply (*Internet. Enjeux juridiques,* 1997: 53).

In the case of criminal activities on the internet, research is in a state of confusion regarding the identification of the author of the offence and the establishment of its constitutive elements. Besides the fact that the illegal message may disappear, the author can always defend him- or herself by maintaining that it was modified, or even distorted and falsified, by a third party (*Internet. Enjeux juridiques,* 1997: 50). What is more, the simple testimony of a person who might have seen the message, or of a user who might have recorded it, does not have the same persuasive force as a verbal trial certifying the offence (*Internet. Enjeux juridiques,* 1997).

Nonetheless, the law has begun to function in order to try to catch up with virtual criminality, and the 250 million people who were linked up to the internet by 2000 (*L'Internet,* 2000: 3). Various countries are trying to control cyberspace, starting with the United States, where the number of homes connected to the internet was supposed to be around 35.2 million by 2000, that is a third of the homes in the country (cf. *Internet. Enjeux juridiques,* 1997: 57). However, a passionate debate has started up in the US, using as a support the first amendment of the American Constitution and freedom of expression, and it seems that self-control of this abstract system is the most attractive approach.

Among the various attempts at regulation in the United States, one should mention those that control pornography. The importance and the visibility of virtual criminality of a pornographic nature, chiefly connected with children, prompted the adoption in February 1996 of the Communications Decency Act. As regards the protection of minors, this law does not only propose the setting up of technical devices in audiovisual programmes, but also the extension of this type of protection to all messages of an 'indecent' nature (*Internet. Enjeux juridiques*, 1997: 57). The Act (Article 223) penalizes with a fine and a prison sentence the distribution of obscene contents aimed at minors. Nevertheless, the legislation does not incriminate the users or the suppliers of services who act on good faith and adopt the necessary measures to limit the contents judged to be obscene. These people are not held responsible for the violation of the first amendment of the Constitution (*Internet. Enjeux juridiques*, 1997: 57). Responsibility is limited to cases where the operator authorizes the use of these infrastructures knowing that they are used for illicit activities (Communications Decency Act, Articles 223a-2 and 223d-2). Furthermore, employers are not held responsible for the acts committed by their employees outside their professional activities (*Internet. Enjeux juridiques*, 1997: 59). The Act has been criticized, however, for undermining freedom of expression and certain provisions have been appealed regarding their constitutionality. The enforcement of its more controversial provisions seems problematic at present (*Internet. Enjeux juridiques*, 1997).

The development of cybercontrol in France leaves it 'at the tail end of the European group', as it is put in the Interministerial Report (*Internet. Enjeux juridiques*, 1997: 9–12). However, a report requested by the *Secretariat d'Etat a l'Industrie* questions the law of July 1996, which opens the telecommunications industry to competition (*Développement technique de l'Internet*, June 1999: *Le Monde*, 20–21 June 1999). At the time, internet issues were not properly taken into account, and the report defends the establishment, for a limited period of time, of certain specific regulations in order to encourage research in this sector. Even if an effort is made to rapidly develop the internet, there is a clear resistance at the heart of French society to this new social space. The establishment of new rules of behaviour has provoked great social and legal concern, especially regarding what is described as the need for a 'new civility' (*Internet. Enjeux juridiques*, 1997). The humanistic commitment to the values that are the basis of the individual's rights and freedom remains fundamental. Unconditional respect for these values means that, at a national level, French law can condemn the online servers as soon as they transmit controversial messages. The new penal code includes controls on 'making, transmitting, diffusing, by any means . . . a message of a violent or pornographic character or of a nature that seriously affects human dignity, or seeks commercial benefit from using images of this nature . . .' (*Code pénal*, Article 227–24; Gras, 1996). According to the French concept, cyberspace must be a space for freedom of expression, but above all it must be 'a tool for progress and enrichment rather than a synonym for danger' (*French Penal Code*).

As regards state cybercontrol, a 'purely national approach is unrealistic' (*Internet. Enjeux juridiques*, 1997: 8). Because of its transnational character, its fleetingness and the volatility of content, cyberspace can only define common operating rules through detailed international cooperation. It is essential to adopt common principles in order to allow for a juridical exchange on a global scale. In Europe, the European Union, is beginning to be seen as having a crucial controlling role as a supranational authority. The EU intends to establish a minimum code of ethics, which would be used as the base for the cybercontrol of each member country (*Internet. Enjeux juridiques*, 1997: 11).

However, cyberspace, because of its structure, its features and the way it functions, is not a space where a priori any type of control can be set up easily. A system of coercive rules to stipulate the type of content that should be respected is not envisaged in cyberspace as it is, for example, in audiovisual material – a comparison which is nevertheless readily made. There are only two moments when cybercontrol can actually be enforced: when services are offered or asked for, by autoregulation; or else a posteriori (*Internet. Enjeux juridiques*, 1997: 9). Autoregulation can be achieved either by self-censorship among suppliers, or by electronic systems that classify services, or by parental filtering (*Internet. Enjeux juridiques*, 1997: 10). As the virtual world progressively occupies a more predominant place in people's lives, and as information and communication come to be at the heart of the social system, families are called on yet again. They are asked to play a central role to control, educate and socialize in the virtual world, despite the explosion of the latter and the fact that it is often better mastered by children than by parents.

It is possible to observe a transformation in the traditional concepts of public and private space. In order to rationalize or to limit the abuses in cyberspace, moral elements are reintroduced in the abstract systems (*Internet. Enjeux juridiques*, 1997: 561). Internet, a 'restored public space', establishes a 'transfigured private space', which limits the former, but is also open to it (Sutter and Zécler, 1998). One seeks private restraints on abuses in the public sphere, a sphere which is a co-constituent of it. This inevitably leads to a debate about cyberdemocracy (Poster, 1997), discussion of which lies beyond the scope of this article. However, one cannot overlook the new canons of this virtual civility, minimum rules concerning the respect of the individual's rights, such as the use of civil language, not encouraging political and sexual violence, stressing consumers' rights, refraining from criminal behaviour. Specialists in the virtual world are invited to work out a code of ethics similar to the codes of conduct that are multiplying, nowadays, in the global environment of industrial, commercial and financial trade. Such a code could establish rules of transparency, accountability and respect for the current legal framework. What tends to happen in France is that certain online servers, aware of the inspections others have undergone, exercise a severe autoregulation censoring from the very roots any sites that might be in any way unlawful (Brault, 1996; cf. also *Le Monde* of 19–20 May 1996).

 In this article I have tried to put forth some comments for a debate on this subject. An in-depth analysis would not, however, have ended here. The impact of these changes on the criminal field and on the field of control questions not only law as a whole, but also and above all, criminological theory, even beyond criminal law. In this field, a change of paradigm must be undertaken to account for this shift towards the immaterial and to underline a modern criminological philosophy, for the 21st century. It is necessary to develop an *abstract systemic paradigm*, without which we will continue to confront a state of virtual chaos.

NOTE

Originally published as 'Un Net Pas Tres Net' in *Archives de Philosophie du Droit* 1999 and translated by Serena Barkham-Huxley.

REFERENCES

Beck, U. (1994) 'D'une théorie critique de la société vers la théorie d'une autocritique sociale' *Déviance et Société* XVIII/3: 333–44.
Bourcier, D. (1998) 'Données sensibles et risque informatique. De l'intimité menacée à l'identité virtuelle', pp. 39–58 in G. Koubi (ed.) *Questions sensibles*. Paris: PUF.
Branscomb, A. W. (1995) 'Anonymity, Autonomy, and Accountability: Challenges to the First Amendment in Cyberspace', *Yale Law Journal* 104 (7 May): 1639–79.
Brault, N. (1996) 'Le Droit applicable à Internet. De l'abîme aux sommets'. *Legicom. Revue Trimestrielle du droit de la communication* 12/2: 101–115.
Capeller, W. (1997) 'La transnationalisation du champ pénal: réflexions sur les mutations du crime et du contrôle', *Droit et société* 35: 61–78.
Ewald, F. (1985) *L'État-providence*. Paris: Grasset.
Giddens, A. (1984) *The Constitution of Society*. Cambridge: Polity Press.
Giddens, A. (1994) *Les conséquences de la modernité*. Paris: L'Harmattan.
Gras, F. (1996) Internet et la responsabilité pénale. *Legicom. Revue Trimestrielle du droit de la communication*, No. 12/2: 95–99.
Grass, F. (1989) 'The "New Bad Future" Robocop and the 1980's Sci-Fi Film', *Science as Culture* 5: 5–70.
Green, N. (1997) Beyond Being Digital: Representation and Virtual Corporeality, pp. 59–98 in Holmes, D. (ed.) *Virtual Politics. Identity and Community in Cyberspace*. London: Sage.
Haas, G. and I. Vassileff (1996) Délinquance Numérique: l'attaque des Stad par les données. *Legicom. Revue Trimestrielle du droit de la communication*, No. 12/2: 43–50.
Hollinger, R. C. (ed.) (1997) *Crime, Deviance and the Computer*. Aldershot: Dartmouth.
Holmes, D. (ed.) (1997) *Virtual Politics. Identity and Community in Cyberspace*. London: Sage.
Internet. Enjeux juridiques (1997) Rapport au ministère délégué à la Poste, aux Télecommunications et à l'Espace et au ministre de la Culture, Mission Interministérielle sur l'Internet présidée par Isabelle Falque-Pierrotin, La Documentation française, Paris.
Lautman, J. (1996) 'Risque et rationalité', *L'Année sociologique* 46(2): 273–85.
L'internet (2000). Special issue of *Cahiers français*, Jean-Yves Capul (ed). Paris: La documentation Française, No 295.
Le Monde: www.lemonde.fr/

242   SOCIAL & LEGAL STUDIES 10(2)

Mann, D. and M. Sutton (1998) 'Netcrime. More Change in the organization of Thieving', *British Journal of Criminology* 38(2): 201–28.

McClellan, J. (1995) 'Cyberspace: Judge Dread'. *The Observer* 29 January.

McMillen, J. and P. Grabosky (1998) 'Internet Gambling', in *Trends and Issues in Crime and Criminal Justice*, Australian Institute of Criminology, No. 88.

Mefford, A. (1997) 'Lex Informatica: Foundations of Law on the Internet', *Indiana Journal of Global Legal Studies* 5(I): 211–37.

Nahikian, J. D. (1996) 'Learning to love "the ultimate peripheral": virtual vices like "cyberprostitution" suggest a new paradigm to regulate online expression', *John Marshall Journal of Computer and Information Law*, 4.

Pinguet, M. (1996) 'La douane et la cyber-délinquance', *La Gazette du Palais* 25 October.

Poster, M. (1997) 'Cyberdemocracy, The Internet and the Public Sphere', pp. 212–27 in D. Holmes (ed.) *Virtual Politics. Identity and Community in Cyberspace.* London: Sage.

Sutter, G. and H. Zécler (1998) 'Internet: espace public, espace privé?', *Revue de la Recherche Juridique Droit Prospectif* No 2: 561–75.

Virilio, P. (1996) *Un paysage d'événements.* Paris: Éd. Galilée.

Walton, Taylor and Young (1973) *The New Criminology.*

Wilson, M. (1997) Community in the Abstract: A Political and Ethical Dilemma? in D. Holmes (ed.) *Virtual Politics. Identity and Community in Cyberspace.* London: Sage.

Worms, F. (1996) Risques communs, protection publique et sentiment de justice. *L'Année sociologique*, 46(2): 287–307.

[5]

VIRTUAL CRIMINALITY: OLD WINE IN NEW BOTTLES?

PETER N. GRABOSKY

Australian Institute of Criminology, Australia

INTRODUCTION

IT HAS become trite to suggest that the convergence of computing and communications has begun to change the way we live, and the way we commit crime. Whether this will necessitate a revision of our philosophical, historical and sociological assumptions, however, is another matter. One must beware of overgeneralization and hyperbole, which characterize a great deal of discourse on the digital age. In the pages that follow, I suggest that 'virtual criminality' is basically the same as the terrestrial crime with which we are familiar. To be sure, some of the manifestations are new. But a great deal of crime committed with or against computers differs only in terms of the medium. While the technology of implementation, and particularly its efficiency, may be without precedent, the crime is fundamentally familiar. It is less a question of something completely different than a recognizable crime committed in a completely different way.

Perhaps the most remarkable developments relating to crime in the digital age are its transnational implications, and the threats to personal privacy posed by new technologies. The speed of electronic transactions allows an offender to inflict loss or damage on the other side of the world, bringing new meaning to the term 'remote control'. In addition, digital technology facilitates surveillance, by public agencies and the private sector, to a degree that is quite revolutionary.

MOTIVATION

Let us look first at motivations of those who would commit computer-related crime. One could perhaps be excused for observing *plus ca change, plus c'est la meme chose*. Computer criminals are driven by time-honoured motivations, the most obvious of which are greed, lust, power, revenge, adventure,

SOCIAL & LEGAL STUDIES 0964 6639 (200106) 10:2 Copyright © 2001
SAGE Publications, London, Thousand Oaks, CA and New Delhi,
Vol. 10(2), 243–249; 017405

244   SOCIAL & LEGAL STUDIES 10(2)

and the desire to taste 'forbidden fruit'. While many criminal acts flow from mixed motives, it is greed that primarily underlies electronic funds transfer fraud, and lust that drives the traffic in child pornography. The ability to make an impact on large systems may, as an act of power, be gratifying in and of itself. The desire to inflict loss or damage on another may also spring from revenge, as when a disgruntled employee shuts down an employer's computer system, or ideology, as when one defaces the web page of the United States Central Intelligence Agency. Much activity that occurs on the electronic frontier entails an element of adventure, the exploration of the unknown. The very fact that some activities in cyberspace are likely to elicit official condemnation is sufficient to attract the defiant, or the irresistibly curious. Given the degree of technical competence required to commit many computer-related crimes, there is one other motivational dimension worth noting here. This, of course, is the intellectual challenge of mastering complex systems.

None of the above motivations is new. The element of novelty resides in the unprecedented capacity of technology to facilitate acting on these motivations.

INTERPERSONAL RELATIONS IN CYBERSPACE

Digital technology has, to some extent, impacted on interpersonal relations. The illusion of anonymity seems to have elicited more candour over the internet than one would expect in face-to-face communications. But whether the role play that occurs in some chatrooms constitutes something completely different from good theatre, in which the actors are immersed in their roles, is open to question. To be sure, some of this role play is extremely aggressive, or otherwise antisocial. But any more so than a performance of Hamlet?

The internet has indeed brought about significant changes in human interaction. Ordinary investors are now able to buy and sell shares online without dealing through intermediaries such as underwriters, brokers and investment advisers. While this may enhance the efficiency of securities markets, it also provides opportunities for criminal exploitation. But the fundamental criminality is still reducible to the basics: misrepresenting the underlying value of a security at the time of the initial public offering, or market manipulation during secondary trading of a security, through the dissemination of false information, or engineering a deceptive pattern of transactions to attract the attention of the unwitting investor.

One hears anecdotes about children who have been lured from the safety of their homes by paedophiles after an initial encounter in an internet chatroom, or women who, after an electronically arranged assignation, meet with foul play at the hands of a predator. But is this really new? Cyberspace serves the same function as the busstop, the schoolyard or the disco.

There is another sense in which digital criminality may be similar to conventional criminality. At the risk of oversimplification, one may divide conventional criminals into two classes: the competent and the incompetent.

Sooner or later, most of the latter wind up in prison. The competent ones avoid detection, or at the very least, prosecution and conviction. So it is with cybercriminals. The most adept are never noticed, much less identified. By contrast the inept cybercriminal leaves his footprints all over cyberspace.

NEW CHALLENGES FOR THE STATE

The digital age has begun to pose new challenges for the state. Blasphemous, seditious, salacious, and otherwise offensive communications have long been the focus of governmental preoccupation. In an era where many governments seek to shed functions and devolve powers, the urge to control digital technology remains strong. And yet the ability of governments and legal systems to adapt to new media for the transmission of offensive content is somewhat limited. Of course, one could always 'pull the plug', and severely restrict citizens' access to cyberspace. But those governments which seek to maximize the economic well-being of their citizenry realize that it is futile to try to hold back the tide of globalization, and that failure to get in on the ground floor of electronic commerce may retard economic development.

The challenges faced by governments are by no means limited to the regulation of online content. In English-speaking societies at the very least, the capacity of public police is now acknowledged to be limited. Most victims of residential burglary are aware that they stand little chance of recovering their lost possessions; they harbour few illusions that 'their' offender will eventually be brought to justice. The role of the police is often limited to that of legitimizing insurance claims and providing a few kind words (and perhaps some crime prevention advice) to the victim. Individuals are, to an extent that few wish to acknowledge openly, largely on their own as far as crime prevention is concerned. And so those who can afford it acquire sophisticated alarm systems and live in 'gated' communities. The necessity of self-reliance in crime control is no less in cyberspace than in one's physical neighbourhood.

PARADOXES OF THE DIGITAL AGE

In addition to the tension between the shrinking state, and the imperative to direct traffic on the information superhighway, the digital age has given rise to other paradoxes. Technologies of anonymity and pseudonymity such as remailers and cryptography can provide a modicum of cover for someone wishing to mask his or her identity and the content of his or her communication. But not everyone avails themselves of such technologies, and capacities of surveillance exceed all but the most determined users.

Cryptography, regarded by law enforcement as a threat, is one of the fundamental pillars of electronic commerce. Without this secure technology, electronic payments, much less the transmittal of one's credit card details, would be that much riskier. Cryptography may be a boon to criminals, but it is arguably an even greater boon to legitimate business.

Arguably, the internet constitutes a greater threat to privacy than was ever thought possible. The possibility of remaining anonymous in cyberspace, far from being endless, appears significantly constrained. Moreover, the threat to privacy may come from private as well as governmental sources. Much is made of so-called 'hacker sites' and chatrooms devoted to 'teensex', many of which are essentially accessible to the public. The fact remains that these can be wonderful sources of intelligence for law enforcement agencies or information security specialists. The annals of law enforcement are expanding with examples of police officers posing as 13-year-old girls who arrange online assignations with those who were once described as 'dirty old men'.

THE PRIVATE THREAT TO PRIVACY

Of perhaps even greater significance is the exploitation of personal information by private commercial interests. The amount of personal information available about individuals' spending patterns and consumer preferences is surprising to many. In the past, information privacy was protected by data dispersion (Clarke, 1988). A great deal of personal information may have been stored here and there in various locations (whether public or private), but aside from major investigations, the cumbersome logistics of sorting through rooms full of forms in one place and another precluded collation on any significant scale. Technologies of data manipulation that permit merging of databases and matching of individual identities now facilitate the aggregation of data from disparate sources (Clarke, 1988). The term 'data mining' is commonly used to refer to such practices. The linkage of disparate data is facilitated by the existence of identification numbers that are common in most industrial societies. The nine-digit Social Security Number in the United States is a classic example. Through the collation of disparate personal details, the whole becomes greater than the sum of its parts.

One suspects that most individuals are not resorting increasingly to anonymity, and that their personal details are accessible in abundance. Moreover, these details are traded freely by marketing firms.

Many people who use electronic mail do so with unusual candour. In the words of Bennahum (1999, 102) 'Email is a truth serum'. But unlike a face-to-face conversation, electronic communications are not evanescent. Records persist, and may return to haunt one or more participants in the communication. Even when a message is erased, it may have been retained by another party to the communication, or it may have been 'backed up' on one or more system files. Moreover, many communications are accessible merely by using readily available search technology. One estranged husband searched the internet for his ex-wife's account name and collected 30 pages of messages that she had posted in chatrooms, not all of which reflected well on her as a parent. Seeking greater visiting rights with his children, he presented them unsuccessfully to the mediator in his custody hearing (Glod, 1999).

THE TRANSNATIONAL DIMENSION

One of the greatest challenges posed by the advent of digital criminality is the enormously enhanced potential for transnational offending. Many, if not most, cybercrimes can now be committed from the other side of the world as easily as from the building next door. Not only will this tend to make identification of the perpetrator somewhat more difficult, it will greatly impede prosecution of the offender.

Despite the hackneyed contention that the world is shrinking, laws differ. Some jurisdictions prohibit unauthorized access to a computer system, while others do not. Some make it a crime to alter or erase data, while others do not. Nations such as Germany make it a crime to disseminate neo-Nazi propaganda. As distasteful as such material may be, the right to do so is protected by the Constitution of the United States of America. Some nations criminalize online gambling, while others see it as a wonderful source of export income.

A degree of common legal ground is required in order to mobilize the law of a foreign state on one's behalf. Without 'dual criminality', assistance of the jurisdiction in which the offender is situated is most unlikely to be forthcoming. But even if there is a degree of consistency, enforcement by officials in the host nation may by no means follow automatically. All law enforcement agencies have their priorities. If I, comfortably situated in Australia, were foolish enough to fall victim to an online investment fraud originating in Albania, the Australian authorities and/or their Albanian counterparts may have more pressing demands. 'My' case may never receive serious investigative consideration by authorities in either jurisdiction.

IMPLICATING THIRD PARTIES

New opportunities for computer-related crime can create new responsibilities for third parties. Consider, for example, the liability of employers for misuse of office computers by employees. If I were to send a co-worker sexually offensive email messages, my employer could be liable for failing to provide a safe working environment. What degree of preventive or reactive response would be required on my employer's part in order to avoid liability?

Companies whose shares are traded on major stock exchanges are generally required by their national laws to ensure that information disclosed about the company and its activities is full and accurate. With the increasing use of the World Wide Web as a medium of corporate public relations come new responsibilities for disclosure. Corporate websites can be hacked or mimicked with uncanny realism. How often should a company's website be checked or updated in order to ensure that the information it contains is correct? What is an unacceptable delay in rectifying misinformation? What is the appropriate course of action for a company that discovers that its website is linked to other websites which themselves may contain inaccuracies about the company in question? The future will no doubt present a number of such scenarios, and it will be interesting to observe how they are resolved. To safeguard against some of these difficulties, many companies have begun to engage the services of consultants who scan the internet for corporate references (Grabosky, Smith and Dempsey, 2001, ch. 6).

CONCLUSION

One of the basic tenets of criminology holds that crime can be explained by three factors: motivation, opportunity, and the absence of a capable guardian. This explanation can apply to an individual incident as well as to long-term trends. Derived initially to explain conventional 'street' crime, it is equally applicable to crime in cyberspace. As we have seen, motives for computer-related crime are nothing new. Technologies may change rapidly, but human nature does not. The Ten Commandments are as relevant today as they were in Biblical times. The thrill of deception characterized the insertion of the original Trojan Horse no less than did the creation of its digital descendants.

By contrast, the variety and number of opportunities for cybercrime are proliferating. The exponential growth in connectivity of computing and communications creates parallel opportunities for prospective offenders, and parallel risks for prospective victims. As the internet becomes increasingly a medium of commerce, it will become increasingly a medium of fraud.

Capable guardianship has evolved over human history, from feudalism, to the rise of the state and the proliferation of public institutions of social control, to the postmodern era in which employees of private security services vastly outnumber sworn police officers in many industrial democracies. The policing of terrestrial space is now very much a pluralistic endeavour. So too is the policing of cyberspace. Responsibilities for the control of computer crime will be similarly shared between agents of the state, information security specialists in the private sector, and individual users. In cyberspace today, as on terrestrial space two millennia ago, the first line of defence will be self-defence.

DISCLAIMER

Opinions expressed in this essay are those of the author, and not necessarily those of the Australian Institute of Criminology or the Australian Government.

REFERENCES

Bennahum, D. (1999) 'Daemon Seed: Old Email Never Dies', *Wired* 7.05 (May) 100–11.

Clarke, R. (1988) Information Technology and Dataveillance. Commun. ACM 31,5 (May 1988) 498–512 http://www.anu.edu.au/people/Roger.Clarke/DV/CAC M88.html (visited 30 December 1999)

Glod, M. (1999) 'Spouses may delete their marriage, but e-mail lives on as evidence', *Seattle Times* 28/4/99. http: //archives.seattletimes.com/cgi-bin/texis.mummy/ web/vortex/display? StoryID = 3733259942 &query = internet+and+privacy (visited 13 June 1999)

Grabosky, P., R. G. Smith and G. Dempsey (2001) *Electronic Theft: Unlawful Acquisition in Cyberspace*. Cambridge: Cambridge University Press.

[6]

SITES OF CRIMINALITY AND SITES OF GOVERNANCE

FRANCIS SNYDER

London School of Economics and Université d'Aix-Marseille III

INTRODUCTION

THIS IS a thought-provoking essay on a highly topical and controversial subject: the rise of virtual criminality and how to control it. We
all have read of global computer viruses, and perhaps experienced
them; but probably few readers of this journal have direct personal experience of cybercrime. Among the many merits of Wanda Capeller's stimulating
article is the identification of some main issues in the matter, pointers to fault
lines in current debates, and suggested avenues of research and policymaking
for the future. Here it is not possible to survey all of this rich tapestry.
Instead, my purpose is to offer some comments on a few selected themes.

THE MYTH OF NEUTRALITY

The ardent amateur of the cyberworld may be surprised to learn that,
according to the author, many people assume that cyberspace is neutral. But
what does 'neutrality' mean in this context? It surely cannot refer to a lack
of social organization. Internet networks may be the modern equivalent of
the early 20th-century anthropologist's stateless societies. However, the
juxtaposition in itself indicates that networks are a type of social organization, as economic organization theorists have often told us. They have a
structure, a distribution of power, norms, and often decision-making procedures.

Nor can 'neutrality' be assumed to mean an absence of values. Every technology, at least in my view, embodies certain assumptions about social
relations. Better, perhaps, it tends to favour or enhance certain types of social
relations and place others at a disadvantage. Technology, in other words, is
social. This means that it cannot be neutral, if by 'neutral' we mean standing
outside society, somehow 'objective' and outside social values.

SOCIAL & LEGAL STUDIES 0964 6639 (200106) 10:2 Copyright © 2001
SAGE Publications, London, Thousand Oaks, CA and New Delhi,
Vol. 10(2), 251–256; 017406

Perhaps by 'neutral' one means the absence of regulation. In this perspective, regulation is considered as embodying the potential of skewing social interaction so as to favour certain interests. To my mind, this is also a dead end. Consider a pure market, if such a thing can be conceived. Even in the absence of regulation, an entirely free market would not be without some form of governance. The latter would, however, be carried out ultimately by the market actors. It seems obvious that, in such a situation, social interaction would ultimately favour some interests and place others at a disadvantage. But even here the state is not absent: regulation is an essential element in the creation and preservation of a market.

One needs then to ask: who has claimed that cyberspace was neutral, and why? Did such a pretence, if it existed, stem merely from the relative lack of technical knowledge that might be characteristic of an early period in the development of new technology? What is the 'supposed' neutrality of cyberspace that appears to be questioned by virtual criminality? Among the principal merits of Wanda Capeller's article is the raising of precisely this question. It helps us to pinpoint, in this new context, what we can call the myth of neutrality of social fields, and then to begin to examine its implications.

A main point in Wanda Capeller's convincing argument is that cyberspace is a specific environment. In other words, it is a social field, though of a particular type. If we approach the internet in this way, we know that the internet has certain shared features as a social field, but at the same time it has distinctive and perhaps unique characteristics. In the general respect, it may not differ from other social fields: each has its distinctive characteristics, which differentiate one social field from another. Few observers, if any, would pretend that any social field was neutral. Viewed as a social field, is the internet any different?

THE OLD AND THE NEW

What is old, and what is new, about the internet, and about virtual criminality? The author points out that risk is not new, but virtual risk is. An increase in the anonymity of social interaction is new. Wanda Capeller identifies a number of elements of continuity, as well as elements that pose novel challenges.

The article argues that, in order to come to grips with virtual criminality, we need to develop an abstract systemic paradigm. It may be that not all readers will know how to give flesh to this skeletal proposal. What does it mean? As I see it, it means first that the internet has distinctive characteristics. Second, it means that the pairs of trust and risk on the one hand, and anonymity and accountability on the other, are of key importance. Third, it implies that regulation must be international, not national. Here I focus on the second point.

Trust, risk, anonymity and accountability would seem to differ in character. At first glance, I suggest that this is so because trust, risk and anonymity are descriptions of fact, whereas accountability may be a description of fact but more importantly for lawyers is also normative. Of course, someone may be accountable for his or her actions, just as they may trust someone or not, be subject to risks or not, and be anonymous or not. But when we talk about accountability, in particular if the 'we' are lawyers, we are interested also in the questions of why and how such accountability is achieved. This brings into play institutions, norms, and possibly dispute resolution processes. It requires a perspective that is different from (or in addition to) the purely individual or actor's perspective.

This shift of perspective is captured to some extent in the article. Wanda Capeller explores nicely some of the implications of trust, risk and anonymity for the institutional and normative structures of accountability. Her principal objective with regard to these issues is to sketch the main lines of discussion and call for wider debate. On these points, her article provides a very useful starting point and foundation for further reflection.

SUPPORT AND ENVIRONMENT

What is distinctive about cybercrime, and how should policy makers react to it? One of the points about Wanda Capeller's article that I found most stimulating was her distinction between cyberspace as a support system on the one hand, and cyberspace as an environment on the other hand. This seems to be the key to the new paradigm that she has in mind, and also to her analysis of potential control strategies.

The sceptic might ask if the distinction between support and environment is unique to the internet: isn't it true of all technologies? This may be the case, but for the moment it is crucial to focus solely on the internet. Capeller's point is precisely that the internet is not simply a technology. That there is a real virtual criminal field, as she points out, is due to the specific characteristics of the internet as an environment. To my mind, the distinction is convincing, even though I would have liked to learn more about her view of the distinctive features of the internet as an environment and their implications both for forms of criminality and for its control.

The distinction hits home, in particular, in Capeller's discussion of the reponse of the European Parliament with regard to cybercrime. She argues, convincingly in my view, that the EP's response focuses on the internet only as a support and neglects its distinctive environmental features. If one searches the article for a list of these distinctive features, however, it appears that they consist of the transmission of innovations in real immediate time, the flexibility of the system and the lack of central control. Do economists' models of the market, or theories of games, help us to appreciate the implications of these features? What other features, if any, are unique to the internet? Or is it the case that the internet environment brings together many features that previously were separate?

I look forward to further analysis of this issue, because I suspect that Wanda Capeller is right in stating that 'Europe deprives itself of a truly effective control system from the beginning, ignoring the specific nature of what

it seeks to master' (236). To provide an analysis of this nature, and if necessary develop new abstract models to highlight its specific features, can be an
important role of sociological and social and legal scholarship.

WHAT KIND OF REGULATION?

All this leads to a key question: how to control cybercrime? There seem to
be four main issues. First, who governs? Second, how and according to what
values? Third, what normative form should regulation take? Fourth, how
should offences be defined? Those familiar with recent debates regarding
European Union law will recognize these old friends. In that field, they have
usually gone under the guise of what level of governance, what balance
between state and market, whether preference should be given to legally
binding measures or to soft law and, in the agricultural field for example,
whether fraud against the community budget should or can be characterized
as an administrative or a penal matter.

This general framework can be more useful if it is reformulated in terms of
a conception of sites of governance (see Snyder, 1999). We can think of sites of
governance as having a structural aspect and a relational aspect. The former
refers to institutions, norms and dispute resolution processes. The latter connotes the way in which a specific site is related to others, for example in a
network, as part of a hierarchy, in a competitive relationship, and so on.This is
especially attractive if our objective is to consider how sites of criminality may
be controlled. It also has the perhaps more substantial advantage in terms of
analytic strategy of ridding us of an outdated notion of multilevel governance.
The latter seems inevitably to involve a state-centred or at least state-based perspective, which is no longer appropriate or helpful in the context of globalization or, as Wanda Capeller points out, when we are dealing with the internet.

Though expressing these issues in a slightly different way, Wanda Capeller's
article provides a helpful survey of some of the main questions with regard to
regulation. It seems clear that control of virtual criminality will need to be
done by means of a site of governance that is not purely national, or at least
through some form of cooperation between different sites. While recognizing
that each site has a different structure, we need now to give more attention to
how they are related, and possibly to developing new types of relationships.
This seems to me to be an important area for future work. Lawyers, sociologists of law and others interested in similar matters have devoted most of their
energy to what I have called the structural aspects of sites. Relatively little
attention has to my knowledge been devoted to the relational aspects; conflicts of law (private international law) or comity principles with regard to
competition policy are important exceptions that would seem to prove the
rule. What cooperative arrangements can we imagine and develop to fill this
increasingly important gap? What protections for the citizen will eventually
be necessary? One has only to consider the development of international
police cooperation to realize that increasing intersite relationships in order to

combat cybercrime can pose novel, difficult issues, for example of human rights, not to mention accountability of these new intersite networks.

Inevitably it will be necessary to confront the difficulty of reconciling divergent approaches of different sites, such as those of the United States and France that are described in the article. Reconciliation does not necessarily mean harmonization, as the European Union panoply of regulatory strategies clearly indicates. What form should virtual governance take? Wanda Capeller describes how, in France, the debate about control of cybercrime is entangled with the debate about the balance between state and market: the idea of opening up the telecommunications sector to competition appears to be linked, for better or worse, to fears about increasing virtual criminality. She points to the resistance in France to the development of the internet. I find this fascinating, and hope that further research will be done on this topic. In France, the state is entrusted with the task of protecting the citizen. One might ask what is specific to the internet here, that is, to what extent does this specific example simply reflect more widely applicable differences in regulatory policy in the USA and France. Note, however, that the role of the state in this context is not uniquely French: witness the 1996 Communications Decency Act in the United States. The differences between the two would appear to be in the all important details, such as the definition of offences, rather than in the form of regulation. Hence the necessity of international cooperation.

With regard to the form of regulation, Wanda Capeller emphasizes the importance of a code of ethics or a code of conduct. In this context, this soft law might be used partly to bolster the framework of state law or other legally binding norms, instead of being entirely on its own. Further reflection on this topic would be well advised to take account of the rapidly growing literature on soft law. This normative form has long been important in public international law. During the past 20 years, it has assumed a high profile in the regulatory system of the European Union (see for example Snyder, 1996). It is becoming increasing important in the governance of international economic and social activities. Attention now needs to be paid to issues of enforcement and compliance. For example, what does compliance mean with regard to soft law? How can enforcement and compliance be negotiated? How do we know whether and when compliance is achieved? To what extent can secondary relationships or the market be enlisted to increase compliance with controls on undesirable activity, such as virtual criminality? These and other questions regarding soft law require further research.

CONCLUSION

Wanda Capeller's article is a stimulating, innovative analysis of an important phenomenon. It identifies some of the main issues and points to ways in which they might be addressed. The notion of an abstract systemic paradigm should be elaborated in more detail. Faced with sites of criminality, we now need to develop further a conception of sites of governance.

256   SOCIAL & LEGAL STUDIES 10(2)

REFERENCES

Snyder, Francis (1996) 'The Effectiveness of European Community Law: Institutions, Processes, Tools and Techniques', *Modern Law Review* 56(1): 19–54.
Snyder, Francis (1999) 'Governing Globalization: Global Legal Pluralism and European Law', *European Law Journal* 5(4): 334–74.

[7]

AN ENDNOTE ON REGULATING CYBERSPACE: ARCHITECTURE VS LAW?

GRAHAM GREENLEAF[*]

I. INTRODUCTION: KING CANUTE'S COMEBACK

About a millennium ago, King Canute became known for issuing executive orders (perhaps because of a lack of time for formal legislation) against forces of nature: to wit, to turn back the waves. His lack of success is notorious.[1]

With such a start, you might reasonably expect this article to proceed to the usual warnings about the futility of governments trying to regulate the unstoppable forces of cyberspace.[2] In fact, my drift will be largely in the opposite direction: regulation of the 'nature' of cyberspace – 'architecture' as it is called later on – may often be the most effective form of regulation, and may sometimes be necessary to preserve important values. We need some King Canutes in cyberspace.[3]

There is relatively little writing about a general theoretical structure for the regulation of cyberspace. Such a theoretical structure is needed to enable us to assess whether current or proposed laws (or the absence of them) are the best or only regulatory options available. This article comments on some of the forms that such a theoretical approach might take and gives examples of its application, including some drawn from Australian law.

Much of this article discusses how governments could legislate to affect or

---

[*]   BA LLB (Syd) MACS; Professor of Law, University of New South Wales.

[1]   Sveynsson, Canute II the Great (995-1035), King of England and Denmark has had a bad press. However, he was probably being ironic if "According to Legend, he proved to flatterers the limits of his powers by demonstrating his inability to induce the waves to recede": *Directory of Royal Genealogical Data*, University of Hull at: <http://www.dcs.hull.ac.uk/cgi-bin/gedlkup/n=royal?royal01548>.

[2]   For example John Perry Barlow, who compared the US Government's attempts to stop the use of strong encryption via the 'Clipper Chip' with 'the folly of King Canute': see JP Barlow, "Jackboots on the Infobahn" *Wired* 2.04 at <http://www.hotwired.com/Lib/Privacy/privacy.barlow.html>; or P Waters and L Carver who say that "the Internet is as inevitable and overwhelming as the incoming tide which confronted King Canute, and renders the traditional approach of regulation and prohibition futile": P Waters and L Carver "The Internet and Telephony: The Impact of Uncontrollable Technology on Traditional Telephony Regulation" Gilbert and Tobin website at <http://www.gtlaw.com.au/gt/bin/frameup.cgi/gt/pubs/telephony.html>.

[3]   These sovereigns will act without irony, their laws will be effective. However, the effectiveness of laws regulating architecture will not necessarily serve benign ends, as is discussed later.

control cyberspace architecture in various situations, and the effects that this might have, but the purpose is not to argue for governments to regulate architecture more extensively. Rather, the aim is to illustrate that architecture is not neutral but embodies choices and values: it reflects the interests of the 'codewriters',[4] and its legitimacy as regulation can and should sometimes be questioned on this basis.

I start by discussing how our views of the nature of cyberspace have changed over the last few years, then outline where we might start to develop a comprehensive approach to assessing regulatory options in cyberspace, and conclude with examples of how it can shed light on current and proposed instances of cyberspace regulation.

II.   THE EVOLVING NATURE OF CYBERSPACE

A.   A Realm of Freedom? The Myths of Digital Libertarianism

Much of the earliest and most influential writing about cyberspace was from a decidedly libertarian perspective, written by people excited by the early pre-commercial Internet's potential to create virtual communities and customs which seemed to have little relation to the nation state or the practices of 'real space'.[5] James Boyle has described this approach as,[6]

> it was not so much that nation states would not want to regulate the Net, it was that they would be unable to do so, forestalled by the *technology of the medium*, the *geographical distribution of its users*, and the *nature of its content*. This tripartite immunity came to be a kind of Internet Holy Trinity, faith in which was a condition of acceptance into the community.

To Boyle's Trinity of famous sayings I have added two more myths of digital libertarianism.[7] A quick comment on each will indicate why cyberspace is developing in a contrary direction. Detailed discussion of some of these examples will be saved until later in the paper.

(i) "On the Internet, no one knows you're a dog" (New Yorker cartoon)[8]

This famous cartoon encapsulated the belief that cyberspace was a realm of anonymity and pseudonymity, where you could browse the web in privacy, or adopt a pseudonym (and new sex or history if you like) for interactions with others. In fact, it is increasingly closer to the truth to say that the default condition of our interactions and communications in real space is anonymity, whereas the

---

4   L Lessig's terminology, discussed later.

5   Or 'meat space' as John Perry Barlow called it.

6   J Boyle, "Foucault in Cyberspace: Surveillance, Sovereignty and Hard-Wired Censors" (1997, draft only): original available at <http://www.wcl.american.edu/pub/faculty/boyle/foucault.htm>); copy available at <http://www2.austlii.edu.au/itlaw/secure/foucault.htm>.

7   The first and last in the following five.

8   'There's a now classic joke about cyberspace that first appeared as a cartoon in the New Yorker magazine: A dog and cat are sitting in front of a computer. Former says to the latter, "On the Internet, no one knows you're a dog" quoted at <http://www.umass.edu/pubaffs/online/archives/96/041596.html>.

1998 *UNSW Law Journal* **595**

default condition of Internet communications is some form of identification,[9] and many businesses and governments are investing in increasing the level of identification.

(ii) "Information wants to be free" (Stewart Brand)[10]

The process of digitisation of works made them infinitely reproducible at virtually no marginal costs, and infinitely distributable via the Internet. The Internet and property in information were widely believed to be incompatible, and technology would win against law and set information free. The reverse process is now underway: technical protections of intellectual property over networks may protect property interests in digital artefacts more comprehensively than has ever been possible in real space, and destroy the public interest elements in intellectual property law in the process. In the worst scenarios, the surveillance mechanisms being developed to do this may also bring about the end of the anonymity of reading. Perhaps the true version of Brand's aphorism will turn out to be "Information wants to be free ... but it wants to keep *you* under surveillance".

(iii) "The Net interprets censorship as damage and routes around it" (John Gilmore)[11]

The Internet's structural resistance to censorship is supported by well-publicised cases of data being moved from one server to the next to continue its availability, and by the numerous routes that can be found to any page on the web by those savvy enough to wish to avoid attempts at censorship. It is also an accurate reflection of the Internet's technical origins, it having been designed to re-route messages around outages caused by nuclear war. However, this resistance to censorship is easily over rated, and the structure of cyberspace may in fact facilitate pervasive censorship (at least for the majority of non-savvy users). There are a number of reasons for this. Technologies such as PICS (Platform for Internet Content Selection) were ostensibly developed to facilitate individual and parental (rather than state) choice and control of 'content selection' through third party content filters. But there is nothing in the technology to stop the content selection (and thus the choice of third party filter) being imposed at a level higher up network hierarchies than that of the individual user.[12] The use of content filters by

---

9   As yet, it is usually only something weaker than true identification, such as unauthenticated pseudonymity. since machine addresses and even email addresses are not unambiguous or non-repudiable: see G Greenleaf "Privacy principles: Irrelevant to Cyberspace?" (1996) 3 *Privacy Law & Policy Reporter* 114. However. others such as Jerry Kang see the same default condition emerging: 'in cyberspace. the exception becomes the norm: Every interaction is like the credit card purchase": J Kang. "Cyberspace Privacy: A Proposal Regarding the Private Sector's Processing of Personal Information Generated in Cyberspace" (1998) *Stanford Law Review* (forthcoming). cited in Lawrence Lessig "The Architecture of Privacy" (Draft 2). *Taiwan Net '98.* Taipei March 1998: <http://cyber.law.harvard.edu/works/lessig/architecture_priv.pdf>.

10   Almost always attributed (without any source) to Stewart Brand. EFF board member. founder of Whole Earth Catalog and the WELL. One list of famous quotes adds "Among others. No telling who really said this first.": <http://world.std.com/~tob/quotes.htm>.

11   That Gilmore. a founder of the Electronic Frontier Foundation. did say this is well attested. but the exact occasion is obscure: see Boyle. note 6 *supra* at <http://www2.austlii.edu.au/itlaw/secure/foucault.htm#N_4_>

12   See Boyle note 6 supra, part III for a brief discussion.

employers, universities and even the state (where international Internet connectivity is through a very limited number of channels) may make Internet censorship pervasive, and sometimes remote. Second, the Internet's potential for surveillance of our browsing habits encourages the self-censorship of the panopticon.

(iv) *"In Cyberspace, the First Amendment is a local ordinance"* (John Perry Barlow)[13]

Barlow's ironic[14] comment was a reminder that cyberspace can be resistant to regulation by any particular local sovereign. Information that the government of Burma may wish to suppress may be untouchable on a server in the USA. Activities such as Internet gambling (and its profits) may be run from a server on some tropical island. There are a number of reasons why the limits of national sovereigns to control the Internet are exaggerated, but the principal one is that nations are increasingly acting in concert to deal with the borderless nature of cyberspace by creating both relatively uniform laws across jurisdictions (for example, the WIPO Copyright Convention and the European Union's privacy Directive), and agreements for international cooperation in surveillance and investigation (for example, the Wassenar Agreement concerning encryption export controls). There is also the fact that those who wish to evade national laws mainly operate at the margins: there are problems in running significant commercial organisations from underdeveloped countries, and in spending the profits thus generated. While not disregarding the Internet as a source of regulatory arbitrage[15], location matters for reasons other than the regulatory climate.

(v) *"A Declaration of the Independence of Cyberspace"*
(John Perry Barlow[16] again)

In Barlow's 1996 'Declaration' he asserted that "[y]our legal concepts of property, expression, identity, movement, and context do not apply to us", and generally gave a pugnacious assertion of the 'keep your hands off our Internet' approach, directed against the nation states and governments of the world. The demand for independence even finds echoes in the judgment of Dalziel J in the original judgment striking down the USA's *Communications Decency Act*[17] as unconstitutional: "As the most participatory form of mass speech yet developed, the Internet deserves the highest protection from government intrusion".[18]

Boyle's critique of digital libertarianism, and particularly its claim to the

---

13   JP Barlow "Leaving the Physical World" presented at Conference on HyperNetworking, Oita, Japan: <http://www.eff.org/pub/Publications/John_Perry_Barlow/HTML/leaving_the_physical_world.html>.

14   The intended irony in Barlow's comment is that the First Amendment protects freedom of communication via Internet in the USA, rather than restricts it, so it is not only prohibitions that have the limitations of locality.

15   cf M Froomkin, "The Internet As A Source of Regulatory Arbitrage" in B Kahin and C Nesson (eds), *Borders in Cyberspace*, MIT Press (1997).

16   <http://www.eff.org/pub/Publications/John_Perry_Barlow/barlow_0296.declaration>.

17   *Communications Decency Act* of 1996, Pub L No 104-104, tit V, 1996 USCCAN (110 Stat) 56, 133; available at <http://www.cdt.org/policy/freespeech/12_21.cda.html>.

18   *American Civil Liberties Union v Reno*, 929 F Supp 824 (ED Pa 1996); available at: <http://www.ciec.org/decision_PA/decision_text.html>.

1998 *UNSW Law Journal* **597**

'independence' of cyberspace, is based on both "its blindness towards the effects of private power, and the less familiar claim that digital libertarianism is also surprisingly blind toward the state's own power in cyberspace".[19] The technological solutions to legal problems preferred by the 'digiterati' (such as PICS and P3P) are not as neutral or benign as they are believed to be, he argues. The paradox is that to 'protect mass speech' and to protect other values, the Internet may sometimes need 'government intrusion', as the rest of this article explores.

Barlow's 'Declaration' may seem like the last gasp of digital libertarianism, but we now hear distorted echoes of this approach in the insistence by some governments that, at least whenever consumer interests such as privacy are involved, voluntary self-regulation by Internet businesses can be trusted to produce an answer.

B. A Realm of Surveillance? A Dystopian View of Cyberspace

In contrast with the digital libertarians is a view of cyberspace which emphasises the likely extent of identification and surveillance in cyberspace, and its potential for misuse. A version of this argument is sketched below.[20] At this stage of the Internet's development, my view is that the jury is still out, and whether the repressive or the liberating potential of the Internet prevails (or some mix of both) depends on political decisions and technical developments yet to occur.

(i) The Pervasiveness of Cyberspace

The twenty first century will see life teeming in cyberspace. Irrespective of their level of computer literacy, education, interest or consent, everyone in at least the advanced industrial economies will spend a significant portion of time 'in' cyberspace by the early years of the twenty first century. People may not always realise that what they are doing is 'on the Internet', but the reality appears from a few simple factors. Transactions with business and government will much more commonly take place via information systems that are connected to the Internet. Many tools that people use in their work, such as inventory control systems, medical diagnostic equipment, will be connected to the Internet as a means of distributing data to remote parts of an organisation. These tools will tend to require information about who their user is, for security and accountability purposes. We will communicate with others in various public, semi-public and private ways via cyberspace, and obtain some portion of our entertainment from it.

(ii) Surveillance by Default

One consequence of our living a large part of our lives in cyberspace is simply that, whether we know or care, large quantities of personal information about each of us will be collected via a pervasive, worldwide-network (and stored on

---

19 Boyle, note 6 *supra*, "Introduction".
20 An earlier version of this section appeared in G Greenleaf, "Privacy and cyberspace: An ambiguous relationship" (1996) 3 *Privacy Law & Policy Reporter* 88.

machines connected to it). This is an event new in world history. The accessibility or interconnectedness of this information is contingent on several factors, including custom, public opinion and law, but is unlikely to be contingent on any serious technical considerations. Because the information will have been collected by processes related to one pervasive network, any impediments to its being found, published, or related to other data elsewhere on the Internet are easily removed if those who control the information wish to remove them. The great protectors of privacy of the past such as cost, distance, incompatibility and undiscoverability , are all disappearing in the face of the Internet and its protocols - the great equalisers of the twenty first century.

Cyberspace interactions are prima facie not anonymous, because we disclose potentially identifying (or interaction-enabling) information[21] such as name, email address or machine address in the act of communicating, unless we make a conscious effort not to do so. Widespread use of digital signatures will make them more strongly identified. In real space the default state of communications has been that they are anonymous unless we choose to identify ourselves or are already known to the other party.

(iii) Identity and Digital Personae

So we will all have a digital persona, which Roger Clarke describes as "a model of an individual's public personality based on data and maintained by transactions, and intended for use as a proxy for the individual",[22] a representation in cyberspace of who and what we are. A digital persona may be active or passive.[23] In fact, we will have multiple digital personae, as each organisation with which we deal will do so on the basis of different data about us available to it. We need to distinguish between those parts of a person's digital personae which are in 'public' spaces in the sense of being able to be found by Internet search engines or other means, and those parts which are in non-public spaces, either 'proprietary' (the databases of a government or company) or 'personal' (information found only on the networked computers of the person the subject of the information, or those that person has provided it to, such as by email). Those who hold parts of our digital personae in proprietary (or 'closed') systems can easily cumulate that information with our total 'public' digital persona, as well as combining it with that held in other proprietary systems to which they have access. From the cumulative effect of our digital personae, others will draw inferences about our personalities and behaviour. The extent to which we will be able (technically and/or legally) to exercise some control over what makes up our digital personae will be an important issue. Whether the use of anonymous or pseudonymous transactions

---

21   As in note 9 *supra*, this is as yet usually only something weaker than true identification. The use of digital signatures, discussed below, may change this.

22   R Clarke, "The Digital Persona and its Application to Data Surveillance" (1994) *The Information Society* March 1994; for abstract only: <http://www.anu.edu.au/people/Roger.Clarke/DV/AbstractDigPersona.html>.

23   Clarke makes a useful distinction between the "passive digital persona", the cumulation of details of our transactions and communications that are discoverable on the Internet (our snail tracks), and the 'active digital persona', the computerised 'agents' of various types that actively affect what information the user receives or discloses (ranging from filters rejecting or classifying or replying to incoming mail, to 'knowbots' regularly trawling for information that the user wants).

will be prohibited, or in some cases will be required, is discussed in the later example 'Building anonymity into architecture'.

(iv) Identification at the Cyberspace / Real Space Interface

We only exist virtually in cyberspace: the digital persona is only a representation of the physical person that exists in real space. Identification occurs at the cyberspace/real space interface. In cyberspace it has often been relatively easy to impersonate someone. Recognising individuals over distance and time without recourse to human memory has always been a key organisational challenge to bureaucracies.[24] Tokens, knowledge and biometrics, or combinations of these, provide the links between the physical person and the file. Identification in cyberspace intensifies the challenge because it removes any physical settings or proximity which assist identification, and it often requires real time responses. The reliability of electronic commerce, or email and other Internet transactions, or the believability of a person's digital persona, depends to a very large extent on the continuing reliability of links between the virtual and physical person.

Biometric identifiers entered directly into networked devices will in the longer run provide a main means of identification. In the more immediate future, smart cards are likely to provide one of the main bridges between physical and virtual identity. They have many potential advantages because they can include in the one token (i) digital representations of value (e-cash or credit); (ii) digital signatures (to provide authentication of messages transmitted); and (iii) digital biometric identifiers (to guarantee security/access to networks). Their portability means they can be the link between mobile people and pervasive networks.

(v) An Encrypted Space: Public Key Infrastructure

Public key (asymmetric) cryptography may be one of the most significant inventions of the twentieth century, information technology's equivalent of the invention of nuclear weapons. A large part of the existence of many people and organisations in cyberspace will be an encrypted one, in that they will be acting via messages and transactions which are encrypted for reasons of confidentiality or authentication or both. Cryptography is likely to be essential for many aspects of the Internet's commercial operations: digital cash; credit transactions; non-repudiation of contracts; authenticity of electronically filed and retrieved documents. Most encrypted transactions will depend upon an infrastructure involving new types of entities such as Certification Authorities. While digital libertarians hailed the potential of encryption to increase privacy of communications, the counterpoint is that the other main use of public key cryptography, authentication through the use of digital signatures, is likely to increase dramatically the extent of strong identification of communications in cyberspace. As with the Internet generally, whether public key cryptography has a repressive or the liberating effect is yet to be determined.

---

24 R Clarke "Human Identification in Information Systems: Management Challenges and Public Policy Issues" (1994) 7 *Information Technology and People* 6:
<http://www.anu.edu.au/people/Roger.Clarke/DV/HumanID.html>.

III.   THEORIES OF CYBERSPACE REGULATION
DIGITAL REALISM NEEDED

Cyberspace does have characteristics that distinguish it from real space, and they make it more difficult for us to develop a coherent approach to how it should (or should not) be regulated by law. A theory of regulation which is capable of taking account of these unique characteristics is needed, and authors such as a Reidenberg, Boyle, Johnson and Post, and Lessig have put forward candidates.

Joel Reidenberg argues that 'the set of rules for information flows imposed by technology and communication networks form a "Lex Informatica" that policy makers must understand, consciously recognise and encourage'.[25] He argues that the 'technological architectures' of networks impose a set of 'rules for the access to and use of information' distinct from law, and that policy choices are available through control of the technology itself, 'through laws that cause technology to exclude possible options, or through laws that cause users to restrict certain actions'. Reidenberg's work contains many valuable examples of the interplay between 'technological architectures' and law as sources of regulation of cyberspace, but does not provide a sufficiently general approach to determining the most effective way of regulating cyberspace in a particular instance (for example, the roles that morality and markets might play), or a political basis for criticising regulatory options.

Johnson and Post argue[26] for what they call 'net federalism' or 'decentralised, emergent law'. Their argument is that the model for the governance of the Internet which is most likely to be successful is 'de facto rules [which] may emerge as a result of the complex interplay of individual decisions' by various types of system administrators and by users. They argue[27] that:

> Net federalism looks very different than what we have become accustomed to, because here individual network systems, rather than territorially-based sovereigns, are the essential governance units. The law of the net has emerged, and we believe can continue to emerge, from the voluntary adherence of large numbers of network administrators to basic rules of law (and dispute resolution systems to adjudicate the inevitable inter-network disputes), with individual users 'voting with their electrons' to join the particular systems they find most congenial.

Johnson and Post's argument is essentially moral and political, rather than a method of analysis of cyberspace regulation: the architecture of the Internet facilitates a form of self-regulation through a 'collective conversation'; we have not yet tried sufficiently to utilise this capacity; but if we do it will produce the

---

25   J Reidenberg, "Lex Informatica" (1998) 76 *Texas Law Review* 553; see also J Reidenberg, "Governing Networks and Rule-Making in Cyberspace" (1996) 45 *Emory Law Journal* 912-30.

26   DR Johnson and D Post "And How Shall the Net be Governed? - A Meditation on the Relative Virtues of Decentralized, Emergent Law": <http://www.cli.org/emdraft.html>; DR Johnson and D Post "Law and Borders: The Rise of Law in Cyberspace" (1996) 48 *Stanford Law Review* 1367; version available at: <http://www.cli.org/X0025_LBFIN.html>; other papers by Johnson and Post are available at the Cyberspace Law Institute site: <http://www.cli.org/>.

27   'Conclusion, David R Johnson & David Post "And How Shall the Net be Governed? - A Meditation on the Relative Virtues of Decentralized, Emergent Law": <http://www.cli.org/emdraft.html>.

most effective form of regulation.[28]

A more comprehensive theoretical approach to cyberspace regulation is advanced by Lawrence Lessig in a number of articles.[29] To summarise, his starting point is that behaviour is regulated by four types of constraints: laws, social norms, markets and 'nature' (or the 'architecture' of real space). However, this 'anti-law' starting point is counterbalanced by emphasis on the extent to which the law indirectly seeks to regulate behaviour by directly influencing the three other constraints: social norms, markets and (sometimes) 'nature'. Applying this analysis to cyberspace, Lessig identifies the equivalent of 'nature' as 'code, or the software that makes cyberspace as it is, ... a set of constraints on how one can behave', and concludes that code is in general more pervasive and effective ('immediate') a constraint in cyberspace than is nature in real space. However, code is also more susceptible to being changed by law (more plastic) than is nature. Therefore, both code and law (in its indirect form) are more important as regulation of cyberspace than many realise or admit. Also, in order to analyse comprehensively the options available to affect particular behaviours, all four types of constraints (and the potential of law to indirectly regulate via the other three) must be considered.

Lessig describes this approach[30] as part of a more general reaction against the University of Chicago Law School's obsession with the limits of law as a regulator. The 'old' Chicago School's anti-law analysis emphasised the effectiveness (in contrast with law) of both markets and social norms as regulators of individual behaviour, and how both markets and norms were relatively impervious to control by law. A third influential anti-law stream arises from Michel Foucault's work,[31] where the fine-grained controls of continuous surveillance through the 'architectures' of social life (including the built environment, and the social institutions that inhabit it) contrast with the coarse controls of law. In summary, these anti-law approaches emphasise the effectiveness of the three other types of constraint – markets, norms, and 'nature'/'architecture' – at the expense of law.

---

28   'We've hardly tried a collective conversation designed to allow responsible participants to set their own rules and to help all concerned - online and off - seek to understand and respect others' vital interests. Yet that kind of conversation is precisely the kind of activity the net itself is designed - thanks to the engineers - to facilitate': *ibid.*

29   Particularly "The Law Of The Horse: What Cyberlaw Might Teach", 11 June 1998 draft available at: <http://cyber.law.harvard.edu/works/lessig/law_horse.pdf> and via the *Stanford Technology Law Review Working Papers* 1997 draft <http://stlr.stanford.edu/STLR/Working_Papers/97_Lessig_1/index.htm>); see also "Constitution and Code" (1996-7) 27 *Cumberland Law Review* 1; "Intellectual Property and Code" (1996) 11 *St John's Journal of Legal Commentary* Issue 3; "Reading the Constitution in Cyberspace" (1997) 45 *Emory L. J.* 869-910: available at <http://www.law.emory.edu/ELJ/volumes/sum96/lessig.html>; "The Architecture of Privacy" (2nd Draft), *Taiwan Net '98*, Taipei March 1998, available at: <http://cyber.law.harvard.edu/works/lessig/architecture_priv.pdf> (visited 15/10/08); Lawrence Lessig and Paul Resnick, "The Architectures of Mandated Access Controls": available at <http://cyber.law.harvard.edu/works/lessig/Tprc98_d.pdf>; see also other papers listed at the Harvard site: <http://cyber.law.harvard.edu/lessigcurres.html>.

30   L Lessig, *ibid* in Part 1 "The Regulation of Real Space'.

31   Particularly M Foucault *Discipline and Punish: The Birth of the Prison*, Peregrine Books (1977) (translated by A Sheridan); see also Boyle, note 6 *supra*, at Part 6 "Foucault & the Jurisprudence of Digital Libertarianism"

Digital libertarianism's arguments, that law is destined to be ineffective in cyberspace - are often a particular application of 'anti-law' arguments to the new frontier of cyberspace, which to a large extent borrows from the earlier anti-law streams. The optimistic versions stress the potential for forms of self-regulation in cyberspace, which is to a large extent an emphasis on social norms as regulation. The pessimistic versions are resigned to a world of uncontrollable surveillance and manipulation driven by market imperatives. Both versions see little positive role for law in cyberspace regulation, and that is where Lessig (and Boyle) are correct in differing from them. A theory that recognises and explains the ability of law to regulate cyberspace both for good and for ill could be called 'digital realism', to contrast with both the extremes of optimism and pessimism that a failure to understand the role of law in cyberspace can lead to.

All of the authors mentioned share an emphasis on the importance of the technical infrastructure of cyberspace – whether they call it 'code' or 'Lex Informatica' or 'Net federalism' – as a source of regulation of cyberspace. In my view Lessig presents the most useful and comprehensive theoretical framework, but as I will explain below it is one which needs significant modification, and leads me to prefer the term 'architecture' to 'code'. The rest of this article supports the view that to understand the control (de facto and de jure) of cyberspace architecture is the key to understanding the regulation of cyberspace.

IV.   CYBERSPACE REGULATION AS A FUNCTION OF FOUR CONSTRAINTS

A good starting point is to consider in more detail the four types of constraint discussed by Lessig,[32] and the operation of each in cyberspace.

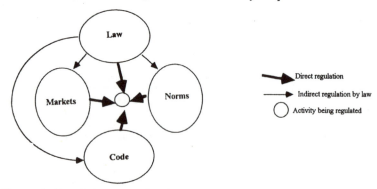

Figure 1: Regulation as a function of four types of constraints (adapted from L Lessig)[33]

---

32   The section derives from the discussion of the four constraints in L Lessig, note 29 *supra*. The examples used are mine except where noted.

33   Figure 1 is a recreation, not as well drawn and with slightly different headings, of L Lessig's diagram in L Lessig, note 29 *supra*.

1998 *UNSW Law Journal* **603**

A. Norms, Morality and Self-Regulation

In real space social norms cause us to frown on racist jokes or sexist language, to tell the truth about our age where concessions might be available, and to observe other conventions both because we have been brought up to feel guilty if we act otherwise, and also because we fear social embarrassment by doing otherwise (at least if caught). Norms also aid the observance of the sanctions of law by making us guilty about breaking laws even if the likelihood of enforcement is next to nil.

In cyberspace norms play similar roles, and some special ones. The observance of the customs of netiquette by individual Internet users means that you avoid responding to email IN FULL CAPITALS even if you are annoyed (just as you don't shout in arguments), and most people don't send 1 MB attachments to discussion lists with thousands of members. If some Internet businesses voluntarily adopt and adhere to self-regulatory schemes such as the Platform for Privacy Preferences (P3P), then their observance would be because they had adopted the norms of P3P (whatever their motivation for so doing). There is also code/architecture which facilitates P3P, but it does not enforce its norms, as discussed later.

The reasons why norms are effective sanctions in cyberspace are however, likely to be significantly difference from real space. Cyberspace 'morality' may become like the morality of the panopticon or the goldfish bowl. The obvious lesson from Foucault[34] is that, to the extent that we fear and assume surveillance of our activities by others in cyberspace (whether in real time or ex post facto), we are likely to condition our actions to adhere to norms relevant to that behaviour, irrespective of the existence of legal sanctions. For example, anyone visiting websites containing pornographic material will do so conscious that their machine address (at least) will be known to wherever they visit, and potentially traceable back to them. The extent of the fear will often be proportional to their proximity to those likely to be carrying out the surveillance. Surveillance of email by employers is a powerful sanction, as is sharing a computer with a spouse. However, cyberspace tends to obliterate such distances even where they seem to exist. The fear of obviously well-targeted email appearing in your local (under surveillance) email inbox generated by unwise visits to websites on the other side of the world is likely to dissuade some people from such visits.[35]

---

34 M Foucault note 31 supra.
35 In fact this will not usually happen unless you have set your browser software to disclose your email address, or unless your machine address is correlated with your email address on some external source. However, many Internet users will not be sophisticated enough to realise this, and that is the point: the fear of inadvertent disclosure is enough to condition behaviour.

B. Markets

Markets constrain behaviours in obvious ways in real space, influenced by property, contract and other laws which regulate those markets. The market constraints in cyberspace are as important as in real space. Unpopular code/architecture can perish where market forces operate. One distinctive feature of their operation in cyberspace is likely to be network effects, described by Lemley and McGowan as "markets in which the value that consumers place on a good increases as others use the good".[36] Many aspects of the Internet are 'archetypal examples of network markets' in □that they 'involve products whose entire value lies in facilitating access between a consumer and others who own the product'. 'The principal characteristics distinguishing such products ... are the absence of material inherent value and the necessity for common standards among goods incorporated into the network'.[37] Market constraints are not the focus of this article, and will be referred to only incidentally in the examples that follow.

C. 'Code', 'Nature' and 'Architecture'

In real space laws criminalising bank robbery are very helpful, but thick walls, bulletproof glass, armed guards and combination locks on safes are the most effective constraints. We don't need a law on larceny of real property. When considering the combination of constraints which make up regulation in real space, it is easy to ignore the roles of the natural environment, the artefacts of the built environment, and human biology, because we so often take them as the 'givens' of the situation being regulated. In many situations this is because they are non-malleable as constraints (rigid plasticity, in Lessig's terminology discussed below).

Lessig describes the equivalent of real space nature as "code, or the software that makes cyberspace as it is, ... a set of constraints on how one can behave". "The substance of these constraints vary, but they are all experienced as conditions on one's access to cyberspace".[38] His examples are whether or not passwords or other identification are required for access, whether encryption is allowed, and whether or not an individual's 'click stream' is tracked. He argues that is code/nature is more important in cyberspace regulation than in real space, for reasons explored in the following section.

D. Law: Direct and Indirect Regulation

Law typically regulates individual behaviour directly, and does so by threatening ex post facto sanctions. However, in real space as well as cyberspace, law also regulates individual behaviour indirectly, by aiming to change markets,

---

36   MA Lemley and D McGowan 'Legal Implications of Network Economic Effects' (1998) 86 *California Law Review* 479.

37   MA Lemley and D McGowan, *ibid* at 488-9.

38   L Lessig, note 29 *supra*.

norms or code. As others have done in different contexts, Lessig argues[39] that the anti-law Chicago School is misleading in that it assumes that the other constraints – markets, norms and code/architecture – are independent of law, but in fact they are in part a product of the law. We have to ask to what extent a particular constraint is created by law, and to what extent it can be changed by law. Law does not only affect individual behaviour directly (for example, by prohibiting certain conduct), but also indirectly by seeking to change markets, norms or architectures.

As in one of Lessig's examples,[40] governments can choose to address the barriers faced by disabled people by forbidding discriminatory conduct (direct regulation by law), by requiring educational institutions to teach children to respect the interests of the disabled (law indirectly regulating norms), or by requiring building codes to allow for access ramps and other physical facilities (law indirectly regulating real space 'code'). In real space, he argues, these indirect regulations are already 'the regulatory technique of choice'.

As will be illustrated later in this paper, law in cyberspace will often be more effective if it regulates code/architecture rather than trying to directly regulate individual behaviour.

V.   FIVE FEATURES OF CYBERSPACE ARCHITECTURE AS REGULATION

There are some important general features of cyberspace code ('architecture' as I will call it), some of which are identified by Lessig.[41] They are explained here and illustrated in the examples that follow.

A.   Architecture is More than Software

Lessig's characterisation of code as software ("code, or the software that makes cyberspace as it is") is an oversimplification. The equivalent of 'nature' in cyberspace needs to be understood as including a number of elements other than software, including at least hardware, Internet protocols and other standards, and aspects of human biology. Lessig is not consistent in limiting code to software, as he refers to "code ... or protocols", and includes in his examples of code both firmware (the 'V-chip') and a proposed protocol (PICS).[42] We need a more comprehensive statement of what is included in this constraint (and a better name).

Most obviously, we must include the hardware that comprises the physical infrastructure of cyberspace networks (such as routers, cabling, satellites). For example, although the Internet's protocols were designed to make particular physical connections irrelevant by allowing messages to route around outages, physical topography is still important in countries where governments only allow international connection to the Internet through a limited number of closely

---

39   *Ibid.*

40   *Ibid.*

41   L Lessig note 29 *supra*; points (ii), (iii) and (iv) in this section follow Lessig's approach, but (i) and (v) differ.

42   Platform for Internet Content Selection.

supervised junctions.

More important are Internet protocols (actual or proposed) such as TCP/IP, PICS, P3P or the Robot Exclusion Standard, not software in themselves but standards which can be implemented in software.[43] Protocols are code developed by participatory processes particular to the Internet, and are of vital importance as non-proprietary code.

Human biology can also be part of code, because various forms of biometrics will provide the 'authenticated' link between individuals and pervasive networks in the near future: identification is the 'real space/cyberspace interface'. Physical tokens (for example smart cards) are also important (at least for the time being), because they provide a portable link between individuals and networks.

If this argument is accepted, then 'code' becomes an inappropriate term, in that one of its usages is a synonym for software and thus is too narrow in its connotations. 'Code' is also far too ambiguous to be useful, since it is used in some contexts to refer to 'codes of conduct' (thus risking confusion with norms), and codification as opposed to less systematic laws (thus risking confusion with law). The term 'architecture' or 'cyberspace architecture' more fully expresses the nature of this constraint, and carries fewer ambiguous connotations. In my view 'architecture' should be used in preference to 'code'. In recent articles, Lessig has started to refer to "the architecture of privacy" and "the architecture of mandated access controls".[44]

The fact that cyberspace architecture has a number of components (software, protocols, hardware etc), is also helpful in explaining some differences in how these components operate as constraints. For example, in relation to the matters discussed below, protocols are usually less plastic than software.

B. Architecture has Immediacy as a Constraint

The directness or immediacy of a constraint ('A constraint is direct when its force gets applied immediately.') is one determinant of its effectiveness, the more direct the better. Real space architecture typically regulates more directly than law, which threatens punishment after the breach. It does not always enforce. directly - 'the constraints of cancer are years away from the puff'.[45] The extent to which directness can be made to vary is a basis for choice between forms of regulation. Cyberspace architecture is often self-executing (for example, passwords and other forms of access controls), but not necessarily so.

C. Most Architecture has High Plasticity

The plasticity of a constraint is the ease with which it can be changed. Plasticity is a major variable in the extent to which law can regulate a constraint, with more plastic constraints more susceptible to change by law. The tides were not plastic at

43 R Clarke, G Dempsey, OC Nee and RF O'Connor 'A Primer on Internet Technology' available at <http://www.anu.edu.au/people/Roger.Clarke/II/IPrimer.html> provides brief explanations of Internet protocols and other standards.
44 See L Lessig, note 29 *supra* for article titles.
45 L Lessig, *ibid*.

all, as King Canute found. Australia's immigration constraints are premised on an absence of land borders with any other country, those of North American countries are not, and there is nothing any of them can do to change this. In other situations, the physical environment is a more plastic constraint. Architecture (in its real space sense) is very plastic while still in the planning stage (less so when built), and thus we have building codes. There is a great deal of choice in the nature and effectiveness of the constraints embodied in various styles of architecture, as Bentham stressed with his 'simple idea in architecture', the Panopticon.[46] In any given context where regulatory choice is being considered, the relative plasticity of the four types of regulation needs consideration.

Cyberspace architecture is inherently relatively plastic, since it is almost entirely a human artefact, whereas real space 'nature' is only partly artefact. This is one reason why law regulating cyberspace architecture is likely to be effective. It is generally possible for law to require changes to software, standards and hardware. Only a few aspects of cyberspace, such as those aspects of human biology with which it interacts, are impervious to law, and relatively few (perhaps some very basic protocols such as TCP/IP) would be very resistant to change by law.

D. The Legitimacy of Architecture Depends on Who Controls It

Recognition of the significance of cyberspace architecture as regulation forces us to look to its origins. Lessig poses the question:[47]

> Once it is plain that code can replace law, the pedigree of the codewriters becomes central. Code in essence becomes an alternative sovereign – since it is in essence an alternative structure of regulation. But who authors this sovereign authority? And with what legitimacy?

Control of cyberspace architecture is at present highly fragmented. Much of the most general architecture of cyberspace, protocols and standards, has been developed and is controlled by a variety of broadly representative and participatory non-government organisations of Internet governance, including the World Wide Web Consortium (W3C), the Internet Engineering Task Force (IETF), the Internet Society, the International Standards Organisation (ISO) and new players such as the gTLD-MoU. The fact that there is now far greater diversity of participants in global networks than when the Internet was a relatively homogenous and more technically-oriented community means that the consensus models of many institution of Internet governance will be under increasing strain, and subjected to increased demands to accommodate public policies,[48] as illustrated by the attempts to develop a new domain name system.

Governments already determine a considerable amount of the cyberspace architecture through legislation, as can be seen in the examples following. Increasingly, private companies such as Microsoft control significant parts of the

---

46 M Foucault, note 31 *supra* at 200-209.
47 L Lessig, note 29 *supra*.
48 Cf Reidenberg, note 25 *supra* at 592.

code of cyberspace through market share of a relatively small number of competing products such as browsers. As mentioned earlier, Boyle argues that digital libertarians have underestimated the extent to which both private power and governments already determine the architecture of cyberspace. Sometimes, the cumulative effect of individual users exercise significant control over architecture through market choices, as illustrated by the widespread usage of the PGP ('Pretty Good Privacy') encryption software. More often, intermediaries such as system operators or Internet Service Providers (ISPs) exercise significant controls over what is and is not possible by individual users.

In any given situation, one of the questions to be asked is whether an existing or proposed form of regulation by architecture is appropriate, given the nature of the regulator.

E. Default Settings Give Regulation by Default

The importance of the default settings in various forms of cyberspace architecture has not yet received sufficient emphasis. Architecture does not only make certain courses of action possible or impossible. It may theoretically leave open a number of possible courses of action in cyberspace, but one option will have the advantage of being set as a default. In real space, doors are lockable, but in houses the default setting is 'open', whereas in prison it may be 'locked'. The significance of default settings in cyberspace is illustrated in the examples following, particularly the example of cookies.

VI.   REGULATION BY AND OF CYBERSPACE ARCHITECTURE: EXAMPLES

Having set out this sketch of a theoretical approach to regulation of cyberspace, the rest of this paper puts forward a number of examples which illustrate both differing aspects of how architecture regulates cyberspace, how cyberspace architecture is already regulated by law, and the regulatory choices that such an analysis can reveal. The work of Lessig, Boyle and Reidenberg provides extensive examples of architecture and its regulation in US law, often with a focus on content regulation and intellectual property. For non-American readers these examples are often complicated and made less relevant by legislative limits imposed by the US Constitution: the First Amendment is a local ordinance, after all. The examples following are drawn from universal Internet technical features, from Australian legislation, and from the German 'Multimedia Law',[49] one of the most extensive European attempts to regulate cyberspace architecture by law.

A. Building Anonymity into Architecture

The extent to which the surveillance capacity of cyberspace is limited, and

---

49 *Information and Communication Services Act* of 1997 (Informations- und Kommunikationsdienste-Gesetz - IuKDG) 1 August 1997- English translation at <http://www.iid.de/iukdg/iukdge.html>; see U Wuermeling, "Multimedia Law - Germany" (1998) 14 *Computer Law & Security Report* 41 for a summary; see also L Bygrave "Germany's Teleservices Data Protection Act" (1998) 5 *Privacy Law & Policy Reporter* 53.

1998 *UNSW Law Journal* **609**

where permitted made controllable by user choice, is perhaps the single key issue in the regulation of cyberspace.

Germany's *Teleservices Data Protection Act*[50] is a leading legislative example in addressing what the Germans call 'systemic data protection' ('Systemdatenschutz'), but we can also call 'legislating code'. The key provision requires the objective of minimising or eliminating the collection and use of personal information to be built into the 'design and selection of technical devices' (hardware and software) and thus into all aspects of cyberspace architecture:

> s3(4) The design and selection of technical devices to be used for teleservices shall be oriented to the goal of collecting, processing and using either no personal data at all or as few data as possible.

It is this design requirement that makes the specific requirement on service providers to provide anonymous and pseudonymous uses of teleservices "to the extent technically feasible and reasonable"[51] a meaningful requirement, because it removes the excuse that systems have not been designed to allow for anonymous or pseudonymous transactions. Here, the control of code by law is both a serious, though general, limitation on the types of Internet systems that may be built, and a necessary precondition for legal sanctions aimed directly at the behaviour of service providers.

(i)   The 'Anonymity Principle' in Australia

In Australia the 'anonymity principle' has been making progress toward becoming a legal requirement of cyberspace architecture. Its local origins lie in Principle 10 of the *Australian Privacy Charter* (1994): 'People should have the option of not identifying themselves when entering transactions'.[52]

In 1998 the Australian Privacy Commissioner's *National Principles for the Fair Handling of Personal Information*[53] included Principle 8 "Wherever it is lawful and practicable, individuals should have the option of not identifying themselves when entering transactions". The Victorian Government proposes to include a legislative formulation of these principles in its *Data Protection Act.*[54] One of the main differences between this formulation and that in the German law is that it does not have the explicit legislative requirement for systems to be designed to allow anonymity and pseudonymity, so it is possible that it may be interpreted to allow the excuse that it is not 'practicable' because the system design makes it technically impossible.

Somewhat more concrete requirements for code to allow anonymity may emerge from the Australian Commonwealth Government's development of standards for

---

50   Article 2 of the *Information and Communications Services Act* of 1997 - see references above.

51   s4(1) The provider shall offer the user anonymous use and payment of teleservices or use and payment under a pseudonym to the extent technically feasible and reasonable. The user shall be informed about these options.

52   Australian Privacy Charter Council (1994) *Australian Privacy Charter*, available at: <http://www.anu.edu.au/people/Roger.Clarke/DV/PrivacyCharter.html>, and explanatory material at <http://www.anu.edu.au/people/Roger.Clarke/DV/PrivChHist.html>.

53   <http://www.privacy.gov.au/news/p6_4_1.html>.

54   See G Greenleaf, "Will Stockdale Break the Privacy Impasse?" (1998) 5 *Privacy Law & Policy Reporter* 21 at 22.

the use of encryption technologies (both for digital signatures and confidentiality) in communications by and with Commonwealth Government agencies. The Government Public Key Authority (GPKA)[55] is considering requiring facilities for anonymity and pseudonymity to be designed in as a condition of accreditation of Certification Authorities (CAs) that wish to operate in the Commonwealth government sector, as part of the Government Public Key Infrastructure (GPKI).[56]

B.   Cookies: Caller ID with Hidden Opt-Out

Cookies are an element of Internet protocols, server software and browser software which allow information to be placed on, and retrieved from, the user's hard disk during browsing of websites. Cookies allow a web server to 'know' such information as whether it has interacted with a particular user before, and to retrieve information from the user's hard disk about those previous interactions.[57] "Cookies are a way for a server to sustain a stateful session by passing information back to a user agent; the user agent returns the information back to the server on its next visit".[58]

Cookies are one of the most significant methods of surveillance of user browsing behaviour on the Internet. They provide a cost effective method of linking one instance of a user's browsing behaviour to another instance, allowing profiles of user behaviour to be created. They also allow the user's own hard disk to be used as a storage device for servers to record how they wish to interact with that user (for example, what type of advertisements to use).

Cookies were apparently an 'undocumented feature' in Netscape Navigator 2, with therefore no user control or knowledge as to when cookies were written or read during browsing. The existence and use of cookies prompted considerable protest by privacy organisations and others[59] from early 1996 onwards.

In Netscape Navigator Gold 3.0 (1996) the only options concerning cookies were (i) to accept all cookies without any warning (the default setting) or (ii) to be presented with an alert box every time before a cookie is accepted. There was no option allowing all cookies to be refused automatically without any alert box required.[60] The alert box is annoying, and responding to it slows down browser performance, so it is likely that many people would not change the default, even if they were aware it was possible to do so. Since the default was set at 'never

---

55   <http://www.gpka.gov.au/>.

56   Personal knowledge, due to the author's membership of the GPKA as a consumer representative. The GPKA has released 3rd Draft Criteria For Accreditation Of Certification Authorities (CAs)/Service Providers, but this element is not included in that draft: see <http://www.gpka.gov.au/working-groups/accreditation-evaluation/public/CAcriteria/CACriteria.htm>.

57   Netscape has described this as "Cookies are a general mechanism which server side connections (such as CGI scripts) can use to both store and retrieve information on the client side of the connection. The addition of a simple, persistent, client-side state significantly extends the capabilities of Web-based client/server applications." See quote at <http://www.epic.org/privacy/internet/cookies/>.

58   DM Kristol: <http://portal.research.bell-labs.com/~dmk/cookie.html>.

59   See 'The Coookies Page' (Electronic Privacy Information Center):
     <http://www.epic.org/privacy/internet/cookies/>.

60   This might mean that the browser could not access some pages, or even that occasional system crashes might result, but many users would prefer to have the option nevertheless.

warn', even the option to change would never be drawn to most users attention. In all these ways, the code conspired to maximise both the overt and covert 'acceptance' of cookies.

In Netscape Communicator 4.01 (1997), although the default setting is still 'Accept all cookies' (and do so without warning), it is now possible for users to choose to not accept cookies at all, or to only accept them after a warning. The result is that the code for cookies in version 4.01 is equivalent to caller-ID in telephony with the default set at opt-out (in secret, not drawn to the user's attention). Only the aware user can opt -out per line ('do not accept') or change the settings to the equivalents of per call opt-in ('warn me before accepting...'). It would be easy enough for the code to change the default setting to opt-in: the browser software would simply require the user to expressly opt in or out of accepting cookies, or (more drastic), change the default setting to 'do not accept'.

Also as Clarke points out,[61] the permission sought is only to write a cookie; cookies are automatically read by any servers who request them and know the ID of the desired cookie. There is a further option in Netscape Communicator 4.01 to accept only cookies that get sent back (only) to the originating server, at least allowing users to exclude cookies that can be read by servers run by third parties (which allows marketers to share user profile information).

Legislatures around the world have used law to regulate the consumer's options in relation to caller-ID. Regulation of the code of cookies presents similar policy choices. Germany's *Teleservices Data Protection Act*[62] deals with cookies in providing that 'in case of automatic processing' the user must be informed of the "type, scope, place and purposes" of collection of personal data "prior to the beginning of the procedure"[63] and also sets out ways by which consent can be given electronically. The overall effect on cookies would seem to be that browser code would have to be changed to accommodate one of the two opt-in approaches discussed above, but whether this has yet affected the operation of the Internet in Germany is not known.

C. Mandatory Surveillance Code: Interceptability and Decryption Ability

Surveillance of telecommunications by the state is an area where governments in Australia and elsewhere have shown little reluctance to legislate directly to require particular architectures for cyberspace. This is law mandating cyberspace architecture.

(i) Interceptability

Lessig gives the example of the 1994 US *Digital Telephony Act*[64] as a

---

61   R Clarke, "Cookies" (Version 1/6/98): <http://www.anu.edu.au/people/Roger.Clarke/II/Cookies.html>.

62   Article 2 of the *Information and Communications Services Act* of 1997 - see note 49 *supra*.

63   Section 3(5) provides in part "The user shall be informed about the type, scope, place and purposes of collection, processing and use of his personal data. In case of automated processing, which permits subsequent identification of the user and which prepares the collection, processing or use of personal data, the user shall be informed prior to the beginning of the procedure." Bygrave considers that the provision does affect cookies, note 49 *supra*.

64   PL NO 103-414.

requirement by Congress "that telephone companies select a network architecture that facilitates wire tapping".[65] In Australia the situation is much the same. The *Telecommunications Act* 1997 (Cth) Part 15 ('Cooperation with agencies') requires that carriers and carriage service providers must comply with obligations concerning interception capability and special assistance capability; must prepare and submit an annual interception capability plan; and must notify the Australian Communications Authority of technological changes affecting the provision of help to agencies in relation to carrying out of various law enforcement obligations under Part 14.[66]

These interception obligations are set by a determination by the Attorney-General, which "must specify an international standard or guidelines (the "international standard"), or the relevant part of the international standard, on which the determination is based" (s 322). The basis of this change resulting from the *Telecommunications Legislation Amendment Act* 1997 (Cth) is that:

> Australia has agreed to the use of International User Requirements at a meeting of the International Law Enforcement Telecommunications Seminar. This Bill will empower the Attorney-General to determine the specifics of interception capability. The capability requirements will be based on the International User Requirements[67]

This provision is therefore an example of cyberspace architecture in Australia being determined to a large degree by international agreements to which Australia is a party.

(ii) Decryption Ability

Although there is no direct prohibition on users sending encrypted messages over telecommunications networks, there are limitations on the extent to which carriers and carriage service providers can provide encryption services. Under the *Telecommunications Act* 1991 (Cth) licensing of network providers through the network service providers licences limited their ability to provide encryption facilities. The *Telecommunications Act* 1997 (Cth), as amended by the *Telecommunications Legislation Amendment Act* 1997 (Cth) also provides for 'special assistance capabilities' to be determined by the Attorney-General on the same basis as interception capability.

Keith Holland notes[68] that these requirements apply to both carriers and to carriage service providers, either of whom could be required "to include the ability to decrypt messages which may have been encrypted *by the carrier or service*

---

65   L Lessig, note 32 *supra*.

66   Summarising s 317 <http://www.austlii.edu.au/au/legis/cth/consol_act/ta1997214/s317.html>.

67   Department of the Parliamentary Library <http://www.aph.gov.au/library/pubs/bd/1997-98/98bd067.htm>: Bills Digest No 67 1997-98 Telecommunications Legislation Amendment Bill 1997. See also N Waters, "Telecommunications interception - extending the reach or maintaining the status quo" (1998) 4 *Privacy Law & Policy Reporter* 110.

68   K Holland. Assistant Secretary. Security Law and Justice Branch. Attorney-General's Department. in 'Recent International Legal Developments in Encryption' (IIR Conferences. 1998) available at: <http://www2.austlii.edu.au/itlaw/articles/Holland.html>. Holland seems to include decryption capacity as part of interception capacity. but the definition of 'interception' (s 320) means that it is more likely that decryption capacity is a 'special assistance capacity'.

provider as part of the normal operation of the service", but "does not, however, require carriers or service providers to decrypt traffic which has been encrypted by customers before being carried over the network". In summary, such restrictions do not prevent individual users from sending encrypted messages, but do limit the encryption services that carriers and service providers can provide. This is an example of law attempting to change cyberspace architecture by focussing on intermediaries (carriers and carriage service providers), while at the same time not attempting to regulate the equivalent activities of the end-users of telecommunications services because to do so would be futile.

D.   Spam Black Holes: Is Law Safe for 'Return To Sender' Architecture?

The fight against unsolicited commercial email (commonly called 'spam') is an example of control of architecture, rather than law, being used to advance consumer and citizen interests rather than commercial interests. There are a variety of strategies and software being used,[69] of which the most extreme is the creation of spam 'black holes' such as that created by the MAPS (the Mail Abuse Protection System) RBL (Realtime Blackhole List)[70] which describes itself as:

> The MAPS RBL is a system for creating intentional network outages for the purpose of limiting the transport of known-to-be-unwanted mass email. The MAPS RBL is a subscription system, such that no one is ever denied connectivity to a non-RBL-subscriber. If your network seems to have been 'blackholed' by us, be aware that the places you cannot reach have deliberately chosen not to exchange traffic with you. We are not the network's police force, but rather, a method to identify likely spam origin.

Mail servers adopting the MAPS RBL refuse to exchange email with any mail servers listed in the MAPS RBL because they have been judged to be the sources of spam or relay spam email. Users of such mail servers find that much of the Internet treats them as a 'black hole' from which mail is not permitted to leave. This is cyberspace architecture which combines some technical features for transmission of information with a set of semi-formalised practices by those controlling email servers.

This is a consumer-controlled aspect of architecture that challenges law. The operators of MAPS RBL state that they have been often threatened with legal actions for conspiracy in restraint of trade[71] but none of the threatened actions has proceeded. This example shows the regulatory choices which are open: an alternative to legislation prohibiting spam is simply to ensure (if necessary) that restraint of trade laws do not impede operators of Internet black hole facilities. Such a choice, though some argue it is too weak a response,[72] would avoid making any individual conduct criminal or tortious (possibly ineffectively), and leaves the matter to code and the 'marketspace' of choices by mail server operators.

---

69   See CAUCE, The Coalition Against Unsolicited Commercial Email - <http://www.cauce.org/>.
70   See statement on MAPS RBL website at <http://maps.vix.com/rbl/>.
71   *Sherman Antitrust Act* actions in the USA.
72   See CAUCE, The Coalition Against Unsolicited Commercial Email - <http://www.cauce.org/>.

E.   Platform For Privacy Preferences (P3P): What Can Protocols Achieve?

The World Wide Web Consortium (W3C) is developing the Platform For Privacy Preferences (P3P),[73] an Internet protocol which attempts to provide a framework to increase trust between web service providers and users of their services. As Roger Clarke explains,[74] the purpose of the P3P specification is to enable:

- websites to specify their personal data use and disclosure practices;
- web users to specify their expectations concerning personal data disclosure practices; and
- software agents to undertake negotiation, on behalf of the parties, in order to reach an agreement concerning the exchange of data between them.

In effect, it is to provide means whereby an individual can have sufficient information that he or she can make an informed decision on whether to permit further use of the data, or decline further use of the data. Moreover, that decision is to be able to be delegated to a software agent acting on behalf of the individual.[75]

P3P is a protocol which is intended to be able to be applied to support negotiations in a variety of Internet contexts, including explicit data provision (for example, answers to questions on web forms), implicit data provision (for example, capture of the 'click stream' or URLs of pages visited in succession), and explicit data provision from third sources (for example, a web user's stored profile of preferences, demographic details etc). How it can be applied to some extensions to basic HTML such as cookies and Java is not yet determined. P3P allows web users to have multiple digital pseudonyms (and therefore multiple digital personae), allowing a user to choose between a 'data-poor' or 'data rich' personality depending on the site visited.[76]

P3P is the first important privacy initiative to have emerged from the consultative and self-regulatory structures of Internet governance (although dominated by W3C staff members), and for that reason alone is of considerable significance. Otherwise, it is simply an example

Clarke compares what P3P is attempting to deliver against the OECD privacy Guidelines,[77] and concludes that it only addresses parts of three of the eight

---

73   See the Platform for Privacy Preferences pages on World Wide Web Consortium website at: <http://www.w3c.org/P3P/>.
74   R Clarke, "Platform for Privacy Preferences: An Overview", which is an excellent, simple overview of P3P: <http://www.anu.edu.au/people/Roger.Clarke/DV/P3POview.html>.
75   *Ibid.*
76   Paragraph summarised from R Clarke, note 74 *supra*.
77   R Clarke 'Platform for Privacy Preferences: A Critique': <http://www.anu.edu.au/people/Roger.Clarke/DV/P3PCrit.html>.

1998 *UNSW Law Journal* **615**

OECD Principles.[78]

The more substantial criticism is that P3P says nothing about measures to ensure that it is complied with. If the web service provider breaches the practices that it has told the user that it adopts during a P3P 'negotiation' what can the user do about it (assuming he or she ever finds out in the first place)? P3P does not require the web service provider to log access and uses of the data it collects. P3P is not a certification scheme, and provides no guarantee of audits or similar protective measures (industry based certification initiatives like TRUSTe could supplement it). There is no guarantee that the P3P framework provides any linkage to a particular country's laws (such as contract laws or data protection laws), as Clarke points out, so P3P 'promises' may be legally meaningless. There is an 'assurance statement' in the Protocol where an attempt could be made to provide either contractually binding or legally descriptive statements, but its use is not compulsory.

P3P could develop as one of many useful forms of privacy protection, but it will be of little value unless it meshes with law and organisational practices. P3P is therefore an instance of where law is necessary to make protections offered by cyberspace architecture meaningful. Until law does that, P3P could be little more than a framework for deception.

The Electronic Privacy Information Center (EPIC) identifies a different danger: it considers P3P as, in effect, a framework for efficient collection of personal information as a condition of entry to websites. The possibility of increasing exclusion of those who value their privacy may make support for this initiative counter-productive to privacy, compared with simply opposing the increased collection of personal information.[79] EPIC's approach is one which would see limited value in law providing a legal framework to support and enforce P3P, and more value in legislation requiring architecture which supports anonymity, such as in the German law.

F. Stopping Searching - Robot Exclusion Standards

Internet-wide search engines such as Alta Vista and HotBot use robots (also known as spiders or webcrawlers)[80] to trawl the Internet, creating complete word occurrence indexes of every web page and every item posted to every News group that the spider is allowed to access.[81] As a result it is now possible to search for occurrences of a name or phrase occurring anywhere in the text of any web page, or in any News posting.

Web spiders and Internet search engines pose issues for copyright and privacy

---

78 It addresses data collection directly from the individual concerned, limitations on use and disclosure, and openness about use and disclosure policies, but does not address other principles relating to collection from third parties, subject access to data held by the web-site operator, retention of data and security. This is not necessarily a criticism, merely a limitation of one tool, but it would seem that some of these matters could be addressed by the same protocol in order to give more comprehensive privacy protection.

79 J Clausing 'Proposed privacy standards fail to please advocates of online privacy' 2 June 1998, *NYT Cybertimes* <http://www.nytimes.com/library/tech/98/06/cyber/articles/02privacy.html>.

80 See 'The Web Robots Page': <http://info.webcrawler.com/mak/projects/robots/robots.html>.

81 Many web robots are also self-limiting and only index sites down to a certain depth, so they are not comprehensive.

policies. It is possible that some Internet search engines might breach copyright laws (at least those which provide not just document titles in search results but short extracts as well), but in most cases the owners of such pages will welcome the extra access to their pages directed there by the search engine. Irrespective of copyright considerations some website operators might simply not want other search engines providing direct access to pages on their site, for reasons such as wanting users to use their own customised search engine instead, or because they do not think that web spiders update their indexes often enough, or because they are concerned that extensive access by robots will degrade performance of their server.

There is also a type of privacy issue. Technically, before robots can index any information on the web or in a newsgroup, it must have been made available to everyone on the Internet.[82] Nevertheless, many who place information on the Internet would not expect that it will be read by anyone outside those with whom they have some common experience, or the information used for purposes completely outside the intended purposes for which it was provided. For example, those involved in creating web pages, or involved in newsgroup discussions, concerning (say) gay and lesbian issues or issues relating to minority religious groups, could find that information about them was being systematically compiled and disseminated so as to harm them. Those who once valued the Internet as an escape from the values of small communities may find there is no longer any escape except behind barricades of secret communications.

Should there be some right not to be indexed? Legislative intervention would probably be dangerous, because this involves freedom of speech and freedom of the press considerations in a new context not just copyright and privacy. However, there are good reasons to accommodate the wishes of those who don't wish their pages to be indexed. Copyright law is likely to prove a very blunt instrument here. If, for example, copyright law was interpreted so that it was a breach of copyright to operate a web spider without obtaining the consent of each site indexed, the result would be that the cost of providing Internet-wide search facilities would rise very sharply, as operators of web spiders would be forced to obtain such consents in relation to millions of web pages. In all probability, only the few largest commercial players would have any prospect of sustaining such facilities, and far fewer pages would be indexed as operators would find it uneconomical to contact site owners who only provided a few pages. As a result the web could easily become unnavigable and impoverished as a source of information.

Can control of architecture provide an answer to this dilemma? There is a customary limitation on the operation of robots, which provides part of the answer. The *Robot Exclusion Protocol (1994)*[83] allows a server administrator to define[84] which parts of a website are not allowed to be indexed by robots (with exceptions for particular robots if desired). The default is assumed that if a site does not choose to exclude robots in this way, the whole of the site is available to

---

82   This must be done either by posting it to a newsgroup or putting it in a public_html directory or equivalent.
83   *A Standard for Robot Exclusion*: <http://info.webcrawler.com/mak/projects/robots/exclusion.html>.
84   In the file on the local URL "/robots.txt".

be indexed. The Protocol is not yet[85] any official Internet standard but rather "a common facility the majority of robot authors offer the WWW community to protect WWW server against unwanted accesses by their robots", and there are no sanctions against web spiders that ignore the Protocol and index sites or parts of sites contrary to instructions.

The authors of the Protocol recognised that it had limits because only a server administrator can maintain the list of pages on the server which are not to be indexed, not the owner of individual pages on the server. The Robots META tag has therefore been developed,[86] so that individual pages can contain information in their header that excludes robot indexing on a page-by-page basis. A tag of the form <META NAME="ROBOTS" CONTENT="NOINDEX, NOFOLLOW"> means that a robot should neither index this document, nor analyse it for links. The extent to which this tag is observed by robots (or used by page owners) is uncertain but seems not yet to be widespread, though its equivalent for Usenet posts is used widely.[87]

If there is near universal observance of the *Robot Exclusion Protocol* and the Robots META tag (when used) then this could be regarded as a reasonable resolution of the issue through a combination of architecture and self-regulation (norms or morality). Although it places the burden of opting out on those who do not wish their servers or pages to be searchable, this may well be a reasonable trade-off against the disastrous consequences for the Internet of requiring consent to be obtained from each individual page owner.

However, code and norms may not be enough. If the Protocol and the tag were ignored widely by robots, then legislation requiring the observance of such requests not to be indexed could be justifiable. This would be legislation requiring the observance of architecture which is not self-executing. On the other side of the coin, it might become necessary for legislation to provide a limited right to index, by ensuring that the transitory copying involved in the operation of a web spider was not prohibited, in which case legislation would be making architecture possible.

G. Electronic Copyright Management Systems (ECMS): 'IP Phone Home'

Digital libertarians expected intellectual property law to be one of the first casualties of cyberspace, because the process of digitisation of works made them infinitely reproducible at virtually no marginal costs, and infinitely distributable via the Internet. 'Everything [you know] about intellectual property is wrong'

---

85 There is now an 'Internet Draft', a working documents of the Internet Engineering Task Force (IETF), "A Method for Web Robots Control" (1996, expired June 1997):
<http://info.webcrawler.com/mak/projects/robots/norobots-rfc.html>.

86 The Robots META tag is explained at:
<http://info.webcrawler.com/mak/projects/robots/exclusion.html>#meta>.

87 Deja News, Alta Vista and some other search facilities allow users to insert the flag 'x-no-archive:yes' at the beginning of each post, and they are then not indexed. Old Internet information presents different problems. 'Living down' old Internet information is still possible. Web indexing engines only maintain details of current versions of pages. Some Usenet indexes such Alta Vista only retain postings for a few weeks or months, but DejaNews intends to archive all Usenet posts as far back as it can. However, it does accept requests for old posts to be deleted - again, an opt-out solution.

claimed John Perry Barlow.[88] As Lessig observes, infinite copies could only be made if "the code permits such copying", and why shouldn't the code be changed to make such copying impossible'?[89] It has only taken a few years for intellectual property to become one of the most controversial areas where cyberspace architecture is said to be replacing law as the most effective method of protection.

The controversy about electronic copyright management systems (ECMS), as copyright-protecting technologies are often called, stems from at least three main concerns:

- The architecture of ECMS need not observe any of the public interest limitations built in to copyright law . These include the right to lend a work for use by others (the basis of libraries, the 'first sale doctrine'), and the various 'fair dealing' rights to copy works or parts thereof for purposes such as 'criticism and review' or 'private study and research'. As Lessig puts it "what the law reserves as an limitation on the property holder's rights the code could ignore".[90] If dealings in relation to intellectual property become direct transactions where it is practical for the intellectual property owner to enter into a contract with the user (unlike the purchase of a book in a store), then such contracts are likely to routinely exclude such public interest exceptions.

- The enforcement of such contracts is also unlike real space contracts, Lessig points out, because whereas the law always takes into account various public and private interests in determining the extent and means by which contracts will be enforced, when contracts are self-enforced by code (for example, by the intellectual property suddenly becoming unusable) these public values are not likely to be taken into account.[91] We might add that when the law enforces a contract there is an independent assessment of whether there has been a breach of the contract, whereas here the enforcement is automated and unilateral, built into the architecture. If 'code contracts' replace law, these are not necessarily the same as 'law contracts', and may not be in the public interest.

- The amount of on-line surveillance of users of intellectual property may be unacceptable, compared with the ways in which we use intellectual property in real space, as discussed below.

There are numerous technologies and products now being developed which will provide different forms of technological protection to intellectual property: digital

---

88   JP Barlow, "Selling Wine Without Bottles: The Economy of Mind on the Global Net" *Wired* 2.03 (1993) at
      86, available at:
      <http://www.eff.org/pub/Publications/John_Perry_Barlow/HTML/idea_economy_article.html>.

89   L Lessig, note 29 *supra* at "Code Replacing Law: Intellectual Property".

90   *Ibid.* Lessig also notes extensive argument in the USA as to whether "the fair use exceptions to copyright
      protection are not affirmative rights against the copyright holder, but instead the consequence of not being able
      to efficiently meter usage. Once that technical limitation is erased, then so to would the fair use rights be
      erased".

91   L Lessig, *ibid* at "Code Replacing Law: Contracts".

watermarks which include irremovable information about rights holders and/or licensees in the copyright work itself; search engines and web spiders routinely scanning the web for copies of identifiable digital works; on-line works that send reports back to a central location whenever they are used or copied ("IP phone home"); and cryptographic 'containers' which allow copies of works to be distributed widely but only used in full once a key has been obtained.

These are all important elements in the architecture that is being developed to protect intellectual property, but they are probably not the key element. What may make architecture replace law as the protection of digital intellectual property is a common framework for the trading of intellectual property rights, both between businesses and to end-users, a set of standards within which all of the particular IP-protective technologies can work.

(i) The Imprimatur Project: Europe's ECMS Code Development

In Europe the Imprimatur project,[92] sponsored by the European Commission, is developing such a model. The actors and inter-relationships in the Imprimatur Business Model, Version 2, are described briefly by Koelman and Bygrave:[93]

> In brief, the role of the creation provider (CP) is analogous to that of a publisher; ie he/she/it packages the original work into a marketable product. The role of the media distributor (MD) is that of a retailer; ie, he/she/it vends various kinds of rights with respect to usage of the product. The role of the unique number issuer (UNI) is analogous to the role of the issuer of ISBN codes; ie, it provides the CP with a unique number to insert in the product as microcode so that the product and its rights-holders can be subsequently identified for the purposes of royalty payments. The role of the IPR database provider is to store basic data on the legal status of the products marketed by the MD. These data concern the identity of each product and its current rights-holder. The main purpose of the database is to provide verification of a product's legal status to potential purchasers of a right with respect to usage of the product. As such, the IPR database is somewhat similar in content and function to a land title register. The role of the monitoring service provider (MSP) is to monitor, on behalf of creators/copyright-holders, what purchasers acquire from MDs. Finally, the certification authority (CA) is intended to assure any party to an ECMS operation of the authenticity of the other parties whom he/she/it deals. Thus, the CA fulfils the role of trusted third party (TTP).

From this brief description, some fundamental changes to the way in which copyright currently operates can be noted:

- Each digital artefact (including copyright works) is issued with a unique identification number,[94] which is then inserted by the content provided as microcode in the work to enable it to be tracked in various situations;

- There is an IPR database, 'somewhat similar in content and function to a land title registry', enabling anyone (particularly potential purchasers) to

---

92 Imprimatur: <http://www.imprimatur.alcs.co.uk/>.

93 K Koelman and L Bygrave, *Privacy, Data Protection and Copyright: Their Interaction in the Context of Electronic Copyright Management Systems,* Institute for Information Law, (June 1998) p 5 (Report commissioned for the Imprimatur project):
    <http://www.imprimatur.alcs.co.uk/IMP_FTP/privreportdef.pdf>.

94 K Koelman and L Bygrave, note 93 *supra,* p 7.

verify a digital artefact's ID and legal status.

- There is a monitoring service provider (MSP) which, on behalf of creators and rights holders, will (though the summary does not say this) monitor transactions, uses and breaches (depending on the technology) of rights in digital artefacts. MSPs will use a variety of mechanisms, including reporting from Media Distributors, and surveillance of the web through the use of search engines, customised web spiders, and digital artefacts that report on their own usage.

- Certification Authorities (CAs) play a major role, as it assumed that both parties to transactions, and the authenticity of communications from them will be routinely identified by digital signatures, and so verification by CAs is needed.

This blueprint for the code in which intellectual property transactions will operate in cyberspace could hardly be more different than the real space code in which IP operates at present, and as regulation this code shares few similarities with IP law. This is not necessarily a criticism, merely an observation of how powerful and different code as regulation will be in intellectual property.

Koelman and Bygrave, while not opposed to ECMS, stress that the surveillance dangers are one of the most significant obstacles to the acceptable operation of ECMS:

> such systems could facilitate the monitoring of what people privately read, listen to, or view, in a manner that is both more fine-grained and automated than previously practised. This surveillance potential may not only weaken the privacy of information consumers but also function as a form for thought control, weighing down citizens with 'the subtle, imponderable pressures of the orthodox', and thereby inhibiting the expression of non-conformist opinions and preferences. In short, an ECMS could function as a kind of digital Panopticon. The attendant, long-term implications of this for the vitality of pluralist, democratic society are obvious.

(ii) The Propagate Project: An Australia's ECMS Development

In Australia the approach taken to ECMS by Imprimatur is being developed further by the Propagate project.[95] The model used by Propagate,[96] when fully developed, 'has the potential to become a standard in its own right and to be directly implemented in software'. Propagate is principally about the development of cyberspace code: at both the standards and software levels for digital

---

95   <http://www.propagate.net/> operated by Access CMC and Impart Corporation, and funded in part by DEETYA.

96   See <http://www.propagate.net/models.html>.

1998 *UNSW Law Journal* **621**

transactions.[97] The differences between the models being developed by Propagate and Imprimatur need not concern us here.

Propagate held its first Consensus Forum[98] in August 1998 with the aim of developing consensus within the Australian 'rights community' and others concerning both the accuracy and completeness of the model and the value of the ECMS approach.[99] Assuming that the model remains non-proprietary, Propagate's 'consensus' approach is obviously valuable in seeking input and consensus from 'stakeholders'. However, the consensus process seems relatively informal and closed, and is not yet a form of representative decision-making. For example, there was little explicit representation at the Forum of the users of copyright works, or of the broader public interests that copyright serves, though it was said that this will be remedied at subsequent meetings. This is simply an example of how, as Lessig put it 'once it is plain that code can replace law, the pedigree of the codewriters becomes central'. A framework for ECMS may become of the most important forms of architecture as regulation. Who controls and who participates in the development of this framework will be important, and might not be a matter on which consensus is easily reached.

H.   Copyright Circumvention Devices: Protecting Architecture

The Australian Attorney-General has confirmed that

> The Government has decided to implement two new enforcement measures. One of the enforcement measures would ban commercial dealings in "black box" or other circumvention devices. There will also be a ban on the removal of copyright information electronically attached to copyright material.[100] (by which was meant 'rights management information').

These provisions will implement Article 11 and Article 12 of the WIPO *Copyright Treaty* 1996.[101] This is an early examples of international agreements being used to regulate cyberspace. Although they will affect use of technologies on CD-ROMs etc, their main effect will be in cyberspace. Both provisions will give legal support to the growing importance of architecture in the protection of

---

97   Propagate's objectives are stated to be: 'Propagate is a project to develop through industry, government and community based consensus a generally applicable conceptual model which describes a flexible system for the trading of intellectual property through the World Wide Web. The model will be propagated through stakeholders who participate in the evolution of the model. The Propagate Conceptual Model will be comprehensive, distributed, component based developed through a process of consensus with all the stakeholders, be they creators, agents, collecting societies, distributors, publishers or end users. It will be media, asset, and channel neutral to allow for flexibility, adaptability and growth. It may be deployed as a specification, discrete application or as an API to an existing application.' See: <http://www.propagate.net/project/objectives.html>.

98   The Consensus Forum details are at <http://www.propagate.net/consensus.html>.

99   Most of the copyright collecting societies and other major rights-holder organisations attended and were actively interested in ECMS development. The discussions at the Forum showed a lively sensitivity to privacy considerations, and recognition of the value of anonymous and pseudonymous transactions, but there were fewer ideas put forward on how to accommodate the 'fair dealing' issues discussed above.

100 Speech by Attorney-General Daryl Williams, "Copyright and the Internet: New Government reforms" para 35, 30 April 1998, Murdoch University - <http://law.gov.au/articles/copyright_internet.html>.

101 See Commonwealth Attorney-General's Discussion Paper *The Digital Agenda* "Part 5 - Proposed scheme for new technological measures and rights management information provisions" <http://law.gov.au/publications/digital.htm#anchor1565870>.

copyright through ECMS systems and other technological means. On the one hand they will make illegal any individual actions that will interfere with copyright management information which is part of the ECMS architecture. On the other hand they will make it illegal to deal in any way in 'black' architecture, hardware or software that could be used to circumvent copyright protections. Such provisions help make the Internet safe for ECMS.

Part II
Cybercrimes

[8]

The Changing Definition and Image of Hackers in Popular Discourse

AMANDA CHANDLER
Department of Sociology and Inter-disciplinary Studies, The Manchester Metropolitan University, U.K.

It seems that with the advent of the computer came the computer hacker — in fact it might even be suggested that the personal computer would never have existed without the computer hacker. As discussed in the next section, Stephen Jobs and Stephen Wozniak established one of the first personal computer companies — a company which began with the manufacture and marketing of 'blue boxes' (a gadget which could be attached to the telephone, which emitted the same tone signal as the telephone and therefore enabled the user to make free telephone calls. This activity was/is known as 'phreaking', and is possibly one of the earliest forms of 'hacking'. This activity and the possession of a 'blue box' was and is obviously illegal. However, the term 'hacker' has not always had criminal connotations. This paper will be looking at the how the term 'hacker' has changed in definition — changes that have occurred with the subsequent generation of computer and computer user. Although the changes in definition have culminated in a negative and criminal image, e.g. 'hackers' being compared to burglars and even murderers, many other images have also been used throughout literature and reporting on this subject — not all of which are necessarily negative. This paper will consider some of the more popular/prevalent images of 'hackers' as portrayed in film, literature, (cyberpunk) fiction and coverage of actual cases as reported in national daily newspapers.

History of the Term 'Hacker'

As Cornwall writes: "(t)he origin of the world is obscure, and the terms has been used to mean rather different things" (1987: 18). In fact it might be

230   *A. Chandler*

suggested that every new generation of computer has spawned a new generation of 'hacker'. Rheingold claims that "(o)riginally the term was a more honorable reference to the virtuosity of some programmers in finding ingenious ways to overcome obstacles" (1991: 178). This concept of an honorable profession, which conflicts with more contemporary notions, is echoed by Hafner & Markoff who state that "(i)n the 1960s and 1970s, to be a computer hacker was to wear a badge of honor. It singled one out as an intellectually restless soul compelled to stay awake for forty hours at a stretch in order to refine a program until it could be refined no more. It signified a dedication to computers that was construed as fanatical by outsiders" (1991: 11). Therefore, even in the early days of computers and computer programming, we find common themes which linger on today, e.g. intellectual, fanatical, though these traits have undergone a rather sinister transformation. According to Sterling, 'hacking', as defined by Stephen Levy in *Hackers* (1984), "can signify the free-wheeling intellectual exploration of the highest and deepest potential of computer systems. Hacking can describe the determination to make access to computers and information as free and open as possible. Hacking can involve the heartfelt conviction that beauty can be found in computers, that the fine aesthetic in a perfect program can liberate the mind and spirit" (1993: 53). This original generation of 'hackers' also developed a code of practice, which Stephen Levy calls the Hacker Ethic, which was founded on two principles, namely the free sharing of information and the prohibition against harming, altering or destroying any information that was discovered through this activity. These themes, particularly the first, are prevalent in any discussion of contemporary 'hacking' and illustrate the central dichotomy of this topic, i.e. the freedom of information versus computer security.

These original 'hackers' are regarded with respect boarding on adulation — "The original hackers were a bunch of technological wizards at MIT (Massachusetts Institute of Technology), all considered among the brightest in their field" (Clough & Mungo 1992: 34) — a respect generated by their contribution to the development of the personal computer:

> (t)he idea of a small, lightweight computer that was cheap enough to be bought by any member of public was revolutionary, and it was seized on by technological radicals as their contribution to the counter-culture. Moving computing power away from the state and large corporations to the people, it was assumed, could only be a good thing. (Clough & Mungo 1992: 27).

These 'technological radicals' formed the 'Homebrew Computer Club', who according to Rheingold "started out as hobbyists and ended up as an industry" (1991: 336) creating "a second computer industry in a niche that the computer giants considered too minuscule" (Rheingold 1991: 336). Two of these 'radicals' and contributors to the counterculture were Stephen Jobs and Stephen Wozniak, the designers and manufacturers of the 'Apple' personal computer system, and as Clough & Mungo write "(t)he story of Apple, ... isn't just the story of two young men who made an enviable amount of money. What Jobs and Wozniak began with their invention was a revolution. While ... 'the summer of love' ... proved to be ephemera, the PC has brought a real change to society" (1992: 32). They quote a promotional video for Apple, "We build a device that gives people the same power over information that large corporations and the government have over people", and as they rightly point out, this "statement ... echoes the 'power to the people' anthem of the Sixties" (1992: 32). Thus the birth of the personal computer industry may be seen as just one of the many aspects of the Sixties counterculture, but it could just as easily be described as illustrative of the success of capitalism, for in 1980, when Apple went public, Jobs was worth £165 million and Wozniak was worth £88 million.

If Jobs and Wozniak can be described as the second generation of 'hackers', then the third generation are "the kids who inherited the gift of the personal computer and were hacking out and selling the first computer games. Their motivation was often a fast buck and their instincts were entirely commercial" (Clough & Mungo 1992: 74). Here, hacking could be defined as the breaking of copyright protection codes thus enabling the games programs to be refined or altered, or simply to facilitate the 'pirating' of the games. However, it could also be taken to mean simply the time-consuming process of writing the definitive games program, a process involving long hours in front of a computer de-bugging home written codes — the latter definition being more in keeping with the original definition.

However, this third generation were rapidly overtaken by the fourth and current generation of 'hackers' who not only share the same obsessions as their predecessors, have inherited the advantages of the personal computer revolution but have taken "'hacking' — previously an honourable trade — and made it into a form of breaking and entering" (Clough & Mungo 1992: 74) thus transforming the term into a synonym for computer criminal. Clough & Mungo reporting on a 'Hackers' Conference' held outside Amsterdam in August 1989, state that the organizers had prepared a declaration for delegates that "the free and unfettered flow of information is an essential part of our fundamental liberties, and shall be upheld in all circumstances ... (and) computer technology shall not be used by government and corporate bodies to control and oppress the people" (1992: 74). These principles echo the sentiments of the first and

232   *A. Chandler*

second generation hackers, but the conversation and demonstrations at the conference contradicted these ethics. Indeed as one visitor, one of the original founders of the Homebrew Computer Club, felt "the fourth generation hackers were 'underage and underdeveloped': they displayed 'negative social attitudes'. Hacking, he said, had degenerated from being a collective mission of exploration into an orgy of self-indulgence" (Clough & Mungo: 1992: 74) which was particularly evidenced by a new aspect of computer programming, i.e. the writing of computer viruses.

Therefore it can be seen that "a new generation appropriated the word 'hacker' and with help from the press, used it to define itself as password pirates and electronic burglars. With that, the public perceptions of hackers changed. Hackers were no longer seen as benign explorers but malicious intruders" (Hafner & Markoff 1991: 11). However, although the definition of 'hacking' may have become synonymous with criminal activity, it is questionable whether the common images or comparisons which are used in various discourses on 'hacking' are as negative, or whether they are not more ambivalent, even positive.

Cowboys and the Electronic Frontier

American literature covering the real events of the Operation Sundevil or 'hacker crackdown'[1] of the late 1980s in America resounds with descriptions of hackers as electronic cowboys, outlaws or renegades. Indeed, Sterling writes "(h)ackers long for recognition as a praiseworthy cultural archetype, the post modern electronic equivalent of the cowboy and mountain man", and furthermore "many hackers actually attempt to live up to this techno-cowboy reputation" (Sterling 1993: 54). This image is also prevalent in Sterling's cyberpunk novel *Neuromancer* in which the 'hero', Case, is described as a computer cowboy. These images of cowboy and outlaw were nowhere more prevalent than in reports of the arrest of Kevin Mitnick in February 1995. A report in *The Times* on 17 February 1995 calls him "a legendary outlaw on the computer frontier", and describes the chase and his eventual arrest as having "all the features of the classic Western: a colourful villain who had evaded the law for years, a loner determined to track him down and cliff-hanging final reel when justice triumphed". In fact the headline to the report — "Phone Ranger Traps Cyberspace Outlaw" — carries all the traditional connotations of 'good guy' versus 'bad guy'. 'Hackers' perceive themselves as "there to push back the frontiers of computing; to explore areas of the new technology that no one had seen before, to test the limits of computer science" (Clough & Mungo 1991: 34).

The use of word 'frontier' with all its American cultural and historical connotations is particularly pertinent with regard to the Electronic

Frontier Foundation. This organization was created as a direct result of the Operation Sundevil crackdown on hackers and was established not so much as to condone the activities of the hackers arrested during the operation, but in order "to raise and disburse funds for education, lobbying, and litigation in the areas relating to digital speech and the extension of the Constitution in Cyberspace" and furthermore to "fund, conduct and support legal efforts to demonstrate that the Secret Service has exercised prior restraint on publications, limited free speech, conducted improper seizure of equipment and data, used undue force, and generally conducted itself in a fashion which is arbitrary, oppressive and unconstitutional" (see Sterling 1993: 24). This Foundation was not intended to be a 'hackers' defence fund' but was aimed at ensuring civil liberties in cyberspace, and it is particularly interesting to note that the principal founders and founders were first and second generation hackers (see above) such as Wozniak and Jobs.

The use of images such as cowboys and pioneers has particular resonance in American culture. "The outlaw, the rebel, the rugged individual, the pioneer, ... the private citizen resisting interference in his pursuit of happiness — these are figures that all Americans recognise and that many will strongly applaud and defend" (Sterling 1993: 55). "The cowboy in various guises is popularly accepted by Americans as a symbol ... He represents rugged individualism ..., unadorned masculinity ... and ultimate heroism" (Savage 1979: 4). The symbol of the cowboy is linked with American western heritage and he "is the last sentinel on the parapet of Americanism" (Savage 1979: 15). The perpetuation of such images through film, documentary and advertising has given the cowboy an elevated yet mythical status — "he is in a real sense First Citizen of the Republic, a guardian, a righter of wrongs, or at the very least, a perceptive and philosophical observer of the human condition" (Savage 1979: 20), and his chief attribute is "the fine middle-class virtue of common sense, and in action at that" (Savage 1979: 20). Thus the cowboy stands for all that is American in Americans.

If the cowboy is the embodiment of Americanism, it is to:

> the frontier the American intellect owes its striking characteristics. That coarseness and strength combined with acuteness and inquisitive-ness; that practical, inventive turn of mind, quick to find expedients; that masterful grasp of material things, lacking in the artistic but powerful to effect great ends; that restless, nervous energy; that dominant individualism, working for good and for evil, and withal that buoyancy and exuberance which comes with freedom — these are traits of the frontier, or traits called out elsewhere because of the existence of the frontier. (Allen 1969: 52–53, citing Turner 1920).

This is a rather romanticized vision of the Wild West and may be regarded as somewhat dated (although relatively contemporaneous with the actual events), and absurd in that American character and intellect is unlikely to have been influenced by one such single factor to the extent that Turner describes, but it illustrates the symbolic importance of the frontier in American culture.

Moreover, Savage writes "The West is a place for fantasies because it is remote in time and space. If its history is brief and bizarre, its landscape is vast and bizarre, often isolating the individual through extremes of geography and climate and forcing him to depend solely upon his own physical and psychological resources" (1979: 61). Hence the cowboy and his environment have come to epitomize and explain Americans and Americanization from a romantic and mythical perspective. The image is used to sell pragmatism, individualism, heroism, clothes, beer, cigarettes, holidays and guns. It is pervasive throughout American economic and cultural thought, and it is therefore not surprising that hackers have tried to adapt this positive heroic model for their own. In some ways, these images are appropriate to the electronic frontier and the pioneering hackers. Once again, they are pitting their wits against a huge and uncharted though nebulous geography — cyberspace.

However, the reality of the Wild West and pioneering is also a useful comparison "The frontier, and the freedom it offered, attracted not only many of the best men but also many of the worst, fugitives from justice and those unable to cope with the responsibilities of life in society, criminals and social misfits. For in one sense the lure of the frontier represented the flight from civilisations and the restraints civilisations imposes on men" (Allen: 1969: 55). These epitaphs — criminals, social misfits — crop up in texts on hackers. As discussed above, not all hackers are criminals, although some are, and their incomprehensible obsessiveness has led to the perception and fear that these are people who cannot cope with normal human relations (see later discussion on computer addiction).

The use of the term 'Wild' West did not only refer to the unchartered spaces but also to the fact that the West was lawless and this was for two reasons — "first, because of the social conditions that obtained there ...; secondly, because the law that was applied there was not made for the conditions that existed and was unsuitable for those conditions" (Allen 1969: 496). Thus, Allen describes how the restraints of the law were ineffectual given the widespread yet isolated population thus "(i)n the absence of the law and in the social conditions that obtained, men worked out an extra-legal code or custom which guided their actions. This custom is often called the code of the West" (Allen 1969: 497). Furthermore, failure to abide by this code did not result in formal punishment but in informal restraint or withdrawal of the protection of the code from the violator. In some ways this is akin to the Hackers Ethic or Code as described by Levy. Given the early lack of regulation of cyberspace, the first and second generation hackers developed their own code which still obtains today. Sterling writes that "truly heavy-duty hackers, those with serious technical skills who had earned the respect of the underground, never stole money or abused credit cards" (1993: 95). In his opinion, the more respected the hacker, the less likely he was to have committed any common, easily prosecutable offence. Their reputations were built on "cleverness and technical mastery" (1993: 95). They believed in 'look but don't touch' and often reported potential breaches of security systems to the relevant authorities (Gold and Schifreen, on discovering the ease with which the Prestel system could be breached, reported this to British Telecom at least 6 months before their arrest); this too was part of the hacker code. Moreover, "(m)ost hackers regard credit card theft as 'poison' to the underground, a sleazy and immoral effort" and hackers committing such activities will be denied access to the most respected bulletin boards (where the best technical information can be found) and will be ostracized by the rest of the electronic community.

> Hackers have their own rules, which separate behaviour that is cool and elite from behaviour that is rodent like, stupid and losing. These 'rules', however, are mostly unwritten and enforced by peer pressure and tribal feelings. (Sterling 1993: 59).

The second aspect of the lawlessness of the Wild West was due to the fact that the laws were enacted in the East under conditions which were totally alien and different to the conditions pertaining in the West, and thus they were inapplicable and unsuitable, e.g. the Homestead law only allowed a man 160 acres of land which was totally impracticable in the West where conditions were arid and water sources few and far between. It was estimated that 2650 acres was the minimum required in the West on which to live and survive. However, this did not find favour with the lawmakers in the East, thus the law in the West had to circumvented if populations were to survive. In a similar fashion, traditional principles of law such as those regarding privacy, property and the protection of information as a commodity are inapplicable in cyberspace and, for this reason, most countries, especially America, have seen a burgeoning increase in the enactment of computer specific legislation outlawing new areas of computer (criminal) activity.

> Hacking had become too important to be left to the hackers. Society (has been) forced to tackle the intangible nature of cyberspace-as-property, cyberspace as privately owned unreal estate. In the new,

severe responsible, high-stakes context of the 'Information Society' of
the 1990s, hacking was called into question. (Sterling 1993: 57–58).

However, the introduction of computer crime legislation has had a
negative effect; hackers perceive the new laws not so much as attempts to
preserve law and order and protect public safety, but "immoral attempts by
soulless corporations to protect their profit margins and to crush
dissidents" (Sterling 1993: 62). Thus not only are traditional legal
principles irrelevant and inapplicable, but modern and specific legislation
is there to be circumvented or ignored as immoral or unsuitable to the
custom of cyberspace — just likes the 'laws' of the Wild West.

In conclusion, therefore, it would seem that both the legend and the
reality of the cowboy and the frontier are useful to the hacker community
as it provides a popular and positive image to which Americans can relate
because, for Americans, they are central to the American way of life. In this
way, hackers may be accepted as the 'guys in the white hats' who are carving
out and protecting a new American territory. It is an image for which the
Americans have a sneaky admiration and creates a useful counterbalance
for other, more sinister, images of hackers which are being perpetrated by
the media, law enforcement agencies and the legal system.

Intellectual Joyriders

It is possible that once computer networks become as commonplace as
our national highway system, we will learn to treat them in much the
same way. Rules of the road will emerge and people will learn to
respect them for their own safety and for the common good. (Hafner
& Markoff 1992: 12).

Comparing the computer networks with highways is another image
which is not only prevalent throughout the discourses on computer
hacking, but one which is particularly useful for the criminal justice system
as it provides a comparison which justifies law making and enforcement.
Michael Colvin, introducing the second reading of the Computer Misuse
Bill, said:

Just as at the beginning of the century, when the first motor cars
appeared on our roads, we had to introduce special laws to govern
their use and misuse, in spite of existing legislation on horse-drawn
carriages, so too are special laws required today to cope with
computers. (Hansard 1990: 1136).

By comparing cyberspace to roads or motorways, it also facilitates
portraying hackers as 'joyriders' and hacking as 'illegal computer

joyriding' (Hafner & Markoff 1992: 200) — very negative images when compared with that of the cowboy as discussed above. This is well illustrated by the case of Strickland and Woods sentenced at Southwark Crown Court in May 1993 who, during the judge's summing up for sentence, described the two defendants as 'intellectual joyriders'; a phrase which was seized on by the media — particularly *The Guardian* (22 May 1993 — "'Intellectual Joyriders' Jailed") who quote the judge as saying "not all joyriders are propped on cushions behind the wheel of a Ford Sierra bombing down a motorway with their mates and a can of Special Brew". Both defendants were given 6 months imprisonment in order to penalize them and deter others (see reports in *The Guardian* 22 May 1993; *The Times* 22 May 1993; *The Mail* 22 May 1993). This was a strong negative image as it could coalesce in the public's mind with another contemporary 'folk devil' — the joy/death rider. There is no time here to analyse the creation of a moral panic over joyriding, but suffice it to say that from the late 1980s onwards the media have been highlighting the escapades of youngsters in stolen high-performance cars (an intentional stereotype used here to illustrate the types of images created by the media). By classifying the two very different activities into one category, the public were alerted to the danger, if not the potential, of computer hackers, i.e. that they might cause the death of innocent people, and hacking took on a wholly negative meaning. It might also be suggested that this negative image was reinforced by media publicity surrounding a book which gave technical information on how to write a virus program. There were calls for a boycott of publication of this book on the grounds that it should be no more acceptable that a DIY guide to joyriding (*The Times*, 12 June 1992 "Virus No Joke").

Car joyriders as a sociological phenomenon have, until recently, received very little attention despite the fact that they have existed since the development of the motor car (as hackers have since the advent of the computer). However, the predominant media image is that they are young, white, working class, unemployed, male juveniles. Allowing for the fact that this is a media-generated stereotype, it contrasts neatly with the reality of computer hackers as portrayed by Sterling, who says of the American hackers caught up in Operation Sundevil, "the actual hackers themselves (were) mostly bespectacled middle-class white suburban teenagers" (1993: 27). Moreover "(h)ackers are generally teenagers and college kids not engaged in earning a living. They often come from fairly well-to-do middle-class backgrounds" (Sterling 1993: 62). Thus, although these hackers may be unemployed in the sense that they are not working. Sterling points out that they are school or college students. Furthermore, reports and analysis of the American cases reveal that if the hackers were no longer students, they were usually employed on computer systems. With reference to the

238   *A. Chandler*

cases of hackers which have come before the British courts: Gold was 25 and a trainee accountant; Schifreen was aged 21; Whitely aged 21 was a computer operator; Woods, although unemployed, was aged 26; Strickland. again unemployed, was aged 22; and the youngest was Bedworth aged 19 (now a degree student in Artificial Intelligence at Edinburgh University). In spite of the fact that two were unemployed, none of these defendants could be described as juveniles.

Car joyriding may be considered a contemporary manifestation of juvenile delinquency and thus traditional sociological theories may be used to explain it. It may be described as delinquency because it is "non-utilitarian, malicious and negativistic" (Colten 1955: 24). Depending on your perspective, hacking can be regarded in the same way. Hackers' 'pranks' are spiteful and deliberately annoying (though for the hacker, it might simply be a message to the system analyst that his security is inadequate). Computer security managers may consider hacking non-utilitarian as investigations of break-ins involve expense and time (whereas hackers may claim that break-ins highlight vulnerable security in important systems). Hacking may be regarded as negativistic in that it is potentially dangerous as data may be deliberately or unintentionally altered (whereas hackers may describe their activities as exploring the 'frontier' or system to its full potential or ensuring that the power of the computer does not reside in the hands of the powerful few).

This last concept of negativism is interesting and it may be here that there is a similarity in explanation. Apter describes this as the "desire to do the opposite of that which is required or expected in a given situation. ... Satisfying such a desire can lead to a thrill of malicious glee" (1992: 97) and that "an important part of the pleasure surely comes from the surge of arousal that goes with the defiant act" (1992: 98) — hence the 'joy' in joyriding, the excitement of driving at high and dangerous speeds. For Apter, "(a)t its best, negativism represents people's refusal to be less than they could be, their obstinate commitment to freedom and self-determination, their unwillingness to be mere ciphers" (1992: 99). This can lead to infringements of the law such as joyriding, but "(n)egativism of the non-violent kind ... can lead the individual to question and challenge, directly or implicitly, the assumptions on which a society is based — its values, ideals and taboos" (1992: 181) and he argues that "negativism enters into creativity and cultural development in every sphere, be it art, science, engineering, business or politics" (1992: 181). Paradoxically, therefore, negativism can be positive in that it leads to attempts to explore beyond what is permissible and accessible resulting in creativity and discovery — the motivation ascribed to computer hackers.

After all, they argue, if Alexander Graham Bell had gone along with the rules of the Western Union telegraph company, there would have been no telephones. If Jobs and Wozniak had believed that IBM was the be-all and end-all, there would have been no personal computers. If Benjamin Franklin and Thomas Jefferson had tried to 'work within the system', there would have been no United States. (Sterling 1992: 60).

On a superficial level, therefore, hacking and joyriding are two very different activities. Joyriding involves experiencing thrills, danger and excitement through very physical action whereas hacking is more cerebral and sedentary — the excitement resulting from many patient hours sitting in front of a computer culminating in cracking the security of a system, and then further hours spent protecting that access for future use. Both are now criminal activities having attracted specific legislation (in the United Kingdom, the Aggravated Vehicle Taking Act 1991, the Computer Misuse Act 1990 — and here it is interesting to note that specific legislation against joyriding took much longer to pass than the law against hacking despite the fact that joyriding had been happening for a considerably longer time. This might be explained by the fact that comparing hackers to joyriders heightened the public's awareness of the dangers of unauthorized computer access, thus these two negative images fed off one another justifying legislation in both areas). Yet on a more analytical level, it may be that both activities can be attributed to the same motivation.

Hackers/Murderers

The media is dominated by accounts of banks, financial institutes and telecommunication organizations as the principal victims of hacking activity, while the public or individual as victim is reserved for reports of the hypothetical ability of hackers to kill. On 25 May 1988, *The Times* quotes an article from Computer Weekly that hospital systems and therefore lives may be at risk ("Computer Hackers 'May Kill'"). This potential for killing came to the fore in media reports surrounding the Michaelangelo virus in March 1992 which, it was warned, could be lurking in computers in hospitals and medical research institutes. Reports at that time warned that not only could viruses lose companies millions but that, in extreme cases, they could kill (*The Mail* 5 March 1992 — "A Plague on Your Computer"), a sentiment echoed in *The Mirror* (6 March 1992 — "Terminators: How the Whizzkids Set Up A Computer Wipeout"). Both reports contain details of the Ethiopia Water Drilling Case in which it is alleged that 1400 lives were lost due to a virus infecting the drill's computer system. This seems to be the only reported case where lives have been lost due to what may be described computer misuse, though it is not alleged that the virus was introduced by a remote hacker.

240   *A. Chandler*

However, the recurrent fear or "standard nightmare scenario, much trumpeted by computer-security experts who fear the computer underground" (Sterling 1993: 40) is that hackers will break into air traffic control computers and cause plane crashes. This hypothetical threat may have been given credibility in the public's mind following a scene in the American film, Die Hard II, where a gang break into the air traffic control computer in order to blackmail authorities into allowing them to rescue a drug baron being extradited into the U.S.A. under armed guard. This 'nightmare scenario' conjures up the worst fears — not only the threat of drugs, but also the potential for blackmail and death that a computer system makes people vulnerable to. It is perhaps interesting to question whether this film or the potential threat has not become confused with the reality. During the second reading of the Computer Misuse Bill 1990, Mr Gary Waller, MP, states that "(t)here are several known instances of people breaking into air traffic control systems. One trembles to think of the dangers of that" (Hansard 1990: 1161). This view is echoed by the Law Commission in its report of who had received reports of such access to systems outside the U.K. (No. 186: 5: 1·26). It must be queried here whether Mr Waller was basing his comments on the findings of the Law Commission because, during the authors' research, no reports of hackers breaking into air traffic control systems have been found. It is true that on 17 September 1991, voice and data communications were cut to Kennedy, La Guardia and Newark airports in the U.S.A. and that, at the time, this attributed to the activities of hackers. However, as Sterling discovered, this was due to a power failure at the local telecommunication company's switching station; the back-up systems had not been switched to due to human error (Sterling 1993: 40–41). However, the reality of air traffic control chaos combined with the hypothetical threats of hackers could lead many to believe that the incident was the responsibility of hackers. However, as the Law Commission reported, "it would be very unusual for unauthorised outside access to be obtained to, or at least to any significant level of, a closed system that because of its nature emphasises security, such as air traffic control" (No. 186: 5: 1·26) and Michael Colvin, MP, was able to allay the fears of the House of Commons during the second reading of the Computer Misuse Bill:

> I have investigated this issue and have been assured that the air traffic control system in the United Kingdom is on a closed circuit and that it is therefore virtually impossible for a hacker to gain access. That is vital, because otherwise one might start a lot of alarmist reporting that would give people the feeling that they were in danger in the air. (Hansard 1990: 1162).

It is interesting to note that the introducer of the Computer Misuse Bill should try and play down one of the common fears expressed about computer misuse (which would obviously have been more supportive of measures to criminalize such activities), and it might be suggested that the loss of revenue to British airports and air travel companies may have been instrumental for similar reassurance is markedly lacking in response to a point raised by Ms Emma Nicholson, MP, who states that "(e)xtremely unpleasant things have happened in the USA, where people have to tried to kill patients in hospital by accessing their drug records and altering their prescriptions on computer" (Hansard 1990: 1153).

It might be that this potential for murder or death is given more credence by the public due to the metaphors used by the press in computer misuse reports. In *The Guardian* (9 February 1989 — "Smart Worms and the Sex.Exe Virus") viruses are likened to AIDS stalking the electronic world's nervous system. It could be argued that by linking two 'folk devils' in this way, lends truth to media speculation and reporting about both because reports on AIDS can now be compared with hacking and vice versa, and in this way spurious evidence becomes corroborative. The link between AIDS and computer crime became further entrenched in December 1989 with the AIDS diskette scandal, in which 10,000 diskettes were mailed from London to various institutes through the U.K. and Europe including hospitals, universities and financial institutes. The diskette purported to contain data on AIDS but on installation it was discovered that it contained a virus which could destroy hard disks if a 'licence' fee was not paid. Media reports at the time suggested that again intensive care patients and air traffic control systems could be put at risk (*The Times* 14 December 1989 — "Computer Disc May Put Patients at Risk") but, as *The Mail* reported (14 December 1989 — "Pay Or Be Wiped Out"), quoting a spokesman for the London Stock Exchange, you would have to be "off your heads to put an unsolicited disc into your machine" (although it is estimated that at least 1000 recipients did just that!). Therefore, it was unlikely that such sensitive systems would be at risk. It was following this incident that Michael Colvin, MP, undertook to introduce the Computer Misuse Bill (*The Times* 16 December 1989 — "MP Takes Up Fight on Computer Tampering") despite the fact that the attempted crime (of writing a malicious program) was poorly thought out and the perpetrator apprehended (although the charges were subsequently dropped as the Crown Prosecution Service accepted that the defendant was unfit to plead). It would be more true to say that this incident clearly illustrates the ease with which viruses can and often are introduced into systems; rather than being planted by hackers, the appearance of viruses are often due to the willingness of system users to load up unchecked software. However, such incidents are reported in such a way as to alert the public to the dangers of hackers rather than to alert computer security managers to the risks likely to result from 'promiscuous' computers (those computers which are exposed to many different floppy disks).

'Mad Hackers'[2]

> Perhaps a medical metaphor (is) better — hackers should be defined as 'sick', as computer addicts unable to control their irresponsible, compulsive behaviour. (Sterling 1993: 58).

Compulsiveness and obsessiveness are very common adjectives in texts on hackers whether they are used to describe the hours sat in front of a computer, the hackers' thirst for exploration and knowledge, hackers' determination to share illicit information and knowledge, their desire to teach others how to hack, or their tendency to confess and implicate others once apprehended.

However, such adjectives may not take on a negative meaning if you are the systems manager employed to track down intruders. For example, Cliff Stoll recounts in his books, *The Cuckoo's Egg*, how his investigation and tracking down of the West German spy ring began because of a 75 cent discrepancy between the normal system accounting and the lab's own charging scheme. According to Hafner & Markoff, "Cliff stayed at work until midnight puzzling over the mysterious seventy-five-cent error, which he suspected might be a computational error" (1991: 170). Both his book and their account detail how he tracked down the intruder after months of setting traps in the system, keeping a detailed diary of events, even sleeping on the floor to maintain surveillance of the intruder. In fact, Hafner & Markoff suggest detection "requires the same skills that the hacker himself employs" (1991: 170).

Much is made of their 'unusual' dress (e.g. they tend to be described as scruffy and oblivious to fashion) and their lack of social life (e.g. no expensive habits, no girlfriends etc.). Hackers are portrayed as being unable to distinguish reality from fiction:

> Hackers perceive hacking as a 'game' ... You can win or lose at hacking, succeed or fail, but it never feels 'real'. It's not simply that imaginative youngsters sometimes have a hard time telling 'make-believe' from 'real life'... Computers simulate reality. (Sterling 1993: 84).

This is particularly true in the context of computer games:

> Simulation games are an unusual hobby; but then hackers are unusual people, and their favorite pastimes tend to be somewhat out of the ordinary. (Sterling 1993: 112).

Computer fantasy games akin to 'Dungeon and Dragons' are technical, detailed and complex and require a 'dungeon master' to create more new and inventive scenarios. Urvile (the pseudonym of one of the hackers caught up in Operation Sundevil) was such a 'dungeon master'. During his arrest and the seizure of his equipment, notes for scenarios were found which were interspersed with details of hacks he had actually committed. This is how Sterling describes Urvile (the following is typical of descriptions of the hackers apprehended in Operation Sundevil, the American crackdown on hackers):

> Not only was it next to impossible to tell Urvile's fantasy game notes from cyberspace 'reality', but Urvile himself barely made this distinc- tion. It's no exaggeration to say that to Urvile it was all a game. Urvile was very bright, highly imaginative, and quite careless of other people's notions of propriety. His connection to 'reality' was not something to which he paid a great deal of attention. Hacking was a game for Urvile ... Urvile was an obsessive young man.(Sterling 1993: 114).

Sterling also cites what he calls a 'colourful tale' of a Californian hacker told to him by Carlton Fitzpatrick, program co-ordinator of the Financial Fraud Institute at the Federal Law Enforcement Training Centre. The hacker had been:

> raiding systems, typing code without a detectable break, for twenty- four, thirty-six hours straight. Not just logged on — but typing. Investigators were baffled. Nobody could do that. Didn't he have to go to the bathroom? Was it some kind of automatic keyboard-whacking device that could actually type code. A raid on the suspect's home revealed a situation of astonishing squalor. The hacker turned out to be a Pakistani computer science student who had flunked out of a California university. He'd gone completely underground as an illegal electronic immigrant and was selling stolen phone service to stay alive. The place was not merely messy and dirty, but in a state of psychotic disorder. Powered by some weird mix of culture shock, computer addiction, and amphetamines, the suspect had in fact been sitting in front of his computer for a day and a half straight, with snacks and drugs at hand on the edge of his desk and a chamber pot under his chair. (Sterling 1993: 221).

The press or media have not been slow in attributing hacking to psychological or psychiatric disorders, for example (*The Guardian* 21 March 1985 — "Who Goes There?") hacking has been described as the 'masturbation of the microcomputer age' and a tendency to voyeurism and trespass are part of the psychological make-up of teenagers. In *The Mail* in 1989 (16 December 1989 — "Doctor is Jailed for Computer Thefts"),

244   *A. Chandler*

there is a rather interesting report of a doctor who stole £58,000 worth of computer equipment to satisfy such a severe craving for hard- and software that, it was alleged, he needed psychiatric treatment. However, the best illustration of the media emphasis on the psychiatric causes of hacking must be in the coverage of the case of Bedworth whose defence of computer addiction was accepted by the jury who acquitted him of hacking. In *The Mirror*'s coverage of the case, it is reported that his mother was powerless to control the 'monster' ("Computers Turned my Boy into a Monster" — 18 March 1993: p. 1) and that Bedworth became violent when she tried to stop him hacking and once even threw her to the floor ("I had to turn Electricity Off to Stop My Computer Mad Son" — 18 March 1993: p. 4–5). Further, Professor James Griffiths-Edwards of London University's National Addiction Centre is quoted as saying that Bedworth was "suffering from a mental disorder. It was an intellectual challenge which obsessed him". Griffiths-Edwards regarded this as "monstrously abnormal behaviour" and declared that there was "something very abnormal about him" ("Mum's Hell over her Robot Boy" — 18 March 1993: cont. from p. 1). The following day, *The Mirror* offered advice to parents in an article headed "Is Your Child a Secret Hacker?" and said that though a child may seem like the ideal teenager — quiet and happy, playing on his computer rather than running with local tearaways — he could be a hacker capable of throwing multi-million pound networks into chaos. The use of words such as 'monster', 'abnormal' and 'robot' render the image of a hacker as something (or someone) which is other than human and therefore frightening; the public, through their concern for the mental health of their sons[3] are made aware of the negative effects and dangers of hacking. The use of psychiatry and psychology as explanations render the activity less criminal and offer the possibility of treatment redeeming the child as normal and human.

This concept of the 'mad' hacker was also used in a storyline in the Australian soap opera, 'Neighbours'. The Gottliebs, a young couple on Ramsay Street, took in a young man as a lodger (without first checking his references). Initially this man, Russell Butler, seemed the ideal lodger; he was quiet, unobtrusive and helpful. However, in a story line reminiscent of 'Pacific Heights' (an American thriller), Butler's behaviour became increasingly strange, manipulative and frightening. There were suggestions that he was secretly hacking into the local hotel's computer system to plant viruses in order that he would be called in as a computer systems analyst to correct the fault. There was an argument over the high telephone bill. He told different people conflicting stories about his past. Finally, it was discovered that he had previously been in a psychiatric unit and had been treated for depression. This storyline contrasted with two earlier stories: one in which a teenager hacked into the school's computer to change examination grades (a popular scenario in both hacker fiction and reality, and one which does not attract the same level of condemnation but rather a secret admiration); and the second, the use of the computer bulletin board system to begin a romance between two teenagers (one of whom was dying). This second story had overtones of romance and heroism in which the computer was non-threatening — indeed it was the instrument of love, a go-between. The later 'Butler' storyline, by contrast, contained all the stereotypical and negative images of hacking, and reflects the public's and media's change in attitude towards computers and hackers. Shown at peak viewing time, it warned both children and adults alike of the dangers of hacking and computers.

But is 'computer addiction' a real psychiatric or psychological disorder? Margaret Shotton, in *Computer Dependency*, discovered through her research that dependency did occur for a small proportion of computer users but that the "effects arising from it were not as dire as suggested in the literature" which feared that computers were dehumanizing and desocializing (Shotton 1989: 235, see also her initial investigations of the existing literature on computer dependency contained in Chapter 1). She argues that "(m)uch of the Dependents' time was spent undertaking activities which were not extrinsically useful and perhaps for that reason their activities were considered unusual; but is dancing useful, or singing or playing football? (1989: 263). Moreover, "(m)any who live the monastic life, or the life of the intellectual, artist or musician, often have little need for others and are frequently admired for their dedication" (1989: ;263). Her interviews "revealed the Dependents on the whole to be a group of middle-class, young, intelligent and well-educated people who were happy with their lot, and invariably very successful if this may be measured by the status of their jobs" (1989: 274) — qualities, she suggests, which are emphasized in modern Western society:

> science is worshipped, art relegated. Western culture is now object and task-centred; the nurturing, caring society seems all but to have disappeared ... Self-need and individuality are fostered at the expense of the group. Life becomes work-centred and many people have no time for others, not even for their families. (Shotton 1989: 275).

Therefore, she argues, the very qualities which stigmatize computer dependents are those very qualities which are presented as being desirable and thus she finds it difficult to understand why the Dependents are regarded as different rather than conformist. She goes on to posit the suggestion that "perhaps our society needs people such as this ... Perhaps we need 'thinkers' and 'doers' if we are to progress" (1989: 275).

From her research, therefore, it would seem that Shotton has found that there is a small minority of people who are computer-dependent but far

246   *A. Chandler*

from this being a dehumanizing or demonizing activity, it can have benefits not only for the individual ["reinforcement, excitement, intellectual stimulation, the feeling of power and potency, unlimited challenges, prestige and self-confidence" (1989: 26)] but for society as a whole. This reality conflicts harshly with the negativity prevalent in the media portrayals and reports.

Tinker, Tailor, Hacker, Spy

The potential ability of hackers to infiltrate national and military defence systems is one of the biggest perceived threats and, to a certain extent, this fear is justified: "(a)lmost every computer system of note has been hacked: the Pentagon, NATO, NASA, universities, military and industrial research laboratories" (Clough & Mungo 1992: 9). However, it is difficult to know or judge to what level the hackers have gained access for details of sensitive systems are unlikely to be given in court in the 'public or national interest'. Moreover, as the Law Commission acknowledged, it would be virtually impossible for hackers to enter a closed system such as a defence weapons system where the emphasis is on security (No. 186: 5: 1·26). Indeed, it has been suggested that any access gained would only be to the most inferior levels. However, the threat of hackers to infiltrate the world's most sensitive military systems is one of the most enduring and popular themes. It was probably brought to the public's attention initially and most forcibly by the 1983 film 'War Games' (a discussion of which no self-respecting text on hacking would omit!). In this film, a teenager hacks into the computer which monitors and controls the nuclear defence system of the U.S.A. Believing that it is simply a games playing machine, the teenager begins a game with the computer. However, the computer believes the 'game' is real and begins the countdown to World War III. This film contains many interesting images; firstly, in the above scenario, it is the machine and not the human who cannot tell reality from fantasy; secondly, the film may be regarded as posing the question 'if a computer is in charge of our nuclear defence, who is in charge of the computer?'; thirdly, the moral of the film could be interpreted as saying that basically computers are stupid machines — humans, despite (or because of) their weaknesses such as irrationality and lack of logic, make better decisions. However, for the purposes of this section, the following exchange between two characters illustrates the reaction and the attitude of authority (adults) towards hackers and spies:

> George Wigan (FBI): "The kid claims he was looking for a toy company. Ha! Ha! That's great!"

> John McKittrick (System Manager): "There is no way a high school

> punk can put a dime in a telephone and break into our system. He has got to be working for someone else. He's got to be!"

> George Wigan: "He does fit the profile perfectly: he is intelligent but an underachiever, alienated from his parents, has few friends, a classic case for recruitment by the Soviets. Now what does this say about the state of our country? Have you got any insight into why a bright boy like this would jeopardise the lives of millions?"

> FBI Agent: " No, Sir, he says he does this sort of thing for fun!"

This extract describes the stereotypical image of a (psychiatrically or psychologically disturbed) teenager hacker but, in this case, these are the very attributes of an American citizen turned Soviet spy. From this point of view, all hackers are spies! It also neatly demonstrates the division between the new generation of computer users and the government or state.

The profound influence of this film on popular perception of hacking is illustrated by the fact that references are made to it during the parliamentary debates on the Computer Misuse Bill (see Hansard 171: 1309) particularly comments made by Mr Colvi, MP:

> it was a frivolous, teenage film, (but) it nevertheless told a very serious story. It contained an element of truth, in that today's teenagers, thanks to the extent to which computers are available in schools, can finish their education fully computer literate. The film highlighted the temptation to stray down the path of trespass and the serious consequences ultimately of that activity. So although 'War Games' was in itself a frivolous movie, it has a serious story to tell. (Hansard 171: 1319)

This fictional scenario became reality in early 1989 when a group of three West German hackers were arrested and charged with selling secrets to the KGB. Media reports at the time suggested that the Russians put pressure on the hackers through their involvement with drugs (*The Guardian* 3 March 1989 — "German Hackers Sold Military Secrets to the East") and later claimed that the hackers were addicted to drugs and alcohol (*The Guardian* 4 March 1989 — "Experts Debate Potential Harm of German Computer Spy Ring"). However, Hafner & Markoff's account is somewhat different from the media reports. They suggest that it was the hackers' idea to approach the Soviets and that the money involved was trivial as was the information passed to the Russians. In fact, they write:

> (o)nce the initial sensation had died down, sceptical journalists began to question just how much damage to national security the group of hackers spies had done? Had highly classified material changed hands?

248   A. Chandler

Or was it merely some harmless public domain software? (Hafner &
Markoff 1991: 229).

Moreover, they suggest that the real issue is:

Why the public outrage when the real menace of computer espionage
is most likely not from the Soviet Union but in sophisticated schemes
perpetrated by both foreign and American corporate spies secretly
tapping into their competitors' systems in search of trade secrets and
market information? (1991: 229).

This sentiment is echoed by Clough & Mungo who state that:

(e)spionage is a curious trade. Those who claim to know how
espionage agencies work say that computer penetration has become a
new and useful tool for latter-day spies. The Americans are said to be
involved, through the NSA, as are the British, through GCHQ, the
General Communications Headquarters, which gathers intelligence
from diverse sources. Hacking, at this rarefied level, becomes a matter
of national security. (Clough & Mungo 1992: 186).

This has particular pertinence given the discussion in the House of
Commons during the third reading of the Computer Misuse Bill (see
Hansard 171, 1289, 1299–1324) with regard to Amendment 7 which was
tabled to ensure that Parliament considered the powers (or restraints on
the power of the Secret Services to hack). According to Mr Cohen, MP, who
tabled the amendment, Section 3 of the Security Services Act 1989
legalized burglary by the Secret Services provided a warrant signed by the
Secretary of State is obtained subject to certain provisos (though that piece
of legislation was passed after much opposition from all parties). Similarly
he argued, the Interception of Communications Act 1985 allows the Secret
Service to 'tap' calls by warrant from the Secretary of State with the proviso
that any intercepted information not needed by the Secret Service would
be erased or destroyed. He had tabled Amendment 7 because whether
these powers could be extended to cover incidents of computer hacking by
the Secret Service was not debated at the time of the passing of the two
Acts. He argues that before the Bill, anyone, including the Secret Service,
could hack because it was not illegal but "now the House is saying, as a
matter or principle, that hacking is not acceptable and is a criminal
offence. Instead of any change being made, the Minister says that as long
as a warrant is obtained hacking can continue" (Hansard 171: 1301)
(under the powers given in Section 3 of the Security Services Act 1989). He
continues:

(l)egalising a criminal activity such as burglary is wrong in principle.

> The security services should not be above the law. There may be circumstances in which they must break the law, but if they are caught they should be subject to the law and court action ... the security services should be subject to proper constraints. (Hansard 171: 1301).

The amendment was added in order that this should be properly debated because he felt it was:

> another example of how the Government keep reducing parliamentary democracy while given unrestricted powers to the security services to do almost what they like. It is the opposite to what has been happening in eastern Europe where the security services' powers have been curtailed and sometimes removed. Attempts are certainly being made there to make them more accountable, whereas our services are less accountable under this Government. (Hansard 171: 1299–1300).

Fears were expressed that the security services could hack and collate information on any individual without independent supervision which, in the report of the Lindop Committee (Section 23·21), ensures that they are "open to the healthy — and often constructive criticism and debate which assures for many public servants that they will not stray beyond their allotted functions" (Hansard 171: 1300–1301). Unfortunately, however, this amendment was not pressed or passed because as Mr Colvin (Sponsor of the Bill) said:

> (t)he passage of the Security Service Act was marked by the most detailed discussion and careful consideration of the various provisions now in force. Therefore, I am reluctant in my Bill, to vary legislation that the House passed with considerable debate so recently.

Therefore, it would seem that the security or Secret Services are able to continue their hacking activities without any restraint or supervision.

Conclusions

It would seem, therefore, that on the whole, representations and images of hackers in the media and film are negative. This is particularly true in Britain where reports and accounts portray their activities as dangerous and potentially subsersive. Such reports not only pose the hacker as a threat to the economic survival of this country, but, through the use of criminal, psychopathic and alien imagery, they have become a danger to the public (and even to themselves). Thus an activity which once attracted sneaky admiration, even respect, is now portrayed as murderous and

250   A. Chandler

treacherous. The prevalent image in the America media is more
ambivalent — the cowboy/Western image is one which members of
American society can relate to and even sympathize with. It is an image
which is part of their history and culture, and therefore not alien or
threatening. However, it would be unfair to suggest that all media coverage
of hacking is negative in perspective. British newspaper coverage of
computer hacking has, in fact, acknowledged the circulation of myth, scare
stories and anecdotal evidence[4] but such reports are in the minority and
are surrounded by headlines containing huge figures which are said to
represent the loss attributable to computer crime, reports giving virus
alerts and 'exposing' the threat to human life, and demands for legislation.
It is, therefore, not surprising that the hacker has joined the rogues gallery
of modern folk devils.

Notes

1 Operation Sundevil was a joint operation carried out by the FBI, CIA and local
   law enforcement agencies over a period of several months which targetted the
   perceived threat of 'hackers'. It was heavily criticized because the law
   enforcement agencies often made armed arrests and, due to their ignorance,
   confiscated equipment which could not even be used for hacking. In one case,
   the agents even confiscated one user's collection of books because they
   contained the word 'cyber' in the titles. For a good account of the events of
   Operation Sundevil, see Hafner & Markoff *Cyberpunk: Outlaws and Hackers on the
   Computer Frontier* (Fourth Estate, London, 1991) or Sterling *The Hacker Crackdown:
   Law and Disorder on the Electronic Frontier* (London, Viking, 1993).
2 This title was chosen for this section because it was the pseudonym used by
   Nicholas Whiteley when hacking into computer systems. This was his 'call sign'
   to alert the systems operator that his security had been breached. Nicholas
   Whitely was convicted of criminal damage as a result of his hacking activity, and
   was sentenced to 12 months imprisonment, 8 months suspended, for four counts
   of damaging disks.
3 I use the terms 'sons' in this instance because all the accounts of hackers,
   whether from the U.S.A., Britain or Europe, concern males (girls and women
   being relegated to the role of girlfriend). The author is not trying to suggest that
   all hackers, or indeed computer users are male, but it should be noted that males
   make up the majority of cyberspace, although more and more females are
   gaining access. This is an area in which more research needs to be
   undertaken.
4 For example: *The Times* (4 November 1986) "Brits £40 million Bill for Hi-Tech
   Fraud" — this report dismissed the notion of teenage computer hackers as
   being a myth, and blamed the careless use of passwords and inadequate security
   for giving employees the opportunity to defraud their employers.

References

Allen, W. (1969) *The Urgent West: The American Myth and Modern Man.* John Baker: London.

Apter, M. (1992) *The Dangerous Edge: The Psychology of Excitement.* MacMillan Free Press: London.

Clough, B. & Mungo, P. (1992) *Approaching Zero: Date Crime and the Computer Underworld.* Faber & Faber: London.

Cohen, A.K. (1955) *Delinquent Boys.* The Free Press: Glencoe.

Cornwall, H. (1987) *Datatheft: Computer Fraud, Industrial Espionage and Information Crime.* Heinemann: London.

Hafner, K. & Markoff, J. (1991) *Cyberpunk: Outlaws and Hackers on the Computer Frontier.* Fourth Estate: London.

Hansard 166 (1990) HMSO: London.

Hansard 171 (1990) HMSO: London.

Law Commission Report (1989) Criminal Law: Computer Misuse. Report No. 186. HMSO: London.

Levy, S. (1984) *Hackers: Heroes of the Computer Revolution.* Penguin Books: London.

Rheingold, H. (1991) *Virtual Reality.* Mandarin: London.

Savage, W. (1979) *The Cowboy Hero: His Image in American History and Culture.* University of Oklahoma Press: London.

Shotton, M. (1989) *Computer Addiction: A Study of Computer Dependency.* Taylor and Francis: London.

Sterling B. (1993) *The Hacker Crackdown: Law and Disorder on the Electronic Frontier.* Viking: London.

Turner, F.J. (1920) *The Frontier in American History.* Holt, Reinhart and Winston, Inc.: New York.

[9]

Computer Crime in the Global Village: Strategies for Control and Regulation — in Defence of the Hacker

LIZ DUFF* and SIMON GARDINER†

*School of Law, University of Westminster and †Anglia Law School, Anglia Polytechnic University, U.K.

Introduction to Cyberspace

Welcome to the final frontier: cyberspace. This is no voyage with Captain Kirk, but one nearer to home. We will be taking the 'electronic information super-highway' into cyberspace where the sub-cultures of 'phreakers', 'breakers', 'hackers', 'cybersurfers', 'techno-anoraks' and 'cyberpunks' roam and probe. This is the world of unlimited dreams, where reality is virtual. Cyberspace as a term has its origins in science fiction. It featured in the 1984 novel by William Gibson, *Neuromancer*, which featured a world called cyberspace, after cyber, the most powerful computer. The world is populated by computer cowboys who roam the space's electronic systems. Today it is seen as the latest in a number of phases in which mass information systems have had a scientific base. The power of writing ruled from the middle ages, electronic entertainment media from around 1900, information technology from the early 1960s and since the mid-1980s, cyberspace has moved to a dominant position. More and more activities in society are taking place within computer systems. Many sectors of industry such as financial services take place virtually completely in cyberspace. This has implications for legal regulation. As Heather (1994) says, "Cyberspace is a rival to natural language which has dominated the subject matter of law from earliest times".

A sector of cyberspace known as the Internet is fast becoming part of our popular consciousness. Over the last 18 months, the U.K. press has bombarded us with discussion of 'The Net' (see Fielding 1994; Freedland 1994; Holderness 1994). It is a largely unplanned, dispersed, decentralized,

0194–6595/96/020211 + 18 $18.00/0

non-hierarchical global network and has its origins in the late 1960s when academics, the U.S. Government and communication experts worked out how to link computers over long distances after the Pentagon became concerned about the vulnerability of fixed computer systems to nuclear attack. This system soon became known to computer enthusiasts and the web quickly expanded with a distinct alternative ethos. Today, 137 countries have access with an estimated 35 million individuals connected, and governments, financial and academic institutions and commercial companies identify its potential. The risk of greater commercialization at the expense of access has been identified by Holderness (1994:4) with the increasing commercial interest in the Internet by global media companies such as AT&T. What has been called "utterly ungovernable anarchy" by Barlow (1993), and "a kind of anarchic socialism" by Holderness (1994), is a system that has no central control and few barriers. Access to the hardware technology is of course required and Freedland (1994:23) identifies the danger of "the evolution of a disconnected underclass, forever lost to cyberspace". Although the clear potential for access and democratization to information exists, there is concern that it allows access to unlawful speech such as computer-generated pornography and hate speech such as pro-Nazi literature. There have been calls for more effective policing, although space where anonymity and pseudonymity is so easy, prospects are limited. The U.S. Government have proposed a device known as the 'Clipper Chip' which will standardize and secure individuals' privacy to their messages obtained from the Internet. The down-side is that Government agencies could monitor who they choose.

Computers and other forms of information technology are the access to cyberspace. They are a central part of the global electronic village. It has the potentiality to enslave or empower. What seems clear is that it has facilitated the spread of techniques of social control. Electronic surveillance is insidiously encompassing our lives. Video cameras follow our movements in public high streets. Databases store evermore personal details. Marx (1988) talks of the "maximum security society", where the link between public and private is blurred and citizens become subject to constant inspection — the 'city of surveillance' or, as Gordon (1990) terms it, the "electronic panopticon".

This article will challenge the development of criminalization of so-called computer crime. Computers have helped make 'white-collar crime' become visible and imaginable in the popular consciousness. The media have had an important role in representing computer crime as a real social problem of the new age. Traditionally in its short history since Sutherland 'invented' the term, white-collar crime has been largely invisible. The criminalizing of unauthorised access to computer systems, hacking, is one step in this process to the city of surveillance. If new technology and the wonders of cyberspace are to be part of the dream of progress and the empowerment of man, electronic super-highways must have few barriers.

White-collar Computer Crime

The computer has existed in a recognizable form for over 40 years. The notion of computer crime first appeared in the 1960s when it was first realized that computers could easily be used to commit a variety of frauds. The second category of computer crime is a more recent phenomenon, with its proliferation being a result of the democratization of computers with the move away from the static mainframe to the dynamic nature of the portable computer. Together with the modem that allows access to remote computer systems from the home through telephone lines, this has enabled the computer to be domesticated and accessible to the home user. This reflects the recent explosion of technology removing the traditional limits on information and entertainment. We are arguably at a crossroads; on the verge of either a liberating brave new world or the technological enslavement of the mind.

How can computer crime be categorized? A simple distinction can be made between the situation where computers are used by individuals as a new, and perhaps more effective, tool for the commission of offences that they would probably have had a propensity to commit anyway. The commission of frauds by individuals who are likely to be insiders to a company would be an example. Some of these activities can be seen as 'computer specific' in that the opportunity to commit the crimes may not have been present until the computer technology was developed. The second area of computer-related crime is where the computer itself or the system is the target. This includes the unauthorized access to a computer system, the alteration of data or the insertion of an outside agent such as a 'virus'. This second category has opened up a whole new area of criminal activity. Other more complex distinctions have been made. Schlozberg (1983) lists: (1) theft, embezzlement and fraud of intangible property; (2) sabotage and vandalism; (3) automatic destruction of data; (4) appropriation of data; (5) theft of computer services; and (6) alteration and modification of data.

An alternative classification of computer crime is to focus on the offender. Wasik (1991) identifies three distinct levels of computer misuse. The first is that of corporate crime where the misuse is central to company policy and carried out by those who hold a structural position. The second level is that of occupational crime where individuals commit offences against their employers in the course of their employment. This includes examples of theft of computer hardware and frauds. The third level is that of misuse by outsiders via unauthorized access. This includes the

214   *L. Duff and S. Gardiner*

perpetration of fraud or the infliction of damage to programs or data held on the computer. Of course, as a preliminary move to the commission of these offences, unauthorized access is required, which may involve browsing through information held on a computer system. However, this conduct, commonly known as hacking, does not automatically fit into the accepted definitions of white-collar crime. Edelhertz (1970:3) defines it as "an illegal act or series of illegal acts committed by non-physical means and by concealment or guile, to obtain money or property, to avoid payment or loss of money or property, or to obtain business or personal advantage".

There are obvious problems in defining an area of criminal activity which has had limited academic and media attention. Edelhertz's definition expressly excludes violence and death from the province of white-collar crime. A major problem which Nelken (1994:355) identifies is that there are few reliable statistics for white-collar crimes and they are not included in the official statistics which serve as a basis for debates about 'the crime problem'. Sutherland's 1949 classic definition fails to clearly distinguish those crimes committed for an organization or business and those where it is the victim carried out at its expense. Since Sutherland's work, there have been many different attempts to either explain white-collar crime as crime that can be explained within general theories of crime, or those that highlight the distinctions between it and general crime and reinforce the specificity of white-collar crime. Clarke (1990:7) argues that the majority of business crime should be dealt with differently to general crime: "pursuing business crime as fraud, through criminal prosecution, though appropriate for a minority of classes, is irrelevant and impossible for the majority".

This limited analysis of the parameters of white-collar crime positively supports the argument that unauthorized access to computer systems should not be a crime because there is no economic motive. Mere unauthorized access to computer systems is one that will invariably lack this motive, where the driving force is the intellectual challenge. Even where the unauthorized access leads to infliction of damage to computer hardware or software, it is not inevitable that there is an economic motive, as it is likely to be carried out through boredom or revenge. So arguably, most forms of computer hacking cannot be seen as white-collar crime.

Costs of Computer Crime

What is the amount of loss through computer misuse? There are great discrepancies in claims made. Definitional problems are one reason. The dark figure of computer crime which is not discovered or reported is unknown. In the 1980s in advanced capitalist societies, there were a number of attempts to estimate the levels of loss by computer misuse. In a comprehensive series of surveys, the Audit Commission indicate that there has been an increase. In 1984, out of 943 public and private organizations, 8% said they had been the victims of computer fraud with a total loss of the rather precise figure of £1,133,487. In 1987, again about 8% of firms reported fraud, but this time the total loss was £2,561,351. These figures have almost universally been seen as underestimates. Other more speculative claims have put the figures at £2 million per day. In 1989, a survey by computer consultants put the annual figure at £2 billion. Interestingly, there have been very few rigorous attempts to measure rates of loss in the last few years, when perhaps the popular focus on crime has moved from high-tech business crime to more orthodox forms of street and property crime. Without being able to estimate the dark figure of computer-related crime accurately, it is impossible to locate the scale of crime within the divergent figures. Such crime is significantly under-reported to the authorities. Commercial bodies perceive many positive reasons for not reporting such crime. Damage may be done to the company's commercial standing and there may be a lack of confidence by potential investors. Financial institutions have been notoriously reticent to admit fraud and especially adamant when computer misuse is involved. In 1986, Barclays bank admitted they had been victim to considerable fraud, but issued a statement 'categorically denying' that it had been a computer fraud. The de-regulation of the City of London and the movement of organized crime into high-tech financial crime, is likely to mean that the reality of the level of computer-facilitated fraud is high.

Hacking: an Honourable Tradition?

Hacking has become a term loved by the media who have both mythologized and demonized the hacker. The discourse of hacking is very powerful in popular consciousness. Interestingly, the term was originally used to describe early pioneers in computer programming who continually refined programs. This progressed, as Sparague (1992:439) states, to the "displaying of feats of ingenuity and cleverness, in a productive manner, involving the use of computer systems". Gaining unauthorized access to computer systems was one way of displaying this expertise. During the 1980s, it extended to a wider body of young computer enthusiasts who developed a compulsion to gain access to computer systems. It is now used to describe all those who attempt to or gain unauthorized access. Indeed the archetypal hacker, the young, bright compulsive whose nocturnal hours are spent in front of a computer screen, is now 'the cyberpunk' — real life meets science fiction.

Hackers display the classical characteristics of sub-cultural groups. They have their own code of ethics although it is true that there are different

216   *L. Duff and S. Gardiner*

perspectives of acceptable behaviour. The vast majority of hackers see unauthorized access as legitimate. Computer hacking has infiltrated the popular consciousness more than any other white-collar crime. The media have had a crucial role in this construction. Along with other activities such as joy-riding and drug abuse, it has been portrayed very much as the activity of a sub-cultural group. The hacker has been identified as the middle class equivalent of the street gang. However, he [and it is identified as predominantly a male activity, but see McClellan (1994*a*)] is involved invariably in a solitary activity. There is contact with other hackers and there is a hierarchy to which access is exclusive. Two recent book written by American and British journalists respectively, Hafner & Markoffs *Cyberpunk: Outlaws and Hackers on the Computer Frontier* and Clough and Mungo's *Approaching Zero: Data Crime and the Computer Underworld,* present powerful imagery of the world of the hacker (also see Rushkoff 1994; Sterling 1994; Quittner & Slatalla 1995).

This phenomenon is one that initially became prominent in the U.S.A. It grew out of phone 'phreakers' who, in the 1960s, began accessing the telephone system so as to get free long-distance phone calls. The early phreakers are identified by Clough & Mungo (1992) as "blind kids" for whom "it was a natural pastime...you didn't need sight to phreak, just hearing and a talent for electronics". The 'Little Blue Box' was developed which reproduced the multi-frequency tones that were used as a dialling command by a telephone. Clough & Mungo (1992) identify a number of the most infamous phreakers who began to communicate creating an underground culture. They created their own conference lines. This was part of the counter-culture against the power and control of the state and was essentially an attempt to liberate technology. One of the most infamous phreakers was John Draper, better known as 'Captain Crunch', so called because of the inclusion of a free whistle in a cereal, 'Cap'n Crunch', which he modified to be used for phreaking. The late 1960s saw the cross-over from phreaking to hacking as it was recognized that computer systems had the same possibilities of exploration and application as the phone system, a computer system in itself. A number of phreakers became involved in writing the early software. The two founders of the Apple Computer Corporation moved into the manufacturing of small 'personal' computers in the late 1970s as an extension of their manufacturing of Little Blue Boxes. As the first company to produce affordable personal computers, it has been one of the most phenomenal success stories in modern business. In 1977, in its first year of operation, it sold $2·5 million worth of PCs. In 1982, this rose to $583 million!

The representation of the hacker is a contested one. The media have had an influential role in constructing how the hacker is popularly identified. Hollinger & Lanza-Kaduce (1988) see that indeed the media have been crucial in the criminalizing process of hacking in Western capitalist societies. Black (1993:67) identifies that there have been three stages in this constructed image. From the late 1970s to the mid-1980s, she sees a negative image of the hacker as deviant obsessives often from broken homes. The academic and computer expert, Donn Parker, is seen as being very influential in this view which analogizes hacking with more obvious constructions of juvenile delinquency such as drug abuse. The second stage is seen by Black (1993:69) as a softening of the negative imagery of hackers. They may still be seen as deviant in some way but as "rather harmless, more of a nerd than malicious". A distinction starts to be made between the harmless hacker and the real computer criminal. However, the emergence of ex-hackers providing their own representation rejects the nerdish notion of outsiders who cannot cope with life and have to retreat to their computers. As Levy (1984:7) explains:

> Beneath their often unimposing exteriors, they were adventurers, visionaries, risk-takers, artists...and the ones who most clearly saw why the computer was a truly revolutionary tool...I came to understand why the true hackers consider the term an appellation of honour rather than a pejorative.

The third stage is seen as the hacker maturing into an individual seen (Black 1993:73) as "useful to society in a number of ways". This began to be recognized in official reports (OECD:1986) in terms of their assistance in improving security. Black believes that this more positive representation of the hacker led to some ambivalence in the debate of whether dedicated legislation was required to criminalize unauthorized access. However, during this period in the late 1980s, there were conflicting representations with the media in comparison to experts, still stressing the inherent danger of hacking. Hollinger & Lanza-Kaduce (1988) stress the tendency of the media to sensationalize the amount and consequences of hacking. This media-constructed image has arguably been assisted by the computer industry. How the subsequent criminalization has effected the contemporary image of hacking and computer crime is open to question (see *Knightmare* 1994 for a recent self-account of hacking). It is too easy to subsume all activities within a criminal umbrella which makes no distinction between those merely involved in unauthorized access and real criminal acts.

However, two sides of the hacker can be clearly identified. As was stated earlier, some forms of hacking cannot be absorbed within a white-collar criminal definition. The good, non-malicious hacker has good motives; it being, as Cornwall (1985) argues," an educational and recreational sport...the process of getting in is much more satisfying than what is discovered in the protected computer files".

218   *L. Duff and S. Gardiner*

Clough & Mungo (1992:214) agree:

> They are mostly explorers, exercising intellectual curiosity. They will
> break into computers, sometimes causing ancillary damage or taking
> up systems time, and probably they will exploit the telecom systems to
> do so. But their intent for the most part is not malicious.

The opposing bad hacker is the dark character who is the electronic
vandal with the use of viruses, logic bombs and computer worms, and the
high-tech thief who abuses the access by syphoning money. He is the one
who the media have labelled as the 'cyberpunk'. The basic distinction is
one of motive — there is a difference between the clever/curious and the
malicious/devious. However, the dominant legal response has been to
criminalize any unauthorized access. This criminalization is endemic of the
extension of the sphere of influence of the state.

Legal Response to Hacking

The history of the legal response to computer crime has largely been a
delayed response to the danger of large-scale fraud. Only with the advent
of the personal computer was it acknowledged that fraud was taking place
and dedicated laws may be needed. The U.S.A. seems to have viewed the
need to introduce dedicated computer misuse legislation at an earlier stage
than European countries. In the late 1970s, Florida and Arizona were the
first states to enact specific legislation. Now all states have their own
dedicated legislation. At the federal level, the U.S. congress has passed the
Counterfeit Access Device and Computer Fraud and Abuse Act 1984,
which was amended by the Computer Fraud and Abuse Act 1986 so as to
clarify the ambiguities in the original legislation (Shackelford 1992). The
federal law is designed to protect computers in Government departments.
It is distinct from the British legislation in that simple 'computer trespass'
or browsing is not prohibited, so unauthorized access, for example of the
computers of the Pentagon to view classified information, is not a specific
crime unless the individual had an intent or reason to believe that the
information will be used to harm the U.S.A. In comparison, overwhelmingly the individual state laws are similar to Britain's laws, in that
they criminalize unauthorized access without the need to have any further
ulterior intent.

In Britain, concern over the perceived limitations of the general criminal
law to regulate computer misuse led to the Law Commission examining the
arguments and need for new legislation (see Law Commission 1988, 1989).
They considered the limitations of the application of the existing law,
specifically the area of theft, fraud and criminal damage. Their recom-

mendation after the consultation period was that new dedicated computer misuse offences should be created. These are found in the Computer Misuse Act 1990. The three offences created were: (5·2) "unauthorized access to a computer with intent to commit or facilitate the commission of a serious crime"; (5·3) "unauthorized modification of computer material"; and, lastly, the controversial, the criminalization of mere (5·1) "unauthorized access to computer". No further intent to commit any other act is required.

Arguments For Criminalization

The Law Commission considered the counter arguments for criminalizing basic hacking. Those in support of the use of the criminal law argue that the civil law is ineffective in regulating such acts. It is argued that unauthorized access will often lead to the commission of criminal acts: fraud, theft and criminal damage. By criminalizing unauthorized access to a computer system at a preparatory stage, individuals will be deterred from commission of these ancillary offences. It is also argued that with unauthorized access, there is an inherent risk of inadvertently damaging or destroying data and causing disruption of work.

The deterrent argument is based on the premise that there will both be a short-term impact reducing such conduct and a longer educative effect reinforcing positive computer ethics. However, this utilitarian aim of reducing crime may in fact be dysfunctional. The fact that it is a criminal act may create a mystique so as to encourage its breaking and, as technology continually develops, the curiosity of hackers may well outweigh any scruples they may have in breaking the law and lead to the law being in disrepute. These deterrent effects of criminalization and punishment have been questioned on grounds of the accuracy of empirical claims that criminals and would-be criminals are dissuaded from crime by an assessment of the risks of conviction and the subsequent punishment. The ability of policy makers to make accurate judgements about the effect of punishment on behaviour can legitimately be questioned. In times of high rates of recidivism, such arguments seem to be limited. Another problem with deterrence is that such utilitarian arguments are based on a notion of protecting others against harm. Applying this Millsian argument to hacking, the reality is that the vast majority of unauthorized access occurs undetected—where is the harm? If any subsequent harm actually does occur, invariably mainstream crimes will be committed.

The other argument for punishing acts considered to be crimes is retribution. Although this philosophical justification has been questioned as a dominant basis for punishment, it remains a powerful ideology. When applied to peripheral offences such as computer hacking, it is far from

220   *L. Duff and S. Gardiner*

convincing. There is a lack of consensus surrounding the moral nature of hacking. The extension of the criminal law, in response to the ever-increasing rapidity of technological developments, will inevitably lack a clear view of violation of ethical norms.

Arguments Against Criminalization

The arguments against unauthorized access being an offence are perhaps less pragmatic and more philosophical. It can be argued, however, that they more accurately reflect traditional parameters of the criminal law. Such access can be allied to trespass. Clearly privacy may well be invaded, but there is no general right of privacy in Britain. There is a tension between a law of privacy and greater rights of access. The two must co-exist in a way that the both oppose and complement each other. A law protecting privacy of information, if accepted as required, should be general and not partial concerning only information held on computers. Another argument considered by the Law Commission was that detection and enforcement would be difficult with such a crime. However, the view was accepted that if an activity is so serious and socially damaging, a criminal sanction should follow whatever the problems of enforcement.

The benign, good hacker is seen as playing a crucial role in identifying lacunas and limitations to security systems before the real criminal exploits them. Log-in codes and passwords are crude mechanisms for restricting access, especially in the way that they are used in practice. Hacking has led to the development, although not always to the implementation, of new security devices. As one barrister specializing in computer law argues (Wasik 1991:74):

> We get a lot of useful information about gaps in security of computer systems from hackers, which are often suppressed by manufacturers. Hackers are made the whipping boys for generally lax computer security.

New security techniques have been developed including encryption techniques, requiring codes and smart cards, and biometric techniques, using fingerprints or retinal patterns of blood vessels in the eyeball. There are, of course, cost implications for such mechanisms and there is a fear that if unauthorized access is criminalized, manufacturers will not consider security as such a crucial matter. The importance of security is recognized by the Computer Crime Unit of the Metropolitan Police Force based at Scotland Yard, who actively encourage businesses to improve their security measures and to take more responsibility for the protection of their data. Indeed, in some European countries, the legislation requires that the offender must have breached a security measure that was in place before there can be liability. If there is no security measure, the unauthorized access is not a crime. This was rejected by the Law Commission, arguing that an analogy would be with a burglar not being liable when he enters through an open door.

The suggestion that the responsibility for security should rest with the party that holds the data is not new. The Data Protection Act 1984 imposes an obligation on the data user to take adequate security measures to ensure that the data they hold is kept secure. So that, in effect, if they do not have adequate security controls to protect data concerning private individuals, they are in breach of the Act. This is also the position in Luxembourg and Denmark where failure to take proper security measures is in itself punishable in the criminal courts. It does appear contradictory that where the data has some economic value, for example to a company, the same rules do not apply. If a computer system has totally inadequate security procedures, the issue of negligence should be considered, rather than absolving the data user/holder from all liability. Therefore, liability will not be passed to the hacker, whose most serious misdemeanour might have been merely to break a password.

Hackers are invariably male, aged 17–25 years, and rarely pursue this activity for any financial gain. The argument that criminalization of this activity will deter such people is at best naive, and at worst a misdirection of limited resources in pursuing such offenders. A positive development has been the greater awareness of the need to generate more precise computer ethics. In the U.S.A., at the end of the 1980s, a group known as the "Electronic Frontier Foundation" was created in response to the crackdown of the U.S. government on computer crime. It is designed to (McClellan 1994*b*) "protect the rights of the ordinary cyberspace user". A similar group has been founded in the U.K. called 'CommUnity'. It was a direct response to an aborted attempt in 1992 to introduce a legislative requirement to have a license to set up a 'bulletin board', and has now developed a general self-help group.

The Enforcement of Law

The Metropolitan Police's Computer Crime Unit has sole responsibility for policing the Computer Misuse Act 1990 in London, and provides expertise and assistance in relevant investigations to other police forces around the country. It comprises of about six officers; a large increase from the one officer from its inception in 1985 up until 1990. The emphasis of their investigations changes over a period of time. Currently, much of their time concerns pursuing individuals who are introducing viruses into other programs. They are also increasingly involved in providing assistance to

222   *L. Duff and S. Gardiner*

other departments within the Metropolitan force, such as the Fraud Squad and Obscene Publications Squad, in dealing with computer-generated pornography.

The officers in the unit are computer literate and undergo quite extensive training. In turn, these officers train other officers in investigating computer crime. Outside expertise is often sought and investigations often involve help from other agencies such as British Telecom. There is a small team of computer engineers who work for the Metropolitan Police.

Little of the Computer Crime Unit's work is pro-active. It relies on information from complaints made by organizations or individuals who claim that their computer system has been accessed by an unauthorized user. The Unit recognizes that many incidents of unauthorized access go unreported for a variety of reasons. These reasons range from the organization involved not wanting to lose the confidence of its clients, or not having confidence in the police investigation, or simply not being able to afford the time involved in an investigation of this nature. These reasons combined with the problems of investigating such crimes have led to a relatively small number of prosecutions under the Act.

One of the few prosecutions for hacking was of student, Paul Bedworth (unreported) (Crown Court), which gained a lot of media attention. He was one of three who were charged with conspiracy to commit offences contrary to Section 3 of the Computer Misuse Act 1990. Bedworth admitted hacking into a large number of computer systems, using the JANET academic network, including the *Financial Times* and the European Organisation for the Research and Treatment of Cancer in Belgium. Nevertheless, Bedworth was acquitted after he successfully claimed that he was addicted to hacking and as a result could not form the necessary intent. The verdict was criticized for creating a licence to hack, and being a clear example of the type of behaviour that the Computer Misuse Act 1990 had intended to criminalize. Rather than charging the accused with the basic summary offence of hacking under Section 1, a major problem was that the Crown Prosecution Service (CPS) decided to prosecute under the more serious charge of conspiracy to commit a Section 3 offence. This is committed when there is unauthorized modification of computer material. There were good reasons for this course of action. Firstly, to provide a full list of all the organizations into which the three had hacked would have entailed an extremely long indictment. In addition, due to the seriousness of the activities, the CPS wanted to charge them with the more serious offences under Section 3, and a conspiracy charge allowed liability to be established if the prosecution could merely establish that there was a plan between the individuals to commit the offence.

Much was made in the trial of the obsessional nature of computer hacking (Charlesworth 1993). It was argued, in Bedworth's defence, that he was a computer addict and that he could not stop his explorations. Hacking like many activities is addictive to some participants. Medical experts have begun to talk of a 'computer tendency syndrome' (see Shotton 1989). There are attractions to this as further ammunition in the argument against criminalization of hacking. However, such defences are worryingly positivistic and obsessionalize hackers. Non-chemical dependency is also an issue fraught with problems, although endocrinic drugs initiated by hacking may have similar effects as external drug use. A stereotyping of the obsessional nature of hackers can be seen from the view of a member of the Computer Crime Unit:

> They want to beat the system. They are thin, spotty face individuals aged between 17 and 25. They have no interest in anything else in the universe apart from computers, and have tremendous egos. When they go into a system they don't care about the problems they may be causing, they just want to get in, or see how far their virus will spread. They are so arrogant. Virus writers, hackers and the Dungeons and Dragon freaks. They're very much of the same ilk. It's a funny sort of breed.

Not so much attention was given to Bedworth's co-defendants, Karl Strickland and Neil Woods, who admitted conspiracy charges and were sentenced to 6 months imprisonment. The judge who sentenced the pair said the sentences were meant to penalize them, and to act as deterrence to others who might be similarly tempted. At the time when sentences were passed (May 1993) on the two men, the Computer Crime Unit claimed that the media interest in the case had brought about a decrease in the amount of hacking in Britain. However, in the first 4 months of 1994, 130 complaints of hacking were reported to the unit under the Computer Misuse Act 1990.

In the U.S.A., during the late 1980s and early 1990s, the Secret Service of the Treasury Department initiated an investigation known as 'Operation Sundevil'. They believed they were involved in investigating a wide conspiracy involving $50 million in telecommunications fraud alone. What resulted was a small number of guilty pleas for accessing the phone system and a small number of minor convictions. One major concern was made over the fact that a number of hacker groups were found to have downloaded the 'E911 file' from the telephone system which contained information relating to installation and maintenance of emergency services. It was later discovered that this was information which was, in fact, publicly available. It had been thought that the investigation would unearth major criminal conspiracies. What they found were disparate groups of individuals, invariably oblivious to any criminal enterprise. If

224   *L. Duff and S. Gardiner*

there was commission of crime, they were minor ones already catered for
by the general law.

The first prosecution in the U.S.A. under the Computer Fraud and
Abuse Act 1986 was against Robert Morris, who created a computer virus.
He was a computer graduate at Cornell University researching into
computer security. He released a 'computer worm' into the Internet. The
worm was a program that was designed to roam, undetected, freely over the
network, and enter computers without altering any existing files or the
operating system. He intended to use this worm to highlight security
aspects of the network. However, due to a programming error, the worm
reproduced itself uncontrollably, jamming computers which it should have
entered harmlessly. Although little permanent damage was caused, it was
estimated that between $5–12 million of down-time and labour costs were
incurred. Morris was convicted of intentionally gaining access to a federal-
interest computer without authorization and was given probation and
fined $10,000. Subsequently, in the small number of convictions under the
act, offenders have been given custodial sentences.

This was also the fate of Kevin Mitnick who was convicted for
unauthorized access of federal government systems (see Hafner & Markoff
1991:15). After a lengthy investigation by the FBI, he was finally traced,
convicted and given a 1-year custodial sentence. A similar argument as that
used by Bedworth was made by Mitnick's lawyer. He was portrayed as a
'computerholic'. Since a period of probation which conditionally denied
him access to any computer, he has disappeared and gone underground.
The FBI have renewed their interest in him under suspicion of continued
hacking activities, and he has been termed 'cyberspace's most wanted
fugitive'. He has a reputation of being able to gain access to any system. It
has been rumoured that he entered NORAD, the North American Air
Defense Command Computer, and could have initiated the go-codes for
intercontinental ballistic missiles. When questioned as to the truth of this
allegation (Sweeney 1994:17), he responded:

> No — that's not true. That's where I draw the line; there is a difference
> between being a joy-rider on the information superhighway and being
> a criminal. The media prints all this rubbish.

Danger: Viruses!

The real danger of hacking, the dark-side, is the emergence of the virus.
Again a term which has its origin in science fiction, it emerged in the mid-
1980s in the form of the 'computer virus'. These programs are used by
computer gangs fighting hacker wars against each other, dropping viruses
and logic bombs into each others' systems. But the nightmare scenario is

that viruses are dropped into other systems, both public and commercial. New strains of viruses are being created all the time. In the late 1980s, Eastern Europe was seen as an increasing source of new viruses, with Bulgaria particularly highlighted. The new centre for their creation seems to be the Far East. Many computer programs purchased in countries such as Thailand have an unwanted extra — a virus. Bulletin boards exist from which they can be selected and down-loaded. Viruses such as Michelangelo have become infamous. This was a doomsday bug which was programmed to wipe out hard disks on 6 March — the anniversary of Michelangelo's birth. It had spread around the world and it was estimated that 5 million machines would be damaged — in fact it resulted in only a few thousand machines being affected, and it is believed by some that it the danger was blown out of proportion by the computer industry. It is estimated by IBM that by the year 2000, 10 million viruses will have been created. A recent virus written by the 'Dark Avenger' based in Bulgaria has been identified as the 'Mutating Engine', which it is believed can disguise itself in 4 billion different ways. Current virus scanners are unlikely to be able to detect them. However, Alan Soloman, who has developed anti-virus programmes under the name, Dr Soloman, believes that the medical metaphor of 'virus' is too emotive and a more appropriate term should be a 'computer weed'. He argues that they can be eradicated and are only an inevitable part and parcel of the developing technology. They should really be seen as 'electronic graffiti'.

Conclusion

Perhaps the overwhelming argument in support of the criminal law's absence is that computers and electronic communication are destined to become the primary means of public expression. Notions of freedom of expression are in danger as this more regulated forum becomes central to public discourse. Social order in the middle ages was based on the enforced ignorance of the masses to the written word. There is a danger of returning to mass exclusion from information. The electronic media must not have any fewer legal immunities than those which currently apply to information. As Foucault (1977) rightly states, "Power is knowledge".

The hacker has been a focus of media interest. The cyberpunk has been constructed as a danger to life as we know it. It is argued that the overwhelming reason for criminalization of unauthorized hacking has been symbolic. It is designed to 'educate', 'moralize' and 'socialize' hackers. The media have, as conveyors of contemporary symbols, had a crucial role in this criminalization. It is middle class youth who have been criminalized as the perpetrators of computer crime; not the disenchanted employee as the insider, or the operations of organized crime. The media

226   *L. Duff and S. Gardiner*

have been highly influential in stressing the moral threat of hacking. As Chambliss & Seidman (1982:315) argue, the one way to identify symbolism in law is to measure the degree of enforcement. If they are not utilized vigorously against the perceived problem, symbolism is likely; indeed, very low investigation and prosecution levels are the reality. The media portray rampant and obsessive abuse. As Hollinger & Lanza-Kaduce (1988:118) argue, "It would appear that computer crime laws were passed, in part, to stigmatise hacking but not the hacker".

The more effective control for the dark side of hacking is likely to be non-legal. The development of positive codes of ethics and acceptable behaviour for those using the information super-highway are needed. An analogy can be made with joy-riding. It has been the subject of special aggravated criminal offences, but the more effective move to control the activity has been to penalize the victim. Insurance companies have focused on the owners and manufacturers of sought-after makes of cars. Again, security is seen as more beneficial.

There is a genuinely held belief with the majority of hackers that all electronically accessible information is essentially in the public domain. The authors support this view as the electronic village is globalized. The onus is on custodians of information to legitimize their restrictions on public access and to use appropriate and effective security methods. There is, of course, a paradox here which is true of most new technology. The ideological message has constantly been that it will liberalize man and open up new horizons. However, increasingly it has been used to control and demarcate information. The criminalization of hacking has resulted in restriction of information. The view that cyberspace will empower individuals, as far as access to knowledge and information, can be criticized as utopian rhetoric and helplessly optimistic. This 'privatization' of knowledge is a microcosm of the insidious re-defining of public space with increased control and exclusion. The story in inner city ghettos is replicated in cyberspace. The re-defining of juridical relationships is also occurring. The trespass of cyberspace has been moved from the traditional civil law area to one of the criminal law in the same way as trespass to land is increasingly being criminalized. The Criminal Justice and Public Order Act 1994 has brought issues of public right to land; in the past, solely a matter of civil law into the domain of the criminal law. In physical space or cyberspace: 'Trespassers really will be prosecuted'!

References

Barlow, J. (1993) *The Net Guide* Penguin: London.
Black, D. (1993) The Computer Hacker—electronic vandal or scout of the networks? *Journal of Information Science* 4.

Chambliss, W. & Seidman, R. (1982) *Law, Order and Power* 2nd ed. Addison-Wesley.

Charlesworth, A. (1993) Addiction and hacking. *New Law Journal* 16 April.

Clarke, M. (1990) The control of insurance fraud: a comparative view. *British Journal of Criminology* **30,** 1–24.

Clough, B. & Mungo, P. (1992) *Approaching Zero: Data Crime and the Computer Underworld.* Faber & Faber: London.

Cornwall, H. (1985) *The New Hacker's Handbook.* Century Communications: London.

Edlehertz, H. (1970) *The Nature, Impact and Prosecution of White Collar Crime.* US Government Printing Office.

Fielding, H. (1994) A non-anorak wearer's guide to the Internet. *The Independent on Sunday* 29 May.

Freedland, J. (1994) A network heaven in your own front room. *The Guardian* 30 April.

Foucault, M. (1977) *Discipline and Punish.* Vintage: New York.

Gibson, W. (1984) *Neuromancer.* Harper Collins: London.

Gordon, D. (1990) *The Justice Juggernaut: Fighting Street Crime, Controlling Citizens.* Rutgers University Press: New Jersey.

Hafner, K. & Markoff, J. (1991) *Cyberpunk: Outlaws and Hackers on the Computer Frontier.* Corgi: London.

Heather, M. (1994) Challenges for the law from cyberspace and virtual worlds. *The Computer and Security Report* **10,** 17–21.

Holderness, M. (1994) Internet: paying the piper. *The Guardian* 14 July.

Hollinger, R. & Lanza-Kaduce (1988) The process of criminalisation: the case of computer crime laws. *Criminology* **26,** 101–126.

Knightmare (1994) *Secrets of a Super Hacker.* Loompanics: Washington.

Law Commission Working Paper No.110 (1988) *Computer Misuse.* HMSO: London.

Law Commission Working Paper No.186 (1989) *Criminal Law — Computer Misuse.* HMSO: London.

Levy, S. (1984) *Hackers: Heroes of the Computer Revolution.* Doubleday: New York.

Marx, G. (1988) *Undercover: Police Surveillance in America.* University of California Press: Berkeley.

McClellan, J. (1994*a*) Cyberspace: cyberfeminist. *The Observer* 24 April.

McClellan, J. (1994*b*) Cyberspace: freedom of speech on-line. *The Observer* 26 June.

Nelken, D. (1994) *White-Collar Crime.* In *The Oxford Handbook of Criminology* (Maguire, M., Morgan, R. & Reiner, R., Eds). Clarendon Press: Oxford.

Organisation for Economic Cooperation and Development (OECD) (1986) *Computer Related Crime: Analysis of Legal Policy.* OECD: Paris.

Parker, D. (1976) *Crime by Computer.* Charles Scribner & Sons: New York.

Quittner, J. & Slatalla, M. (1995) *Matters of Deception.* Vintage: London.

Rushkoff, D. (1994) *Cyberia: Life in the Trenches of Hyperspace.* Harper Collins: London.

Schlozberg, S. (1983) *Computers and Penal Legislation.* Norwegian Research Centre for Computers and Law. Universitetsforlaget: Oslo.

228   *L. Duff and S. Gardiner*

Shakelford, S. (1992) Computer-Related Crime. *Texas International Law Journal* **27**, 479–505.

Shotton, M. (1989) *Computer Addiction? A Study of Computer Dependency.* Taylor & Francis: London.

Sparague, R. (1992) Computer crime: a review of Cyberpunk. *Rutgers Computer and Technology Law Journal* **18**, 439.

Sterling, B. (1994) *The Hacker Crackdown.* Penguin: London.

Sutherland, E. (1949) *White Collar Crime.* Holt Rinehart & Winston: New York.

Sweeney, J. (1994) To Catch a Hacker. *The Observer* 4 September.

Wasik, M. (1991) *Crime and the Computer.* Clarendon Press: Oxford.

[10]

A sociology of hackers

Tim Jordan and Paul Taylor

Abstract

Illicit computer intruders, or hackers, are often thought of as pathological individuals rather than as members of a community. However, hackers exist within social groups that provide expertise, support, training, journals and conferences. This article outlines this community to establish the nature of hacking within 'information societies'. To delineate a 'sociology of hackers', an introduction is provided to the nature of computer-mediated communication and the act of computer intrusion, the hack. Following this the hacking community is explored in three sections. First, a profile of the number of hackers and hacks is provided by exploring available demographics. Second, an outline of its culture is provided through a discussion of six different aspects of the hacking community. The six aspects are technology, secrecy, anonymity, membership fluidity, male dominance and motivations. Third, an exploration of the community's construction of a boundary, albeit fluid, between itself and its other, the computer security industry, is provided. This boundary is constructed through metaphors whose central role is to establish the ethical nature of hacking. Finally, a conclusion that rejects any pathologisation of hackers is offered.

Introduction[1]

The growth of a world-wide computer network and its increasing use both for the construction of online communities and for the reconstruction of existing societies means that unauthorised computer intrusion, or hacking, has wide significance. The 1996 report of a computer raid on Citibank that netted around $10 million indicates the potential seriousness of computer intrusion. Other, perhaps more whimsical, examples are the attacks on the CIA

Tim Jordan and Paul Taylor

world-wide web site, in which its title was changed from Central Intelligence Agency to Central Stupidity Agency, or the attack on the British Labour Party's web-site, in which titles like 'Road to the Manifesto' were changed to 'Road to Nowhere'. These hacks indicate the vulnerability of increasingly important computer networks and the anarchistic, or perhaps destructive, world-view of computer intruders (Miller, 1996; Gow and Norton-Taylor, 1996). It is correct to talk of a world-view because computer intrusions come not from random, obsessed individuals but from a community that offers networks and support, such as the long running magazines *Phrack* and *2600*. A present there is no detailed sociological investigation of this community, despite a growing number of racy accounts of hacker adventures.[2] To delineate a sociology of hackers, an introduction is needed to the nature of computer-mediated communication and of the act of computer intrusion, the hack. Following this the hacking community will be explored in three sections: first, a profile of the number of hackers and hacks; second, an outline of its culture through the discussion of six different aspects of the hacking community; and third, an exploration of the community's construction of a boundary, albeit fluid, between itself and its other, the computer security industry.[3] Finally, a conclusion that briefly considers the significance of our analysis will be offered.

In the early 1970s, technologies that allowed people to use decentred, distributed networks of computers to communicate with each other globally were developed.[4] By the early 1990s a new means of organising and accessing information contained on computer networks was developed that utilised multi-media 'point and click' methods, the World-Wide Web. The Web made using computer networks intuitive and underpinned their entry into mass use. The size of this global community of computer communicators is difficult to measure[5] but in January 1998 there were at least 40 million (Hafner and Lyons, 1996; Quarterman, 1990; Jordan, 1998a; Rickard, 1995; Quarterman, 1993). Computer communication has also become key to many industries, not just through the Internet but also through private networks, such as those that underpin automated teller services. The financial industry is the clearest example of this, as John Perry Barlow says 'cyberspace is where your money is'. Taken together, all the different computer networks that currently exist control and tie together vital institutions of modern societies; including telecommunications, finance, globally distributed production and the media (Castells, 1996; Jordan, 1998a). Analysis of the community which attempts to illicitly use these networks can begin with a definition of the 'hack'.

A sociology of hackers

Means of gaining unauthorised access to computer networks include guessing, randomly generating or stealing a password. For example, in the Prestel hack, which resulted in the Duke of Edinburgh's mail-box becoming vulnerable, the hacker simply guessed an all too obvious password (222222 1234) (Schifreen, hacker, interview). Alternatively, some computers and software programmes have known flaws that can be exploited. One of the most complex of these is 'IP spoofing' in which a computer connected to the Internet can be tricked about the identity of another computer during the process of receiving data from that computer (Felten *et al.*, 1996; Shimomura, 1996; Littman, 1996). Perhaps most important of all is the ability to 'social engineer'. This can be as simple as talking people into giving out their passwords by impersonating someone, stealing garbage in the hope of gaining illicit information (trashing) or looking over someone's shoulder as they use their password (shoulder surfing). However, what makes an intrusion a hack or an intruder a hacker is not the fact of gaining illegitimate access to computers by any of these means but a set of principles about the nature of such intrusions. Turkle identifies three tenets that define a good hack: simplicity, the act has to be simple but impressive; mastery, however simple it is the act must derive from a sophisticated technical expertise; and, illicit, the act must be against some legal, institutional or even just perceived rules (Turkle, 1984: 232).[6] Dutch hacker Ralph used the example of stealing free telephone time to explain the hack:

> It depends on how you do it, the thing is that you've got your
> guys that think up these things, they consider the technological
> elements of a phone-booth, and they think, 'hey wait a minute, if
> I do this, this could work', so as an experiment, they cut the wire
> and it works, now *they're hackers*. Okay, so it's been published, so
> Joe Bloggs reads this and says, 'hey, great, I have to phone my
> folks up in Australia', so he goes out, cuts the wire, makes phone
> calls. He's a stupid ignoramus, yeah? (Ralph, hacker, interview)

A second example would be the Citibank hack. In this hack, the expertise to gain unauthorised control of a bank was developed by a group of Russian hackers who were uninterested in taking financial advantage. The hacker ethic to these intruders was one of exploration and not robbery. But, drunk and depressed, one of the hackers sold the secret for $100 and two bottles of vodka, allowing organised criminals to gain the expertise to steal $10 million (Gow and

Tim Jordan and Paul Taylor

Norton-Taylor, 1996). Here the difference between hacking and criminality lay in the communally held ethic that glorified being able to hack Citibank but stigmatised using that knowledge to steal. A hack is an event that has an original moment and, though it can be copied, it loses its status as a hack the more it is copied. Further, the good hack is the object in-itself that hackers desire, not the result of the hack (Cornwall, 1985: vii).

The key to understanding computer intrusion in a world increasingly reliant on computer-mediated communication lies in understanding a community whose aim is the hack. It is this community that makes complex computer intrusion possible and a never ending threat, through the limitless search for a good hack. It is this community that stands forever intentionally poised both at the forefront of computer communications and on the wrong side of what hackers see as dominant social and cultural norms.

Computer underground: demographics

Analysing any intentionally illicit community poses difficulties for the researcher. The global and anonymous nature of computer-mediated communication exacerbates such problems because generating a research population from the computer underground necessitates self-selection by subjects and it will be difficult to check the credentials of each subject. Further methodological difficulties involved in examining a self-styled 'outlaw' community that exists in cyberspace are indicated by the Prestel hacker.

> There used to be a hacking community in the UK, the hackers I used to deal with 8 or 9 years ago were all based in North London where I used to live and there were 12 of us around the table at the local Chinese restaurant of a Friday night . . . within about 20 minutes of me and my colleague Steve Gold being arrested: end of hacking community. An awful lot of phone calls went around, a lot of discs got buried in the garden, and a lot of people became ex-hackers and there's really no-one who'll talk now (Schifreen, hacker, interview).

Demographic data is particularly difficult to collect from an underground community.[7] However, some statistics are available. Following presentation of these, an in-depth exploration of the hacking community on the basis of qualitative research will be pre-

A sociology of hackers

sented. After investigating the US police force's crackdown on the computer underground in the early 1990s, Sterling estimated there were 5,000 active hackers with only around 100 in the elite who would be 'skilled enough to penetrate sophisticated systems' (Sterling, 1992: 76–77). For the same period, Clough and Mungo estimated there were 2,000 of 'the really dedicated, experienced, probably obsessed computer freaks' and possibly 10,000 others aspiring to this status (Clough and Mungo, 1992: 218).[8] Though no more than an indication, the best, indeed only, estimates for the size of the hacking community or computer underground are given by these figures.

Another means of measuring the size of the computer underground is by its effects. Though this cannot hope to indicate the actual number of hackers, as one hacker can be responsible for extensive illicit adventures, measuring the extent of hacking allows one indication of the underground's level of activity. Three surveys are available that generate evidence from the 'hacked' rather than hackers: the 1990 UK Audit Commission's survey, the 1993 survey conducted as part of this research project, and the 1996 War Room Research, information systems security survey.[9] Results from all three sources will be presented, focusing on the amount of hacking.

The 1990 UK Audit Commission surveyed 1,500 academic, commercial and public service organisations in the United Kingdom. This survey found 5% of academic, 14% of commercial and 11.5% of public service organisations had suffered computer intrusion (Audit Commission, 1990). A survey was conducted as part of this research project (hereafter referred to as the Taylor survey) and received 200[10] responses, of which 64.5% had experienced a hack, 18.5% a virus only and 17% no detected illicit activity (Taylor, 1993). The 1996 WarRoom survey received 236 responses from commercial USA firms (Fortune 1,000 companies) of which 58% reported attempts by outsiders to gain computer access in the 12 months prior to July 1996, 29.8% did not know and 12.2% reported no such attempts. The types of intrusions can be categorised as 38.3% malicious, 46.5% unidentifiable as malicious or benign and 15.1% benign[11] (WarRoom, 1996).

The level of hacking activity reported in these surveys varies greatly between the Audit Commission on the one hand and the Taylor and WarRoom surveys on the other. A number of possibilities explain this. The lower level of hacking comes from a survey of UK organisations, while Taylor was over half from the USA and a

Tim Jordan and Paul Taylor

third UK and WarRoom was solely USA. This might suggest a higher level of hacking into USA organisations, though this says nothing about the national source of a hack. Second, the Audit Commission survey has a much larger sample population and consequently should be more reliable. However, third, the WarRoom and Taylor surveys stressed the confidentiality of respondents. This is a key issue as organisations show a consistently high level of caution in reporting hacks. The WarRoom survey found that 37% of organisations would only report computer intrusion if required by law, that 22% would report only if 'everybody else did', that 30% would only report if they could do so anonymously and only 7% would report anytime intrusion was detected (WarRoom, 1996). From this perspective the Audit Commission survey may have under-reported hacking because it did not place sufficient emphasis on the confidentiality of responses. Fourth, the Taylor and WarRoom surveys were conducted later than the Audit Commission survey and may reflect rising levels of or rising awareness of hacking. Unfortunately, there is no way of deciding which of these factors explain the differences in reported levels of hacking.

The available statistics suggest the computer underground may not be very large, particularly in the number of elite hackers, but may be having a significant effect on a range of organisations. If the Taylor and WarRoom surveys are accurate nearly two-thirds of organisations are suffering hacks. To grasp the nature of hackers requires turning to the qualitative fieldwork conducted in this project.

Internal factors: technology, secrecy, and anonymity, membership fluidity, male dominance and motivations

> To find 'hacker culture' you have to take a very wide view of the cyberspace terrain and watch the interactions among physically diversified people who have in common a mania for machines and software. What you will find will be a gossamer framework of culture. (Marotta, hacker, interview)

The 'imagined community' that hackers create and maintain can be outlined through the following elements: technology, secrecy, anonymity, boundary fluidity, male dominance and motivations. Community is here understood as the collective identity that members of a social group construct or, in a related way, as the 'collective imagination' of a social group. Both a collective identity and imagination allow individuals to recognise in each other membership of the same community. The computer underground, or at least the hacking part of it, can be in this way understood as a community that offers certain forms of identity through which membership and social norms are negotiated. Even though some of these forms are externally imposed, the nature of Internet technology for example, the way these forms are understood allows individuals to recognise in each other a common commitment to an ethic, community or way of life. This theorisation draws on Anderson's concept of the imagined community and on social movement theories that see movements as dispersed networks of individuals, groups and organisations that combine through a collectively articulated identity. Anderson names the power of an imagined identity to bind people, who may never meet each other, together in allegiance to a common cause. Social movement theories grasp the way movements rely on divergent networks that are not hierarchically or bureaucratically unified but are negotiated between actors through an identity that is itself the subject of much of the negotiation (Jordan, 1995; Diani, 1992; Anderson, 1991). These perspectives allow us to grasp a hacking community that can use computer mediated communication to exist world-wide and in which individuals often never physically meet.[12]

Technology

The hacking community is characterised by an easy, if not all-consuming, relationship with technology, in particular with computer and communications technology.

> We are confronted with . . . a generation that has lived with computers virtually from the cradle, and therefore have no trace of fear, not even a trace of reverence. (Professor Herschberg, academic, interview)

Hackers share a certain appreciation of or attitude to technology in the assumption that technology can be turned to new and unexpected uses. This attitude need not be confined to computer mediated communication. Dutch hacker Dell claimed to have explored the subterranean tunnels and elevator shafts of Amsterdam, including government fall-out shelters (Dell, hacker, interview), while

Tim Jordan and Paul Taylor

Utrecht hacker Ralph argued hacking 'pertains to any field of technology. Like, if you haven't got a kettle to boil water with and you use your coffee machine to boil water with, then that in my mind is a hack, because you are using technology in a way that it's not supposed to be used' (Ralph, hacker, interview). It is the belief that technology can be bent to new, unanticipated purposes that underpins hackers' collective imagination.

Secrecy

Hackers demonstrate an ambivalent relationship to secrecy. A hack demands secrecy, because it is illicit, but the need to share information and gain recognition demands publicity. Sharing information is key in the development of hackers, though it makes keeping illicit acts hidden from law enforcement difficult. Hackers often hack in groups, both in the sense of physically being in the same room while hacking and of hacking separately but being in a group that physically meets, that frequents bulletin boards, on-line places to talk and exchanges information. It is a rare story of a hacker's education that does not include being trained by more experienced hackers or drawing on the collective wisdom of the hacking community through on-line information. Gaining recognition is also important to hackers. A member of the Zoetermeer hacking group noted 'Hacking can be rewarding in itself, because it can give you a real kick sometimes. But it can give you a lot more satisfaction and recognition if you share your experiences with others. . . . Without this group I would never have spent so much time behind the terminals digging into the operating system' (Zoetermeer, hackers, interview). A good hack is a bigger thrill when shared and can contribute to a hacker gaining status and access to more communal expertise. For example, access to certain bulletin boards is only given to those proven worthy.

A tension between the need to keep illicit acts away from the eyes of police and other authority figures but in front of the eyes of peers or even the general public defines hackers' relationship to secrecy. No hack exemplifies this more than a World-Wide Web hack where the object is to alter an internationally accessible form of public communication but at the same time not be caught. In the case of the Labour Party hack, the hacker managed to be quoted on the front page of UK national newspapers, by ringing up the newspapers to tell them to look at the hack before it was removed, but also kept his/her identity secret. A further example is that many hackers take trophies in the

764

A sociology of hackers

form of copied documents or pieces of software because a trophy proves to the hacking community that the hacker 'was there'. The problem is that a trophy is one of the few solid bases for prosecuting hackers. Ambivalence toward secrecy is also the source of the often-noted fact that hackers are odd criminals, seeking publicity. As Gail Thackeray, one-time police nemesis of hackers, noted 'What other group of criminals . . . publishes newsletters and hold conventions?' (Thackeray, cited in Sterling, 1992: 181).[13]

Anonymity

The third component of the hacking community is anonymity. As with technology what is distinctive is not so much the fact of online anonymity, as this is a widely remarked aspect of computer-mediated communication (Dery, 1993: 561), but the particular understanding of anonymity that hackers take up. Anonymity is closely related to secrecy but is also distinct. Secrecy relates to the secrecy of the hack, whereas anonymity relates to the secrecy of a hacker's offline identity. Netta Gilboa notes one complex version of this interplay of named and hidden identity on an on-line chat channel for hackers.

> Hackers can log into the #hack channel using software . . . that allows them to come in from several sites and be on as many separate connections, appearing to be different people. One of these identities might then message you privately as a friend while another is being cruel to you in public. (Gilboa, 1996: 102–103)

Gilboa experienced the construction of a number of public identities all intended to mask the 'real' identity of a hacker. A second example of this interplay of anonymity and publicity is the names or 'handles' hackers give themselves and their groups. These are some of the handles encountered in this research: Hack-Tic (group), Zoetermeer (group), Altenkirch (German), Eric Bloodaxe, Faustus, Maelstrom, Mercury, Mofo. Sterling notes a long list of group names – such as Kaos Inc., Knights of Shadow, Master Hackers, MAD!, Legion of Doom, Farmers of Doom, the Phirm, Inner Circle I and Inner Circle II. Hackers use names to sign their hacks (sometimes even leaving messages for the hacked computer's usual users), to meet on-line and to bolster their self-image as masters of the hack, all the while keeping their offline identity secret.[14]

Tim Jordan and Paul Taylor

Membership fluidity

The fourth quality of the hacking community is the speed at which membership changes. Hacking shares the characteristics ascribed to many social movements of being an informal network rather than a formally constituted organisation and, as such, its boundaries are highly permeable (Jordan, 1995; Diani, 1992). There are no formal ceremonies to pass or ruling bodies to satisfy to become a hacker. The informal and networked nature of the hacking community, combined with its illicit and sometimes obsessional nature means that a high turnover of hackers occurs (Clough and Mungo, 1992: 18). Hackers form groups within the loose overall structure of the hacking community and these may aspire to be formally organised, however the pressures of law enforcement means that any successful hacking group is likely to attract sustained attention at some point (Quittner and Slatalla, 1995).

> People come and go pretty often and if you lay off for a few months and then come back, almost everyone is new. There are always those who have been around for years . . . I would con-sider the hacking community a very informal one. It is pretty much anarchy as far as rule-making goes. . . . The community was structured only within the framework of different hacking 'groups'. Legion of Doom would be one example of this. A group creates its own rules and usually doesn't have a leader . . . The groups I've been in have voted on accepting new members, kicking people out, etc. (Eric Bloodaxe, hacker, member of Legion of Doom, interview)

Gilboa claims that the future of hacking will be a split between life-long hackers, often unable to quit because of police records and sus-picion, and 90% of hackers who will move on 'when they get a job they care about or a girlfriend who sucks up their time' (Gilboa, 1996: 111). A more prosaic, but equally potent, reason why the hacking community's membership is fluid is given by hacker Mike 'if you stop, if you don't do it for one week then things change, the network always changes. It changes very quickly and you have to keep up and you have to learn all the tricks by heart, the default passwords, the bugs you need' (Mike, hacker, interview). The sheer speed at which computer communications technology changes requires a powerful commitment from hackers.

A sociology of hackers

Male dominance

The fifth component of hacking culture is male dominance and an associated misogyny. Research for this project and literature on hackers fails to uncover any significant evidence of female hackers (Taylor, 1993: 92). Gilboa states 'I have met more than a thousand male hackers in person but less than a dozen of them women' (Gilboa, 1996: 106). This imbalance is disproportionate even in the field of computer mediated communication (Spertus, 1991: i). A number of factors explain the paucity of women generally in the computer sciences: childhood socialisation, where boys are taught to relate to technology more easily than girls; education in computers occurs in a masculine environment; and, a gender bias towards men in the language used in computer science (Spertus, 1991; Turkle, 1984; Taylor, 1993: 91–103). With these factors producing a general bias towards males in relation to computers, the drive towards the good hack exacerbates this as it involves a macho, competitive attitude (Keller, 1988: 58). Hackers construct a more intensely masculine version of the already existing male bias in the computer sciences.

> When Adam delved and Eve span . . . who was then the gentleman? Well, we see that Adam delves into the workings of computers and networks and meanwhile Eve spins, what? Programmes? Again, my wife programmes and she has the skills of a hacker. She has had to crack security in order to do her job. But she does it as her job, not for the abstract thrill of discovering the unknown. Even spins. Females who compute would rather spend their time building a good system, than breaking into someone else's system. (Mercury, hacker, interview)

Whether Mercury's understanding of differences between men and women is accurate or not, the fact that he, and many other hackers, have such attitudes means the hacking community will almost certainly feel hostile to women. Added to these assumptions of, at best, separate spheres of male and female expertise in computing is the problem that anonymity often fuels sexual harassment. 'The fact that many networks allow a user to hide his real name . . . seems to cause many males to drop all semblance of civilisation. Sexual harassment by email is not uncommon' (Freiss, hacker, interview). Gilboa, a woman, recounts an epic tale of harassment that included hackers using her on-line magazine as a 'tutorial' example of how to

Tim Jordan and Paul Taylor

charge phone calls to someone else, taking over her magazine entirely and launching a fake version, being called a prostitute, child molester and drug dealer, having her phone calls listened to, her phone re-routed or made to sound constantly engaged and having her email read. One answer to Gilboa's puzzlement at her treatment lies in the collective identity hackers share and construct that is in part misogynist.

Motivations

Finally, hackers often discuss their motivations for hacking. They are aware of, and often glory in, the fact that the life of a dedicated hacker seems alien to those outside the hacking community. One result of this is that hackers discuss their motivations. These are sometimes couched as self-justifications, sometimes as explanations and sometimes as agonised struggles with personal obsessions and failures. However, whatever the content of such discussions, it is the fact of an ongoing discourse around the motivation to hack that builds the hacking community. These discussions are one more way that hackers can recognise in each other a common identity that provides a collective basis for their community. A number of recurring elements to these discussions can be identified.

First, hackers often confess to an addiction to computers and/or to computer networks, a feeling that they are compelled to hack. Second, curiosity as to what can be found on the world-wide network is also a frequent topic of discussion. Third, hackers often claim their offline life is boring compared to the thrill of illicit searches in online life. Fourth, the ability to gain power over computer systems, such as NASA, Citibank or the CIA web site, is an attraction. Fifth, peer recognition from other hackers or friends is a reward and goal for many hackers, signifying acceptance into the community and offering places in a hierarchy of more advanced hackers. Finally, hackers often discuss the service to future computer users or to society they are offering because they identify security loopholes in computer networks. Hackers articulate their collective identity, and construct a sense of community, by discussing this array of different motivations.

> I just do it because it makes me feel good, as in better than anything else that I've ever experienced . . . the adrenaline rush I get when I'm trying to evade authority, the thrill I get from having written a program that does something that was supposed

A sociology of hackers

> to be impossible to do, and the ability to have social relations
> with other hackers are all very addictive . . . For a long time, I
> was extremely shy around others, and I am able to let my
> thoughts run free when I am alone with my computer and a
> modem hooked up to it. I consider myself addicted to hacking
> . . . I will have no moral or ethical qualms about system hacking
> until accounts are available to the general public for free . . . Peer
> recognition was very important, when you were recognised you
> had access to more. (Maelstrom, hacker, interview)

Maelstrom explores almost the whole range of motivations including curiosity, the thrill of the illicit, boredom, peer recognition and
the social need for free or cheap access. By developing his own interpretation out of the themes of motivation, he can simultaneously
define his own drives and develop a sense of community. It is this
double movement in which individual motivations express the
nature of a community, that makes the discussions of motivations
important for hackers. Finally, the motivations offered by perhaps
the most famous of all hackers, Kevin Mitnick, provides another
common articulation of reasons for hacking.

> You get a better understanding of cyberspace, the computer
> systems, the operating systems, how the computer systems
> interact with one another, that basically was my motivation
> behind my hacking activity in the past. It was just from the gain
> of knowledge and the thrill of adventure, nothing that was well
> and truly sinister as trying to get any type of monetary gain or
> anything. (Mitnick, hacker, interviewer)

Internal factors: conclusion

These six factors all function largely between hackers, allowing
them a common language and a number of resources through which
they can recognise each other as hackers and through which newcomers can become hackers. These are resources internal to the
hacking community, not because they do not affect or include non-
hackers but because their significance is largely for other hackers.
Put another way, these are the resources hackers use to discuss their
status as hackers with other hackers, they are collectively negotiated
within the boundaries of the hacker community. This raises the
issue of how an external boundary is constructed and maintained.
How do hackers recognise a distinction between inside and outside?

Tim Jordan and Paul Taylor

How do hackers adjust, reinvent and maintain such a distinction? This is the subject of the third and final section of this definition of the hacker community.

External factors: the boundary between computer underground and the computer security industry

Hackers negotiate a boundary around their community by relating to other social groups. For example, hackers have an often spectacular relationship to the media. Undoubtedly the most important relationship to another community or group is their intimate and antagonistic bond to the computer security industry (CSI). This relationship is constitutive of the hacking community in a way that no other is. Put another way, there is no other social group whose existence is necessary to the existence of the hacking community. Here is a sample of views of hackers from members of CSI.

> Hackers are like kids putting a 10 pence piece on a railway line to see if the train can bend it, not realising that they risk derailing the whole train. (Mike Jones, security awareness division, Department of Trade and Industry, UK, interview)

> Electronic vandalism. (Warman, London Business School, interview)

> Somewhere near vermin. (Zmudsinski, system engineer/manager, USA, interview)

Naturally, hackers often voice a similar appreciation of members of CSI. For example, while admitting psychotic tendencies exist in the hacking community Mofo notes:

> my experience has shown me that the actions of 'those in charge' of computer systems and networks have similar 'power trips' which need to be fulfilled. Whether this psychotic need is developed or entrenched before one's association with computers is irrelevant. (Mofo, hacker, interview)

However, the boundary between these two communities is not as clear as such attitudes might suggest. This can be seen in relation to membership of the communities and the actions members take.

Hackers often suggest the dream that their skills should be used by CSI to explore security faults, thereby giving hackers jobs and

A sociology of hackers

legitimacy to pursue the hack by making them members of CSI. The example of a leading member of one of the most famous hacker groups, the Legion of Doom, is instructive. Eric Bloodaxe, aka Chris Goggans, became a leading member of the hacking community before helping to set up a computer security firm, Comsec, and later moving to become senior network security engineer for WheelGroup a network security company (Quittner and Slatalla, 1995: 145–147 and 160–160). On the CSI side, there have been fierce debates over whether hackers might be useful because they identify security problems (Spafford, 1990; Denning, 1990). Most striking, a number of CSI agencies conduct hacking attacks to test security. IBM employ a group of hackers who can be hired to attack computer systems and the UK government has asked 'intelligence agents' to hack its secure email system for government ministers (Lohr, 1997; Hencke, 1998).[15] In the IBM case, an attempt at differentiating the hired hackers from criminal hackers is made by hiring only hackers without criminal records (a practice akin to turning criminals who have not been caught into police) (Lohr, 1997). Both sides try to assure themselves of radical differences because they undertake similar actions. For example, Bernie Cosell was a USA commercial computer systems manager and one of the most vehement anti-hackers encountered in this study, yet he admitted he hacked

> once or twice over the years. I recall one incident where I was working over the weekend and the master source hierarchy was left read-protected, and I really needed to look at it to finish what I was doing, and this on a system where I was not a privileged user, so I 'broke into' the system enough to give myself enough privileges to be able to override the file protections and get done what I needed . . . at which point I put it all back and told the systems administrator about the security hole. (Cosell, USA systems manager, interview)

More famous is the catalogue of hacks Clifford Stoll had to perpetrate in his pursuit of a hacker, which included borrowing other people's computers without permission and monitoring other people's electronic communications without permission (Stoll, 1989; Thomas, 1990). Such examples mean that differences between the two communities cannot be expressed through differences in what they do but must focus on the meaning of actions. Delineating these meanings is chiefly done through ethical debates about the nature of

Tim Jordan and Paul Taylor

hacking conducted through analogies drawn between cyberspace and non-virtual or real space.

CSI professionals often draw analogies between computer intrusion and a range of widely understood crimes. These analogies draw on the claim that a computer is something like a bank, car or house that can be 'got into'. Using this analogy makes it easy to understand the danger of hackers, people who break into banks, schools or houses usually do so for nefarious purposes. The ethical differences between hackers and the CSI become clearly drawn. The problem with such analogies is that, on further reflection, hackers seem strange burglars. How often does a burglar leave behind an exact copy of the video recorder they have stolen? But this unreal situation is a more accurate description of theft in cyberspace because taking in cyberspace overwhelmingly means copying. Further, hacker culture leads hackers to publicise their break-ins, sometimes even stressing the utility of their break-ins for identifying system weaknesses. What bank robbers ring up a bank to complain of lax security? The simple analogy of theft breaks down when it is examined and must be complicated to begin to make sense of what hackers do.

> There is a great difference between trespassing on my property and breaking into my computer. A better analogy might be finding a trespasser in your high-rise office building at 3am and learning that his back-pack contained some tools, some wire, a timer and a couple of detonation caps. He could claim that he wasn't planting a bomb, but how can you be sure? (Cosell, USA systems manager, interview)

Cosell's analogy continues to draw on real world or physically based images of buildings being entered but tries to come closer to the reality of how hackers operate. However, the ethical component of the analogy has been weakened because the damage hackers cause becomes implied, where is the bomb?[16] Cosell cannot claim there will definitely be a bomb, only that it is possible. If all possible illegal actions were prohibited then many things would become illegal, such as driving because it is possible to speed and then hurt someone in an accident. The analogy of breaking and entering is now strong on implied dangers but weak on the certainty of danger. The analogies CSI professionals use continue to change if they try to be accurate. 'My analogy is walking into an office building, asking a secretary which way it is to the records room and making some

Xerox copies of them. Far different than breaking and entering someone's home' (Cohen, CSI, interview). Clearly there is some ethical content here, some notion of theft of information, but it is ethically far muddier than the analogy burglar offers. At this point, the analogy breaks down entirely because the ethical content can be reversed to one that supports hackers as 'whistle-blowers' of secret abuses everyone should know about.

> The concept of privacy is something that is very important to a hacker. This is so because hackers know how fragile privacy is in today's world. . . . In 1984 hackers were instrumental in showing the world how TRW kept credit files on millions of Americans. Most people had not even heard of a credit file until this happened . . . More recently, hackers found that MCI's 'Friends and Family' programme allowed anybody to call an 800 number and find out the numbers of everyone in a customer's 'calling circle'. As a bonus, you could also find out how these numbers were related to the customer . . . In both the TRW and MCI cases, hackers were ironically accused of being the ones to invade privacy. What they really did was help to educate the American consumer. (Goldstein, 1993)

The central analogy of CSI has now lost its ethical content. Goldstein reverses the good and bad to argue that the correct principled action is to broadcast hidden information. If there is some greater social good to be served by broadcasting secrets, then perhaps hackers are no longer robbers and burglars but socially responsible whistle blowers. In the face of such complexities, CSI professionals sometimes abandon the analogy of breaking and entering altogether; 'it is no more a valid justification to attack systems because they are vulnerable than it is valid to beat up babies because they can't defend themselves' (Cohen, CSI, interview). Here many people's instinctive reaction would be to side with the babies, but a moment's thought reveals that in substance Cohen's analogy changes little. A computer system is not human and if information in it is needed by wider society, perhaps it should be attacked.

The twists and turns of these analogies show that CSI professionals use them not so much to clearly define hacking and its problems, but to establish clear ethical differences between themselves and hackers. The analogies of baby-bashing and robbery all try to establish hacking as wrong. The key point is that while these analogies work in an ethical and community building sense, they do not work

Tim Jordan and Paul Taylor

in clearly grasping the nature of hacking because analogies between real and virtual space cannot be made as simply as CSI professionals would like to assume.

> Physical (and biological) analogies are often misleading as they appeal to an understanding from an area in which different laws hold. . . . Many users (and even 'experts') think of a password as a 'key' despite the fact that you can easily guess the password, while it is difficult to do the equivalent for a key. (Brunnstein, academic, Hamburg University, interview)

The process of boundary formation between the hacking and CSI communities occurs in the creation of analogies by CSI professionals to establish ethical differences between the communities and their reinterpretation by hackers. However, this does not exclude hackers from making their own analogies.

> Computer security is like a chess-game, and all these people that say breaking into my computer systems is like breaking into my house: bull-shit, because securing your house is a very simple thing, you just put locks on the doors and bars on the windows and then only brute force can get into your house, like smashing a window. But a computer has a hundred thousand intricate ways to get in, and it's a chess game with the people that secure a computer. (Gongrijp, Dutch hacker, interview)

Other hackers offer similar analogies that stress hacking is an intellectual pursuit. 'I was bored if I didn't do anything . . . I mean why do people do crosswords? It's the same thing with hackers (J.C. van Winkel, hacker, interview). Gongrijp and van Winkel also form boundaries through ethical analogy. Of course, it is an odd game of chess or crossword that results in the winner receiving thousands of people's credit records or access to their letters. Hackers' elision of the fact that a game of chess has no result but a winner and a loser at a game of chess whereas hacking often results in access to privileged information, means their analogies are both inaccurate and present hacking as a harmless, intellectual pursuit. It is on the basis of such analogies and discussions that the famed 'hacker ethic' is often invoked by hackers. Rather than hackers learning the tenets of the hacker ethic, as seminally defined by Steven Levy, they negotiate a common understanding of the meaning of hacking of which the hacker ethic provides a ready articulation.[17] Many see the hacker

A sociology of hackers

ethic as a foundation of the hacker community, whereas we see the hacker ethic as the result of the complex construction of a collective identity.

The social process here is the use of analogies to physical space by CSI and hackers to establish a clear distinction between the two groups. In these processes can be seen the construction by both sides of boundaries between communities that are based on different ethical interpretations of computer intrusion, in a situation where other boundaries, such as typical actions or membership, are highly fluid.

Conclusion

The nature of the hacking community needs to be explored in order to grasp the social basis that produces hacking as a facet of computer networks. The figures given previously and the rise of the World-Wide Web hack, offering as it does both spectacular publicity and anonymity, point to the endemic nature of hackers now that world-wide computer networks are an inescapable reality. Hackers show that living in a networked world means living in a risky world. The community found by this research articulates itself in two key directions. First there are a number of components that are the subject of ongoing discussion and negotiation by hackers with other hackers. In defining and redefining their attitudes to technology, secrecy, anonymity, membership change, male dominance and personal motivations, hackers create an imagined community. Second, hackers define the boundaries of their community primarily in relation to the Computer Security Industry. These boundaries stress an ethical interpretation of hacking because it can be difficult to clearly distinguish the activities or membership of the two communities. Such ethics emerge most clearly through analogies used by members of each community to explain hacking.

Hackers are often pathologised as obsessed, isolated young men. The alien nature of online life allows people to believe hackers more easily communicate with machines than humans, despite hackers' constant use of computers to communicate with other humans. Fear of the power of computers over our own lives underpins this terror. The very anonymity that makes their community difficult to study, equally makes hackers an easy target for pathologising. For example, Gilboa's experience of harassment outlined earlier led her to pathologise hackers, suggesting work must be done exploring the

Tim Jordan and Paul Taylor

characteristics of hackers she identified – such as lack of fathers or parental figures, severe depression and admittance to mental institutions (Gilboa, 1996: 112). Similar interpretations of hackers are offered from within their community, 'All the hackers I know in France have (or have had) serious problems with their parents' (Condat, hacker, interview). Our research strongly suggests that psychological interpretations of hackers that individualise hackers as mentally unstable are severely limited because they miss the social basis of hacking. Gilboa's experience is no less unpleasant but all the more understandable when the male dominance of the hacking community is grasped.

The fear many have of the power of computers over their lives easily translates into the demonisation of those who manipulate computers outside of society's legitimate institutions. Journalist Jon Littman once asked hacker Kevin Mitnick if he thought he was being demonised because new and different fears had arisen with society becoming increasingly dependent on computers and communications. Mitnick replied 'Yeah . . . That's why they're instilling fear of the unknown. That's why they're scared of me. Not because of what I've done, but because I have the capability to wreak havoc' (Mitnick, cited in Littman, 1996: 205). The pathological interpretation of hackers is attractive because it is based on the fear of computers controlling our lives. What else could someone be but mad, if s/he is willing to play for fun on computer systems that control air traffic, dams or emergency phones? The interpretation of hackers as members of an outlaw community that negotiates its collective identity through a range of clearly recognisable resources does not submit to the fear of computers. It gains a clearer view of hackers, who have become the nightmare of information societies despite very few documented cases of upheaval caused by hackers. Hacking cannot be clearly grasped unless fears are put aside to try and understand the community of hackers, the digital underground. From within this community, hackers begin to lose their pathological features in favour of collective principles, allegiances and identities.

University of East London   Received 6 August 1997
                                                  Finally accepted 23 June 1998

Notes

1 Thanks to Sally Wyatt, Alan White, Ian Taylor and two anonymous referees for comments on this piece.

A sociology of hackers

2 Meyer and Thomas (1989) and Sterling, (1992) provide useful outlines of the computer underground, while Rosteck (1994) provides an interesting interpretation of hackers as a social movement. Previous accounts lack detailed survey work.

3 This analysis draws on extensive fieldwork consisting of both a quantitative questionnaire (200 respondents) that outlines the extent and nature of hacking and 80 semi-structured interviews with hackers (30), computer security professionals (30) and other interested parties (20). A full methodology and list of interviewees is available in Taylor, (1993). All notes of the following form (Schifreen, hacker, interview) indicate that Schifreen was a hacker interviewed for this project.

4 It is of course impossible to provide an adequate history of computer networking here and would distract from the main purpose of present arguments. A summary and full references for such a history can be found in Jordan, (1998a).

5 See Jordan, (1998a) for a full discussion of methodologies for counting Internet users.

6 The concept of a 'hacker' has had several manifestations, with at least four other possibilities than a computer intruder. This paper is concerned solely with hacker in the sense of a computer intruder, though see Taylor, (1993) for further discussion (Levy, 1984; Coupland, 1995). It should also be noted that hacking makes most sense within a society in which knowledge has become extensively commodified and is subject to a process in which it can be extensively copied (Mosco and Wasco, 1988).

7 One indication of these difficulties is that the passage of the Computer Misuse Act 1990 in the UK meant it was difficult to persuade UK hackers to discuss their activities but a lack of comparable legislation in the Netherlands removed one barrier to several Dutch hackers allowing interviews to go ahead. For an extensive discussion of the difficulties and advantages of this research methodology, see Taylor, (1993: chapter 2). For a general discussion of such difficulties see Jupp (1989).

8 Professional security consultants, whose interests are best served by a large underground, have placed the number of hackers as high as 50,000 or 35,000 (Sterling, 1992: 77; Gilboa, 1996: 98).

9 A fourth survey exists, the 1991 UK National Computing Centre Survey, but investigates 'logical breaches' (disruption to computer systems) and only provides tangential evidence of hacking. We became aware of John Howard's work too late for inclusion in this analysis (Howard, 1997).

10 Academic (39.5%), commercial (41%), public service organisations (2.5%), other (14%) and some combination of the above (3%).

11 The following categories from the WarRoom survey were joined to create categories of clearly malicious, neither malicious nor benign, and clearly benign: malicious – manipulated data integrity (6.8), introduced virus (10.6), denied use of service (6.3), compromised trade secrets (9.8), stole/diverted money (0.3), harassed personnel (4.5); neither – installed sniffer (6.6), stole password files (5.6), trojan logons (5.8), IP spoofing (4.8), downloaded data (8.1), compromised email/documents (12.6), other (3.0); and, benign – probing/scanning of system (14.6), publicised intrusion (0.5). It is of course possible to argue that any intrusion is malicious and to dispute the division given above.

12 Much more, of course, could be said about the nature of community and the theories referred to here. To prevent this paper becoming a theoretical exposition of well-known work, the understanding of community will be left here.

Tim Jordan and Paul Taylor

13 Hackers do indeed hold conferences, such as HoHoCon, SummerCon, PumpCon and DefCon (Rosteck, 1994). See Littman, (1996: 41–44) for a description of such a conference.

14 Anonymity also enables some of the darker fears that emerge about hackers. Finding fearsomely named gangs of hackers running amok in supposedly secure systems can give rise to exaggerated fears, which hackers are often happy to live up to, at least rhetorically (Barlow, 1990).

15 Our research also leads us to believe that CSI uses teams of hackers to test security far more often than CSI professionals publicly admit.

16 Other CSI professionals offered similar analogies, such as finding someone looking at a car or aeroplane engine.

17 Steven Levy distilled a hacker ethic from the early, non-computer intruder, hackers. This ethic is often invoked by all types of hackers and Levy defines the tenets as: all information should be free; mistrust authority, promote decentralisation; hackers should be judged by their hacking, not by bogus criteria such as degrees, age, race or position; you can create art and beauty on a computer; and, computers can change your life for the better (Levy, 1984: 40–45).

References

Anderson, B., (1991), *Imagined Communities*, second edition, London: Verso.

Audit Commission, (1990), 'Survey of Computer Fraud and Abuse', Audit Commission.

Barlow, J.P., (1990), 'Crime and Puzzlement', *Whole Earth Review*, Fall 1990, 44–57.

Castells, M., (1996), *The Rise of the Network Society: the information age, volume 1*, Oxford: Blackwell.

Cherny, L. and Weise, E., (eds), (1996), *Wired Women: gender and new realities in cyberspace*, Seattle: Seal Press.

Clough, B. and Mungo, P., (1992), *Approaching Zero: data crime and the computer underworld*, London: Faber and Faber.

Coupland, D., (1995), *Microserfs*, London: HarperCollins.

deamon9/route/infinity, (1996), 'IP-Spoofing Demystified', *Phrack*, 7 (48), also available at http://www.geocities.com/CapeCanaveral/3498/.

Denning, P., (ed.), (1990), *Computers Under Attack: intruders, worms and viruses*, New York: Addison-Wesley.

Dery, M., (ed.), (1993), *Flame Wars*, London: Duke University Press.

Diani, M., (1992), 'The Concept of a Social Movement', *The Sociological Review*, 40 (1): 1–25.

Dreyfus, S., (1997), *Underground: tales of hacking, madness and obsession on the electronic frontier*, Kew: Mandarin.

Felten, E., Balfanz, D., Dean, D. and Wallack, D., (1996), 'Web-Spoofing: an Internet con game', *Technical Report 540-96*, Department of Computer Science, Princeton University, also at http://www.cs.princeton.edu/sip.

Gilboa, N., (1996), 'Elites, Lamers, Narcs and Whores: exploring the computer underground', in Cherny, L. and Weise, E. (eds), (1996), 98–113.

Goldstein, E., (1993), 'Hacker Testimony to House Sub-committee Largely Unheard', *Computer Underground Digest*, 5.43.

Godell, J., (1996), *The Cyberthief and the Samurai: the true story of Kevin Mitnick and the man who hunted him down*, New York: Dell.

A sociology of hackers

Gow, D. and Norton-Taylor, R., (1996), 'Surfing Superhighwaymen', *The Guardian* newspaper, 7/12/1996, 28.

Hafner, K. and Lyons, M., (1996), *Where Wizards Stay Up Late: the origins of the Internet*, New York: Simon and Schuster.

Hafner, K. and Markoff, J., (1991), *Cyberpunk: outlaws and hackers on the computer frontier*, London: Corgi.

Harasim, L., (ed.), (1993), *Global Networks: computers and international communication*, Cambridge: MIT Press.

Hencke, D., (1998), 'Whitehall Attempts to Foil Net Hackers', *Guardian Weekly*, 26 April, 8.

Howard, J., (1997), 'Information Security', unpublished PhD dissertation, Carnegie Mellon University, available at http://www.cert.org.

Jordan, T., (1995), 'The Unity of Social Movements', *The Sociological Review*, 43 (4): 675–692.

Jordan, T., (1998a), *Cyberpower: a sociology and politics of cyberspace and the Internet*, London: Routledge.

Jordan, T., (1998b), 'New Space? New Politics: cyberpolitics and the Electronic Frontier Foundation', in Jordan, T. and Lent, A. (eds), (1998).

Jordan, T. and Lent, A., (eds), (1998), *Storming the Millennium: the new politics of change*, London: Lawrence and Wishart.

Jupp, C., (1989), *Methods of Criminological Research*, London: Unwin Hyman.

Keller, L., (1988), 'Machismo and the Hacker Mentality: some personal observations and speculations', paper presented to WiC (Women in Computing) Conference.

Levy, S., (1984), *Hackers: heroes of the computer revolution*, Harmondsworth: Penguin.

Littman, J., (1996), *The Fugitive Game: online with Kevin Mitnick, the inside story of the great cyberchase*, Boston: Little, Brown and Co.

Ludlow, P., (ed.), (1996), *High Noon on the Electronic Frontier*, Cambridge: MIT Press.

NCC, (1991), 'Survey of Security Breaches', National Computing Centre.

Meyer, G. and Thomas, J., (1989), 'The Baudy World of the Byte: a post-modernist interpretation of the Computer Underground', paper presented at the American Society of Criminology annual meeting, Reno, November 1989.

Miller, S., (1996), 'Hacker takes over Labour's cyberspace', *The Guardian* newspaper, 10/12/1996, 1.

Mosco, V. and Wasko, M., (eds), (1988), *The Political Economy of Information*, Wisconsin: University of Wisconsin Press.

Quarterman, J., (1990), *The Matrix: computer networks and conferencing systems worldwide*, Bedford: Digital Press.

Quarterman, J., (1993), 'The Global Matrix of Minds', in Harasim, L. (ed.), 1993, 35–56.

Quittner, J. and Slatalla, M., (1995), *Masters of Deception: the gang that ruled cyberspace*, London: Vintage.

Ross, A., (1991), *Strange Weather*, London: Verso.

Rosteck, T., (1994), 'Computer Hackers: rebels with a cause', honours thesis. Sociology and Anthropology, Concordia University, Montreal, also at http://www.geocities.com/CapeCanaveral/3498/.

Shimomura, R., (1996), *Takedown: the pursuit and capture of Kevin Mitnick, the world's most notorious cybercriminal – by the man who did it*, with John Markoff, London: Secker and Warburg.

Tim Jordan and Paul Taylor

Spafford, E., (1990), 'Are Computer Hacker Break-Ins Ethical?', Princeton University Technical Report, CSD-TR-994, Princeton.

Spertus, E., (1991), 'Why are there so few female computer scientists?', unpublished paper, MIT.

Sterling, B., (1992), *The Hacker Crackdown: law and disorder on the electronic frontier*, London: Viking.

Sterling, B., (1994), 'The Hacker Crackdown three years later', only published electronically, available at http://www.uel.ac.uk/research/nprg.

Stoll, C., (1989), *The Cuckoo's Egg: tracking a spy through the maze of counter-espionage*, New York: Simon and Schuster.

Taylor, P., (1993), 'Hackers: a case-study of the social shaping of computing', unpublished PhD dissertation, University of Edinburgh.

Thomas, J., (1990), 'Review of The Cuckoo's Egg', *Computer Underground Digest*, 1.06.

Turkle, S., (1984), *The Second Self: computers and the human spirit*, London: Granada.

WarRoom, (1996), '1996 Information Systems Security Survey', WarRoom Research, LLC, available at http://www.infowar.com/.

[11]

>> NETCRIME

More Change in the Organization of Thieving

DAVID MANN and MIKE SUTTON*

This paper is primarily concerned with criminal activities in the publicly accessible areas of the Internet known as newsgroups. Findings are presented from a small scale exploratory study of two Internet newsgroups and a tentative model of the structure of these newsgroups is proposed. Members of both newsgroups disseminated information and products to those who might wish to commit crimes. One newsgroup focused upon hacking encrypted satellite television services and the other was a locksmithing group with members interested in picking locks and understanding more about safes and other security devices. The Internet is a particularly effective medium for criminal recruitment and the dissemination of criminal techniques. Whilst it is possible that it will bring an increase in crime and create new problems for those concerned with crime control and criminality prevention, it is too early to tell whether the Internet or high technology crime will cause major problems for law and order in the future. However, with the expansion of the Net, various NetCrimes may become high volume crimes. If this happens, existing approaches for dealing with and seeking to understand the reasons for high volume crime will have to be widened and new ones developed to meet the challenge of crimes facilitated by, or taking place in, a radically different environment.

Perhaps the most important theme to emerge from this study is the susceptibility of high-technology devices, such as smart-cards, to ingenious or systematic hacking attempts. Moreover, once 'cracked', rapid dissemination via the Internet of a new security breach can, in a matter of hours, render obsolete previously crime proof systems.

This paper is divided into three main parts, plus a glossary. The first part describes the origins, structure and characteristics of the Internet (Net)[1] then, with a brief review of the literature, goes on to look at current concerns regarding crime on the Internet and related media. This includes observations and opinions of criminologists, journalists, authors, police officers and other users of the Internet.

*The authors are respectively Higher Scientific Officer and Senior Research Officer, Home Office Research and Statistics Directorate.

For several years, those with responsibility for national security, criminal investigation and crime control have been developing methods for monitoring and policing crime on the Internet. It is hoped that this paper will go some way towards creating a wider body of knowledge that will eventually make their work easier and more effective. Particular thanks, for their advice and active encouragement, are due to: Keith Buzzard CESG, Mike Cochrane—Defence Research Agency, and Inspector David Davis—West Midlands Constabulary. The authors would also like to thank: Chris Nuttall; Chris Lewis; Peter Grove; John Graham; Pat Mayhew; Tom Ellis; Peter Marshall, Ed Mortimer, Paul Ekblom—Home Office Research and Statistics Directorate; Joanna Shapland—University of Sheffield; Howard Parker—University of Manchester; Rebecca Hart—Home Office Librarian; Heather Lockwood and J. L. Cheetham.

The views expressed in this paper are those of the authors and do not necessarily represent those of the Home Office or any other Government department.

[1] It is accepted practice to use Internet and Net interchangeably.

201

DAVID MANN AND MIKE SUTTON

The second part of this paper describes and discusses findings from an observational study of two Internet newsgroups, beginning with a European satellite pay-TV hacking group. The people looked at in this group were very active in illegally obtaining satellite TV services. This involved compiling illicit hardware and software, distributing it for free, selling it, purchasing it or finding out how to get it without paying. The other newsgroup examined was primarily North American, and its members are interested in locksmithing (the Locksmiths). It is a smaller group and was studied to test the generality of the findings from the first newsgroup. The Locksmiths is a strangely Tartuffian[2] newsgroup. Many members said they were professional locksmiths and claimed that they would not answer requests on how to make and use lock picks, or how to break combination locks. Yet such information was regularly given out by the group and disseminated over the whole Internet.[3]

The third part of this paper looks at some current approaches for studying and dealing with high volume crimes and discusses their suitability for understanding and controlling crime on the Net. This is followed by some recommendations for future research and implications for policy.

This paper also includes two new terms: *NetCrime*—meaning any criminal offence committed via the Internet; and *NetOffenders*—to describe those who initiate such crimes, or take up criminal opportunities on the Net. NetOffenders are not necessarily specialists in NetCrime. The term applies to anyone using the Net for criminal purposes—either in a planned and deliberate way or opportunistically.

Problems caused by such groups as the satellite TV hackers looked at in this paper have already reached such proportions that the Council of Europe has produced at least two publications dealing with them (1995*a*, 1995*b*). Although the Council of Europe handbook (1995*a*) does not produce any separate figures for the costs to industry of illegal satellite hacking it includes this activity within a general description of audio visual piracy:

In 1994, audio visual piracy (videos, unauthorized broadcasting of films, unlawful transmissions, piracy of decoding equipment) represented about 10 million (US) dollars in countries such as Austria, Bulgaria, Portugal, Switzerland; 20 million dollars in Romania; 50 million dollars in France, Germany, Greece and Spain, roughly 100 million dollars in the United Kingdom; more than 200 million dollars in Italy.

These figures are startling. In Britain, it has been estimated that illegal distribution of satellite smart-cards has cost one service provider (Sat-TV[4]) well in excess of £300,000[5] (Sylvester 1996).

The Net provides a uniquely safe environment for many people to acquire illegal benefit from the enterprise of others. Making illegal profit from the latest innovations of industry is nothing new (e.g. forgery and coin clipping). However, the main

---

[2] Certain members hypocritically pretending to be deeply pious.
[3] The authors have been careful not to include in this paper any information regarding how to open locks, safes, or how to overcome other security devices.
[4] Pseudonym used in this paper for a European satellite TV service provider.
[5] The cost of developing, manufacturing and distributing each new generation of smart-cards, to replace those defeated, would increase this sum considerably. This is merely a conservative estimate of 'lost' subscriptions.

difference is that the Net is a relatively new technology that has facilitated a means of providing an immediate and constant supply of illicit techniques, services and products as soon as they are available.

Background to the Internet

The revolution in communications sweeping the planet—a revolution in which the Internet plays a crucial part—will eventually prove as potent a political force as the rise of industrial mass production. It will change the ways in which people relate to each other individually and in groups; it will change the ways in which we define the public sphere; it will change the distribution of power in the workplace and in society at large. (Morton 1996)

The Internet is an open interconnection of computers developed in the 1970s as a resilient military network. Lack of central control and flexibility were specifically built into the system. These features enabled it to grow into an international, publicly accessible network. No one owns the Net because each computer and 'connecting medium' (copper cable, satellite, optical fibre etc.) can have a different owner. The Net is available in 150 countries and there are an estimated 60 million users world wide. By early 1996, more than 60,000 networks and five million computers were connected via the Net. At the current rate of growth, with thousands of newcomers every day, more than 100 million computers will be connected via the Net by the year 2000.

Users of the Net have come to describe this medium of communication as 'cyberspace', a term first used in the science fiction book *Neuromancer* (Gibson 1986). The term cyberspace is used in this paper as it is now commonly understood to mean: the non-physical place which comprises the whole Internet system.[6]

Many newcomers to the Net mistakenly regard the World Wide Web (*Web* or *WWW*) as the entire Internet, because it is the most easily accessible and most widely 'hyped up' application. It is the 'glossy front-end'—primarily a means of advertising, disseminating or publishing information. Web pages may have links to other Web pages stored at any other 'place' on the Net.[7]

Another relatively new means of communication on the Net is *Internet Relay Chat* (IRC). Rather than posting messages and waiting for responses, IRC allows users to interact via text on the Net in 'real time' and most closely resembles an on-line 'conversation'. The user types a line of text which is then immediately visible to other users on that 'channel'. The ephemeral nature of IRC makes monitoring very difficult. Some of the hackers who were observed as part of this study used IRC to exchange news and ideas about hacking Sat-TV for a few hours on Friday nights.

The most familiar, and certainly the most widely used application for one-to-one communication is *email*. Email has been around for a number of years and is much slower than IRC. Email lists expand email from 'one-to-one' to 'one-to-many' recipients, facilitating the creation of information groups or discussion groups.

---

[6] It is the ether of communication, brought into being by computers on the Net, their links and the applications they support (satellites, microwaves, radio waves, infrared, wire and fibre optic cable etc.). It is also a symbolic 'place' (see pp. 222–4).

[7] It is this network of links that gives the Web its name.

DAVID MANN AND MIKE SUTTON

Then there are newsgroups,[8] which are the main object of this study. These are similar to email lists, but more open. At the time of writing, there are more than 20,000 newsgroups. They are almost all unmoderated[9] and their ease of access and openness make them ideal places to collect and disseminate information with like-minded people. If desired, various degrees of anonymity can be achieved through *remailers, spoofing* or using anonymous accounts. In most cases, explicitly criminal discussions are rare, due to the public nature of newsgroups. Hackers, paedophiles and others wishing to use or disseminate highly illicit information or images generally set up alternative and complementary means of communicating with each other using either IRC, private email or *bulletin board systems* (BBS) (Sterling 1992, Durkin and Bryant 1995).

In newsgroups, individuals can be exposed to the views and beliefs of numerous strangers, associates or friends. Participants have the ability to disseminate information or opinions to a far wider group than would normally be possible by traditional means. It is possible to read discussions from several weeks ago or as they are actually taking place and anyone can take part in, or initiate, discussions. As with most organizations there are rules, but the non-physical nature of newsgroups provides an arena in which people are freed from many of the normal rules governing interactions, and consequently things are inherently more anarchic: *flames* that might invite a punch on the nose in the physical world are common; responses to ignorant newcomers (*newbies*) vary from abuse to a warm welcome; there are no visible police officers, no elected officials, and no rules apart from *netiquette*. Any number of single conversations may develop and grow over weeks rather than minutes, branching off into new *threads* and attracting or losing participants along the way.

Deviance on the Internet: A Review of the Literature

The global village

In 1964 Marshall McLuhan wrote:

After three thousand years of specialist explosion and of increasing specialism and alienation in the technological extensions of our bodies, our world has become compressional by dramatic reversal. As electrically contracted, the globe is no more than a village.

The term global village has now entered our general vocabulary and the Internet is without doubt the best example yet of how electrical media such as the telephone, radio and television have seemingly made the world a smaller place by transmitting news and ideas regularly between cities, countries and continents. Writing at a time when the modern Internet was hardly conceivable, McLuhan (1964: 5) saw the changes brought about by such media exposing the user to previously marginalized groups.

It is this implosive factor that alters the position of the Negro, the teen-ager, and some other groups. They can no longer be contained, in the political sense of limited association. They are now involved in our lives, as we are in theirs, thanks to the electric media.

---

[8] For a good description of how newsgroups are set up, and how—for instance—paedophile newsgroups have been 'accepted' on the Net, see Moore (1995: 176–7).

[9] Not censored.

>>NETCRIME

The Internet is anarchic. Although in principle national laws apply in 'cyberspace' as they do elsewhere, the Internet has not been regulated, and possibly cannot be controlled, in the same way as, for example, television and radio. Not everyone who uses the Net behaves 'responsibly'. For example, paedophile and so called *race hate* groups on the Net have their own agendas which clearly deny the rights of others.

The medium is the message

McLuhan's most popularly quoted phrase 'the medium is the message' describes how the technology (e.g. automation) itself—and not just the way it is used—determines the essence of the thing which shapes our lives (McLuhan 1964: 7):

... the personal and social consequences of any medium—that is, of any extension of ourselves—result from the new scale that is introduced into our affairs by each extension of ourselves, or by any new technology.

We are extended by the global and immediate nature of Internet applications such as emails, newsgroups and IRC. Obviously this has an undoubted potential to deliver a *big message*.[10] Amongst other things, the Internet is potentially a huge growth area for research into criminal and deviant behaviour. However, it is relatively new and so, not surprisingly, research is sparse. What has been written on criminal activity facilitated by the Internet and electronic networks reveals a number of concerns. Most of these concerns are not with the WWW but with IRC, BBS and newsgroups. By allowing a multitude of previously unconnected people to communicate easily with each other,[11] these three elements of the Net represent a new and unparalleled social dimension. Much of what has been written about crime in these areas of the Net focuses upon the speed and freedom of information exchanged and the existence, in this 'environment', of 'communities' of people who would not otherwise meet (Durkin and Bryant 1995).

The national press have been characteristically apocalyptic, highlighting concerns about pornography and crime. Some headlines conjure up barely believable images of corruption, depravity and lawlessness:

Virtual anarchy: Cyberspace was meant to be a place of wonder and freedom, but the reality is monstrous: a cesspool of all that is worst in human nature. (*The Guardian*, 30 January 1996)

Elsewhere, other writers have focused upon 'the hacker problem' and have set out to explain why hackers hack (Landreth 1985; Sterling 1994; Best and Luckenbill 1994). While 'old style' hackers characteristically become involved in computer intrusion for the challenge, Sterling (1994) believes that there is a new and growing problem in the shift away from such nominally profitless hi-tech crimes towards those that offer definite financial rewards:

---

[10] The Internet was designed to be bomb-proof in the event of nuclear war. It grew organically, independently of state controls, international treaties and other regulations. As it grew its very independence and self regulation were held up as virtues which allow untrammelled freedom of information and exchange of ideas. The Internet is a world without hierarchy of access, but it gives voice to devils and angels alike. The medium is the message as McLuhan explains (McLuhan 1964: 8) ... the 'message' of any medium or technology is the change of scale or pace or pattern that it introduces into human affairs.

[11] Overcoming limits previously imposed by time and geography.

DAVID MANN AND MIKE SUTTON

My own assessment is that computer intrusion as a non-profit act of intellectual exploration and mastery, is in slow decline, at least in the United States; but electronic fraud, especially telecommunication crime, is growing by leaps and bounds.

Similar conclusions were reached in a research study by Coutorie (1995) which asked both non-traditional 'experts' (hackers) and traditional 'experts' to forecast the future nature of high technology crime. Coutorie found a high level of consensus that radio/satellite attacks and electronic counterfeiting were likely to be rapidly growing areas. Both sets of 'experts' in his study believed: '. . . high technology crimes are going to be more sophisticated in the future and that law and law enforcement agencies will be ill-prepared to meet this challenge.' These fears could be explained away as just another *moral panic* (Cohen 1973). However, there is an alternative view held by some who believe things will never be the same again, with information exchanged without regard to national borders or class distinction, and that the nature of such exchange represents enormous implications for the police and policing:

If the future is as bleak as some would have it, then policing the real streets as well as the Super-Highway will present many challenges . . . The development of personnel to deal with the Super-Highways must happen despite it always being difficult to divert money and training facilities from today's pressing problems, towards even more pressing problems coming along.[12] (Blakey 1995)

Wall (1997) provides an excellent overview of the organizations involved in policing the Internet, their various responses to NetCrime and the strategies they employ. He explains why particular strategies will need to be changed and recommends what some of these changes should be.

Curiously, some writers portray hackers as inheriting a new frontier which shares much of the romance associated with images of the old Wild West, and some so called 'Netizens' appear to see themselves in a similar light:

Hackers of all kinds are absolutely soaked through with heroic antibureaucratic sentiment. Hackers long for recognition as a praiseworthy cultural archetype, the postmodern electronic equivalent of the cowboy and mountain man. Whether they deserve such a reputation is something for history to decide. But many hackers—including those outlaw hackers who are computer intruders and whose activities are defined as criminal—actually attempt to live up to this techno-cowboy reputation. (Sterling 1992)

More work is needed before it will be possible satisfactorily to attempt to determine the extent to which existing theories and approaches can be used to explain NetCrime. However, preliminary inroads have already been made in a study of *hackers* and *phreakers* (Meyer 1989). Meyer looked at less public communications channels (BBS, voice boxes, email and telephone conversations) and found that social interactions between members of the computer underground fit well with Best and Luckenbill's (1982) typology of collegial associations:

Mutual association is an indicator of organizational sophistication in deviant associations. Its presence in the computer underground indicates that on a social organization level phreakers/hackers act as 'colleagues' . . . Hackers, phreakers and pirates face practical problems. For example, in order to

---

[12] However, elsewhere in his paper Blakey points out that this is not a call for the police to monitor and proactively 'patrol' the Net.

pursue their activities they require equipment and knowledge. The problem of acquiring the latter must be solved, and, additionally they must devise ways to prevent discovery, apprehension and sanctioning by social control agents.[13]

At the time of writing, very few (if any) other observational studies have been undertaken of Internet newsgroups. Social scientists are beginning to catch up, but it seems that journalists are well ahead of the game (Durkin and Bryant 1995):

The mass media and popular press are providing glimpses of the larger social dimensions of computer deviance, especially sexual deviance, but the phenomenon awaits systematic research by sociologists and other behavioural scientists.

There are few writers specializing in the field of high technology crime, but they appear to be unanimously of the opinion that such crimes are increasing or set to increase. This suggests that researchers from a broad range of disciplines, such as anthropology, sociology, criminology, law, operational research, psychology etc., and those responsible for policy, legislation and law enforcement should look at this area in greater depth.

Background to the Study

To view subscription-only satellite TV programmes legally involves using a decoder device—a black box which normally sits on top of the television and requires a smart-card supplied by the satellite television company. This smart-card allows the decoder to decrypt a satellite television signal received by way of a dish usually attached to the customer's home. Customers may choose to pay to view all the service provider's channels—e.g. movies, sports and soft-porn—or they can pay a lesser amount for a limited number of channels. The smart-card determines which channels can be seen. To view satellite TV programmes illegally, it is possible to purchase stolen smart-cards, although the service provider can quickly deactivate these cards via a signal from the satellite once the loss has been reported.[14] Subscribers can also sell their valid cards whilst informing the service provider that it was stolen, a replacement card will be issued and the old card will be deactivated soon after. It is also possible to buy a *cloned*, pirate card from illicit commercial companies.

This study began in August 1995 with a chance meeting where the authors discovered that it was possible illegally to view subscription-only satellite television programmes for free by using yet another method. The method involved using a dummy smart-card in the decoder connected via a cable to a personal computer running software designed by hackers to emulate a valid smart-card. The Internet had been used to disseminate information on how to make, or alternatively where to buy, the necessary peripherals. Since the software, known as Season9, was made available for free on the Net, money did not appear to be a primary motive[15] for those involved in developing this method.

[13] See also Best and Luckenbill (1994).
[14] Although blocking equipment developed by hackers can be employed while the card is in use to prevent this from happening.
[15] However, copies of the dummy card and associated software could be purchased for less than £20 from other individuals advertising on the Net and in Satellite TV magazines.

DAVID MANN AND MIKE SUTTON

This is not the place to explore, in any depth, arguments over the legality of producing such software and hardware to decrypt subscription satellite TV services, or the manufacture and distribution, sale and use of hardware and software to do so. It is sufficient to say that in the UK many of these activities fall under the Copyright, Designs and Publications Act 1988. Section 297 of this Act refers to the fraudulent use of programmes provided for the UK and describes dishonestly receiving a programme as a criminal offence. This includes cable and satellite television services. Section 297a covers unauthorized decoders or apparatus to decode or adapt, while section 296 covers devices to circumvent copy protection. Section 6(2) is particularly important: 'An encrypted transmission shall be regarded as capable of being lawfully received by members of the public only if decoding equipment has been made available to members of the public by or with the authority of the person making the transmission or the person providing the contents of the transmission.'

The individual who demonstrated to the authors how the dummy smart card and decryption software worked had never used the Net and neither had his friends and relatives who also had one. All of them had purchased the equipment and software for £18 from the same person, a 30-year-old computer engineer who was connected to the Net at his place of work.

The authors were loaned the equipment and the software to take away with the aim of finding out more about the motives of whoever was involved in the creation and dissemination of this decryption method. Additional files on the software disk referred to a newsgroup address where the authors of the Season9 software could be contacted. After observing this newsgroup for several weeks a definite structure and hierarchy began to emerge. A tentative-model of members' roles was outlined and presented on 17 May 1996 at a Home Office seminar on Internet crime. In the belief that their model could be applied to other newsgroups, the authors were referred to a locksmithing group which was then studied using the same methods (see below). The Satellite TV newsgroup was studied for a period of eight months and the Locksmiths for two months. The results of these two small-scale exploratory studies are discussed with an aim to develop a systematic framework for studying newsgroups on the Net.

Satellite Hackers and Locksmiths: The Newsgroups

Research method

As the satellite television newsgroup address was supplied with the illicit decryption software it was a simple process to find it on the local *news server* and then down load all messages from the previous four weeks.

At this stage, the authors' knowledge, garnered from previous *lurking* on other newsgroups, precipitated a search for a small number of members who would be playing an influential role in maintaining the main aims of the group. There were many messages and some of these contained technical details about how encrypted television signals could be hacked, but these were buried amongst many other discussions ranging from satellite dishes and legitimate decoding equipment, to the scheduling of favourite programmes. Therefore, it was impossible to determine what the main aims of the

>>NETCRIME

group were, or whether it had a definite structure or hierarchy. In an attempt to overcome this problem, a computer program was written to create a list of those members who had posted most frequently to the group since the start of the study (which was at this time into its seventh week). However, after checking the messages from the list of most active members, it was found that those posting the most did not actually appear to be performing any core functions, nor were they particularly interested in hacking satellite TV services. For example, the member who maintained the group *FAQ*[16] (a particularly influential role) had rarely posted during this period.[17] It was later found that the Hackers were using IRC and a private email list to communicate with each other about how to hack Sat-TV. This would explain why—while the newsgroup revolved around their efforts—they rarely posted to the newsgroup. Therefore, to identify those specifically interested in hacking satellite TV broadcasts, information surrounding the group, such as members' names, WWW pages and documents including the FAQ, were collated and analysed. As the author of the FAQ provided his name, it was an easy matter to search the newsgroup for his other contributions on previous weeks.

The newsgroup messages were then searched for key phrases found in the FAQ, such as: *Season; latest hack; Season9; Season10;* and *Sat-TV*. From this search, a list of important members' names was compiled (the sub-group). In addition, a *search engine* was used to search all newsgroups on the Internet to provide some insight into the wider activities and interests of the sub-group members. They were named the SatHackers for the purposes of this study. As the FAQ explained and the search engine confirmed, the SatHackers had at their core a small group of hackers who had successfully *reverse engineered* and broken the encryption used by each new generation of Sat-TV's smart-cards.

The next step was to read the entire database of satellite TV newsgroup postings to find contributions from SatHackers and observe their interactions with the whole newsgroup. This involved systematically reading, printing, and sorting all posts into emerging categories. Therefore, an inductive process of moving from individual observations to generalizations was adopted, and the categories were defined by a number of factors including: attitudes, and the function, role, or service members were providing or seeking to provide. The main aim was to categorize the members according to how it seemed the rest of the newsgroup were responding to them.[18]

Due to the sheer size of the main satellite TV newsgroup, and the number of postings on marginal technical points, a decision was taken that the satellite newsgroup research should focus solely upon the SatHacker sub-group. This decision was justified several weeks after the study began when the SatHackers themselves decided to take the radical action of forming a new newsgroup and leaving behind in the original 'community' those who were mainly interested in the wider legitimate aspects of satellite television—such as TV programmes and different types of legitimate hardware.

---

[16] Acronym for 'frequently asked questions'—provides answers for newcomers—see Glossary.

[17] Neither had others (found later on a more efficient search) who appeared to be hackers of satellite TV encryption systems.

[18] At a later date, the Locksmiths group was studied in the same way. While its size, structure and organization was found to be slightly different there were many similarities with the SatHackers.

DAVID MANN AND MIKE SUTTON

Validity

The study was based upon principles used in traditional observational studies. While there are similarities between social settings in the so called 'real' world and cyberspace, there are also many differences. Perhaps the most important distinction is that the environment of the Net is not as vivid and colourful as the traditional 'built' environment. Compared to traditional observational research, of which there are many famous examples (Matza 1964; Cohen 1973; Parker 1974; Foster 1990), observation of Internet newsgroups is literally two-dimensional. Newsgroups do, however, provide plenty of rich detail and insight into the structure, organization and motives of participants. Such information is provided by the participants themselves, because newsgroups often resemble a kind of marathon focused discussion group (see Moore 1995).

Members of the newsgroups looked at in this study did not 'suffer fools gladly'. Walter Mitty type characters were rare because when they surfaced they were rapidly identified and *flamed* with considerable ridicule and vitriol. The SatHackers had successfully hacked satellite TV encrypted systems in the past and this history of authenticity[19] was crucial for the research, as it established that most of what was being discussed was valid.

Research on the Net is also better suited to validity checks, which are particularly important in observational studies, as Mays and Pope (1985) point out:

... the validity of observational accounts relies on the truthful and systematic representation of the research. In many ways it is honesty which separates the observational account from the novel.

With observational studies of newsgroups, establishing validity is less of a problem because the entire focus of the observation (all the newsgroup's postings) can be easily archived and copied. This means that researchers can answer any criticism of subjectivity by handing over copies of the messages for secondary analysis. In this respect, observational research of newsgroups is similar to archeology in that a properly preserved site is open to inspection for others to investigate and draw their own conclusions.

Advantages

There are many advantages to doing observational research on the Net. Traditional observational research in the social sciences relies upon the researcher as the research 'instrument' to describe and analyse what has been seen and this is still true in cyberspace. However, on the Net there is no need to be present at the time when important postings, discussions or events actually happen. Also, with newsgroups, there are no real problems with gaining access to the setting—in contrast to other areas of the Net such as *mailing lists* and BBS which may employ security measures to deter the outsider. Useful research can be undertaken without the need to interact with the group, as is done in more traditional research, and running the risk of participating in illegal activity (Parker 1974), or influencing the behaviour of the group (Roethlisberger 1939; Whyte 1955). There is no need to strike up a rapport, or establish empathy with the group. Consequently, there is less risk of 'going native'.

---

[19] As mentioned above, the authors had been shown how the illicit smart-card and software worked.

Ethics

The Net is constantly progressing and evolving, and this study was helped at various stages by the arrival on the Net of a new generation of efficient search engines which were used (as described above) to search for specific individuals, groups, or subject matter across all WWW pages and newsgroups. This was important because newsgroups are characteristically transient and multi-participatory.

A decision was made at the outset of the research not to interact with the newsgroups studied in any way. This was not traditional non-participant observation because the authors were completely invisible to the group. Normally, there are ethical considerations in carrying out covert research of this nature (Holdaway 1983; Wexler 1990)—particularly what to do if you are aware of a serious crime being planned (Monti 1994). However, there are at least three reasons why this does not necessarily apply to the Net. First, participants in newsgroups are fully aware that their conversations are being watched by many people who do not reveal themselves. Indeed, netiquette requires newcomers to *lurk* until they have something worthwhile to add, and this is the basis of the *FAQ* convention. Secondly, some members believe they are actually being monitored by the police or other officials. Indeed, some members of the satellite hackers group suspected that the group was being monitored by Sat-TV and so they openly taunted imagined *lurking* Sat-TV employees. Thirdly, it is not always possible to infer from a participant's email address the jurisdiction in which they are located, and so it is often impossible to determine if a crime has actually been committed in the participant's locality (see Wall 1997).[20] Despite such arguments it is anticipated that the issue of covert studies, which involve cross referencing the activities of particular individuals and then using what they have written on the Net for research purposes, will generate considerable debate amongst members of the research community in the future.

Findings

Classification of newsgroup members

At best, studies of single newsgroups can identify and characterize the roles of members and create typologies which may also apply to other newsgroups. But there is little to be gained from developing classification systems and typologies without seeking to understand how the roles and behaviour of people in the newly defined categories explain their involvement and continuing participation in whatever is being studied. Used in this way, typologies have heuristic value in criminology:

> They can make it easier for the theorist to see analogies between different kinds of criminal behaviour, or similarities between different kinds of offender, and thus make it easier for him (sic) to trace the causal processes which apply to them. (Hood and Sparks 1970)

[20] See also: European Scrambling Systems FAQ Version 2.0.

Participating members in both the SatHackers and Locksmiths newsgroups were identified, using the research methods described above, and the various roles of core members were characterized and classified (see Figure 1) under the following headings:

Hacker Gurus (Found in the SatHackers only) Possess an acknowledged ability to crack encrypted TV signals and smart-cards. They also communicated with each other on a private, 'invitation only' email list outside of the newsgroup. They rarely posted in the public forum of the newsgroup.

Parasites Seek to acquire products or services from the group, often without due deference. Individual Parasites post infrequently and often give up after being flamed or ignored. Parasites are likely to be strangers to other core members. However, they fulfil a role which is inextricably linked to the roles of other members, particularly Growlers and Acolytes. Therefore, they have been classified as core members of the group.

Acolytes (found in the SatHackers only) Glorifiers or followers of the Hacker Gurus. These members mainly seek to cushion Hacker Gurus from demands of Parasites. They appear to do this because they value the Hacker's products so highly and fear the Hacker Gurus may become offended and no longer share newly developed illicit software.

Information Providers Collate and disseminate background information which they may also use to produce the group FAQ. They usually respond to, and encourage, Newbies. Along with the Hacker Gurus (in the SatHackers) they provide the products around which the newsgroup is based.

Prophets and Warners Perhaps the most loosely defined group, and should be thought of as a sub-type of Information Provider—the main difference being that they have a more pessimistic outlook and their posts are never particularly technical. They are analogous to 'look-out men', watching for both opportunities and threats—warning of scams and legal issues.

Growlers Protect the group from disruption. Often responding to Abuser attacks and sometimes 'flaming' Parasites. Growlers differ from Acolytes in that they seek to protect the order and well-being of the group as a whole, while Acolytes seem preoccupied with the well being of their heroes: the Hacker Gurus.

Jostlers Apparently aspiring to a valued role in the group, Jostlers are essentially the 'wannabes' of the newsgroups. They appear to want to be either Hacker Gurus or Information Providers. It seems that some even want to be Acolytes. Jostlers are more than simple newbies, but they are unlikely to have secured their own place in the group. After lurking in the group for a while, some try cutting their teeth on relatively simple technical problems, but often their questions and suggestions are either ignored or flamed. Jostlers can be distinguished from the more established Acolytes by the way they frequently seek to define what the group should be doing and by the flames these suggestions attract from other core members.

Abusers Intentionally abuse or sometimes threaten the group for virtually any reason. It seems fair to say that Abusers just abuse—for them it seems to be a cathartic sport.

212

>> NETCRIME

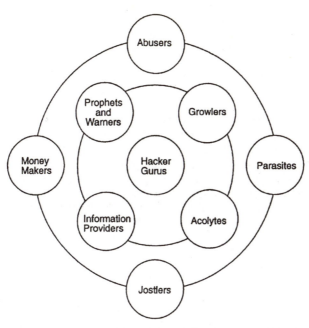

F I G . 1   Structure and characteristics of core members: the Sat Hackers group

Money Makers Seek to acquire products from the group for commercial gain or aim to sell specific products and services to group members. In the SatHackers group, they used the Hacker Guru's insights to create cloned smart-cards. They posted adverts and sold specialist equipment to group members. Some advertised their more popular products in a magazine. Many had WWW sites and pay to access BBSs. Some of these held details on how to buy all the products necessary to view Sat-TV and a number of pornographic European stations without subscribing.

Honest Enquirers Seek to acquire knowledge from the group for worthy and legitimate reasons. This category was found only in the Locksmiths where members attempted to differentiate between requests for information from the hobbyist, amateur locksmith (Honest Enquirer), and those with possibly criminal motives. This was not an issue in the SatHackers group where everyone knew that using Season software to watch Sat-TV without paying was illegal.

Membership Issues

Some newsgroup 'members' were like members of a club or social group in the 'traditional' sense. However, others were hardly members at all. It could be argued that they were more like tourists or occasional visitors—generally lurking and only posting once or twice a year. This was true of some Hacker Gurus as well as Parasites. Some members were difficult to classify. For example, in the Locksmiths group, some members did not fulfil just one role but several—possibly due to the smaller size of the group which meant there was a need to 'double-up' and provide more than one core function.

Although the aim of this study was not to quantify the number of different newsgroup members, it is useful at this point to provide an indication of the composition of the main newsgroup studied. In the first four weeks of the study, before the SatHackers split from their 'mother' newsgroup, there were numerous SatHacker posts from: seven Hacker Gurus, five Acolytes, five Jostlers, five Money Makers, four Growlers, four Prophets and Warners, one Abuser, six Information Providers and eight Parasites.[21] This gives only an indication of the group composition as it became apparent that many members were lurking and not participating in the discussions (e.g. see: Herz 1994). Over a short period there is no way of telling how many members are lurking. The group became much 'busier' after they formed their own newsgroup and once Season10 was introduced. It seems reasonable to speculate that the number of Parasites lurking on the group would have increased enormously in the following weeks as they would be looking for information on how to get the new Season software.

Main Themes

Two main themes emerged from studying the interaction of these particular newsgroup members: *Demand and Supply* and the *Apprentice Work-Ethic*. These are discussed in turn.

The demand for and the supply of illicit services and products

Three weeks after the study began, Sat-TV moved one jump ahead in the continuous series of races between themselves and the SatHackers by broadcasting new encrypted signals and supplying its paying customers with a new generation of smart-cards (Season10). This made the old Season9 software obsolete and some group members appeared to be quite desperate for a solution. This event created an opportunity to witness key aspects of the relationship between different members of the group and to understand more about the dynamics of supply and demand for illicit services and products (Sutton 1995).

A few days after the Season9 smart-card was replaced, the SatHackers became busy with a large number of posts—revealing an extensive demand for illicit smart-cards and decrypting software to overcome Season10. The Acolytes were not happy with the 'tone' of some Parasites who were regularly troubling their heroes the Hacker Gurus with petty requests:

Parasite: Does anyone know when the hack of the 0A[22] cards is coming out? Please post your answer. Thanks in advance.

---

[21] In fact, the number of core members in this group was well suited to the study. Had the group been as large as some notorious hacker newsgroups it would have been considerably more difficult to analyse the posts.

[22] Hexadecimal for 10. Used here to mean Season10. More commonly used as a convenient way of representing the binary code of a computer.

Acolyte: If anyone did know that the 0A program was due by a particular date I think they would post the information without some idiot needing to ask! There are thousands of people waiting for these codes and yet there are a countless number of complete pratts who seem to think that the hackers have got time to deal with individual enquiries. Jesus!

At other times unwary Parasites asking for the latest Season hack were mercilessly flamed:

Parasite: Are this that the new season left for January 1996 for [Sat-TV] (new code)

Abuser: Speak English pal. Are this is left January for that for [Sat-TV]? What the hell are you talking about you smelly Frenchman? When you find out let me know.[23]

Frustration at the lack of supply appeared to become so great that some became suspicious and abusive. In this example from the SatHackers, a Growler sought to protect the group from further abuse by identifying an abuser who was using an *anonymous remailer* incorrectly:

Abuser: GET FUCKED ALL YOU GREEDY PIC CHIP HACKERS! THE REASON NONE OF THE SOURCE CODES ARE AVAILABLE IS BECAUSE YOUR [SIC] GREEDY TWATS. WHAT GOES AROUND COMES AROUND.

Growler: Please note the post address of this chappie is [. . .] a few messages to his service provider telling them what an awfully good chap he is might help him.

After Sat had produced the latest smart-card and a hack had not been forthcoming, a number of bogus hacks and other scams were offered for sale by Money Makers and other people. Prophets and Warners sought to inform members of the dangers:

There was a company advertising in [. . .]—a device called the Predator—basically a Season interface and software . . . Note—here is an interesting example of how the free-hack gets sold . . . if they really do have series 10 cards cracked, I think they will be inundated with sales. Caveat Emptor! As we have not heard anything concrete in this newsgroup, it would appear . . . well . . . suspect!

And

It seems likely that this is a con! It would be interesting! If someone could get it demonstrated. I suspect the con involves connecting a valid card or just the chip into the interface, hidden of course. . . . BE VERY CAREFUL OF THIS DEVICE.

In the following example from the SatHackers, three weeks after Sat-TV introduced Season10, a Jostler desperately tries to rally the Hacker Gurus into action:

Jostler: It's quite obvious that [Sat-TV] learned how long it would take us to find a hack. I read last time that it took three months before the season program came out. They have evidently released 0A at the end of Oct 1995 so that it will take at least three months to do the same again. This means we are going to miss all the films and some of them look very good over Christmas. To say boo to the system, we should really try to have a proper hack sorted before Christmas so that they know that we are invincible. Can we all start work on it . . . ?

---

[23] Following this episode a group of French members debated setting up a Satellite newsgroup of their own to avoid such xenophobia!

215

Acolyte: Who is the 'we' you keep referring to, are you meaning this in the Royal *we* meaning everyone else or are you already some way into solving the problem and need assistance to finish it. Don't you think WE started on it as soon as the series 0a card was released and have been/are working very hard on the problem, and for nothing, and why should they release the result of their labours to an unappreciative public. Someone else could take your remarks as being a bit offensive and I am sure you don't want to really piss off all the really clever guys that are doing their best to bring about the means of enjoying [Sat-TV] to the rest (read majority) of the people who don't have the ability to do this. A bit of encouragement and praise for their efforts might help keep them going. Of course if you really want to view all these good films over Xmas you could take the radical approach to the problem and take out a subscription.

Naturally, at this time, Money Makers also took the opportunity to try to profit from those waiting for the new Sat-TV hack:

Money Maker: CTX can now offer the full [Sat-TV] package on real [Sat-TV] cards. These cards are NOT PIRATE cards and are fully paid up for 12 months. These cards are not intended for the UK or Irish market. We guarantee the [Sat-TV] card for 1 year even if [Sat-TV] change their card again as a new legal card will then be sent out.

Information Provider: One little detail was missing . . . 449 pounds should put a damper on things.

Blatant, clumsy requests for illicit information were frequently (though not always) ignored or denied. For example, someone entering the SatHackers group and asking 'Hey Dudes, how do I watch Sat-TV movies without paying?' would have been seen by established members of the group as a parasite and their overtly criminal request as a threat to the group existence.[24] The Locksmiths generally appeared more 'respectable'—at least on the surface. Members of the Locksmiths were *never* observed asking how they could do something obviously illegal, and simply asking how to get a set of lock picks would often result in a good flaming:

Parasite: What are some of the ways of getting your hands on a set of picks?

Growler: It is against the law to have picks if you are not a locksmith. Since you are not a locksmith you shouldn't be concerned with 'getting your hands on a set of picks'.

The apprentice work ethic

The Hacker Gurus in the SatHackers were able to provide the group with a free product, namely the latest Season hack, as well as expert knowledge regarding how to hack satellite TV smart-cards. The Information Providers in the Locksmiths also had a free product to offer their group—the information contained in their comprehensive FAQ. In addition, they shared their 'expert' or amateur locksmith knowledge. As the study progressed it became clear that, in both groups, some members were regulating the exchange of products and ideas. This unwillingness to share information with

---

[24] Like the stranger who walks into a pub frequented by criminals and asks in a loud voice how he could buy a stolen computer. He would either be totally ignored or asked by the landlord to leave—and to go down to a computer store and pay retail the same as everybody else.

216

everyone can be usefully explored within the framework of deviant exchange outlined by Best and Luckenbill (1994):

> Like individual deviance, deviant exchange is socially organized. Participants in an exchange share a cognitive perspective which shapes their actions. Each participant also affects the other; together, they must come to terms over the conditions for the exchange, including their divisions of labour and respective payoffs, and they must coordinate their actions. The participants also work together to avoid detection and apprehension by social control agents. Deviant exchange is more complex than individual deviance because it requires at least two participants who cooperate in reciprocal roles.

Distinguishing between two main types of deviant exchange, Best and Luckenbill (1994) describe those based on *sales* (money) and those based on *trades* (exchange of deviant tasks—e.g. forbidden sexual services). They explain how those who enter deviant trades do so as equals with a minimal division of authority. However, their explanation of deviant trades needs to be expanded to account for the new form of social organization that has recently emerged in newsgroups on the Net. According to Best and Luckenbill, each participant can decide whether or not to trade with a particular individual and then decide who gets what. On the Net it is different. Once information has been posted onto a newsgroup—usually in response to a request from one individual—it is then freely available for any reader of that newsgroup to use.[25] This results in a clear lack of equity between those who develop products (e.g. illicit software), or have specialist knowledge, and those who want that product or wish to acquire more knowledge.

While it seemed that Hacker Gurus and Information Providers were usually prepared to give away their newsgroup products, they were sometimes reluctant to pass on their own hard won expertise to anyone—*just for the asking*. Ideally, they would rather trade with 'likeminded' people who could assist in their own learning or with other projects they were working on. However newsgroups are an open forum, and it was in an attempt to restore equity to the current situation—where so many information-hungry newbies (Parasites) are arriving—that an *apprentice work ethic* was observed. This involved some members conveying strong messages that other members should be prepared to 'put in some work' and not expect to 'get something for nothing'. This served not only to restore equity, it also slowed down the flow of information and provided, where necessary, a convenient smokescreen to conceal the exchange of overtly criminal information.[26]

In practice, the apprentice work ethic meant that while the SatHackers' FAQ gave out information on how to watch Sat-TV without paying, and the Locksmith FAQ provided detailed instructions on how to make lock picks and crack certain combination locks, the Growlers in both groups frequently flamed Parasites asking for such information. This was a particularly surprising discovery because it contradicts the widely propagated view that the Net is an information goldmine which is free for all to excavate.

---

[25] And information is regularly cross-posted to different newsgroups and Web sites.

[26] This may in effect stymie the original intention of the Net: the dissemination of information without regard to class boundaries or professional hierarchy etc.

DAVID MANN AND MIKE SUTTON

In the two groups studied some Parasites learned very little, while those who took the trouble to lurk, learn the 'language' and respect the idiosyncrasies of core members, found what they came for. In the SatHacker group, Hacker Gurus sometimes expected a particularly high level of technical competence:

Parasite: Is there any software out there which is not *key* or *dongle* protected that will enable me to copy the information/codes from one series 10 card and transfer it to another series 10 card?

Hacker Guru: Try it yourself. Its quite difficult at first, but you'll learn a lot.—Translate one of the widely available 'maccess' like pic-sources into 68hc05sc21 code (same as 68hc05b6). Then obtain the sources from 'getrom'—they come with the program portions that generate the digital signature (otherwise the packets become rejected) and send them to the smart card . . . Anyway, you have to make sure that the card you want to reprogram is still capable of nano code parsing (i.e. does 'renumber' work?) (Sat-TV sent kill commands to all 09 cards within Sept./Oct.) bis denn . . .

While it was beyond the scope of this study to determine if such Parasites eventually became accepted as apprentice hackers and graduated to Hacker Guru status, it seems most likely that this was happening. In contrast, to the highly technical knowledge that is required to even begin hacking a satellite TV system, lock picking could be learned with less demanding entry-level 'qualifications'. The Locksmiths' FAQ gave some brief instructions on how to make lock picks from scratch, and suggested that all picks should be made by hand by the person who is going to use them. New members who asked the group for help in this respect were immediately seen as *Honest Enquirers*, and actually received enough tuition from the *experts* to begin making lock picks:

Honest Enquirer: Could someone offer detailed help on how to make lock picks? Preferably only using hand tools as I don't have legal access to a machine shop. Thank you.

Information Provider: A machine shop isn't necessary if you are willing to take some extra time. If you have access to a power drill (a hand power drill of the usual home type) you can buy a small grindstone (perhaps two inches in diameter) mounted on a metal shaft (usually one quarter inch diameter) which you can put into the chuck of a drill. This will do a good job of removing metal—in fact you'll have to work slowly to keep from overheating the steel (it should never get too hot to hold.) Then you take your starting piece of steel (clock spring, street sweeper bristle . . .) and grind it to the shape you want . . .

Newcomers to the Locksmiths, who wanted to be seen as Honest Enquirers to increase the likelihood that members would share their expert information, fared best if they could demonstrate two things. First, that they were prepared to put some effort into learning the 'craft' and second, as the following post demonstrates, provide the group with some background details[27] explaining their interest:

Honest Enquirer: Hi all. I work for an auto dealer and found myself fooling with locks more and more and have now decided to learn how to pick pin tumbler (and other types) locks as well as wafer type. I bought a deadbolt as suggested in the FAQ, own a good set of picks, and open this cheesy deadbolt with either clockwise *or* counterclockwise tension. I am, however, still having little success with mounted locks on doors. I have locked (not yet unlocked) both my front door and a lock at work (everyone thinks I'm cuckoo at work, but they tolerate me and my new hobby) . . . I obviously need a

---

[27] Which may, or may not, be a fictional cover story—it is impossible to be sure.

little more practice, but my practice lock ain't cuttin' the mustard. Also, is it true, as it seems, that most locks will bind pin 5 first while unlocking pin 1. What next, guys?

Information Provider: Well, I wouldn't feel too bad about the locks you haven't opened. I consider myself a pretty good picker, but there are still some locks that *ought* to be easy that I have never been able to open. My front door is one of them. In general, I have found it helpful to buy about a dozen different locks and wear them out practising. Keep on practising and try to keep a positive attitude about opening the lock. If you start getting frustrated, walk away for a while and try again later. (Also, the main problem I had when first learning to pick was too much tension on the tension-wrench).

On other occasions, members of the Locksmiths group became much more suspicious. 'Dubious' questions frequently received an off-handed response because the background details were not believed.

Parasite: I'm locked out of my van. I can get in to the front and passenger seats, but the back is separated from the front (like in cop cars). I need to get into the back part where all of my important stuff is, but for a reason I can't recall it's opened by a different key only. What is an easy way to open it w/o calling a locksmith.

Growler: Obtain one very large rock from your local roadside. Throw rock at window with great force, release lock from inside; open door!!! This will work at very low initial cost, end cost however is higher than you would have paid for a service call from your local locksmith professional.

However, responses were inconsistent and sometimes just about any story would do:

Honest Enquirer: My brother is taking a locksmith course and is having a small problem. He is supposed to soot a blank key and put it into a warded lock in order to make an impression. The problem is that when he twists the key in order to mark the soot, it doesn't seem to make a mark. Any experts have an idea how to help him. I will forward it to him since he does not reside on the Net. Thanx.

Expert Information Provider: The course should have given him an idea of how the lock works, so he should know where the marks will be—just at the edge of the key where it hits the wards. If simply turning it back and forth doesn't leave a visible mark, he could try twisting and pulling slightly to scrape off the soot. The ward would be at the end of the scrape closest to the bow of the key.

Overall, both the SatHackers and the Locksmiths frequently required members who did not wish to be treated like Parasites to take the trouble to demonstrate a familiarity with the group, or display a minimum level of technical knowledge. Both newsgroups encouraged members to produce the commodities they wanted from the group for themselves, rather than simply relying upon others to do the work for them.

Discussion

Project Crime

The concept of Project Crime was first introduced in Mary McIntosh's 'Changes in the Organization of Thieving' (McIntosh 1971). It provides a useful starting point for discussing the way particular NetCrimes are carried out:

. . . when large amounts of valuables are being stolen, and owners improve their ways of protecting them, each theft becomes a complicated job, often involving a more elaborate technology than craft crime, and nearly always involving special advance planning and taking of greater risks—each theft becomes a project in itself . . .

Hence, the need to learn and develop lock picking skills was described as one of the characteristics of *Project Thieving* (McIntosh 1971):

Since Elizabethan days, strong-box locks with other locks had been vulnerable to the Black Art of skeleton keys and pick-locks. But this was defeated when the warded lock was replaced by the lever or tumbler lock. In turn techniques were developed for forcing locks off and for defending against this; for drilling holes in locks by various means and for defending against these; for dynamiting locks and defending against this, and so on.

It is clear that certain 'areas' of the Net might be regarded as the latest of many frontiers in the technological war between criminals and the security industry. The organization of the SatHackers group and the sophistication of their enterprise in overcoming new advances in smart-card security, which necessitated Sat-TV's introduction of Season10, shares remarkable similarities with the project crimes described by McIntosh (1971):

. . . it is not simply the size of stealable holdings or the level of protective technology that accounts for project theft. These factors tend to lead to a continually advancing technology of theft, as owners and thieves struggle to outwit one another, and it is the need for frequent innovation that makes each theft a separate project. And each job may (therefore) require a different assortment of somewhat specialized skills, one calling for an expert in alarm systems, another for a driver of a get-away car, one for a safe-cracker, another for a strong-arm man.

The similarities between these descriptions of project crime and the structure and organization of the SatHackers are seemingly self evident—although of course the specialist roles are 'miles apart'. Rather than needing strong-arm men, lookouts and get-away drivers, newsgroups like the SatHackers need Growlers, Prophets and Warners and Information Providers. However, there are important differences. For example, McIntosh's project criminals did not work together on a regular basis.

Deviant newsgroups as gangs

In many ways, the structure and organization of the newsgroups in this study resemble earlier descriptions of street gangs (see Spergel 1995 for an overview). Young people have formed themselves into gangs throughout history, so the same thing should not be entirely unexpected on the Internet.

In the United States, gangs have already spread from the inner-cities to suburbia (Monti 1994). It seems likely that cyberspace is just another 'place' where gangs will develop and certain deviant newsgroups will come to be described as cybergangs:

When places as different as inner-city slums and suburban townships have gangs, one must submit that either persons in both places share the same values and moral vision or that their unique views about what is right or wrong cannot tell us much about where gangs will develop. (Monti 1994)

Criminal Recruitment and Rapid Dissemination Threats

It is worth noting that some full-time criminals specialize in locks (Mack 1964), and that in the past at least, lock picking was seen as an essential craft for would-be expert burglars (Benney 1936). It seems reasonable to suggest that in the future newsgroups like the Locksmiths might play an increasing, if somewhat unwitting, role in the recruitment and education of property offenders.

Technological improvements in the design of safes, alarms and locks have resulted in an increasing movement towards entrepreneurial crimes.[28] However, not all thieves are equipped with the necessary ambition, connections and discipline to exploit these new opportunities:

Robbery of persons at ATM machines has increased in frequency. Today's persistent thieves continue to pursue old forms of crime not only because they are incapable of exploiting or unwilling to exploit the new opportunities but also because there is a bountiful supply of the older ones providing returns that, seen through their eyes, are satisfactory albeit far from optimal. (Shover 1996)

It is not only thieves who are interested in picking locks. As computer security has become more sophisticated, hackers have adopted other, 'off-line', techniques known as *social engineering* and *human engineering* to discover passwords to get access to 'interesting' computer systems. Hacker newsgroups and Web pages also regularly refer members to the Locksmiths' FAQ to pick up tips on how to gain access to large computer systems by breaking into the buildings housing them and overcoming physical security systems (Delham 1995).

Picking locks requires craft skills. Wear, damage and intra-lock variation can mean that two locks of the same type may not both be pickable. Therefore, the dissemination of *traditional* lock picking information over the Net by the Locksmiths does not share the same potential as the dissemination of electronic hacking information, of the type supplied by the SatHackers, *for rendering all security systems of a particular type instantaneously obsolete*. However, dissemination of information about combination locks and locks involving electronics may create more problems because weaknesses in a lock's design can be found and exploited so that all locks of a certain type can be opened. Indeed, the Locksmiths' FAQ contained details on how to break into particular locks by cleverly exploiting a design fault to work out the combination.

Crime, Place and Cyberspace

Currently, most crime prevention schemes focus heavily upon the importance of both place and target (Sutton 1996), generally considered to be part of the situational crime prevention approach (Clark 1980). These are designed to reduce crime by limiting offending opportunities through target hardening methods such as locks and alarms while increasing the offenders' perceived risk of being caught, particularly through the use of CCTV and neighbourhood watch schemes. This approach is commonly used to

---

[28] Low level organized crime e.g.: scams involving setting up dummy ATM machines to capture the credit card details of unsuspecting victims (see Shover 1996).

reduce crimes such as vandalism, burglary, car theft and robbery. On the Net, situational crime prevention methods would need to be capable of going beyond this present focus, because in most cases the object, offender and victim (see Brantingham and Brantingham 1981) may never actually come together. Therefore, we have to move beyond physical anti-crime measures such as street lights, locks and bolts, 'eyes on the street' (Jacobs 1965) and improved architecture (Newman 1973; Coleman 1985).

The need to develop crime prevention approaches for the virtual 'spaces' of the Net will undoubtedly create a new criminological challenge, not least because environmental criminology, so far, has concentrated on the physical meaning of place. Although the Net is not viewed by users as having extent in physical space its 'virtual' spaces are nevertheless seen as physical in character. As Slouka (1996) explains, cyberspace is:

... not a space in the standard, three dimensional sense of the word, but a metaphor, a symbolic 'place' we 'inhabit' but are not present in physically. The telephone is an obvious, if primitive example. When we make a telephone call we, and the party at the other end meet in a sort of symbolic space. We communicate—share information, emotions, and so on—yet are not physically present.

Users will 'visit' a WWW site, 'drop into' an IRC channel, or regularly 'hang out' in a Newsgroup. In addition, there is a well-defined hacker subculture which embraces the concept of cyberspace as a *place*—a new frontier—that should ideally be beyond the constraints of existing social control structures.

Despite these distinctions, NetCrime also shares certain similarities with more 'traditional' high-volume crimes, such as the large number of readily available opportunities to participate. Indeed, almost limitless criminal opportunities are emerging 'indoors' fuelled by the huge growth in ownership of personal computers—an increase within the European Union of 88 per cent in 1994–95 (*The Economist* 1995). Unlike any previous communication medium, the Net can provide direct access to a number of criminal opportunities such as: accessing (down loading) and distributing (posting) obscene images of children; posting information on how to consume and manufacture controlled drugs; distribution of bomb making instructions; incitement to racial hatred; swopping and selling illegally obtained credit card numbers (see Sterling 1992) and the distribution of pirated software. There is also unregulated gambling with companies owned and operated abroad, which require nothing more than the provision of credit card details to open an account. All of these things can be done from your workplace desktop or from the comfort of your own home. Furthermore, particular newsgroups seem to provide a ready made, accessible and experienced deviant peer group. And such groups have always played an important part in explaining take-up, frequency and continuation of offending amongst young people (e.g. Miller 1958; Matza 1964).

Unreality

NetOffenders can commit offences on the Net without the need to physically interact with either their victim or co-offenders. The very nature of doing things in such a remote way (by keyboard and computer screen) is characteristically *unreal*. A merely curious user down loading on to disk an obscene image, just to see what all the fuss in the newspapers is about, may have committed a crime.[29] And yet doing so from a computer, by simply tapping the mouse and keyboard will not feel as criminal as buying the same material on the street or even ordering it from abroad and having it drop through the letterbox. Slouka (1996) describes how this separation of an advanced cyberspace from the physical world is likely to cause problems:

... Human culture depends on the shared evidence of the senses, always has; we can communicate with one another because a hurled rock will always break skin, a soap bubble always burst. A technology capable of providing an alternate world—abstract, yet fully inhabitable, real to our senses yet accessible only through a computer screen—would take away this common ground and replace it with one manufactured for us by the technologists ... reality has been and continues to be the great touchstone of the world's ethical systems. Because, simply put, the world provides context, and without context, ethical behaviour is impossible ... Virtual systems, by offering us a reality divorced from the world, from the limits and responsibilities of presence, offer us a glimpse of an utterly amoral universe. (pp. 11–12)

This 'unreal' phenomenon seduces users into suspending normalized and generally accepted codes of moral and ethical practice without offering any replacement other than the good manners of netiquette. Perhaps the most conclusive evidence of this unreality is the number of people providing illicit information to newsgroups, or inciting others to commit crimes while providing clearly visible personal details such as their name, address, company address and telephone numbers—which could easily lead to them being identified and perhaps prosecuted or dismissed from work.

Future Research and Implications for Policy

Although the Net can be a particularly powerful and unique medium for the dissemination of criminal techniques and recruitment of others into criminal activity, there is as yet no way to accurately measure what its effect is. For example, the number of people acting on information obtained from newsgroups is completely unknown. Without a more comprehensive research study to determine who participates in crime on the Net—who provides demand and who supplies illicit services and products—we are not really in any position to speculate about typical NetOffenders.

Police officers are already attributing the reported increase in child prostitution and paedophile rings to Internet activity (Kearney 1996; Bridge 1996). While little overall impact has been made to date, one or two police forces have conducted notable operations. For instance, Operation Starburst (a Europe-wide police crackdown on paedophiles using the Net), led to the arrest and conviction of members of a loosely connected international network of paedophiles. In the UK, the Internet Watch Foundation (IWF) has recently been established to rate the content of material on the Net. The foundation established a hotline in December 1996 to enable users to report the presence of illegal material, such as child pornography, in a newsgroup. Service providers are asked to remove the offending material and details are passed to the police. In the six months since its inception, the IWF hotline received a total of 374

---

[29] Indeed merely viewing it on their computer screen may be illegal: Criminal Justice Act 1988.

DAVID MANN AND MIKE SUTTON

reports of which 257 related to child pornography. Only nine reports relate to material originating in the UK; the vast majority originate in the USA.

At the European Ministerial Conference at Bonn (1997), Ministers stressed the role of the private sector in protecting the interests of consumers and respecting ethical standards, and strongly supported the EU Council Resolution of 17 February 1997 on illegal and harmful content on the Internet. In addition, there is a current European Commission Green paper on 'The Protection of Minors and Human Dignity in Audio-Visual Information Services' which also deals with the problem of unsuitable material on the Internet. And an OECD report on the Internet—comparing national best practices, identifying issues and proposing solutions—is due in October 1997.

Yet, overall, resources remain scarce and there has been little external pressure to investigate or prevent NetCrime. Coutorie writes that most law enforcement agencies in the United States have not begun to address the problem in proportion to its scope:

> The idea that a department can depend on its computer hobbyist to carry them through must be discarded and a specialty investigative area recognized and supported. Who would expect their department's most avid reader of Agatha Christie to be their best homicide investigator?

This limited law enforcement on the Net is partly due to the support for deviancy which exists within the Internet community. There is an overwhelming ethos of free speech on the Net, which means that many Netizens vigorously campaign against new regulatory legislation which is seen as censorship. They seem loath to act against NetOffenders, possibly because in doing so they would be simultaneously inviting external control. In addition, there are other structural supports for deviance which are similar to those described by Best and Luckenbill in relation to crime in the wider environment (1994: 253–54):

> The most familiar examples are urban: the nineteenth-century English rookery—a neighbourhood of thieves, prostitutes, and other deviants rarely entered by the police ... the red light section informally set aside by the police as a vice district ... or the safe city, where local authorities agree to leave fugitive criminals alone so long as they commit their crimes elsewhere. Other examples involve rural areas, such as forest or mountain camps where bandits and other outlaws hide ... These examples suggest that deviants obtain geographic control by default, when the respectable society cannot enforce its norms throughout its domain. Thus piracy flourished when there were too few naval vessels to patrol the seas ... Geographic control often reflects such limited resources of social control agents. When agencies gain sufficient resources, they usually try to extend their control over these regions and suppress deviance.

The parallels here are quite clear. Some BBS and other areas of the Net are already, in some ways, like the old rookeries of London. Police officers lack familiarity with the strange 'territory', while confusion surrounds aspects of both jurisdiction and duty. A key element in Operation Starburst's success was the ability of the investigators to understand the applications and culture of the Net, and then conduct an operation that could, where necessary, transcend physical geography.

Newsgroups such as the SatHackers provide hackers with a forum where they can discuss techniques and brag about their accomplishments with like minded people. Newsgroups can encourage, justify, and seek to normalize deviant behaviour. Whilst more research is needed to determine why the core members of certain newsgroups do what they do, it seems reasonable to assume that, at the very least, being part of the core membership provides a sense of belonging and importance. There is also an element of banditry (see Hobsbawm 1969) where some newsgroup core members see themselves as champions of the Internet community, from whom they get support, in the fight against what they see as the *greed* of big business corporations such as the Sat-TV empire.

It does not seem too fantastic to imagine that parts of the Net will soon develop into a new 'improved' underworld—albeit for a new generation of thieves who may not necessarily live in the kind of urban milieu that has for so long been the home of violent robbers and serious property offenders. And motives may be different—while Money Makers were present in both of the newsgroups studied, there is no evidence that either Hacker Gurus or Expert Information Providers were personally making money from their involvement in these groups. In the light of what has already been written about why hackers hack (Landreth 1985; Sterling 1992; Best and Luckenbill 1994), it seems that the SatHackers *primarily* did it for the challenge of solving a puzzle and taking limited risks—not for financial gain.

There were striking similarities in the structure and organization of both newsgroups in this study. However, it must be emphasized that this is small-scale exploratory research, and the typologies proposed are relatively crude. Considerably more research is needed and it is hoped that this paper will encourage others to study newsgroups on the Net to develop this work further.

There is no doubt that some criminologists will find cyberspace a new challenge. They should perhaps first concentrate upon the diversity and number of criminal opportunities available. An audit of crime on the Net should be undertaken. It is hoped that some of the methods developed for this study, and its findings, will inform such an exercise.

At the moment it is possible to watch any number of Internet newsgroups and observe crimes as they unfold. It is currently possible to do observational research without encountering the sort of hazards that have traditionally confronted those who wish to study crime in the making, but it is hard to tell how long this situation will remain. NetOffenders may become much more elusive in the future.

This paper has touched on many important issues that cannot be examined in detail here. From a practical perspective, the most important finding from this study was the potential vulnerability of high-tech security systems that rely upon smart-card technology. The Net provides a forum that facilitates organized, concerted and systematic hacking projects, and also provides the means to disseminate any successful hacks. Once 'cracked', rapid dissemination of the new hack over the Internet can, in a matter of hours, render previously crime proof systems obsolete. Before the expansion of the Internet, manufacturers had always enjoyed a time-lag between the moment when a new crime technique was first found to be effective and widespread adoption of the new method (e.g.: half a tennis ball struck hard to burst open central locking systems on cars, or electronic 'grabbers' to capture codes of mobile telephones and remote car locks). And thieves conveyed such information to others in prison or, presumably, over a few beers, but . . . slowly. It does not require much imagination to guess what will happen if such time-lags disappear when more offenders begin to 'surf the net' for the latest 'crack' or to tell others what they know. It also seems unlikely that the Apprentice Work Ethic will be strong enough to hold back a steady stream of information that will enable others to commit crimes more easily—particularly given the common practice of cross-posting information between different newsgroups, the relaxation of moral codes on-line, the lack of practical inhibitors and the temptations of large financial gains.

DAVID MANN AND MIKE SUTTON

As we approach the new millennium and begin to enjoy the fruits of the information revolution, NetCrime challenges the way we have traditionally come to understand and seek to control crime.[30] For example, the semiconductor chips[31] that Sat-TV placed in the Season10 smart-cards are reputed to be among the most secure available. Five months after the card's release the general view held in the SatHackers group was that a hack would not be possible in the foreseeable future. However, in April 1996 an illicit commercial company produced a smart-card capable of emulating the legitimate Season10 card. This card did not meet the requirements of the SatHackers who were looking to produce a free hack. To this end, in December 1996, a prominent Hacker Guru from the SatHackers—who had progressed to post-graduate studies— co-authored a paper detailing a theoretical attack that could, according to the authors, compromise this and other smart-card chips.

Such expertise, in the wrong hands, could cause immense problems for private individuals and financial institutions given the increasing number of high security systems incorporating smart-cards. The vulnerability of smart-cards to sustained or novel hacker attacks is unlikely to go away. At the very least, high technology security systems would be more secure if they utilized unhacked or bespoke computer chips, such as the one used in Season10. In addition, other highly technical protective measures that prudent designers might consider include error detection and multiple encryption with voting (Anderson and Kuhn 1996). Although such measures may increase the cost of smart-cards systems, these costs might be outweighed by a considerable reduction in lost revenue.

It should be noted that a full hack of the Season10 card was never announced. However, by early 1997 postings suggested that it had been severely compromised. Pay-to-view[32] transmissions were being hacked and Sat-TV's ability to permanently deactivate illicit cards had been overcome. Within weeks, Sat-TV launched a new smart-card. This made all Season10 cards obsolete. Now, at the time of writing, the SatHackers are trying to crack Season11.

Glossary

Anonymous remailer (or remailers)—An intermediate computer which conceals the sender's identity and forwards their message to its destination.

BBS (Bulletin Board System)—A remote computer serving as an information and message-passing centre, typically owned by an individual and accessed via a modem.

CCC-list—A mailing list on the Internet.

Clone—To make a functionally equivalent copy of a hardware product. Usually for re-sale.

Cyberspace—The non-physical place 'inside' computers, which includes the Internet system.

Down loading—Taking information from a computer, the Internet or a BBS.

Email—Electronic mail. To receive Email you need an Email address which will have to be known to the sender.

---

[30] With regard to the law itself, the issues are probably less complex. For example copyright infringement will be deemed to have taken place by whoever sends, receives and possibly even provides a service where pirated programs are disseminated. Similarly, laws relating to obscenity, race relations and defamation will apply (See Martin 1995).

[31] Siemens 8051 Smart-card Micro controller in combination with an application specific integrated circuit (ASIC).

[32] Extra sporting events requiring additional one-off payments.

>>NETCRIME

FAQ (Frequently Asked Questions)—Most newsgroups should have a FAQ which provides answers so that newcomers don't make a nuisance of themselves by filling the newsgroup with the same tedious questions. A comprehensive collection of FAQs can be found at ftp://rtfm.mit.edu/pub/usenet-by-group/

Flames—Written insult or ridicule.

Flame war—Abusive arguments between two or more members of a group.

Hackers—Infiltrate computer systems without permission. Also used to describe people who compromise hardware or software security. Sometimes used to mean 'old-style' computer experts able to overcome technical problems by systematic or ingenious methods.

Human engineering—To solicit information from others that might be useful for hacking purposes. Often done by devious means.

IRC (Internet Relay Chat)—An application allowing many people to exchange messages live, in 'real time'. Analogous to telephone chat lines.

Lurking—Reading postings without participating (not a derogatory term).

Mailing list—A group of subscribers who all receive email messages posted to the list address. Analogous to a closed newsgroup.

NetCrime—Any criminal offences committed via the Net.

Netiquette—Internet etiquette. A full description can be found on the net in the document RFC1855.

Netizens—A responsible, active member of the internet community.

NetOffenders—those who initiate crimes or take up criminal opportunities on the Net.

Newbies—Newcomers on the Net. 'Noun, often preceded by the epithet "'clueless"' . . . Depending on where they show up and how they behave, newbies may be patiently tolerated or mercilessly hazed' (Herz 1994).

News server—Computer on the Net that stores and distributes newsgroup posts.

Newsgroups—Databases of messages arranged by subject which constitute forums for discussion or dissemination. Rather than sending an email to an individual it can be sent to a newsgroup for anyone interested in the subject to read.

Phreakers—Hackers of the telephone or other telecommunications systems.

Posting—Sending information such as an email to a newsgroup or mailing list.

Remailer—see anonymous remailer above.

Reverse engineer—Taking apart and understanding a piece of hardware or software, usually for the purposes of cloning.

Search engine—Computer system able to search the Net for individuals, or specific words. Vitally important for finding information on the Net.

Smart-card—a plastic card like a bankers card fitted with a microprocessor (including memory) rather than a magnetic strip, used in commercial transactions, telecommunication etc. Its design is intended to combat fraud [Chambers dictionary].

Social engineering—see Human engineering.

Spoofing—Concealing your identity by appearing to be someone else.

Surf/Surfing—Moving between WWW documents, not necessarily with the aim of finding any specific information. The implication of speed in the term can be misleading.

Threads—(See Herz 1994): 'A chain of commands linked by the follow protocol. Threads are ostensibly linked by a common topic, but the subject matter of a given thread tends to drift as it gets longer.'

Voice boxes—digitized spoken messages.

Wannabes—Those who 'want to be' in a respected or prestigious position such as Hacker Guru. Usually used as a derogatory term implying ignorance.

DAVID MANN AND MIKE SUTTON

WWW (World Wide Web) (The Web)—A vast collection of documents which may contain links to other related documents and can incorporate images and sound. Accessible via 'browsers' such as Netscape, Mosaic or Internet Explorer.

REFERENCES

ANDERSON, R. J. and KUHN, M. G. (1996), Improved Differential Fault Analysis. Published on the Internet: *Mail: Cypherpunks*.

BENNEY, M. (1936), *Low Company: Describing the Evolution of a Burglar*. London: Peter Davies.

BEST, J. and LUCKENBILL, D. F. (1982), *Organizing Deviance*. New Jersey: Prentice-Hall.

—— (1994), *Organizing Deviance*, 2nd edition. New Jersey: Prentice-Hall.

BLAKEY, D. (1995), 'Tackling Computer Crime and the Internet—Policy Approaches of the UK Police', paper presented at: *Computer Crime and the Internet*, QMW Public Policy Seminar, 16 November, London.

BRANTINGHAM, P. J. and BRANTINGHAM, P. L. (1981), *Environmental Criminology*. London: Sage Publications.

BRIDGE, A. (1996), 'The world takes a first step to halt abuse of its children', *The Independent*, 28 August, 1.

COHEN, S. (1973), *Folk Devils and Moral Panics*. London: Paladin.

COLEMAN, A. (1985) *Utopia on Trial: Vision and Reality in Planned Housing*. London: Hilary Shipman.

COUNCIL OF EUROPE (1995a), *The Fight against Sound and Audiovisual Piracy*, handbook. Council of Europe Publishing.

—— (1995b), *The legal protection of encrypted television services*, Recommendation No. R (91) 14 and explanatory memorandum. Council of Europe Press.

COUTORIE, L. E. (1995), 'The Future of High-Technology Crime: a parallel Delphi study', *Journal of Criminal Justice*, 23/1: 13–27.

CLARKE, R. V. G. (1980), 'Situational Crime Prevention Theory and Practice', *British Journal of Criminology*, 20/2: 136–47.

DELHAM, DR (1995), '*Infiltrating Disney*' 2600: The Hacker Quarterly, Winter 1995–96.

DURKIN, K. F. and BRYANT, C. D. (1995), 'Log on to sex: some notes on the carnal computer and erotic cyberspace as an emerging research frontier', *Deviant Behaviour: An Interdisciplinary Journal*, 16: 179–200.

FOSTER, J. (1990), *Villains: Crime and Community in the Inner City*. London: Routledge.

GIBSON, W. (1986) *Neuromancer*. London: Grafton Books.

HERZ, J. C. (1994), *Surfing on the Internet: A Net-Head's Adventures On-Line*. London: Abacus.

HOBSBAWM, E. J. (1969), *Bandits*. New York, Delacorte.

HOOD, R. and SPARKS, R. (1970), *Key Issues in Criminology*. London: World University Library, Weidenfeld and Nicolson.

HOLDAWAY, S. (1983), *Inside the British Police*. Oxford: Blackwell.

JACOBS, J. (1965), *The Death and Life of Great American Cities*. Penguin: Harmondsworth.

KEARNEY, M. (1996), 'They're just kids from middle-class families, yet they sell sex on the street', *Evening Standard*, 21 August: 22.

LANDRETH, B. with RHEINGOLD, H. (1985), *Out of the Inner Circle: a Hackers Guide to Computer Security*. Bellevue, Washington: Microsoft Press.

LANGFORD, D. (1995), 'Law and Disorder in Netville,' *New Scientist*, 17 June.

McINTOSH, M. (1971), 'Changes in the Organisation of Thieving', in S. Cohen, ed., *Images of Deviance*, 98–133. England: Penguin Books.

MACK, J. (1964), 'Full-Time Miscreants, Delinquent Neighbourhoods and Criminal Networks', *British Journal of Sociology*, 15: 38–53.

MARTIN, D. (1995), 'Internet law comes of age', *Internet Research: Electronic Networking Applications and Policy*, 5/3: 11–14.

MATZA, D. (1964), *Delinquency and Drift*. Englewood Cliffs, NJ: Prentice Hall.

MAYS, N. and POPE, C. (1995), 'Observational methods in health care settings', *British Medical Journal*, 311: 182–84.

McLUHAN, M. (1964), *Understanding Media: The Extensions of Man*. London: Routledge.

MEYER, G. R. (1989), 'The Social Organization of the Computer Underground', unpublished MA thesis. Department of Sociology, Northern Illinois University.

MONTI, D. (1994), *Wannabe Gangs in Suburbs and Schools*. Cambridge, MA: Blackwell.

MOORE, D. W. (1995), *The Emperor's Virtual Clothes: The Naked Truth about Internet Culture*. Chapel Hill, NC: Algonquin Books.

MORTON, O. (1996), 'Beware Censorship says Oliver Morton, editor of Wired magazine', *The Independent*, 24 September, s. 2: 3.

MILLER, W. B. (1958), 'Lower-class culture as a generating milieu of gang delinquency', *Journal of Social Issues*, 15: 5–9.

NEWMAN, O. (1973), *Defensible Space*. London: Architectural Press.

PARKER, H. (1974), *View from the Boys: a Sociology of Down-Town Adolescents*. London: David and Charles.

ROETHLISBERGER, F. J. and DICKSON, W. J. (1939), *Management and the Worker*. Harvard University Press.

SHOVER, N. (1996), *Great Pretenders: Pursuits and Careers of Persistent Thieves*. Boulder, CO: Westview Press.

SLOUKA, M. (1996), *War of the Worlds: The Assault on Reality*. London: Abacus.

SPERGEL, L. (1995), *The Youth Gang Problem: A Community Approach*. New York: Oxford University Press.

STEFFENSMEIER, D. J. (1986), *The Fence: In the Shadow of Two Worlds*. New Jersey: Rowman and Littlefield.

STERLING, B. (1992), *The Hacker Crackdown: Law and Disorder on the Electronic Frontier*. London: Penguin Books.

SUTTON, M. (1995), 'Supply by Theft: Does the market for stolen goods play a role in keeping crime figures high?', *British Journal of Criminology*, 35/3: 400–16.

—— (1996), *Implementing Crime Prevention Schemes in a Multi-agency Setting: Aspects of Process in the Safer Cities Programme*, Home Office Research Study No. 160. London: Home Office.

SYLVESTER, R. (1996), 'Sky high cost of TV hackers', *The Sunday Telegraph*, 4 February: 12.

The Economist (1995), 1 July. Taken from Coutorie, L. E. (1995), 'The Future of High-Technology Crime: a parallel Delphi study', *Journal of Criminal Justice*, 23/1: 13–27.

The Economist (1995), 'The Internet Survey', 1 July.

WALL, D. (1997), 'Policing The Virtual Community: The Internet, cybercrimes and policing cyberspace', in P. Francis, P. Davies, and V. Jupp, *Policing Futures*. London: Macmillan.

WEXLER, S. (1990), 'Ethical Obligations and Social Research', in K. L. Kempf, ed., *Measurement Issues in Criminology*, 78–107. New York: Springer-Verlag.

WHYTE, W. F. (1955), *Street Corner Society: The Social Structure of an Italian Slum*. Chicago: Chicago University Press.

[12]

Cyberterrorism: The Logic Bomb versus the Truck Bomb

DOROTHY E. DENNING

In 1996, a computer hacker allegedly associated with the white supremacist movement temporarily disabled a Massachusetts Internet service provider and damaged part of its record-keeping system. The service provider had attempted to stop the hacker from sending out racist messages worldwide under its name. The hacker signed off with the threat, "You have yet to see true electronic terrorism. This is a promise."

The hacker apparently never made good on his promise, but the threat of a cyberterrorist attack has many people worried. The highly acclaimed *Computers at Risk* report (1991) from the US National Research Council concludes, "Tomorrow's terrorist may be able to do more with a keyboard than with a bomb." *Cybercrime, Cyberterrorism, and Cyberwarfare* (1998) from the Washington-based Global Organized Crime Project of the Center for Strategic and International Studies says, "Cyberterrorists, acting for rogue states or groups that have declared holy war against the United States, are known to be plotting America's demise as a superpower."

Dorothy E. Denning is professor of computer science at Georgetown University and director of the Georgetown Institute for Information Assurance. She has been working on cyberspace threats and defences for almost thirty years and is the author of Information Warfare and Security *(Addison Wesley, 1998). Her paper is an extension of testimony given in May 2000 to the US House Armed Services Committee Special Oversight Panel on Terrorism.*

Defining Cyberterrorism

Cyberterrorism is the convergence of cyberspace and terrorism. It refers to unlawful attacks and threats of attack against computers, networks and the information stored therein that are carried out to intimidate or coerce a country's government or citizens in furtherance of political or social objectives. Further, to qualify as cyberterrorism, an attack should result in violence against persons or property, or at least cause enough harm to generate fear. Attacks that lead to death or bodily injury, explosions, or severe economic losses would be examples. Serious attacks against crucial infrastructures could count as acts of cyberterrorism, depending on their impact. Attacks that disrupt non-essential services or that are mainly a costly nuisance would not.

Numerous cyberterrorism scenarios have been suggested. In one, a cyberterrorist attacks the computer systems that control a large regional power grid. Power is lost for a sustained period of time and people die. In another, the cyberterrorist breaks into an air-traffic control system and tampers with it. Two large civilian aircraft collide. In a third, the cyberterrorist disrupts banking operations, international financial transactions and stock exchanges. Economic systems grind to a halt, the public loses confidence, and destabilisation is achieved. While none of these or similar scenarios has yet occurred, many believe it is not a question of "if" but "when".

Exploiting Cyberspace

Terrorists have moved into cyberspace to facilitate traditional forms of terrorism such as bombings. They use the Internet to communicate, co-ordinate events and advance their agenda. While such activity does not constitute cyberterrorism in the strict sense, it does show that terrorists have some competency in using the new information technologies.

By 1996, the headquarters of terrorist financier Osama bin Laden in Afghanistan were equipped with computers and communications equipment. Egyptian computer experts were said to have helped devise for bin Laden a communications network that used the World Wide Web, e-mail and electronic bulletin boards. Activists of the Palestinian group Hamas have been said to use chat rooms and e-mail to plan operations and co-ordinate activities, making it difficult for Israeli security officials to trace their messages and decode their contents. The Revolutionary Armed Forces of Columbia use e-mail to field inquiries from the press.

The Web is especially popular as a medium for reaching a global audience. For example, after the Peruvian terrorist group Tupac Amaru stormed the Japanese ambassador's residence in Lima in December 1996, taking hostage four hundred diplomatic, military and political officials, sympathisers in the United States and Canada put up solidarity websites. One site included detailed drawings of the residence and assault plans.

In February 1998, the Lebanese group Hizbollah was operating three websites: one for its central press office (www.hizbollah.org), another to describe its attacks on Israeli targets (www.moqawama.org), and the third for news and information (www.almanar.com.lb). That month, Clark Staten, executive director of the Emergency Response and Research Institute

(ERRI) in Chicago, testified before a US Senate subcommittee that "even small terrorist groups are now using the Internet to broadcast their message and misdirect/misinform the general population in multiple nations simultaneously". He gave the subcommittee copies of both domestic and international messages containing anti-American and anti-Israeli propaganda and threats, including a widely distributed extremist call for "jihad" (holy war) against the United States and the United Kingdom.

In June 1998, *U.S. News & World Report* noted that twelve of the thirty groups on the US State Department's list of terrorist organisations were on the Web. Today it appears that virtually every US-designated terrorist group has a website. Forcing them off the Web is impossible, because they can set up their sites in countries with free speech laws. The government of Sri Lanka, for example, banned the separatist Liberation Tigers of Tamil Eelam, but it did not even attempt to have their London-based website closed.

Even in democracies, however, there are limits to what terrorists can post on the Net. After a group of anti-abortionists put up a website terrorising doctors who perform abortions, a federal jury ordered that the pages be taken down and damages of more than $100 million paid. The "Nuremberg Files" site had listed the names of about two hundred abortion providers under the heading of "baby butchers". Readers were invited to send in such personal details as the doctors' home addresses, licence plate numbers and the names of their children. Three doctors whose names appeared on the list were killed, and after each murder the doctor's name was promptly crossed out. Doctors named on the site testified that they lived in constant fear and used disguises, bodyguards and bulletproof vests for protection. In ordering the site closed, the federal jury said the site and "wanted" posters amounted to death threats against the doctors.

Many terrorists are using encryption to conceal their communications and stored files, compounding the difficulties of counter-terrorism efforts. Hamas, for example, has reportedly used encrypted Internet communications to transmit maps, pictures and other information pertaining to terrorist attacks. Ramzi Ahmed Yousef, a member of the international terrorist group responsible for bombing the World Trade Center in 1993, encrypted files on his laptop computer. The files, which US government officials decrypted, contained information concerning plans to blow up twelve US-owned commercial airliners in the Far East. The Aum Shinrikyo cult, which nerve-gassed the Tokyo subway in March 1995, killing twelve people and injuring six thousand more, also used encryption to protect its computerised records, which included plans to deploy weapons of mass destruction in Japan and the United States.

Cyberspace Violence

Cyberspace is constantly under assault. Cyberspies, thieves, saboteurs and thrill seekers break into computer systems, steal personal data and commercial secrets, vandalise websites, disrupt service, sabotage data and systems, launch computer viruses and worms, conduct fraudulent transactions and harass individuals and companies. These attacks are facilitated by increasingly powerful and easy-to-use software tools, which are readily available for free from thousands of websites on the Internet.

Many of the attacks are serious and costly. For example, the ILOVEYOU virus and variants, launched in May 2000, were estimated to have hit tens of millions of users worldwide and cost billions of dollars in damage. Denial-of-service attacks against Yahoo, CNN, eBay and other e-commerce websites are estimated to have caused more than $1 billion in losses. They also shook the confidence of businesses and individuals in e-commerce.

Governments are particularly concerned about terrorist and state-sponsored attacks against the vital infrastructures that constitute the national life-support systems of their countries. The Clinton administration has defined eight such systems: telecommunications, banking and finance, electrical power, oil and gas distribution and storage, water supply, transportation, emergency services and government services.

There have been numerous attacks against such infrastructures in the United States. Although they cannot strictly be described as terrorist in nature, they reveal the vulnerability of modern society to cybercrime and the possibilities open to cyberterrorists. Thus, hackers have invaded the public phone networks, compromising nearly every category of activity, including switching and operations, administration, maintenance and provisioning (OAM&P). They have crashed or disrupted signal transfer points and switches and other network elements. They have planted "time bomb" programs designed to shut down major switching hubs, disrupted emergency 911 phone services throughout the eastern seaboard and boasted that they have the capability to bring down all switches in Manhattan. They have installed wiretaps, re-routed phone calls, changed the greetings on voice-mail systems, taken over voice mailboxes and made free long-distance calls at their victims' expense, leaving some victims with phone bills of hundreds of thousands of dollars. When they cannot crack the technology, they use "social engineering" to trick employees into giving them access.

In March 1997, one teenage hacker penetrated and disabled a telephone company computer that serviced Worcester Airport in Massachusetts. As a result, the telephone service to
the Federal Aviation Administration control
tower, the airport fire department, airport
security, the weather service and various private airfreight companies was cut off for six
hours. Later in the day, the juvenile disabled
another telephone company computer, this
time causing an outage in the Rutland area.
The outage caused financial losses and threatened public health and public safety. On a separate occasion, the hacker allegedly broke into
a pharmacist's computer and accessed files
containing prescriptions.

Banks and financial systems are a popular
target of cybercriminals. The usual motive is
money, and perpetrators have stolen or
attempted to steal tens of millions of dollars.
In one case of sabotage, a computer operator
at Reuters in Hong Kong tampered with the
dealing room systems of five of the company's bank clients. In November 1996, he
programmed the systems to delete key operating system files after a delay long enough to
allow him to leave the building. When the
"time bombs" exploded, the systems crashed.
They were partially restored by the next
morning, but it took another day before they
were fully operational. However, the banks
said the tampering did not significantly affect
trading and that neither they nor their clients
experienced losses.

In another act of sabotage against a crucial
infrastructure, a fired employee of Chevron's
emergency alert network disabled the firm's
alert system by hacking into computers in New
York and San José, California, and reconfiguring them so they would crash. The vandalism
was not discovered until an emergency arose at
the Chevron refinery in Richmond, California,
and the system could not be used to notify the
adjacent community of the release of a nox-
ious substance. During the ten-hour period in
1992 when the system was down, thousands of
people in twenty-two states and six unspecified areas of Canada were put at risk.

An overflow of raw sewage on the Sunshine Coast of Australia in June 2000 was
linked to a 49-year-old Brisbane man who
allegedly penetrated the Maroochy Shire
Council's computer system and used radio
transmissions to create the overflows. The man
was charged with 370 offences, including
stealing, computer hacking and using radio
communications equipment without authority.

Government computers, particularly US
Department of Defence computers, are a regular target of attack. Detected attacks against
unclassified DoD computers rose from 780 in
1997 to 5,844 in 1998 and 22,144 in 1999.

The most damaging and costly attacks
have been carried out for reasons other than
the pursuit of terrorist goals. As the above
cases illustrate, they have been motivated by
greed, revenge, thrill seeking, the desire for
notoriety, and other non-ideological factors.
They are properly classified as cybercrimes,
not cyberterrorism.

Ideologically Motivated Cyberattacks

Terrorism is normally associated with
attacks perpetrated in furtherance of political
and social objectives. Numerous cyberattacks
have been so motivated. For example, in 1998
ethnic Tamil guerrillas swamped Sri Lankan
embassies with eight hundred e-mails a day
over a two-week period. The messages read:
"We are the Internet Black Tigers and we're
doing this to disrupt your communications."
Intelligence authorities characterised it as the
first known attack by terrorists against a
country's computer systems.

Also in 1998, Spanish protesters bombarded the San Francisco–based Institute for Global Communications (IGC)—an Internet service provider—with thousands of bogus e-mail messages (a practice known as "spamming"). E-mail was tied up and undeliverable to IGC's users, and support lines were clogged with people who could not get their mail. The protesters also spammed IGC staff and member accounts, swamped IGC's Web page with bogus credit card orders, and threatened to employ the same tactics against organisations using IGC services. They demanded that IGC stop hosting the website of the *Euskal Herria Journal*, a New York–based publication supporting Basque independence. Protesters said IGC supported terrorism because a section of the Web pages contained material on the Basque terrorist group ETA, which claimed responsibility for assassinations of Spanish political and security officials, and attacks on Spanish military installations. IGC finally relented and pulled the site because of the "mail bombings".

During the Kosovo conflict in 1999, computers of the North Atlantic Treaty Organisation were blasted with e-mail bombs and hit with denial-of-service attacks by "hacktivists" protesting against Nato's bombing of Serbia. In addition, Western businesses, public organisations and academic institutes reportedly received highly politicised, anti-Nato, virus-laden e-mails from a range of eastern European countries. Web defacements were also common. After a US plane accidentally bombed the Chinese embassy in Belgrade, Chinese hacktivists posted on US government websites messages such as, "We won't stop attacking until the war stops!"

Since December 1997, the Electronic Disturbance Theater (EDT), a New York–based activist group, has been conducting Web sit-ins against various sites in support of Mexico's Zapatista guerrillas. At a designated time, thousands of protesters point their browsers to a target site using software that floods the target with rapid and repeated download requests. EDT's software has also been used by animal rights groups against organisations said to abuse animals. Electrohippies, another group of hacktivists, conducted Web sit-ins against the World Trade Organisation when it met in Seattle in late 1999. These sit-ins all require mass participation to have much effect, and thus are more suited to use by activists than by relatively small groups of terrorists operating in secrecy.

While the above incidents had social and political motivations, it is hard to judge whether they were sufficiently harmful or frightening to be classified as cyberterrorism. To the best of my knowledge, no attack so far has led to violence or injury to persons, although some may have intimidated their victims. Both the EDT and the Electrohippies view their operations as acts of civil disobedience, analogous to street protests and physical sit-ins, not as acts of violence or terrorism. This is an important distinction. Most activists, whether participating in a street march or Web sit-in, are not terrorists.

However, there are a few indications that some terrorist groups are pursuing cyberterrorism, either solely or in conjunction with acts of physical violence. In February 1998, the ERRI's Clark Staten told a US Senate Judiciary Committee Subcommittee on Technology, Terrorism and Government Information that it was believed that "members of some Islamic extremist organizations have been attempting to develop a 'hacker network' to support their computer activities and even engage in offensive information warfare attacks in the future".

In November 1998, the *Detroit News* reported that Khalid Ibrahim, who claimed to be a member of the militant Indian separatist group Harkat-ul-Ansar, had tried to buy military software from hackers who had stolen it from US Department of Defence computers they had penetrated. The attempted purchase was discovered when an 18-year-old hacker calling himself Chameleon attempted to cash a $1,000 cheque from Ibrahim. Chameleon said he did not have the software and had not given it to Ibrahim, but Ibrahim may have obtained it or other sensitive information from one of the many other hackers he approached. Harkat-ul-Ansar declared war on the United States following the August 1998 cruise-missile attack on a suspected terrorist training camp in Afghanistan run by Osama bin Laden, which allegedly killed nine of their members.

The Provisional Irish Republican Army employed the services of contract hackers to penetrate computers in order to acquire the home addresses of British law enforcement and intelligence officers. The data was used to draw up plans to kill the officers in a single "night of the long knives" if the British government did not meet terms for a new ceasefire. As this case illustrates, terrorists may use hacking as a way of acquiring intelligence in support of physical violence, even if they do not use it to wreak havoc in cyberspace.

Terrorists might also engage in computer network attacks as a way of financing physical operations. For example, they could penetrate an e-commerce website and steal credit card numbers, conduct fraudulent transactions against an Internet bank, or extort money from victims by threatening electronic sabotage.

How Real a Threat?

To understand the potential threat of cyberterrorism, two factors must be considered: first, whether there are targets that are vulnerable to attacks that could lead to violence or severe harm; and second, whether there are actors with the capability and motivation to carry them out.

Looking first at vulnerabilities, several studies have shown that vital infrastructures are potentially open to cyberterrorist attack. "Eligible Receiver", a no-warning exercise conducted by the US Department of Defence in 1997, found that power grid and emergency 911 systems had weaknesses that could be exploited by an adversary using only tools publicly available on the Internet. Although neither of these systems was actually attacked, study members concluded that the services these systems provide could be disrupted. Also in 1997, President Clinton's Commission on Critical Infrastructure Protection issued its report warning that through mutual dependencies and interconnectedness, vital infrastructures could be vulnerable in new ways. The report said that vulnerabilities were steadily increasing, while the costs of attack were decreasing.

Although many of the weaknesses in computerised systems can be corrected, it is effectively impossible to eliminate all of them. Even if the technology itself offers good security, it is frequently configured or used in ways that leave it open to attack. In addition, there is always the possibility that insiders, acting alone or in concert with other terrorists, will misuse their access capabilities. According to Colonel Konstantin Machabeli of Russia's Interior Ministry, the state-run gas monopoly Gazprom was hit in 1999 by hackers who collaborated with a Gazprom insider. The hackers allegedly used a Trojan horse to gain control of the central switchboard, which controls gas flows in pipelines. Gazprom, the world's largest natural gas producer and the largest gas supplier to western Europe, denied the report.

Consultants and contractors are frequently in a position to cause grave harm. In March 2000, Japan's Metropolitan Police Department reported that a software system it had procured to track 150 police vehicles, including unmarked cars, had been developed by the Aum Shinrikyo cult. At the time of the discovery, the cult had received classified tracking data on 115 vehicles. Further, the cult had developed software for at least eighty Japanese firms and ten government agencies. It had worked as a subcontractor for other firms, making it almost impossible for them to know who was developing their software. As a subcontractor, the cult could have installed Trojan horses to launch or facilitate cyberterrorist attacks at a later date. Fearing a Trojan horse of its own, the US State Department last February sent an urgent cable to about 170 embassies asking them to remove software which it belatedly realised had been written by citizens of the former Soviet Union.

If we assume, then, that vital infrastructures *are* vulnerable to cyberterrorist attack, the question becomes one of whether there are actors with the capability and motivation to carry out such operations. While many hackers have the knowledge, skills and tools to attack computer systems, they generally lack the motivation to cause violence or severe economic or social harm. Conversely, terrorists who are motivated to cause violence seem to lack the capability or motivation to cause damage in cyberspace.

Looking Ahead

In August 1999, the Center for the Study of Terrorism and Irregular Warfare at the Naval Postgraduate School in Monterey, California, issued a report entitled "Cyberterror: Prospects and Implications". The report assessed the likelihood of terrorist organisa-

tions pursuing cyberterrorism. It concluded that the barrier to entry for anyone other than nuisance hackers was quite high, and that terrorists generally lacked the wherewithal and human capital needed to mount a meaningful operation. Cyberterrorism, the report argued, was a thing of the future, although it might be pursued as an ancillary tool.

The Monterey team defined three levels of cyberterror capability. The first is the "simple-unstructured" capability to conduct basic hacks against individual systems using tools created by someone else. Organisations at this level possess negligible target analysis, command and control functions, or learning ability.

The second level is the "advanced-structured" capability to conduct more sophisticated attacks against multiple systems or networks, and possibly to modify or create basic hacking tools. Organisations at this level possess elementary target analysis, command and control functions and learning ability.

The third level is the "complex-co-ordinated" capability to carry out a co-ordinated attack capable of causing mass disruption against integrated, heterogeneous defences (including cryptography). An organisation operating at this level would be able to create sophisticated hacking tools. It would possess significant target analysis, command and control functions and learning ability.

The Monterey team estimated that it would take a group starting from scratch two to four years to reach the advanced-structured level and six to ten years to reach the complex-co-ordinated level, although some groups might get to these levels sooner or turn to outsourcing or sponsorship to extend their capability.

The study examined five terrorist group types: religious, New Age, ethno-nationalist separatist, revolutionary, and far-right extremist. It determined that only the religious groups were likely to seek the most damaging capability level, as it is consistent with their indiscriminate application of violence. New Age or single-issue terrorists, such as the Animal Liberation Front, pose the most immediate threat, but are more likely to accept disruption as a substitute for destruction. Revolutionary groups and ethno-nationalist separatists are both likely to seek an advanced-structured capability. Far-right extremists are likely to settle for a simple-unstructured capability, as cyberterror offers neither the intimacy nor the cathartic effects that are central to the psychology of far-right terrorism. The study also determined that hacker groups are psychologically and organisationally ill suited to cyberterrorism, and that it would be against their interests to cause mass disruption of the information infrastructure.

Thus, at this time, cyberterrorism does not seem to pose an imminent threat. This could change. For a terrorist, cyberterrorism has some advantages over physical methods. It can be conducted remotely and anonymously, and does not involve the handling of explosives or a suicide mission. It would probably attract extensive media coverage, as journalists and the public alike are fascinated by practically any kind of computer attack. Indeed, cyberterrorism could be immensely appealing to terrorists precisely because of the tremendous attention given to it by governments and the media.

Yet cyberterrorism also has its drawbacks. Systems are complex, so it may be harder to control an attack and achieve a desired level of damage than it is by using physical weapons. Unless people are injured, there is also less drama and emotional appeal for the terrorist. Further, terrorists may be disinclined to try new methods unless they see their old ones as inadequate, particularly when the new methods

require considerable knowledge and skill to use effectively. Terrorists generally stick with tried and true methods. Novelty and sophistication of attack may be much less important than the assurance that a mission will be operationally successful. Indeed, the risk of operational failure could be a deterrent to terrorists. For now, the truck bomb poses a much greater threat than the logic bomb.

The next generation of terrorists will grow up in a digital world, with ever more powerful and easy-to-use hacking tools at their disposal. They might see greater potential for cyberterrorism than the terrorists of today, and their level of knowledge and skill relating to hacking will be greater. Hackers and insiders might be recruited by terrorists or become self-recruiting cyberterrorists, the Timothy McVeighs of cyberspace. Some might be moved to action by cyber policy issues, making cyberspace an attractive venue for carrying out an attack. Cyberterrorism could also become more attractive as the real and virtual worlds become more closely coupled, with a greater number of physical devices attached to the Internet. Some of these may be remotely controlled. Terrorists, for example, might target the robots used in telesurgery. Unless such systems are carefully secured, carrying out a cyberattack that physically harms someone may be easy as penetrating a website is today.

Although the violent pursuit of political goals using exclusively electronic methods is likely to be at least a few years into the future, the more general threat of cybercrime is very much a part of the digital landscape today. In addition to cyberattacks against digital data and systems, many people are being "terrorised" on the Internet today with threats of physical violence. Online stalking, death threats and hate messages are abundant. These crimes are serious and must be addressed. In so doing, we will be in a better position to prevent and respond to cyberterrorism if and when the threat becomes more serious. ❑

[13]

Redefining borders: The challenges of cybercrime *

DAVID L. SPEER
Marquette University, Political Science Department, Milwankee, WI 53201-1881, USA
(e-mail: david.speer@marquette.edu)

Abstract. Cybercrime is the newest security threat in the world today, and is distinct from any other threat facing the world. This paper attempts to place cybercrime in relation to other security threats, as well as illustrate the unique characteristics of cybercrime. First, an investigation of the major elements of cybercrime will be conducted. After the parameters of cybercrime have been laid out, cybercrime will be analyzed as a security threat on both domestic and international levels. Finally, current security structures will be examined for their effectiveness in controlling the threat posed by cybercrime.

Introduction

In the aftermath of the Cold War, domestic and international security agencies began to retool their focus towards transnational criminal threats such as drug trafficking and organized crime. However, none of their efforts have prepared the security structures and enforcement agencies to deal with the challenges posed by cybercrime. The institutionalized focus of security and law enforcement agencies on tracking the physical location and sources of security threats is a major impediment towards successfully combating cybercrime. More important, the exact nature of cybercrime remains underspecified in the policy and scholarly debates over the magnitude of the problem and its solutions.

Recently, the United States has taken steps to establish new security structures and upgrade existing structures, but these steps are just the beginning of what needs to be done. The impetus for this initiative has come from President Clinton, Janet Reno, and individuals that have witnessed the destructive power of cybercrime. Agencies involved in fighting cybercrime must look at three major factors. First, the nature of the cybercrime must be understood, as there are many different classifications of the crimes depending on the offender and the victim. Next, the crimes need to be understood in relation to how they fit into current means of analyzing a security threat. The final area is how security structures can best counter cybercrimes.

* I would like to thank my mentor Dr H. Richard Friman for his comments and support on this paper.

The nature of cybercrimes

Cybercrimes are activities in which computers, telephones, cellular equipment, and other technological devices are used for illicit purposes such as fraud, theft, electronic vandalism, violating intellectual properties rights, and breaking and entering into computer systems and networks. A term that is related to cybercrime is information warfare, which includes war-related activities carried out by individuals, organizations, and governments. These activities are implemented against the infrastructure and computer systems of other organizations and governments using the same skills and equipment that are used in cybercrimes (Cilluffo, Berkowitz, and Lanz 8, 1998). These two terms are often used synonymously, but are quite different. More importantly, applying the term information warfare to cybercrimes, often sensationalizes crimes that are unimportant on the levels of national or international security.

With these definitions in mind, it is necessary to examine the nature of the cybercrime. This section examines four major elements of cybercrime: the location of the criminal in relation to the crime, the victim, the offender, and what is being done to eliminate the threat. Addressing the nature of cybercrime is the first step towards comparing this issue to other security threats.

Location

The location of the offender in relation to the scene of the crime is the characteristic of cybercrime that differentiates itself most from others. In more traditional threats, the criminal is physically present at the crime scene. Therefore, enforcement officials can apprehend the criminal and bring him or her to justice. This is not the case with cybercrimes, as the criminal usually is not present at the crime scene thus making apprehension difficult. Not only are the offenders not present, but many times they are in another state or country. As a result cooperation between various enforcement officials is necessary. Recently, efforts have been made toward cooperation as illustrated by the apprehension of an Israeli hacker with the alias of "analyzer" who helped two teenagers in California interfere with military deployments in the Persian Gulf (Cilluffo, Berkowitz, and Lanz XV, 1998). However, cooperation can be inhibited by problems of jurisdiction and whether an enforcement agency will be able to cross borders in order to apprehend a criminal. Again the "analyzer" example illustrates this point because Israeli, not United States, authorities arrested this hacker ("Ehud Tenebaum" 1, 18 Mar. 1998).

Victims

Beyond the cooperation and jurisdictional difficulties faced by enforcement agencies is the problem of dealing with a large variety of victims of cybercrimes. The primary victims are governments and their various agencies, corporations, and organizations. These institutions each have different agendas that often times are opposed to each other, which hinders progress toward the common goal of elimination of cybercrime. Additionally, a large percentage of cybercrime is committed against individuals, but there has been limited emphasis on the individuals in conferences and summits, due to the fact that they have limited power and influence over governments.

Cybercrime legislation has been slowed by competing demands of the victims' lobbies. For example, the United States government has established the Federal Intrusion Detection Network or FIDNET which is an agency designed to fight cybercrime by monitoring government computers for security breaches. There have been attempts to centralize FIDNET under the Federal Bureau of Investigation (FBI). Organizations, corporations, and individuals are all very opposed to this type of control because they feel it would be an invasion of their privacy and has great potential for abuse. The reason these groups feel this way is because the access would be regulated by the FBI, which would "create a de facto 'desktop surveillance' network" (Markoff 1, 1 Oct. 1999). As a result of these strong feelings, many lobbyists are working against this type of law enforcement.

Additionally, each of these potential targets has internal protection and security enforcement measures already in place. For example, Sun Microsystems Incorporated has a company rule about their employees not having modems attached to their computers, to prevent hackers from breaking into the company network using an idle modem. This is such a serious threat that Sun will immediately fire anyone that breaks the rule ("Modem" 1, 18 Mar 1998).

Some firms are taking more drastic action against hackers by employing vigilante tactics. Many institutions, including major corporations and the Pentagon have installed counteroffensive computer programs. These programs will attack a hacker's computer once a breach of security has occurred. These types of programs fall into a gray area of legislation because they are not illegal, yet many law enforcement officials feel that these programs can cause more problems than they prevent. According to Schwartau, many law enforcement agencies unofficially say to these institutions, "We can't handle the problem. It's too big. If you take care of things yourself, we will look in the other direction. Just be careful." (8, 11 Jan 1999) Unfortunately, many hackers that fall victim to these programs often want revenge and will work even harder to destroy an institution's computer systems.

262   DAVID L. SPEER

On an international level, the countries that are the most vulnerable to these threats are the United States, Japan, and member states of the European Union. At the time of this writing, very little data is available on the number of cybercrimes committed in these countries. An interesting paradox exists in these cases. These are the countries in the world that are the most reliant on computers and technological devices to support and control their infrastructures. This makes them the most vulnerable to cybercrime threats and information warfare. Yet because these countries have invested the most into their technological equipment, they also have the best security for these systems. Therefore, the less technological equipment a country has, the less vulnerable it is to this type of threat. Unfortunately, without this equipment it is virtually impossible to compete in the international economy.

Offender

The other part of the threat equation is the offender and his or her motives and intentions. This is one of the most unique areas of cybercrime. In some instances the criminal is a teenager trespassing on someone else's computer for fun or to prove themselves in the face of their peers. In other cases, the offender is an adult looking to vandalize computers or steal sensitive information and sell it. Conversely, the offenders in information warfare are governments or individuals acting against other governments and the target country's infrastructure. The intent of information warfare is national defense, or to weaken the opponent by disabling key computer systems.

Beyond clear examples of crimes such as these, there are many gray areas in cybercrime. For example, individuals and groups commit crimes that they may not know are crimes or may not understand the potential consequences of their actions. An example of this is people pirating software from a friend, this is particularly true with people that are new to the computer world. This illegal transfer of software occurs both over the telephone with the use of a modem or physically by exchanging diskettes. In this type of cybercrime, there is a very definite overlap with intellectual property rights and laws governing these rights. Therefore many new legal precedents must be set as well as new legislation to determine the proper punishment for these various crimes. Additionally, the international community needs to set standards for dealing with these crimes and how an offender in one country will be punished by the legal system in the victims' countries.

A related issue to the offender is the dual-use skills and abilities that are pocessed by many individuals that work for corporations and governments. The same skills are used to program a new and useful program as to program a virus designed to ruin entire computer networks. Therefore, it is very difficult to monitor individuals with the potential to commit cybercrimes. This is an area that many corporations and governments are extremely concerned about, because they employ individuals with these skills. Furthermore, a large portion of cybercrimes are committed by people inside an organization because it is easier to gain access to the system.

Eliminating the threat

These aspects of cybercrime have lead to discussions of the threat at a number of conferences dealing with transnational crime. Both the G8 and European Union have held conferences about international crime with cybercrime as an area of focus. These conferences have been surprisingly similar in the manner in which cybercrime is being discussed as well as the measures to prevent it. The most recent conference with cybercrime as a topic was the 1998 G8 summit in Birmingham, United Kingdom. This conference took most of its initiative from the 1997 G8 summit in Denver, Colorado. At the 1997 summit, many calls to action were primarily placed by the United States, but no treaty or agreement was signed (G8 Denver Summit, 1997). Once again, in the 1998 summit, nothing binding was signed by the participating countries because most of the participants were unwilling to delegate the authority of their domestic security structures (G8 Birmingham Summit, 1998). In both of these summits, the United States was the country arguing most strongly for a prohibition regime on cybercrime. These summits generated a list of ten steps that needed to be carried out by the participants, including modifying existing domestic regulations and working toward international standards and cooperation (Communiqué Annex Action Plan, 1, 1997). The United States is not the only country that is concerned about the new threats from technology. In 1995, the European Union held its own conference about setting up standards for dealing with cybercrime threats. These talks had obvious influence on the 1997 and 1998 summits, as the topics were very similar with cooperation internationally and among the member states being extremely important (EU Recommendation, 1995). In addition to the conferences held by countries are those held by corporations and organizations. The impetus for the conferences is the feeling that governments are not dealing with these threats in a timely manner. For example, the annual RSA Data Security, Inc. data security conference and expo is a forum for corporations, organizations, individuals, and government agencies to discuss security and encryption. Here, these actors attempt to initiate standards and develop norms for the security world (RSA Conference, 1999).

As a result of these conferences, new legislation is developing, as is a classification system for the various crimes. In the United States, the classification system consists of four classifications of cybercrimes and computer crimes. The first category is that of "computer as target", here computers are the targets of crimes such as vandalism, trespassing, and information theft (Carter 1, 4 Nov. 1999). The information theft is the biggest concern for most corporations, as thefts of detailed plans about a new product's design or marketing campaign could ruin the company. Next is that of "Computer As the Instrumentality of the Crime", where the offender modifies the processes of a system or piece of equipment or alters a device's primary licit use to something illicit (Carter 2, 4 Nov. 1999). This type of crime mostly consists of fraud, and stealing information such as credit card numbers or cellular phone billing codes. Third are crimes that occur when the "Computer Is Incidental to Other Crime" (Carter 3, 4 Nov. 1999). In these cases, the computer is not necessary to commit the crime, but facilitates the process of committing the crime. Examples of this type of crime are money-laundering or the spread of child pornography over the internet. The final category of cybercrime, "Crimes Associated With the Prevalence of Computers", are crimes that are related to the computer and its peripheral equipment. This category covers software piracy, copyright violations, and counterfeiting of both software and hardware (Carter 4, 4 Nov. 1999).

With this new set of classifications, the United States has begun to establish an international prohibition regime which is a set of "norms and the processes by which they are enforced" on a global scale (Nadelmann 479, 1990). Nadelmann further argues that prohibition regimes are established only when crimes exhibit a "strong transnational dimension", excluding many types of crime which are left to the domestic enforcement agencies to handle (Nadelmann 481, 1990). Cybercrime fits quite well into the framework established by Nadelmann because it is a threat that exists in every country of the world that relies on computers. Furthermore, the perpetrators of these crimes are often in other countries than the scene of the crime creating a "transnational dimension". Nadelmann developed a set of five stages through which a prohibition regime must go through to be successful at eliminating a given problem or threat. Cybercrime falls into the third stage of this process. At this point the regime proponents, which include governments and moral entrepreneurs, begin to push for the "suppression and criminalization of the activity by all states and the formation of international conventions" (Nadelmann 485, 1990). Usually, the moral entrepreneurs, or the people that try to establish a prohibition regime, are individuals or members of nongovernment organizations. In the case of cybercrime, corporations join the list of moral entrepreneurs fighting against cybercrime because of the high level of risk that the corporations face. With corporations supporting the prohibition regime, it is likely that the regime will be established, if not succeed at its goal of eliminating cybercrime.

Analysis of the security threat

The single biggest factor in determining what does and what does not constitute a security threat are boundaries. These boundaries serve as indicators of what is secure or needs to be made secure. According to Lipschutz, these "boundaries are always under challenge and they must always be reestablished, not only on the ground but also in the mind" (224, 1995). Nowhere is this more true than in the realm of cyberspace, where new threats are constantly emerging and pushing boundaries of security. Until recently, many people did not consider cybercrimes a major threat, and as a result very little was modified in the security structures of the domestic and international complexes. Additionally, during the Cold War period the threats and their origins were known and understood (Lipschutz, 2, 1995). Now the problem lies in the fact that the source of the threat is unknown, as is the reasoning of the instigating actors.

For the analysis of cybercrimes and information warfare as a security threat, the pattern established by Buzan, Wæver, and de Wilde (1998) is useful. First, the cybercrime threat is a heterogeneous complex, that is a number of different actors are interacting in many different sectors. By comparison, in a homogeneous complex, the threat is confined to a few actors in one or two sectors. As a result, the dangers of cybercrime can come from any number of actors in numerous sectors ranging from military to societal sectors. Beyond the heterogeneous nature of the cybercrime complex, there is both an objective and a subjective threat embodied in this area. The objective threat has already been demonstrated by the numerous incidents of hackers breaking into the computers of governments, corporations, and organizations. The subjective threat is the basis for the information warfare arguments: that the potential for attack on key government and infrastructure systems is quite real.

The information warfare complex also has an objective side that has been demonstrated through tests conducted by governments working with hackers to test their computer systems. That hackers were able to enter the government and infrastructure systems suggests the potential to plant viruses or shut down the system entirely (Cilluffo, Berkowitz, and Lanz, 20, 1998). To this date, there has been very little information warfare, with the first incidents being practiced against the United States in the Persian Gulf, by the two teenagers in California in the "analyzer" example above. The number of information warfare attacks like this are growing. During the air raids on Kosovo, the United States "cyberwarriors" were trying to "drain the assets or alter banking records" of Slobodan Milosevic and other top officials. During this period the United States also detected many attempts to break into United States' computers (Becker 1, 1 Oct. 1999).

Beyond the heterogeneous versus homogeneous and objective versus sub-jective arguments there are the three major pieces of a security complex: referent objects, securitizing actors, and functional actors. The cybercrime threat fits into these three pieces, but there are some areas that are not fully covered by this typology. For Buzan, Wæver and de Wilde the referent ob-jects, or the "things that are being existentially threatened", are generally states or nations (Buzan, Wæver, and de Wilde 36, 1998). In some cases the economy or the environment fit into their referent object category, but the au-thors fail to discuss the place of corporations and organizations. Corporations and organizations are frequent targets of cybercrimals, particularly from com-peting entities stealing research secrets and confidential information. This is a very clear example of an existential threat, therefore, the referent object category needs to be expanded to include more than just states, economies, and the environment.

Securitizing actors are "actors who securitize issues by declaring some-thing – a referent object" (Buzan, Wæver, and de Wilde 36, 1998). Buzan, Wæver, and de Wilde's argument that government officials, lobbyists, bureau-cracies, and other individuals are generally the securitizing actors fits well with cybercrimes. These actors usually have to speak in terms of interna-tional, national, or social security to have their message accepted, even if the threat would only affect a small portion of that population (Buzan, Wæver, and de Wilde 40, 1998). The terms international, national, and social security have to be used by some securitizing actors to amplify small threats. The threat may not affect the majority of the population, which would result in the issue not receiving the attention that the actor feels it deserves. This pattern extends itself into cybercrimes because these are the same actors that are trying to securitize computers, the internet, and the users of these devices. Lastly functional actors "affect the dynamics of a sector" (Buzan, Wæver, and de Wilde 36, 1998). This category includes those who try to enforce the laws and those that break the laws. This is the category that truly distinguishes the cybercrime threat from other possible security violations. Functional actors can be identified by their actions within a given sector. For example, in the drug threat, the movement of Pablo Escobar up through the ranks to kingpin of the Medellín cartel has been traced by many law enforcement officials and scholars. The functional actors in cybercrimes are not as easily identified. Ob-viously the control and enforcement officials and the victims of cybercrimes can be identified. The perpetrators of these crimes are very difficult to distin-guish because they have many false identities that they use online. Therefore, when they are offline, the perpetrators have no connection to their online iden-tities or crimes. Thus it is very difficult to identify, arrest, and prosecute these criminals. Additionally, many times the criminals act from areas outside the jurisdiction of many enforcement officials. This makes arresting the offender very difficult, especially given the fact that no international treaties have been signed to facilitate the capture of these criminals.

Security structures

Most law enforcement and security structures are directed toward physical security threats with very little, if any, focus on cybercrime or information warfare threats. This problem is occurring at domestic and international levels, with most existing governments and enforcement agencies being slow to react to the threat. On a domestic level, most governments have been slow to pass legislation specifically targeting cybercrimes. Currently, the governments of developed countries throughout the world have passed some legislation dealing with cybercrime, but this legislation is slow and this threat is very dynamic. For example, one of the most important pieces of legislation dealing with cybercrime in the United States is the Computer Fraud and Abuse Act of 1986, now fourteen years old. Furthermore, this act deals primarily with federal computers, leaving out privately owned computers and networks. Another is example is the Computer Misuse Act of 1990 in the United Kingdom. This piece of legislation is more comprehensive than the United States act above because it applies to all computers, rather than just federal computers. Unfortunately, this document is almost ten years old and speaks in generalities about computers. The crimes are moving faster than the legislation, thus loopholes in the legislation can be found, because the laws do not exactly apply to many of the crimes.

Beyond the slow and somewhat ineffective legislation are problems with the enforcement agencies. Many local police do not have the knowledge nor the equipment necessary to enforce laws against cybercrimes. In many national enforcement agencies the cybercrime department has just recently been started or does not exist at all. The United States Federal Bureau of Investigation has a cybercrime unit that has been growing continuously since its inception. Recently, the FBI asked for $74 million to improve their information technology equipment as well as train more agents to effectively fight cybercrime (Tillett, 1, 24 March 1999). In Great Britain, the National Crime Intelligence Service is launching a cybercrime squad, that will be assisted by the MI5 Intelligence service and the GCHQ, the British spy center. This squad will fight against computer aided money laundering, fraud, and will share information about hacking, pedophilia, and counterfeiting (NCIS, 1, 17 Jan 2000). Cybercrime departments in enforcement agencies are not only occurring in developed nations, but also in developing nations. For example, in India the Central Bureau of Investigation (CBI) is introducing the Information Technology bill to "help check computer crime and legalize electronic transactions" (India, 1, 25 Feb 1999). Moreover, Indian officials realize that they are behind in adopting computer systems, but want Indian enforcement agents to be able to effectively use a computer and fight cybercrime in the future. Furthermore, these organizations have limited staffs that cannot track all the cybercrimes that have been committed. To avoid this problem the United States Securities Exchange Commission (SEC) has obtained the help of 125 volunteer agents that will help investigate potentially fraudulent activities. Additionally, the SEC relies on other individuals and institutions to provide approximately 120 tips per day about activities and individuals that need to be investigated (Woody, 1, 16 Nov 1998).

Internationally, the security structures to combat cybercrime are worse than those at the domestic level. The international security structures are virtually non-existent because the high levels of cooperation between countries necessary have not been forthcoming. To apprehend many of the more dangerous criminals, international cooperation is vital. Countries around the world see that this cooperation is necessary, and, as mentioned above, have been holding conferences. Loose agreements are the only thing that have come of these conferences thus far because cooperation infringes upon state power and sovereignty. Governments realize that as the world becomes more interdependent, they will lose more of their sovereignty to international organizations and treaties. Therefore, opposition to cooperation is prevalent, but as the cybercrime threat continues to grow, more agreements and cooperation will occur. One of the few examples of international cooperation is between the United States and India. The United States has been helping India establish a cybercrime division in the CBI ("India", 1, 25 Feb 1999).

At this point in time, cybercrime is seen as a lesser threat on the international level, much like the threats presented by money laundering and trafficking in women for the international sex trade. These three types of transnational crime, all are growing in importance and the level of attention that they command, yet are still not on the same level of importance as arms trafficking and the drug trade. When cybercrime becomes a greater threat, most likely due to a major incident or attack, the level of cooperation will increase. Cybercrime will then be more comparable to the drug trade or trafficking arms, both of which command much greater levels of international cooperation.

Many things need to be done in order to improve the security structures so that they will be effective in combating cybercrime. Domestically, the most necessary improvement to the system would be funding. With additional funding security agencies and local police would be able to buy new equipment and train officers to handle cybercrime threats. This necessary funding is now just beginning to be provided as the number of cybercrimes continues to increase at a rapid rate. For example, the United States is now giving scholarships for students studying information technology and computer security. In exchange for the scholarships, the students will work for the federal government in the Federal Cyber Services division for a set period of time (Brewin, 1, 17 Jan 2000).

When increasing enforcement agencies, the potential for corruption also increases. The number of officers fighting cybercrime that will become corrupt is much lower than with other criminal activities, such as drug trafficking, because there is much less money involved in cybercrime. Furthermore, education of the civilian population about what is and is not legal when dealing with computers is necessary. With an educated population, less ordinary people would commit cybercrimes, thus reducing the work load for the national agencies. Not only would the work load be reduced, but the gray areas surrounding cybercrimes would also be lessened.

Internationally, the single biggest improvement to the security structure would be working multilateral agreements, particularly between the developed nations. These multilateral agreements would allow for high levels of cooperation between countries and their enforcement agencies. Additionally, many of the jurisdiction difficulties between countries would be eliminated. The first example of a multilateral agreement is beginning to take shape in the European Union with the data privacy directive. This directive is designed to establish "a common regulatory framework for data transmission, to ensure both a high level of privacy for the individual and free movement of data within the EU (de Bony, 1, 17 Jan 2000)." By October 1998 all fifteen member nations were to have implemented this directive, but only six of the nations met this deadline. Another four nations complied by August 1999. France, Germany, Ireland, Luxembourg, and the Netherlands all have yet to implement the directive, as a result, the European Commission is taking these countries to the European Court of Justice to have the matter resolved. The lack of implementation by some of the most powerful countries in the European Union illustrates some of the difficulties with establishing multilateral agreements dealing with cybercrime.

Another possibility to enhance the security structure would be an international organization dealing specifically with cybercrimes. This type of organization would possibly be an extension of the United Nations (UN), the North Atlantic Treaty Organization (NATO), Interpol, or would be independent. Such an organization would help facilitate cooperation in the apprehension of cybercriminals and building secure computer networks. If the organization was part of the United Nations, it would often be bogged down by the politics of competing nations within the UN, and not be as effective as possible.

Additionally, this organization does not seem as though it would have a place within the UN. A more positive aspect of being part of the UN would be the jurisdictional reach the structure would have in all parts of the world. If such a security structure was part of NATO, it would be much more limited in jurisdictional reach given fewer countries are NATO members. Additionally, many governments might be concerned about the fact that NATO is a military organization and the potential for abuse of sensitive information and power for military or other purposes would exist. If the concerns about abuse could be overcome, this structure could become quite effective because of the resources available to it through NATO. Interpol would be the best choice for the structure because the jurisdictional reach would be large and the concerns about military abuse of information would not be an issue. If such a security structure was independent, it would face many difficulties because few governments would trust a new organization. Therefore, much of the organization's initial years would be spent building political trust and clout rather than serving as a means to deter cybercrime.

The CERT® Coordination Center at Carnegie Mellon University has been working with the United States government and many corporations since 1988 after a cybercrime has been committed. This organization was initially a computer incident response unit. An incident is defined by the organization as "the act of violating an explicit or implied security policy" (CERT (4) 6 Dec. 1999). The CERT® Coordination Center has now branched out beyond this task to help start other incident response teams and coordinate large scale operations between many teams. Additionally, this team has been researching the causes and prevention methods of security vulnerabilities, as well as improvement of security systems. This organization could be an example from which to build an international security complex. Furthermore, the need for such an organization is very evident by looking at statistics produced by the CERT® Coordination Team. In 1988, the team handled six incidents, ten years later in 1998 they dealt with 3,734 incidents. This number has almost doubled in the first three quarters of 1999, with 6,844 incidents handled (CERT (3) 6 Dec. 1999).

Conclusion

Unfortunately, most of the necessary modifications and additions to the cybercrime security structure will not occur until after a major attack on a government system takes place. A large number of attacks on critical corporations and industries within a country also could trigger support. If these attacks occur, it would be very difficult to build an effective defense because many new perpetrators would attack after seeing that there is a poor defense system. The damage that would have to be done to the government or corporations of a country would have to be devastating, causing a shut down in the computer systems of the victim to generate the support to build a security structure. The necessary levels of destruction, damage, and loss of valuable resources to bring cybercrime to the forefront of security threats is nearing. In 1999 spending on eradication and protection against computer viruses as well as lost productivity around the world totaled $12.1 billion (Fonseca, 1, 18 Jan 2000). As figures like these continue to grow, more countries will take notice and start taking more action against cybercrime. Additionally, once one or two developed nations establish strong security structures, many other countries will follow their lead and develop their own structures. Again, this would further assist cooperation between nations. After a major attack has transpired, funding will become readily available for building a strong security structure. Until that time, funding will continue to be limited, as will support for the agencies currently fighting the cybercrime threat.

The new threats of cybercrime and information warfare have not yet become a major security issue in most countries. In the near future, as the threat grows and more examples of cybercrime and information warfare are seen, this will become a major security issue. When governments and corporations take this threat seriously, many resources will be directed toward eliminating it. These resources should be used to modify existing security structures and create new ones. Additionally, the resources must be used on an international level to create multilateral agreements between nations about cooperation and jurisdiction issues. Not only must these areas be addressed, but efforts must be put forth to understand why these criminals commit these crimes, and what measures can be taken to stop them. Overall, the threat of cybercrime is very large now, and will only continue to grow as more of the world becomes knowledgeable about computers and other technological equipment. This threat can be curbed now in its early phase, or later when the threat is much larger. This depends on what actions the governments and corporations of the world decide to take now.

References

Becker, Elizabeth, "Pentagon Sets Up New Center for Waging Cyberwarfare," *New York Times* 1 Oct 1999.

Brewin, Bob, "Government Wooing Best and Brightest for Cyberdefense Mission," *Federal Computer Week* 17 Jan 1999.

Buzan, Barry, Wæver, Ole, and de Wilde, Jaap, *Security: A New Framework for Analysis* (Boulder, CO: Lynne Rienner Publishers, 1998).

Carter, David L., *Computer Crime Categories: How Techno-criminals Operate*. Accessed 4 Nov. 1999. http://nsi.org/Library/Compsec/crimecom.html.

272   DAVID L. SPEER

CERT® Coordination Center, Homepage and other pages. Accessed 6 Dec. 1999.
    (1) http://www.cert.org, (2) www.cert.org/nav/aboutcert.html,
    (3) www.cert.org/stats/cert_stats.html,
    (4) www.cert.org/tech_tips/incident_response.html.
Cilluffo, Frank J., Berkowitz, Bruce D., Lanz, Stephanie, *Cybercrime ... Cyberterrorism ...
    Cyberwarfare ...: Averting an Electronic Waterloo* (Washington, D.C.: The CSIS Press,
    1998).
Computer Fraud and Abuse Act 1986 (US) 18 USC 1030. Accessed 7 Dec. 1999.
    http://www.austlii.edu.au/au/other/crime/123.html.
Computer Misuse Act 1990 (UK) Accessed 7 Dec.
    1999. http://www.austlli.edu.au/au/other/crime/125.html.
de Bony, Elizabeth, *EC Takes Countries to Court on Data Privacy* 17 Jan 1999. Accessed 18
    Jan. 1999. http://www.idg.net.
Denning, Dorothy E., *Information Warfare and Security* (New York: ACM Press; Reading,
    MA: Addison-Wesley, 1999).
Ehud Tenebaum (AKA "analyzer") Arrested in Israel Associated Press 18 Mar 1998.
European Union, Committee of Ministers to the Member States. "Recommendation No. R
    (95) 13" 11 Sept 1995. http://www.usdoj.gov/criminal/cybercrime/cryoe.htm .
Federal Bureau of Investigation Nation Computer Crime Squad. Home Page. Accessed 4 Nov.
    1999. http://www.fbi.gov.
Fijnaut, Cyrille, Marx, Gary T. *Undercover: Police Surveillance in Comparative Perspective*
    (The Hague: Kluwer Law International, 1995).
Friman, Richard H., Andreas, Peter, *The Illicit Global Economy and State Power* (Lanham:
    Rowman & Littlefield Publishers Inc., 1999).
Fonseca, Brian. "$12.1 billion reportedly spent to ward off computer viruses in 1999,"
    InfoWorld 18 Jan 1999.
G8 Birmingham Summit 1998. Homepage. Accessed 4 Nov 1999.
    http://www.g8summit.gov.uk/
G8 Denver Summit 1997 document, *Communiqué Annex: Action Plan to Combat High-Tech
    Crime* Accessed 4 Nov 1999. http://www.usdoj.gov/criminal/cybercrime/action.htm.
G8 Denver Summit 1997 document, *Communiqué Annex: Principles to Combat High-Tech
    Crime* Accessed 4 Nov 1999. http://www.usdoj.gov/criminal/cybercrime/principles.htm.
"India to Police Internet Abuse, Cyber Crimes," *Reuters* 25 Feb 1999.
Joubert, Chantal, Bevers, Hans, *Schengen Investigated* (The Hague: Kluwer Law International,
    1996).
Lipschitz, Ronnie D., *On Security* (New York: Colombia University Press, 1995).
Markoff, John "New Center Will Combat Computer Security Threats," *New York Times* 1 Oct
    1999.
Meeting of the Justice and Interior Ministers of the Eight December 9–10, 1997, *Communiqué*
    Accessed 4 Nov 1999. http://www.usdoj.gov/criminal/cybercrime/communique.htm.
"Modem on the Desk Earns a Pink Slip at Sun," *Network Week* 18 Mar 1998.
Nadelmann, Ethan A, *Cops Across Borders: the Internationalization or US Criminal Law
    Enforcement* (University Park, PA: Pennsylvania State University Press, 1993).
Nadelmann, Ethan A, "Global Prohibition Regimes: the Evolution of Norms in International
    Security," *International Organization* Autumn 1990, 479–526.
Platt, Charles, *Anarchy Online: Net Crime/Net Sex* (New York: HaperPaperbacks, 1996).
RSA convention, Homepage. Accessed 4 Nov 1999.
    http://www.rsa.com/conf99/overview.html.

REDEFINING BORDERS: THE CHALLENGES OF CYBERCRIME 273

Schwartau, Winn, "Striking Back Corporate Vigilantes go on the Offensive to Hunt Down Hackers," *Network World* 11 Jan 1999.

Tillett, L. Scott, "IT Key to FBI's Future," *Federal Computer Week* 24 Mar 1999. http://www.idg.net accessed 19 Jan 2000.

"UK Reportedly to Launch National Cybercrime Squad," *Reuters* 17 Jan 1999.

Woody, Todd, "The SEC's Internet Ranger John Reed Stark, Internet Enforcement Chief, Surfs the Web for Scams," www.thestandard.com 16 Nov. 1998. Accessed 18 Jan. 1999.

[14]

GEORGE SMITH

An Electronic Pearl Harbor? Not Likely

The government's evidence about U.S. vulnerability to cyber attack is shaky at best.

Information warfare: The term conjures up a vision of unseen enemies, armed only with laptop personal computers connected to the global computer network, launching untraceable electronic attacks against the United States. Blackouts occur nationwide, the digital information that constitutes the national treasury is looted electronically, telephones stop ringing, and emergency services become unresponsive.

But is such an electronic Pearl Harbor possible? Although the media are full of scary-sounding stories about violated military Web sites and broken security on public and corporate networks, the menacing scenarios have remained just that—only scenarios. Information warfare may be, for many, the hip topic of the moment, but a factually solid knowledge of it remains elusive.

There are a number of reasons why this is so. The private sector will not disclose much information about any potential vulnerabilities, even confidentially to the government. The Pentagon and other government agencies maintain that a problem exists

but say that the information is too sensitive to be disclosed. Meanwhile, most of the people who know something about the subject are on the government payroll or in the business of selling computer security devices and in no position to serve as objective sources.

There may indeed be a problem. But the only basis on which we have to judge that at the moment is the sketchy information that the government has thus far provided. An examination of that evidence casts a great deal of doubt on the claims.

Computer-age ghost stories

Hoaxes and myths about info-war and computer security—the modern equivalent of ghost stories—contaminate everything from newspaper stories to official reports. Media accounts are so distorted or error-ridden that they are useless as a barometer of the problem. The result has been predictable: confusion over what is real and what is not.

A fairly common example of the type of misinformation that circulates on the topic is illustrated by an article published in the December 1996 issue of the FBI's *Law & Enforcement Bulletin*. Entitled "Computer Crime: An Emerging Challenge for Law Enforcement," the piece was written by academics from Michigan State and Wichita State Universities.

George Smith of Pasadena, California, edits *The Crypt Newsletter*, an Internet publication dealing with computer security. He is the author of *The Virus Creation Labs: A Journey into the Underground* (American Eagle, 1994).

INFORMATION WARFARE

Written as an introduction to computer crime and the psychology of hackers, the article presented a number of computer viruses as examples of digital vandals' tools.

A virus called "Clinton," wrote the authors, "is designed to infect programs, but . . . eradicates itself when it cannot decide which program to infect." Both the authors and the FBI were embarrassed to be informed later that there was no such virus as "Clinton." It was a joke, as were all the other examples of viruses cited in the article. They had all been originally published in an April Fool's Day column of a computer magazine.

The FBI article was a condensed version of a longer scholarly paper presented by the authors at a meeting of the Academy of Criminal Justice Sciences in Las Vegas in 1996. Entitled "Trends and Experiences in Computer-Related Crime: Findings from a National Study," the paper told of a government dragnet in which federal agents arrested a dangerously successful gang of hackers. "The hackers reportedly broke into a NASA computer responsible for controlling the Hubble telescope and are also known to have rerouted telephone calls from the White House to Marcel Marceau University, a miming institute," wrote the authors of their findings. This anecdote, too, was a rather obvious April Fool's joke that the authors had unwittingly taken seriously.

The FBI eventually recognized the errors in its journal and performed a half-hearted edit of the paper posted on its Web site. Nevertheless, the damage was done. The FBI magazine had already been sent to 55,000 law enforcement professionals, some of them decisionmakers and policy analysts. Because the article was written for those new to the subject, it is reasonable to assume that it was taken very seriously by those who read it.

Hoaxes about computer viruses have propagated much more successfully than the real things. The myths reach into every corner of modern computing society, and no one is immune. Even those we take to be authoritative on the subject can be unreliable. In 1997, members of a government commission headed by Sen. Daniel Moynihan (D-N.Y.), which included former directors of the Central Intelligence Agency and the National Reconnaissance Office, were surprised to find that a hoax had contaminated a chapter addressing computer security in their report on reducing government secrecy. "One company whose

officials met with the commission warned its employees against reading an e-mail entitled Penpal Greetings," the Moynihan commission report stated. "Although the message appeared to be a friendly letter, it contained a virus that could infect the hard drive and destroy all data present. The virus was self-replicating, which meant that once the message was read, it would automatically forward itself to any e-mail address stored in the recipient's in-box."

Penpal Greetings and dozens of other nonexistent variations on the same theme are believed to be real to such an extent that many computer security experts and antivirus software developers find themselves spending more time defusing the hoaxes than educating people about the real thing. In the case of Penpal, these are the facts: A computer virus is a very small program designed to spread by attaching itself to other bits of executable program code, which act as hosts for it. The host code can be office applications, utility programs, games, or special documents created by Microsoft Word that contain embedded computer instructions called macro commands—but not standard text electronic mail. For Penpal to be real would require all electronic mail to contain executable code automatically run when someone opens an e-mail message. Penpal could not have done what was claimed.

That said, there is still plenty of opportunity for malicious meddling, and because of it, thousands of destructive computer viruses have been written for the PC by bored teenagers, college students, computer science undergraduates, and disgruntled programmers during the past decade. It does not take a great leap of logic to realize that the popular myths such as Penpal have contributed to the sense, often mentioned by those writing about information warfare, that viruses can be used as weapons of mass destruction.

Virus writers have been avidly thinking about this mythical capability for years, and many viruses have been written with malicious intent. None have shown any utility as weapons. Most attempts to make viruses for use as directed weapons fail for easily understandable reasons. First, it is almost impossible for even the most expert virus writer to anticipate the sheer complexity and heterogeneity of systems the virus will encounter. Second, simple human error is always present. It is an unpleasant fact of life that all software, no matter how well-behaved, harbors errors often unnoticed by its authors. Computer viruses are no exception. They usually contain errors, frequently such spectacular ones that they barely function at all.

Of course, it is still possible to posit a small team of dedicated professionals employed by a military organization that could achieve far more success than some alienated teen hackers. But assembling such a team would not be easy. Even though it's not that difficult for those with basic programming skills to write malicious software, writing a really sophisticated computer virus requires some intimate knowledge of the operating system it is written to work within and the hardware it will be expected to encounter. Those facts narrow the field of potential professional virus designers considerably.

Next, our virus-writing team leader would have to come to grips with the reality, if he's working in the free world, that the pay for productive work in the private sector is a lot more attractive than anything he can offer. Motivation—in terms of remuneration, professional satisfaction, and the recognition that one is actually making something other people can use—would be a big problem for any virus-writing effort attempting to operate in a professional or military setting. Another factor our virus developer would need to consider is that there are no schools turning out information technology professionals who have been trained in virus writing.

And computer viruses come with a feature that is anathema to a military mind. In an era of smart bombs, computer viruses are hardly precision-guided munitions. Those that spread do so unpredictably and are as likely to infect the computers of friends and allies as enemies. With militaries around the world using commercial off-the-shelf technology, there simply is no haven safe from potential blow-back by one's creation. What can infect your enemy can infect you. In addition, any military commander envisioning the use of computer viruses would have to plan for a reaction by the international antivirus industry, which is well positioned after years of development to provide an antidote to any emerging computer virus.

To be successful, computer viruses must be able to spread unnoticed. Those that do have payloads that

Hoaxes and myths about information warfare contaminate everything from official reports to newspaper stories.

go off with a bang or cause poor performance on an infected system get noticed and immediately eliminated. Our virus-writing pros would have to spend a lot of time on intelligence, gaining intimate knowledge of the targeted systems and the ways in which they are used, so their viruses could be written to be maximally compatible. To get that kind of information, the team would need an insider or insiders. But with insiders, computer viruses become irrelevant. In such a situation, it becomes far easier and far more final to have the inside agent use a hammer on the network server at an inopportune moment.

But what if, with all the caveats attached, computer viruses were still deployed as weapons in a future war? The answer might be, "So what?" Computer viruses are already blamed, wrongly, for many of the mysterious software conflicts, inexplicable system crashes, and losses of data and operability that make up the general background noise of modern personal computing. In such a world, if someone launched a few extra computer viruses into the mix, it's quite likely that no one would notice.

Hackers as nuisances

What about the direct effects of system-hacking intruders? To examine this issue, it is worth examining in detail one series of intrusions by two young British men at the Air Force's Rome Labs in Rome, New York, in 1994. This break-in became the centerpiece of a U.S. General Accounting Office (GAO) report on network intrusions at the Department of Defense (DOD) and was much discussed during congressional hearings on hacker break-ins the same year. The ramifications of the Rome break-ins are still being felt in 1998.

One of the men, Richard Pryce, was originally noticed on Rome computers on March 28, 1994, when personnel discovered a program called a "sniffer" he had placed on one of the Air Force systems to capture passwords and user log-ins to the network. A team of computer scientists was promptly sent to Rome to investigate and trace those responsible. They soon found that Pryce had a partner named Matthew Bevan.

Since the monitoring was of limited value in determining the whereabouts of Pryce and Bevan, investigators resorted to questioning informants they found on the Net. They sought hacker groupies, usually other young men wishing to be associated with those more skilled at hacking and even more eager to brag about their associations. Gossip from one of these Net stoolies revealed that Pryce was a 16-year-old hacker from Britain who ran a home-based bulletin board system; its telephone number was given to the Air Force. Air Force investigators subsequently contacted New Scotland Yard, which found out where Pryce lived.

By mid-April 1994, Air Force investigators had agreed that the intruders would be allowed to continue so their comings and goings could be used as a learning experience. On April 14, Bevan logged on to the Goddard Space Center in Greenbelt, Maryland, from a system in Latvia and copied data from it to the Baltic country. According to one Air Force report, the worst was assumed: Someone in an eastern European country was making a grab for sensitive information. The connection was broken. As it turned out, the Latvian computer was just another system that the British hackers were using as a stepping stone.

On May 12, not long after Pryce had penetrated a system in South Korea and copied material off a facility called the Korean Atomic Research Institute to an Air Force computer in Rome, British authorities finally arrested him. Pryce admitted to the Air Force break-ins as well as others. He was charged with 12 separate offenses under the British Computer Misuse Act. Eventually he pleaded guilty to minor charges in connection with the break-ins and was fined 1,200 English pounds. Bevan was arrested in 1996 after information on him was recovered from Pryce's computer. In late 1997, he walked out of a south London Crown Court when English prosecutors conceded it wasn't worth trying him on the basis of evidence submitted by the Air Force. He was deemed no threat to national computer security.

Pryce and Bevan had accomplished very little on their joyride through the Internet. Although they had made it into congressional hearings and been the object of much worried editorializing in the mainstream press, they had nothing to show for it except legal bills, some fines, and a reputation for shady behavior. Like the subculture of virus writers, they were little more than time-wasting petty nuisances.

But could a team of dedicated computer saboteurs accomplish more? Could such a team plant mis-

information or contaminate a logistical database so that operations dependent on information supplied by the system would be adversely influenced? Maybe, maybe not. As in the case of the writing of malicious software for a targeted computer system, a limiting factor not often discussed is knowledge about the system they are attacking. With little or no inside knowledge, the answer is no. The saboteurs would find themselves in the position of Pryce and Bevan, joyriding through a system they know little about.

Altering a database or issuing reports and commands that would withstand harsh scrutiny of an invaded system's users without raising eyebrows requires intelligence that can only be supplied by an insider. An inside agent nullifies the need for a remote computer saboteur or information warrior. He can disrupt the system himself.

The implications of the Pryce/Bevan experience, however, were not lost on Air Force computer scientists. What was valuable about the Rome intrusions is that they forced those sent to stop the hackers into dealing with technical issues very quickly. As a result, Air Force Information Warfare Center computer scientists were able to develop a complete set of software tools to handle such intrusions. And although little of this was discussed in the media or in congressional meetings, the software and techniques developed gave the Air Force the capability of conducting real-time perimeter defense on its Internet sites should it choose to do so.

The computer scientists involved eventually left the military for the private sector and took their software, now dubbed NetRanger, with them. As a company called WheelGroup, bought earlier this year by Cisco Systems, they sell NetRanger and Net security services to DOD clients.

Inflated numbers

A less beneficial product of the incidents at Rome Labs was the circulation of a figure that has been used as an indicator of computer break-ins at DOD since 1996. The figure, furnished by the Defense Information Systems Agency (DISA) and published in the GAO report on the Rome Labs case, quoted a figure of 250,000 hacker intrusions into DOD computers in 1995. Taken at face value, this would seem to be a very alarming figure, suggesting that Pentagon computers are under almost continuous assault by malefactors. This number has shown up literally hundreds of times since then in magazines, newspapers, and reports.

But the figure is not and has never been a real number. It is a guess, based on a much smaller number of recorded intrusions in 1995. And the smaller number is usually never mentioned when the alarming figure is cited. At a recent Pentagon press conference, DOD spokesman Kenneth H. Bacon acknowledged that the DISA figure was an estimate and that DISA received reports of about 500 actual incidents in 1995. Because DISA believed that only 0.2 percent of all intrusions are reported, it multiplied its figure by 500 and came up with 250,000.

Kevin Ziese, the computer scientist who led the Rome Labs investigation, called the figure bogus in a January 1998 interview with Time Inc.'s *Netly News*. Ziese said that the original DISA figure was inflated by instances of legitimate user screwups and unexplained but harmless probes sent to DOD computers. But since 1995, the figure has been continually misrepresented as a solid metric of intrusions on U.S. military networks and has been very successful in selling the point that the nation's computers are vulnerable to attack.

In late February 1998, Deputy Secretary of Defense John Hamre made news when he announced that DOD appeared to be under a cyber attack. Although a great deal of publicity was generated by the announcement, when the dust cleared the intrusions were no more serious than the Rome Labs break-ins in 1994. Once again it was two teenagers, this time from northern California, who had been successful at a handful of nuisance penetrations. In the period between when the media focused on the affair and the FBI began its investigation, the teens strutted and bragged for *Anti-Online*, an Internet-based hacker fanzine, exaggerating their abilities for journalists.

Not everyone was impressed. Ziese dismissed the hackers as "ankle-biters" in the *Wall Street Journal*. Another computer security analyst, quoted in the same article, called them the virtual equivalent of a "kid walking into the Pentagon cafeteria."

> *The time and effort spent dreaming up scary info-war scenarios would be better spent bolstering basic computer security.*

Why, then, had there been such an uproar? Part of the explanation lies in DOD's apparently short institutional memory. Attempts to interview Hamre or a DOD subordinate in June 1998 to discuss and contrast the differences between the Rome incidents in 1994 and the more recent intrusions were turned down. Why? Astonishingly, it was simply because no current top DOD official currently dealing with the issue had been serving in that same position in 1994, according to a Pentagon spokesperson.

Info-war myths

Another example of the jump from alarming scenario to done deal was presented in the National Security Agency (NSA) exercise known as "Eligible Receiver." As a war game designed to simulate vulnerability to electronic attack, one phase of it posited that an Internet message claiming that the 911 system had failed had been e-mailed to as many people as possible. The NSA information warriors took for granted that everyone reading it would immediately panic and call 911, causing a nationwide overload and system crash. It's a naïve assumption that ignores a number of rather obvious realities, each capable of derailing it. First, a true nationwide problem with the 911 system would be more likely to be reported on TV than the on Internet, which penetrates far fewer households. Second, many Internet users, already familiar with an assortment of Internet hoaxes and mean-spirited practical jokes, would not be fooled and would take their own steps to debunk it. Finally, a significant portion of U.S. inner-city populations reliant on 911 service are not hooked to the Internet and cannot be reached by e-mail spoofs. Nevertheless, "It can probably be done, this sort of an attack, by a handful of folks working together," claimed one NSA representative in the Atlanta *Constitution*. As far as info-war scenarios went, it was bogus.

However, with regard to other specific methods employed in Eligible Receiver, the Pentagon has remained vague. In a speech in Aspen, Colorado, in late July 1998, the Pentagon's Hamre said that the exercise demonstrated that a small team of computer attackers could take down the country's power system. The Pentagon has consistently refused to provide substantive proof, other than its say-so, that such a feat is possible, claiming that it must protect sensitive information. The Pentagon's stance is in stark contrast to the wide-open discussions of computer security vulnerabilities that reign on the Internet. On the Net, even the most obscure flaws in computer operating system software are immediately thrust into the public domain, where they are debated, tested, almost instantly distributed from hacker Web sites, and exposed to sophisticated academic scrutiny. Until DOD becomes more open, claims such as those presented by Eligible Receiver must be treated with a high degree of skepticism.

In the same vein, computer viruses and software used by hackers are not weapons of mass destruction. It is overreaching for the Pentagon to classify such things with nuclear weapons and nerve gas. They can't reduce cities to cinders. Insisting on classifying them as such suggests that the countless American teenagers who offer viruses and hacker tools on the Web are terrorists on a par with Hezbollah, a ludicrous assumption.

Seeking objectivity

Another reason to be skeptical of the warnings about information warfare is that those who are most alarmed are often the people who will benefit from government spending to combat the threat. A primary author of a January 1997 Defense Science Board report on information warfare, which recommended an immediate $580-million investment in private sector R&D for hardware and software to implement computer security, was Duane Andrews, executive vice president of SAIC, a computer security vendor and supplier of information warfare consulting services.

Assessments of the threats to the nation's computer security should not be furnished by the same firms and vendors who supply hardware, software, and consulting services to counter the "threat." Instead, an independent group should be set up to provide such assessments and evaluate the claims of computer security software and hardware vendors. Its assessments, evaluations, and war game results should not be classified.

Although there have been steps taken in this direction by the National Institute of Standards and

Technology, a handful of other military agencies, and some independent academic groups, they are still not enough. NSA also performs such an evaluative function, but its mandate for secrecy and classification too often means that its findings are inaccessible to those who need them or, even worse, useless because NSA members are not free to discuss them in detail.

The time and effort expended on dreaming up potentially catastrophic information warfare scenarios could be better spent implementing consistent and widespread policies and practices in basic computer security. Although computer security is the problem of everyone who works with computers, it is still practiced half-heartedly throughout much of the military, the government, and corporate America. If organizations don't intend to be serious about security, they simply should not be hooking their computers to the Internet. DOD in particular would be better served if it stopped wasting time trying to develop offensive info-war capabilities and put more effort into basic computer security practices.

It is far from proven that the country is at the mercy of possible devastating computerized attacks. On the other hand, even the small number of examples of malicious behavior examined here demonstrate that computer security issues in our increasingly technological world will be of primary concern well into the foreseeable future. These two statements are not mutually exclusive, and policymakers must be skeptical of the Chicken Littles, the unsupported claim pushing a product, and the hoaxes and electronic ghost stories of our time.

Recommended reading

Computer Underground Digest
    (http://www.soci.niu.edu/~cudigest) and RISKS
    Journal (http://catless.ncl.uk/Risks/VL.IS.html).
President's Commission on Critical Infrastructure Protection, *Critical Foundations: Protecting America's Infrastructure* (http://www. pccip.gov).
The Federation of American Scientists' Information
    Warfare on the Web clearinghouse (http://www.
    fas.org/irp/wwwinfo.html).
Clifford Stoll, *Silicon Snake Oil: Second Thoughts on
    the Information Highway*. New York: Doubleday,
    1995.
Virus Myths: Web site (http://www.kumite.com/myths).

[15]

The Worldwide Search for Techno-thieves: International Competition v. International Co-operation

HEDIEH NASHERI and TIMOTHY J O'HEARN

ABSTRACT *In an age of explosive worldwide growth of electronic data storage and communications, many vital interests require the effective protection of information. Today's information age requires businesses to compete on a worldwide basis, sharing sensitive information with appropriate parties while protecting that information against competitors, vandals, suppliers, customers, and foreign governments. Elements of the US civilian infrastructure, such as the banking system, the electric power grid, the public switched telecommunications network, and the air traffic control system, are central to so many dimensions of modern life that protecting these elements must have a high priority. Governments have an important stake in assuring that rival nations do not appropriate technology.*

The rapid growth of computing and communications technologies (collectively known as 'information technologies') and the increasingly global nature of commerce and business apparently have caused an increase in economic espionage.[1] The objective of this article is to examine the law enforcement policies and practices relating to economic espionage in the USA.

The significance of economic espionage is evident from recent developments in the USA. In the first part of this decade, there was anxiety among economists, politicians and members of the news media over the apparent decline in living standards in America in the last quarter of a century. In response, the Clinton administration emphasized the importance of securing the continued development of technologically sophisticated jobs so that the standard of living would not be dragged down by the competition and cheap labor of less developed countries.

Technological advances are making the leakage of technology through corporate spying and theft of 'intellectual capital' both easier and cheaper. Economic espionage is carried out to gain access to corporate strategic plans, to research and development information, and to manufacturing process data. The power of computer technology has increased the means available for the theft and transfer of trade secret information. Modern communications

Correspondence: H Nasheri, Justice Studies at Kent State University, Kent, Ohio, USA, and T J O'Hearn, Intellectual Property Practice, Jones, Day, Reavis & Pogue, Cleveland, Ohio, USA.

ISSN 1369-0869 Print; 1364-6885 Online/99/030373-10 © 1999 Taylor & Francis Ltd

connectivity, commercial enterprise activities, and the posting and accessibility of corporate data on computer systems have made it easier to copy and transfer valuable trade secret information. In remarks to the US Chamber of Commerce on Corporate Vulnerability to Economic Espionage, FBI Director, Louis Freeh, talked about two examples of recent high-tech crime cases. The first involved an individual, who was sitting at home in Russia, with a laptop computer, which he used to break into a New York City bank. He stole, or attempted to steal, several millions of dollars. It apparently took some time for the defense mechanism and detection mechanism of the renowned bank to identify the problem and prevent most of the loss. The second case involved another individual in another country, entertaining himself on his laptop computer, which he used to hack his way into a computer in Northern Florida and started to shut down for several hours each, in various communities, the 911 systems, which are the police, fire and rescue emergency telephone systems. According to the FBI, these cases are representative of many other computer intrusion cases.[2]

The Need for Global Action

The importance of this topic in the international arena was discussed at length in a Manual published by the United Nations entitled: *International Review of Criminal Policy—United Nations Manual on the Prevention and Control of Computer-Related Crime*.[3] This and other publications recognize the ever-increasing threat of economic espionage to global security and sustainability. For example, the Annual Report to Congress on Foreign Economic Collection and Industrial Espionage reported the following 'Key Findings':

- Despite the adoption [in the US] of the Economic Espionage Act of 1996, many foreign countries, including some traditional US allies, continue their attempt to acquire US trade secret information and critical technologies for military and commercial application, through both legal and illegal means.
- Updated information, as reported by the US Intelligence Community, reaffirms the findings of the 1997 Annual Report to Congress on Foreign Economic Collection and Industrial Espionage to include the origin of the threat, collection targets, and methods of operation.
- Analysis of updated information indicates that eight countries are most actively targeting US proprietary economic information, trade secrets, and critical technologies.
- Collection efforts continue to be driven by military force modernization, economic competition, and commercial modernization using technologies with dual-use applications.
- Clandestine collection efforts continue; however, consistent with traditional espionage operations, a significant majority to foreign intelligence collection is initially conducted through legal and open means and may be a precursor to economic espionage.[4]

According to the Center for Strategic and International Studies, cyber-terrorists, high-tech crooks and mischievous hackers present a growing threat to America's economic, social, governmental and defense institutions. As the Center's report stated, 'bytes, not bullets, are the new ammo'. The report noted the growing threat of international electronic crime, citing FBI information that nearly all the Fortune 500 corporations 'have been penetrated electronically by cyber-criminals', who are stealing an estimated $10 billion a year. Arnaud De Borchgrave, a former newspaper and magazine publisher who directed the study, reports that at least 30 countries, 'including some very close to the United States', have attempted to break into sensitive American computer systems.[5]

As these government and private sector investigations indicate, the spy of the future is less likely to resemble James Bond, whose chief assets were his fists, than the engineer who lives quietly down the street and never does anything more violent than turn a page of a manual or flick on his computer.[6] The ground rules have changed, and the battlefield among competing nations is now economic rather than ideological.

Espionage in the 1990s is enhanced by the ruins of the cold war spy regimes. Newly configured, the secret operations of America's enemies (and friends) threaten to hollow out the economy and siphon away some of the jobs and technologies needed to remain competitive in the 21st century. The techno-thieves have many tools, but their principal weapon is the openness of American society, and the defenders are hobbled by victim companies too embarrassed to complain, as well as by laws aimed at nineteenth-century threats.[7]

International Co-operation vs International Competition

There are a number of complex issues to confront, given the multiplicity of countries potentially involved in economic espionage. These include issues such as the determination of which country the crime was actually committed in and who should have jurisdiction to prosecute. Countering computer crimes committed from a distance, and having an increasing range of international targets (such as country of commission of the crime, the number of actors and victims involved, and the range of potential consequences) will require a well-developed network of inter-state co-operation to attain effective investigation and prosecution. In light of the technicalities of international interaction, co-operation between nations in criminal matters is crucial. These issues need to be addressed by all countries, whether they be producers, users or consumers of the new information technologies, because the technologies are an integral part of the economic, social and cultural development.[8]

In an age of increased economic competition among industrialized nations, however, the hope of international co-operation may be naive. For the most part, foreign information collectors do not distinguish between military technology, civilian technology, proprietary information, and trade secrets—they simply collect what they find to be of value. Increasing economic competition has redefined the context for espionage as nations link their national security to their economic security. Intelligence services are expanding from their primary focus on military secrets to include the collection of economic intelligence. The US is particularly vulnerable to the changing focus of foreign collection since American corporations and research centers rely heavily on communications systems, computer networks, and electronic equipment to process and store information. Executives are being warned that hotel rooms and first-class sections of foreign airlines are being bugged. Luggage is secretly searched at airports. Laptop computers are stolen.[9] The espionage threat is particularly troubling when the capabilities or experience of a foreign intelligence service support a US corporation's foreign competitor.

A number of foreign countries, including some traditional US allies, continue their collection efforts against the US. In 1998, eight countries were identified as the nations most actively involved in the collection of US proprietary economic and industrial information.[10] These countries do not reflect the entire picture of targeting against US interests—only the most serious threat. A threat to US economic and industrial interests entails both intent and capability. All countries on this year's Priority Country List have the intent and capability to engage in economic collection and economic espionage. Hostile intent involves a willingness to effectively conduct economic espionage against the US and the capacity to do so. An effective foreign collection program focuses on technology and information that can be used by a country's indigenous commercial and defense industries. In addition, a close relationship between government and business exists among many of the most active economic collector countries—a factor that helps to establish targeting priorities and promote effective dissemination of information. In addition, to have a sufficient negative effect on US industry, a foreign country must have the capability to exploit stolen technology and a base for profiting from it, such as a large economy, an advanced industrial sector, or a third-country buyer.

Many questions remain unanswered, however, including questions about the true nature and extent of such crimes. The various law enforcement and private sector organizations that are concerned with this topic bring different perspectives and may have hidden agendas. As one survey report involving Fortune 1000 companies in the US observed: 'Notably, the top six most significant threats [as ranked by the survey respondents] are primarily "internal" security issues [within the company] ... . These findings are in contrast to the more traditional focus upon 'external' threats [from outside the company] such as property crime, terrorism and executive protection which seem to attract more public attention.'[11]

It is difficult to assess the dollar loss as a result of economic espionage and the theft of trade secrets. The US intelligence community has not systemically evaluated the costs. Pacific Northwest National Laboratory, under contract by the FBI, recently developed a methodology to assess and determine the scope of economic loss resulting from the theft of intellectual property. This Economic Loss Model was first applied to the facts of a case involving the theft of intellectual property from a US corporation by a foreign competitor who, as a result of the theft, captured the market. Using this tool, the misappropriation of intellectual property in this case was estimated to have resulted in over $600 million in lost sales, the direct loss of 2600 full-time jobs, and a resulting loss of 9542 jobs for the economy as a whole over a 14-year time frame. The analysis also determined that the US trade balance was negatively impacted by $714 million and lost tax revenues totaled $129 million. The Economic Loss Model will continue to be used on a case-by-case basis and may be used for court purposes to produce loss estimates.[12]

Of the wide variety of information risks facing US companies operating internationally, those resulting from electronic vulnerabilities appear to be the most significant. The National Counterintelligence Center (NACIC), an arm of the US intelligence community established in 1994 by presidential directive, concluded that specialized technical operations (including computer intrusions, telecommunications targeting and intercept, and private-sector encryption weaknesses) account for the largest portion of economic and industrial information lost by US corporations. Specifically, the NACIC noted that, because they are so easily accessed and intercepted, corporate telecommunications, particularly international telecommunications, provide a highly vulnerable and lucrative source for anyone interested in obtaining trade secrets or competitive information.

Because of the increased use of these links for bulk computer data transmission and electronic mail, intelligence collectors find telecommunications intercepts cost-effective. For example, foreign intelligence collectors can intercept facsimile transmissions through government-owned telephone companies. The stakes are large because approximately half of all overseas telecommunications are facsimile transmissions. Innovative 'hackers' connected to computers containing competitive information evade the controls and access companies' information. In addition, many American companies have begun using electronic data interchange, a system of transferring corporate bidding, invoice, and pricing data electronically overseas. Foreign government and corporate intelligence collectors find this information invaluable.[13]

Foreign collection efforts continue to be driven by military force modernization, economic competition, and commercial modernization using technologies with dual-use applications. Targeting duel-use technology provides foreign collectors with a high return on investment and a low probability that the US will detect any diversion from its stated end use. A majority of collected information is restricted, sensitive and/or proprietary and its loss is detrimental to US economic interests. A smaller portion of collected information is 'classified'.

According to the Defense Security Service 'DSS', US defense industry reporting of suspicious activity during 1997 revealed that foreign government and commercially sponsored entities continued to target weapon components, developing technologies, and technical information more intensely than complete weapon systems and military equipment. Less developed countries seek older technologies that cost less but will still improve their military capabilities. More developed nations appear to seek more advanced technical information to copy or counter US military systems. A review of reported incidents of suspected targeting against critical technologies in 1997 has reaffirmed that all 18 categories of the DoD's Military Critical Technology List (MCTL) continue to be the subject of foreign interest for military and/or economic exploitation. The majority of MCTL categories are dual-use and are included in Appendix 'A'.[14]

Economic espionage cannot be eliminated through the use of any single tool. For example, it is impossible to prevent, with technical means alone, a party authorized to view information from improperly disclosing that information to someone else. The problems of information vulnerability, and the legitimacy of various national interests, point to the need for a concerted effort to protect vital information assets.

United States Government's Response

An example of American reaction to these concerns can be seen in the Economic Espionage Act of 1996, which culminated a nearly two-year effort by the FBI and US industry professionals to strengthen criminal prohibitions on trade secret theft. The EEA contains two central provisions. The first provision, Section 1831, is directed toward foreign economic espionage and applies only where the theft of a trade secret is carried out to benefit a foreign government, instrumentality, or agent. The second provision, Section 1832, criminalizes the theft of trade secrets regardless of who benefits. Due to the perception that foreign economic espionage is more heinous, an individual convicted of violating Section 1831 can be imprisoned for up to 15 years and fined $500,000 or both, and corporations and other organizations convicted of violating Section 1831 can be fined up to $10 million. In contrast, a defendant convicted under Section 1832 can be imprisoned for up to 10 years and fined $500,000 or both.

The EEA is intended to address both the general need for a federal criminal deterrence against trade secret theft, and the apparent threat of industrial espionage sponsored by foreign governments.[15] The EEA 'establishes a comprehensive and systemic approach to trade secret theft and economic espionage, facilitating investigations and prosecutions' by federal authorities.[16]

The EEA amounts to unprecedented federal statutory support in the US for the protection of intellectual property rights.[17] Before its passage, the relevant legal structures sometimes failed to deter trade-secret misappropriation. 'When a San Jose Company had learned that outsiders had downloaded a sensitive business proposal and run off to New Mexico, the US Attorney's Office refused to go after the culprits.'[18] The passage of the EEA reflects Congress' recognition of the need to remedy such problems. The Act also applies to offenses committed outside the US, if the offender is a citizen or permanent resident alien of the US, if the corporation or other organization was incorporated or organized in the US or if an act in furtherance of the offense was committed in the USA.[19]

According to the CIA's Annual Report to Congress, foreign collection continues to focus on US trade secrets and science and technology information. In its 1997 comments, the CIA said the US Economic Espionage Act, 'represented an important step toward safeguarding valuable intellectual and proprietary information'.[20]

As a matter of policy, the FBI reportedly does not *officially* identify governments that sponsor economic espionage.[21] Nonetheless, according to a news report in the *Los Angeles Times* on 12 January 1998, the FBI has identified Israel as one of the major players in the economic espionage that threatened $300 billion of technology in 1997. Governments of at least 23 countries, ranging from Germany to China, are targeting US firms, according to the FBI.[22] More than 1100 documented incidents of economic espionage, and 550 suspected incidents that could not be fully documented, were reported in 1997 by major companies in a survey conducted by ASIS. The 1997 survey disclosed that high-tech companies, especially in Silicon Valley, are the most frequent targets of foreign spies, followed by manufacturing and service industries. France, Germany, Israel, China, Russia, and South Korea were named as major offenders in an article by Edwin Fraumann, a New York-based FBI agent. The FBI confirmed Fraumann's report that more than 700 foreign counterintelligence investigations involving economic espionage were pending before the bureau.[23] The ASIS's periodic surveys, which FBI Director Louis Freeh has cited in congressional testimony, provide the federal government with its only estimate of potential damage from economic espionage. France, intelligence sources say, is among the worst offenders and at one time targeted more than 70 US corporations, including Boeing, IBM, Texas Instruments and Corning Glass.[24] According to Fraumann, France has even spied on US companies by wiretapping US businessmen flying on Air France between New York and Paris. France also has used such clandestine methods as surveillance of business personnel and communications inside France, including telephone conversations and faxes.[25]

Fraumann's article listed a series of 'intrusive methods' used by foreign countries, including: eavesdropping by wiretapping, bugging offices or capturing cellular telephone conversations, penetrating computer networks, stealing proprietary information contained in drawings and documents and on floppy disks and CD ROMs, using an attractive man or woman to form a close personal relationship with an employee with access to trade secrets, hiring a competitor's employee who has valuable knowledge, bribing a supplier or employee, planting an agent or 'mole' in a company with the mission to compromise key employees, tapping into computer databases and intercepting communications to ferret out confidential research, technologies and other information.[26]

Recent Economic Espionage Enforcement Activities

An example of the tension between international competition and enforcement of economic espionage laws can be seen in a recent case involving biotechnology. The FBI recently arrested Dr Yoichi Iota, a 32 year old researcher who held a two-year prestigious fellowship at the Mayo Clinic Laboratory. Iota was accused of stealing research data. The FBI's court documents allege that Iota downloaded several years' worth of research information to magnetic-optical disks, photographed Mayo's laboratory for research on cartilage and connective tissue, and took tissue samples, gene sequencing data and research books that were critical to the laboratory's work.

Iota left a post at Osaka City University in 1997 for at two-year stint at Mayo according to an FBI affidavit. Upon his arrival at Mayo, he requested a large-capacity hard drive for his computer. When his request was denied, he bought the drive on his own. According to the affidavit, the suspicion about his use of the hard drive surfaced a few days before he left for his wedding in Hawaii on 19 March 1999. The affidavit describes that a laboratory supervisor saw Iota download data to magnetic optical disks, and that another researcher said Iota's data on gene sequencing was missing from the laboratory's central computer. The supervisor then found the research books and other laboratory materials were missing and that Iota's hard drive contained large files of data from the laboratory's main computer, including proprietary research data dating back to 1990. Another research fellow told investigators that Iota had periodically shipped packages to Japan during his last two weeks in Minneapolis then, on the eve of his departure, a Mayo security officer found him in the laboratory taking photographs. Iota was charged with committing fraud by computer, punishable by up to five years in prison and a $250,000 fine. US Magistrate Judge John Mason in St Paul ordered him to surrender his passport and remain in Minnesota.[27] It is unclear at this time whether this was motivated solely by personal gain or whether it had the sponsorship of either a governmental or private-sector entity in Japan. The case highlights the risks that result from the open contact and discourse in the American scientific community.

The above action was brought to court based on the Fraud by Computer statutory provision, even though this case is a perfect example of an economic espionage case. Most likely this case has not yet been brought under the EEA because the Attorney General Janet Reno has been reluctant to use the law, bringing fewer than a handful of economic espionage cases to date, due to the fact that Reno must personally review each case and approve each prosecution. The legislative history around the Act shows that there was concern expressed by members of Congress that prosecutions of these types of cases would stifle competition.

A more common variety of US-based industrial espionage can be seen in the recent case of David B. Kern. In January of 1999, Mr Kern, 45, was the first person in California to be charged under the EEA. The case was filed in Sacramento federal court in California. According to the court documents, Kern stole instructions about how to maintain, repair and calibrate million-dollar radiation therapy machines manufactured for the treatment of cancer by Varian Associates Inc. of Palo Alto. According to the US Attorney, the confidential methods and procedures for maintaining the machines are set forth in Varian's service manuals and bulletins and those materials constitute trade secrets. Kern worked for Varian's Oncology Systems division as an installation service manager from 1991 through 1994. He then went to work in 1995 as head of Engineering for Radiological Associates of Sacramento Medical Group, which competes with Varian for service contracts when the one-year warranties have expired on Varian machines in Northern California hospitals and treatment centers. Upon completing a service call in October or November 1996, a Varian technician inadvertently left behind at Sacramento's Mercy General Hospital a laptop computer containing software with Varian's maintenance technology on it. Kern helped himself to the laptop and copied the confidential files, according to the information. When Radiological Associates discovered what Kern had done, it was reported to Varian. The FBI was then brought in to investigate the matter.

The Kern case represents the more typical kind of information theft. According to Richard J Hefferenan, a security consultant, in an era of downsizing and diminished corporate loyalty close to two-thirds of all US intellectual property losses can be traced to insiders, 'people are always looking for somebody who looks different, when a great deal of the theft is committed by insiders who walk and talk just like you and me'.[28] Most of the cases brought so far under the EEA do not involve foreign nationals, but rather companies that were approached by a competitor's employee who offered them trade secret information.

The Avery Dennison case is the first case in which the government has used the EEA to indict a company in addition to individual defendants. A Taipei-based company, Four Pillars Enterprises Co., Ltd., was accused of trying to steal trade secrets from Pasadena, California-based Avery Dennison Corp., an adhesives manufacturer. Avery Dennison instigated the charges against Four Pillars' CEO Dr Yang by reporting to the FBI that Dr Yang was stealing 'proprietary information' via an Avery Dennison employee, Victor Lee. Pin Yen Yang, 72, President of Four Pillars Co., Ltd. of Taiwan, and his daughter, Hwei Chen 'Sally' Yang, 40, were accused of taking secrets from Avery Dennison through one of the company's researchers in Ohio. The Yangs pleaded innocent to charges of economic espionage, conspiracy, mail fraud, wire fraud, money laundering and receipt of stolen goods. The money laundering charge carries the longest possible prison sentence of 20 years. According to the FBI, the Yangs paid about $150,000 to Ten Hong Lee, also known as Victor Lee, a research engineer at an Avery Dennison lab in Ohio. In return, Lee shipped them trade secrets related to products such as self-stick postage stamps, name labels, diaper tape and battery labels from 1989 to 1997, when the Yangs were indicted in Cleveland, Ohio in September of 1997. The case went to trial and the jury returned guilty verdicts.

The FBI continues to expand its enforcement efforts. The FBI and the U.S. Chamber of Commerce joined efforts in February 1999 to fight economic espionage. According to FBI Director Louis Freeh, FBI has the legal tools to combat economic espionage and protect trade secret information, however, a private sector-law enforcement joint effort is fundamental to success against those who criminally target proprietary information. This collaboration calls for:

(1) a system to alert businesses to espionage threats,
(2) strategies to identify and implement steps to combat economic espionage, and
(3) a clearinghouse for information between the two agencies.

The FBI also plans to work with the 84 U.S. Chambers of Commerce abroad to press the need for a global approach to intellectual property theft.[29]

Conclusion

The growth of information technology makes the emergence of information theft inevitable worldwide. Law enforcement officials in the US, apparently viewing the US economy as the most likely target, have begun to focus on this new form of crime and US Congress has handed them a new enforcement tool in the EEA. This law, while relatively new, has far-ranging international implications. It is a trap for unwary foreign competitors who compete aggressively with US-based companies. It also may serve as a model that will be followed by other nations with similar legislative or law enforcement initiatives. In those countries where the government plays a role in encouraging industrial activity, the conflict between economic nationalism and international competition will be an ongoing problem. It remains to be seen whether US initiatives in this area will be the start of an international trend or whether the US will stand alone in its effort to combat techno-crime.

Notes and References

1 National Counterintelligence Center (NACIC), *1998 Annual Report to Congress on Foreign Economic Collection and Industrial Espionage.*

2 Remarks by FBI Director Louis Freeh to Chamber of Commerce Foundation Symposium on Corporate Vulnerability to Economic Espionage, Washington, D.C., *FDCH Political Transcripts* 9 February 1999.

3 See e.g. 'International Review of Criminal Policy' *United Nations Manual on the Prevention and Control of Computer-Related Crime*, Nos 43 and 44, 1994.

4 See e.g. *1998 Annual Report to Congress on Foreign Economic Collection and Industrial Espionage.*

5 Otto Kreisher 'Report warns of dangerous results of cyber-attacks', *Copley News Services*, 15 December 1998.

6 Alvin Toffler 'Power shift: knowledge, wealth and violence at the edge of the 21st century' in John J Fialka *War by Other Means: Economic Espionage in America*, 1997, p 66

7 Fialka, *Ibid.*

8 See e.g. 'International Review', *op. cit.*, note 3.

9 Del Jones 'FBI—spies cost U.S. firms $2B a month' *USA Today* 10 February 1999, p 2B.

10 *Op. cit.*, note 4.

11 1998 Pinkerton Security Threats Survey, *Top Security Threats facing Corporate America, 1998 Survey of Fortune 1000 Companies.*

12 *Op. cit.*, note 4.

13 'The eight who dig out secrets' *Intelligence Newsletter* No 348, 10 December 1998. Also see 'Even allies commit economic espionage against U.S.' *South Bend Tribune* 15 November 1998, p b14. For more information on NACIC, visit their website, < http://www.nacic.gov >.

14 *Op. cit.*, note 4.

15 For more detailed discussion, see Hedieh Nasheri and Timothy J O'Hearn, 'Crime and technology: new rules in a new world' *Information & Communications Technology Law* Vol 7, No 2, 1998, p 145 and also see Hedieh Nasheri and Timothy J O'Hearn 'High-tech crimes and the American economic machine' *International Review of Law Computers & Technology Law* Vol 13, No 1, 1999, p 7.

16 Chaim A Levin, 'Trade secret thieves face fines' *Prosecution, National Law Journal* 27 January 1997 at TCC12 (quoting remarks of President Clinton, 32 Weekly Comp. Pres. Doc. 2040, 11 October 1996).

17 *Ibid.*

18 Dan Goodin, 'Busting industrial spies' *The Recorder* 25 September, 1996, p 1.

19 R Mark Hallihan, 'The recently enacted Economic Espionage Act' *The National Law Journal* 9 December 1996, p B6.

20 'U.S. Intelligence Agencies size up the world' *Defense Week* Vol 18, No 48, 8 December 1997.

21 'Foreign spies hurt American business' *News Day*, 13 January 1998, p A43.

22 '*LA Times*: FBI suspects Israel of industrial espionage' *Jerusalem Post* 13 January 1998, p 1.

23 *Ibid.*

24 *Op. cit.*, note 21.

25 Edwin Fraumann 'Economic espionage: security missions redefined' *Public Administration Review* Vol 57, No 4, July/August 1997, p 303.

382   *H Nasheri & T J O'Hearn*

26 Jack Nelson 'Spies took $300-billion toll on U.S. firms in '97' *Los Angeles Times* 12 January 1998, p 1.
27 Sharon Schmicke 'Hightech theft case at Mayo reflects a new worry' *Star Tribune* 31 March 1999, p 1A.
28 Daniel Eisenberg, 'Eyeing the competition' *Time* 22 March 1999, p 58.
29 Heidi Przybyla 'FBI-industry inititiative urges to fight economic spying' *Journal of Commerce* 11 February 1999, p 4A.

[16]

The Extension of the Criminal Law to Protecting Confidential Commercial Information: Comments on the Issues and the Cyber-Context

C DAVID FREEDMAN

ABSTRACT *Confidential commercial information is an increasingly valuable commodity and commercial resource which may be inadequately protected by the traditional approach of English criminal law against misappropriation. This paper reviews the nature of the problem and some of the relevant legal issues. Notwithstanding that a global reform of the law in this area is probably not on the cards, the position advocated here is that the direct application of the criminal law is indeed an appropriate vehicle through which to deter the misappropriation of confidential commercial information. However, the scope of any new law must be carefully circumscribed—if it is drawn too wide, the law runs the danger of acting outside of the articulated rationale for criminal liability and endangering other legitimate interests (particularly in the cyberspace context). If it is drawn too narrow, any new law may very well prove ineffective. It is suggested that there are a number of difficulties, both doctrinal and practical, that must be resolved prior to enacting new legislation in this area. Some observations are presented upon the more critical issues for those interested in the implications of law reform in this area for cyberspace.*

Introduction

Constructing civil remedies and criminal laws to deal with the misappropriation of confidential information has always presented conceptual and practical difficulties for the law. Much has been done in recent years with respect to protecting personal data against interference, but much remains to be done in the area of confidential commercial information. It is clear that whilst the economic value of such information may justify its legal protection, its very nature makes the application of legal principles to it problematic. The approach to civil liability for misappropriation in English law has sought to avoid these complications by adopting an indirect approach to protection, focusing on the enforcement of obligations of confidence arising in law or equity in relation to such information rather

Correspondence, C D Freedman, Emmanuel College, Cambridge, CB2 3AP; E-mail < cdf25@cam.ac.uk >.

1369-0869/99/020147-16 © 1999 Taylor & Francis Ltd

than the information itself. The criminal law has been applied in an even more hesitating fashion. Criminal liability is contingent on the misappropriative act itself being incidentally proscribed by law, and there are significant gaps in the present scope of criminal law coverage. The release in late 1997 of a consultation paper by the Law Commission with its provisional recommendations for a new criminal offence of misuse of trade secrets,[1] is but the latest development highlighting the inadequate application of the criminal law in this area.

In this paper, I shall review the nature of the problem and some of the relevant legal issues. The best response to the present state of the law on these issues would be a complete revision of civil and criminal liability to offer a comprehensive model of protection. Notwithstanding that such global reform of the law in this area is probably not on the cards, the position advocated here is that the criminal law is indeed an appropriate vehicle through which to deter the misappropriation of confidential commercial information. However, the scope of any new law must be carefully circumscribed—if it is drawn too wide, the law runs the danger of acting outside of the articulated rationale for criminal liability and endangering other legitimate interests (particularly in the cyberspace context). If it is drawn too narrow, any new law may very well prove ineffective. I would suggest that there are a number of difficulties, both doctrinal and practical, that must be resolved prior to enacting new legislation in this area and will present a few observations upon the more critical issues for those interested in the implications for cyberspace.

The Need for Effective Legal Protection in the Modern Technological Context

Confidential Commercial Information: Definitional Problems and Functional Descriptionp

The commercial value of *confidential commercial information*[2] has traditionally provided the primary justification for civil remedies and criminal sanctions to deter misappropriative activity in English law and elsewhere.[3] This is reflective of the fact that such information, in the form of trade secrets or 'know-how' or otherwise, has always been an important business asset. In the contemporary context, the need to protect such information is made even more acute as innovation has become the central feature of post-industrial developed economies,[4] making knowledge-based assets increasingly critical economic resources in such economies. In this sense it is clear that threats to the security of confidential commercial information fit within the convergence of two technology-related trends: the rise in value of intellectual property and information in post-industrial economies arising from innovations in technology, and the rise in economic crime as a phenomenon in national and international commercial life itself stemming partly from technological innovation.[5] Before turning to the state of the law and how it might be reformed, it is useful to say a brief word respecting the nature and economic function of confidential commercial information in the modern technological context.

If one tries to create a definitive typology of confidential commercial information, the exercise seems doomed to failure.[6] Not only does the intangible and indivisible nature of information make the task difficult,[7] but the myriad forms that confidential information can take in a commercial context—from technical pre-patent schematics to more gener- alised know-how and operational procedures—renders any attempt at an exhaustive definition practically meaningless.[8] In short, exhaustive classification is an unproductive exercise that is best avoided. One can, however, seek to describe the function and importance of confidential commercial information in economic terms, and draw appropriate conclusions to be used in constructing legal models protective of such information.

Basic economic principles suggest that the law ought to provide a degree of protection to confidential commercial information in order to encourage sufficient investment in the creation of new knowledge-based assets, whilst at the same time avoiding the creation of an artificial scarcity of such resources through over-protection.[9] This balance between the protection of information to encourage investment in development with adequate access to information is a delicate one—economic efficiency in information will not be achieved through over-investment in the creation of informational resources or through duplication of resources to create the same information resources.[10] Moreover, individuals ought be guided by the clear availability of suitable legal remedies in determining the level of private resources, if any, that ought to be dedicated to providing additional protection for such information so that these private expenditures may be optimised.[11] On a global level, then, it is the task of law-makers to achieve this fine balance between protection through legal remedies and self-help and access through appropriately constructed laws.

Regulation and the Modern Technological Context

This basic economic paradigm must be viewed in the contemporary context; a context in which the innovation of new knowledge-based products is increasingly important to post-industrial developed economies. The process of innovation is itself often a joint and serial activity; a process in which developers share and exploit resources and build on each other's work in an attempt to create new products and wealth. In this sense, confidential commercial information in its various forms functions within this cycle of innovation as both a commodity (valuable in itself) and as a resource (to be exploited by commercial actors).[12] Central to the success in exploiting such informational resources is the ability to share the information without risk of destroying its value through illicit acquisition, use or disclosure. This need to be able to exploit valuable informational resources in partnership is critical to the ongoing refinement of technologies; the exchange of confidential information in this sense is, to use one judge's phrase, 'both necessary and expected'.[13]

Having said that confidential business information is increasingly valuable in the modern technological context, one can also add that this context itself has changed the nature of commerce with implications for any attempt at regulation in this area. As the Alberta Law Reform Institute reported when it looked at the protection of trade secrets in Canadian law:[14]

... technology has changed the nature of modern business in a number of respects. [first] Business has become a race against time. Technology is volatile and short lived. The increasing pace of technological change means that perfectly good ideas and inventions may be obsolete before they can be patented and brought to the market place. This problem is complicated by the fact that different parts of a product may have different development rates ... Today the business advantage lies in technology. The business pressures to know what competitors are doing are therefore intense ... [second] employee mobility is greater than any time in history ... [third] technology has made espionage so much simpler. There is now an array of sophisticated equipment, much of it derived from military developments, which makes espionage within even well run enterprises a real threat.

150   *C D Freedman*

The modern technological context, then, is a business environment where information is critical in different stages of product development, is quickly out of date, and is susceptible to misuse or unauthorised disclosure by those having had control over it or being able to acquire it illicitly. The presence of a global networking environment highlights these problems and makes the need for effective legal treatment even more critical.[15] In such circumstances, I would suggest, there is a need for effective deterrents against misappropriative acts both to maintain the value of informational assets and to protect the integrity of the innovation cycle.

The Present State of the Law

Problems in Ascertaining the Precise Nature of the Mischief to be Remedied

To follow correct form in evaluating the merits of criminalising certain acts in relation to confidential information, the discussion ought properly to begin with a detailed analysis of the mischief to be remedied, identify those specific acts which ought to be proscribed, and consider the public policy implications of proscribing such acts. Unfortunately such a traditional approach is made difficult by the lack of sufficiently independent data upon which to base such an analysis, a point that I shall return to later. One should recognise at the outset that considering new regulation without such an independent review of the nature of the mischief to be remedied will undoubtedly run into trouble at some stage.

Notwithstanding the lack of data respecting misappropriative activity, what can be said in general terms is this: confidential commercial information is primarily at risk in two types of scenarios—situations in which information is acquired through illicit means and without the complicity of one rightfully in possession, and, situations in which the information is obtained from one rightfully in possession but in breach of that person's obligations. The first scenario is essentially variations on the theme of industrial espionage; acts which can themselves be characterised as purely private activity (whether local or trans-national) or as state-sponsored acts.[16] The second set of scenarios encompass matters ranging from simple disclosure by ex-employees to new employers to deliberate disclosure by present confidants claimed to be in the public interest.

Property in Confidential Information and the Approach to Civil Liability

With some hesitation, it seems necessary to include some recognition of the traditional debate respecting proprietary rights in confidential information within this discussion.

Despite the fact that, as one scholar put it, '[t]here is a natural and deep-seated tendency ... to treat confidential information in proprietary terms',[17] the inability to exclude others from its use or possession as is required in the normal legal sense of *ownership*[18] would seem to deny it proprietary status as a result. Whilst the issue has not been definitively settled in English law,[19] the great weight of judicial[20] and academic[21] comment is inconsistent with ascribing to such information a property characterisation and as such the normal criminal law of theft is inapplicable.[22] In American law,[23] by comparison, it is clear that specified types of commercial information in the form of trade secrets may be property for both the purposes of certain civil actions[24] and criminal offences.[25] Given that the balance of rights achieved in a ready-made form by property law is seemingly unavailable in this exercise, the challenge for the English criminal law is to identify those matters of private consequence that are in the public interest to protect, and how those interests might be furthered through the availability of criminal sanctions.

In private English law, confidential information is indirectly protected from unauthorised use or disclosure through the enforcement of obligations of confidentiality in relation to such information. Obligations may be expressly or implicitly agreed to, or judicially constructed in appropriate circumstances, as between the parties. It has been said that the protection of confidential information in the form of the equitable action of breach of confidence, the primary vehicle for civil liability outside contract, is *sui generis* in the sense that it has arisen in a multi-jurisdictional fashion, emanating from principles of property, contract, and equity.[26] It seems sufficiently clear now that the action for breach of confidence falls completely outside tort.[27] Others would put the action in none of these jurisdictional pigeonholes in a contemporary context, seeing it as but another manifestation of the law of restitution.[28] Whatever one's view of the evolutionary antecedents or the jurisdictional basis of the action, it is now sufficiently clear that there exists an independent jurisdiction in equity arising on principles of good faith and conscience to restrain unauthorised use or disclosure of confidential information.[29]

Whilst the existence of this independent jurisdiction can now be seen as definitively settled, its scope and extent is still not fully developed. In a general sense, the contours of the action will depend very much on the nature of the information sought to be protected, the parties to the action, and the circumstances claimed to give rise to an enforceable obligation between the parties. Uncertainty respecting the parameters of this developing jurisdiction naturally colours attempts to introduce criminal law provisions into the same area.

The First Scenario: Conduct-based Liability for Illicit Acquisition

The first scenario identified above respecting misappropriation is in those situations where one not properly in possession of the information in question seeks to acquire it without the complicity of one properly in possession of the information. Conventional ploys like bribing and suborning employees are essentially variants on breach of confidence relying on receipt-based principles of liability, which I shall turn to below. The issue here is whether liability may follow based directly on the nature or method of acquisition, which is obviously relevant in technological contexts.

There is an obvious need to balance policy interests in this area; whilst business people have a legitimate interest in securing as much information as possible on competitors and their products, it is in no one's interest to have a completely unregulated marketplace. The Younger Commission described this fundamental consideration in these terms:[30]

The main difficulty in considering the acquisition of industrial and commercial information is deciding where to draw the line between methods which consist of painstaking and legitimate gathering of business information and those which the law should treat as illegal. Most people would agree that it is part of the normal function of an efficient business man to be well-informed on his competitor's products, prices, sales promotions, and so forth; and most people would agree that it would be quite wrong for him to steal his rival's test samples or suborn his employees; but there are grey areas.

The lack of property in confidential information has resulted in an approach to liability in both civil and criminal law in this area that is highly unsatisfactory.

Criminal liability does not proceed from a generalised approach based on misappropri-ation directly; the lack of property takes the misappropriative act outside the law of theft.[31] Liability, then, is conditioned on the act itself being incidentally proscribed under statute (for example, under the *Interception of Communications Act 1985*, the *Copyright, Designs and Patent Act 1988*, the *Computer Misuse Act 1990*, or the *Trade Marks Act 1994*) or common law (primarily the offence of conspiracy to defraud), with each area having its own deficiencies.

Whilst it is beyond the scope of this paper to attempt an exhaustive analysis of the various criminal law proscriptions relevant to the remedy of the mischief identified, I would suggest, much as the Law Commission recently advised,[32] that there are significant gaps in this incidental application of the criminal law. For example, 'van Eck' reception devices used to capture the radiation from computer screens from public vantage points would not seem to run foul of the *Computer Misuse Act 1990*, as neither would reading confidential information off the screen directly, provided one has not caused the computer to perform a function within the meaning of that statute. Perhaps a more significant problem is that of the person who has authority to use the computer in question, but acts outside his or her authority in accessing confidential information.[33] This is an undesirable state of affairs. One would think that the criminal law ought to be able to relieve the 'decent and reputable trader's sense of helplessness'[34] in such circumstances.

What then of civil liability? It would seem natural to look to private law for norms of actionable conduct that might be useful in determining complementary criminal standards. Unfortunately, this is an area in which civil liability is most uncertain.

First, English law traditionally disfavours an approach that speaks to norms of 'unfair competition' directly. [35]

Secondly, there are a number of inconsistent authorities as to whether a jurisdiction exists to find liability based on an acquisitive method standing alone, and what the test to find such liability ought to be. Various conduct-based standards have been proposed in the context of the equitable action of breach of confidence—amongst them that the act of acquisition was itself unlawful,[36] surreptitious,[37] reprehensible,[38] unconscionable,[39] wrong-ful,[40] and on the basis that the act falls under some generalised principle of liability grounded in the flexible nature of the equitable jurisdiction itself.[41] Many respected authorities argue that liability based on any such approach implicitly raises the spectre of liability imposed on highly idiosyncratic judicial views of general or commercial morality.[42] This is a criticism that is not unique to breach of confidence claims but reflects a fundamental tension that has been at the root of the long-standing judicial reluctance to import equitable doctrines into the commercial context.[43] On the other hand, one might argue that this trend seems to have abated somewhat in recent years as equity has undergone a period of revitalisation, especially in commercial contexts. Clearly the point is most uncertain.

The Second Scenario: Receipt-based Liability for Breach of Confidence

With respect to the second set of scenarios, this is an area where private law has developed sophisticated receipt-based principles of civil liability in law and equity. The question for the criminal law in this area is whether criminal laws can be fashioned where civil liability is itself insufficient—for example, where the defendant is judgement-proof.

The Law Commission's 1997 provisional recommendation supports the creation of a new offence of misuse of trade secrets that is exactly on point and would appear to be an appropriate way forward in this area. The model advocated restricts application of the law to offensive conduct in relation to unauthorised use or disclosure of a functionally defined subset of confidential commercial information, 'trade secrets'. The orientation of the provisional draft law is to punish an offender who knowingly misappropriates valuable information that is not 'generally known'. The offence is not overly broad in scope and the Law Commission intends actual prosecutions to be instigated only the worst cases and where the availability of civil remedies is inadequate in the circumstances of individual cases. The most appropriate use of such sanctions would be to punish employees, co-venturers, consultants and others who rightfully acquire information, but then knowingly and intentionally misuse it. The scope of the provisional model deliberately does not speak to illicit modes of acquisition or the question of industrial espionage.

The cyberspace interest in this area does not so much lie in the methods by which the proscribed act of misappropriation is accomplished, but with the shape of cyberspace itself. It seems clear that certain types of employees are now increasingly mobile in modern information economies. This is especially true in respect of the services of technical experts and specialised managers who are active in the technology sectors.[44] There is a strong economic interest in making the skills of these experts available in the market-place on demand. However, as these same people work with the kinds of valuable confidential commercial information that is often the primary asset of their employers, there is an economic interest in ensuring that confidential information provided by employers remains confidential especially as against industry rivals. Over-protection of information through broad criminal liability in this area may very well inhibit necessary employee mobility and slow the natural pace of innovation unjustifiably.

Some Observations on Criminalisation and the Cyberspace Context

It seems appropriate to open this section of the discussion with some comments on the term 'cyberspace'. Whilst I have used the term somewhat freely in this paper, I have purposely not sought to define it. It would appear that the use of the expression (itself from William Gibson's seminal science fiction novel, *Neuromancer*) in both the academic literature and in the media is most popularly associated with the Internet, and perhaps exclusively so. It seems to me that this is an unduly restrictive definition of the term given that we are still in the infancy of the information age and our conceptions of cyberspace are equally in their early stages. I would suggest that given both the continually evolving nature of information technology and the increasingly inter-connectivity of information handling devices, cyberspace is more than merely the virtual space created by a global network of computer networks and I have used the term here in a broader sense. Whitaker has recently described cyberspace in this sense as a new world of 'technological fusion' which itself 'exists nowhere and everywhere ... forever a *tabula rasa* in the sense that it is constantly being constructed and reconstructed, written and rewritten'.[45] This seems an apt characterisation in my view.

I suggest that new criminal laws enacted to protect confidential commercial information will impact on cyberspace generally in two respects. Obviously regulation will impact upon the use of information technologies to commit acts that may be proscribed by law. In this sense, it is the definition of the subject-matter to be protected and the breadth of the proscription on activity that is all important. If the scope of regulation is overly broad, new laws may prove detrimental to the optimal exploitation of technologies such as the Internet. Regulation will also have an impact on the development of information technologies themselves, and in this sense it is again of critical importance that the scope of regulation be drawn with care else we risk an over-protection of information and a hindrance on the mobility of the specialised labour force that creates those technologies that are cyberspace.

Having presented some thoughts on the problem of misappropriation of confidential commercial information and its inadequate legal treatment at present, the following remarks are directed to some of the issues relevant in the process of constructing new laws to protect confidential commercial information in the 'information society' and some of the implications for cyberspace.

The Need to Develop a General Model Providing Comprehensive and Complementary Liability Rules in Private and Criminal Law

Intellectual property rights are of increasing economic importance in national and global economies. As such, the law must respond to the need for liability rules that provide adequate protection to maintain sufficient investment to encourage continued development without over-protecting these rights. In general terms, traditional rights such as copyright and patent have developed sophisticated structures which I would suggest will be able to respond to society's on-going needs.

The law respecting the protection of confidential information is very much an aspect of intellectual property law that is in need of revision. In the 19th century, a jurisdiction in equity was created to enable such information to be protected based on the enforcement of actual or constructive obligations of confidentiality. Whilst these principles have seen radical development in the United States in the ensuing years in both the fields of intellectual property law (the law respecting trade secrets, in both common law and statutory forms) and constitutional law (the recognition of privacy rights), English law has been content with a conservative process of refinement that may not adequately meet our present and future needs. This is particularly so where liability is sought to be recognised based on conduct of the defendant in acquiring the information as the primary basis of liability, rather than through the traditional relational context.

In approaching the question of a new criminal law presence in this area, I would suggest that it is of the utmost importance that fragmentary and context-specific strategies be abandoned in favour of the development of generalised principles.[46] What is needed is a principled and comprehensive model of protection that offers complementary civil and criminal liability in respect of confidential commercial information. By not adopting a more principled approach both at civil and criminal law, we risk over-regulation and inconsistent application of present models of liability.

For example, whilst there are distinctions now made between government, commercial and personal information within the equitable action of breach of confidence, such a distinction has not been as strongly made in the incidental application of criminal law. The rationale for protecting these various types of information is quite different, as is the proper scope of legal protections. Certainly no reasonable person would suggest that confidential information as it relates to corporations and individuals is the same, yet these distinctions fail to inform the criminal law. If we are to offer protection to confidential commercial information without unduly impinging on other legitimate interests (for example, civil liberties), it would seem prudent to draft new laws to ensure that they are not applied outside the context of their articulated rationale. In this sense, we ought recognise that liability rules in respect of confidential information have the ability to act as methods of private censorship, as was attempted in the *Scientology* cases in the United States.[47] Beyond this, it seems odd to limit protection of that which is considered properly protectable, to acts of use or disclosure but not acquisition. Surely it is the nature of the misappropriative act itself that is culpable, whilst the nature of the information merely demarcates the appropriate breadth of the proscription.

Defining an Appropriate Role for Criminal Sanctions

The Law Commission has taken the provisional position that criminal law in this area should be narrowly applied and ought to follow civil liability.[48] As civil liability is essentially receipt-based liability in this area, the implicit position is that the criminal law ought to refrain from introducing new standards of conduct-based liability. This is to say that the criminal law should restrict itself to breach of confidence situations where the threat of civil liability in the circumstances is insufficient to promote compliance with express or implicit obligations of confidentiality. This approach is reflective of the traditional reluctance in English law to construct models of direct liability for unfair competition.

I have suggested that the law should offer comprehensive protection for confidential commercial information. I would further suggest that the criminal law in this area may fulfil three functions: to set minimum standards of acceptable commercial behaviour, to deter the breach of private obligations of confidence in appropriate circumstances as envisaged by the Law Commission, and to bring domestic treatment in line with emerging international standards respecting the protection of intellectual property through more liberalised unfair competition norms. This is relevant in the cyberspace context as we are presently engaged in setting out the principles that will govern the conduct of commerce in cyberspace (like the standard and method of encryption necessary to allow commercial transactions to be conducted on the Internet). We ought to confront the need to set appropriate standards of commercial behaviour in relation to confidential commercial information in this area as one might reasonably expect misappropriation to be accomplished through the use of emerging technologies.

With respect to the first point, the function of the criminal law in the commercial context is, at a minimum, to define the outer limits of tolerable commercial behaviour.[49] In this sense, the criminal law plays a role that civil remedies cannot: it serves a declaratory and educational function in supporting appropriate standards of commercial behaviour. The difficulty, of course, lies in applying criminal sanctions where civil liability is uncertain,[50] and where it is unclear as to whether the conduct in question is truly worthy of blame.[51] However, it is clear that one legitimate function for new criminal laws in this area is to set a threshold standard for commercial behaviour, below which criminal liability may be incurred.

Secondly, the criminal law is able to provide general deterrence against wrongful acts where civil liability is inadequate; for example, where the defendant is judgement-proof or the plaintiff is without the resources or sophistication to bring an action (or even has been driven into bankruptcy as a result of the acts in question). In such circumstances, the proscribed act still attracts liability and consequences. This is useful in enforcing commercial morality in the sense of deterring certain wilful breaches of obligations of confidence in cyberspace or elsewhere.

Thirdly, national criminal laws can also act internationally in the sense of working towards harmonisation of national laws, and creating a global response to such transnational problems as money laundering. It may be that such an approach is the best way of protecting intellectual property across borders, and perhaps the solution to the transnational problem of industrial espionage.[52] I would suggest that on a criminal law level, it would seem reasonable to proceed in part on the basis of enacting legislation aimed at eradicating 'dishonest commercial practices' in relation to the misappropriation of valuable commercial information where the nature of the conduct is sufficiently offensive. Such an approach allows one to confront competitors who obtain confidential information illicitly through conventional methods (such as suborning employees) and through the use of technological means to surreptitiously acquire their rival's secrets. I would suggest that such a standard would dovetail nicely with the standards agreed upon in the TRIPs Agreement, itself building on the incorporated provisions of the Paris Convention for the Protection of Industrial Property, Art. 10*bis*,[53] which establishes a regime against unfair competition practices which is now enforceable under TRIPs through the World Trade Organisation.

The Need for More and Better Data Respecting Misappropriative Acts

Criminal laws must be sufficiently precise to enable people to know whether they risk criminal liability for a contemplated course of conduct, and avoid inefficient enforcement of the criminal law through flawed prosecutions. Lawmakers considering the problem of misappropriation are faced with creating new laws without a detailed and independent review of the nature of the problem. Whilst one might be able to develop the main principles of a protective model that speaks to the relevant public policy interests in a more global sense, there is a serious lack of sufficiently reliable data to determine those acts themselves which ought be proscribed in any new law. I would suggest two points in this regard.

First, the present lack of comprehensive civil and criminal sanctions necessarily affects the reporting of misappropriative activity as existing legal remedies do not cover the acts subject of a potential complaint. Moreover, even where there are remedies available at law, trade secret cases traditionally suffer from a reluctance on the part of victims to extend losses and suffer crises of investor confidence by engaging the legal process for redress of their complaints.[54] That there are few complaints should not be taken to mean that misappropriative activity does not occur.

Secondly, such evidence as does exist in the forms of statistics or studies that document the problem of misappropriation tend to grow out of proprietary surveys conducted by industry groups, like the American Society for Industrial Security.[55] The problem in relying on these types of studies is that they are geared towards producing lists of industry losses rather than detailing types of conduct. The loss figures themselves are not actual losses, but estimates and projections based on subjective criteria. Such projected losses may make interesting journalism,[56] but law-makers ought to be wary of legislating based on the expectation of the looming economic disaster these estimates tend to engender. However, even when viewed critically, these figures do point at a serious problem that threatens to become larger if it remains unchecked.

Sadly, there are few academic studies. The most recent is by Professor Burr who looked at misappropriation of trade secrets in the American state of New Mexico and found that misappropriation of trade secrets mainly involved confidants (employees, government inspectors, etc.) but also extended to third party theft. Whilst this study was limited in scope and volume of data, it is one of the very few sources of publicly available and independent data in this area. The sample was taken from a pool of small to medium sized corporations and did not sample large or trans-national corporations, whose orientation seems to be traditional industrial manufacturing rather than economic activities tied to newer technologies and informational products. The study also seems to be directed at the question of civil redress rather than willingness to pursue criminal complaints.[57]

The risk that is run is that in enacting laws that seek to remedy the mischief of misappropriation without a very clear idea of which acts ought be proscribed, one runs the risk of over-regulation. In the context of a global communications environment, such as the Internet, this is not just a matter of national concern. It is clear that in some cases, local regulation of cyberspace can have international implications. Such was the case in the claim by German prosecutors against CompuServe, resulting in the blocking of certain news-groups to its world-wide subscribers.[58] In this sense, it is important to get the national balance right.

I suggest that governments would be well advised to take the lead in commissioning further research on this point if laws are to achieve their potential in addressing real-world needs. What is required is both an accurate estimate of the nature and scope of misappro-priative activities, and, procedural reform to encourage complainants to come forward to engage the legal process whilst maintaining the security of their informational assets during the course of litigation (civil and criminal).

Incorporating Technological Solutions into Legal Models

American law has traditionally required protective measures in trade secrets law. The present model of civil liability in English law for breach of confidence does not require that an information owner take reasonable steps to protect his or her information (though such efforts may be relevant in recognising the information in question as that having 'the necessary quality of confidence'[59]),[60] a position that the Law Commission provisionally advocates for the criminal law.[61] The popular objection against such a requirement is the analogy to the homeowner who suffers a burglary—ought we make criminal liability of the burglar contingent on the doors and windows of the house being locked? With respect, for the following reasons it is my submission that this position is quite wrong.

First, intangible information is not the same as household electronics equipment and jewellery. In the area of confidential information, where the subject-matter might itself be no longer protectable by the desire of the owner to place it in the public domain, it would appear that such a requirement is useful in limiting the scope of any legal protection to that which is in fact relatively secret and of commercial value.

Secondly, there is a public interest in encouraging the prudent use of technology in handling informational assets. Those who use information technology to deal with their sensitive information ought to be encouraged to act wisely.

Thirdly, and perhaps most importantly, by not making the law more clearly predictable information owners are placed in a position where they must go beyond taking *reasonable* protective measures and must take maximum protective measures consistent with their perceptions of the value of the information in question. Rational actors will take protective measures on a cost–benefit basis, but the efficiency of such measures in economic terms is not addressed by the state of the law and seemingly a policy of encouraging economic inefficiency is adopted.[62] Is it really better to require traders with valuable information to operate by the law of the jungle rather than merely act as reasonably prudent business people?

I would suggest that the adoption of such a requirement very much reflects the reality of cyberspace. Technologies like software-based encryption of information are useful in both attracting legal protection to certain types of information as well as assisting information owners in the efficient exploitation of the Internet to handle information.

Conclusion

Abraham Lincoln famously remarked upon the utility of the patent concept in words that apply with equal force to all protected forms of intellectual property. He described the benefit of legal protection as promoting innovation by adding 'the fuel of interest to the fire of genius'.[63] The law has different reasons for protecting differing varieties of such property, each having its proper limits and each seeking to further the innovative process by balancing private and public interests in knowledge-based assets. In our own time, as intellectual property rights are of critical economic importance, there is a greater willingness to employ the blunt instrument of the criminal law to safeguard such rights. It is my suggestion that in the area of confidential commercial information, there is a need to revise present models and offer comprehensive and complementary protection through both receipt-based and conduct-based standards of liability. The complicating feature is the effect such remedies and proscriptions may have on individual and commercial exploitation of information technologies. I would counsel caution in drafting new laws and encourage more extensive study of the mischief to be remedied, especially the creation of suitably independent data on the nature of misappropriative activity, and encourage law-makers to look beyond national borders to the international context and implications of domestic regulation.

Notes and References

1 Law Commission for England and Wales *Legislating the Criminal Code: Misuse of Trade Secrets,* Law Com CP 150, 1997, hereinafter *Consultation Paper on Misuse of Trade Secrets.*

2 I am using the phrase 'confidential commercial information' in this paper in a generic sense, purposely avoiding other descriptions which often have specialised or inconsistent meanings both within English law and in other legal systems—for example, 'know-how'; compare *Income and Corporations Tax Act 1988*, s 533(7), *EC Technology Transfer Regulation*, Art 10(1), and *Poly Linn Ltd v Finch* [1995] FSR 751. An alternative description might be that used in the *Agreement on Trade-Related Aspects of Intellectual Property Rights*, Art 39'; with respect to this formulation, see R Krasser 'The protection of trade secrets in the TRIPs Agreement' in F-K Beier and G Schricker (eds) *From GATT to TRIPs—The Agreement on Trade-Related Aspects of Intellectual Property Rights, IIC Studies in Industrial and Copyright Law,* Vol 18, Max Planck Institute, Munich, 1996, pp 216–225; F Dessemontet 'Protection of trade secrets and confidential information' in C A Correa and A A Yusuf *Intellectual Property and International Trade: The TRIPs Agreement,* Kluwer, 1998, p 237 and authorities cited therein at fn 2.

3 *Consultation Paper on Misuse of Trade Secrets,* para 3.1; F Gurry *Breach of Confidence,* Clarendon Press, Oxford, 1984, pp 7–8; J Hull *Commercial Secrecy: Law and Practice,* Sweet & Maxwell, London, 1998, pp 3–4; R Dean *Law of Trade Secrets,* Law Book Company, Sydney, 1990, pp 8–10; J Pooley *Trade Secrets,* Law Journal Seminars Press, New York, 1997, §1.03[3]; M F Jager *Trade Secrets Law,* West Group, 1996, §1.04.

4 C Arup *Innovation, Policy and Law,* Cambridge University Press, 1993, p 123.

5 See R B Davies and G Saltmarsh 'An international overview of the incidence of economic crime' in J Reuvid (ed.) *The Regulation and Prevention of Economic Crime Internationally,* Kogan Page, London, 1995, pp 91–112.

6 See generally on the problem of definition: J A Thorburn 'Defining confidential business information' *SPG International Law Practicum*, Vol 9, pp 6–8, 1996; K G Fairbairn and J A Thorburn *Law of Confidential Business Information*, Canada Law Book, Aurora, 1998, ch. 3.

7 Primarily by denying information a true proprietary characterisation; see below.

8 *Faccenda Chicken Ltd v Fowler* [1986] 1 All ER 617, 627; B S DuVal, 'The occasions of secrecy' *University of Pittsburgh Law Review* Vol 47, p 579 at p 588, 1986.

9 C Arup *op. cit.*, p 126.

10 See W Landes, R Posner and D Friedman 'Some economics of trade secret law' *Journal of Economic Perspectives* Vol 5, p 61, 1991.

11 'Trade secret misappropriation: a cost–benefit response to the Fourth Amendment analogy' *Harvard Law Review* Vol 106, p 461, 1992.

12 C Arup *op. cit.*, pp 125–130.

13 *Lac Minerals Ltd v International Corona Resources Ltd* (1989), 61 DLR. (4th) 14, 47 (SCC) per LaForest J.

14 Institute of Law Research and Reform and a Federal Provincial Working Party, *Trade Secrets* (Report No 46, 1986), para 2.10–2.12.

15 B Atkins 'Trading secrets in the information age: can trade secret law survive *The Internet?*' *University of Illinois Law Review* Vol 4, p 1151 at pp 1152–1154, 1996; V A Cundiff 'Trade secrets and *The Internet*: a practical perspective' *Computer Law* Vol 14, p 6 at p 7, 1997.

16 These latter situations are more appropriately addressed in a political forum between governments and can be excluded from this discussion, see D E Denning *Information Warfare and Security*, ACM Press, New York, 1999; E Fraumann 'Economic espionage: security missions redefined' *Public Administration Review*, Vol 57, p 303, 1997; G Mossinghoff, J D Mason and D Oblon 'The Economic Espionage Act: a new federal regime of trade secret protection' *Journal of the Patent Office and Trademark Society* Vol 79, p 191 at pp 192–193, 1997; S Porteous 'Economic/commercial interests and intelligence services' Commentary No 59 CSIS, Ottawa, 1995; 'Economic security', CSIS, Ottawa, 1996. For an economic treatment of these issues, see M Whitney and J Gaisford 'Economic espionage as strategic trade policy' *Canadian Journal of Economics*, Special Issue, p 627, 1996.

17 A S Weinrib 'Information and property' *University of Toronto Law Journal* Vol 36, p 117 at p 133, 1988. For example, *Murray v Yorkshire Fund Managers Ltd* [1998] 1 W L R 951; *Boardman v Phipps* [1967] 2 AC 46, 107.

18 J E Penner *The Idea of Property in Law*, Clarendon Press, Oxford, 1997, p 119.

19 The matter was left open by the House of Lords in the *Spycatcher* litigation; *Attorney General v Guardian Newspapers Ltd* (No 2) [1990] 1 AC 109, 281 per Lord Goff.

20 *Oxford v Moss* (1978), 68 Cr App R 183; *Absolom* (*The Times*, 14 September 1983); *Jeffreys v Boosey* (1854), 4 H L C 814; *Nicrotherm Electrical Co Ltd v Percy* [1957] R P C 207; *Stewart* [1988] 50 D L R (4th) 1 (SCC).

21 For a general review of the law on this point, see D Fisch Nigri 'Theft of information and the concept of property in the information age' in J W Harris (ed.), *Property Problems, From Genes to Pensions*, Kluwer, London, 1997, pp 48–60; R Dean *The Law of Trade Secrets*, pp 53–83; S Ricketson 'Confidential information—a new proprietary interest', *Melbourne University Law Review* Vol 11, pp 223–245 (Part I) and pp 289–315 (Part II), 1977; A S Weinrib 'Information and property', p. 117; J E Stuckey 'The equitable action for Breach of confidence: is information ever property?', *Sydney Law Review* Vol 9, p 402, 1981; S J Soltysinski 'Are trade secrets property?', *International Review of Industrial Property & Copyright Law* Vol 3, p 331, 1986.

22 *Oxford v Moss* (1979), 68 Cr App R 183; *Stewart* [1988] 50 D L R (4th) 1 (SCC); R G Hammond 'Theft of information', *Law Quarterly Review* Vol 100, p 252, 1984.

23 For a general review of the American position, see R T Nimmer and P A Krauthaus 'Information as a commodity: new imperatives of commercial law', *Law & Contemporary Problems* Vol 55, p 103, 1992; A Beckerman-Rodau 'Are ideas within the traditional definition of property: a jurisprudential analysis', *Arkansas Law Review* Vol 47, p 603, 1994.

160 *C D Freedman*

24 *Ruckelhaus v Monsanto Co*, 467 US 986 (1984). See R Milgrim *Trade Secrets*, §1.7 for the authoritative American position respecting the incorporation of both proprietary and tort approaches to the protection of trade secrets. Also, M Jager *Trade Secrets Law*, §4–15; E Kitch 'The law and economics of rights in valuable information', *Journal of Legal Studies* Vol 13, p 683, 1980; M Deutch 'The property concept of trade secrets in anglo-American law: an ongoing debate', *University of Richmond Law Review* Vol 31, p 313, 1997.

25 *Carpenter v US*, 484 US 19 (1984); *US v Seidlitz*, 589 F 2d 152 (4th Circ, 1978).

26 Gurry *Breach of Confidence*, pp 58–61; G Jones 'Restitution of benefits obtained in breach of another's confidence', *Law Quarterly Review* Vol 86, p 63 at p 464, 1970; *Cadbury Schweppes Inc v FBI Foods Inc* (1999), 167 DLR (4th) 577; *Lac Minerals Ltd v International Corona Resources Ltd* (1989), 61 DLR (4th) 14, 47 (SCC); *Aquaculture Corp. v. New Zealand Green Mussel Co. Ltd* (1985), 5 IPR 353 (NZCA); *Moorgate Tobacco Co. Lt. v Philip Morris (No.2)* (1984), 156 CLR 414 (Aust HC).

27 *Kitechnology B V v Unicor Gmbh* [1995] FSR 765; R P Meagher, W M C Gummow and J R F Lehane *Equity Doctrines and Remedies* 3rd edn, Butterworths, Sydney, 1992, para 4103.

28 Lord Goff and G Jones *The Law of Restitution* 4th edn, Sweet & Maxwell, London, 1993, ch 35–36; P Birks *An Introduction to the Law of Restitution*, Clarendon Press, Oxford, 1989, pp 343–346; D Friedmann 'Restitution for wrongs: the basis of liability' in W R Cornish, R Nolan, J O'Sullivan, and G Virgo (eds) *Restitution: Past, Present and Future*, Hart Publishing, Oxford, 1998, pp 133–154 at p 150.

29 *Attorney General v Guardian Newspapers Ltd (No 2)* [1990] 1 A.C. 109; *Seager v Copydex* [1967] 1 W L R 923; *House of Spring Gardens v Point Blank* [1984] I R 611.

30 *Report of the Commission on Privacy* (1972, Cmnd 5012), para 489.

31 See J T Cross 'Protecting confidential information under the criminal law of theft and fraud', *Oxford Journal of Legal Studies* Vol 11, p 264, 1991.

32 *Consultation Paper on Misuse of Trade Secrets*, para 1.24.

33 *D P P v Bignall* [1998] Crim. L R 53 (QB); but see R v. Bow Street Metropolitan Stipendiary Magistrate, ex parte Government of the United States of America [1999] 3 W.L.R. 620 (HL).

34 V Tunkel 'Industrial espionage: what can the law do?', *Denning Law Journal* p 99 at p 103, 1995.

35 English law knows no tort of unfair competition; *Bulmer Ltd v Bollinger SA* [1977] 2 CMLR 625; *Moorgate Tobacco v Philip Morris Ltd* [1985] RPC 219 (Aust HC); *Erven Warnink B V v J Townend & Sons (Hull) Ltd* [1980] RPC 31; *Hodgkinson & Corby Ltd and Roho Inc v Wards Mobility Services Ltd* [1995] FSR 169; *Mogul Steamship Co v McGregor & Co* (1889), 23 QBD 598; A Kamperman Sanders *Unfair Competition Law*, Clarendon Press, Oxford, 1997, pp 52–54. Interestingly, modern American law in this area is built on the acceptance of unfair competition norms and has been so recognised since the first *Restatement of Torts* (1939), §757. For a review of early American common law on the point, see J L Hopkins *The Law of Unfair Trade, including Trade-Marks, Trade Secrets and Good-Will*, Callaghan & Co., Chicago, 1900, pp 153–165; *International News Service v Associated Press*, 248 US 215 (1918).

36 *Francome v Mirror Group Newspapers Ltd* [1984] 1 WLR 892; *ITC Film Distributors v Video Exchange* [1982] ch 431; *Distillers Co (Biochemicals) Ltd v Times Newspapers Ltd* [1975] QB 613, 621; G Wei 'Surreptitious takings of confidential information', *Legal Studies* Vol 12, p 302, 1992.

37 *Lord Ashburton v Pape* [1913] 2 ch 469; *Argyll v Argyll* [1965] 1 All ER 611, 627; *Butler v Board of Trade* [1971] ch 680; *Commonwealth v John Fairfax & Sons* (1980), 147 CLR 39, 50 (Aust. HC); *Webster v James Chapman & Co.* [1989] 3 All E.R. 939; R P Meagher, W M C Gummow & J R F Lehane *Equity Doctrines and Remedies*, para. 4109; M Richardson 'Breach of confidence, surreptitiously or accidentally obtained information and privacy: theory versus law', *Melbourne University Law Review* Vol 19, p 673, 1994; M Richardson and J Stuckey-Clarke 'Breach of confidence' in P Parkinson (ed) *Principles of Equity*, LBC Information Services, North Ryde, 1996.

38 G Jones 'Restitution of benefits obtained in breach of another's confidence' p. 463.

39 *Franklin v Giddens* [1978] Qd. R. 72; R Wacks *Privacy and Press Freedom*, Blackstone Press, London, 1995, p 61.

40 *Restatement of Torts* (1939), §757; *Restatement of Unfair Competition* (Third) (1995), §43. See also *Ansell Rubber Co. Pty Ltd v Allied Rubber Industries Pty Ltd* [1967] V.R. 37.

41 *Creation Records Ltd v The News Group* [1997] E.M.L.R. 444; *Shelley Films Limited v Rex Features Limited* [1994] *Entertainment and Media Law Review* 134; *Linda Chih Ling Koo v Lam Tai Hing* [1993] 2 H.K.C. 1. See R Wacks *Privacy and Press Freedom*, p 63.

42 W R Cornish 'Protection of confidential information in English law', *International Review of Industrial Property & Copyright Law* Vol 6, p43 at pp 50, 53, 1975.

43 See *Moorgate Tobacco Co. Ltd v Philip Morris* (No.2) (1984), 156 C.L.R. 414 (Aust HC), where the claim was raised in relation to breach of confidence as well as being advanced on the purported tort of unfair competition.

44 See E Kitch 'The expansion of trade secrecy protection and the mobility of management employees: a new problem for the law', *South Carolina Law Review* Vol. 47, p 659, 1996.

45 R Whitaker *The End of Privacy*, WW Norton, New York, 1999, p 55.

46 See generally H Cornwall *Data Theft: Computer Fraud, Industrial Espionage and Information Crime*, Heinemann, 1987.

47 *RTC and Bridge Publications Inc. v FACT NET Inc., Wollersheim and Penny*, 901 F. Supp. 1519 (D Colo., 1995) and 901 F. Supp. 1528 (D. Colo., 1995); *RTC v Lerma*, 908 F. Supp. 1353 (ED Va, 1995). See N Hanlon-Leh 'Lessons from cyberspace and outerspace: the scientology cases', *Summer Brief* Vol 17, p 48, 1998.

48 *Consultation Paper on Misuse of Trade Secrets*, para. 3.28. This is essentially an *ultima ratio* policy similar to the position recommended by the Council of Europe in relation to interference with protected personal data; see Recommendation R(89)9 (13 September 1989) and the position advocated to the Council by the Select Committee of Experts on Computer-Related Crime of the Committee on Crime Problems. In general terms, the Law Commission's provisional model is a narrow one which builds upon its recommendations respecting the equitable action of breach of confidence made in 1981; see *Report on Breach of Confidence* (Law Com. No. 110) in which it was recommended that a statutory tort be enacted to replace the current common law and equitable regime. The Law Commission recognises that whilst the government of the day accepted its recommendations in 1989, there was no political will to legislate in the area; *Consultation Paper on Misuse of Trade Secrets*, para. 2.13.

49 G E Lynch 'The role of the criminal law in policing corporate misconduct', *Law & Contemporary Problems* Vol 60, p 23 at p 64, 1997.

50 C Steele and A Trenton 'Trade secrets: the need for criminal liability', *European Intellectual Property Law Review* Vol 20, No5, p 188 at p 192, 1998.

51 R G Bone 'A new look at trade secrets law: doctrine in search of justification', *University of California Law Review* Vol 86, p 241 at p 296, 1998.

52 See L L Hicks and J R Holbein 'Convergence of national intellectual property norms in international trading arrangements', *American University Journal of International Law & Policy* Vol 12, p 769, 1997; J H Reichman 'Beyond the historical lines of demarcation: competition law, intellectual property rights, and international trade after GATT's Uruguay Round', *Brooklyn Journal of International Law* Vol 20, p 75 at p 76, 1993.

53 *Paris Convention for the Protection of Industrial Property* (Stockholm Act of 14 July 1967 of the Paris Convention for the Protection of Industrial Property), Art 10*bis* provides for member states to have effective protection against unfair competition covering 'any act of competition contrary to honest practices in industrial and commercial matters' with specific examples; see G H C Bodenhausen *Guide to the Paris Convention for the Protection of Industrial Property*, BIRPA, Geneva, 1968, p 145, who presents a history of the Convention and these provisions from the original 1883 Convention.

54 Institute of Law Research and Reform and a Federal Provincial Working Party, *Trade Secrets* (Report No 46, 1986), para 2.13. Similar views were expressed in the Judiciary Committee, House of Representatives report to the US Congress with the tabling of the bill that became the *Economic Espionage Act of 1996*; Report No 104–788, 104th Congress (2nd Session); also the

Senate Report, No 104–359. Similarly, the *Annual Report to Congress on Foreign Collection and Industrial Espionage* by the President under the *Intelligence Authorization Act for Fiscal Year 1995*, s.809(b).

55 ASIS conducts research on industrial property losses; see the 1998 Report, covering 1996–1997, by R Heffernan and D Swartwood ASIS, 1998. A similar survey is the 1996 Information Systems Security Survey in S M Shaker and M P Gembicki *The WarRoom Guide to Competitive Intelligence*, McGraw Hill, New York, 1999, pp 223–228.

56 For example, J Fialka *War by Other Means: Economic Espionage in America*, WW Norton & Co, New York, 1997, and 'Stealing the spark: why economic espionage works in America', *Washington Quarterly* Vol 19, p 175, 1996; I Winkler *Corporate Espionage*, Prima Publishing, 1997; B. Parad, *Commercial Espionage: 79 Ways Competitors Can Get Any Business Secret*, Global Connection, Skokie, 1997, are just a few of the books recently published.

57 See S L Burr 'Protecting business secrets in national and international commerce', *Science Communication* Vol 17, p 274, 1996. See also L F Mock and D Rosenbaum 'A study of trade secrets theft in high technology industries', US National Institute of Justice, Washington, 1988.

58 See I C Ballon 'The law of The Internet: developing a framework for making new law (II)', *Cyberspace Law* Vol 10, p 16, 1997; S M Hanley 'International internet regulation: a multinational approach', *John Marshall Journal of Computer & Information Law* Vol 16, p 997, 1998.

59 *Saltman Engineering Co Ltd v Campbell Engineering Co Ltd* [1948] R.P.C. 203, 215.

60 *Faccenda Chicken v Fowler* [1987] ch 117, 137–138.

61 *Consultation Paper on Misuse of Trade Secrets*, para. 4.22.

62 'Trade secret misappropriation: a cost–benefit response to the Fourth Amendment analogy' p 461.

63 *Lecture on Discoveries and Inventions*, in R P Basler, M D Pratt and L A Dunlap *The Collected Works of Abraham Lincoln*, Rutgers University Press, New Brunswick, 1953, supplemented.

[17]

Cyberstalking: The Regulation of Harassment on the Internet

By Louise Ellison
Lecturer in Law, University of Reading

and Yaman Akdeniz*
Ph.D. student at the Cyberlaw Research Unit, Centre for Criminal Justice Studies, Department of Law, University of Leeds

Summary: *This paper highlights the issues surrounding on-line harassment and asks whether potential victims are adequately protected by existing national laws. It also examines the unique law enforcement problems which the Internet presents as well as addressing the implications legal regulations of the Internet may have for free speech and privacy on-line. Non-legal means of tackling harassment on the Internet are also explored.*

Introduction

Recent years have seen a series of "moral panics" regarding information accessible on the Internet and its use for criminal activity. These include the availability of sexually explicit material,[1] the use of the Internet by paedophiles to distribute child pornography,[2] the use of the Internet by Neo-Nazis and other racist groups,[3] the availability of hate speech and bomb-making instructions[4] and the use of encryption technology to secure private communications by terrorists and

---

* The authors would like to thank Professor Clive Walker, Director of Centre for Criminal Justice Studies, University of Leeds for his comments on this article.

[1] See P. Elmer-Dewitt "On a screen near you: Cyberporn", *Time*, July 3, 1995: M., Rimm, "Marketing Pornography on the Information Superhighway" [1995] 83 *Georgetown Law Journal* 1839. Note that Marty Rimm's 18-month study was later found to be misleading because it was based upon the many adult-oriented BBSs all around the U.S. but not the Internet. For a critique of the Rimm study see J. Wallace and M. Mangan *Sex, Laws, and Cyberspace: Freedom and Censorship on the Frontiers of the Online Revolution* (New York: Henry Holt & Company, 1996).

[2] See "Paedophiles use encoding devices to make secret use of Internet", *The Times*, November 21, 1995; "Two jailed for child porn on Internet", *The Daily Telegraph*, May 25, 1996; "Use of Computer Network for Child Sex Sets off Raids", *New York Times*, September 14, 1995; "Minister calls for Internet controls", *The Daily Telegraph*, March 22, 1996; "Six years for priest who broadcast abuse of boys to Internet paedophiles", *The Daily Telegraph*, November 13, 1996.

[3] See U.S. Anti-Defamation League Report, *High-Tech Hate: Extremist Use of the Internet*, October 1997.

[4] See "Youths held after pipe-bomb blasts", *The Daily Telegraph*, March 5, 1998.

organised crime.[5] In reality, these fears are largely misplaced; while the Internet tends to produce extreme versions of problems, it rarely produces genuinely new ones.

The phenomenon of cyberstalking and on-line harassment looks set to be the focus of the next Internet-related moral panic. In the United States, a number of states have already introduced specific cyberstalking legislation. In the United Kingdom, extensive press coverage of stalking cases, which focused upon the bizarre and menacing behaviour of stalkers and the devastating effect stalking had on the lives of victims, ensured its place as the crime of the nineties.[6] The stalking debate within the United Kingdom was fuelled by a number of high-profile acquittals which served to highlight the deficiencies of both civil and criminal law in dealing with those who engage in stalking activity.[7] In March 1996, Charles Wilson was found not guilty of intentional harassment, having allegedly plagued Charlotte Sell for two years. The magistrate in the case, Geoffrey Breen, stated that while Sell had clearly been caused considerable alarm and distress by the defendant's actions, what the defendant had done amounted to stalking but stalking was not a criminal offence.[8] Dennis Chambers allegedly waged a campaign of harassment against Margaret Bent for four years but was acquitted of causing grievous bodily harm in September 1996, on the grounds that there was no evidence of intention to cause psychological injury.[9] At this time there were also important developments in both the criminal and civil law responding to the problem of stalking.[10] Concern that existing laws did not adequately protect victims of stalking finally led to the enactment of the Protection from Harassment Act 1997.[11]

This paper sets out the case against the introduction of further legal measures to deal with on-line harassment. It argues that fears about on-line activity and content which prompt calls for heavy-handed legislation are often founded on misconceptions as to the nature and the scale of the problem. Such calls also invariably belie a certain naivety with regards to the unique law enforcement problems created by

[5] See D. E. Denning and W. E. Baugh Jr., "Cases Involving Encryption in Crime and Terrorism," October 1997, http://guru.cosc.georgetown.edu/~denning/crypto/cases.html. But see also Global Internet Liberty Campaign, *Cryptography and Liberty*, 1998, at http://www.gilc.org/crypto/crypto-survey.html, Y. Akdeniz, "No Chance for Key Recovery: Encryption and International Principles of Human and Political Rights" [1998] *Web JCLI* 1.

[6] M. Goode, "Stalking: The Crime of the Nineties" (1995) 19 *Cambridge Law Journal* 21.

[7] See *The Independent*, January 23, 1995; *The Guardian*, October 24, 1996.

[8] See "Law on stalking may change to protect women", *The Daily Telegraph*, March 6, 1996.

[9] See "Victim is left alone with fear as jury clears stalker", *The Daily Telegraph*, September 18, 1996.

[10] As regards criminal law, see *Ireland, Burstow* [1997] 3 W.L.R. 534. In *Ireland*, the defendant made repeated silent telephone calls to three women who suffered anxiety and depressive disorders as a result. He was convicted of assault occasioning actual bodily harm contrary to s.47 of the Offences Against the Person Act 1861 and sentenced to three years' imprisonment. In *Burstow*, the defendant was convicted of maliciously inflicting grievous bodily harm, contrary to s.20 of the 1861 Act. Burstow waged a campaign of harassment against Tracy Slant during which he made abusive telephone calls to her, watcher her house, stole clothing from her washing line and scattered condoms in her garden. See M. Allen, "Look Who's Stalking: Seeking a Solution to the Problem of Stalking" [1996] *Web JCLI* 4, C. Wells, "Stalking: The Criminal Law Response" [1997] Crim.L.R. 463.

[11] See Home Office, *Stalking—The Solutions: A Consultation Paper* (London: HMSO, 1996).

Cyberstalking: The Regulation of Harassment on the Internet 31

the Internet. In the case of on-line harassment, there are the difficulties of tracing the cyberstalker who remains anonymous and problems of dealing with harassment that crosses national boundaries. The borderless nature of the Internet also means that actions by individual governments and international organisations can have a profound effect on the rights of the law-abiding Internet users, or "netizens", around the world. Legal regulation of the Internet, this article contends, should not be achieved at the significant expense of fundamental rights such as freedom of speech and privacy of on-line users around the globe.

What is on-line harassment?

Harassment on the Internet can take a variety of guises.[12] A direct form of Internet harassment may involve the sending of unwanted e-mails which are abusive, threatening or obscene from one person to another.[13] It may involve electronic sabotage, in the form of sending the victim hundreds or thousands of junk e-mail messages (the activity known as "spamming") or sending computer viruses. Indirect forms of harassment may involve a cyberstalker impersonating his or her victim on-line and sending abusive e-mails or fraudulent spams in the victim's name.[14] Victims may be subscribed without their permission to a number of mailing lists with the result that they receive hundreds of unwanted e-mails everyday. One victim of cyberstalking in the United States, Cynthia Armistead, received thousands of offensive telephone calls after her stalker posted a phoney advertisement on a USENET discussion group offering her services as a prostitute and providing her home address and telephone number.[15] In another case, again in the United States, a woman who complained about a literacy agency on-line found that her home address and telephone number were posted on alt.sex. USENET discussion groups.[16] Being the victim of on-line harassment undoubtedly causes considerable anxiety as well as annoyance. The real fear, however, is that offensive and threatening behaviour that originates on-line will escalate into "real-life" stalking. If the name of the victim is known to the stalker, then it is relatively easy to find out further personal details such as the victim's address and telephone number. In the case of Cynthia Armistead, offensive e-mails were soon followed by abusive telephone calls. Fears in the United States have been fuelled by a number of cases of Internet dating which have been linked to assaults, stalking incidents, and even murders.[17] The arrival in Britain of a controversial new computer database,

[handwritten margin note: cyber-harassment similiar to cyber bullying - more likely in adults.]

---

[12] D. Nelson, *Cyberstalking*, at http://www.tccmweb.com/swcm/may97/stalk.htm.

[13] D. McGraw, "Sexual Harassment in Cyberspace: The Problem of Unwelcome E-mail" [1995] *Rutgers Computer and Technology Law Journal* 492.

[14] See for example the case of *Zeran v. America Online, Inc.*, 958 F.Supp. (1997), U.S. Court of Appeals, 4th Circuit, 129 F.2d 327 (1997); U.S. Supreme Court, Cert. Pet. 97–1488.

[15] See http://www.mindspring.com/~technomom/harassed/.

[16] Jayne Hitchcock wanted to let other writers know about a New York agency asking for $225 to review her book, so she posted a warning on the Internet. Before long, she was "mail bombed" with more than 200 electronic mail missives. Her name, telephone number and address appeared on racist and sex newsgroups, inviting suitors to call her or come to her home day or night. See "Author's real-life story is cyberspace nightmare", *The Washington Times*, February 19, 1998.

[17] "Mainers log on, looking for love in cyberspace despite the dangers sometimes associated with anonymous, online romance, hundreds take the chance," *Portland Press Herald*, March 30, 1997.

192.com, which enables users to obtain an address and telephone number simply by typing in a name promises to make life even easier for stalkers.[18] The National Anti-Stalking and Harassment Campaign reports that between January 1994 and November 1995, 7,000 victims of stalking telephoned their helpline.[19] It is clear that stalking is a major real-life problem but whether the Internet is to prove an attractive picking ground for stalkers remains to be seen.

Legal regulation

There have been calls in the United States for specific cyberstalking legislation.[20] It is argued that victims of cyberstalking are inadequately protected as existing laws are too inflexible to cover on-line harassment.[21] Since its experiences in regard to the Internet tend to be more advanced than those in the United Kingdom, this section briefly examines the difficulties experienced in the United States in the legal regulation of e-mail harassment but argues that such problems are unlikely to be encountered in the United Kingdom.

United States

All United States states now have legislation designed to deal with real-life stalking, but there have proved to be a number of difficulties in applying these state laws to e-mail harassment. California was the first state to pass a stalking law in 1990, and all the other states have since followed. The first United States state to include on-line communications in its statutes against stalking was Michigan in 1993.[22] Under the Michigan Criminal Code, "harassment" means conduct directed toward a victim that includes repeated or continuing unconsented contact, that would cause a reasonable individual to suffer emotional distress, and that actually causes the victim to suffer emotional distress. Unconsented contact under the Michigan Code specifically includes sending mail or electronic communications to that individual. A number of other United States states besides Michigan have anti-stalking laws that include electronic harassment.[23] These states include: Arizona,[24] Alaska,[25] Connecticut,[26] New York,[27] Oklahoma[28] and Wyoming.[29]

---

[18] See "Stalker fears over phones database disk", *The Scotsman*, October 28, 1997.

[19] See Home Office (1996), *op. cit.* See also P. Tjaden and N. Thoennes "Stalking in America: Findings From the National Violence Against Women Survey," Research in Brief, April 1998.

[20] See "As Online Harassment Grows, Calls for New Laws Follow," *The New York Times*, April 2, 1997.

[21] See G. Barton "Cyberstalking: Crime, Enforcement and Personal Responsibility in the On-line World" (1996) at http://www.ucla.edu/Classes/Archives/S96/340/cyberlaw.htm.

[22] Michigan Criminal Code, Stalking: s.28.643(8). Definitions. 1993. s.411h.

[23] See CyberAngels, "Cyberstalking and the Law," http://www.cyberangels.org/stalking/stalk3.html.

[24] Arizona Criminal Code (1995): 13–2921.

[25] Alaska Criminal Law s.11.41.270.

[26] Connecticut Penal Code s.53a–183.

[27] New York Penal Code § 240.30.

[28] Oklahoma Code (1996) § 21–1173.

[29] Wyoming Code, s.6–2–506.

Cyberstalking: The Regulation of Harassment on the Internet 33

In the United States, the constitutionality of state anti-stalking legislation remains undecided.[30] Anti-stalking legislation has been challenged on the grounds of being too vague and too broad.[31] Michigan was the first state to charge someone with on-line stalking. Andrew Armchambeau refused to stop sending e-mail messages to a woman he met through a computer dating agency and was charged under Michigan stalking laws in May 1994. Archambeau's lawyers sought to challenge the constitutionality of the anti-stalking laws. In January 1996, Armchambeau however pleaded no contest to the stalking charge.[32]

McGraw highlights further difficulties in using anti-stalking legislation to combat on-line harassment.[33] In a number of states, McGraw explains, the language of the statute requires physical activity, thus exempting e-mail harassment. Some state statutes also require a "credible threat" of serious physical injury or death.[34] In such states, e-mail harassment is unlikely to meet this standard. This was true in the Jake Baker case. Using the pseudonym "Jake Baker", Abraham Jacob Alkhabaz, a student at the University of Michigan, posted stories to a newgroup called "alt.sex.stories". One of Baker's stories described the rape, torture and murder of a woman.[35] Baker used the real name of a fellow student from the University of Michigan for the victim. Baker also corresponded with a reader of the story via e-mail who used a pseudonym of "Arthur Gonda" in Canada. In over 40 e-mails both men discussed their desire to abduct and physically injure women in their local area. Baker was arrested and held without bail and was charged with the interstate transmission of a threat to kidnap or injure another. Though most described Baker as a quiet "computer geek" with no history of violence, the stories he posted on the Internet were horrific and disturbing. A United States District Court judge dismissed the case against Baker, ruling that the threats lacked a specific intent to act or a specific target required under the Michigan stalking law.[36] It was the American Civil Liberties Union's ("ACLU") submission that his was a case of "pure speech"[37]: "No immediate harm results from the expression of a desire to commit a crime. The only warrant for proscribing such expression is the possibility that it will produce harm, should the speaker act on his desire, in the future."[38] ACLU also quoted Brandeis J. in *Whitney v. California*: "Fear of serious injury cannot alone justify suppression of free speech . . . To justify suppression of free

---

[30] See K. Boychuk, "Are Stalking Law Unconstitutionally Vague or Overbroad?" (1994) 88 Nw.U.L.Rev. 769, J. Hueter, "Will Washington Stalking Laws Survive Constitutional Scrutiny?" (1997) 72 Wash. L.Rev. 213.

[31] B. Jensen, "Cyberstalking: Crime, Enforcement and Personal Responsibility in the On-line World," http://www.law.ucla.edu/Classes/Archive/S96/340/cyberlaw.htm.

[32] See "Man pleads no contest in stalking case", *The Detroit News*, January 25, 1996.

[33] D. McGraw (1995) *loc.cit.*

[34] See generally for verbal threats, J. T. Nockleby, "Hate Speech in Context: The Case of Verbal Threats" (1994) 42 Buff.L.Rev. 653.

[35] H. Brook-Szachta, "U.S. v. Jake Baker: The Role of Unique Features of Electronic Mail in a 'True Threat' Analysis," http://www.libraries.wayne.edu/~jlitman/pbrooks.html.

[36] See *U.S. v. Baker*, 890 F. Supp. 1375 (1995). See also Jake Baker Information Page at http://www.mit.edu:8001/activities/safe/safe/cases/umich-baker-story/Baker/Jake_Baker.html.

[37] See ACLU amicus brief in *U.S. v. Jake Baker & Arthur Gonda* at http://www.aclu.org/court/baker.html. See also *Watts v. United States*, 394 U.S. 705, 707 (1969).

[38] *ibid.*

speech there must be reasonable ground to fear that serious evil will result if free speech is practiced. There must be reasonable ground to believe that the danger apprehended is imminent."[39] It was ruled that the sadistic fantasies contained in Baker's posting to USENET were protected by the First Amendment.[40]

In the United States, there are also difficulties in applying federal and state telephone harassment laws to e-mail harassment. According to Barton, few state telephone harassment laws presently apply to e-mail. Barton argues that e-mail harassment is best tackled by such telephone harassment laws, rather than by anti-stalking legislation, and therefore calls for their amendment by adding electronic communication provisions which adequately address the characteristics and scope of e-mail harassment.[41]

United Kingdom

In contrast to the situation described in the United States, existing United Kingdom laws are sufficiently flexible to encompass on-line stalking and e-mail harassment. The Telecommunications Act 1984, s.43, for example, makes it an offence to send by means of a public telecommunications system[42] a message or other matter that is grossly offensive or of an indecent, obscene or menacing character. For the purposes of the Act, a public telecommunication system is any telecommunications system so designated by the Secretary of State and is not confined to British Telecom's telephone system.[43] The Act therefore potentially covers the sending of offensive e-mail messages in some instances.[44] The Act will not apply, however, in cases where the data is transmitted by using a local area

---

[39] 274 U.S. 357 at 376–377 (1927).

[40] See 18 USC §875(c). See J. Wallace, and M. Mangan (1996) *op. cit.*, F. S. Haiman, *Speech Acts and the First Amendment* (Southern Illinois University Press, 1993); F. S. Haiman *Speech and Law in a Free Society* (University of Chicago Press, 1981), C. E. Baker, *Human Liberty and Freedom of Speech* (Oxford University Press, 1989).

[41] In October 1996, a Texas District judge issued one of the first restraining orders to an on-line stalker which was itself delivered by e-mail and posted in newsgroups. Kevin Massey was accused of the on-line harassment of Teresa Maynard, co-founder of the ISP, Internet America. The temporary restraining order was granted following allegations that Massey had made "vulgar" posting to newsgroups which referred to Maynard and sent "lewd" and "insulting" e-mail messages. See "In Harassment Case, Judge Issues Injunction via the Net," *The New York Times*, October 17, 1997.

[42] A "telecommunications system" is defined in s.4(1) of the Telecommunications Act 1984 as "a system for the conveyance, through the agency of electric, magnetic, electro-magnetic, electro-chemical or electro-mechanical energy, of: (a) Speech, music and other sounds. (b) Visual images. (c) Signals serving for the impartation . . . of any matter otherwise than in the form of sounds or visual images . . . "

[43] Telecommunication Act 1984, s.9(1). See also House of Commons, Home Affairs Committee, *First Report on Computer Pornography*, (1993–1994 H.C. 126) Appendix 2: Memorandum by the Crown Prosecution Service, at p.27, para. 66.

[44] The Criminal Justice and Public Order Act 1994, s.92 increased the maximum fine for an offence under s.43 to level 5 from level 3 and made it an imprisonable offence with a maximum term of six months. The new sentencing powers bring the penalty more into line with the maximum sentence for transmitting indecent or obscene material through the post (which is 12 months' imprisonment) contrary to s.11(2) of the Post Office Act 1953. See C. Manchester, "CJPOA 1994: Obscenity, Pornography and Videos" [1995] Crim.L.R. 123 at 127.

network unless part of the transmission is routed through a public telecommunications system.[45] So, whether the Act applies to e-mail harassment will depend upon the telecommunications network used, but the Act is not limited to voice communications.

The Protection from Harassment Act 1997 may also be invoked in cases of on-line harassment. This Act provides a combination of civil and criminal measures to deal with stalking.[46] It creates two criminal offences, the summary offence of criminal harassment[47] and an indictable offence involving fear of violence.[48] Under section 2 it is an offence to pursue a course of conduct which amounts to the harassment of another where the accused knew or ought to have known that the course of conduct amounts to harassment.[49] A person commits an offence under section 4 if he pursues a course of conduct which causes another to fear, on at least two occasions, that violence will be used against him. It is sufficient that the accused ought to have known that his course of conduct would cause the other to so fear on each of those occasions. The Act also gives courts the power to impose restraining orders on convicted defendants, prohibiting them from further conduct which may be injurious to the victim.[50] Breach of such an order caries a potential sentence of five years' imprisonment. Harassment includes alarm and distress.[51] Harassment, alarm and distress are not defined in the Act. These terms are to be given their ordinary meaning. The range of behaviour covered by the Act is thus potentially extremely wide. The sending of abusive, threatening e-mails or the posting of offensive material would constitute an offence under section 2 of the Act as long as it amounts to a course of conduct (for example, more than one e-mail must be sent) and the offender knew or ought to have known that his conduct amounted to harassment. According to Home Office Minister Alun Michael, there have been 504 prosecutions under section 2 of the 1997 Act, which have resulted in 247 convictions.[52] None of these prosecutions were Internet related and the majority dealt with neighbourhood nuisance issues rather than stalking activity.[53]

Although existing United Kingdom laws may potentially provide better protection from on-line harassment than that afforded, for example, by United States anti-stalking legislation, the use of these laws will be necessarily limited to relatively straightforward cases of an identifiable offender sending obscene, offensive or

---

[45] Also note that the Malicious Communications Act 1988, s.1 creates an offence of sending letters which convey, *inter alia*, threats with the purpose of causing distress or anxiety. The Act does not however cover telecommunications messages. See C. P. Walker, "Criminal Libel," in P. Milmo and W. V. H. Rogers, *Gatley on Libel and Slander* (London: Sweet & Maxwell, 1988) at 22.17.

[46] See for example S. Gibbsons, "Freedom from Fear of Stalking" (1998) 6 *European Journal on Criminal Policy and Research* 133–141.

[47] A person guilty of this offence is liable to imprisonment for a term not exceeding six months: s.2(2).

[48] A person guilty of this offence is liable to imprisonment for a term not exceeding five years: s.4(4).

[49] "Conduct" includes speech (s.7(4)) and "course of conduct" is defined as conduct on at least two occasions (s.7(3)).

[50] s.5.

[51] s.7(2).

[52] In addition, 171 cautions have been recorded provisionally for the offence. See House of Commons Written Answers, Protection from Harassment Act, col. 298, June 18, 1998.

[53] See for example the cases of *Huntingdon Life Sciences Ltd v. Curtin, The Times*, December 11, 1997; *McGlennan v. McKinnon*, 1998 S.L.T. 494.

threatening e-mails within the United Kingdom. This is because of the unique enforcement problems involved in the legal regulation of the Internet. The Protection from Harassment Act 1997 may not, for example, avail the victim of on-line harassment when the offender is outside the United Kingdom or if the offender chooses to remain anonymous.

Enforcement problems

"Even with the most carefully crafted legislation, enforcing a law in a virtual community creates unique problems never before faced by law enforcement agencies."[54]

These problems pertain mainly to international aspects of the Internet. It is a medium that can be accessed by anyone throughout the globe with a computer and modem. This means, as explained below, that a potential offender may not be within the jurisdiction where an offence is committed. Anonymous use of the Internet, though beneficial in many instances, also promises to create challenges for law enforcement authorities.

The international stalker

The Internet is a global medium regardless of frontiers, and this creates new possibilities for the so-called cyberstalker. Cheap and easy access to the Internet means that distance is no obstacle to the cyberstalker. A user in the United Kingdom may be stalked by someone on the other side of the world by the click of a mouse. The Internet is not a "lawless place",[55] but there are difficulties in applying laws that are made for specific nation states and this would be also true of applying national harassment and stalking laws to the Internet.

For example, under section 43 of the Telecommunications Act 1984, an offence is not committed where a telecommunication system located outside the jurisdiction is used to send offensive materials into the United Kingdom.[56] Even if the 1984 Act covered telecommunication systems located outside the jurisdiction, there would have been difficulties for prosecuting a foreign cyberstalker. First, the act of the cyberstalker might not constitute an offence within the country of origin; and even if it did so there may be problems of extradition. There would also be problems in cross-border policing.

The United Kingdom Government recently dealt with the problem of cross-border policing in the context of transnational child abuse with the Sexual Offences (Conspiracy and Incitement) Act 1996. The Act deals with British sex offenders abroad, and section 2 of the 1996 Act makes it an offence to incite another person to commit certain sexual acts against children abroad. The scope of incitement for the purpose of section 2 extends to the use of Internet, and any incitement will be deemed to take place in the United Kingdom if the message is received in the

---

[54] B. Jensen, "Cyberstalking: Crime, Enforcement and Personal Responsibility in the On-Line World," http://www.law.ucla.edu/Classes/Archive/S96/340/cyberlaw.htm.

[55] See J. R. Reidenberg, "Governing Networks and Cyberspace Rule-Making" (1996) 45 *Emory Law Journal* 911.

[56] House of Commons, Home Affairs Committee: *First Report on Computer Pornography* (1993–1994) H.C. 126) Appendix 2: Memorandum by the Crown Prosecution Service at p.27, paras 67 and 68.

United Kingdom.[57] The same principles could apply if the 1997 Protection from Harassment Act were to be extended to British offenders who live abroad. This would only be a limited and partial solution, however, to the problem of international stalkers. In addition, recent criticism from police officers of the 1996 Act casts doubt upon the effectiveness of this kind of extraterritorial legislation.[58]

The anonymous stalker

Internet technology creates possibilities for anonymous communications and hence for anonymous cyberstalking. The identity of a cyberstalker may, therefore, not be revealed or found. The fluidity of identity on the Internet has been described as one of its chief attractions.[59] The Internet facilitates experimentation with different identities. Users may adopt an on-line persona which bears little, if any, resemblance to his or her real identity. Pseudonymity is achieved by simply forging or "spoofing" an e-mail header so as to create an on-line digital persona. For example, Alice can create a new persona for her on-line participation in USENET discussion groups with an e-mail address such as Billy-Kid@compuserve.com rather than using her real e-mail address, alice@compuserve.com. Impersonation of other users may also be possible by faking the header of an e-mail message to make it appear as if it originates from the victim's account. Anonymity on the Internet can be achieved by using an anonymous re-mailer. Re-mailers are computer services which cloak the identity of users who send messages through them by stripping all identifying information from an e-mail and assigning a random replacement header. The most sophisticated re-mailer technology is called MixMaster[60] which uses public key cryptography, granting unprecedented anonymity to users who wish to communicate in complete privacy. A user who chains together several re-mailers could send communications safe in the knowledge that the trail created would be so complex that it would be impossible to follow.[61] According to Ball, true anonymous re-mailers maintain no database of addresses:

"When messages are resent from a truly anonymous re-mailer, the header information is set either to a deliberately misleading address, or to randomly generated characters. There is no record of the connection between the sending address and the destination address. For greater security, many users program messages to pass through five to twenty re-mailers before the message arrives at its final destination. This technique, known as chaining, assures greater

---

[57] See also the Sex Offenders Act 1997, s.7 which deals with sexual offences committed outside the U.K. See P. Alldridge, "Sexual Offences (Conspiracy and Incitement) Act 1996, Sex Offenders Act 1997" [1997] Crim.L.R. 655.

[58] No prosecution has been achieved under this law within the U.K. since its enactment. See I. Burrell, "Child-sex tourists escape UK law," *The Independent,* July 13, 1998.

[59] See R. Wacks, "Privacy in Cyberspace: Personal Information, Free Speech, and the Internet" in P. Birks (ed.), *Privacy and Loyalty* (Oxford: Clarendon Press, 1997), at p.93.

[60] Lance Cottrel, Mixmaster FAQ, http://www.obscura.com/~loki/re-mailer/mixmaster-faq.html.

[61] Some re-mailers keep a record of the original e-mail address and thus senders are traceable. See L. Detweiler, "Identity, Privacy and Anonymity on the Internet" (1993) at http://www.rewi.hu-berlin.de/Datenschutz/Netze/privint.html; S. Greenberg "Threats, Harassment and Hate On-line: Recent Development" (1997) 6 *Boston Public Interest Journal* 673; M. Froomkin, "Anonymity and its Enmities" [1995] *Journal of Online Law* article 4 at http://www.law.cornell.edu/j/froomkin.htm.

security than sending through a single re-mailer. Even if some re-mailers keep secret records of their transactions, a single honest re-mailing system will protect the user. One disadvantage is that unless the sender has identified herself in the body of the message, the recipient has no way to reply to an anonymously sent message."[62]

The ease with which users can send anonymous messages would render legal regulation of on-line harassment a difficult, if not impossible task. Tracing a cyberstalker may prove an insurmountable obstacle to any legal action where the electronic footprints which users leave behind are effectively eliminated by re-mailer technology.

Given these enforcement problems, some commentators have called for the prohibition of anonymous communications while others have called for restrictions to be placed on anonymity.[63] Opponents of anonymity argue that it facilitates illegal or reprehensible conduct and allows perpetrators to evade the consequences of their actions.[64] Arguments based on the social psychology of anonymity have been used.[65] Anonymity, it is alleged, lowers social inhibitions and encourages anti-social behaviour and aggression.[66] People will say and do things on the Internet, it is maintained, that they would never seriously entertain doing in real life.[67] Those who call for the prohibition of anonymous remailers or other restrictions on on-line anonymity may, however, fail to recognise the cost of such action to the on-line community in terms of fundamental freedoms. Placing restrictions upon anonymity on-line would have serious negative repercussions for freedom of expression and privacy on the Internet, as shall now be described.[68]

Freedom of speech

"Freedom of speech and privacy are frequently conceived as rights or interests of the individual, and as rights or interests of the community as a whole."[69]

Free speech can be facilitated by anonymity on-line. It allows human rights activists, political dissidents, and whistle-blowers throughout the world to engage in confidential communications free from intrusion.[70] It is also essential for political

---

[62] See affidavit of witness Patrick Ball in *ACLU v. Miller*, January, 1997, http://www. aclu.org./issues/cyber/censor/gapbaffidavit.html.

[63] M. Kabay, "Anonymity and Pseudonymity in Cyberspace: Deindividuation, Incivility and Lawlessness Versus Freedom and Privacy," paper presented at the Annual Conference of the European Institute for Computer Anti-virus Research, March 1998.

[64] L. Detweiler (1993), *op. cit.*

[65] V. Bell, and D. de la Rue, *Gender Harassment on the Internet*, http://www.gsu.edu/~lawppw/lawand.papers/harass.html.

[66] M. Kabay (1998), *op. cit.*

[67] S. Greenberg (1997), *op. cit.*

[68] Report of the Committee on Privacy and Related Matters, Chairman David Calcutt Q.C. (Cmnd. 1102, London: HMSO, 1990), para. 3.12, p.7.

[69] R. Wacks, (1997), *op. cit.* at p.103.

[70] See D. Banisar "Bug Off! A Primer on Electronic Surveillance for Human Rights Organizations" *International Privacy Bulletin*, October 1995.

Cyberstalking: The Regulation of Harassment on the Internet   39

discussion and some special subject interest groups who deal with sensitive issues. Users seeking access to information on AIDS, for example, or seeking guidance from the Samaritans clearly benefit from remaining anonymous. One of the best-known anonymous re-mailers on the Internet, anon.penet.fi, was offered for more than three years by Johann Helsingius.[71-72] Among its users were Amnesty International, the Samaritans,[73] and the West Mercia Police who used it as the basis of their "Crimestoppers" scheme. Anonymity also allows users to by-pass class, race and gender stereotypes. As one commentator states, "I may have a good idea you will not consider if you know my name. Or I may individually fear retaliation if my identity is revealed. Anonymity is therefore good, because it encourages greater diversity of speech."[74]

In the United States, attempts to control anonymity on the Internet have been ruled unconstitutional.[75] In *ACLU v. Miller*,[76] the Federal District Court agreed with the ACLU, that a recent Georgia statute is unconstitutionally vague and over-broad because it bars on-line users from using pseudonyms or communicating anonymously over the Internet. Judge Shoob noted that Georgia's law, "sweeps innocent, protected speech within its scope." "The Court recognised that anonymity is the passport for entry into cyberspace for many persons," according to Gerald Weber, Legal Director of the ACLU of Georgia. "Without anonymity, victims of domestic violence, persons in Alcoholics Anonymous, people with AIDS and so many others would fear using the Internet to seek information and support."[77]

There is no express constitutional guarantee for freedom of speech in Britain because of the absence of a comprehensive bill of rights. Although the European Convention on Human Rights, which protects the freedom of expression in Article 10, does bind the United Kingdom in international law as an external bill of rights, it has not been directly implemented in the national laws. This situation is however set to change following the introduction of the Human Rights Bill 1997–1998[78] which will incorporate the ECHR into the United Kingdom legal systems. Article 10 of the ECHR states that:

[71-72] See E. Dyson, *Release 2.0: A Design for Living in the Digital Age* (London: Viking, 1997), p.236; J. Wallace and M. Mangan (1996), *op. cit.* See also *the Church of Scientology vs. anon.penet.fi* pages at http://www.xs4all.nl/~kspaink/rnewman/anon/penet/html.

[73] The Samaritans now use another anonymous re-mailer service (samaritans@anon.twwells.com). See http://www.samaritans.org.uk/sams.html/contact2.html.

[74] See J. Wallace, "Mrs. McIntyre in Cyberspace: Some thoughts on anonymity," *The Ethical Spectacle*, May 1997 at http://www.spectacle.org/597/mcintyre.html.

[75] *NAACP v. Alabama ex rel. Patterson*, 357 U.S. 449 (1958) and more recently *McIntyre v. Ohio Elections Commission*, 514 U.S. 334 (1995); 115 S.Ct. 1511 (1995). See A. Branscomb, "Anonymity, Autonomy, and Accountability: Challenges to the First Amendment in Cyberspaces" (1995) 104 Yale L.J. 1639 at 1642.

[76] See *American Civil Liberties Union of Georgia v. Miller*, 977 F. Supp. 1228 (N.D. Ga. 1997) (preliminary injunction), permanent injunction entered, 1997 U.S. Dist. LEXIS 14972 (August 7, 1997).

[77] ACLU press release, "ACLU Wins First-Ever Challenge to a State Internet Censorship Law in Georgia," June 20, 1997, http://www.aclu.org/news/n062097b.html.

[78] 1997–78 H.C. No. 219. See House of Commons Library Research Paper, *The Human Rights Bill [HL], Bill 119 of 1997/98: Some constitutional and legislative aspects* (No: 98/27, 1998).

"1. Everyone has the right to freedom of expression. This right should include freedom to hold opinions and to receive and impart information and ideas without interference by public authority and regardless of frontiers . . .

2. The exercise of these freedoms, since it carries with it duties and responsibilities, may be subject to such formalities, conditions, restrictions or penalties as are prescribed by law and are necessary in a democratic society, in the interests of national security, territorial integrity or public safety, for the prevention of disorder or crime, for the protection of health or morals, for the protection of the reputation or rights of others, for preventing the disclosure if information received in confidence, or for maintaining the authority and impartiality of the judiciary."

The importance of anonymity as a facilitator of free speech has been affirmed by the European Court of Human Rights in *Goodwin v. U.K.*.[79] The Court recognised that the press has a vital watchdog role in a healthy democratic society and that this function could be undermined if journalists are not reasonably allowed to keep confidential the sources of their information. In this case, the Court concluded that the application of the law of contempt to a recalcitrant journalist was not necessary where the subject of the damaging story had already obtained an injunction against publication. It is not clear that the same level of protection of anonymity would be afforded by the European Court to the idle gossip of non-press speakers such as is common on the Internet,[80] but anonymous "political speech" would deserve higher protection.[81] Moreover, there may also be instances where Internet postings may lead to persecution if the identity of the individual is known.[82–83] The Supreme Court in *NAACP v. Alabama ex rel. Patterson*[84] stated that "inviolability of privacy in group association may in many circumstances be indispensable to preservation of freedom of association".[85] However, the lead it has given in regard to "public" speech is important and is not yet reflected by the English courts, as illustrated by the later case of *Camelot v. Centaur Communications* in which the Court of Appeal demanded disclosure in circumstances not dissimilar to *Goodwin*.[86] Hopefully, the

---

[79] Application No. 17488/90, Reports of Judgments and Decisions 1996, II, 7, (1996) 22 E.H.R.R. 123. See further *X v. Morgan-Grampian* [1990] 2 W.L.R. 1000; S. Palmer, "Protecting Journalists' Sources" [1992] P.L. 61; I. Cram, "When the Interests of Justice Outweigh Freedom of Expression" [1992] M.L.R. 400.

[80] See also the support for disclosure on grounds of private and family life in *Gaskin v. U.K.* Application No. 10454/83, Series A Vol. 160, 1 (1989) 12 E.H.R.R. 36.

[81] See *McIntyre v. Ohio Elections Commission*, 115 S.Ct. 1511 (1995). The Supreme Court stated that: "an author's decision to remain anonymous, like other decisions concerning omissions or additions to the content of a publication, is an aspect of the freedom of speech protected by the First Amendment" and "the anonymity of an author is not ordinarily a sufficient reason to exclude her work product from the protections of the First Amendment."

[82–83] See the written evidence submitted by the Christian Action Research and Education (CARE) to the House of Lords, Select Committee on Science and Technology, Fifth Report on *Information Society: Agenda for Action in the UK* (1995–1996 H.L. 77, London: HMSO), p.187.

[84] 357 U.S. 449 (1958).

[85] *ibid.* at 462.

[86] [1998] 2 W.L.R. 379.

Cyberstalking: The Regulation of Harassment on the Internet   41

Human Rights Act, when passed, will prompt some re-evaluation by the judges of the importance to free speech of anonymity.

Anonymity and privacy

Anonymity, apart from facilitating free speech, can also facilitate the protection of privacy on the Internet. Many users are unaware that every time they surf the Internet, information about the websites they have visited is logged and stored. The Center for Democracy and Technology ("CDT") has an on-line demonstration entitled "Who's Watching You and What are You Telling Them?"[87-90] which allows users to view their personal on-line biography. CDT's websites notes that:

> "Many people surf the web under the illusion that their actions are private and anonymous. Unfortunately, there is more information collected about you than you might think. Every time you visit a site, you leave a calling card that reveals where you're coming from, what kind of computer you have, and many other details. Most sites keep logs of all visitors."

There are Internet-based marketing organisations who build comprehensive profiles of users and then sell on the information. With the right equipment, a user's e-mail address together with files viewed and other detailed information can be obtained by web systems even though no information is supplied directly to a website. The Electronic Privacy Information Center ("EPIC") reviewed 100 of the most frequently visited websites on the Internet in the summer of 1997. EPIC found that few websites have explicit privacy policies (only 17 of their sample), and none of the top 100 websites met basic standards for privacy protection.[91] On-line users can currently use web-based services such as the Anonymizer to surf the web anonymously.[92] The Anonymizer shields a user's personal information from the other websites that he or she visits. On visiting the Anonymizer website a user is assigned an anonymous identity and is thus able to surf the web without revealing his or her true identity.

Anonymity enables users to prevent surveillance and monitoring of their activities on the Internet not only from commercial companies but also from government intrusion. In Britain, the DTI Consultation Paper, "Licensing of Trusted Third Parties for the Provision of Encryption Services",[93] which may have been expected to address privacy and anonymity on the Internet, devoted no space to the issue.[94]

[87-90] See http://www.13x.com/cgi-bin/cdt/snoop.pl.

[91] See Electronic Privacy Information Center report, *Surfer Beware: Personal Privay and the Internet*, Washington, D.C., June 1997 at http://www.epic.org/reports/surfer-beware.html.

[92] See http://www.anonymizer.com.

[93] Department of Trade and Industry, Consultation Paper, "Licensing of Trusted Third Parties for the Provision of Encryption Services," March 1997, http://www.dti.gov.uk/pubs. This followed up the earlier "Paper On Regulatory Intent Concerning Use of Encryption On Public Networks," June 10, 1996, http://dtiinfol.dti.gov.uk/cii/encrypt. See Y. Akdeniz, *et al.*, "Cryptography and Liberty: Can the Trusted Third Parties be Trusted? A Critique of the Recent UK Proposals" (1997) 2 *Journal of Information, Law and Technology*; Y. Akdeniz, "UK Government Encryption Policy" [1997] *Web JCLI* 1; Y. Akdeniz and C. Walker "UK Government policy on encryption: trust is the key?" (1998) 3 *Journal of Civil Liberties* 110.

[94] See Y. Akdeniz, "No Chance for Key Recovery: Encryption and International Principles of Human and Political Rights" [1998] *Web JCLI* 1.

The Internet Watch Foundation (formerly known as Safety-Net),[95] endorsed by the United Kingdom Government, sees anonymity on the Internet as a danger, proposing that[96]:

"... [A]nonymous servers that operate in the UK [should] record details of identity and make this available to the Police, when needed, under Section 28(3) of the Data Protection Act (which deals with the disclosure of information for the purpose of prevention of crime)."

A key aspect of the Safety-Net approach is making users take responsibility for material they post on the Internet; stressing the importance of being able to trace the originators of child pornography and other illegal material.[97] For this purpose, the Safety-Net document proposed that the Internet Service Providers should not provide their users with anonymous accounts. ISPs must ensure that they know who all their customers are. This approach is in contrast with European Union initiatives. The benefits of anonymity on-line were recognised at the recent "Global Information Networks, Ministerial Conference," in Bonn, in July 1997. At the Bonn Ministerial Conference, the Ministers declared that:

"Ministers recognise the principle that where the user can choose to remain anonymous off-line, that choice should also be available on-line. Ministers urge industry to implement technical means for ensuring privacy and protecting personal data on the Global Information Networks, such as anonymous browsing, e-mail and payment facilities."[98]

An express right to privacy in United Kingdom law will be granted for the first time once the Human Rights Bill is passed and comes into force. Article 8 of the European Convention on Human Rights demands "respect for ... private and family life ... home and ... correspondence", and this undoubtedly requires a greater recognition of the value of privacy than has hitherto been forthcoming from English judges or Parliament.[99] In particular, it will be noted that Article 8 expressly protects "correspondence", and this has been applied by the European Court of Human Rights to curtail unregulated police access to telephone conversations as well as other forms of electronic surveillance.[1] "Correspondence' on the Internet is

---

[95] The Internet Watch Foundation ("IWF"), was announced on September 23, 1996. IWF has an e-mail, telephone and fax hotline so that on-line users are able to report materials related to child pornography and other obscene materials. See the Safety-Net proposal, "Rating, Reporting, Responsibility, For Child Pornography and Illegal Material on the Internet" adopted and recommended by the Executive Committee of Internet Services Providers Association ("ISPA"), London Internet Exchange ("LINX") and the IWF at http://dtiinfol.dtigov.uk/safety-net/r3.htm.

[96] Safety-Net proposal 1996, para. 30.

[97] See DTI, "Rating, Reporting, Responsibility, For Child Pornography and Illegal Material on the Internet," September 1996, at http://dtiinfol.dti.gov.uk/safety-net/r3.htm para 29–30.

[98] See the "Bonn Declaration" at http://www2.echo.lu/bonn/final.html.

[99] See House of Commons Library Research Paper, *The Human Rights Bill [HL], Bill 119 of 1997/98: Privacy and the Press*, No: 98/25 (London: 1998); Lord Bingham, "Should there be a law to protect rights of personal privacy?" [1996] E.H.R.L.R. 250.

[1] See *Malone v. U.K.*, application No. 8691/79, judgment of Court Series A, Vol. 82 (1984); *Halford v. U.K.*, Application No. 20605/92 *The Times*, July 3, 1997; P. B. Carter, "Evidence Obtained by the Use of a Covert Listening Device" (1997) 113 L.Q.R. 467.

deserving of at least an equal degree of protection, though whether the importance of anonymity on the Internet both to free speech and to privacy will ultimately be recognised and, in turn, influence the shape of future regulatory initiatives remains to be seen.

Non-legal solutions

This article has highlighted the limitations of legal regulation of on-line harassment in cases which involve anonymous and international cyberstalkers. These limitations in legal regulation are, to some extent, compensated for by the availability of non-legal solutions to on-line harassment. A number of more suitable ways in which users can both empower and protect themselves from on-line harassment are discussed below.

Self-protection

The education of users is the first step towards self-protection from Internet harassment. There are many websites and books which provide information for self-protection from cyberstalkers for on-lines users.[2] In general, women are advised where possible, to adopt either a male or gender neutral user name. Passwords, it is advised, should ideally be a meaningless combination of letters and numbers and changed frequently. Passwords should never be given out and should never be sent out via simple e-mail messages as these are the equivalent of sending traditional "postcards" via snail mail. It is recommended that personal information divulged on-line be kept to a minimum. Users should regularly check their on-line profile (finger files) or biography to see what information is available to a potential stalker. To guard against on-line impersonation, users are also advised to use strong encryption programmes such as the Pretty Good Privacy ("PGP")[3] to ensure complete private communications. Strong encryption can provide confidentiality, integrity and authenticity of the information transferred via on-line communications. Strong encryption and use of such software as PGP is the only solution for having truly private communications over the Internet. Using strong encryption would put your electronic "postcard" in a secure envelope and seal it.

A number of self-appointed Internet patrollers have been involved in tracking the senders of offensive e-mail messages. Among the organisations offering assistance in tracking down stalkers are CyberAngels,[4] a branch of the New York based Guardian Angels, Cybertrackers,[5] and Women Halting On-line Abuse ("WHOA").[6] Once the

---

[2] For example see *Women Halting Online Abuse*, http://whoa.femail.com, CyberAngels at http://www.cyberangels.org/stalking/index.html. Cnet News.Com special, "Cybstalkers: What to do if you are harassed or stalked," July 1997, http://www.cnet.com/Content/Features/Dlife/Dark/ss01c.html; Online Harassmment Resources at http://www.io.com/~barton/harassment/html; *Women, Take Back The Net!: An Online Guide to Reporting E-Harassment* at http://www.virtual.net/Projects/Take-Back-the-Net. Information on real-life stalking can be found in Stalking Victims' Sanctuary at http://www.ccon.com/stalkvictim/ and at the U.S. National Victim Center's Helpful Guide for Stalking Victims, http://www.nvc.org/ddir/info44.htm. See also R. B. Gelman, *et al, Protecting Yourself Online: The Definitive Resource on Safety, Freedom, and Privacy in Cyberspace* (New York: HarperCollins, 1998), A. Sherman, *Cybergrrl! A Woman's Guide to the World Wide Web* (USA: Ballantine, 1998).

[3] See http://www.pgp.com.

[4] See http://www.cyberangels.org.

[5] See http://www.alyssa.com/cyber.htm.

[6] See http://whoa.femail.com/.

perpetrator is identified, a message through e-mail calling for an end to the harassing behaviour is sent out to the perpetrator. These self-policing activities may help in some instances but their overall effectiveness remains to be determined.

Role of the Internet Service Providers

Access to the Internet is possible through Internet Service Providers ("ISPs"). An individual who receives unwanted e-mail or finds that offensive information about them has been posted on the Internet should contact the offender's ISP who may eliminate his or her account. As mentioned above, the ISPs in Britain do not provide their customers with anonymous accounts, and every single Internet user through the British ISPs or ISPs that provide services within Britain should have identifiable customers. These precautions may assist the police in cases in which they are trying to find the identity of a cyberstalker who may be accessing the Internet and conducting his or her cyberstalking activities through a British ISP. These pre-cautions may not be of help in cases in which the offender is untraceable, *e.g.* when he or she uses anonymous re-mailers or where the cyberstalker is not a customer of the ISP in question or has posted messages from outside the jurisdiction.

Some of these issues were discussed in a recent United States defamation case involving America Online, *Kenneth M. Zeran v. America Online, Inc.*[7] On April 25, 1995, six days after 168 people were killed in the Oklahoma City bombing, an unidentified America Online user posted an advertisement on one of AOL's bulletin boards for "Naughty Oklahoma" T-shirts and bumper stickers, all of which contained offensive slogans. The advertisements asked interested parties to contact "Ken" and gave Kenneth Zeran's telephone number in Seattle Washington. Death threats to Zeran started immediately after the initial postings. Zeran, who was not at all responsible for the posting and did not even have an AOL account, decided to sue AOL, arguing that the company had unreasonably delayed in removing the defamatory messages and had failed to screen for similar postings thereafter.

A District Court found that section 230 of the Communications Decency Act 1996,[8] which "creates a federal immunity to any cause of action that would make service providers liable for information originating with a third-party user," barred Zeran's suit. This was also confirmed by the United States Court of Appeals.[9] The court further stated that tort-based lawsuits would have an "obvious chilling effect" on the Internet and on Internet Service Providers. As a result, the controversial CDA 1996[10] now offers more protection to ISPs than any other media but falls short of granting "common carrier" status enjoyed by telephone companies. This may even go too far: according to David Sobel of EPIC, "there should be some degree of accountability on the part of online services as there is for other forms of media."[11]

---

[7] See U.S. District Court, E.D. Virginia, 958 S.Supp. (1997); U.S. Court of Appeals, 4th Circuit, CA–96–1564–A, 129 F.2d 327 (1997); U.S. Supreme Court, Cert. Pet. 97–1488, denied.

[8] 47 USC s.223.

[9] *Kenneth M. Zeran v. America Online, Inc.*, U.S. Court of Appeals, 4th Circuit, CA–96–1564–A, 129 F.2d 327 (1997).

[10] See also *ACLU v. Reno*, 117 S.Ct. 2329 (1997).

[11] J. Kornblum, "Supreme Court backs AOL," *Cnet News.Com*, June 22, 1998.

Software

New and innovative software programs which enable users to control the information they receive are being developed.[12] There are, for example, technical means by which users may block unwanted communications. Tools available include "kill" files and bozo files which delete incoming e-mail messages from individuals specified by the user, and such tools are included with most of the available e-mail software packages. There is also specially designed software to filter or block unwanted e-mail messages. These tools such as CyberSitter[13] and Netnanny[14] are designed mainly to block the access of children to sexually explicit websites and newsgroups, but they can be used to filter out and block e-mail communications. Some of this software can also filter words through the incoming and outgoing e-mail messages. The mandatory use of such software, especially at access level, by libraries and ISPs is criticised[15] within the United States because the decisions taken to block certain websites are arbitrary and within the discretion of the private companies that develop these systems.[16] They are also defective since most of them block such websites as the Middlesex County Club or the Mars Explorer while trying to block the word "sex" or they block websites by looking at the keywords in the meta-tags offered by the individual html files.[17] But these tools may be of some use to victims of cyberstalkers to filter out unwanted messages. In the future, advanced filtering systems which recognise insulting e-mail may also be available.

Conclusion

This article has sought to highlight the issues surrounding legal regulation of the Internet to on-line harassment. It is suggested that " . . . the Internet is in its infancy and lawmakers should exercise caution in attempting to regulate this new technology whose potential none of us can fully comprehend."[18] The most famous attempt at legal regulation of the Internet was the United States Communications Decency Act of 1996 which attempted to limit the availability of "indecent speech" on the Internet.[19] Judge Dalzell in *ACLU v. Reno* stated that:

---

[12] E. Spertus, "Social and Technical Means for Fighting Online Harassment" (Presented at Virtue and Virtuality: Gender, Law, and Cyberspace—MIT Artificial Intelligence Laboratory, May 5, 1996, http://www.ai.mit.edu/people/ellens/Gender/glc/.

[13] See http://www.solidaok.com/.

[14] See http://www.netnanny.com/netnanny.

[15] See the ACLU complaint in *Mainstream Loudoun et al. v. Board of Trustees of the Loudoun County Library*, Case No. 97–2049–A, at http://www.aclu.org/court/loudoncocomplaint.html. See also Judge Brinkema's Opinion in the *Loudoun Blocking Software* case at http://www.techlawjournal.com/courts/loudon/80407mem.htm.

[16] See American Civil Liberties Union, "Fahrenheit 451.2: Is Cyberspace Burning? How Rating and Blocking Proposals May Torch Free Speech on the Internet," August 1997, at http://www.aclu.org/issues/cyber/burning.html; Cyber-Rights and Cyber-Liberties (U.K.), "Who Watches the Watchmen: Internet Content Rating Systems, and privatised censorship," November 1997, at http://www.leeds.ac.uk/law/pgs/yaman/watchmen.htm.

[17] See generally Electronic Privacy Information Center, "Faulty Filters: How Content Filters Block Access to Kid-Friendly Information on the Internet," Washington, December 1997, at http://www2.epic.org/reports/filter-report.html.

[18] S. Greenberg (1997), *op. cit.*

[19] See *ACLU v. Janet Reno*, 929 F. Supp. 824 (1996), and *ACLU v. Reno*, 117 S.Ct. 2329 (1997).

"As the most participatory form of mass speech yet developed, the Internet deserves the highest protection from government intrusion. Just as the strength of the Internet is chaos, so the strength of our liberty depends upon the chaos and cacophony of the unfettered speech the First Amendment protects."[20]

The indecency provisions of the CDA were struck down by the United States Supreme Court in the summer of 1997, and this was also seen as an end to regulatory initiatives by single nation states. We are now witnessing a move towards self-regulatory solutions especially for Internet content regulation.[21] There are also many initiatives at a supranational European level[22] and elsewhere which again suggest that legal regulation of the Internet at a national level is futile and also undesirable. The House of Lords Select Committee on Science and Technology in its paper, *Information Society*[23] stated that where "government intervention is needed, it is also clear that as much as possible should be agreed internationally" and that "there are issues here which must be resolved internationally, to ensure that the defence and law enforcement agencies of national governments are not emasculated by the growth of the Information Society."[24] According to a recent House of Commons Select Committee on Culture Report, "The Multi-Media Revolution," international initiatives will have an important impact on national Internet regulation, but at the same time "the question is whether such attempts at regulation can be anything more than optimistically indicative rather than genuinely effective."[25] This does not mean that laws cannot be applied to the Internet and that individuals cannot be protected from so called cybercrimes. It means that a new multi-layered governance approach will be necessary. The new governance will involve both public and private bodies at both national and supranational level. New self-regulatory solutions will also be sought. In this new way of thinking "self" may both mean as an individual solution (*e.g.* individual protection from cybercrimes such as cyberstalking), or as a more collective solution (*e.g.* codes of conduct for ISPs or the introduction of hotlines and user organisations).

The moral panics that the Internet has witnessed regarding on-line activity, largely the result of misreporting by the media, cloud the fact that it is only a small minority of users who engage in illegal activity such as cyberstalking and only a

---

[20] *per* Judge Dozzell, *ACLU v. Janet Reno*, 929 F. Supp. 824 at 883 (1996).

[21] See House of Lords, Select Committee on Science and Technology, *Information Society: Agenda for Action in the UK* (1995–1996) H.L. 77), para. 5.50 and also Minister for Science Energy and Industry, John Battle, "HMG strategy for the Internet", March 18, 1998 at http://www.dti.gov/Minspeech/btlspch3.htm.

[22] See Communication from the Commission to the European Parliament, the Council, the Economic and Social Committee and the Committee of the Regions, Action Plan on promoting safe use of the Internet, November 1997. See also Y. Akdeniz, "The European Union and Illegal and Harmful Content on the Internet" (1998) 3 *Journal of Civil Liberties* 31.

[23] House of Lords, Select Committee on Science and Technology, *Information Society: Agenda for Action in the UK* (1995–1996 H.L. 77). See also the Government's Response (Cm. 3450, London: HMSO, 1996).

[24] *ibid.* para. 5.45.

[25] House of Commons Select Committee on Culture, *The Multi-Media Revolution—Volume I*, (1997–1998 H.C. 520–I), para. 108. See also the Government Response to "The Multimedia Revolution" (H.C. 520–521), July 1998. see also Cyber-Rights and Cyber-Liberties (UK) Report: "Who Watches the Watchmen: Part II—Accountability and Effective Self-Regulation in the Information Age," September 1998 at http://www.cyber-rights.org/watchmen-ii.htm.

Cyberstalking: The Regulation of Harassment on the Internet 47

small portion of the Internet contains illegal content "The peccadilloes of the few, however, should not be permitted to override the beneficial uses of these computer-mediated communications systems. They are only a small portion of what is actually happening."[26] The beneficial uses of the Internet far outweigh its abuses and the few problems created by the use of the Internet by a small proportion of the Internet community should be dealt with through self-regulatory solutions at both private and public levels together with the improvement of good practices for Internet usage.

[26] A. Branscomb (1995), *op. cit.* at p.1677.

[18]

Virtually Criminal: Discourse, Deviance and Anxiety Within Virtual Communities

MATTHEW WILLIAMS

ABSTRACT *While it would be appropriate to state that criminologists and those in legal disciplines have recently discovered that new technologies are worthy of research, they have yet to tap into growing concerns over sub-criminal activity within increasing populated virtual environments. As a result we find new forms of sociopathic behaviour, which present themselves in abundance, being disregarded due to their 'virtual status', while similar crimes in the real world are subject to intensive investigation. This study considers forms of 'virtual deviance' that manifest themselves within online communities as viable forms of inquiry. Through a multi-method approach, including ethnographic methods, linguistic, case source and discourse analysis, this research project aims to unravel the link between the aetiology of online deviance and the discourses of surveillance, regulation and mediation. It is hoped that the analysis will provide for a virtual regulatory model that curtails disruptive behaviour within online environments while simultaneously maintaining relevant justice models and forms of human/avatar rights.*

Introduction

With the advent of each new technology concerns arise about its misuse. History has seen the use of technology to illicitly appropriate funds, as a tool to aid in illegal practices, and more recently to take forms of derisory discourse into the virtual arena. While it has became widely accepted that 'high tech'[1] crimes are intruding into both social and legalistic practices, little is known about other forms of deviance that manifest within increasingly populated online environments. Credit card fraud, computer hacking and the dissemination of child pornography over computer networks are but a few of the 'high tech' crimes reported on and sensationalized by the media. Yet what is to be made of these other forms of deviance that are performed on a daily basis within virtual environments whose legal status remains dubious? The acts of harassment and even rape have arguably been re-engineered from their 'physical' manifestations into derisory and harmful textual performances that are present within online community interaction. Those who misuse computer-

Correspondence: Matthew Williams, School of Social Sciences, Cardiff University, Glamorgan Building, King Edward VII Avenue, Cardiff CF10 3AT, UK; e-mail < WilliamsM7@cardiff.ac.uk >.

ISSN 1369-0869 Print; 1364-6885 Online/00/010095-10 © 2000 Taylor & Francis Ltd

mediated communication to disrupt online social interaction are beginning to be labelled as deviants and criminals, who have as their source of derision their online victims. Unlike other 'high tech' crimes, both the practice and the consequences of these acts of deviance take place within the virtual environment, making these deviant performances unique in both aetiology and motivation. Arguably the interpretation of conventional 'high tech' crime has been met with relative ease; the adaptation of the Criminal Justice and Public Order Act of 1994 to widen the definition of a publication to include a computer transmission is a typical example from the UK. However, while the conventional 'high tech' crimes which rely on the presence of a physical space have been rapidly met with both social and legal responses, those which exist in virtual space escape any form of social or legalistic rationalization.

In a similar fashion the academic community has yet to acknowledge forms of online sociopathic behaviour as either 'valid' forms of criminality or inquiry. To take the former, it is questionable whether forms of online derision from within virtual environments could constitute either harassment or libel in legal terms. While the law in many parts of the western world has incorporated prophylactic measures that aim to ensure redress for libellous cases concerning harassment via telecommunications networks,[2] legal systems have yet to address equally damaging sub-criminal behaviour that can fragment online community cohesion. Yet, the reverse of this argument centres around the desire for online communities to remain isolated from 'actual' legal systems, favouring their own methods of mediation to curtail sociopathic behaviour. More so, instances of 'virtual rape'[3] seem beyond any legal classification or rationalization and require alternative virtual methods of punishment to ensure forms of justice based on the virtual environment. In the latter, it seems that most attention to the existence of virtual environments and their encroachment upon offline social and political practices rests comfortably within the disciplines of media and communications studies. Research in the area of computer-mediated communication (CMC) has clearly been shaped by this bias often characterized by a lack of insight into more criminological matters of deviance, regulation and forms of online justice. It is at this point where both the disciplines of law and criminology can inject fruitful analysis into the study of CMC and online deviance.

The current study seeks to acknowledge these unfamiliar forms of deviance and in doing so filling the gap mentioned above. By understanding the medium and method of deviance within virtual environments it is hoped that insight will be gained into online anxiety over victimization and forms of regulation, surveillance and mediation. The existence of both a unique communications medium and a graphical 3D environment found in modern online communities[4] results in the adoption of a multi-method approach. Observations of online behaviour compliment a linguistic and discursive analysis of narrative gained from online interaction and virtual focus groups. In tandem with the analysis of individual case information recorded by the online regulatory agencies of each community the study will provide a detailed insight into the varying forms of disruption that plague many online social interactions.

The Study in Context

New forms of communication technology, such as the internet, have allowed through their complex global matrix of interactive tools for the growth of online relationships between individuals. Furthermore, the existence of thousands of electronically linked individuals has come to be known as a 'virtual' or 'online community'. Rheingold[5] was first to ascribe the term community to a group of individuals brought together by computer-mediated communication. Subsequent to this, a debate developed over whether it was appropriate for Rheingold to call such a collective a community.[6] What is important is that we acknowledge that these collectives which are present on the internet are forms that demonstrate the ability to govern themselves via various mechanisms of membership, hierarchical organization based on esoteric knowledge, ability and technological mechanisms. Once it is recognized that forms of power, control and governance are a part of the everyday life of 'netizens', it becomes evident that rules have been instituted to govern conduct within each online community. These rules may be informed by conduct that is deemed appropriate in the 'real' world, while others may be more specific to the nature of the online community itself.

Essentially, a hybrid set of rules and accepted ways of conduct are in operation. The collective that exists in a virtual environment is 'phantasmagoric', a 'space penetrated by and shaped in terms of social influences quite distant'.[7] Individuals who transcend rules are subject to whatever means the community deems necessary to reconsolidate the inappropriate action. This may take the form of reintegrative shaming[8] or more punitive measures such as expulsion from the community or legal proceedings in the offline world. Online deviance is thus a transcendence of rules, values or morals set out by a particular community. Methods of curtailing sociopathic instances are dependent upon and specific to each community. Online collectives can then be seen as virtual gated communities, with their own methods of control and government.

To paint a more vivid picture, examples of sociopathic instances within online communities can be detailed. Of most prominence within the field of deviance and new technologies, is the case of Jake Baker, a young man who posted a lurid and salaciously graphic depiction of rape of a fellow classmate. The threatening story was placed on the Michigan University Bulletin Board, normally used for campus wide dissemination of information to students and staff. Resulting from this perceived 'threat' or 'harassment', Jake Baker was expelled form the university and arrested for threatening behaviour over a telecommunications network. Subsequent to the acquittal of Baker, MacKinnon, contested commenting:

> Words are never only words, but constitute acts in response to which authorities have an obligation to exercise sanctions against 'offenders' despite the civil protections usually accorded to citizens in real life.[9]

Here we can see two mechanisms of control in operation, the non-legalistic expulsion of Baker from the University and the subsequent legal arrest. To expand on this dual process of mediation a clearer picture of online community control and punitive measures can be seen in the Mr Bungle case. A number of chat and role-playing sites have been noted for explicitly sexual activity between consenting participants, so called 'cybersex' or 'cybering'. Some participants employ their programming skills, particularly through 'move' commands and aggressive and sexually explicit verbiage, to 'spam' unwitting participants in ways that might be legally actionable in real life. In the most notable case of such abuse, an accomplished programmer with the persona Mr Bungle devised certain commands that allowed him to isolate and immobilize female participants in order to spam them abusively. Detailed accounts of the incident revealed not only the consequences of the pernicious form of spam inflicted by one player on another, but also how the community was forced to address questions of standards and to create some form of mediation. As a consequence the physical act of rape had been re-engineered as a textual form, connoting a meaning that represented the relational dyad of offender and victim within the actual, in a virtual space:

virtual rape ... is defined ... as a sexually related act of a violent or acutely debasing or profoundly humiliating nature against a character who has not explicitly consented to the interaction. Any act which explicitly references the non-consensual, involuntary exposure, manipulation, or touching of sexual organs of or by a character is considered an act of this nature.[10]

The linguistic injury was forced to draw its vocabulary from physical injury. Further similarities can be found in the metaphor 'words that wound' in Matsuda's work.[11] 'Wound' suggests that a linguistic inference or text can act in ways that parallel the infliction of pain and injury (see later section on linguistic agency). Subsequent punitive measures involved a combination of expulsion and shaming in an attempt to mediate the deviance and injury. Ostracism and social admonition were available and were generally an effective means for enforcing community standards of behaviour.[12] Yet it is important to understand that a virtual punishment, such as non-re-integrative shaming, will only be successful if the existence of the punished persona matters to the computer user who created it. Unlike the Baker case, Mr Bungle was not subjected to any legal proceedings. It is very doubtful that the law could have grappled successfully with this case. Not only is the act of virtual rape questionable in law, but it is doubtful whether Mr Bungle's physical self could be identified and apprehended. Membership to these communities is characterized by a socially fluid and eclectic population, drawn from a global pool of connected internet users, hidden by a veil of anonymity. Moreover, external interference by the state is often unwelcome within virtual communities, preferring their own methods of mediation to curtail deviance.[13]

Research Setting

The setting to be studied can be explained in several ways. Initially it is useful to describe the online community as it appears visually to its members. To take an example, CyberWorlds is a computer program that allows individuals to log-on to several virtual communities where multiple users can 'chat' and socialize. Chat is enabled by typing words or sentences into an interface. The program also allows the participant to view others behaviour through graphical representations of community members, known as avatars. This visual interface also allows for movement within the environment enabling virtual face to face interaction, even though both participants may be separated by thousands of miles in the offline world. What primarily defines the field of study is the mode of communication—the linguistic or textual performances and environmental discourses of surveillance, regulation and mediation.

Linguistic Agency

At the linguistic level it would be prudent to ascertain, if possible, what speech or text could be deemed as offensive. However, any attempt to map the pains of verbal or textual performances, in terms of individual susceptibility and the multitude of contexts derisory speech can take would be fruitless. For this reason a broader approach can be adopted to identify wider frameworks of derisory speech, theorizing the mechanics which allow for such agency in language. By adopting a broader approach, it is possible to identify a bifurcation in forms of language, particularly speech or text of a derisory content. Austin[14] delineates illocutionary and perlocutionary speech acts. Although a clumsy dyad, with a substantial 'grey' area between them, this way of proceeding can be beneficial in under-standing forms of online derision. The illocutionary speech performance is one where at the same time as what is being said, something is also being done; the policeman stating 'I am charging you with assault' is not saying something which has a delayed consequence, the consequence is immediate.[15] The speech is the act of doing. Perlocutionary acts however have a delayed effect, what is said at one point in time may have a consequence that is temporarily distant. The reason for the disparity in speech acts derives from social and linguistic conventions. The illocutionary speech act is only so due to its ability to refer and draw from convention and ritual in society at points in time. Instances of failed speech performances can help explain the illocutionary acts reliance on the temporal social milieu.

These forms of language also exist within the speech of online community members, although some of the conventions used to explain these acts in the actual world are suppressed and expanded. Traditional forms of violent behaviour (e.g. forms of physical or actual violence within a non-virtual environment) that have been re-engineered to operate as textual violent performances can be seen as illocutionary acts. The previous example of virtual rape can be understood from this perspective. When the assailant, Mr Bungle, forced his victim to 'eat his/her own pubic hair'[16] the textual act bore a two-fold performance; the act of 'eating pubic hair' occurred at the same time as the assailant's utterance or act. Virtual perceptions of time and environment (where what is said often has no temporal lag to what is done) mean that such textual performances have immediate consequences. The illocutionary nature of internet interaction is due to both the sponta-neity and immediacy of social speech and the permanence of writing within the virtual environment.[17] The illocutionary act of virtual rape draws its agency from the possibility for the utterance to immediately subordinate the victim in a hierarchical structure. As Butler states, drawing from the work of Matsuda:

> Speech does not merely *reflect* a relation of social domination; speech *enacts* domination, becoming the vehicle through which that social structure is reinstated ... hate speech *constitutes* its addressee at the moment of its utterance; it does not describe an injury or produce one as a consequence; it is, in the very speaking of such speech, the performance of the injury itself, where the injury is understood as social subordination.[18]

Both the hierarchy and ritual that exist within virtual communities allow for agency in the form of illocutionary speech, and hence the possibility for subordination and victimization of community members. The very nature of interaction inherent within computer-mediated communication has forged a convention that allocates more 'functions' to text than usually created in the actual world. Within virtual environments, text functions as dialogue, action, description and emotion which, when combined, makes context. Such a burden on text arguably leaves it susceptible to misuse, being employed as an effective vehicle for derision.

Environment

Of most prominence and significance to the study is the discourse of behavioural regu-lation, surveillance and mediation that permeates and characterizes online community interaction. Most online communities have developed a set of rules governing conduct, in tandem with deterrence mechanisms to dissuade any 'inappropriate' action. These ways of ensuring acceptable conduct primarily face what has been identified, in psychological terms, a disinhibiting effect—behaviour that is ignorant of any self-consciousness, anxiety over social situations or worries about public evaluation—that accompanies online communication.[19] It is from this point that the study aims to understand how the disinhibiting nature of online environments can effect behaviour and discourses of surveillance, regulation and mediation. Arguably the notion of 'risk taking' can aid in forging a link between disinhibiting characteristics and these discursive practices.

The idea of virtual or cyber risks is not a completely new concept. In his seminal work 'Risk Society' Beck[20] writes of the increasing risk associated with nuclear, reproductive and genetic technologies, in doing so, identifying certain consequences of new technologies in modern society. In a similar vein the risk-society thesis can be applied to 'the' virtual environment. Encapsulated within the notion of 'the' virtual environment are technologies of information and communication, and those who employ such tools are running a myriad of risks. Common examples include the invasion of the computer virus, computer fraud, internet addiction, cyber cults or other deviant groups such as paedophile rings and the rapid spread of moral panics and irrational fear facilitated by scare stories such as genetically modified foods. These risks, however, work on a reciprocal plane— consequences of the virtual often manifesting themselves in the actual. The computer virus aims to destroy data and disrupt actual life and time; other risks involve the computer being used as an instrument of gain; while the spread of moral panics manifest themselves in 'actual' political consequences. It is this reciprocity that distinguishes between two kinds of cyber risk, the other which is evident within online communities. This kind of cyber risk holds a more tenuous relationship with the 'actual' world. In other terms, these kinds of cyber risks are engineered out of the virtual environment within which they seek to rage their consequences. An example would be the risk of having one's avatar appearance or name attacked in a derisory manner. This is not to say that the real person who created the avatar would be immune to these consequences, it is more the argument that these risks are truly virtual in that they are engineered from within the online environment. Without the existence of 'the' virtual environment these cyber risks would have no breeding ground.

Anonymity, which is granted to every community member, forms part of the disinhibiting environment, and as such assessments of 'risk taking' and 'being at risk' have to be altered in light this characteristic. Those wishing to take the risk of hurling abuse at a fellow community member are more likely to do so in a virtual environment than one that makes the offender 'directly' liable for their actions. Some individuals within virtual communities remind themselves of the distance between them and their partners in conversation, and in doing so disassociate themselves with accountability and self-control. Indeed, the possibility for reprisals, apart from a severe virtual tongue-lashing, is minimal given the degree of anonymity granted to the offender. Theorizing 'the' virtual environment in this way shows how chat groups have arguably become susceptible to varying degrees of disruption. What is evident is that users do seem to be less inhibited by conventions seen in everyday life, be it due to anonymity or any of the other features of the disinhibiting environment. They can be seen to be more intimate or more hostile with each other than would be socially acceptable in the real community. Yet ultimately, when hostility beckons, users are comforted by the thousands of kilometres between them and the object of their derision.

It becomes clear that risk is suspended for those seeking to disrupt community life. This period of suspension is evidently a temporary phenomenon; at some point community members must re-enter the offline world. Some may argue, then, that there should be a higher prevalence of deviance on the net given the notion of risk suspension. Yet such commentators are ignorant of the day-to-day infraction of community rules and etiquette. The rule breaking may not be as serious as those accounts previously detailed (see the account of virtual rape), yet the ignorance of community values and morals may be enough to challenge its integrity and call for mechanisms of mediation.

As previously mentioned the discourses of surveillance, regulation and mediation are common in virtual community practice. Most notably the medieval practice of charivari in 13th- and 14th-century France bares similar characteristics with discipline and punishment within virtual communities.[21] Charivari involved the public ridicule and physical taunting of an individual who had transcended community rules. Similarly the mediation of deviance within online environments often involves the use of shaming via textual performances. Very often technical means of regulation can fail if the aggressor has access to esoteric knowledge such as inside information on the programming language that created the community.[22] Even if banished from the community, anonymity allows for an avenue where the deviant can re-enter as another avatar. It is for these reasons that the community turns to modes of public ridicule that are intended to humiliate the virtual offender. A common example of ritual shaming can be seen in the practice of 'toading', often found in Multi-User Domains (MUD). The process usually involves the system administrator, or the person at the peak of the community hierarchical scale, altering the appearance and/or description of the offender's persona into something shameful (commonly a toad, which can be traced back to fantasy gaming and the Dungeons and Dragons role-playing genre). A process of public ridicule then begins with the victims and other sympathetic community members venting their anger upon the offender via derisory speech. However, the question of reciprocity between the 'actual' and the 'virtual' as previously mentioned has to be addressed. Even though the system administrator or equivalent has the power to control the offender's behaviour and identity, thus enabling the process of shaming, what effect does this have on the 'actual' person behind the deviant persona? As mentioned below, if those who are being victimized need not suffer by exiting the online community then neither does the offender have to suffer any reprisal. If the link between the online persona and the 'actual' person is tenuous, then arguably no form of shaming can have the desired effect of rehabilitation or exclusion. This leaves the question of public ridicule as punishment. In the offline world, the mode of punishment as spectacle[23] was successful in the 18th and 19th century due to the offenders constant residence amongst their community peers, allowing the shaming to have a sustained effect. Yet shaming in a virtual environment is short-lived. This means the purpose of public ridicule can be found in a justice based on the alleviation of the feelings of those harmed. The chief concern then is to protect the community's integrity and to expel anything that threatens its solidarity, while simultaneously repairing the harm done via a process of retribution. However, this process of justice may have the opposite effect; by encouraging community members to taunt and abuse other members, hatred and derisory performances are given a free and legitimate reign, encouraging a lack of trust and interdependence. Without these, a community becomes fragmented where members grow ever more anxious over the possibilities of victimization and the eventual demise of their online environment.

Online Anxiety

Anxieties over the risks of 'virtual' victimization are inextricably linked to both the environmental and textual area of computer-mediated communication. The disinhibiting nature of the online environment, while creating at atmosphere of free abandon, can conversely create an air of tension and uncertainty.[24] While the environment may be responsible for some degree of 'general' or 'low-level' anxiety among some community members (especially those members whose children also visit the same community), this explanation can not account for the possibility of 'focused' experiences of fear online. It is at this level of analysis that the issue of 'power play' enters the relations between the offender, victim and the deviant act. At the linguistic level, Butler[25] eluded to the anxiety provoking nature of derisory utterances in the 'actual' world. The most anxiety provoking utterances were those that threatened a person's identity within the linguistic and social system, thereby challenging the initial process of interpellation. Further, Matsuda's[26] notion of social subordination via hate speech adds to the overall theory of linguistic agency. At the empirical level, it may be possible to envisage the power and consequences of linguistic agency. At one level, the offender can call into question the identity of another person, while at another, the system administrator enables the process of shaming via the transformation of the offender's identity (see above for an example of 'toading'). At both levels anxiety may present itself as a consequence of the threat to an avatar's existence. The 'power play' between the assailant and the victim clearly manifests itself as a process of subordination. To repeat Matusda,[27] the assailant calls into play the social system and attempts, via the agency in language, to recast the object of derision in an undesirable light, in so doing altering their position in the social hierarchy. Such recasting arguably induces certain levels of anxiety. However, while it is clear that anxiety is a consequence of these linguistic processes in the 'actual' world, it may be less lucid when theorizing linguistic agency and anxiety within online communities. Indeed, several inconsistencies that are present within the online community may alter the way anxieties are experienced and managed.

Firstly, the online community as a locale is structured not just by its 'visual', 'textual' or 'auditory' immediate environment, but also by distanced relations, from the experiences of participants in the real world, and the influences of the real world itself. Anxiety is thus a hybrid of the locale and the distanced. Those who have direct or indirect experiences of virtual victimization may experience anxiety that is a product of modern society, where space and place no longer coincide.[28] Secondly, social hierarchies that have been engineered within the online community could be said to incorporate both products of 'actual' hierarchies—such as the supremacy of esoteric knowledge—and the needs of the immediate virtual environment. With this in mind, the application of Matsuda's[29] theory of subordination becomes slightly clumsier. In attempting to understand anxiety through subordination within the virtual environment it is pertinent to be aware of the social structure outside of the online community as well as those operating inside. Any theory of subordination through derisory language must then consider these relations in tandem. Lastly, moving away from linguistic agency, the notion of cyber risk has to be considered if anxiety is to be theorized in the traditional framework—anxiety as a by-product of being cognitively aware of one's, or another's, risk of being victimized.

Understanding anxiety and risk within the virtual environment can be understood in one of many ways. At two extremes, users of communications technology may both over- and underestimate the power and influence such technology has over institutions and individuals. Those who are ignorant to cyber crimes and virtual harassment obviously fear nothing. Yet those who are aware of their existence may over predict the risk of becoming a victim and be subject to disproportionate levels of anxiety. More so, those who are ignorant may experience various forms of abuse without being prepared. Arguably this would have the undesirable effect of community fragmentation, with new members fleeing the virtual environment. Both cases hold unattractive consequences for online community life.

Conclusion

The difficulty in rationalizing forms of online derision within virtual environments, due to their esoteric nature, means that their interpretation and understanding has yet to be achieved. As a result we find new forms of sociopathic behaviour, which present themselves in abundance, being disregarded due to their 'virtual status', while similar crimes in the real world are subject to intensive investigation. The research project at hand seeks to change the focus from deviance in the actual world to derisory behaviour in the equally significant virtual world. The importance of the study rests in the fact that increasingly populated online environments[30] are having to incorporate justice models, regulatory frameworks and security patrols in order to curtail any disruptive or potentially harmful behaviour. These structures, in tandem with the aetiology of online deviance and anxiety, deserve thorough investigation by those qualified in both legal and criminological disciplines. If the virtual environment is to become a 'second home' for a large proportion of the population, as is the case for many already, then structures that protect their fundamental rights in the actual world must be duplicated in the virtual. By unravelling the tie between the motivations of virtual deviance and regulatory practices it is hoped that enhanced methods of governance that incorporate elements of justice and fundamental human/avatar rights can be delineated, in doing so, reducing levels of online anxiety and maintaining community integrity.

Notes and References

1 High tech crimes are those offences that involve the use of technology in its various forms for illicit purposes of acquisition, espionage, criminal collaboration and more recently acts of harassment and stalking.

2 E S Ross 'E-mail stalking: is adequate legal protection available?', *John Marshall Journal of Computer and Information Law*, Vol 13, pp 405–432, 1995.

3 R C MacKinnon 'Punishing the persona: correctional strategies for the virtual offender' in S Jones (ed) *Virtual Cultures: Identity and Communication in Cybersociety*, Sage, London, 1997a, pp 206–235; R C Mackinnon 'Virtual rape', *Journal of Computer Mediated Communication*, Vol 2, No 4, 1997b. Available online at < http://www.ascusc.org/jcmc/vol2/issue4/mackinnon.html > .

4 See R Schroeder 'Networked worlds: social aspects of multi-user virtual reality technology', *Social Research Online*, Vol 2, No 4, 1997. Available online at < http://www.socresonline.org.uk/socresonline/2/4/5.html > .

5 H Rheingold *Virtual Reality*, Secker & Warburg, London, 1991.

6 Arguably a space has manifested itself resembling something like a community on computer networks, at a time when forms of 'real life' community are subject to erosion. Debates over what constitutes a community, e.g. physical proximity, shared history, shared value system, shared language etc have come under scrutiny. Needless to say the intrusion of new communications technology has complicated the issue further. Therefore, in this paper, I take the liberty of using the term 'community' in a broad and shifting way, in doing so acknowledging the 'stalemate' that seems to exist over its definition.

7 A Giddens *The Consequences of Modernity*, Polity Press, Oxford, 1990, p 19.

8 J Braithwaite *Crime, Shame and Reintegration*, Cambridge University Press, Cambridge, 1989.

9 MacKinnon, *op. cit.*, 1997a, p 217.

10 *Virtual Rape Consequences*, 1994. Available online at < http://vesta.physics.ucla.edu/~smolin/lambda/laws_and_history/failed/antirape.html > .

104   *M Williams*

11 M J Matsuda, C R Lawrence, R Delgado and K W Crenshaw, *Words That Wound: Critical Race Theory, Assaultive Speech, and the First Amendment*, Westview Press, Boulder, 1993.

12 R C Mackinnon 'Searching for the Leviathan in Usenet', in S Jones (ed) *Cyber Society: Computer Mediated Communication and Community*, Sage, Thousand Oaks, CA, 1995. E Reid 'Virtual worlds: culture and imagination', in S Jones (ed) *op. cit*, 1995.

13 Mackinnon, *op. cit.*, 1997b.

14 J L Austin *How to do Things With Words*, Harvard University Press, Cambridge, Mass, 1962.

15 *Ibid.*

16 MacKinnon, *op. cit.*, 1997a, pp 206–235.

17 B Kolko and E Reid 'Dissolution and fragmentation: problems in online communities', in S Jones (ed) *Cyber Society 2.0: Revisiting Computer Mediated Communication and Community*, Sage, Thousand Oaks, CA, 1998, pp 212–231.

18 J Butler *Excitable Speech: A Politics of the Performative*, Routledge, London, 1997.

19 A Joinson 'Causes and implications of disinhibited behaviour on the internet', in J Gackenbach (ed.) *Psychology of the Internet: Intrapersonal, Interpersonal, and Transpersonal Implications*, Academic Press, New York, 1998.

20 U Beck *Risk Society: Towards a New Modernity*, Sage, London, 1992.

21 E Reid 'The self and the internet: variations on the illusion of one self', in J Gackenbach (ed) *Psychology of the Internet: Intrapersonal, Interpersonal, and Transpersonal Implications*, Academic Press, New York, 1998.

22 MacKinnon, *op. cit.*, 1997a.

23 M Foucault, *Discipline and Punish: The Birth of the Prison*, A Sheridan (Trans.), Penguin, Harmondsworth, Middlesex, 1986.

24 Reid, *op. cit., 1998.*

25 Butler, *op. cit.*

26 Matsuda *et al., op. cit.*

27 *Ibid.*

28 Giddens, *op. cit.*

29 Matsuda *et al., op. cit.*

30 *Five hundred million people are expected to have Internet access by 2003*, NUA Internet Surveys. Available online at < http://www.nua.ie/surveys >.

[19]

Cybercrimes v. Cyberliberties[1]

NADINE STROSSEN[2]

ABSTRACT   *The broad topic of 'crime and cyberliberties' encompasses two major subtopics: firstly, the extent to which online expression may be punished under new criminal laws, even if it would be lawful in the traditional print media; and secondly, the extent to which online privacy may be restricted to facilitate enforcement of existing criminal laws. In both contexts, many law enforcement officials argue that we have to make trade-offs between, on the one hand, individual rights and, on the other hand, public safety. In fact, though, the alleged dichotomy is oversimplified and misleading. Claims about the alleged unique dangers of online expression are exaggerated, and the types of criminal laws and law enforcement strategies that have worked effectively in other media are also effective in cyberspace. For example, children should be protected from exploitation in the production of child pornography through the same measures, regardless of whether the material is distributed through postal mail or e-mail. Indeed, individuals and organizations who are devoted to protecting children from exploitation and abuse—whether for the production of child pornography or any other purpose—have expressed frustration that resources that should be used to enforce existing laws are being diverted toward efforts to create new cyberspeech crimes, such as the two US laws criminalizing online material that is 'indecent,' 'patently offensive', or 'harmful to minors'. The many judges who have ruled on these laws—including the entire US Supreme Court—have agreed that they violate free expression rights and are not necessary for their stated purpose of protecting children. The battle to preserve online privacy has not been as successful in the US, where the government restricts strong encryption despite the vigorous objections of not only cyberlibertarians, but also the business community. Moreover, even some law enforcement and other government officials have concluded that, on balance, security concerns are aided, not undermined, by strong encryption, since it protects innocent individuals and legitimate businesses from cybercriminals, and it also protects governments and vital infrastructures from cyberterrorism. Most governments apparently recognize these facts since they have not joined the US in restricting encryption technology.*

Correspondence: Nadine Strossen, New York Law School, 57 Worth Street, New York, NY 10013, USA.

ISSN 1369-0869 Print; 1364-6885 Online/00/010011-14 © 2000 Taylor & Francis Ltd

12   *N Strossen*

Introduction

I am delighted and honoured to address this important conference. I want to thank the members of the Cyberlaw Research Unit at the University of Leeds not only for organizing this conference and inviting me to participate in it, but also for their pathbreaking work on cyberlaw and cyberliberties. They have been wonderful colleagues of mine and of the American Civil Liberties Union (ACLU) in both scholarly and advocacy endeavours.

I am proud that the ACLU, which is America's largest and oldest civil liberties organization, has been at the forefront of the newest civil liberties frontier, in cyberspace—not only throughout the US, but also, in collaboration with other organizations around the world, on a global basis. We are spearheading an international coalition called the Global Internet Liberty Campaign, or 'GILC'.[3] And a couple of our most active, effective coalition partners are in Britain and Ireland, including Cyber-Rights & Cyber-Liberties (UK),[4] which was founded by Yaman Akdeniz of the Leeds Cyberlaw Unit. In this international conference, it is important to stress the international scope of our cyberliberties work. Of course, cyberspace is an inherently global medium. And cybercrime and terrorism are worldwide concerns. Likewise, though, preserving human rights in cyberspace is also an international concern.

I have been asked to discuss the legal developments in the US, where we have had more legislation and litigation in this area than any other country. Our courts' rulings have been grounded specifically on US law—in particular, the free speech guarantee of the First Amendment to our Constitution and our constitutional right of privacy. However, those same freedoms are also guaranteed under international human rights law, under regional human rights instruments, including the European Convention on Human Rights, and under the domestic law of nations around the world.[5] Therefore, the principles that have guided legal developments in the US should be relevant in the British Isles and elsewhere, just as developments in Britain and in other parts of the world are also relevant in the US.

Overview of the Interrelationship between Cybercrime and Cyberliberties

The conference organizers asked me to outline the interrelationships between cybercrime and cyberliberties. This broad subject encompasses two major subtopics: first, the extent to which the exercise of certain liberties—notably, free expression—may be criminalized online even if it would be lawful in the traditional print media; and second, the extent to which online liberties—notably, privacy—may be restricted to facilitate punishment of established crimes, such as trafficking in child pornography or engaging in information terrorism. In other words, the first subtopic concerns whether government may restrict our cyberliberties in order to create new crimes, peculiar to cyberspace; and the second concerns whether government may restrict our cyberliberties in order to prosecute existing crimes, common to all media, more effectively.

In both contexts, many officials argue that we have to make trade-offs between, on the one hand, individual rights and, on the other hand, public safety. In fact, though, this alleged tension is oversimplified and misleading. In terms of advancing public safety, measures that stifle cyberliberties are often at best ineffective, and at worst counterproductive. This doubly-flawed nature of laws limiting cyberliberties shows the sadly prophetic nature of a statement that Thomas Jefferson made to James Madison more than 200 years ago, when these two American founders were corresponding about the Bill of Rights to the

US Constitution. Jefferson warned that 'A society that will trade a little liberty for a little order will deserve neither and will lose both'.[6]

This statement is right on the mark concerning the current debates about cybercrimes and cyberliberties, for several reasons. First, claims about the alleged unique dangers of online expression are exaggerated. Second, the types of criminal laws and enforcement strategies that have worked effectively in other media are also effective in cyberspace. Third, far from harming minors, much of the online expression that has been targeted for censorship is affirmatively beneficial for them.

For these reasons, even those who specialize in protecting young people from sexual exploitation and violence—indeed, especially those experts—oppose Internet censorship. This is true, for example, of Ernie Allen, the Director of the National Center for Missing & Exploited Children in the US, which works closely with the Federal Bureau of Investigation and local police agencies around our country. Mr Allen and his colleagues understand that the political obsession with suppressing ideas and images that are allegedly harmful to children's minds is a dangerous distraction and diversion from constructive efforts to protect actual children from tangible harm.[7] In short, cybercensorship does no more good for the safety and welfare of young people than it does for the free speech rights of everyone—and I say 'everyone' advisedly, since young people have free speech rights of their own.[8]

The same false tension between liberty and security also marks too much of the political rhetoric about protecting online privacy through such measures as strong encryption or cryptography and anonymous communications. To be sure, law enforcement would to some extent be aided if officials could easily gain access to online communications, just as law enforcement would receive some benefits if officials could readily spy on all communications of any type. But such pervasive surveillance would violate internationally respected, fundamental privacy rights.[9] The consensus of the international community is that this would be too high a price to pay for reducing crime. After all, what would be the point of limiting our fellow citizens' interference with our personal security, only at the price of increasing police officers' interference with the very same security?[10] This point was eloquently stated by a great former Justice of the US Supreme Court, Louis Brandeis, who was one of the architects of the legal right to privacy even before he ascended to the high Court.[11]

> Decency, security and liberty alike demand that government officials shall be subjected to the same rules of conduct that are commands to the citizen ... . Our Government is the potent, the omnipresent teacher ... . Crime is contagious. If the Government becomes a lawbreaker it breeds contempt for law ... . To declare that in the administration of the criminal law the end justifies the means—... that the Government may commit crimes in order to secure the conviction of a private criminal—would bring terrible retribution.[12]

Just as weakened privacy protections would let government officials access online communications by ordinary, law-abiding citizens, these same weakened protections would also enhance access to online communications by cybercriminals and terrorists. They will not comply with government restrictions on encryption. To the contrary, they will take all available measures to secure their own communications, including illegal measures. Meanwhile, thanks to legal limits on encryption, cybercriminals will more easily prey on law-abiding individuals and businesses, and vital infrastructures will be more vulnerable to cyberterrorists. For these reasons, even some government officials have joined with cyberlibertarians in opposing limits on encryption. They concur that, on balance, such limits do more harm than good to public safety.[13]

That, in a nutshell, is my broad overview of the relationship between cyberliberties and crime control: namely, that this relationship, far from being inherently antagonistic, is often mutually reinforcing. In many respects, law and public policy are developing in a way that is consistent with this perspective. In the US, the courts consistently have struck down new laws that seek to criminalize online expression that would be legal in other media. Many judges who have ruled on such laws have agreed with the ACLU and other cyberlibertarians that the laws are not in fact well-designed for protecting children, which is their asserted goal. These judges include the entire US Supreme Court, ruling in the landmark 1997 case striking down the first federal Internet censorship law in the US, the Communications Decency Act, or 'CDA',[14] in *Reno v. ACLU*.[15]

Now we have to call that case *ACLU v. Reno I*, since the US federal government recently enacted its second cybercensorship law, the so-called 'Child Online Protection Act' or 'COPA',[16] which we are now fighting in a case called *ACLU v. Reno II*.[17] With a name like the 'Child Online Protection Act', it is not surprising that few politicians had the political courage to oppose this law. Fortunately, though, the only judge to rule on the law to date has agreed with us that it is not only unconstitutional, but also unwise and misnamed since it does not really protect children. Indeed, he concluded his opinion on this note: '[P]erhaps we do the minors of this country harm if First Amendment protections, which they will with age inherit fully, are chipped away in the name of their protection.'[18]

When we turn from online free speech to privacy, the US courts have likewise been supportive of our arguments that restricting cyberliberties cannot be justified in terms of the alleged countervailing law enforcement concerns. For example, in *ACLU v. Miller*,[19] we successfully challenged a state law that prohibited anonymous and pseudonymous online communications. There have, though, been fewer rulings concerning privacy than free speech in the online context, they have only been issued by lower-level courts, and they have not been as consistently supportive of the cyberliberties positions.[20]

In the US, the battle over online privacy and encryption is being waged mostly in the legislative and executive branches of government, rather than in the courts, with the Clinton Administration steadily opposing strong encryption, but with many members of Congress, from both major political parties, on the other side. Thus far, at least, the US government is quite isolated in the international community in this respect, since most other countries allow strong encryption.[21] That is certainly true in Europe, which in general has stronger legal protections for privacy of communications and data than we have in the US.[22] However, the Clinton Administration is working hard to export its anti-privacy, anti-encryption stance around the world,[23] and it has gained support from some officials here in Britain, for example. Therefore, it is essential to understand why this stance is as inimical to public safety as it is to personal privacy.

Criminalizing Sexually-Oriented Online Expression

Now that I have sketched out the general picture concerning the relationship between cyberliberties and cybercrime, I would like to spend the rest of my time filling in some of the details. Let me start with the area where we have had the most legislation and litigation in the US, since this is also an area of great concern in other countries, including right here in Britain: namely, criminalizing online expression that is sexually oriented. In fact, Yaman

Akdeniz and I are co-authoring a book chapter on this topic, focusing on this aspect of cyberlaw in both the UK and the US.[24]

In the US, from the moment that cyberspace first hit the public radar screen, we immediately saw political and media hysteria about 'cyberporn' and efforts to censor online expression of a sexual nature. This reaction was not surprising. Despite Americans' general commitment to free speech, throughout our history, any sexually-oriented expression in any medium has always been suspect. That is because of my country's Puritanical heritage—which, of course, we share with the British Isles. One of America's most popular humorists, Garrison Keillor, put it this way: 'My ancestors were Puritans from England [who] arrived in America in 1648 in the hope of finding greater restrictions than were permissible under English law at the time.'[25] Consistent with this long-standing American tradition, we are seeing many efforts to stifle online sexual expression, all over the US, at all levels of government, from the US Congress and Clinton Administration to local school boards and library boards.[26] From a free speech perspective, that is the bad news about sexually-oriented expression online.

But there is good news too. Just as elected officials have mostly supported censorship of sexually-oriented online material, the courts have provided a welcome contrast, as I have indicated. So far, the ACLU has brought constitutional challenges to seven new laws censoring sexually-oriented material online: the two federal statutes I already mentioned;[27] four state laws (in New York,[28] Virginia,[29] New Mexico[30] and Michigan[31]); and one local law (in Loudoun County, Virginia[32]). And so far, we have won every single one of these challenges, with only one recent exception, which I do not think is too significant for cyberliberties (as I will explain in a moment). Moreover, these decisions affirming freedom of cyberspeech have been joined in by 19 different judges who span a broad ideological spectrum, having been appointed by the last six US Presidents, going all the way back to Richard Nixon (including four Republicans and two Democrats). In short, the ACLU position on online free speech is essentially the position that is now enshrined in First Amendment law.

The one recent setback is an intermediate appellate court ruling on a Virginia state law restricting government employees' access to sexually-oriented online material.[33] The US Supreme Court has held that the government, when it acts as employer, may impose more limits on its employees' expression than the government, when it acts as sovereign, may impose on its citizens' expression.[34] Nevertheless, the lower court agreed with us that Virginia's law violated even the reduced free speech rights of government employees.[35] In contrast, the intermediate appellate court overturned that decision in February, 1999 on the broad rationale that government employees have no free speech rights concerning any communications in any medium whenever they act primarily in their role as employees.[36] So, this court was not imposing special restrictions on expression in cyberspace as opposed to other media. Rather, it was imposing special restrictions on expression by government employees, regardless of the medium. We think this ruling was wrong, and hope to overturn it on further appeal. In any event, though, it really does not have any special impact specifically on *cyber*law or *cyber*liberties.

In contrast, our two most recent victories in cybercensorship cases do have broad positive implications for online free speech, so I would like to describe those. First, let me tell you a bit more about our lower court victory in February, 1999 in *ACLU v. Reno II*, against the second federal cybercensorship law, COPA. In response to the Supreme Court's decision striking down the CDA in *ACLU I*,[37] Congress wrote a somewhat less sweeping law the second time around. The CDA had criminalized any online expression that is 'patently offensive'[38] or 'indecent'.[39] In contrast, COPA outlaws any online communication 'for commercial purposes'[40] that 'includes any material that is harmful to minors'.[41] Both of COPA's critical terms are defined broadly. First, a communication is 'for commercial purposes' if it is made 'as a regular course of ... trade or business, with the objective of earning a profit', even if no profit is actually made.[42] Therefore, COPA applies to many not-for-profit Websites, which provide information completely free—including the ACLU's own Website. Second, material is 'harmful to minors' if it satisfies US law's three-part obscenity definition specifically as to minors—namely, if it appeals to the prurient interest in sex, is patently offensive, and lacks serious value, from a minor's perspective.[43]

I should note that the ACLU opposes the obscenity exception that the US Supreme Court has carved out of the First Amendment (over the dissenting votes of many respected Justices).[44] However, we have not used our cybercensorship cases as occasions for challenging that exception. In other words, we have not challenged these new laws to the extent that they simply transplant to cyberspace existing free speech exceptions, which have been upheld in other media—in particular, obscenity, child pornography, and solicitation of a minor for sexual purposes. Rather, what we have actively opposed in these new laws is their creation of new, broader categories of expression that is unprotected specifically online, even though it would be constitutionally protected in traditional print media. So, with that perspective, let me turn back to *ACLU* v. *Reno II*. On 1 February 1999, a federal judge, Lowell Reed, granted our motion for a preliminary injunction.[45] He enjoined the government from enforcing COPA pending the trial on the merits. Judge Reed held that we had shown the necessary 'likelihood of success' on the merits of our claim that COPA violates the First Amendment for many of the same reasons that CDA did.

Since COPA regulates expression that is protected 'at least as to adults',[46] Judge Reed ruled, it is presumptively unconstitutional unless the government can satisfy the demanding 'strict scrutiny' test. It has to show both that the law's purpose is to promote an interest of 'compelling' importance and that the law is narrowly tailored to promote that purpose— in other words, that there are no 'less restrictive alternative' measures, which would be less burdensome on free speech.[47] Judge Reed concluded that the government does have a compelling interest in shielding minors even from materials that are not obscene by adult standards.[48] However, Judge Reed also concluded that the government was unlikely to be able to show that COPA is the least restrictive means of achieving this goal.[49] For example, Judge Reed noted that the evidence before him 'reveals that blocking or filtering technology may be at least as successful as COPA would be in restricting minors' access to harmful material online without imposing the burden on constitutionally protected speech that COPA imposes on adult users or Web site operators'.[50] The government has appealed from Judge Reed's ruling.[51] Quite likely, this case will go all the way to the US Supreme Court, which has only issued one decision on the 'harmful to minors' doctrine, which was more than 30 years ago.[52]

Now let me turn to our second recent victory, in another important cyberspeech case, which is also still working its way through the court system. This case is called *Mainstream Loudoun* v. *Loudoun County Library*,[53] and it is so far the only court ruling on the burgeoning controversy over filtering and blocking software. Ever since it became clear that the CDA and other direct censorial measures were facing constitutional difficulties, advocates of suppressing online sexual expression stepped up their promotion of rating and filtering systems, which would also bar access to the same expression. The ACLU has issued two reports explaining why all these systems are problematic for many reasons.[54]

For one thing, the filtering software is inevitably both under-inclusive and over-inclusive, in terms of blocking all the material it purports to, and only that material. Therefore, while individual Internet users certainly have the right to install software on their own computers that blocks out material they consider contrary to their values, there is still a problem. Almost all manufacturers of blocking software refuse to disclose either the sites they block or the criteria they use to determine which sites they will block. Consequently, the manufacturers are imposing their value choices on their customers. They are not facilitating the customers' exercise of their own freedom of choice. In short, this is really more of a consumer protection problem than a free speech problem. However, there is a serious free speech problem when the filtering software is installed not as a matter of choice on the part of individual users, but rather, by government officials who control the computers—in public institutions. Across the US, officials are busily installing or advocating blocking software on computers in public libraries, schools, and universities.[55] Therefore, individual choice is stripped from the many members of the public whose only access to the Internet is through such computers. For them, the installation of filtering software on, say, library computers has the same censorial impact as the removal of books from library shelves. And book banning is precisely the analogy that was invoked by the only court that has ruled on this issue to date. In November 1998, federal judge Leonie Brinkema upheld a First Amendment challenge to mandatory filtering software that had been installed in the Loudoun County, Virginia public libraries.[56] Pursuant to a 'Policy on Internet Sexual Harassment', the library officials required software to block 'child pornography and obscene material', as well as material deemed 'harmful to juveniles' under state law.[57]

As an aside—but an important one—I want to note the distorted, overbroad concept of sexual harassment that is reflected in this policy, along with too many others. The policy assumes that the presence of sexually oriented expression on library computer terminals *ipso facto* constitutes illegal sexual harassment. But that assumption is patently incorrect. As the US Supreme Court has held, expression does not give rise to a sexual harassment claim merely because a person at whom it is directed considers it offensive.[58]

Even beyond the library's misguided concept of sexual harassment, it also implemented its policy in a way that violated online First Amendment rights, and that was the focus of Judge Brinkema's ruling. Specifically, the library installed a commercial software product called 'X-Stop'. Judge Brinkema held that the filtering requirement operated as a presumptively unconstitutional 'prior restraint' on expression. Therefore, it had to withstand the same type of strict judicial scrutiny that has also been applied to other censorial laws, such as CDA and COPA.[59]

Judge Brinkema assumed for the sake of argument that the government's asserted interests were of compelling importance—namely, its interests in minimizing access to obscenity and child pornography, and in avoiding the creation of a sexually hostile environment.[60] However, Judge Brinkema concluded that the blocking policy was unconstitutional on several, independently sufficient, grounds: (1) it is not necessary to further the government's asserted interests; (2) it 'is not narrowly tailored'; (3) it limits adult patrons to accessing only material that is fit for minors; (4) it 'provides inadequate standards for restricting access'; and (5) it 'provides inadequate procedural safeguards to ensure prompt judicial review'.[61]

One particularly interesting feature of Judge Brinkema's analysis is her catalogue of 'less restrictive means' that Loudoun County could have used to pursue its asserted interests: installing privacy screens; charging library staff with casual monitoring of Internet use; installing filtering software only on some Internet terminals, and limiting minors to those terminals; and installing filtering software that could be turned off when an adult is using the terminal.[62] Significantly, Judge Brinkema cautioned that while all of the foregoing alternatives are less restrictive than the challenged mandatory filtering policy, she did not 'find that any of them would necessarily be constitutional', since that question was not before her.[63] Loudoun County officials decided not to appeal from Judge Brinkema's ruling.[64] Of course, the constitutional questions involved will not be settled until the US Supreme Court rules on them in another filtering controversy.[65]

Debates about Online Privacy and Cryptography

In the following sections, I would like to amplify a bit on the second major aspect of the cyberliberties/crime debate that I outlined earlier: the controversy about online privacy and encryption or cryptography. Advocates of restricting encryption argue that, as the price for barring criminals and terrorists from using effective cryptography, we must also bar law-abiding citizens and businesses from doing so. This rationale was effectively debunked in an excellent report that Cyber-Rights and Cyber-Liberties (UK) issued in September 1998 and entitled 'Cyber-crime and Information Terrorism'[66]: 'Many things are valuable to criminals and terrorists but this alone does not provide a reason for imposing controls ... . [C]riminals find cars useful but society doesn't control the supply of cars because of this.'[67]

In light of this passage, it is ironic to note that when the automobile was first invented, law enforcement officials did seek to restrict its usage, precisely because they did fear that it would facilitate criminal activities.[68] Today that argument seems ludicrous, but, at bottom, it is precisely the same as the one that is now being offered in an attempt to justify restrictions on cryptography. This is the argument that is being made by the Clinton Administration in the US. The Clinton Administration insists that the only kind of encryption technology that should be available is 'key recovery' or 'key escrow' cryptography. Yet this type of encryption is inherently insecure, since it is expressly designed to give covert access to the plaintext of encrypted data to a third party—in particular, the government.

Although some government officials contend that there is a conflict between cyberliberties and cybercrime or cyberterrorism, in fact, that is not so. To the contrary, this situation vividly illustrates Thomas Jefferson's observation I previously quoted: about liberty and security concerns working in tandem, rather than in tension, with each other. Indeed, it is particularly apt to refer to Jefferson's communications with Madison in the cryptography context; when these two American founders corresponded prior to the signing of the Declaration of Independence, they encoded all their messages—in short, they used 18th-century-style encryption![69] Notwithstanding the Clinton Administration's adamant official position, individual officers and agencies in the US government have broken ranks. One important example is a high-level US government committee: the National Research Council (NRC) committee on cryptography. In its 1996 report, this committee concluded that strong encryption is essential for promoting law enforcement and national security:

> If cryptography can protect the trade secrets and proprietary information of businesses and thereby reduce economic espionage (which it can), it also supports in a most important manner the job of law enforcement. If cryptography can help protect nationally critical information systems and networks against unauthorized penetration (which it can), it also supports the national security of the United States.[70]

Accordingly, even though this NRC report recognized that restricting encryption would strengthen some law enforcement efforts, it nevertheless concluded that '[o]n balance, the advantages of more widespread use of cryptography outweigh the disadvantages'.[71] Some of the reasons for this conclusion were outlined as follows in a September 1998 GILC report that focused specifically on the precise type of cryptography regulation that has been enforced and advocated by the US—export restrictions:

[E]xport controls on cryptography hurt law-abiding companies and citizens without having any significant impact on the ability of criminals, terrorists or belligerent nations to obtain any cryptographic products they wish;

[E]xport restrictions imposed by the major cryptography-exporting states limit the ability of other nations to defend themselves against electronic warfare attacks on vital infrastructure;

[F]ailure to protect the free use and distribution of cryptographic software will jeopardize the life and freedom of human rights activists, journalists and political activists all over the world;

[A]ny restriction on the use of cryptographic programs will be unenforceable in practice, since the basic mathematical and algorithmic methods for strong encryption are widely published and can easily be implemented in software by any person skilled in the art;

[T]he increasingly common use of public networks to electronically distribute such products in intangible form reinforces the unenforceability of export controls.[72]

For the foregoing reasons, restrictions on encryption are not even effective, let alone necessary, in countering cybercrime. On this ground alone, such restrictions should be rejected. But there are also additional grounds for this conclusion. For one thing, the government cannot show that there is in fact a substantial danger of the specific type of crime that is claimed most urgently to warrant restrictions on cryptography—namely, information terrorism. Fortunately, claims about this potential problem turn out to be greatly overblown. This was shown, for example, by a recent study, published in the Fall 1998 Internet publication, *Issues in Science and Technology Online*. Its title effectively summarizes its conclusion: 'An Electronic Pearl Harbor? Not Likely'. The study was written by George Smith, an expert on computer crime, security and information warfare.[73] He dismissed government and media descriptions of the dangers of cyberterrorism as 'myths',[74] 'hoaxes'[75] and 'the electronic ghost stories of our time'.[76] Although the Smith study focused on the US, no doubt it is relevant for other countries too. Here is its conclusion:

The government's evidence about U.S. vulnerability to cyber attack is shaky at best. ... Although the media are full of scary-sounding stories about violated military Web sites and broken security on public and corporate networks, the menacing scenarios have remained just that—only scenarios. ... [An examination of the] sketchy information that the government has ... provided ... casts a great deal of doubt on the claims.[77]

Precisely the same conclusion was reached by a report by a commission appointed by President Clinton on 'Critical Infrastructure Protection'.[78] The Commission was charged with analysing the danger that information terrorists could pose to our nation's infrastructure—communications lines, power grids and transportation networks. The Commission's members consisted largely of military and intelligence officials. Therefore, the Commission was, presumably, especially sympathetic toward government claims of law enforcement and national security threats. Yet even this group was forced to acknowledge that there was no evidence of an 'impending cyber attack which could have a debilitating effect on the nation's critical infrastructure'.[79]

Nonetheless, that recognition did not deter the commission from seizing upon the fear of cyberterrorism to press for government measures that constrict individual rights, including key recovery encryption. Indeed, the Commission was so eager to leverage public concerns about info-terrorism into heightened government surveillance over the public, that it disregarded the countervailing dangers that key recovery encryption poses to the very infrastructure that the Commission was created to protect![80] Those dangers were well-described, for example, in the recent report by Cyber-Rights & Cyber-Liberties (UK), on 'Cyber-crime and Information Terrorism':

> Increasingly, the economies of the developed and developing nations are dependent on networked computing resources. Irrespective of whether it is communications, electrical power generation, road, rail or air transport, stock exchanges, banks, finance houses, agriculture, hospitals or a host of other infrastructures, all now depend on regular and continuous information exchanges between networked computer systems for their continuing safe operation. In the absence of effective cryptographic protection the computer systems that keep these·infrastructures operating are wide open to attacks by terrorist and criminal organizations using only modest resources. Cryptographic ... controls are preventing the protection of these civil infrastructures and rendering them easy and tempting targets for international terrorists and criminals. Far from impeding crime and terrorism, therefore, controls on cryptography are having precisely the opposite impact.[81]

These same dangers had been heralded in a May 1997 report by 'an Ad Hoc Group of Cryptographers and Computer Scientists', 'The Risks of Key Recovery, Key Escrow, and Trusted Third Party Encryption':

> Any key recovery infrastructure, by its very nature, introduces a new and vulnerable path to the unauthorized recovery of data where one did not otherwise exist. This ... creates new concentrations of decryption information that are high-value targets for criminals or other attackers ... . The key recovery infrastructure will tend to create extremely valuable targets, more likely to be worth the cost and risk of attack.[82]

In sum, not only are claims about the dangers of cyberterrorism exaggerated, but also, the proposed counter-measures—notably, restrictions on cryptography—far from being necessary to respond to any such dangers, are not even effective; to the contrary, they are counterproductive.

A number of recent government reports have reached precisely the same conclusions. For example, last September, a European Parliament report called for rejecting encryption controls, including those advocated by the US.[83] Significantly, this report was issued in the wake of increasing evidence of unjustified surveillance by law enforcement agencies in various European countries. Indeed, the vast majority of governments that have considered the issue have opposed restrictions on encryption. This pattern was documented by a comprehensive report that GILC issued in February 1998, entitled 'Cryptography and Liberty'.[84] It surveyed the cryptography policies of all countries in the world, based on direct communications with their governments. It concluded that, in most countries, cryptography may be freely used, manufactured, and sold without restriction. As the GILC report concluded that '[f]or those [countries] that have considered the topics, interests in electronic commerce and privacy ... outweigh the concerns expressed by law enforcement'.[85]

Conclusion

In conclusion, everyone who values human life—and human rights—must of course be vigilant against the fear, insecurity, and manipulation caused by terrorists and other criminals. But we must also be vigilant against the fear, insecurity, and manipulation caused by those who seek to fight against criminals. In a classic 1927 opinion, the great US Supreme Court Justice Louis Brandeis cautioned against ceding our hard-won freedoms to even well-intentioned government agents. Tellingly, that opinion warned against electronic surveillance and restrictions on free speech and privacy with respect to the then-newest communication technology—the telephone—despite claims about the urgent need to fight against telephonic crime. Justice Brandeis's stirring, prophetic words apply fully to electronic surveillance and restrictions on free speech and privacy with respect to the now-newest communication technology—cyberspace—despite claims about the urgent need to fight against cybercrimes and information terrorism. As Justice Brandeis warned:

> Experience should teach us to be most on our guard to protect liberty when the government's purposes are beneficent .... The greatest dangers to liberty lurk in insidious encroachment by men of zeal, well-meaning but without understanding.[86]

Notes and References

1 Keynote Address presented to 'Cyberspace 1999: Crime, Criminal Justice and the Internet', 14th BILETA Annual Conference, York, March 29, 1999. For research assistance with this essay, including drafting the footnotes, Professor Strossen gratefully acknowledges her Chief Aide, Amy L. Tenney, and her Research Assistant, César de Castro. The footnotes were added through the efforts of Professor Strossen's staff who thereby have earned both the credit and the responsibility for these notes (which Professor Strossen has not reviewed, and for which she disclaims both credit and responsibility). Finally, she would like to thank the conference organiser Dr David Wall and also Yaman Akdeniz, Cyberrights and Cyberliberties, UK, for inviting her to address the conference.

2 Professor of Law, New York Law School; President, American Civil Liberties Union.

3 Global Internet Liberty Campaign. Online. Available online at <http://www.gilc.org> (21 June 1999).

4 Cyber-Rights & Cyber-Liberties (UK). Available online at <http://www.cyber-rights.org> (2 June 1999).

5 Global Internet Liberty Campaign *Regardless of Frontiers: Protecting the Human Right to Freedom of Expression on the Global Internet*, 1998. Available online at <http://www.gilc.org/speech/report> (20 September 1999); Global Internet Liberty Campaign *Privacy and Human Rights: An International Survey of Privacy Laws and Practice*, 1998. Available online at <http://www.gilc.org/privacy/survey/intro.html> (13 September 1999).

6 *Williams* v. *Garrett*, 722 F. Supp. 254, 256 (W.D. Va. 1989) (quoting Thomas Jefferson).

7 N Strossen and E Allen 'Megan's Law and the Protection of the Child in the On-Line Age', *American Criminal Law Review*, Vol 35, pp 1319–1341, 1998. In a related vein, Professor Frederick Schauer of Harvard University testified against the Child Pornography Prevention Act of 1996, a federal law punishing anyone who possesses any work that depicts someone who appears to be a minor engaged in 'sexually explicit conduct'. Schauer stated that the law would ' "wind up hurting rather than helping the cause of prosecuting the ... individuals who exploit children" by diverting resources away from actual prosecution of child molesters'. N Strossen *Bang the Tin Drum No More*, 1997. Available online at <http://www.intellectualcapital.com/issues/issue97/item2462.asp> (21 June 1999).

8 *Erznoznik* v. *City of Jacksonville*, 422 US 205, 212 (1975) ('[M]inors are entitled to a significant measure of First Amendment protection.'); *Tinker* v. *Des Moines Indep. Community Sch. Dist.*, 393 US 503, 506 (1969) ('First Amendment rights ... are available to ... students.'); United

   Nations Children's Fund *Convention on the Rights of the Child,* 1989. Available online at
   < http://www.unicef.org/crc/part1.htm > (21 June 1999), Article 13 ('The child shall have the
   right to freedom of expression; this right shall include freedom to seek, receive and impart
   information and ideas of all kinds, regardless of frontiers, either orally, in writing or in print, in
   the form of art, or through any other media of the child's choice.').

9 Electronic Privacy Information Center, *Cryptography and Liberty 1999: An International Survey
   of Encryption Policy,* 1999. Available online at < http://www2.epic.org/reports/
   crypto1999.html > (24 July 1999), p 8.

10 The concept of the right to privacy as personal security against unwarranted intrusion by others
   is embodied in many legal guarantees of that right, including the Fourth Amendment to the US
   Constitution, which provides, in pertinent part: 'The right of the people to be secure in their
   persons, houses, papers, and effects, against unreasonable searches and seizures, shall not be
   violated ... .' Indeed, many individuals feel particularly threatened by governmental intrusions.

11 S D Warren and L D Brandeis 'The right to privacy', *Harvard Law Review,* Vol 4, p 193, 1890.

12 *Olmstead* v. *US,* 277 U.S. 438, 485 (1928) (Brandeis, J. dissenting), overruled by *Katz* v. *United
   States,* 389 US 347 (1967).

13 National Research Council *Cryptography's Role in Securing the Information Society,* 1996.
   Available online at < http://www.nap.edu/readingroom/books/crisis/ > (29 September 1999).

14 47 U.S.C. § 223 (a, d) (1999).

15 *Reno* v. *American Civil Liberties Union,* 521 U.S. 844 (1997).

16 47 U.S.C. § 231 (1999).

17 *American Civil Liberties Union* v. *Reno,* 31 F. Supp. 2d 473 (E.D. Pa. 1999).

18 *Ibid.* at 498.

19 *American Civil Liberties Union* v. *Miller,* 977 F. Supp. 1228 (N.D. Ga. 1997).

20 *Bernstein* v. *US,* 974 F. Supp. 1288 (N.D. Ca. 1997), *aff'd,*176 F.3d 1132 (9th Cir. May 6, 1999)
   (holding that encryption regulations were an unconstitutional prior restraint in violation of the
   First Amendment). *But c.f., Junger* v. *Dale,* 8 F.Supp. 2d 708, 715 (N.D. Oh. 1998) (holding that
   'although encryption source code may occasionally be expressive, its export is not protected
   conduct under the First Amendment'); *Karn* v. *US Department of State,* 925 F. Supp. 1 (D.D.C.
   1996) (rejecting First Amendment challenge to encryption export regulations). In mid-September
   1999, the Clinton Administration announced that it will relax encryption export controls. J
   Clausing 'In a reversal, White House will end data-encryption export curbs', *New York Times,*
   17 September 1999, C1. However, even with the Clinton Administration's recent pronouncement,
   civil libertarians continue to point out the problems with encryption regulations—namely, that
   export control laws on encryption are unconstitutional prior restraints on speech, and that the
   new proposed regulations apply only to commercial, not academic, work. Electronic Frontier
   Foundation *Latest Governmental Encryption Scheme Still Unconstitutional: EFF-Sponsored
   Legal Challenge Will Proceed,* 1999. Available online at < http://www.eff.org/
   91699_crypto_release.html > (16 September 1999). Shortly before this article went to press, the
   Ninth Circuit withdrew the three-judge panel decision in *Bernstein* and ordered the case to be
   reheard *en banc. Bernstein* v. *US,* No. 97–16686, 1999 US App. LEXIS 24324 (9th Cir. 30
   September 1999).

21 Global Internet Liberty Campaign *Cryptography and Liberty An International Survey of
   Encryption Policy,* 1998. Available online at < http://www.gilc.org/crypto/crypto-survey.html >
   (20 September 1999), p 5.

22 *Ibid.* at 5.

23 *Ibid.* at 6.

24 Y Akdeniz and N Strossen 'Obscene and indecent speech' in C Walker, Y Akdeniz and D Wall
   (eds) *The Internet, Law and Society,* London, Addison Wesley Longman, forthcoming.

25 Garrison Keillor, Statement to the Senate Subcommittee on Education, 29 March 1990 (Testimony
   on NEA Grant Funding and Restrictions) 136 Cong. Rec. E. 993 (1990).

26 American Civil Liberties Union: Cyberliberties. Available online at < http://www.aclu.org/
   issues/cyber/hmcl.html > (28 August 1999).

27 *Reno v. American Civil Liberties Union,* 521 U.S. 844 (1997); *American Civil Liberties Union v. Reno,* 31 F. Supp. 2d 473 (E.D. Pa. 1999).

28 *American Library Ass'n v. Pataki,* 969 F. Supp. 160 (S.D.N.Y. 1997).

29 *Urofsky v. Allen,* 995 F. Supp. 634 (E.D. Va. 1998), overruled by *Urofsky v. Gilmore,* 167 F.3d 191 (4th Cir. 1999).

30 *American Civil Liberties Union v. Johnson,* 4 F. Supp. 2d 1029 (D.N.M. 1998).

31 *Cyberspace v. Engler,* 55 F. Supp. 2d 737 (E.D. Mich. 1999).

32 *Mainstream Loudoun v. Loudoun County Library,* 24 F. Supp. 2d 552 (E.D. Va. 1998).

33 *Urofsky v. Gilmore,* 167 F.3d 191 (4th Cir. 1999).

34 *Waters v. Churchhill,* 511 U.S. 661, 674–75 (1994); *Pickery v. Board of Educ.,* 391 U.S. 563, 568 (1968).

35 *Urofsky v. Allen,* 995 F. Supp. 634 (E.D. Va. 1998).

36 *Urofsky v. Gilmore,* 167 F.3d 191, 196 (4th Cir. 1999).

37 *Reno v. American Civil Liberties Union,* 521 U.S. 844 (1997).

38 47 U.S.C. § 223(d)(1)(B).

39 47 U.S.C. § 223(a)(1)(B)(ii)

40 47 U.S.C. § 231(a)(1).

41 *Ibid.*

42 47 U.S.C. § 231(e)(2)(B).

43 47 U.S.C. § 231(e)(6).

44 N Strossen *Defending Pornography: Free Speech, Sex, and the Fight for Women's Rights,* New York, Scribner, 1995, p 57–58.

45 *American Civil Liberties Union v. R eno,* 31 F.Supp. 2d 473 (E.D. Pa. 1999).

46 *Ibid.* at 492.

47 E Chemerinsky *Constitutional Law: Principles and Policies,* New York, Aspen Law & Business, 1997, p 416.

48 *American Civil Liberties Union v. Reno,* 31 F.Supp. 2d 473, 495 (E.D. Pa. 1999).

49 *Ibid.* at 497.

50 *Ibid.*

51 American Civil Liberties Union, *Internet Censorship BattleMoves to Appeals Court,* 1999. Available online at < http://www.aclu.org/features/f101698a.html > (28 August 1999).

52 *Ginsberg v. New York,* 390 US 629 (1968).

53 *Mainstream Loudoun v. Loudoun County Library,* 24 F.Supp. 2d 552 (E.D. Va. 1998).

54 American Civil Liberties Union, *Fahrenheit 451.2: Is Cyberspace Burning?,* 1997. Available online at < http://www.aclu.org/issues/cyber/burning.html > (28 August 1999); American Civil Liberties Union, *Censorship In a Box,* 1998. Available online at < http://www.aclu.org/issues/cyber/box.html > (28 August 1999).

55 American Civil Liberties Union *Censorship In A Box,* 1998. Available online at < http://www.aclu.org/issues/cyber/box.html > (28 August 1999), pp 9–10.

56 *Mainstream Loudoun v. Loudoun County Library,* 24 F. Supp. 2d 552 (E.D. Va. 1998).

57 *Ibid.* at 567.

58 *Harris v. Forklift Sys. Inc.,* 510 US 17, 21 (1993); N Strossen *Defending Pornography: Free Speech, Sex, and the Fight for Women's Rights,* New York, Scribner, 1995, Chapter 6, pp 119–140.

59 *Mainstream Loudoun v. Loudoun County Library,* 24 F.Supp. 2d 552, 564–65 (E.D. Va. 1998).

60 *Ibid.* at 564.

61 *Ibid.* at 570.

62 *Ibid.* at 567.

63 *Ibid.*

64 D Hedgpeth 'Libraries abandon court fight; board won't appeal internet policy rulings', *Washington Post,* 22 April 1999, V03.

65 For detailed information on all of these cases, including the parties' litigation papers and the courts' rulings, see the ACLU's website. American Civil Liberties Union. Available online at < http://www.aclu.org/issues/cyber/hmcl.html > (28 August 1999).

66 B Gladman *Wassenaar Controls, Cyber-Crime and Information Terrorism*, 1998. Available online at < http://www.cyber-rights.org/crypto/wassenaar.htm > (29 September 1999), pp 4–5.

67 *Ibid.*

68 National Public Radio 'Feds say e-mail scrambler is a weapon', National Public Radio Morning Edition, 14 April 1995.

69 J Fraser 'The use of encrypted, coded and secret communications is an 'ancient liberty' protected by the US Constitution', *Virginia Journal of Law and Technology*, Vol 2, p 25, n 123, 1997.

70 National Research Council *Cryptography's Role in Securing the Information Society*, 1996. Available online at < http://www.nap.edu/readingroom/books/crisis/ > (29 September 1999), p 24.

71 *Ibid.* at 27.

72 Global Internet Liberty Campaign *Cryptography is a Defensive Tool, Not a Weapon*, 1998. Available online at < http://www.gilc.org/crypto/wassenaar/gilc-statement-998.html > (30 September 1999), p 2.

73 G Smith *An Electronic Pearl Harbor? Not Likely*, 1998. Available online at < http://www.nap.edu/issues/15.1/smith.htm > (20 September 1999).

74 *Ibid.* at 1.

75 *Ibid.* at 2.

76 *Ibid.* at 9.

77 *Ibid.* at 1.

78 The President's Commission on Critical Infrastructure Protection *Critical Foundations; Report Summary*, 1997. Available online at < http://www.info-sec.com/pccip/web/summary.html > (10 October 1999).

79 A Oram *A Sacrifice to the War Against Cyber-Terrorism*, 1997. Available online at < http://www.oreilly.com/people/staff/andyo/ar/terror_pub.html > (quoting the report issued by the President's Commission on Critical Infrastructure Protection on 13 October 1997 and presented by its Chairman Robert T. Marsh, before a Congressional Committee on 5 November 1997).

80 Electronic Privacy Information Center *White Paper: The Clinton Administration's Policy on Critical Infrastructure Protection: Presidential Decision Directive 63*, 1998. Available online at < http://www.epic.org/security/infowar/cip_white_paper.html > (20 September 1999).

81 B Gladman *Wassenaar Controls, Cyber-Crime and Information Terrorism*, 1998. Available online at < http://www.cyber-rights.org/crypto/wassenaar.htm > (29 September 1999), pp 4–5.

82 Ad Hoc Group of Cryptographers and Computer Scientists *The Risks of Key Recovery, Key Escrow, and Trusted Third Party Encryption*, 1998. Available online at < http://www.cdt.org/crypto/risks98 > (29 September 1999), p 15–16.

83 Omega Foundation *An Appraisal of the Technologies of Political Control*, 1998. Available online at < http://www.jya.com/stoa-atpc-so.htm > (8 October 1999).

84 Global Internet Liberty Campaign *Cryptography and Liberty 1998*, 1998. Available online at < http://www.gilc.org/crypto/crypto-survey.html > (29 September 1999). Shortly before this article went to press, EPIC published the 1999 update to this report. Electronic Privacy Information Center *Cryptography and Liberty 1999: An International Survey of Encryption Policy*, 1999. Available online at < http://www2.epic.org/reports/crypto1999.html > (24 July 1999).

85 Global Internet Liberty Campaign *Cryptography and Liberty 1998*, 1998. Available online at < http://www.gilc.org/crypto/crypto-survey.html > (29 September 1999), p 7.

86 *Olmstead* v. *US*, 277 US 438, 479 (1928) (Brandeis, J. dissenting), overruled by *Katz* v. *US*, 389 US 347 (1967).

"subsidiarity" in the Maastricht Treaty of European Union of 1992.[13] In this way, fragmentation in order to preserve rather than to regiment social and cultural texture has become a constitutional article of faith within the European Union. Further pressures to respect difference can be expected to flow from the commitment at the recent Amsterdam Summit to expand the Union into Eastern Europe.[14]

At Member State level within the European Union, there is no doubt that there is a strong commitment, based on global economic competition but equally political populism, to embrace in principle "the age of the Information Society".[15] Yet, because of cultural, historical and sociopolitical diversity, there will inevitably be divergent approaches to the growth and governance of the Internet in different European societies. For example, while the German Government has political fears and sensitivities about the use of the Internet by Neo-Nazis, the United Kingdom takes a more relaxed attitude to the dangers of racism but conversely has a long cultural tradition of repression towards the availability of sexually explicit material. It is then for the European Union to try to reflect these differences. The legitimate and predominant constitutional concerns of the European institutions are the working and openness of the Internal Market. The regulation (or non-regulation) of the Internet by individual Member States may create risks of distortions of competition (such as through the potential liabilities of the Internet Service Providers) and thereby hamper the free circulation of these services, and lead to a distortion and loss of competivity externally of the Internal Market producers.

Faced with the fragmentation of both the Internet and the all-purpose nation state, and having regard to the cardinal principles of respect for difference and subsidiarity, it is not surprising that both nation Member States within Western Europe and the European Union have each avoided domineering stances and the imposition of monopolistic forms of governmentality. This does not mean that the Internet is a "lawless place."[16] Rather, in the current stage of modern, or late modern society, one can expect a trend towards "governance" rather than the "government", in which the role of the nation state is no longer ascendant. The nation state must abjure the traditional monopolisation of the policing function not only on political and philosophical grounds associated with growth of neo-Liberalism or new Conservatism,[17] but also because of the pragmatic difficulties in doing otherwise in a situation of instantaneous, mass participation and global

[13] Cm. 1934, HMSO, London, 1992, art. 3a. See House of Commons Foreign Affairs Committee, *Europe after Maastricht* (1992–1993 HC 642); R. Dehousse, *Europe after Maastricht: An Ever Closer Union?* (Law Books in Europe, Munich, 1994).

[14] Treaty for Europe (Cm. 3780, Stationery Office, London, 1997). See A. Duff, *The Treaty of Amsterdam* (Federal Trust, Sweet & Maxwell, London, 1997); House of Commons Foreign Affairs Committee, *The Treaty of Amsterdam* (1997–1998 HC 305).

[15] See House of Lords Select Committee on Science and Technology, *Information Society* (1995–1996 HL 77, HMSO, London), paras 1.1, 1.6 (the *Government Response* is at Cm. 3450, 1996); European Commission Communication, *The Information Society and Development: the Role of the European Union* (COM (97) 351, Brussels-Luxembourg, 1997).

[16] J. R. Reidenberg, "Governing Networks and Cyberspace Rule-Making" (1996) 45 *Emory Law Journal* 911.

[17] See J. Habermas, *The New Conservatism* (Polity Press, Cambridge, 1989); A. Gamble, "The Political Economy of Freedom" in R. Levitas (ed.), *The Ideology of the New Right* (Polity Press, Cambridge, 1986); J. Sheptycki, "Policing, Postmodernism and Transnationalism" (1998) 38 *British Journal of Criminology* 485.

modes of Internet communication.[18] It therefore seeks further sustenance by the activation of more varied levels of power at second hand. In this way, laws, regulations, and standards will affect the development of the Internet (and, one might say, self-reflexively, vice versa), and this is also true for self-regulatory solutions introduced for the availability of certain types of content on the Internet. So[19]: "Rules and rule-making do exist. However, the identities of the rule makers and the instruments used to establish rules will not conform to classic patterns of regulation."

The result is that there appears not to be a single, harmonised site for the regulation of illegal and harmful content on the Internet. Even where the formal mechanisms for harmonisation exist in an enforceable and sanctionable form (in other words within the European Union), the approach has been discursive rather than directive. This hesitancy is understandable since the condemnation of content is itself culturally and politically specific[20] and even where there is some commonality, such as with the outlawing of child pornography, one finds that the exact definition of offences varies markedly from one country to another. The European Commission issued last year a Communication Paper in which it concurred that "each country may reach its own conclusion in defining the borderline between what is permissible and not permissible."[21] This "margin of appreciation" between Member States is of course very much in line the approach fostered by the Council of Europe's European Court of Human Rights.[22]

Therefore, a multi-layered solution seems a suitable response to the altered states of virtual reality, though many of the proposed levels of governance entail their own problems, so that the effect is often to localise rather than to solve disputes about state coercive powers. Nevertheless, one might predict that the framework of multi-layered governance of the Internet, at least in so far as it applies in Western Europe, will eventually comprise a neo-corporatist[23] mixture of:

- Global international regulatory solutions by the likes of OECD and the United Nations.
- Regional supranational legislation such as by the European Union.
- Regulations by the individual governments at national or local level, such as through specialist police squads and customs control units.

---

[18] D. Garland, "The Limits of the Sovereign State" (1996) 35 *British Journal of Criminology* 445; C. Walker "Cyber-Contempt: Fair Trials and the Internet" (1997) 3 *Yearbook of Media and Entertainment Law* 1.

[19] J. R. Reidenberg, "Governing Networks and Cyberspace Rule-Making" (1996) 45 *Emory Law Journal* 911 at 911–912.

[20] A good example is the tolerance of the English law offence of blasphemy which protects only the Christian religion: *Gay News and Lemon v. U.K.*, Application No. 8710/79, D.R. 28, p.77.

[21] See European Commission Communication to the European Parliament, the Council, the Economic and Social Committee and the Committee of the Regions, *Illegal and Harmful Content on the Internet* (COM (96) 487, Brussels-Luxembourg, October 16, 1996). An on-line copy is available at http://www2.echo.lu/legal/en/internet/communic.html.

[22] *Handyside v. U.K.*, Application No. 5493/72, Series A Vol. 24 (1976) 1 E.H.R.R. 737. See T. H. Jones, "The Devaluation of Rights under the European Convention" [1995] *Public Law* 430.

[23] See J. Habermas, *The New Conservatism* (Polity Press, Cambridge, 1989), p.61.

- Self-imposed regulation by the ISPs[24] with the creation of industry-wide codes of conduct[25]—these may cut across the above boundaries since ISPs (such as America Online and CompuServe) can operate at a global level.
- Representation of on-line users through national and transnational pressure groups at both national and international level.
- Rating systems such as Platform for Internet Content Selection ("PICS")[26] and Recreational Software Advisory Council on the Internet ("RSACi")[27]— again, the precise siting of these interventions remains debatable.
- Self-imposed regulation, such as through software filters, to be used by end-users, whether individually (especially by parents and by teachers in schools) or collectively (especially by social rules within network communities such as discussion groups).[28]
- Hotlines and pressure organisations to report illegal content such as child pornography on the Internet. The leading example in the United Kingdom is the Internet Watch Foundation.[29] The Internet Watch Foundation ("IWF") was announced in September 1996 initially as a hotline to deal with the existence of illegal content on the Internet. But the IWF also fosters the development of rating systems at a United Kingdom level, and in February 1998 it recommended these systems as the best way to fosters the availability of harmful Internet content especially for minors.[30] The Department of Trade and Industry and the Home Office played key roles in the establishment of the body, and have since endorsed its work on a number of occasions[31] as well as undertaking a review of its achievements to date.[32]

In total, these levels of intervention reflect late modernity in that there is a dispersal of regulatory power not only in regard to levels of governance but also in the shifting

---

[24] See R. L. Dunne, "Deterring Unauthorized Access to Computers: Controlling Behaviour in Cyberspace through a Contract Law Paradigm" (1994) 35 *Jurimetrics J.* 1.

[25] For proposals at a E.U. level see European Council, Recommendation on the development of the competitiveness of the European audiovisual and information services industry by promoting national frameworks aimed at achieving a comparable and effective level of protection of minors and human dignity (Brussels-Luxembourg, May 28, 1998 at http://europa.eu.int/comm/dg10/avpolicy/new_srv/recom-protec_en.pdf).

[26] See http://www.w3.org/pub/www/pics/. PICS has been developed by the World Wide Web Consortium, an association of academics, public interest groups and computer companies. See further R. Whittle "Internet Censorship, Access Control and Content Regulation" (http://www.ozemail.com.au/~firstpr/contreg/).

[27] See http://www.rsac.org/homepage.asp. The (non-governmental) Recreational Software Advisory Council has developed a content advisory system which has been integrated within web browsers.

[28] The House of Lords Select Committee emphasised self-regulation, especially by end-users, as the "best hope" of controlling undesirable materials: *Information Society* (1995–1996 HL 77, HMSO, London), para. 5.50. See also Government Response to the House of Lords Select Committee on Science and Technology, *Information Society* (Cm. 3450, HMSO, London, 1996), para. 6.10.

[29] See http://www.internetwatch.co.uk. For a critique of its activities, see Y. Akdeniz, "Child Pornography on the Internet" (1998) 148 *New Law Journal* 451.

[30] See *Rating and Filtering Internet Content—A United Kingdom Perspective* at http://www.internetwatch.org.uk/annual.html.

[31] See Government Response to the House of Lords Select Committee on Science and Technology, *Information Society* (Cm. 3450, HMSO, London, 1996), p.6; Barbara Roche, HC Debs. Vol. 296, col. 615 (Written Answers), June 26, 1997.

[32] See http://www.coi.gov.uk/coi/depts/GTI/coi8435d.ok.

boundary between the public and the private, with the latter taking a strong role in policing.[33] In so far as they point towards self-governance and the mobilisation of concerned and active groups, there may also be some rationale and impetus provided by the communitarian movement.[34] Applied to the availability of illegal and harmful materials on the Internet, it might be argued that it is ultimately up to good "Netizens" to sustain the voice of communal morality rather than expecting some state law enforcer to surf in to clean up the virtual town.[35] However, the success of such an appeal to the localised governance of crime or anti-social behaviour will itself raise profound questions as to the constitution of "community", the choice of moral precepts which are to prevail and democratic accountability.[36] So, such appeals to a communal spirit should not be allowed to mask the fact that repression will continue, whether through traditional policing institutions or through the tyranny of societal standards.

Legislative history of the E.U. initiatives

The foregoing model of a mixed political economy has been recognised by the European Commission, which suggested in a recent Communication Paper on illegal and harmful content that[37]: " . . . the answer to the challenge will be a combination of self-control of the service providers, new technical solutions such as rating systems and filtering software, awareness actions for parents and teachers, information on risks and possibilities to limit these risks and of international co-operation." The Communication Paper emanated as a response to calls for the regulation of the Internet within the European Union in early 1996. The Communication Paper was launched together with a Green Paper on the Protection of Minors and Human Dignity in Audio-visual and Information Services in October 1996.[38] The European Commission documents follow the resolution adopted by the Telecommunications Council of Ministers in September 1996, on preventing the dissemination of illegal content on the Internet, especially child pornography. While the Communication gives policy options for immediate action to fight against harmful and illegal content on the Internet, the Green Paper sets out to examine the broader challenges that society faces in ensuring that these issues of overriding

---

[33] N. Rose and P. Miller, "Political Power beyond the State" (1992) 43 *British Journal of Sociology* 173; T. Jones and T. Newburn, *Private Security and Public Policing* (Clarendon Press, Oxford, 1998).

[34] A. Etzioni, *The Spirit of Community* (Simon Schuster, New York, 1993).

[35] J. Braithwaite and P. Pettit, *Not Just Deserts: A Republican Theory of Criminal Justice* (Oxford University Press); P. Selznick, *Moral Commonwealth* (University of California Press, Berkley, 1995); H. Strang, "Replacing Courts with Conferences" (1995) 11 *Policing* 212; C. Leadbeter, *The Self Policing Society* (Demos, London, 1996).

[36] See A. Crawford, *The Local Governance of Crime* (Clarendon Press, Oxford, 1997); D. Wall, "Policing and the Regulation of the Internet", below, p.79.

[37] See European Commission Communication to the European Parliament, the Council, the Economic and Social Committee and the Committee of the *Regions, Illegal and Harmful Content on the Internet* (COM (96) 487, Brussels-Luxembourg, October 16, 1996. An on-line copy is available at http://www2/echo.lu/legal/en/internet/communic.html.

[38] See European Commission, *Green Paper on the Protection of Minors and Human Dignity in Audiovisual and Information Services* (COM (96) 483 final, Brussels-Luxembourg, October 16, 1996). An on-line copy is available at http://europa.eu.int/en/record/green/gp9610/protec.htm.

public interest are inadequately taken into account in the rapidly evolving world of audiovisual and information services. It suggests that[39]:

> "If such mechanisms of international governance and re-regulation are to be initiated then the role of nation states is pivotal. Nation states are now simply one class of powers and political agencies in a complex system of power from world to local levels but they have a centrality because of their relationship to territory and population."

The United Kingdom Government welcomed the E.U. Communication with its emphasis on multi-layered governance as entirely consistent with the United Kingdom's approach, which would emphasise self-governance at a national level[40]: "The UK strongly agrees with the Commission that since a legal framework for regulation of the Internet already exists in Member States, new laws or regulations are unnecessary." More recently, Chris Smith, the Secretary of State for Culture, Media and Sport stated that:

> "It is vital . . . in considering how best to address [the problem of illegal and harmful content on the Internet], that we bear in mind that only a small fraction of the material available to the public poses a threat to the protection of minors or human dignity. It will be important, therefore, not to impose hasty regulation upon these new services and thereby constrain their development and the educational, commercial and social opportunities and other benefits they can engender."[41]

The Communication and the Green Paper were followed by the European Commission Working Party Report[42] in early November 1996. According to the Working Party Report, a self-regulatory system, including representatives of industry and users, to advise on whether or not a breach of the Code of Conduct has occurred, should be developed. The next stage in the discussion was that the European Parliament adopted a resolution on the Commission Communication Paper in April 1997.[43] According to the European Commissioner for industrial affairs and information and telecommunications technologies, Martin Bangemann, it is difficult to pass legislation at international level on "harmful" content on the Internet, but there is less cultural difference in what is "illegal", and the response must be global.[44]

Taking up that wider perspective, in a resolution adopted at the meeting of October 1996, the Council of Ministers of the European Union has recognised the

---

[39] P. Hirst and G. Thompson, "Globalization and the Future of the Nation State" (1995) 24 *Economy and Society* 408 at 430.

[40] House of Commons Select Committee on European Legislation Fourth Report (1996–1997 H.C. 36), para. 14.8.

[41] See House of Commons Select Committee on European Legislation, Second Report (1997–1998 H.C. 155–ii). See particularly "The Information Society and Protection of Human Dignity" at para. 60.

[42] European Commission Working Party Report, *Illegal and Harmful Content on the Internet* (1996) at http://www2.echo.lu/legal/en/internet/content/wpen.html.

[43] See European Commission, *Communication on Illegal and Harmful Content on the Internet* (COM (96) 0487—C4–0592/96) Committee on Civil Liberties and Internal Affairs, March 20, 1997, available at http://www/europarl.eu.int/dg1/a4-97/a4-0098/htm.

[44] *ibid.*

need for further analysis of the issues underlying development of information society policy internationally with a view to reaching a common understanding on means and conditions governing the use of global information networks. The Council of Ministers stressed the need for co-ordination between initiatives relating to the subjects, both in the Union framework and in other international fora. These issues were discussed at the "Global Information Networks, Ministerial Conference," in Bonn, in July 1997.[45] The resultant "Bonn Declaration"[46] underlined the importance of clearly defining the relevant legal rules on responsibility for content of the various actors in the chain between creation and use. The Ministers recognised the need to make a clear distinction between the responsibility of those who produce and place content in circulation and that of intermediaries such as the Internet Service Providers, thus beginning to accept that it is producers and users who must exercise normative choice and discernment and that carriers are not in a position to act as content guardians in this medium. Despite these calls and initiatives, the manager of CompuServe Germany, Felix Somm was successfully prosecuted in May 1998 for the dissemination of child pornography to its customers in Germany.[47]

The E.U. ministers also declared at the Bonn Conference "their intention to co-operate fully within the Council of Europe, the OECD, the WTO and other appropriate international fora, in order to identify and dismantle existing obstacles to the use of new services on global information networks, to prevent the establishment of new barriers, and to establish a clear and predictable legal framework at national and, where appropriate, European and global levels." This statement serves to emphasise that Internet-related problems deserve not only national and supranational attention but also global levels of governance because the Internet remains beyond the control of any single nation state or even the E.U. Member States combined.

The Bonn Declaration was followed in September 1997 by Martin Bangemann's call for an Internet charter, which would focus on issues to do with technical standards, illegal content, licences, encryption and data privacy[48]:

> "The current situation may lead to the adoption of isolated global rules with different countries signing up to different rules agreed under the auspices of different international organisations. An international charter would provide a suitable answer."

The idea was given further substance when Martin Bangemann and fellow Commissioner, Sir Leon Brittan, launched a proposed framework for international policy co-operation and sought to start a process which could lead to the adoption

---

[45] See the "Global Information Networks, Ministerial Conference," Bonn July 6–8, 1997, http://www2.echo.lu/bonn/conference.html.

[46] See http://www2.echo.lu/bonn/final.html.

[47] See G. Leong, "Computer Child Pornography—the Liability of Distributors?", below p.19; http://www.cyber-rights.org/isps/somm-dec.htm.

[48] See "A New World Order for Global Communications," a speech by Martin Bangemann to Telecom Inter@ctive '97, ITU Geneva, September 8, 1997 at http://www.ispo.cec.be/infosoc/promo/speech/geneva.html.

of an International Communications Charter for the Internet in February 1998.[49]

In November 1997, the European Commission adopted a new proposal for an Action Plan, promoting the safe use of the Internet, which would cover a three-year period between 1998 to 2001.[50] The new Action Plan recognised that the Internet does not exist in a "legal vacuum". However, because of the global nature of the Internet, the E.U. prefers self-regulatory solutions for the regulation of illegal and harmful content. The Action Plan, therefore, encourages the creation of a European network of hot lines to report illegal content such as child pornography by on-line users, the development of self-regulatory and content-monitoring schemes by access providers, and content providers for combating illegal content. It also seeks the development of internationally compatible and interoperable rating and filtering schemes to protect users (especially children at risk from harmful content), and measures to increase awareness of the possibilities available among parents, teachers, children and other consumers to help these groups to use the networks whilst choosing the appropriate content and exercising a reasonable amount of parental control. The Commission's Action Plan was adopted by a decision of the Council and the European Parliament in September 1998.[51] It now returns to the European Parliament for second reading under the co-decision procedure.

Critique of the E.U. initiatives

While all these initiatives appear attractive to concerned users, there are certain matters which should be carefully addressed before developing the suggested solutions.

First, although the new E.U. Action Plan suggests that "harmful content needs to be treated differently from illegal content", what is "illegal" or "harmful" is not clearly defined. The Action Plan states that illegal content is related to a wide variety of issues such as instructions on bomb-making (national security), pornography (protection of minors), incitement to racial hatred (protection of human dignity) and libel (protection of reputation). But none of those issues listed is necessarily "illegal content", nor even considered as "harmful content" (a concept probably undefinable in a global context) by many European countries.[52] Such laxity in the

---

[49] See the European Commission, Communication on International Charter: The need for strengthened international co-ordination—Communication from the Commission to the European Parliament, the Council, the Economic and Social Committee and the Committee of the Regions (COM (98) 50, Brussels-Luxembourg, at http://www.ispo.cec.be/eif/policy/com9850en.html). See also E. Tucker, "Internet: EU Tries to Forge System of Rules," *Financial Times*, February 5, 1998.

[50] See Communication from the Commission to the European Parliament, the Council, the Economic and Social Committee and the Committee of the Regions, *Action Plan on Promoting Safe Use of the Internet* (Brussels-Luxembourg, November 1997). An on-line version is available at http://www2/echo.lu/legal/en/internet/actplan.html.

[51] European Parliament and Council, Decision No. 10182/98/EC adopting a Multiannual Community Action Plan on promoting safer use of the Internet by combating illegal and harmful content on global networks (Brussels-Luxembourg, September 16, 1998 at http://www2.echo.lu/iap/position/en.html.

[52] See further the European Commission, *Interim Report on Initiatives in EU Member States with respect to Combating Illegal and Harmful Content on the Internet, Version 7* (Brussels-Luxembourg, June 4, 1997, at http://www2.echo.lu/legal/en/internet/wp2en.html.

use of language was at the core of the successful challenge to the United States Communications Decency Act 1996 in the United States Supreme Court,[53] and states within Western Europe should especially avoid pandering to the lowest common denominator where the least tolerant can set the pace. The European Court of Human Rights in its judgment in *Handyside*[54] stated that the steps necessary in a democratic society for the protection of morals will depend on the type of morality to which a country is committed. Therefore, "harm" is a criterion which will depend upon cultural differences.[55] This emphasis on freedom of trans-frontier expression is prescient, especially if territorial expressions about rights or otherwise are under attack.

Secondly, as well as concerns about standards to be enforced, one should also examine closely the viability of the chosen mechanism. The creation and use of hotlines for reporting illegal content is encouraged by the E.U. Action Plan, and according to the United Kingdom's Internet Watch Foundation's annual report of March 1998 (which covers the period between December 1996 and November 1997), there have been 781 reports to the Foundation from on-line users and in 248 of them action was taken (206 involved child pornography, 16 adult pornography, 12 financial scams and 9 other). These reports resulted in the review of 4,324 items, and the Foundation has taken action in 2,215 of them (2,183 referred to the police and 2,000 to ISPs). 1,394 of these originated from the United States, while only 125 of the items originated from the United Kingdom.[56] Yet, these figures tell us little, as the actual amount of child pornography on the Internet is unknown[57] so it is difficult to judge how successful the United Kingdom hotline has been. Another downside is that the efforts of the organisation are concentrated on the newsgroups carried by the United Kingdom ISPs. This means that while illegal material is removed from the United Kingdom servers, the same material will continue to be available on the Internet carried by the foreign ISPs in their own servers. The expensive monitoring of the Internet at a national level is of limited value as the few problems created by the Internet remain global ones and thus require global solutions.

While the E.U. Action Plan emphasises self-regulatory solutions, these may result in the privatised censorship of "controversial speech by banishing it to the farthest

[53] *ACLU v. Reno*, 117 S. Ct. 2329 (1997); Y. Akdeniz, "Censorship on the Internet" (1997) 147 *New Law Journal* 1003.

[54] *Handyside v. U.K.*, App. No. 5493/72, Series A Vol. 24 (1976) 1 E.H.R.R. 737.

[55] European Commission Working Document, Protection of minors and human dignity in audiovisual and information services: Consultations on the Green Paper (SEC(97) 1203, Brussels-Luxembourg, June 13, 1997 at http://www2.echo.lu/legal/en/internet/gpconsult.html).

[56] See the IWF statistics at http://www.internetwatch.org.uk/stats.html and the annual report at http://www.internetwatch.org.uk/annual.html.

[57] But see the survey in the (Irish) Department of Justice, Equality and Law Reform, *Illegal and Harmful Use of the Internet* (Pn.5231, Dublin, 1998), pp.34–35, which suggests that 0.07 per cent of the 40,000 newsgroups carry "child erotica" or "pornography", plus 238 (out of around 50 million web pages) "girl-related child pornography or erotica" web sites (an unspecified larger number were boy-related). The definitions used are far from tight (see p.30), and claims that this source of child pornography is either "major" or "increasing" are unsubstantiated in the absence of earlier measures or measures of other forms of trafficking.

corners of cyberspace with blocking and rating schemes".[58] Rating and filtering products claim to empower users to block unwanted material from their personal systems. The most sophisticated and widely recognised of these systems is the Platform for Internet Content Selection ("PICS"), introduced by the World Wide Web Consortium.[59] European governments have been especially enthusiastic about this projected self-regulatory solution to Internet content. But according to a recent American Civil Liberties Union (ACLU) paper, third-party ratings systems pose significant free speech problems, creating a "cloud of smoke."[60] Therefore, with few third-party rating products currently available, the potential for arbitrary censorship increases. According to the ACLU paper, "it is not too late for the Internet community to slowly and carefully examine these proposals and to reject those that will transform the Internet from a true marketplace of ideas into just another mainstream, lifeless medium."

In July 1998, the Economic and Social Committee of the European Commission published its opinion on the E.U. Action Plan.[61] Although favourably disposed in general, the Committee noted that very little attention has been given to illegal content in relation to protection of intellectual property, human dignity, and privacy or to offences relating to national and economic security.[62] Furthermore, the Committee was not convinced that the technological solution proposed by the Commission on harmful Internet content is the most effective way of tackling a social problem. One of the dangers noted by the Committee with this approach is that, the use of filtering tools may create a false sense of security for parents and teachers, while children will quickly find any loopholes.[63] The Committee further questioned the claim that PICS will turn the Internet into an environment free of harmful content.[64] More importantly, the Committee was worried that the possibility of Internet Service Providers using filtering and rating systems at the level of entry would render these systems, dubbed as "user empowering", an instrument of control, "actually taking choice out of citizens' hands."[65] Therefore the Committee stated that[66]:

> "The Committee supports the Commission in its view that cultural and social diversity based on freedom of expression is a thing of great value which must not be compromised by efforts to achieve a safe Internet; also that, in deciding what is harmful and what is not, the onus must be on the individual, whether or not in his capacity as educator."

[58] *per* B. Steinhardt, Associate Director of the ACLU, see American Civil Liberties Union, *Fahrenheit 451.2: Is Cyberspace Burning? How Rating and Blocking Proposals May Torch Free Speech on the Internet*, 1997 at http://www.aclu.org/issues/cyber/burning.html.

[59] See above.

[60] See WASHINGTON POST editorial, "Filters and Free Speech," *The Washington Post*, November 24, 1997.

[61] Economic and Social Committee of the European Commission, Opinion on the Proposal for a Council Decision adopting a Multiannual Community Action Plan on promoting safe use of the Internet (OJEC, 98/C 214/08, Brussels-Luxembourg, July 10, 1998), pp.29–32.

[62] *ibid.* para. 3.1.1.1.

[63] *ibid.* para. 3.2.1.

[64] *ibid.* para. 3.3.1.

[65] *ibid.* para. 3.4.

[66] *ibid.* para. 3.4.

Overall, the Committee felt that the Action Plan was over-ambitious. The Committee considered it highly unlikely that the proposed measures will in the long term result in a safe Internet[67] with the rating and classification of all information on the Internet being "impracticable". The Committee, therefore, "sees little future in the active promotion of filtering systems based on rating."[68] In the view of the Committee, the scope of the Action Plan should be restricted to combating illegal content, and a lower priority should be assigned to the development of means of combating harmful content. It may be noted that the Civil Liberties Committee of the European Parliament has also adopted a report on the Action Plan which concluded that combating Internet content which is liable to prosecution is a matter for the Member States.[69]

A third point of critique of the Commission's initiatives is that there are some overarching principles which are in danger of being lost from sight.

In political terms, these first include respect for national sensitivities and difference, so that most regulation must be pursued, if at all, at a localised level (the principle of subsidiarity). One might compare here the European standard-setting in the field of data protection,[70] where the problem was much narrower and where regional harmonisation was seen to be in furtherance of rights and mainly in conflict with other interests (economic or governmental) rather than other rights.

A second political principle tends in the opposite direction—towards universalisation. This consideration is the constant demand for respect for individual rights, which, as expressed through the Council of Europe's European Convention on Human Rights and Fundamental Freedoms of 1950.[71] Much of the text of this "external bill of rights" is shortly to be incorporated into United Kingdom law by the Human Rights Bill 1997–1998.[72] Amongst its many provisions relevant to criminal law and process[73] is a strong (though not absolute) statement in favour of free expression in Article 10(1)[74]: "(1) Everyone has the right to freedom of expression. This right shall include freedom to hold opinions and to receive and impart information and ideas without interference by public authority and regardless of frontiers . . . ". According to a European Commission working party report, "respect for the principles of the protection of minors and human dignity is a *sine*

---

[67] *ibid.* para. 4.1.

[68] *ibid.* para. 4.1.1.

[69] European Parliament, News report, "Promote use of Internet but crack down on illegal content," June 8, 1998, at http://www.europarl.eu.int/dg3/sdp/newsrp/en/n980608.htm.

[70] See Council of Europe Convention on Data Protection 1980; European Communities, Directive on Data Protection, 95/46/EC, O.J. L281, November 23, 1995 (http://www2.echo.lu/legal/en/dataprot/dataprot.html). The Directive is now reflected in the Data Protection Act 1998.

[71] Cmd. 8969. See M. O'Boyle, D. Harris and C. Warbrick *Law of the European Convention on Human Rights* (Butterworths, London, 1995).

[72] 1997–1998 H.C. No. 219. See the House of Commons Library Research Paper, *The Human Rights Bill [HL], Bill 119 of 1997/98: Some constitutional and legislative aspects* (No. 98/27, 1998).

[73] See L. H. Leigh, "The Influence of the European Convention on Human Rights on English Criminal Law and Procedure" (1993) 1 E.J.C., C.L. & C.J. 3; C. Ovey, "The European Convention on Human Rights and the Criminal Lawyer: An Introduction" [1998] Crim.L.R. 4.

[74] Note also the requirement of respect for privacy of communications in Article 8(1), as recognised in *Malone v. U.K.*, Application No. 8691/79, Judgment of Court Series A, Vol. 82 (1984); *Halford v. U.K.*, Application No. 20605/92 *The Times*, July 3, 1997.

qua non for the development of the new services."[75] But there are problems related to the use of rating systems and filtering software[76] not necessarily addressed by the E.U. initiatives. Far from empowering individual users or supervisors (such as parents), systems such as PICS are reliant upon a centralised system of classification of material content. But this classification process clearly takes control away from end-users and imposes standards which most do not have the time, inclination or knowledge to question (or even notice). The classification process also imposes forms of cultural hegemony which are most undesirable. What is illegal and harmful depends on cultural differences, and there are significant variations in different societies. There is even diversity in the most common example of child pornography. The definition of a "child" varies in different countries and also the creation and possession of computer generated (pseudo-photographs)[77] images of children are not always a crime. It is therefore imperative that international initiatives take into account different ethical standards in different countries in order to explore appropriate rules to protect people against offensive material. In this context it might be useful to quote from one of the more recent judgments of the European Court of Human Rights at Strasbourg stating that[78]:

" . . . freedom of expression constitutes one of the essential foundations of a democratic society, one of the basic conditions for its progress. Subject to paragraph 2 of Article 10 [of the European Convention on Human Rights], it is applicable not only to 'information' or 'ideas' that are favourably received or regarded as inoffensive or as a matter of indifference, but also to those that offend, shock or disturb. Such are the demands of that pluralism, tolerance or broadmindedness without which there is no democratic society."

Next, there are also economic ground-rules. It is often the commercial exploitation of the Internet which predominates in governmental thinking.[79] However, inappropriate regulation of content may threaten the growth of the information technology and result in loss of market share and investment to competitors such as the United States or in the Far East.

---

[75] European Commission Working Document, *Protection of minors and human dignity in audiovisual and information services: Consultations on the Green Paper* (SEC(97) 1203, June 13, 1997).

[76] See American Civil Liberties Union, *Fahrenheit 451.2: Is Cyberspace Burning? How Rating and Blocking Proposals May Torch Free Speech on the Internet* (August 1997, http://www.aclu.org/issues/cyber/burning.html); Cyber-Rights and Cyber-Liberties (UK) Report, *Who Watches the Watchmen: Internet Content Rating Systems, and Privatised Censorship* (November 1997 at http://www.leeds.ac.uk/law/pgs/yaman/watchmen.htm).

[77] Criminal Justice and Public Order Act 1994, s.84.

[78] *Castells v. Spain*, Application No. 11798/85, Series A, Vol. 236 (1992) 14 E.H.R.R. 445, § 42. See also *Lingens v. Austria*, Application No. 9815/82, Series A, Vol. 103 (1986) 8 E.H.R.R. 407; *Demicoli v. Malta*, Application No. 13057/87, Series A, Vol. 210 (1992) 14 E.H.R.R. 47; *Oberschlick v. Austria*, Application No. 11662/85, Series A, Vol. 204 (1995) 19 E.H.R.R. 389; *Jersild v. Denmark*, Application No. 15890/88, Series A, Vol. 298 (1995) 19 E.H.R.R. 1.

[79] See DTI, *Converging Technologies* (http://www.dti.gov.uk/future-unit (1998)); European Commission, Green Paper on the Convergence of the telecommunications, media and Information Technology Sectors, and the Implications for regulation towards an Information Society Approach (COM (97) 623); European Commission Directorate-General XIII, Communication on the Need for Strengthened International Coordination (COM (98) 50).

Conclusion

By providing quick and cheap access to any kind of information, the Internet is the first truly interactive "mass" medium. It should not be surprising that governments around the globe are anxious to control this new medium,[80] and the Internet seems to be sharing some patterns common to the regulation of any new media. Most of the people concerned about the Internet are non-users of it, and there is exploitation of their concerns both by politicians and by the mass media.[81] The full potential of the development of the Internet will depend upon society accentuating its opportunities for speech, information and education, whilst empowering, but not demanding, very localised forms of policing (often at the level of individual user) to permit or block any message according to content.[82] The political and social diversity of Europe and the innovative technical openness and boundlessness of the Internet make other approaches virtually impossible and certainly undesirable.

[80] Human Rights Watch, "Silencing The Net: The Threat to Freedom of Expression On-line" [1996] 8(2) *Monitors: A Journal of Human Rights and Technology* at 'http://www.cwrl. utexas.edu/~monitors/.

[81] Y. Akdeniz, "Governance of Pornography and Child Pornography on the Global Internet: A Multi-Layered Approach," in L. Edwards and C. Waelde (eds), *Law and the Internet: Regulating Cyberspace* (Hart Publishing, Oxford, 1997).

[82] Compare (Canadian) Information Highway Advisory Council, *Preparing Canada for a Digital World* (1997, at http://strategis.ic.gc.ca/SSG/ih01650e.html); (French) Conseil D'Etat, *Internet et les réseaux numériques*, 1998 at http://www.internet.gouv.fr/francais/textesref/ rapce98/accueil.htm; (Irish) Department of Justice, Equality and Law Reform, *Illegal and Harmful Use of the Internet* (Pn.5231, Dublin, 1998), paras. 5.1.3, 5.2, 5.3, 5.5.

[21]

Marketing Pornography on the Information Superhighway: A Survey of 917,410 Images, Descriptions, Short Stories, and Animations Downloaded 8.5 Million Times by Consumers in Over 2000 Cities in Forty Countries, Provinces, and Territories

MARTY RIMM*

I. OVERVIEW

A. PORNOGRAPHY[1] ON COMPUTER NETWORKS

As Americans become increasingly computer literate, they are discover-

---

* Researcher and Principal Investigator, College of Engineering, Carnegie Mellon University. This interdisciplinary project was made possible by four grants from Carnegie Mellon University. The author [hereinafter "principal investigator"] wishes to thank members of the research team for their encouragement, patience, and support. Principal faculty advisor: Dr. Marvin Sirbu, Department of Engineering and Public Policy. Faculty advisors: Dr. David Banks, Department of Statistics; Dr. Timothy McGuire, Dean, Charles H. Lundquist School of Business, University of Oregon; Dr. Nancy Melone, Associate Professor of Management, Charles H. Lundquist School of Business, University of Oregon; Carolyn Speranza, Artist/Lecturer, Department of Art; Dr. Edward Zuckerman, Department of Psychology. Senior Programmer: Hal Wine. Programmers: Adam Epstein, Ted Irani. Research Assistants: Patrick Abouyon, Paul Bordallo, G. Alexander Flett, Christopher Reeve, Melissa Rosenstock. Administrative Assistant: Timothy J. Burritt. Administrative Support: Dr. Chris Hendrickson, Associate Dean, Carnegie Institute of Technology; Robert P. Kail, Associate Dean, Carnegie Institute of Technology; Barbara Lazarus, Ph.D., Associate Provost for Academic Projects; Jessie Ramey, Director, SURG. Contributors: Lisa Sigel, C.J. Taylor, Erikas Napjas, John Gardner Myers. Special thanks to Ron Rohrer, Wilkoff University Professor, Department of Electrical and Computer Engineering; and Daniel Weitzner, Deputy Director, Center for Democracy and Technology, for review of the legal notes.

In an effort to present an informative and balanced report, members of the Carnegie Mellon research team (the principal investigator, his faculty advisors, and research assistants) have consulted with organizations and experts who hold a wide variety of viewpoints about pornography, although the overwhelming majority of contacts have been with the pornography industry itself. While this article discusses a number of different viewpoints on significant legal and policy issues related to the regulation of pornographic material, the research team does not advocate or endorse any particular viewpoint or course of action concerning pornography on the Information Superhighway.

1. "Pornography" stems from the Greek words, porno, meaning prostitutes, and graphos, meaning writing. Over the course of history, it has assumed many definitions and meanings. *See generally* LYNN HUNT, THE INVENTION OF PORNOGRAPHY (1993). Many historians have commented on the difficulty of defining pornography. *See, e.g.,* WALTER KENDRICK, THE SECRET MUSEUM: PORNOGRAPHY IN MODERN CULTURE (1987). The Carnegie Mellon study adopts the "definition" utilized in current everyday practice by computer pornographers. Accordingly, "pornography" is defined here to include the depiction of actual sexual contact

ing an unusual and exploding repertoire of pornographic imagery on computer networks.[2] Every time consumers log on, their transactions assist

---

[hereinafter "hard-core"] and depiction of mere nudity or lascivious exhibition [hereinafter "soft-core"]. The courts and numerous statutes concur with the distinction presented here between "hard-core" and "soft-core." *See, e.g.*, Miller v. California, 413 U.S. 15, 24 (1973); Ballew v. Georgia, 435 U.S. 223, 228 (1978); ARK. CODE ANN. § 5-68-302(2) (Michie 1987); LA. REV. STAT. ANN. § 106 (West 1994). By this definition, not all pornography meets the legal test for obscenity, nor should all depictions of sexual activity be construed as pornographic. Accordingly, data was collected for this article only from bulletin board systems (BBS) which clearly marketed their image portfolios as "adult" rather than "artistic." Any BBS or World Wide Web site which made even a modest attempt to promote itself as "artistic" or "informational" was excluded.

"Pornographer" is defined to include BBS operators who do any of the following: commission photographers to provide new pornographic images; scan pornographic images from magazines; pirate pornographic images from other boards; or purchase adult CD-ROMs for distribution via modem to their customers. "Adult" is the term used by most BBS system operators who market pornography.

2. The question of whether a sexually explicit image enjoys First Amendment protection is the subject of much controversy and reflects a fundamental tension in contemporary constitutional jurisprudence. While this article discusses only the content and consumption patterns of sexual imagery currently available on the Internet and "adult" BBS, the law enforcement and constitutional implications are obvious. Thus, it is necessary to briefly discuss the constitutional status of sexually explicit images.

Obscene material does not enjoy First Amendment protection. *See* Roth v. United States, 354 U.S. 476 (1957); Miller v. California, 413 U.S. 15 (1973). In *Miller*, the Supreme Court established the current tripartite definition for obscenity. In order to be obscene, and therefore outside the protection of the First Amendment, an image must (1) appeal to a prurient (i.e., unhealthy or shameful) interest in sexual activity, (2) depict real or simulated sexual conduct in a manner that, according to an average community member, offends contemporary community standards, and (3) according to a reasonable person, lack serious literary, artistic, political, or scientific value. *Id.* at 25-27; *see also* Pope v. Illinois, 481 U.S. 497, 500-01 (1987) (rejecting "ordinary member of given community" test, in favor of "reasonable person" standard for purposes of determining whether work at issue lacks literary, artistic, political, or scientific value); Pinkus v. United States, 436 U.S. 293, 298-301 (1978) (excluding children from "community" for purpose of determining obscenity, but allowing inclusion of "sensitive persons" in the "community"); Ginzburg v. United States, 383 U.S. 463, 471-74 (1966) (allowing courts to examine circumstances of dissemination to determine existence of literary, artistic, political, or scientific value); *see also* United States v. Orito, 413 U.S. 139, 143 (1973) (holding that constitutionally protected zone of privacy for obscenity does not extend beyond the home).

To complicate matters, all adult pornographic material is initially presumed to be nonobscene. *Cf.* Fort Wayne Books, Inc. v. Indiana, 489 U.S. 46, 62 (1989) (requiring judicial determination of obscenity before taking publication out of circulation); Marcus v. Search Warrant, 367 U.S. 717, 730-31 (1961) (requiring procedures for seizure of obscenity which give police adequate guidance regarding the definition of obscenity to ensure no infringement on dissemination of constitutionally protected speech). Accordingly, law enforcers and prosecutors attempting to pursue an obscenity investigation or prosecution face constitutionally mandated procedural obstacles not present in other criminal matters. *See* New York v. P.J. Videos, Inc., 475 U.S. 868 (1986). For instance, the so-called "plain view" exception to the Fourth Amendment warrant requirement, whereby contraband plainly visible to a law enforcement officer may be seized, does not apply to allegedly obscene material because, prior to a judicial determination, nothing is obscene and therefore, *a fortiori*, nothing be can be considered contraband. *See* Lo-Ji Sales, Inc. v. New York, 442 U.S. 319, 325 (1979) (requiring that search warrants contain specific description of allegedly obscene items to be seized).

pornographers in compiling databases of information about their buying habits and sexual tastes. The more sophisticated computer pornographers are using these databases to develop mathematical models to determine which images they should try to market aggressively. They are paying close attention to all forms of paraphilia, including pedophilic, bestiality, and urophilic images, believing these markets to be among the most lucrative. They are using the Usenet and World Wide Web to advertise their products and maintaining detailed records of which images are downloaded most frequently.

In addition, the market for computer pornography is evolving rapidly. A decade ago, few people had access to the technology necessary to store, transmit, or receive pornographic images on computers. During the past few years, however, pornographers have begun to utilize computer networks—and the unprecedented distribution channels they offer—to penetrate markets throughout the world where public access to pornography has been historically restricted, including China, Saudi Arabia, Malaysia and Turkey.[3]

Computer pornographers are also moving from a market saturation policy to a market segmentation, or even individualized, marketing phase. Until now, most have saturated customers with tens of thousands of images, reasoning that their customers would inevitably find material that they liked. However, few customers have the patience or technical resources to perform the extensive database analysis necessary to quickly download only the images they prefer. Pornographers now have sufficient information to dramatically shrink the size of their portfolios, while at the same time increasing their subscriber revenues. A few have already begun to do so.

In addition to obscenity, one other type of sexually explicit material does not enjoy constitutional protection. In New York v. Ferber, 458 U.S. 747 (1982), the Supreme Court explicitly removed pornography depicting minors from the protective aegis of the First Amendment. That is, obscene or not, visual depictions of children engaged in sexual conduct are not constitutionally protected. Because the government interest identified by the Supreme Court as justifying removing child pornography from the protection of the First Amendment is more urgent than the government interest which justifies denying protection to obscenity, and because the child pornography standard is far less vague than the obscenity standard, law enforcers and prosecutors are not bound by any unique procedural burdens here. *See* United States v. Weigand, 812 F.2d 1239 (9th Cir.), *cert. denied*, 484 U.S. 856 (1987).

In sum, the constitutional regime that the Supreme Court has established for pornography creates two distinct categories of sexually explicit imagery that are not protected by the First Amendment. While ascertaining whether a particular digital image contains a minor is not a Herculean labor, ascertaining whether a particular digital image is obscene in the abstract is well-neigh impossible. Accordingly, the research team will not attempt to pass on the question of obscenity as it applies to the digital images that are the subject of this article.

3. China, for example, recently executed a man found guilty of producing and selling pornographic books. *See China Executes Man for Selling Pornographic Books*, REUTERS WORLD SERVICE (Beijing), Feb. 25, 1995 *available in* LEXIS Library, Reutrs File.

It is clear that pornography is being vigorously marketed in increasingly sophisticated ways and has now found a receptive audience in a wide variety of computer environments. According to industry experts,[4] and the pornographers themselves,[5] there are at least five factors, in addition to an increased focus on paraphilic content, which account for this recent explosion of pornography via computer networks. First, consumers enjoy considerable privacy on computer networks and can easily avoid the potential embarrassment of walking into an "adult" store to acquire pornography. Second, consumers have the ability to download only those images that they find most sexually arousing. Previously, a consumer had to purchase an entire magazine or video in order to gain access to a few desired depictions. Third, easy, discrete storage of pornographic images on a computer enables consumers to conceal them from family members, friends, and associates.[6] Fourth, the prevalence and fear of AIDS and other sexually transmitted diseases has helped pornographers to successfully market "modem sex" and autoeroticism as "safe" and viable alternatives to the dangers of "real" sex. Finally, new and highly advanced computer technologies are quickly being absorbed into the mainstream, permitting an ever-expanding audience to gain access to digitized pornography available on the "Information Superhighway."[7]

B. SCOPE OF CURRENT STUDY AND ARTICLE[8]

The research team at Carnegie Mellon University has undertaken the

---

4. *See* PHILLIP ROBINSON & NANCY TAMOSAITIS, THE JOY OF CYBERSEX (1993).

5. The first three points noted were advertised on the introductory menus of several BBS.

6. Encryption technology also allows pedophiles to conceal their sexually explicit images of children from law enforcers. Even after child pornographic GIFs or JPEGs (image files) are located and seized, they may be unreadable. Due to increasing availability of sophisticated encryption technology, all computer files, including GIFs, can be "scrambled" so thoroughly that they are virtually impossible for law enforcers to unscramble. *See* Ivars Peterson, *Encrypting Controversy*, 143 SCI. NEWS 394 (1993). There is evidence that pedophiles and child pornography consumers are increasingly using "public key" encryption technology to avoid detection individually and when sending images to (or communicating with) one another. A child molester recently thwarted efforts to identify his victims when he stored their names in an encrypted computer file. *See* Steven Levy, *Battle of the Clipper Chip: The Cypherpunks vs. Uncle Sam*, N.Y. TIMES, June 12, 1994, § 6 (Magazine), at 44.

Public key encryption involves utilizing one of a few commonly available software encryption programs which will scramble/encode the contents of a computer file. Every user has two keys, a public one and a private one, which are created unique to their owner. Users can distribute their public keys to other computer users without compromising the security of their private key. Those users can then use the public key to encrypt a message or image which will be sent to the original owner of the public key. Only the original owner can then decode the message with his private key. *Id.*

7. "Information Superhighway" and "Cyberspace" are used to refer to any of the following: Internet, Usenet, World Wide Web, BBS, other multimedia telephone, computer, and cable networks.

8. "Study" hereinafter refers to all data collected by the research team, whereas "article" refers only to those findings reported here.

first systematic study of pornography on the Information Superhighway. Computer networks and technology enable researchers, for the first time, to acquire vast amounts of information about the distribution and consumption of pornography on a scale hundreds of times larger than previously established methods. Each "adult" computer bulletin board system (BBS) can be analyzed according to region, age, size, number of calls, and number of subscribers. Because BBS pornographers rely primarily upon written descriptions to market their images, researchers can develop computer programs that classify these descriptions according to category (e.g., oral, anal, vaginal, sadomasochism). The descriptions may be sorted by frequency of downloads (consumer demand), image file size, and the date on which each image was first posted onto the bulletin boards. More usefully, the data can be easily reanalyzed under many different sets of definitions and assumptions.[9] This multidimensional method of characterizing digital pornography enables researchers to provide new and unbiased information to those involved in the heated public policy debate over pornography.

For the Carnegie Mellon study, the research team downloaded all available pornographic images from five popular Usenet boards over a four month period. In addition, the team obtained descriptive listings from sixty-eight commercial "adult" BBS containing 450,620 pornographic images, animations, and text files that had been downloaded by consumers 6.4 million times;[10] six "adult" BBS with approximately 75,000 files for which only partial download information was available; and another twenty-seven "adult" BBS containing 391,790 files for which no consumer download information was available. Thus, a total of 917,410 descriptive listings were analyzed for content by the research team. Finally, approximately 10,000 actual images were randomly downloaded or obtained via adult BBS, the Usenet, or CD-ROM. These images were used to verify the accuracy of the written descriptions provided in the listings.

The research team's content survey of the images and descriptions for which all, only partial, or no download information was available suggests no substantive differences between the datasets. Accordingly, this article

---

9. As a result of federal legal action against a few well known "adult" BBS operators, including Robert and Carleen Thomas (Amateur Action) and Robert Copella (Pequena Panacha), some systems have removed their paraphilic, pedophilic, and hebephilic imagery from public display. This has created a thriving underground market for "private collections" and anonymous ftp sites on the Internet, which cannot be studied systematically. Thus, it may be difficult for researchers to repeat this study, as much valuable data is no longer publicly available. *See infra* notes 89-95 and accompanying text.

10. The original number of downloads tabulated was 6.4 million. A total of 5.5 million downloads are analyzed here; the other 0.9 million concern animations, text, and other miscellaneous files. Information concerning an additional 2.1 million downloads was later obtained from the market leader, Amateur Action BBS. Thus, the total number of downloads tabulated is 8.5 million.

focuses on the 450,620 files for which complete download information was available. Of these, animations, text files, and images which were either ambiguously described or not described at all, were excluded. A total of 292,114 image descriptions remained and are discussed here. At least 36% of the images studied were identified as having been distributed by two or more "adult" BBS. These "duplicates"[11] enable researchers to compare how identical imagery is consumed on commercial BBS in different regions of the country.

With respect to users, the Carnegie Mellon research team was able to identify consumers of pedophilic and paraphilic pornography via computer in more than 2000 cities in all fifty states in the United States, most Canadian provinces, and forty countries, provinces, and territories around the world.

Part II of this article addresses three issues concerning pornography on the Usenet: (1) the percentage of all images available on the Usenet that are pornographic; (2) the popularity of pornographic boards in comparison to non-pornographic boards, at both a university studied and worldwide; and (3) the origins of pornographic imagery on the Usenet.

Part III, an analysis of commercial "adult" BBS, comprises the major portion of this article. It examines: (1) the availability and demand for hard-core, soft-core, paraphilic, pedophilic, and hebephilic imagery; (2) the concentration of market leaders; (3) market forces common to all "adult" BBS; (4) "adult" BBS demographics; and (5) the image portfolio and marketing strategies of the Amateur Action BBS as a case study.

Two important aspects of reliability and validity are carefully considered. First, how well do the written descriptions of the pornographic images correspond to the study's classifications? Second, how well do the written descriptions marketed by the pornographers correspond to the actual images? The linguistic parsing software developed at Carnegie Mellon University was found to offer a highly reliable estimate of the proportion of different types of pornographic images available on commercial "adult" BBS. Moreover, upon performing extensive validity testing, a panel of judges found a high correspondence between the pornographers' marketing descriptions and the activities depicted in the actual images.

Part IV presents a more informal discussion of the data including: the relationship between images and the words that describe them; the wide circulation of paraphilic imagery; the importance of descriptive lists; the sophistication of modern pornographers; privacy concerns; and a brief comparison between the Marquis de Sade and the market leader of computer pornography.

---

11. Any description with the same name and approximate file size (to +/-1,024 bytes) was identified as a duplicate. A random sampling of 100 suspected duplicates was downloaded to confirm the validity of this method, with one important limitation; if pornographers change the image names, the process becomes far more complex. Thus, 36% is a minimum estimate.

All BBS data was collected in May and June, 1994, unless otherwise noted. This article begins to address, but by no means exhausts, the breadth and depth of the data collected during the research.

C. COMPARISON TO OTHER STUDIES

Two perspectives help inform this study of pornography: that of the pornographer and that of the consumer. This study explores pornography from the perspective of the pornographer by performing a content analysis of the written descriptions provided by the pornographers.[12] It explores pornography from the perspective of the consumer by examining consumer download habits for various classifications of images.

Numerous behavioral studies, conducted in field and laboratory settings, have previously attempted to determine various effects of pornography on its consumers.[13] However, the literature has largely neglected the study of actual consumption because little reliable data has been available. The accuracy of all prior studies has depended upon the honesty of replies people give when surveyed about their sexual tastes. In contrast, this study focuses entirely upon what people actually consume, not what they say they consume; it thus provides a more accurate measure of actual consumption.[14] This methodology is particularly important when analyzing such taboo imagery as incest, bestiality, coprophilia, urophilia, and torture.

---

12. Content analysis studies have depended upon classification schemes developed by researchers or law enforcers, rather than pornographers. While pornographers lack the formal tools necessary to perform reliability and validity testing on their written descriptions, they make their profits satisfying their customers, and one could argue that their financial success suggests no small modicum of understanding of the images they market.

13. *See, e.g.*, U.S. PUBLIC HEALTH SERVICE, REPORT OF THE SURGEON GENERAL'S WORKSHOP ON PORNOGRAPHY AND PUBLIC HEALTH (1986) (suggesting links between childhood involvement in pornography, continued use of violent pornography, and uncommon sexual practices); EDWARD DONNERSTEIN ET AL., THE QUESTION OF PORNOGRAPHY: RESEARCH FINDINGS AND POLICY IMPLICATIONS (1987) (cataloguing various experiments attempting to study the possible link between exposure to pornography and antisocial behavior); Neil M. Malamuth & Joseph Ceniti, *Repeated Exposure to Violent and Nonviolent Pornography: Likelihood of Raping Ratings and Laboratory Aggression Against Women*, 12 AGGRESSIVE BEHAV. 129-37 (1986) (finding no significant link between continued exposure to violent and nonviolent pornography and laboratory aggression toward women); Dolf Zillmann & Jennings Bryant, *Pornography, Sexual Callousness and the Trivialization of Rape*, J. COMM., Autumn 1982, at 10 (noting changes in attitude toward rape, women's "liberation" movement, and callousness towards women, with prolonged exposure to pornography); Dolf Zillmann, *Effects of Prolonged Consumption of Pornography*, in PORNOGRAPHY: RESEARCH ADVANCES AND POLICY CONSIDERATIONS (Dolf Zillmann & Jennings Bryant eds., 1989) 127-57 (linking prolonged use of pornography with trivialization of rape and sexual child abuse as criminal offenses); J.V.P. Check & T.H. Guloien, *Reported Proclivity for Coercive Sex Following Repeated Exposure to Sexually Violent Pornography, Nonviolent Dehumanizing Pornography & Erotica*, in PORNOGRAPHY: RESEARCH ADVANCES AND POLICY CONSIDERATIONS, *supra* at 159-84 (distinguishing between types of pornography which are sexually violent, nonviolent but dehumanizing, and nonviolent but erotic in their effect on user's subsequent behavior).

14. "Consumption" is defined by this study merely as the purchase or download of pornographic products. The issue of consumption admittedly goes further than mere down-

The Carnegie Mellon study is also illuminating because its sample size is several orders of magnitude larger than previously published studies of either pornographic content or consumption.[15] Because the data is in many respects exhaustive, statistical techniques and assumptions that are commonly invoked to impute general consumer behavior are not necessary for this dataset. Thus, the research team considers the inferences drawn highly robust.

The study results suggest a tremendous rift between the sexual activities in which Americans claim to engage, as reported most recently by the

---

loads to include why they are purchased (or pirated), and how they are utilized by the receiver. While the notion of consumption has been explored in the area of the written word by Umberto Eco, Janice Radway, and Wolfgang Iser, among many others, no known studies focus on Cyberspace. No data was available to indicate whether such materials are consumed for erotic, curiosity, or other purposes.

15. The results of the largest content-based study of pornography known to have been conducted were published in 1988. Park Elliot Dietz & Alan E. Sears, *Pornography and Obscenity Sold in "Adult Bookstores": A Survey of 5132 Books, Magazines, and Films in Four American Cities*, 21 U. MICH. J.L. REF. 7 (1987-88) [hereinafter Dietz-Sears]. Comparing the present study and the Dietz-Sears study illustrates the manner in which powerful new technologies have transformed the pornographic landscape in the past seven years:

> The current study [hereinafter Carnegie Mellon study] is considerably larger than the Dietz-Sears study. The Carnegie Mellon study examines 917,410 images, image descriptions, short stories, and short films, whereas the Dietz-Sears study examined 5132 book, magazine, and film covers, as evidenced by its title.
>
> The Dietz-Sears images were selected by a stratified random method. *Id.* at 12. The Carnegie Mellon study examines all of the suppliers meeting minimum scale criteria.
>
> The Dietz-Sears study described what was offered for sale; it did not attempt to indicate which products the customers actually purchased, and in what quantities. *Id.* at 9.
>
> The Dietz-Sears study did not address any changes in pornographic image repertoires and purchases over time. *Id.* at 11-12. The Carnegie Mellon study tracks image repertoires over a fourteen-year period.
>
> The Dietz-Sears study concentrated only on four cities. *Id.* at 11 n.11. The Carnegie Mellon study covers pornography offered in thirty-two states representing all regions of the country, both urban and rural.
>
> The Carnegie Mellon study uses largely objective measures, rather than the subjective criteria of many researchers, to classify the images. It makes no attempt, for instance, to determine what is, or what is not, "degrading" in pornography. This enables independent organizations and policymakers to examine the data "raw"(as provided directly by the pornographers) and draw their own conclusions.
>
> The Dietz-Sears study, in examining only box or magazine covers, gave little indication to what extent the contents deviate from the cover. *Id.* at 12. The covers could conceal or exaggerate the contents.

A number of criticisms of the Dietz-Sears study, and of content analysis of pornography in general, were suggested in Daniel Linz & Edward Donnerstein, *Methodological Issues in the Content Analysis of Pornography*, 21 U. MICH. J.L. REF. 47 (1987-88). The Carnegie Mellon research team carefully considered these criticisms in preparation of this article. There are difficulties inherent in a much smaller dataset, as with Dietz-Sears. *See also infra* notes 65-76 and accompanying text for discussion of the reliability and validity procedures utilized for the Carnegie Mellon study.

study *Sex in America*,[16] and the sexually explicit activities presented in images that many Americans consume.[17]

D. IMPLICATIONS OF STUDY

The Carnegie Mellon research team has compiled a very large dataset, with implications across a wide range of disciplines, including business, telecommunications policy, psychology, sociology, and law. The study's implications are most appropriately divided into two categories: those that relate specifically to pornography and those that are generic to computer networks.

1. Implications of Study Related to Pornography

The study's findings may have serious implications for legal theory and public policy related to pornography. Among the ultimate findings of this study are that digitized pornographic images are widely circulated in all areas of the country and that, due to market forces, digitized pornographic images treat themes such as bestiality and pedophilia, which are not otherwise widely available. Neither statutory nor constitutional law has yet fully advanced to address pornography and obscenity issues in the context of electronic transmission, although legislators are increasingly focusing on this issue.[18] The most complex legal questions concern child pornography, limiting access to minors, and obscenity standards. Each is briefly outlined here:

Child Pornography:[19] On a practical level, the ease of copying and disseminating digitized child pornography presents unique law enforcement challenges because the seizure and eventual destruction of computerized child pornography may no longer appreciably reduce the amount of child pornographic imagery existing in the pedophile underground. Moreover, current bans on child pornography are justified in part as necessary to protect the actual child depicted in the photographs or videos. If

---

16. ROBERT T. MICHAEL ET AL., SEX IN AMERICA: A DEFINITIVE SURVEY (1994).

17. One theory may help explain the differing results. The Carnegie Mellon study presents an exhaustive analysis of the consumption habits of a subset of the general population, whereas the recent *Sex in America* study bases its results on a random sampling of the reported sexual activities of the entire population. This is because the demographics of computer users do not currently mirror those of the general population. The average age of the consumer population in this study is thirty-one, and the vast majority are male. "Adult" BBS system operators report that of those subscribers that are female, many (and in some cases all) are paid by their BBS to "chat" online with male customers. About half the BBS studied offered women free access.

One of the more intriguing questions raised by this study is whether the general population will demand the same types of imagery currently in high demand among computer users.

18. For example, Senator Jim Exon (D-Neb.) has succeeded in persuading the U.S. Senate Commerce Committee to address access to pornography on computer networks as part of the pending telecommunications reform legislation. S. 314, 104th Cong., 1st Sess. (1995).

19. *See infra* note 20 and accompanying text.

technology advances, as it surely will, to allow the creation of pornographic images that do not depict actual children, this justification for prohibiting the dissemination of these images may no longer be compelling.[20]

Limiting Access by Minors: The widespread availability of pornography on computer networks may have a profound effect on those who wish to utilize the emerging National Information Infrastructure for non-pornographic purposes. For instance, primary and secondary schools are increasingly connecting their students to broader national and international computer networks, where pornography permeates the digital landscape. Given the current structure of the Internet, which often permits multiple routes around a blockade, there appears to be no simple practical solution to limiting access by minors to computer pornography.[21] Accordingly,

---

20. Child pornography must now contain visual depiction of an actual child. *See* New York v. Ferber, 458 U.S. 747 (1982). Thus, the sexual abuse or exploitation of an actual child has necessarily occurred. It is possible that a visual depiction, generated entirely by computer, of a "child" engaged in sexual conduct (without the use of an actual child) could enjoy First Amendment protection. *Cf.* John C. Scheller, Note, *PC Peep Show: Computers, Privacy and Child Pornography*, 27 J. MARSHALL L. REV. 989 (1994) (arguing that the state's interest in prohibiting child pornography extends beyond protection of the initial victim, and includes protection of potential future victims, obviating the need for the presence of an actual victim to prosecute those in possession of child pornography).

However, there is language in *Ferber* and Osborne v. Ohio, 495 U.S. 103 (1990), which would support the notion that child pornography produced entirely by digital imaging technology may not be protected by the First Amendment. In both decisions, the Supreme Court used, as a secondary justification for denying constitutional protection to child pornography, the role that child pornography often plays in the molestation of a child. In *Osborne*, the Supreme Court noted that child pornography is often used to lower the sexual inhibitions of children. 495 U.S. at 109-10. *See also Ferber*, 458 U.S. at 759; T. Christopher Donnelly, *Protection of Children from Use in Pornography: Toward Constitutionally Enforceable Legislation*, 12 U. MICH. J.L. REF. 295, 300-04 (1979) (noting the use of child pornography in child molestation, both to arouse the molester and the child, and to overcome the child's inhibitions); W.D. Erickson et al., *Behavior Patterns of Child Molesters*, 17 ARCHIVES SEXUAL BEHAV. 77-78 (1988).

21. The question of whether access by minors to pornography can be effectively limited has been the subject of much debate among members of the research team and many network administrators. There are currently many ways for minors (and adults) to access Usenet newsgroups which have been "banned" or are not carried by a user's host site. The issue is particularly difficult in light of First Amendment and privacy considerations.

A popular electronic pamphlet, "How to Receive Banned Newsgroups Frequently Asked Questions (FAQ)," which is posted monthly on the Usenet illustrates many of the difficulties. Users may access "banned" Usenet newsgroups through any of the following means:

Not-for-profit news providers: Users may telnet to various hosts, such as Freenet, Hermes, Nyx, Prairienet, Um-m-net, or UNC BBS. From there, they can easily access Usenet newsgroups directly.

Commercial news providers: If users have difficulty with not-for-profit news providers, they can turn to commercial news providers. These news providers will provide shell access, news, dialup lines, and more. There are many national service providers both in the U.S. and around the world.

Open netnews transfer protocol (nntp) sites: If users do not want to use a not-for-profit or commercial news provider, there are open nntp sites that allow almost anyone with shell access and a news reader to read from and post to Usenet newsgroups.

Gopher: Usenet newsgroups are available through gopher. To find them, users may search for "Usenet news -t7" in veronica, or use sites recommended in the FAQ.

Mail to news gateways: Mail to news gateways are sites that will take any article given to them and forward it to Usenet newsgroups. These are listed in the FAQ.

Internet services list: This is not a direct way to access Usenet newsgroups, but it does list many places, and it changes often. To get the Internet services list, users may look in alt.internet.services, comp.misc, biz.comp.services, alt.bbs.internet, news.answers, comp.answers, alt.answers, or ftp to rtfm.mit.edu or archie for inet.services.txt.

Telnet: With telnet, users can access any of the free services listed above. They can also access one of the many gopher servers that will allow them to read Usenet newsgroups. These are listed in the Internet services list. They can also access the World Wide Web via telnet.

Email: Many Usenet newsgroups are mirrored in a mailing list. In addition, some sites have ftp archives. Users may determine whether the group they are interested in has this service by checking the FAQ; these FAQs are available through the ftp site rftm.mit.edu.

Ftp: Ftp service is available through e-mail. For information on ftp-through-mail, users may look in the Internet services list.

Perl Scripts: It is also possible for one user to mail another user the contents of certain Usenet newsgroups with a simple Perl script, provided they have access to a shell account.

Mailing Lists: Users may also subscribe to mailing lists that mirror Usenet newsgroups. To get a list of these, they can ftp to rtfm.mit.edu and get /pub/Usenet/news.answers/mail/news-gateway/partX, where "X" is the number of separate parts.

Archived Newsgroups: Many Usenet newsgroups are archived. Users can often examine the FAQ for that group, available at rtfm.mit.edu.

These user "work arounds" are relevant principally to Usenet access providers (commonly referred to as "host sites"), which do not wish to act as a republisher or prevent users from exploring alternate avenues for retrieving pornography. Most of the "work arounds" discussed here also assume that the host is providing unlimited general internet (IP) access to off site locations which might contain pornographic Usenet newsgroups or gopher sites. Parents and schools are not obliged to provide unlimited access to arbitrary IP addresses and port numbers. They can implement IP address filters which limit access only to known, acceptable locations. They can also implement filter programs which will look for the string "alt.sex.*" and either drop the connection or log a child's access for the parents to deal with later. Accordingly, while acting *in locus parentis*, schools may be justified in logging all actions by minors at their computers. This would create an "after the fact" method of determining what students are doing. It is possible that employers may also attempt to monitor their employees' logfiles as a means of insuring that company equipment is utilized for business, as opposed to recreational, purposes.

To complicate matters, however, these strings might block desired informational newsgroups such as alt.sex.safe. Many network observers argue that such a strategy thwarts the most fundamental benefits of the Internet. Moreover, the research team and many network administrators have discovered pornography on alt.test and other supposedly "general interest" newsgroups. Given the approximately 50 new World Wide Web sites and 20 new Usenet groups announced each day, the cost in administering restrictive access may be prohibitive. Administrators would have to check each of the new sites and newsgroups daily and make decisions concerning access. They would then need to propogate the restrictions to every machine or account on the local net. Though technically possible, such filter programs are computationally expensive and do not resolve encryption issues (very common with PGP and other PEM products) or protocols that do not use standard ASCII.

In general, primary and secondary schools, as well as most parents, do not have the capability or resources to implement these safeguards. These difficulties might necessitate the review of thousands of newsgroups on a case by case basis, which has led some network analysts to suggest that a national or international rating system be established. *See infra* note 137. At least one third party vendor has begun to provide such blocking services, but it is not clear to what extent the services will be effective. *See* Carla Koehl et al., *Policing for Porn*, NEWSWEEK, May 22, 1995, at 8. Furthermore, consumers can usually block access to 900 numbers at no cost, and they may be angered at the prospect of having to pay for services (and software updates) which attempt to filter out pornography from their home.

policymakers, as well as parents and educators, may have to reconcile the unprecedented educational and cultural benefits offered by computer networks with their concerns about children's access to pornography.

Obscenity Standards: One of the most intriguing implications for criminal law is whether the computer transmission of obscene material is sufficiently similar to the transmission of obscenity through the mails or common carriers to apply the traditional analytical regimen to digitized pornography. In Cyberspace, this issue extends beyond the borders of the United States: the research team was able to identify consumers of paraphilic and pedophilic computer pornography from countries as diverse as China, Saudi Arabia, Turkey, South Africa, Chile, Malaysia, Hungary, Trinidad and Tobago, New Zealand, Hong Kong, Nigeria, and Japan. While the results discussed here may to some extent dispel the notion that hard-core pornography is consumed primarily in Western nations, the results also raise significant questions as to whether obscenity standards can be implemented on an international scale.

In the final analysis, if the application of digital imaging technology to pornography has any recurring theme, it is that traditional constitutional

---

At the present time, it is also difficult to make distinctions between multiple users at a given site. For instance, a university could not easily set up filters so that the same public cluster machines could be used by persons of legal age to access anything, while at the same time restricting access to certain groups by minors.

Whatever procedures are implemented, many users may develop increasingly innovative techniques to bypass such blockades and trade pornography through underground channels. Although typical firewalls would block most (but not all) of the alternative paths discussed here, they raise additional concerns that those who manage the firewalls could act as censors by determining what their users can and cannot access. Routers could be programmed to restrict any traffic from a given site, but this implies a very large administrative cost to keep such blockage up to date, perhaps as many as several full-time staff per Internet node. Moreover, because current generation routers were not designed for restricting traffic, they may not have enough capacity for enough filters to block all restricted sites.

An intriguing solution to the difficulties raised here may involve some promising new technologies currently being developed at several universities and research labs, including the IBM Almaden Research Center. *See* Will Equitz & Wayne Niblack, *Retrieving Images from a Database Using Texture-Algorithms from the QBIC System*, RESEARCH REPORT, IBM RESEARCH DIVISION (1994). Researchers are currently developing algorithms which would automatically scan through large online image databases to identify specific colors, texture (including contrast, coarseness, and directionality), and patterns. Dubbed "Query by Image Content (QBIC)," the technology might assist network administrators in locating the presence of nudity, genitalia, breasts, ejaculate, feces, and various activities in the images that might suggest sexually explicit content.

Even if the method were only moderately reliable, it might substantially narrow the number of suspected images a human monitor would need to sift through to locate pornography. While it may not be possible in the next decade for such technology to automatically classify images with the same precision as the Carnegie Mellon linguistic parsing software, it does not appear exceedingly difficult to develop algorithms that scan through images and check for textures and colors that might suggest sexual explicitness. However, such technology may not work if the images are encrypted, and significant privacy issues are also implicated.

and law enforcement assumptions and conclusions must adapt to a new technology.

2. Other Implications

In addition to the study of pornography distribution, consumption, and regulation, this study has ramifications for other fields of research and regulation. In a world in which people and institutions are increasingly connected by computer, and vast amounts of personal information are exchanged via computer daily, broad privacy issues are implicated. Moreover, as companies establish World Wide Web sites and offer goods and services online, they are beginning to realize that the misuse of the information they maintain about each consumer "can have a major strategic impact on a company, damaging its reputation and limiting the amount of trust it can foster in relationships with customers, employees, channel members, and competitors."[22]

In addition, portions of the methodology utilized by the Carnegie Mellon study may also be applied to the study of products other than pornography that are marketed and distributed by computer. One could also use computer networks to study other activities sometimes considered threats to society, such as how to make a bomb or how to break into a "secure" computer system. Other issues, such as encryption technology, content flags, and authentication procedures, are discussed in this article.

E. RESEARCH INTERESTS OF THE CARNEGIE MELLON TEAM

More than two dozen faculty, staff, graduate and undergraduate students at Carnegie Mellon University contributed in some manner to this study.[23] After a year of exploring the Internet, Usenet, World Wide Web, and computer Bulletin Board Systems (BBS), the research team discovered that one of the largest (if not the largest) recreational applications of users of computer networks was the distribution and consumption of sexually explicit imagery. The research team was attracted to the current dataset for its unprecedented capacity to provide objective information about a subject which has rarely been treated objectively.

An unusual amount of data was freely available from commercial "adult" BBS, primarily as a consequence of the evolution of the online industry. Large commercial BBS such as America Online, CompuServe, and Prodigy do not carry hard-core pornographic imagery, either for legal or policy reasons. As a consequence, several thousand comparatively small "adult" BBS have sprung up across the country. For many entrepreneurs willing to

22. Paul N. Bloom et al., *Avoiding Misuse of New Information Technologies: Legal and Societal Considerations*, J. MARKETING, Jan. 1994, at 98.
23. Some members assisted on the condition of anonymity and are not listed in the biographical footnote.

risk violating local and federal obscenity statutes, these "adult" BBS have proven quite lucrative. In many instances, the research team was able to persuade the owners of these BBS to provide information about subscriber consumption habits.

The principal investigator, an electrical engineer with a background in broadband communications, began with an interest in digital image manipulation and the transmission of multimedia applications over computer networks in real-time. Other interests include examining how computer networks challenge researchers to develop new methodologies to monitor consumption habits, marketing techniques, and reliability and validity methods for the analysis of vast quantities of data. Indeed, in the coming decade, the modeling of consumer behavior on computer networks will likely prove fertile ground for market researchers, as businesses begin to reap the enormous potential of advertising and distributing goods and services online.[24]

An analysis of pornography in cyberspace provides a fascinating case study of many of the computer network-related legal and technological issues confronting businesses and policymakers today.

F. A BRIEF SKETCH OF THE "INFORMATION SUPERHIGHWAY"[25]

This section is provided as a brief overview for those who have little familiarity with the Usenet, Internet, and commercial "adult" BBS.

1. Overview of the Internet and Usenet

The Internet is an international computer network which links more than 40,000 independently managed computer networks together. Until recently, it was primarily focused on connecting thousands of academic and government computer networks to a common system for exchange of data information. It is increasingly being utilized by commercial enterprises, including pornographers.

Usenet is a collection of over 14,000 newsgroups that are created and maintained by users at sites throughout the United States and the world. In many message systems, including those at Carnegie Mellon, Usenet newsgroups appear as bulletin boards (bboards) under the node "net-

---

24. Three leading market research firms, Nielsen Media Research, Yankelovich Partners, and ASI Market Research, have recently formed a joint venture to analyze online services. *See Research Firms Team Up to Analyze Cyberspace-Paper*, May 17, 1995, *posted to* clari.tw. new_media.

25. This article assumes that the reader has a basic understanding of Usenet and BBS. Only the technical aspects of BBS which relate to pornography will be explained in detail. Many fine books deal extensively with the technical aspects of the Information Superhighway. *See, e.g,* PAUL ABRAMS & BRUCE LARSON, UNIX FOR THE IMPATIENT (1992); ALAN D. BRYANT, CREATING SUCCESSFUL BULLETIN BOARD SYSTEMS (1994); ADAM C. ENGST, INTERNET STARTER KIT (1993). The reader is also referred to *Boardwatch* magazine, a monthly guide to electronic bulletin boards and the Internet.

news." Usenet is also a protocol (method) for exchanging articles identified as belonging to one or more newsgroups. Usenet articles are transmitted both over the Internet and over the public phone system. Thus, Usenet and Internet overlap, but neither are proper subsets of each other. There are, however, many mail gateways to Usenet. These allow people to read and post articles to Usenet newsgroups even if they only have an e-mail account, and no direct Usenet access. Usenet is also a complicated cooperative system that allows for management at various levels.

Of particular interest to this study is the manner in which sites can exchange information. Each major site both receives and provides "feeds" to other sites. The actual newsgroups in either an incoming or outgoing feed are subject to administration. For example, home sites connected via dial-up connections may only receive ten or so newsgroups. In addition, some newsgroups are geographically based. Because some sites are primarily major feed sites, the presence of a certain newsgroup on a site has no relation to whether or not anyone at that site actually reads that newsgroup.

Another interesting and important facet of Usenet is the administration of the various hierarchies. A hierarchy is determined by the leading portion of the newsgroup name. For instance, sci.* denotes the science hierarchy. A more pertinent example for the study's purposes is alt.*, or the "alternative" hierarchy. Most of the sexually explicit images on the Usenet are located in the alt.* hierarchy. All hierarchies, except the alt.* hierarchy, have a quasi-formal procedure for creating a new newsgroup. The alt.* hierarchy, by design, is less formal, and anyone, in essence, can create a newsgroup at any time. How widely a newsgroup is distributed or read is another matter entirely (e.g., it is not uncommon to see new newsgroups with the name "alt.rosanne.flame.flame" "created"). It is therefore extremely difficult to obtain informative numbers when analyzing the number or percentage of groups or traffic, except at a particular site.

2. Commercial Bulletin Board Systems (BBS)

The first BBS was established in 1978 following the advent of the Hayes modem and the FCC's *Registration* decision,[26] which eliminated the need to rent from AT&T a costly Data Access Arrangement. A few years later, with the introduction of the IBM PC and commercial BBS software, thousands of BBS (commercial and non-commercial) began springing up across the country.

Bulletin board systems differ from the Usenet in a number of ways. First, unlike the Usenet's diffuse configuration of newsgroups, BBS usually operate from a central locus. More centralized control of BBS files permits

---

26. *Proposals for New or Revised Classes of Interstate and Foreign MTS and Wats*, 56 F.C.C.2d 593 (1975).

BBS operators to charge for their services, and this opportunity for profit
has motivated a number of pornographers to operate "adult" BBS. This is
another important contrast between the Usenet and BBS: while access to
files on the Usenet is often free (particularly for academic users), a user
must subscribe to a BBS in order to gain access to its files.

The reader should note that most of the commercial "adult" BBS
discussed in this article did not offer their subscribers access to the
Internet or Usenet at the time data was collected. However, in the past
year, many BBS have begun to offer such access as part of their service,
and some BBS can now also be accessed through the Internet via telnet.
The leading "adult" BBS have recently formed a "BBS Direct" Network,
which enables users from anywhere in the United States to pay only $30
per month for unlimited access to their BBS, pornographic image files, and
the Internet.[27]

3. Downloading and Viewing Images

Current technology allows millions of personal computer users to utilize
a home computer, color video monitor, and modem to download and
display pornographic images easily. Most images are stored in common
computer graphic formats, which can be easily opened and viewed on
virtually any computer sold today. The two most popular formats for
representing images on a computer are the Graphics Interchange Format
(GIF) and Joint Photographic Experts Group (JPEG) formats, indicated
by the .gif or .jpg file extensions. These image files can be viewed on any
computer with an appropriate viewer.

Encoding/decoding programs can take an image file in GIF or JPEG
format and convert it into files of ASCII characters. Once the file has been
converted, each part can be posted as though it were a text message on a
Usenet newsgroup for free access by other users around the world. Anyone with the decoding program can copy the messages from the board onto
their computer and feed them to the decoding program. The text is
converted back to a GIF or JPEG file and can again be viewed with the
graphics viewer software. Images are much easier to view when obtained
from private computer bulletin board systems because they do not need to
be encoded or decoded, as the viewer can view them while online or
download them for a collection or later viewing.

While widespread use of the Information Superhighway by the larger
consumer market is still in its infancy, tools that make connecting to,
navigating, and understanding complex international networks are developing rapidly. Many software programs which automatically cut, paste, and
decode Usenet images are now available.

---

27. BBS DIRECT, BROCHURE (on file with *The Georgetown Law Journal*).

on the following five Usenet newsgroups:[32]

> alt.binaries.pictures.erotica
> alt.binaries.pictures.bestiality
> alt.sex.fetish.watersports
> alt.binaries.pictures.female
> alt.binaries.pictures.tasteless

Between April and July of 1994, the research team downloaded all available images (3254) from these five newsgroups. The team encountered technical difficulties with 13% of these images, which were incorrectly encoded or incorrectly uploaded by the poster.[33] This left a total of 2830 images for analysis. The images were then decoded from the format used for transmission into image files.

The research team classified images into two main categories: pornography which originated from "adult" BBS and pornography which did not. The images were said to originate from "adult" BBS if the name, logo, and telephone number of the BBS appeared next to or within the image.[34] Images with no BBS logo were classified in the second category. A third category was added to include individual portraits of women (and occasionally men), with varying degrees of nudity, but no sexual contact or lascivious exhibition. By most standards "PG" or "R" rated, this category was introduced in such a way as to enable those who do not consider such images "soft-core" pornography to exclude them from the final calculations. This study presents the results under both sets of assumptions.

B. RESULTS

1. Intensity of Activity With Respect to Pornographic Imagery

The results suggest that Usenet pornography should be studied according to intensity of activity, not according to quantity of newsgroups, which is relatively small.[35] Seventeen of the thirty-two alt.binaries newsgroups located on the Usenet contained pornographic imagery. Among the non-pornographic newsgroups, 827 image posts were counted during the seven day period. Among the pornographic newsgroups, 4206 image posts were counted, or 83.5% of the total posts.

As discussed later in this article, multimedia applications that combine

---

32. These were the largest available at the research site.

33. The poster is the person who initially sends the image to the newsgroup site.

34. Also included were images with identifiable cropped logos or telephone numbers.

35. The same holds true for "adult" BBS, which *Boardwatch* magazine estimates at 5% of the total number of BBS in the country. *Top 100 B.Boards*, BOARDWATCH, Sept. 1994, at 32-33. Indeed, in a somewhat unscientific survey, at least 23 of the top 100 BBS listed by *Boardwatch* magazine were found to contain "adult" materials. *Id.*

text, sound, and interactive graphics are currently being developed. These applications will no doubt increase the percentage of imagery, including pornography, found on the Usenet.[36]

It is informative, but difficult, to estimate the extent to which the Internet is being used to carry pornographic images. Unfortunately, no reliable data is available to answer this question. The Internet is a network of networks, and traffic between neighboring institutions may go over regional networks. Moreover, much of what a user sends from his or her computer never leaves the corporate or campus network from which it originates.

At one time, the NSFNet, supported by the National Science Foundation, served as a common backbone interconnecting all regional networks. That began to change in 1990 when the first commercial Internet backbone providers emerged, and on May 5, 1995, the NSFNet was fully decommissioned. As of the summer of 1994, when data was initially collected for this study, available statistics indicated by proportion the traffic that utilized the NSFNet backbone. Figure 1 makes this clear.

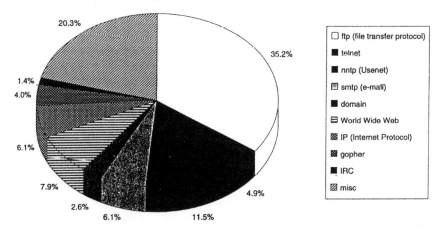

FIGURE 1.   Percentage of Internet Backbone Traffic, August, 1994.

---

36. According to *New Media* magazine, "[m]ultimedia is the first phenomenon in the history of computing to be driven by the consumer—not corporate—markets." Peter Jerram, *Who's Using Multimedia,* NEW MEDIA, Oct. 1994, at 48, 49. A study by Dataquest, *Demand for Multimedia in Large Business,* placed the consumer market for multimedia technology at $16 billion, which dwarfs the $2 billion business market. *Id.* Given that 83.5% of all current Usenet imagery is pornographic, such commercial and entertainment software may be used largely for pornographic purposes. "I am frequently patted on the back by CEOs of companies privately," said James Erlich, creator of Penthouse Interactive Virtual Photo Shoot, "because their hardware sales have gone through the roof since our titles have been released." David Landis, *Regulating Porn: Does It Compute,* USA TODAY, Aug. 9, 1994, at D1.

Within each of these categories, it is difficult to estimate the current percentage of traffic that may be pornographic.[37] The best data concerning network pornography consumption comes from the Usenet, which itself constitutes only 11.5% of Internet traffic. Of this 11.5%, approximately 3% by message count, but 22% by byte count (e.g., 2.5% of total Internet backbone traffic), is associated with Usenet newsgroups containing pornographic imagery.[38] However, as this study makes clear, studying pornography according to consumption, as opposed to availability, provides a much more revealing picture of the marketplace.

Most notably, the percentage of World Wide Web traffic passing through the Internet backbone has more than tripled, to 26.25% as of April, 1995. Accordingly, the research team undertook an initial survey of pornography on the World Wide Web (commonly referred to as the "Web"), which is included in Appendix C. It is essential to note that Usenet and the World Wide Web are merely different protocols.[39] Thus, studying the Usenet in combination with commercial "adult" BBS is highly informative of the broader picture and provides an excellent means of following the potential growth of pornography on computer networks.

2. Popularity of Pornographic vs. Non-pornographic Newsgroups

Two sets of results will be presented here: the worldwide statistics and those at the university studied.

University Results. In an effort to present relatively current information, the results from August 1994 are analyzed here.[40] In broad terms, the

---

37. Heavy pornography traffic over the Internet was reported at a University of Delft computer site. More than 10,000 users from around the world were found to obtain approximately 30,000 images a day using ftp. Other pornography collections obtained or distributed via ftp were reported at the U.S. Department of Energy's Lawrence Livermore National Laboratory, and at France's National Conservatory of Arts and Crafts. *See* Jared Sandberg, *This Is the Tale Of a Mad Scientist And His 'Sex Machine', The Reason Why He's Mad: Voyeurs by the Thousands Overloaded His Program*, WALL ST. J. EUR., Feb. 8, 1995, at 1.

38. These numbers were calculated from data collected at a sample of 453 sites by Brian Reid and reported in the Usenet newsgroup news.lists for March 1995.

39. The Usenet protocol is nntp and the World Wide Web protocol is http. Usenet and World Wide Web refer to the "service" which consists of client software, host software, data residing at hosts, and protocols for moving data between clients and hosts; or, in the case of Usenet, between hosts and other hosts.

40. The research team consulted with several privacy experts and opted not to report detailed demographics of the university population of computer pornography consumers. These demographics included age, sex, nationality, marital status, position (faculty, staff, student), and department. Although the research team obtained such demographics by means available to any authorized user of the campus network, reporting them would raise complex ethical and privacy issues. The data would have to be disguised in a manner that could not be reconstructed to identify individual users.

research indicated that pornographic newsgroups are accessed more frequently during the school year than during summer recess. This suggests that, in comparison to teachers, faculty, and staff, a disproportionately large number of students access Usenet pornography.

Approximately 3600 Usenet newsgroups were available to the users studied. Of these, 104, or 2.88%, were identified as pornographic. Thirteen of the forty (32.5%) most frequently accessed newsgroups were identified as pornographic. The following is a list of the top forty newsgroups. (The newsgroups identified as having pornographic content are in bold):[41]

TABLE 1

TOP FORTY USENET NEWSGROUPS AT A UNIVERSITY STUDIED

Rank	Readers	Group	Reading	Active	Name
1	**633**	**14%**	**9%**	**6%**	**alt.sex.stories**
2	**369**	**8%**	**5%**	**3%**	**alt.binaries.pictures. erotica**
3	273	6%	4%	2%	clari.sports.football
4	258	6%	3%	2%	clari.sports.baseball
5	225	5%	3%	2%	clari.local.xxxxxxxxx
6	216	5%	3%	2%	rec.humor.funny
7	**207**	**4%**	**3%**	**2%**	**alt.sex**
8	**206**	**4%**	**3%**	**2%**	**alt.binaries.pictures. erotica.female**
9	205	4%	3%	2%	xxxxx.forsale
10	201	4%	3%	2%	clari.sports.basketball
11	197	4%	3%	1%	xxxxx.food
12	194	4%	3%	1%	rec.food.recipes
13	180	4%	2%	1%	rec.arts.erotica
14	174	4%	2%	1%	xxxxx.general
15	171	4%	2%	1%	clari.sports.hockey
16	**170**	**4%**	**2%**	**1%**	**alt.binaries.pictures. supermodels**
17	**169**	**3%**	**2%**	**1%**	**alt.binaries.pictures. erotica.orientals**

---

41. One must be careful to distinguish between a newsgroup reader who *subscribes to* a newsgroup and a newsgroup reader who *accesses* a newsgroup. Those who subscribe may or may not read the board, whereas those who access the board may or may not subscribe.

It should also be noted that Usenet names tend to be euphemistic. The bulletin board alt.binaries.pictures.erotica contained, in addition to soft-core and hard-core imagery as defined by this study, the following paraphilias: pedophilia, hebephilia, fisting, B&D/S&M, coprophilia, urophilia, transvestite, and transsexual. The commercial bulletin board clari. news.sex was clearly not pornographic, although sex-related. The newsgroups identified as pornographic include images, as well as written material and offers for sale of pornographic products.

1995] PORNOGRAPHY ON INFORMATION SUPERHIGHWAY 1871

Rank	Readers	Group	Reading	Active	Name
18	**158**	**3%**	**2%**	**1%**	**alt.binaries.pictures.erotica.blondes**
19	148	3%	2%	1%	internet.listserv.letterman-top-ten
20	142	3%	2%	1%	clari.sports.baseball.games
21	136	3%	2%	1%	clari.sports.football.games
21	**136**	**3%**	**2%**	**1%**	**alt.sex.movies**
23	134	3%	2%	1%	clari.tw.computers
24	131	3%	2%	1%	clari.news.briefs
25	**128**	**3%**	**1%**	**1%**	**alt.sex.erotica.market-place**
26	127	3%	1%	1%	clari.news.sex
27	120	2%	1%	1%	clari.nb.apple
27	120	2%	2%	1%	xxxxx.apartments
29	114	2%	1%	1%	clari.news.urgent
29	**114**	**2%**	**1%**	**1%**	**alt.sex.bondage**
31	**111**	**2%**	**1%**	**1%**	**alt.sex.masturbation**
32	**105**	**2%**	**1%**	**1%**	**alt.binaries.pictures.tasteless**
33	104	2%	1%	1%	clari.sports.basketball.college
33	104	2%	1%	1%	misc.jobs.offered
35	103	2%	1%	1%	clari.sports.football.college
35	103	2%	1%	1%	alt.tasteless.jokes
37	**102**	**2%**	**1%**	**1%**	**alt.sex.stories.d**
38	101	2%	1%	1%	clari.news.top
39	99	2%	1%	0%	clari.tw.science
40	99	2%	1%	0%	rec.arts.movies.reviews

The fact that alt.sex.stories is currently more popular than alt.sex.pictures. binaries.erotica has been often misinterpreted as an indication that stories are more popular than images. It is likely that users have been discouraged by the burdensome encoding and decoding tools necessary to transmit imagery over the e-mail network. As new tools become more refined and easier to use, binaries may overtake stories as the top pornographic choice.

Worldwide Results. The worldwide statistics suggest that Usenet hosts appear less willing to offer their readers access to pornographic newsgroups than other types of newsgroups. 81.2% of the sites offer access to non-pornographic newsgroups, whereas only 55.8% of the sites offered their readers access to the pornographic newsgroups. Of the forty most popular newsgroups worldwide, only one—alt.binaries.pictures.erotica— contained encoded pornographic images. Three others of the top forty contained sexually explicit stories and discussion. The top forty worldwide newsgroups are summarized in Table 2.

TABLE 2
TOP FORTY NEWSGROUPS IN ORDER OF POPULARITY, WORLDWIDE

Rank	World-wide Readers Estimate	Readers Sampled	Sites Receiving Group	Messages Per Month	Mbytes Per Month	Cross Posting %	Cost Ratio	Share: % of News Readers	Name
1	800000	6658	92%	37	0.4	43%	0.00	13.5%	news.announce.newusers
2	360000	3193	88%	1584	0.2	100%	0.00	6.5%	news.answers
3	340000	3170	82%	48	0.1	0%	0.00	6.4%	rec.humor.funny
4	**290000**	**3715**	**60%**	**4867**	**6.3**	**19%**	**0.02**	**7.5%**	**alt.sex**
5	290000	2785	79%	3954	9.8	4%	0.04	5.6%	rec.humor
6	290000	2757	81%	5385	5.0	31%	0.02	5.6%	misc.forsale
7	290000	2698	82%	8992	13.9	18%	0.05	5.5%	misc.jobs.offered
8	280000	2490	86%	1517	2.5	15%	0.01	5.0%	comp.unix.questions
9	**270000**	**3976**	**53%**	**2283**	**22.2**	**5%**	**0.06**	**8.0%**	**alt.sex.stories**
10	**260000**	**3709**	**53%**	**8772**	**405.8**	**1%**	**1.10**	**7.5%**	**alt.binaries.pictures.erotica**
11	260000	2327	87%	2965	4.6	8%	0.02	4.7%	comp.lang.c
12	250000	2727	70%	60	0.7	4%	0.00	5.5%	rec.arts.erotica
13	250000	2154	88%	—	—	—	—	4.4%	news.announce.important
14	250000	2123	90%	2392	4.0	17%	0.02	4.3%	news.groups
15	230000	1958	90%	143	0.9	10%	0.00	4.0%	news.announce.newgroups
16	210000	1811	89%	1929	3.3	3%	0.02	3.7%	news.newusers.questions
17	200000	1824	83%	13	0.3	0%	0.00	3.7%	comp.risks
18	190000	1707	84%	1385	2.7	13%	0.02	3.5%	comp.graphics
19	190000	1699	86%	3454	5.2	11%	0.03	3.4%	comp.lang.c++
20	**180000**	**2373**	**57%**	**4722**	**10.9**	**5%**	**0.05**	**4.8%**	**alt.sex.bondage**
21	180000	1804	78%	1631	2.4	8%	0.01	3.6%	rec.video
22	170000	1670	78%	913	0.7	40%	0.00	3.4%	misc.wanted
23	170000	1526	87%	212	1.8	3%	0.01	3.1%	news.announce.conferences
24	160000	1884	63%	1699	3.5	59%	0.02	3.8%	alt.activism
25	160000	1608	77%	7646	15.3	3%	0.10	3.3%	rec.arts.movies
26	160000	1384	87%	2637	4.0	3%	0.03	2.8%	comp.dcom.modems
27	160000	1352	89%	70	1.9	21%	0.01	2.7%	news.lists
28	150000	1526	77%	5122	7.0	8%	0.05	3.1%	rec.travel
29	150000	1481	80%	1262	1.9	24%	0.01	3.0%	misc.jobs.misc
30	150000	1447	80%	97	4.1	0%	0.03	2.9%	comp.binaries.ibm.pc
31	150000	1413	79%	3590	4.2	34%	0.03	2.9%	misc.jobs.contract
32	150000	1383	82%	545	1.3	38%	0.01	2.8%	comp.ai
33	150000	1371	83%	4772	6.1	14%	0.05	2.8%	comp.sys.mac.hardware
34	150000	1291	86%	1545	2.5	16%	0.02	2.6%	comp.windows.x
35	140000	1645	66%	6652	9.1	14%	0.06	3.3%	alt.folklore.urban
36	140000	1473	75%	81	0.5	1%	0.00	3.0%	rec.arts.movies.reviews
37	140000	1473	74%	830	1.4	38%	0.01	3.0%	misc.education
38	140000	1447	72%	4386	10.3	13%	0.07	2.9%	soc.culture.indian
39	140000	1366	77%	2905	4.3	15%	0.03	2.8%	rec.music.misc
40	140000	1359	76%	114	0.6	6%	0.00	2.7%	comp.os.linux.announce

The newsgroups are ranked in Table 2 by the estimated total number of readers worldwide. However, when the data is classified by percent of news readers who subscribe to the newsgroups, three of the five most popular newsgroups are pornographic.[42] Moreover, 20,644 of the 101,211 monthly Usenet posts in the top forty newsgroups, or 20.4%, are pornographic.

Comparisons: University and Worldwide Results. Six of the top forty newsgroups at the University are composed of encoded graphical images, all of which are pornographic. This is true for only one of the top forty Usenet groups worldwide. None of the top forty newsgroups at the University were geared toward new users, whereas three of the top ten Usenet newsgroups worldwide are designed to assist new users or answer general technical questions about the Usenet.

Policymakers might be equally interested in comparing the cost of pornographic and non-pornographic newsgroups. The primary cost factor in maintaining a newsgroup is the amount of storage space required. Image files require considerably more storage space per image posting than a text story or comment. The following chart lists the top forty Usenet newsgroups by volume:

TABLE 3

TOP FORTY NEWSGROUPS IN ORDER OF TRAFFIC VOLUME, WORLDWIDE

Rank	World-wide Readers Estimate	Read-ers Sam-pled	Sites Receiv-ing Group	Mes-sages Per Month	Mbytes Per Month	Cross Post-ing %	Cost Ratio	Share: % of News Readers	Name
1	260000	3709	53%	8772	405.8	1%	1.10	7.5%	alt.binaries.pictures.erotica
2	130000	1779	55%	3623	127.5	14%	0.74	3.6%	alt.binaries.pictures.misc
3	74000	1045	54%	1540	82.0	9%	0.82	2.1%	alt.binaries.sounds.misc
4	97000	1757	42%	2935	76.3	2%	0.46	3.6%	alt.binaries.pictures.supermodels
5	19000	422	34%	837	63.5	4%	1.60	0.9%	alt.binaries.sounds.tv
6	51000	1165	34%	757	50.0	1%	0.45	2.4%	alt.binaries.pictures.erotica.orientals
7	67000	963	53%	1061	45.5	4%	0.50	1.9%	alt.binaries.multi-media
8	29000	535	42%	1504	44.0	4%	0.87	1.1%	alt.binaries.pictures.erotica.male
9	71000	1115	49%	1181	38.3	5%	0.36	2.3%	alt.binaries.pictures
10	16000	360	34%	1384	37.2	7%	1.10	0.7%	alt.binaries.sounds.mods
11	25000	354	53%	12875	31.7	1%	0.92	0.7%	rec.games.deck-master

42. Some network analysts have interpreted this to indicate that more people are likely to read pornographic bulletin boards if they are given as easy access to them as to non-pornographic bulletin boards.

Rank	World-wide Readers Estimate	Read-ers Sam-pled	Sites Receiv-ing Group	Mes-sages Per Month	Mbytes Per Month	Cross Post-ing %	Cost Ratio	Share: % of News Readers	Name
12	39000	560	53%	24443	31.0	0%	0.58	1.1%	alt.chinese.text
13	98000	1752	43%	625	26.7	10%	0.16	3.5%	alt.binaries.pictures.erotica.female
14	120000	1274	74%	14647	24.3	3%	0.20	2.6%	rec.sport.soccer
15	8400	267	24%	708	24.3	7%	0.95	0.5%	alt.binaries.pictures.anime
16	270000	3976	53%	2283	22.2	5%	0.06	8.0%	alt.sex.stories
17	95000	1380	53%	1360	20.4	7%	0.15	2.8%	alt.binaries.pictures.utilities
18	78000	1256	48%	886	20.4	3%	0.17	2.5%	alt.binaries.pictures.tasteless
19	31000	372	64%	6226	18.4	3%	0.52	0.8%	alt.test
20	3500	204	13%	706	16.1	13%	0.83	0.4%	de.alt.binaries.pictures.female
21	54000	737	56%	10796	15.9	44%	0.22	1.5%	alt.fan.rush.limbaugh
22	64000	666	74%	9086	15.8	0%	0.25	1.3%	rec.arts.tv.soaps
23	160000	1608	77%	7646	15.3	3%	0.10	3.3%	rec.arts.movies
24	20000	443	34%	422	14.0	12%	0.32	0.9%	alt.binaries.sounds.movies
25	290000	2698	82%	8992	13.9	18%	0.05	5.5%	misc.jobs.offered
26	110000	1111	77%	6199	12.3	2%	0.12	2.2%	misc.kids
27	88000	1091	62%	5503	12.3	19%	0.12	2.2%	alt.atheism
28	120000	1259	73%	5901	12.1	6%	0.10	2.5%	rec.arts.startrek.current
29	86000	964	68%	6977	12.1	33%	0.13	1.9%	talk.politics.guns
30	55000	615	69%	3310	11.6	1%	0.20	1.2%	soc.culture.vietnamese
31	17000	302	44%	6362	11.4	2%	0.41	0.6%	alt.society.generation-x
32	46000	641	55%	7735	11.3	56%	0.18	1.3%	alt.politics.clinton
33	35000	726	36%	530	11.3	10%	0.16	1.5%	alt.binaries.pictures.cartoons
34	12000	322	29%	581	11.1	4%	0.37	0.7%	alt.binaries.doom
35	100000	1051	73%	4935	11.0	4%	0.11	2.1%	soc.culture.jewish
36	43000	405	82%	451	11.0	0%	0.29	0.8%	comp.mail.maps
37	19000	307	47%	4722	11.0	1%	0.37	0.6%	alt.chinese.text.big5
38	180000	2373	57%	4722	10.9	5%	0.05	4.8%	alt.sex.bondage
39	84000	846	76%	6583	10.9	3%	0.13	1.7%	rec.motorcycles
40	130000	1387	72%	6769	10.4	12%	0.08	2.8%	soc.motss

In the top forty newsgroups, the percentage of total cost used for pornographic newsgroups is 34.2%. Of total space taken for image newsgroups, 76% of the space is used for pornographic images. Of total space taken for text newsgroups, 9.8% are pornographic.

3. Origins of Pornographic Imagery on the Usenet

Having examined the popularity of pornographic imagery on the Usenet, the origins of such imagery are now considered. 71%, or 1671 of the 2354 pornographic images downloaded from the five Usenet newsgroups studied over a four month period, originated from "adult" BBS. For those who consider pornography to include the additional 476 "PG" or "R" rated

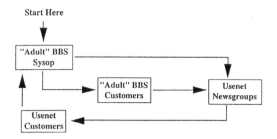

FIGURE 2.   Relationship Between Pornography on the Usenet and Commercial BBS.

images[43] defined in the methodology section, 59% of all Usenet images originate from "adult" BBS.

Many of the ninety-two "adult" BBS identified on the Usenet were unabashedly advertising their products, posting "teaser" images on the Usenet as an essential part of their marketing strategy. However, the precise number could not be determined, because the research team could not distinguish between the posting of an image (or enthusiastic comments) from a subscriber and a posting by a BBS sysop.

Figure 2 illustrates the various paths of pornographic images along the Information Superhighway: The diagram can be elucidated in the following manner. An "adult" BBS sysop commissions photographers for original images; finds the images in magazines; purchases "adult" CD-ROMs; or pirates the images from other BBS. Where necessary, the sysop uses a color scanner to convert them to digital form, and adds his logo and telephone number using a software image manipulation package. After posting the images on his BBS, he writes a brief description of each image, which is included in his complete list of files. He may also upload them onto the Usenet or his customers may upload them onto the Usenet, with or without his knowledge and consent. The Usenet subscribers then download these images from the newsgroups indicated earlier and may then decide to call the BBS if they find the images appealing. When these new subscribers first log on, the menu asks where they heard of the BBS. This enables BBS to determine the extent to which the Usenet serves as an effective advertising outlet.

While such data was not available for this study, most BBS sysops with whom members of the research team "chatted" indicated no objection to

---

43. These images are not actually rated in any official way; the research team has merely chosen "PG" and "R" to describe material that would not *generally* be considered pornographic but which some viewers *might* identify as pornographic. *See supra* text accompanying notes 29-34 for discussion of how this methodology was selected.

their customers posting their images on the Usenet.[44] A BBS with an image portfolio of 10,000 can easily afford to give away a few of its images at no cost. Indeed, the Amateur Action BBS imprints "DISTRIBUTE FREELY!!" on many of its images and even encourages its subscribers to upload them onto other newsgroups.

The results from Part II demonstrate that pornography is widely accessed on the Usenet, and that commercial "adult" BBS are the Usenet's primary source of pornography. These commercial "adult" BBS, which comprise the major portion of the Carnegie Mellon study, will now be discussed.

III. PORNOGRAPHIC "ADULT" COMMERCIAL BBS

This portion of the study analyzes a total of 450,620 files that are classified into four major categories: (1) PARAPHILIA, (2) PEDO/HEBE-PHILIA, (3) HARD-CORE (non-paraphilic), and (4) SOFT-CORE. The findings with respect to the images in each category will be presented in the next subsection. This subsection describes in detail the methodology that the research team used to select and define the four descriptive categories.

A. METHODOLOGY

1. Locating and Selecting "Adult" BBS

The research team took a number of steps in compiling and analyzing the vast amount of data available from adult BBS. First, the team located BBS that offered "adult" material. Then the team either subscribed to, or logged on as a new user or guest, to a number of representative pornographic BBS and collected descriptive lists of the files offered by each. Altogether, these lists contained descriptions of the more than 900,000 encoded pornographic images, short films, and text files available through the various BBS contacted. Consequently, in order to analyze this immense data set, the research team constructed a linguistic classification system to sort and analyze the lists. Each of these steps is described in more detail below.

---

44. The posting of potentially illegal images by BBS users raises complex issues regarding Usenet liability when those images are later downloaded or otherwise transmitted. In such a circumstance, sysops may attempt to allege they lack the requisite scienter to have violated either obscenity or child pornography laws, and that the imposition of criminal liability would thus chill protected expression. *See* Smith v. California, 361 U.S. 147 (1959) (holding that the First Amendment prohibits imposition of criminal liability without scienter in context of obscenity); United States v. X-Citement Video, 115 S. Ct. 464 (1994) (holding that federal child pornography laws do not raise First Amendment concerns with respect to scienter because they include an express requirement); Cubby, Inc. v. Compuserve Inc., 776 F. Supp. 135 (S.D.N.Y. 1991) (holding that computer service company that provided its subscribers with access to electronic library of third party publications was a mere distribution of information and could not be held liable for disseminating defamatory publications absent showing that it knew or had reason to know of defamation).

In order to locate the commercial "adult" boards, the research team obtained listings of more than 5000 computer bulletin board services from *Boardwatch* magazine, *BBS Monthly*, the Usenet, and the bulletin boards themselves. The team eliminated all boards that did not advertise an "adult" selection. This narrowed the list to about 500 boards that focused primarily on marketing "adult" pornographic images, or general boards with large "adult" sections in addition to other general interest material. Two recently published texts identified another 500 "adult" BBS.[45] The research team did not discover any other authoritative list of active "adult" BBS in the United States.

The research team contacted each of these approximately 1000 boards by modem or voice telephone. About half had gone out of business, leaving roughly 500 active boards for further study. Many of these were primarily "chat" boards, which customers use to communicate live with other customers. Still others had only one or two telephone lines and transmitted at 1200 or 2400 baud, suggesting they were smaller, more transient operations.[46]

Consequently, the research team decided that a BBS had to meet the following criteria to be included in this research project: (1) have been in business at least twenty-four months; (2) have at least four telephone lines for use by customers; (3) transmit at 14,400 baud or better; and (4) have at least 1000 "adult" images available for downloading. Because of the expenses involved in operating this type of large BBS, these criteria greatly decreased the likelihood that any BBS examined would have been a transient operation.[47] Exceptions were made in the following two cases: (1) if the BBS was located in a remote region of the United States where it was difficult to find another local source of computer pornography; and (2) if the BBS, based upon its new user menu, appeared to be aggressively expanding its customer base.[48] To the best of the research team's knowledge, the BBS included in this study comprise most of the medium- and large-sized "adult" BBS in the country that existed at the time of the research.

In order to collect descriptive lists of the pornographic images available on each BBS, as well as a representative sampling of the images them-

---

45. *See* ROBINSON & TAMOSAITIS, *supra* note 4; BILLY WILDHACK, THE "ADULT" BBS GUIDEBOOK (1993).

46. Baud is a measure of modem communications and transfer speed.

47. Regrettably, due to a lack of hard-disk space, time, and available funds, the research team was unable to maintain detailed records on some smaller or newer BBS excluded from this study. This data may have indicated the growth or contraction of the industry, as well as the estimated number of boards in the United States.

48. These small but aggressive BBS are important to an understanding of the dissemination of digitized pornography. Because their hard disk space is limited to 500-1000 images, these operators must take special care to provide only those pornographic images that they believe will maximize download revenues. Often, they concentrate on a single market niche, such as bondage, anal, or urophilic images.

1878   THE GEORGETOWN LAW JOURNAL   [Vol. 83:1849

selves, the research team placed more than 300 hours in long distance telephone calls to the "adult" BBS selected by the team. Every BBS asked the members of the research team to provide a real name, address, business and home phone numbers, date of birth, password, and type of computer and modem. Most asked where the members of the research team had heard about their BBS, and approximately half of them required photocopies of a driver's license with proof of age before granting further access to their systems.[49] Still others asked for the user's mother's maiden name (purportedly in case the password was forgotten) and required users to read legal disclaimers related to pornographic files.[50] Members of the research team did not, as a rule, identify themselves as researchers.

2. Developing the Linguistic Classification Scheme for Analyzing Consumption of Pornographic Images

Pornographic "adult" BBS catalogue their images in lists of files that describe each of the available images. In order to select images that appeal to them, customers either browse through the descriptions of pornographic images online, or they download an "allfiles" listing of these descriptions, which they can then peruse offline with standard word processing software. Customers usually prefer the second approach, because it permits them to browse leisurely without paying long distance telephone or connect time charges. The listing for a pornographic image is typically structured as shown in Figure 3.[51]

---

49. Whether board operators attempt to identify and then refuse access to minors raises constitutional questions. The Supreme Court has held that government may limit availability of pornographic images, even though they are protected by the Constitution, in order to prevent minors from gaining access to material which society deems inappropriate for the young. *See* Ginsberg v. New York, 390 U.S. 629 (1968). However, the application of this principle is limited where its effect is to prevent adults, as well as children, from gaining access to constitutionally protected sexual expression. *See* Butler v. Michigan, 352 U.S. 380 (1957) (finding the prohibition of general distribution of a book because of its potentially deleterious effect on children to be an impermissible restriction on freedom of speech).

   Determining whether an image is obscene partly depends on its appeal and effect on a hypothetical "average person." *See* Miller v. California 413 U.S. 15, 24 (discussed *supra* note 2). The average person standard stands in stark contrast to an older approach to obscenity which tested whether a pornographic image impacted the most susceptible, rather than the average person. Regina v. Hicklin, 3 L.R.B.Q. 360 (1868). *Cf.* Commonwealth v. Friede, 171 N.E. 472 (1930) (focusing standard for determination of obscenity on whether it tends to corrupt youth).

   50. For instance, a particularly aggressive BBS—Amateur Action—displayed a message to each user which asserted that the e-mail messages contained on the BBS were protected under the Privacy Protection Act of 1980, 42 U.S.C. §2000aa *et seq.* Section 2000aa protects electronically stored "work product" from search or seizure by law enforcement. The Amateur Action BBS alleged that e-mail constituted protected "work product" and threatened harsh reprisals against law enforcers or others who might surreptitiously read protected e-mail.

   51. While this was the primary format, fourteen other formats were encountered, and had to be converted to this standard form. The record format is determined by the software package used by an operator.

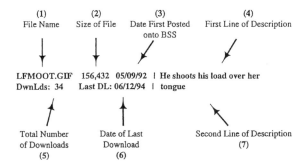

FIGURE 3.   Structure of a Typical BBS Record Listing.

This listing structure provides considerable information about pornography consumption patterns. First, based on the number of downloads (5), it can be determined which images were the most popular. Second, the linguistic description, identified by numbers (4) and (7), permits the images to be classified into categories of certain sexual behaviors. In the above example, the linguistic description denotes fellatio. Third, based on the original posting date (3), researchers can trace over time the manner in which the BBS sysops increased or decreased their offerings of various categories of images, presumably in response to consumer demand. Fourth, while the name of the record (1) usually gave no indication of the content, it often did give an indication of the original source of the image. For instance, an image from the Amateur Action BBS always began with "AA-," followed by a number. An image from the now defunct Windy City Freedom Fortress BBS[52] always began with "WC," followed by a number. This was particularly helpful in determining how many of the images from larger BBS were "pirated"[53] and redistributed by smaller BBS in different regions of the country. Fifth, the date of the last download (6) indicates whether the older images are downloaded as frequently as the newer ones. And finally, the size of the file (2) made it possible to determine the maximum number of images a customer could download over time.[54]

It should be noted that the manner in which the record is presented to the customer often differs from the above sample record, which is presented in "double line" format. Many BBS either hide this information

---

52. Windy City Freedom Fortress is the only defunct BBS included in this study.

53. Many sysops acknowledged that at least some of their images were pirated.

54. Most BBS limit their customers' downloads to a certain number of kilobytes per day. Taking the average number of kilobytes per file, this could be converted to the number of downloaded images. For instance, a $40.00, six month subscription on Amateur Action BBS bought 600 kilobytes per day; with each image an average of 211 kilobytes, the customer could download an (average) maximum of 2.85 images per day, 19.9 images per week, and 85.3 images per month. As will be reported later, based upon information provided by sysops, most customers downloaded substantially less than the maximum number of images permitted by the BBS to which they subscribed.

from their customers or do not provide it because of space or software limitations. For instance, the list of one file from Amateur Action BBS reads as follows:[55]

AA-2438 92K Cody is having an ORGASM! Fingers hole!

In these instances, members of the research team either screen captured the "allfiles" list in double line format, or persuaded the sysop to provide the list privately. In order to study the vast listings of images obtained, the research team decided to construct a classification scheme that would sort the pornographic images by the different types of behavior they depicted. This proved to be no small task, given that it was impossible to sort the enormous volume of records manually. Because the descriptive listing for each pornographic image contained terms that could be mapped to specific categories defining different depictions or interests in pornography, the research team created a computerized dictionary of these terms that sorted the image descriptions into categories. Developing the dictionary required five steps. First, a classification scheme that paired terms and categories was established. Second, because of the nature of the English language, certain categories were given precedence over others. Third, certain categories were permitted to overlap with others. Fourth, images which the dictionary could not classify (e.g., none of the words used to describe the image were contained in the dictionary) were identified. Fifth, an exceptions category was created to deal with further quirks in the descriptions. Each of these steps is described in turn below.

Classification Scheme.   The initial image description classification scheme was adopted from the Dietz-Sears study.[56] However, the Dietz-Sears categories were often found to be either too general or too specific for the current study. For instance, Dietz-Sears divides "B&D/S&M" images into twenty different subcategories.[57] While this is useful in studying different types of "B&D/S&M" as an individual phenomenon, its effect is to diffuse the "B&D/S&M" imagery within the entire pornographic landscape. The Carnegie Mellon study therefore tabulates the twenty "B&D/S&M" subcategories as one category.[58] The criteria for adding additional categories to the Dietz-Sears model were that: (1) a particular word in the description described a sexual act which could not be included in the previously established categories; and (2) that word was repeated more than once in

---

55. Conspicuously absent from this "single line" format are the posting dates and download information.

56. *See supra* note 15 and accompanying text.

57. *See* Dietz-Sears, *supra* note 15, at 19.

58. This is further supported by the number of BBS discovered which have "B&D/S&M" portfolios of 50% or more. *See infra* notes 68-72 and accompanying text.

FIGURE 4. Description Strategies Utilized to Market Pornography.

the list. The added categories include: INCEST, HAIR COLOR, OBESE, PEDO/ HEBEPHILE,[59] "AMAZING," DOGSTYLE, SWING, MUSCULAR, SIXTY-NINE, EMOTIONS, SHOWER, OUTDOOR, PETTING, PANTIES, and WHORE.[60]

When completed, the computer "dictionary" included 3823 words spanning sixty-three basic categories. It is significant to note that pornographers rely not only on activities in identifying an image, but also on attributes (for example, hair color, muscularity) and emotions (for example, pleasure and pain) to market their images. For instance, in the following description, the pornographer intersects the sexual activity with the subject's hair color and body structure to market the image: "Brunette coed has tiny boobs! 3 inch wide cock in her ass." Similarly, pornographers use the intersection of certain sexual activities with sensations of pleasure or pain. "She swallows his whole cock! She is choking!" and "Cody is having an ORGASM! Fingers hole!" are two examples of this technique. Figure 4 makes this clear.

Prioritization Scheme. Because pornographers described images with multiple words, prioritization schemes became necessary to avoid false categorizations. For instance, if the word "fucks" was assumed to imply the vaginal category, the computer dictionary would have classified such descriptions as "he fucks her ass" or "he fucks her mouth" or "she fucks herself with a dildo" as vaginal, when clearly they were not. The research team

---

59. Consider the description "Young girl with no boobs and no pussy hair gets fucked hard!" Although the judges supported this description as PEDOPHILE, the actual image more closely approximated HEBEPHILE, or even YOUNG "ADULT." The most well known computer portfolio of hebephile images came from the now defunct Windy City Freedom Fortress BBS, referred to by consumers as the "Junior Miss Series," or simply "JMIS," in "My Private Collection," or simply "MPC." They are now among the most frequently posted genre of pornographic images on the Usenet. The Carnegie Mellon study cannot always differentiate between pedophilic and hebephilic imagery because of the ambiguous manner in which pornographers market their images. Accordingly, the term "pedophilic" is used in this article, whenever the research team, through linguistic analysis and extensive validity testing of actual images, conclusively identified images of pre-pubescent children, as opposed to adolescents. Otherwise, the term pedo/hebephilic is invoked.

60. *See* Appendix A for a list of many final categories and their definitions.

therefore established a priority scheme that checked for the word "fucks" appearing with the words "ass" or "face" or "dildo;" otherwise the image was classified as "vaginal." Without such a prioritization scheme, the word "fucks" would need to be excluded from the dictionary as too ambiguous. Under such exclusion, the percentage of vaginal sex images recorded would have been greatly and unrealistically diminished because there were relatively few other words describing vaginal sex. The only alternative would have been to require a human judge to review each description that contained the word "fucks" and classify it, which would have been inefficient given the large number of records to be examined. Problems that arose with other words and categories were handled in a similar manner.

Overlap. Overlap was permitted among categories that had the same precedence level. For instance, the following categories were identified in the same precedence level: ORGY, ASIAN, FISTING, LESBIAN. A description such as "She fists her girlfriend's pussy," was thus classified as both a LESBIAN and a FISTING image, while "Three Asians going at it in bed," was classified as both an ASIAN and an ORGY image. Without some overlap, the classification scheme would have proven less insightful.[61] However, the Dietz-Sears model permitted overlap in all cases, which could be misleading.[62] "She gets fucked by a horse" was classified by this study under BESTIALITY, not VAGINAL INTERCOURSE, while "He sucks his boyfriend's dick" depicts HOMOSEXUAL activity, and was not classified by this study as a FELLATIO image.[63] A more difficult description to categorize is, "She licks her girlfriend's asshole." The image could be classified as ORAL, ANAL, or LESBIAN, but the computer classified it as LESBIAN, because lesbian is a more general term which may describe a variety of sexual acts, including oral, vaginal, and anal acts. Thus, general terms were given precedence over particular terms.

Uncategorized Images. An UNCATEGORIZED category was created to identify image descriptions that the dictionary could not sort effectively. Uncategorized images accounted for the fewest number of downloads, probably because when pornographers failed to provide clear content descriptions, they did not effectively market their images. The absence of a description or the use of ambiguous words simply does not entice the customer to download the image. Therefore, there is no reason to believe the presence of these uncategorized images distorted this study's results. Nevertheless, the research team tried to decrease the number of uncategorized images to

---

61. 11% of the images studied "overlapped" into two or more categories.

62. *See* Dietz-Sears, *supra* note 15, at 18.

63. It can thus be assumed that all other classifications depict some form of heterosexual or lesbian activity. This was done to simplify the data for the study and is not meant to suggest any value judgments concerning homosexual imagery.

as low a percentage as practicable by repeatedly fine-tuning the dictionary and developing new categories until the number of uncategorized images fell below 16.1%, or 6.5% of images weighted by number of downloads. There were three reasons an image remained uncategorized. First, the description portion of the record was left blank. Blank descriptions accounted for 72% of what remained uncategorized. Second, the description contained deliberate or accidental misspellings, such as "She socks his cock," which the computer could not identify.[64] Third, descriptions such as "Blonde getting a cheeky dinner plate" were too ambiguous to assign.

Exceptions to Standard Methodology.   Finally, an EXCEPTIONS category was created to account for double meanings and idiosyncrasies in the English language. For instance "Bo Derek walks her dog on the beach," is clearly a portrait of a movie star, not a bestiality image. A manual operator identified exceptions among a random sampling of 40,000 descriptions, then assigned the descriptions to the proper category. The total percentage of exceptions was 1.5%.

3. Reliability and Validity of the Category Dictionary[65]

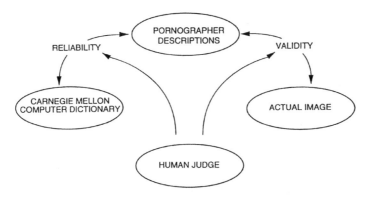

FIGURE 5.   Validation and Reliability Procedure.

Reliability.   The research team implemented a number of checking mechanisms in order to establish the accuracy of the classification scheme before finalizing it. First, four members of the research team checked a random

---

64. Every effort was made to correct as many of these as possible.
65. It should be noted that neither Dietz-Sears, nor any other study known to the research team, has adequately resolved the methodological problems of image classification. The research team views such classifications merely as a convenient way of discussing and describing the availability of, and demand for, computer pornography. Other classification schemes are possible with the current data. *See generally* DAVID LYONS & JOHN ANDERSON, THE PSYCHOLOGICAL AND SOCIAL CONSEQUENCES OF PORNOGRAPHY: RESULTS OF A SYSTEMATIC REVIEW (1993).

sample of 10,000 descriptions and their classification by the computer dictionary. The researchers checked descriptions and classifications in groups of 2500 each, until the fourth group achieved what they considered a high degree of agreement between the computer dictionary and the researchers.

Next, two judges performed formal "reliability" tests. Reliability tests measured how accurately the computer classification scheme had sorted the linguistic image descriptions. The judges were trained in three practice runs of twenty descriptions each to clarify several points of procedure and definitions. They were to decide separately and without discussion whether the description and its classification matched (was accurate), did not match (was inaccurate or erroneous), or partially matched. They developed several rating rules. First, a match occurred when the major idea of the description corresponded to the definition of the classification. Second, a partial match was scored if there was at least one element described which was included in the definition. Sources of partial disagreement typically included descriptions such as the following: "He spreads her ass cheeks," which may or may not match ANAL sex; or, "Two hot blondes kiss each other and suck cock," which may partially match LESBIAN, but is also matched with ORGY. Third, a non-match ocurred when the description had no correspondence to the classification definitions. For example, "She goes down on his love snake," which does not match BESTIALITY; or, "Lady in black gets fucked doggy style," which does not match INTER-RACIAL.

The judges were given a stratified random list of 500 image descriptions, twenty from each of twenty-five categories. The judges strongly confirmed the reliability of the computer classification scheme for PEDO/HEBEPHILE (92.6%) and most of the PARAPHILIA classifications (83.6%). However, because of overlap, the reliability was not as great for classifications such as FELLATIO (73.8%), LESBIAN (78.2%), and PORTRAITS (75%).[66] The judges had difficulty agreeing, for instance, whether an image described as "She sucks his cock while fisting her girlfriend's pussy," was most appropriately classified as FELLATIO, ORGY, LESBIAN, or FISTING.

In the course of research, the team had the opportunity to discuss how pornography is marketed with many computer pornographers. The broader distinction they draw is between the "action" clearly depicted in hard-core materials (oral, vaginal, or anal penetration) and the display of nudity without clearly visible penetration or consummation of the sexual act in soft-core materials. Thus, the classification and prioritization scheme was revised to group the categories into four aggregate classes. The judges

---

66. This should not be interpreted as a limitation of the Carnegie Mellon methodology. Since reliability procedures were completed in September 1994, the research team has continued to fine tune the computer dictionary with considerable success. The individual classifications may be presented with further statistical analysis in a later paper.

were then provided with a second stratified random list of 200 image descriptions, fifty from each of the following four classes.[67]

(1) PARAPHILIA, which included transvestite, transsexual, sadomasochism (B&D/S&M), fisting, urophilia, coprophilia, foreign objects, voyeurism,[68] bestiality, and incest.

(2) PEDO/HEBEPHILE, which included both nude portraits of young children in pre-pubescence, and hard-core sex acts involving young-looking boys and girls.

(3) HARD-CORE, (non-paraphilic), which included explicit sexual contact or penetration between two or more individuals, such as fellatio, vaginal intercourse, or anal penetration.

(4) SOFT-CORE, which included nude and semi-nude portraits emphasizing large breasts, genitalia, or famous models, but with no penetration or erect penis visible.[69]

The reliability for categorizing HARD-CORE (96.5%) and SOFT-CORE (95.5%) imagery rose considerably using this methodology.[70] Thus, analyzing the

---

67. The paraphilia classifications were adapted from an authoritative psychiatric text. AMERICAN PSYCHIATRIC ASSOCIATION, DIAGNOSTIC AND STATISTICAL MANUAL OF MENTAL DISORDERS 522-32 (4th ed. 1994) [hereinafter DSM-IV].

68. Voyeurism did not account for a significant number of downloads and thus could be discarded without any notable effect. However, voyeurism provides an excellent example of how information collected by both pornographers and researchers will be utilized (although not necessarily by linguistic parsing) in the coming years when studying marketing on the Information Superhighway. The description "He watches a hot blonde get fucked" is illustrative. Strictly following DSM-IV, this description would be classified as paraphilic because it contains the word "watches." However, without the introduction of more sophisticated analytic techniques, it would not be clear which of the following three keywords were the reason a customer downloaded the image: "watches," "blonde," or "fucked." It would also not be clear whether those three words *in combination* were what especially attracted the consumer.

There are numerous techniques a researcher or pornographer could apply to answer this question. First, one could obtain from the BBS the log file which indicates the download habits for each consumer. Thus, if the word "watches" were the reason for the download, the consumer would indicate a pattern of having downloaded other images which were described as "watches" (or "blondes" or "fucks"). The log file, which is kept privately by most BBS operators, is the best way to develop profiles of individual consumer habits. However, researchers (or sophisticated pornographers) might be more interested in analyzing segments or market niches; this would enable them to draw general conclusions about the industry independent of a few "unusual" customers. Second, if the log file were not available (and it is expected that in most cases it would not be) there would remain at least two other powerful techniques researchers could apply to answer such questions: cluster analysis and contingency table analysis. For a contingency table analysis, one could separately count the percentage of images which contained each of the three words and then predict the expected number of cases of overlap. This expected number could then be compared to the actual number to determine whether an unusually high or low degree of activity were present.

69. For an explanation of the distinction in definitions utilized in this study between "hard-core" and "soft-core," see *supra* note 1.

70. The presentation of kappa values, which indicate the agreement or disagreement among the judges, was considered unnecessary because of the high level of reliability.

data in these four classes presents a highly reliable means of exploring the explosive growth of pornography on the Information Superhighway.[71] Figure 6 presents a flow chart of the final precedence scheme utilized in this study.

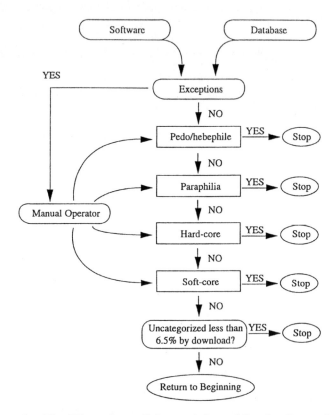

FIGURE 6.   Final Precedence Scheme Adopted for the Carnegie Mellon Study.

---

71. Additional interjudge comments: "INCEST" is entirely a marketing technique, and its true accuracy cannot be determined by any interjudge reliability test. If the pornographer decides to market a particular image as father-daughter, brother-sister, or sister-sister, it is to assist the consumer in achieving a certain level of fantasy. "AMAZING" was found to be another marketing ploy. When the pornographer does not have in mind a good, quick description, he will often try to sell his customer with words such as "amazing" or phrases such as "you won't believe this one!" What makes an image intrinsically "amazing" is entirely subjective. FAMOUS MODELS: any time a name was used, rather than the pronouns "she" or "her," an image was classified as FAMOUS MODELS. The judges, however, were not avid consumers of pornography and thus did not recognize names of particular pornographic "stars." It should be noted here that FAMOUS MODELS was defined broadly, to include a great number of "local" stars from BBS across the United States. HEBEPHILE included images of young, "flat-chested" females, their genitalia shaved, clad in pigtails and bobby socks, and

The final precedence scheme reflects both consumer demand patterns and the differing legal definitions recognized for different materials. Because statutes and the courts have regulated much pedo/hebephilic imagery[72] according to a more easily recognized *per se* standard,[73] this study gives terms suggesting pedophilia and hebephilia the highest precedence in order to more easily identify them. In addition, during its preliminary data collection, the research team was somewhat surprised by the volume and degree of paraphilic material widely available and consumed on commercial "adult" BBS. Correspondingly, the precedence scheme identifies this material separately from hard-core materials, allowing the research team to identify the overall relevance of paraphilic material as defined by *DSM-IV*.[74]

The distinction in the final precedence scheme between hard-core and soft-core pornography merely acknowledges a dividing line drawn by many pornographers, statutes, and courts.[75]

Table 4 offers an example from each of the four classifications, and how the computer program classified them.

TABLE 4

PRECEDENCE SCHEME EXAMPLE, CARNEGIE MELLON PARSING SOFTWARE

Classification	Sample Description
PEDO/HEBEPHILE	Junior teen with no tits spreads legs
PARAPHILIA	Girl with big tits gets fucked by horse
HARD-CORE	Girl with big tits gets fucked by guy
SOFT-CORE	Girl with big tits spreads legs

In addition to the four major classifications, the numbers for vaginal intercourse will be presented in this article, defined both "narrowly" and "broadly." When defined narrowly, no overlap was permitted of vaginal intercourse with other hard-core or paraphilic categories. When defined broadly, overlap was permitted with other hard-core and paraphilic catego-

---

sometimes surrounded by stuffed animals. Thus, they may be, or appear to be, adolescents. The emphasis of this study, as noted earlier, is to determine how many images the pornographers market as pedo/hebephile, an important area which has not been adequately addressed by the legal system. B&D/S&M: When a rope or harness or whip is visible in the image, it was classified under B&D/S&M. However, the "pain and torture" category caused the most difficulty. Pornographers often market anal sex and fisting images as "She screams in pain as he fucks her ass," or "She is tortured as her girlfriend fists her pussy." It was necessary to permit overlap in these cases. Thus, the former image would be classified both as ANAL and B&D/S&M, and the latter would be classified as FISTING and B&D/S&M.

72. Courts and statutes do not distinguish between pre- and post-pubescence. Child pornography is defined as depicting persons under age 18. *See* 18 U.S.C.A. § 2256 (West 1995).

73. *See* New York v. Ferber, 458 U.S. 747 (1982); Osborne v. Ohio, 495 U.S. 103 (1990).

74. *See* DSM-IV, *supra* note 67.

75. *See supra* note 1.

rics, with the exception of bestiality. In both instances, vaginal intercourse has been counted as a subset of hard-core.

Validity.   In addition to assessing the reliability of the classification scheme, the research team assessed the validity of the descriptions. This study defines validity as the extent to which the written descriptions correspond to the actual pornographic images. Reliability alone is sufficient if we are concerned only with categorizing how images are *marketed*; if we wish to make statements about the images themselves using linguistic categorization, we must also verify the *validity* of the descriptions. The use of verbal descriptions to classify images themselves would be invalid if pornographers are often mistaken in their verbal descriptions, or if they deliberately exaggerate or conceal the nature of their images.

There are at least two types of validity tests that could be performed on the Carnegie Mellon dataset. The more obvious validity test would be to have a panel of judges examine the actual images and determine the extent to which they match their classifications. However, such a test is limited to the categorization scheme adopted. As a rule, pornographers do not force images into categories; instead, they force images into words. Accordingly, a second validity test would be to have a panel of judges examine the actual images and determine the extent to which they match their descriptions, independent of the adopted classification schemes. Such a validity test is generic and enables policymakers to answer a broader question: to what extent do pornographers accurately describe their images? The research team decided to adopt the second approach; it thus preserves the world of pornographers and consumers, and makes no attempt to establish "intrinsic" or "absolute" classifications of images independent of the empirical data collected. However, because the validity was high, one may reasonably extrapolate that the images also correspond to the classifications discussed here to the extent that they were found reliable.

For the Usenet portion of this study, it was necessary to examine approximately 3500 actual images. For the commercial BBS portion, another 1500 actual images were examined. The research team found nearly 100% correspondence between the descriptions and the images for those images obtained from the Usenet, but these procedures would be appropriately defined as "informal."[76] Accordingly, a panel of three human judges invoked formal validity procedures. They were given a stratified random set of 400 images, 200 from the market leader, Amateur Action BBS, and

---

76. Images obtained from the Usenet that had a BBS logo were compared to their corresponding descriptions in the "allfiles" listings of the commercial BBS where they originated. These procedures are defined as informal because the researchers, having seldom encountered images which did not correspond to their descriptions, did not keep exact records in this respect. The main task of the Usenet portion of the study was merely to determine what percentage of Usenet pornography originates from "adult" BBS.

200 from the other thirty-four "adult" BBS, fifty of which were described by pornographers to depict vaginal intercourse. As with the reliability procedure, the judges were trained in three practice runs of twenty images each to clarify separately and without discussion whether the image and the description matched, did not match, or partially matched.

Of particular importance, from a legal perspective, is whether *real* men and women are depicted in sexual acts with *actual* animals (or other acts, which based on their descriptions, may be difficult for the reader to accept as having genuinely occurred). The judges took special care to be precise in their judgments by viewing the images on a twenty-inch color monitor and zooming in on certain areas when necessary. However, there is not always enough room in the description area to describe all aspects of the image; the pornographers then decide to emphasize those aspects of an image they believe the customer will find most arousing. For instance, upon examining the image described as, "BRUNETTE IS ON HER KNEES! SEXY REDHEAD FISTS HER ASSHOLE!" it was discovered that one woman was being fisted by another while fellating a man. In this case, the pornographer may have understood that the primary appeal of the image was rectal fisting, and that other possible classifications, such as fellatio, were only of secondary interest to the customer.

Accordingly, the judges developed several rating rules: First, a match occurred when each of the major ideas of the description corresponded to what was visible on the image. Some tolerance of wording was acceptable but nothing which contradicted the description was permitted. Second, a partial match was scored when at least one major element was described which did not appear in the image. Sources of partial disagreement typically included descriptions such as the following: "SHE FINISHES SHIT-TING! SHE HAS SHIT SPECS ON HER ASSHOLE!" (although a close-up of the rectum, one of the judges unable to perceive fecal matter); or "SHE CHOKES ON THICK DOG COCK! DOG SPERM ON HER SEXY LIPS!" (although a depiction of a woman performing fellatio on a dog, two of the judges unable to perceive the ejaculate); or "Brunette has big boobs! She pisses on her girlfriend's face!" (although a urophilic image, two of the judges concluded that the urine was aimed at the chest, not the face). Third, a non-match occurred when there was more than one major element which did not appear in the image. Fourth, the pornographers used code words which did not correspond to standard English. Accordingly, their usage pattern was accepted, because it would be known to those using the BBS. For example, the phrase "junior teen," when invoked by the market leader, Amateur Action BBS, described pre-pubescent children, rather than post-pubescent teenagers. Fifth, the judges also disregarded incestuous references, such as father, mother, daughter, and sister, as irrelevant because there was no way to establish the validity of these relationships. Finally, the judges considered a description accurate if it also contained some form of marketing braggadocio: "She is horny! Sucks thick horse cock like a vacuum cleaner!" (the judges agreeing that a woman was depicted performing fellatio on a horse but ignored the phrase "like a vacuum cleaner").

For the imagery from all thirty-five "adult" BBS, the judges unanimously agreed with the pornographers' descriptions on 84.5% of the images. They agreed partially with 12% of the images and disagreed unanimously with the remaining 3.5%. For the Amateur Action BBS imagery, the judges unanimously agreed with the pornographers' descriptions on 91.5% of the images. They were in partial agreement with the remaining 8.5%, of which 60% were unanimous and 40% suggested some disagreement among the judges. The judges suspected that two of the four hundred images examined may have been digitally manipulated. It is significant to note that none of the judges disagreed with any of the descriptions from Amateur Action BBS.

In sum, validity was very high, suggesting that pornographers, as a rule, take special care to describe their images with the high degree of accuracy they consider necessary to satisfy their customers.

B. RESULTS

Using the classification scheme described above to analyze the thirty-five "adult" BBS lists for which complete download information was available, the research team found that:

(1) The "adult" BBS market is driven largely by the demand for paraphilic and pedo/hebephilic imagery. The availability[77] of, and demand for, vaginal sex imagery is relatively small.

(2) A relatively small number of pornographic "adult" BBS dominate the market at the present time.[78] However, the widespread proliferation of CD-ROM technology now enables "start-up" BBS to accumulate large pornographic portfolios (50,000-plus images) at little cost.

(3) Among the most successful "adult" BBS, a tremendous gap exists between the availability of, and consumption patterns for, the four classifications of imagery. In particular, availability of hard-core and soft-core images exceeds the demand for these types of images, while demand for paraphilic and pedo/hebephilic images exceeds their availabil-

---

77. The term "availability" seems more appropriate than "supply," because electronic images can be easily reproduced, and could be in unlimited supply. However, they may be available only through a limited number of outlets.

78. This article assumes that the market for digital pornography is, for the most part, free and open. Significantly, the high level of demand and small number of suppliers could lead to a less competitive market if a relatively small number of suppliers were to tacitly or overtly agree to fix prices or otherwise hinder upstart competitors. However, the limited barriers to entry should inhibit horizontal concentration in any digital image transmission market.

ity. The data suggests that computer pornographers have not yet optimized their image portfolios according to consumer demand patterns.

(4) Regular mathematical relationships exist between the size of the BBS and their download activity for each of the four major classifications outlined in this study.

(5) Changes in the portfolio of Amateur Action BBS, the market leader for pedo/hebephilic imagery and a leading supplier of the paraphilias, graphically illustrates the market forces common to all "adult" BBS.

1. Findings of "Adult" BBS Generally

First, the availability of and demand for the various classes of pornographic images will be discussed. Table 5 and Figure 7 show the total number and proportion of files and downloads for each of the four major classifications.

TABLE 5

TOTAL SURVEYED "ADULT" BBS FILES AND DOWNLOADS BY
CLASSIFICATION

	Total Files	Total Downloads
HARD-CORE	133,180 (45.6%)	2,102,329 (37.9%)
SOFT-CORE	75,659 (25.9%)	760,009 (13.7%)
PARAPHILIA	63,232 (21.6%)	1,821,444 (32.8%)
PEDO/HEBEPHILIA	20,043 (6.9%)	864,333 (15.6%)

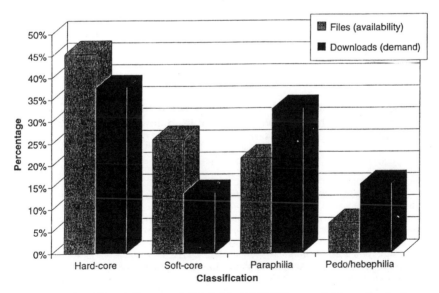

FIGURE 7.   Total Surveyed "Adult" BBS Files and Downloads by
Percentage.

Some important observations can be drawn from the underlying data:

(1) Pedo/hebephilic and paraphilic imagery accounts for 2,685,777 downloads, or 48.4%, of all downloads from commercial "adult" BBS.[79]

(2) For hard-core and soft-core images, availability exceeds demand, while for paraphilic and pedo/hebephilic images, demand exceeds availability.[80]

(3) The supply of vaginal sex imagery exceeds the demand. The total availability of vaginal sex imagery (a subset of the hard-core classification), defined narrowly,[81] was 6.9%, while the demand was even lower, at 4.6%. The availability of vaginal sex imagery, defined broadly[82] with overlap, was 10.1%, while the demand was again lower at 8.3%.

Compared to other forms (print, video) of pornography, the market for computer pornography is driven by a strong demand for pedo/hebephilic and paraphilic imagery. These types of pornography, which are frequently unavailable or difficult to purchase through traditional outlets, are increasingly available and sought after via computer. Further, when subsets of the four classifications are examined, it is clear that material many people historically associate with the term "pornography," including depictions of vaginal intercourse, comprises only a small portion of the images available.

2. Top Five Commercial "Adult" BBS

In order to illustrate more clearly the major trends in the "adult" BBS pornography market, the research team isolated data on the top five market leaders in the industry. The "adult" BBS industry is unevenly distributed among BBS, with five of the thirty-five boards accounting for 81.3% of all downloads.[83] This data, combined with the demographics reported below, indicates that despite the cost of toll calls, leading "adult" BBS serve a national, as opposed to local, market.

These five leading "adult" BBS were studied in further detail. Hard-core imagery was the most widely available, followed by soft-core, paraphilia and pedo/hebephilia. Figure 8 makes this pattern clear.

---

79. The remaining downloads involved text and animation files which were not analyzed for this study.

80. Histograms which examined the number of downloads per file for each BBS for each of the four major classifications strongly support this conclusion.

81. *See supra* text following Table 4 for a narrow definition of vaginal sex imagery.

82. *See id.* for a broad definition of vaginal sex imagery.

83. Recall that this data covers only those BBS for which download data was available. The research team estimates there are approximately another half-dozen equally large "adult" BBS not analyzed in this article because no or only partial download information was available.

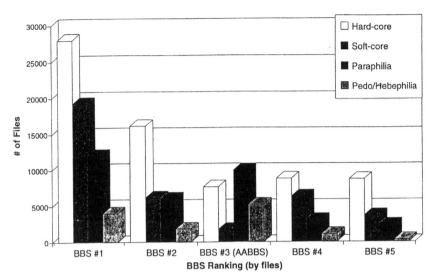

FIGURE 8. Top Five "Adult" BBS by Availability Statistics.

The exception to this general pattern is Amateur Action BBS, which offers an unusually high proportion of paraphilic and pedophilic imagery.

However, these availability figures should be compared to actual consumer consumption statistics for the four classifications of imagery, shown in Figure 9.

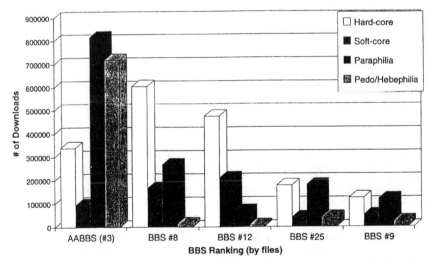

FIGURE 9. Top Five "Adult" BBS by Consumption Statistics.

Hard-core is in the greatest demand by consumers among top "adult" BBS, followed by paraphilia, pedo/hebephilia, and soft-core. It is significant to note that paraphilia, which the courts generally regulate according to community standards,[84] increased from third to second, and that pedo/hebephilic imagery, which is *per se* illegal in light of *New York v. Ferber,*[85] outmarketed the soft-core imagery despite (or perhaps because of) the difficulty in obtaining the former and widespread availability of the latter.

Even among the most successful "adult" BBS, a tremendous gap exists between the availability of and demand for each the four classifications of imagery. The data suggests that computer pornographers have not yet optimized their image portfolios according to consumer demand or capitalized on statistical techniques used by other industries to market their products.[86]

3. Market Forces Common to All Commercial "Adult" BBS

Before the data was analyzed according to the four major classifications, there appeared to be little correlation between the number of files offered by an "adult" BBS and the number of downloads generated. Figure 9 makes clear that the five boards which accounted for the greatest number of downloads were ranked 3, 8, 12, 25, and 9, respectively, out of the thirty-five boards surveyed, according to number of files offered. For instance, the Windy City Freedom Fortress BBS generated more than one million downloads with only 12,000 files, whereas many "adult" BBS with image portfolios exceeding 50,000 files have generated fewer than 20,000 downloads. Many of these newer "adult" BBS are those which have obtained a large percentage of their portfolios from CD-ROM.

The research team then performed a statistical analysis on the data, which revealed that the largest "adult" BBS are not disproportionate to their competitors, but simply reflect the diversity in size that one expects among similar companies in a free market. The results suggest that the

---

84. Paraphilic pornography not depicting children is analyzed under the *Miller* obscenity standard, which requires proof that an allegedly obscene image offends community standards. 413 U.S. 15, 24-27 (1973).

85. 458 U.S. 747 (1982).

86. Four explanations offer possible answers for this disparity. First, it may be that in the case of pedophilic imagery, such images are not widely available, and thus one would expect demand to exceed availability in most instances. However, based on detailed conversations the principal investigator has had with many prominent "adult" BBS sysops, three other explanations appear more viable. First, because the research team has found pedo/hebephilic and paraphilic imagery to be widely available on CD-ROMs and computer networks, many sysops may not provide such imagery out of fear of prosecution. Second, sysops such as Robert Thomas have indicated that they want to give their subscribers a "variety" of choices, regardless of demand for particular classifications. These sysops often view their BBS as extensions of their own interests in pornography. Third, many sysops have indicated either a general ignorance of the power of their data or a lack of adequate time and resources to perform such analysis.

Amateur Action BBS, far from being an anomaly, is merely the most graphic instance of market forces common to all "adult" BBS.[87]

4. "Adult" BBS Demographics

The research team obtained demographics from several leading "adult" BBS which indicate the age, sex, and city of origin of subscribers. These demographics were based on verified credit card information and were obtained either directly from the logfiles of "adult" BBS or various methodologies developed by the research team programmers.[88] Because such demographics are exceedingly difficult to obtain, the research team devoted the bulk of its resources to obtaining demographics from the market leaders who provide pedophilic and paraphilic imagery. Many of these subscribers were found to be system operators of other "adult" BBS, who download the images for redistribution to their own customers in various regions of the world. None of the system operators with whom the research team conversed by phone or "chatted" online indicated they advertise overseas. Given that 71% of the pornography on the Usenet was found to originate from these "adult" BBS, it appears that the vast majority of foreign consumers learn of these American "adult" BBS by downloading images from the Usenet.

As noted in the introduction, the Carnegie Mellon research team was able to identify consumers of pedophilic and paraphilic pornography via computer in more than 2000 cities in all fifty states in the United States, most Canadian provinces, and forty countries, provinces, and territories around the world. Appendix D contains a complete list of cities and countries where these consumers were identified. The demographics should not be understood as exhaustive; they merely indicate a floor of the extent to which pedophilic and paraphilic imagery pervades the digital landscape.

---

87. To determine whether market forces common to all "adult" BBS exist, the research team generated scatterplots that examine the number of files offered by each BBS versus number of downloads, for each of the four classifications. The patterns on these scatterplots were muddled, with most "adult" BBS clustering near the origin. The data was then transformed, with the natural logarithm of the number of downloads plotted against the natural logarithm of the number of files. In this scale the muddle disappeared, suggesting that the transformation reflects implicit market forces and is the natural perspective from which to seek structure in the data. For pedophilia, the null hypothesis of no linear relationship between the transformed variables was rejected with a significance probability of 0.0002; for paraphilia, 0.0077; for hard-core, 0.049; and for soft-core, 0.264.

Before transformation, the Amateur Action BBS pedo/hebephile portfolio appears to differ substantially from other "adult" BBS, but on the logarithmic scale it is not an exceptional data point.

88. Because of the sensitive nature of the consumer data, the research team consulted privacy experts before submitting this article for review and publication. It was decided that once the demographics were tabulated and independently confirmed by two reviewers, the names of all consumers would be permanently deleted from the Carnegie Mellon database. This was done to protect the privacy of consumers in the United States and abroad.

5. "Adult" BBS Market Leader: Amateur Action BBS—A Case Study

The Amateur Action BBS provides an ideal case study, not only because it is a market leader among "adult" BBS, but also because its owners, Robert and Carleen Thomas, were recently convicted of ten counts of using a facility of interstate commerce (a computer) to distribute obscene materials.[89] Legal experts expect this case or a similar one to make its way to the United States Supreme Court.[90] The *Thomas* case highlights an important aspect of the current constitutional test for obscenity. As noted earlier, in *Miller v. California*, the Supreme Court held that whether pornography is "obscene," and therefore unprotected by the Constitution, is partly a question of whether it offends contemporary "community standards."[91] The Supreme Court reasoned that such a standard, although vague, permits communities that desire to maintain certain standards to insulate themselves from pornography that might be considered permissible in other areas with different community standards.[92] When pornography is purchased in a book store or received through the mail, the material is assessed according to the standards of the community where the pornography was purchased or received.

The intriguing questions the *Thomas* case raises are somewhat similar: can communities that desire to maintain certain standards still insulate themselves from pornography when it is distributed via computer? Will a fundamentally different test for obscenity be established in the future, given the significant changes in the means of pornography distribution, which is increasingly facilitated by computer networks?[93] Lastly, what will

---

89. United States v. Robert Thomas et al., No. CR-94-20019-G (W.D. Tenn. filed Jan. 25, 1994). *See* James Crawley, *Memphis Porn Decision is Far-reaching: Ruling Raises Concerns About Rights of Online Computer Users*, SAN DIEGO UNION TRIB., Aug. 16, 1994, at 9.

90. *See* Joshua Quittner, *Computers in the 1990s: Life in Cyberspace*, N.Y. NEWSDAY, Aug. 16, 1994, at B27. At the intermediate appellate level, the case has already attracted the attention of several amici interested in the development of Cyberspace. *See, e.g.*, Electronic Frontier Foundation AABBS Amicus Brief in Support of the Thomases (Appellants), April 19, 1995, *posted to* comp.org.eff.news.

91. 413 U.S. 15, 25-27 (1973).

92. 413 U.S. at 30-34.

93. There are at least two visions of pornography regulation which compete with the traditional test the Supreme Court established in *Miller*. The most fundamentally different perspective has been proposed by feminist legal scholars. *See, e.g.*, Catharine A. MacKinnon, *Not a Moral Issue*, 2 YALE L. & POL'Y REV. 321 (1984). According to this view, pornography is seen as causing and perpetuating patriarchal domination and antiwoman violence and is a practice of sex discrimination. Adopting this approach, two cities attempted to define pornography strictly in terms of the manner in which women are purportedly harmed. *See* ATT'Y GEN. COMM'N ON PORNOGRAPHY, FINAL REPORT 392 (1986). These efforts were provisionally rejected by the courts. *See* American Booksellers Assoc., Inc. v. Hudnut, 771 F.2d 323 (7th Cir. 1985), *summarily aff'd*, 475 U.S. 1001 (1986). Another competing vision consists of a revised version of the *Miller* standard. Instead of using community standards, the proponents of the revised *Miller* standard advocate the creation of a per se list of sexual activities which are automatically and irrevocably deemed obscene. *See* Bruce A. Taylor, *A Proposal for a Per Se Standard*, 21 U. MICH. J.L. REF. 255 (1987-88).

be the impact of such a test on communities which desire a different standard?[94]

In addition to these questions, it is significant to note that 116 Amateur Action BBS images were recently discovered on the Usenet. Two of these images reposted on the Usenet were among those recently found obscene by a Tennessee jury.[95]

The computer dictionary developed for this study was able to classify 99.4% of the 22,319 Amateur Action BBS images, which were downloaded 1.6 million times. The Amateur Action BBS images[96] were also analyzed according to a mean popularity index, which indicates the average number of times each file in each category was downloaded. This index is useful in determining whether a category is in low availability but high demand, or the reverse. The mean popularity indices show that the paraphilias were far more popular than any of the hard-core or soft-core classifications—in other words, the demand for the paraphilias exceeded the availability.

---

94. This question goes to the heart of the *Miller* standard. In *Miller*, the Supreme Court approved the notion that communities desiring to exclude marginally valuable sexual expression should be able to do so without regard to the status of similar expression in other communities. *Miller*, 413 U.S. at 30-34. Implicit in the concept of community, as it relates to obscenity, is the idea that a community necessarily involves a geographic limitation. Whether this geographic limitation should be discarded in the context of cyberspace poses an intriguing set of questions. If, for instance, Cyberspace were held to be a separate and distinct community and that even the most graphic sexual images do not violate Cyberspace community standards, will the traditional, geographically defined community then be compelled to permit such images? This would clearly thwart the *Miller* Court's attempt to protect geographically defined communities' ability to regulate marginally valuable sexually explicit expression. Conversely, if Cyberspace community standards prove to be more restrictive than the standards of the geographic community where a pornographic image is downloaded, should the government be confined to Cyberspace community standards?

This dilemma is made more complex by the Supreme Court's decision in Stanley v. Georgia, 394 U.S. 557 (1969). In *Stanley*, the Court identified a penumbral privacy right to possess obscene material within the confines of one's home. Since computer transmitted pornography most often comes directly into the home, it is at least arguable that *Stanley* operates to immunize computer-transmitted pornographers from criminal liability. If this argument were accepted, the idea that Cyberspace should be considered an independent community would, oddly, be one of boudoirs and bedrooms connected to one another only by telephones.

Lastly, if one chooses to view computer acquisition of obscenity as merely one method, among many, of obtaining obscene material, another logical view is that Cyberspace does not constitute a community at all. A philosophical discussion of "community" is beyond the scope of this article. In sum, the entire conception of community and community standards may be revisited by federal courts as digital pornography becomes more prevalent.

95. The fact that other Amateur Action digitized images have not been adjudicated obscene does not mean that these images are conclusively non-obscene. Rather, federal prosecutors simply selected a cross-section of representative images available on Amateur Action to bring to trial. Thus, it is probable that a number of Amateur Action images constitute obscenity, but have not as yet been adjudicated as such.

96. Although it is common for other BBS to offer menus which divide images into basic categories, such as vaginal, anal and lesbian, Thomas purposely avoided any classification of his portfolio. The principal investigator, who has spoken personally with Thomas, will explore the reasons for this in a future paper.

1898   THE GEORGETOWN LAW JOURNAL   [Vol. 83:1849

Finally, the research team developed numerous histograms to divide these categories in increments of ten percent, according to number of downloads. The histograms reveal that most of Thomas's files were in high demand, and suggest that forcing Thomas to remove a few "objectionable" files will have no measurable effect on his subscriber download habits or interest in his board.

Amateur Action BBS relies on three powerful marketing techniques to attract and maintain its large clientele, which ranged from 3500 to 10,700 individuals over a typical six month period. These techniques include a) portraying a "power imbalance" between the sexes, including a disproportionate representation of women in acts which may be considered degrading; b) deceitful marketing; and c) exploitation of children.[97] Examples of each technique are offered below.

The Power Imbalance: Fellatio-Choking.   The power imbalance between the sexes is among the most debated and controversial subjects in Western culture. Imagery which may help define the acceptable boundaries of relationships between the sexes has also been the focus of heated discussion.[98] It is beyond the scope of this article to present an exhaustive analysis of sadomasochistic imagery discovered on computer networks. At present, Carnegie Mellon researchers are developing more than two dozen computer dictionaries that explore sub-classifications of B&D/S&M imagery.

One of these sub-classifications, which links fellatio with B&D/S&M imagery provides a salient example of how Thomas (and pornographers in general) may transform the same sexual act from "hard-core" pornography into "paraphilia" material, and thereby increase download activity.[99] Thomas markets 1113 images depicting some form of fellatio. These images were downloaded 38,611 times, for a mean popularity index of 34.7:1.[100] Clearly, fellatio is a relatively unpopular category on Thomas's

---

97. Amateur Action BBS is not a market leader for B&D/S&M imagery. Of the 35 "adult" BBS discussed here, Amateur Action BBS accounted for only 6.1% of available B&D/S&M imagery.

98. *See, e.g.,* CATHARINE A. MACKINNON, FEMINISM UNMODIFIED: DISCOURSES ON LIFE AND LAW (1987); ANDREA DWORKIN, LETTERS FROM A WAR ZONE: WRITINGS, 1976–1989 (1989); Carlin Meyer, *Sex, Sin, and Women's Liberation: Against Porn-Suppression,* 72 TEX. L. REV. 1097 (1994).

99. Distinctions between different types of sexually explicit imagery and their impact have been made in the past by many observers. The distinction between "erotica" and "pornography" was first made by Gloria Steinem in 1978. *See* Gloria Steinem, *Erotica and Pornography: A Clear and Present Difference,* Ms. MAG., Nov. 1978, at 53. Steinem suggested that while "erotica" depicts "mutually pleasurable, sexual expression between people who have enough power to be there by positive choice," "pornography" depicts "domination and violence against women . . . unequal power that spells coercion . . . sex being used to reinforce some inequality." *Id* at 54.

100. The mean popularity index indicates the average number of times an image from a particular classification has been downloaded.

board, accounting for only 5% of all images available and 2.4% of all downloads. When Thomas describes an image as "Horny sexy blonde sucks cock! She is rubbing her wet pussy!"[101] he generates an unusually low number of downloads.[102] Whenever he uses the word "choke" in his fellatio descriptions, however, he doubles his downloads. The mean popularity index for fellatio-choking imagery increases to 65:1. These results suggest at least some correlation between increased power imbalance between the sexes (man over woman) and increased consumption. The results also remind us that our classification of images is dependent upon how pornographers market them.[103]

The Power Imbalance: Degradation-Bestiality. Degradation of women is one of the most challenging issues for a researcher to define, because the term is emotionally and politically charged. However, the *disproportion* of imagery depicting women engaged in acts that would be considered degrading in most communities can be definitively established.[104] Because it is beyond the scope of this study to address such issues exhaustively—a computer dictionary needs to be developed for each category—only one instance will be examined in detail.[105] The research team chose to examine bestiality because demand for these types of images more than quadrupled in the six months following the obscenity convictions of Robert and Carleen Thomas.

Thomas offers 852 bestiality images, which were downloaded 122,057 times, making bestiality the second most popular image category on his BBS. The mean popularity index for bestiality was 143.2:1, the highest of all categories. The resolution (picture clarity) of these images ranges from very poor to exceptional, but the validity was near 100%.

The pie chart in Figure 10 illustrates the variety of animals engaged in sexual acts with humans, the most popular of which was "BRUNETTE

---

101. AA-11412; one download.

102. The reader should keep in mind that due to the precedence scheme used, this low number reports fellatio only as it overlaps with other hard-core classifications, but not with pedo/hebephile and paraphilia. Thus, the actual number of images involving fellatio is slightly higher. The exclusion turns out to be useful because the bestiality image cited *infra* note 107 does not directly relate to the power imbalance between the sexes. *See infra* notes 104-10 and accompanying text (describing possible degradation of women in pornography).

103. More study is needed to determine what effect such marketing techniques have on how consumers perceive or fantasize about the images.

104. This assumes, of course, that bestiality is a "degrading" act. On several Usenet boards, including alt.soc.feminism, the research team encountered many who insisted that such acts are not degrading, and that at least some women enjoy cohabiting with beasts. It should be noted that the Dietz-Sears study found it necessary to identify three views of degradation: traditional, moderate, and liberal. Dietz-Sears, *supra* note 15, at 30-33. According to Dietz-Sears, even the most liberal view would find bestiality degrading. *Id.* at 33. The research team takes no position on this issue.

105. A preliminary analysis on urophilia, coprophilia, fisting, B&D/S&M, and enema suggests a similar disproportion.

1900   THE GEORGETOWN LAW JOURNAL   [Vol. 83:1849

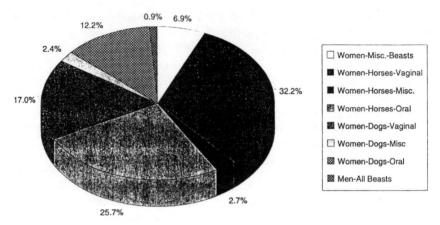

FIGURE 10.   Amateur Action BBS Bestiality Portfolio. 852 Images,
122,057 Downloads; Chart Indicates % by Downloads.

SLUT TAKES A HUGE HORSE COCK IN HER TIGHT PUSSY!"[106] The most popular image depicting a woman and a dog was "Super slut! Sucks dog cock and gets cum on her cute face!"[107] More importantly, 99.1% of the images depicted women engaged in sexual acts with animals, whereas only 0.9% depicted men engaged in sexual acts with animals. Even the most popular bestiality image involving a man had the following description: "He holds the big erect dog cock! Makes cute blonde suck it!"[108] Bestiality images involving only men and animals had the lowest mean popularity index. Thomas apparently realized that his customers did not want man-bestiality imagery after a series of such images that were posted in September 1993 failed to generate a significant number of downloads.[109] Not surprisingly, the least popular bestiality image involved

---

106. AA-8630; 672 downloads. Many additional pages could be devoted to discussing this particular image. Specifically, Thomas cleverly interweaves physical attributes, such as hair color; demeaning language, such as "slut;" and value-neutral words indicating magnitude, such as "huge" and "tight."

107. AA-7806; 597 downloads.

108. AA-9854; 153 downloads.

109. With forty telephone lines, each connected to a 28,800 bps modem, Thomas generates approximately 1400 downloads per day. Curiously, there does not appear to be a clear correlation between the number of telephone lines maintained by a BBS and the number of downloads. The Windy City Freedom Fortress BBS generated more than one million downloads with only eleven telephone lines. This may be due to the fact that its operator, Robert Copella, former vice-president of research and development for the Rand-McNally Corporation, devised a means of maximizing customer calls while minimizing the number of available telephone lines. Mr. Coppella is currently in jail in New Jersey, charged with several federal child pornography offenses and awaiting trial related to his alleged operation of a child pornography BBS in Mexico.

a man: "Horny black guy fucks a young blonde! Big dog licks his ass!"[110] Animals other than dogs and horses depicted in sexual acts with women include monkeys, donkeys, snakes, goats, pigs, and cows.

Bestiality is a typical, but by no means extreme, example of Thomas's shrewd implementation of this marketing technique. Although nearly one-half of his entire portfolio depicts at least one man engaged in sexual acts with women, Thomas has not posted any man-bestiality images since September 1993. He continued to meet the intense demand for women-bestiality images up until the time of this study.

Deceitful Marketing. Verbal descriptions enable Thomas to market his portfolio as somewhat more taboo than may be the case.[111] Indeed, Thomas is one of the few sysops in the country to exploit fully the remarkable power of verbal descriptions to fulfill customer fantasies. The best illustration of this technique is provided by "incest" imagery. Thomas described 1234 images as sexual or highly suggestive acts among family members. These "incest" images were downloaded 167,534 times and accounted for 10.3% of all the downloads. The mean popularity index for "incest" images from Amateur Action BBS was 135.8:1. A second computer dictionary was developed for incest imagery, which was found to overlap considerably with other paraphilias. For instance, the most popular mother-daughter image involved bestiality: "She holds the dog cock! Inserts it in her daughter's ass!"[112] Thomas offers a triple-paraphilic combination with this popular image: "Mother watches daughter fuck herself with a screwdriver!"[113] The most popular father-daughter image was also the most popular sister-sister: "She is fisting her sister's cunt! Father fucks her asshole!"[114] The most popular mother-son image was also among the most popular father-daughter: "She sucks her son's cock! Father is fucking his daughter!"[115]

Because it is not clear whether the images depict sexual acts between genuine family members, Thomas services his clientele with a shrewd blend of exaggeration and deceit. Curiously, Thomas's descriptions of other categories achieved the highest reliability rating from the panel of judges, suggesting that his is among the most meticulously designed boards in the country.

---

110. AA-16996; 21 downloads.

111. Thomas does not make it clear whether his promotional descriptions are intended to be taken as truth, fantasy, or both. It should be noted that the First Amendment may not protect his misleading advertisements. States are permitted to regulate commercial speech which is false, deceptive, or misleading. *See* Virginia State Bd. of Pharmacy v. Virginia Citizens Consumers Council, Inc., 425 U.S. 748, 771 (1976).

112. AA-16590; 365 downloads.

113. AA-7480; 219 downloads; paraphilias: voyeurism, foreign objects, incest.

114. AA-8506; 228 downloads.

115. AA-8589; 214 downloads.

Exploitation of Children.[116] Thomas has attempted to push the parameters and current interpretation of child pornography law. By offering more than 5000 images featuring the exhibition of genital areas of children,[117] being careful not to depict hard-core sex acts with pre-pubescent children, and terming many of the images "nudist" material, Thomas has attempted to skirt the attention of law enforcement. He repeatedly used marketing language in an attempt to convince his subscribers that his material depicting children was both sexually enticing and legal. At the same time, he boasts that his BBS is the "nastiest place on earth."[118]

The demand for soft-core pedophilic imagery exceeded availability by more than 25%, whereas availability exceeded demand for hard-core and most of the paraphilias.[119] Thomas is fully aware of this imbalance as evidenced by his use of a sophisticated third layer of category abstraction.[120] Most of the hard-core and paraphilic descriptions overlap with the following five sub-classifications: virgin, genital exhibition, no pubic hair, no breast development, and "nudist." For the sub-classification "genital exhibition," for instance, the computer dictionary identified 1361 lascivious descriptions of young girls which contained the following words: spread, spreads, spreading, close-up, kinky, kinkiest, candid, poses, posing, and open-leg. The most popular of these was "TENDER BRUNETTE JUN-

---

116. Because child pornography necessarily entails the direct sexual abuse or calculated sexual exploitation of a child, the U. S. Supreme Court has ruled that child pornography can be prohibited regardless of community standards. New York v. Ferber, 458 U.S. 747 (1982). In order for material to be legally proscribed under child pornography laws, it must be 1) a visual depiction; 2) depicting a minor; 3) engaged in sexually explicit conduct. 18 U.S.C. § 2256 defines the phrase "sexually explicit conduct." Under § 2256, sexually explicit conduct includes actual or simulated intercourse, actual or simulated masturbation, and lascivious exhibition of the genitals. The concept of lascivious exhibition has recently been the subject of some debate. *See, e.g.,* United States v. Knox, 32 F.3d 733, 744 (3d Cir. 1994), *cert. denied,* 115 S. Ct. 897 (1995) (holding the exhibition of a child's covered genitalia may violate federal law because "lascivious exhibition" does not require child nudity).

Robert Thomas is presently under federal indictment in the District of Utah for allegedly selling child pornography over his Amateur Action BBS and is awaiting trial. United States v. Thomas, No. 94-CR-107J (D. Utah filed July 20, 1994).

117. The research team found that the vast majority of pedo/hebephilic imagery on Amateur Action BBS were of pre-pubescent children. Thus, the term "pedophilic" is used here.

118. Since his indictment and conviction on obscenity charges in Memphis, Thomas has made changes to his *textual* descriptions of at least 196 images available on Amateur Action BBS, including many which depict pre-pubescent children. In broad terms, these descriptive changes attempt to deemphasize the focus of these images on the children's genitals or the sexually explicit nature of the images. The actual content of the images themselves have not changed.

119. This may be due to the fact that pedophiles believe Thomas is practicing "deceitful marketing" whenever he markets hebephilic-hard-core imagery as pedophilic. The significant possibility of law enforcement action is another possible reason why Thomas's pedophile clients choose the soft-core images of children.

120. The first level comprises the four major classifications. The second layer comprises the specific categories (e.g., orgy, fisting, etc.).

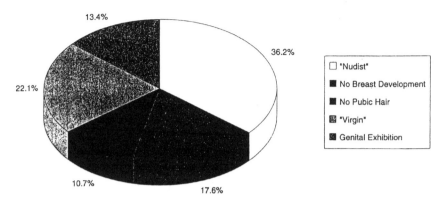

FIGURE 11. Amateur Action BBS Pedophile Portfolio. 5214 Images, 717,896 Downloads; Chart Indicates % by Downloads.

IOR TEEN! NO TITS! SHE IS SPREADING!"[121] Another such image, "INNOCENT BLONDE JUNIOR TEEN! NO TITS! NO PUSSY HAIR! GREAT!"[122] was widely distributed on the Usenet and via so-called drop or underground ftp sites.[123] The entire genital exhibition portfolio accounted for 216,672 downloads. For the subclassification "virgin," 2249 image descriptions contained the following words: sweet, tender, sprouting, budding, virgin, and innocent. These images accounted for 357,192 downloads. Thomas also relies heavily on overlapping descriptions within this third layer (e.g., no pubic hair and no breast development, nudist and sprouting, tender and spreading, etc.). Figure 11 shows the breakdown of how Thomas markets his pedophilic imagery to consumers.

Appendix B, which lists the most popular files for each of the Amateur Action BBS categories, indicates that of the 22,319 image descriptions analyzed, the following generated the most downloads: "Young amateur teen! No tits at all! She spreads her pussy!"[124] An analysis of Thomas's use of five of these terms—young, amateur, teen, no tits, spreads—revealed that this and similar combinations generated unusually intense download activity.

Clientele Distinctions Among Amateur Action BBS Subscribers. Thomas clearly understands that his BBS caters to a variety of clienteles. While he cleverly mixes incest with other paraphilias in any number of combina-

---

121. AA-12330; 1495 downloads.
122. AA-12542; 1024 downloads.
123. Usenet bulletin boards also serve as a vehicle for computer users to make requests for trades away from public traffic. These trades may involve the use of "drop" or "underground" sites without the owner's knowledge or consent. This may also be done with the full consent of the owner, who wants knowledge of the existence of the site restricted.
124. AA-042; 1687 downloads.

1904   THE GEORGETOWN LAW JOURNAL   [Vol. 83:1849

tions, as noted above, he carefully avoids explicit overlap between pedophilia and the other paraphilias.[125] There is substantial evidence, based upon a contingency table analysis of category overlap, to suggest that Thomas caters to at least three separate classes of clientele: paraphilic, pedophilic, and hard-core. For instance, when posting a bestiality image, Thomas takes special care not to describe the female in pedophilic terms (for example, "teen," "young," "virgin," "budding," "no tits," "no pussy hair"). He is keenly aware that customers who seek bestiality (and more generally, paraphilic) images do not seek pedophilic images, and the converse.[126]

The number of subscribers to the Amateur Action BBS has varied significantly during the past year. In May 1994, when the first dataset was collected, Thomas had 3621 active subscribers. As of May 15, 1995, he had 10,687 subscribers[127] and had logged more than 1.16 million calls. 98.9% of

---

125. *See supra* note 2 for discussion of the difference between obscenity and child pornography and the lack of legal overlap.

126. A contingency table analysis of pedo/hebephile and bestiality confirmed that Thomas carefully avoids paraphilic descriptions when marketing images to pedophiles.

127. Because Amateur Action BBS has been in business for more than four years, its cumulative number of subscribers is higher. Other "adult" BBS sysops report the average number of images downloaded by a subscriber to be between 75-150, but no data was available regarding the standard deviation. If one were to assume an average of 112 images downloaded per customer, Thomas would have had a total of 35,644 customers (3,700,000/112). However, some of these may be the same subscribers who renewed their subscriptions. Thus, the estimate of 35,644 cumulative subscribers should be taken only as a very rough approximation of the total number of subscribers to the Amateur Action BBS.

Applying a similar analysis to the other 34 "adult" BBS suggests a very rough estimate of 75,892 subscribers whose consumption patterns were analyzed for this article. This does not include the other 33 "adult" BBS for which no download information was available, including one of the largest "adult" BBS discovered, Event Horizons, which reports more than 30,000 active subscribers. This also does not include those who obtain pornographic images via the Usenet, ftp sites, private trades, or other "adult" BBS.

Usenet statistics estimate the number of active users of alt.pictures.binaries.erotica at 260,000 worldwide. *See supra* Table 2. Due to overlap of readers within the .binaries hierarchy, there is no way of determining the total number of readers of pornographic Usenet newsgroups, but it appears to be notably higher. *See, e.g., supra* text accompanying note 126, which suggests that pornography consumers often comprise mutually exclusive subsets according to sexual tastes. Moreover, because this article demonstrates that pornography consumption at at least one university is substantially higher than among the general population, *see supra* section entitled *Comparisons: Univerisity and Worldwide Results*, it may be that the worldwide sampling underreports the total number of readers of pornographic Usenet newsgroups because it undersamples university sites. However, because "adult" BBS were found to use the Usenet to advertise their products, the subscribers to commercial "adult" BBS may merely be a subset of those accessing pornography via the Usenet. *See supra* section entitled *Origins of Usenet Pornographic Imagery*.

Finally, the "adult" BBS market, as with the BBS market in general, appears to be expanding rapidly. This article reports data from commercial BBS as of June 1, 1994. The most recent editions of *Joy of Cybersex, The Adult BBS Guidebook*, and the alt.bbs hierarchy of the Usenet contain listings of many "adult" BBS which opened in the past twelve months and were not included in this article. For instance, six months after the first dataset was collected for this study, the research team obtained a list of new BBS in the Chicago area.

the subscribers are male, and 1.1% are female. Many of these subscribers are system operators of other "adult" BBS, who download the images for redistribution to their own customers in various regions of the U.S.[128]

Although no definitive numbers are available, there is at least some evidence to suggest that Thomas's BBS is designed to be an advertising lure for his lucrative video business featuring nude children and paraphilic activities. The strong appeal of his BBS to tens of thousands of online consumers and Usenet aficionados around the world highlights the importance of computers as a medium of choice for the distribution and marketing of pedophilic and paraphilic imagery.[129]

IV. CONCLUSION

A. IMAGES? OR ONLY DESCRIPTIONS?

This is as much a study of words as of images, of words that describe images, of words that are as revealing in their accuracy as in their failures to describe an image accurately. Consider the description, "She has one fist in her girlfriend's asshole and another fist in her pussy." Examination of the image revealed that only two fingers were in the anus; the research team interjudge reliability test did not classify this as anal fisting. However, the customer who has a fetish for anal fisting of women and who downloads an image whose description is the one described may not be upset to discover that only two fingers, and not the entire hand, are inserted in the anus. In fact, it may serve as the starting point of another fantasy; the divergence between word and image suggests a certain flux, such that two fingers are in the anus *now*, and the entire fist will be in the anus *later*. The dichotomy between now and later is an extremely clever way for the pornographer to make a still image assume a certain kind of *motion*. In the

---

Twenty-three were advertised as "adult," but none of them had been available for inclusion in the original dataset. In sum, while the reader is cautioned against interpreting the 8.5 million downloads discussed here as alarmingly high, he or she is equally cautioned against attributing the total number of downloads of sexually explicit materials in Cyberspace, both reported and unreported by this article, to a disproportionately small percentage of the computer literate population.

128. Thus, the total number of people who consume AABBS images is higher. Until "pirating" images in this fashion became commonplace, Thomas used to license each image to other "adult" BBS for $10 each. Last year he indicated to the principal investigator that he no longer had any objections to redistribution without a licensing fee, because it was "good advertising." It is interesting to note that Thomas claims to own copyrights to many images which members of the research team obtained independently from computer sources around the world, many of which were scanned directly from previously copyrighted magazines.

129. When Thomas was tried in Memphis for transmitting obscenity, prosecutors elected not to charge him with computer transmission of child pornography. Instead, he was charged with receipt of child pornography through the mails after postal inspectors delivered a child pornography magazine to him, allegedly at Thomas's request. This was the sole count for which he was found not guilty. *See* Quittner, *supra* note 90, at B27.

viewer's mind, it may even become a movie. What he actually sees, and what the words promised he would see, must converge in his mind; they must synthesize into a new form of imagery.

Because of this ability to play to consumer desires through the interplay of images and descriptions, the title of this study is "*Marketing* Pornography on the Information Superhighway." The description, "She hangs from the ceiling as weights are suspended from her pussy lips and nipples" may describe an inherently painful act; however, it is not marketed primarily as a painful act, but as one of restraint. There are many other B&D/S&M images that observers might categorize as painful, based upon their own impressions, but they are not marketed as such and thus not classified in this study as such. When the pornographers want to market an image as painful, when they want to emphasize its torturous aspects, they do so by using words such as pain, torture, abuse, torment, hurt, and suffer. When one actually views many of these images, moreover, there may be some ambiguity as to whether the model is actually in pain or merely acting.

B. PHENOMENOLOGY OF A PORNGEIST[130]

In the past, wherever one lived, it was extremely difficult, if not impossible, to obtain coprophilia or bestiality images, even through underground channels. Computers and modems are profoundly redefining the pornographic landscape by saturating the market with an endless variety of what only a decade ago mainstream America defined as "perverse" or "deviant."[131] What is perhaps even more peculiar, the very same bestiality and

---

130. The Carnegie Mellon research data suggests that paraphilic pornography has been "democratized" and rendered ubiquitous by computer networks in the late 1980s and early 1990s. According to Lynn Hunt, Annenberg Professor of History at the University of Pennsylvania: "Although desire, sensuality, eroticism and even the explicit depiction of sexual organs can be found in many, if not all, times and places, pornography as a legal and artistic category seems to be an especially Western idea with a specific chronology and geography." LYNN HUNT, THE INVENTION OF PORNOGRAPHY 10 (1993). While computer networks may seem at first glimpse as merely an extension of this chronology (e.g., the printing press, photograph, magazine, video, and computer technologies) and geography (globalization), there appears to be little historical precedent for the widespread availability of paraphilic pornography. Most "explicit" depictions discovered among ancient ruins of Greece and Rome would be classified by this study as "hard-core," not paraphilic. For instance, representations of Priapus, known for his gigantic erect phallus, were excavated from the ruins of Pompei, and were often declared "obscene" by the cultures responsible for such excavation. *See* WALTER KENDRICK, THE SECRET MUSEUM: PORNOGRAPHY IN MODERN CULTURE 8 (1987). Although statues such as one "representing a satyr in sexual congress with an apparently undaunted goat," were also excavated from Pompei, it does not appear that such works were widely produced or consumed in a fashion analogous to modern pornographic consumption. *Id.* at 6.

131. One of the suggestions of the 1986 Attorney General's Commission on Pornography was that pornography had, in comparison to previous decades, become increasingly violent, especially in its depiction of women. ATT'Y GEN. COMM'N ON PORNOGRAPHY, FINAL REPORT 386 (1986). While the computer pornography studied here is heavily paraphilic, the research team has not yet determined the extent pornographers rely on violence against women to

coprophilia images are selling briskly across the United States. Yet the mainstream is loath to embrace the frequently downloaded images as best-sellers. One animation, entitled "birra," depicted a woman urinating into the mouth of another. Made in Italy,[132] it was discovered on seventeen "adult" BBS in the United States and downloaded more than 500 times. There are many other notorious and extremely lurid images, such as HBO6.GIF, a crystal clear Harper's Bizarre Series image of a woman defecating into a man's mouth.[133] It was posted twenty-three times on the Usenet over a six month period. Indeed, when an enterprising upstart company advertised on the Usenet to imprint color images onto T-shirts, a half-serious poster from Harvard quipped, "HBO6.GIF anyone?" No description was necessary; it was a comment addressed only to those "in the loop" about computer porn, for whom the lurid image—even the title— had achieved some degree of cultural significance.

Ten years ago, college students could not type a few commands from their dormitory computers and receive instant access, via the Usenet, to thousands of bestiality images and stories. Until the recent explosion of World Wide Web sites, which enable users to view images with the click of a button, college students were among the first computer afficionados to have access to image decoders, powerful UNIX-based software and machines, and most advantageously, free and unlimited advice concerning the technical problems associated with downloading, cutting, and pasting these images. As mentioned in the introduction, the pervasiveness of digital pornography may have a profound effect on primary and secondary schools interested in offering their students access to computer networks. Yet, attempts at regulation may be ineffective; "the net interprets censorship as damage and routes around it" is a well known expression among Usenet enthusiasts. The current structure of the Usenet requires that individual sites choose between an "All things not expressly permitted are prohibited policy," or conversely, "All things not expressly prohibited are permitted."[134] A middle ground does not appear viable.

---

market their imagery. Such an undertaking would first require agreement on what constitutes a "violent" act. For instance, "She screams in pain as he fucks her pussy with a bat" might convince most judges to classify the image as violent. However, "She smiles as he fists her virgin asshole" poses more complicated questions (e.g., whether the model is really smiling, or really enjoying the act). A dictionary could be developed which identifies and tabulates the frequency of such words as pain, torture, abuse, etc. This data could further be sorted according to gender, race, and ethnic origin. Because there may be some discrepancy between what the judge and the pornographer or model considers a violent act, multiple dictionaries which consider different points of view would likely have to be developed.

132. The animation was initially distributed by (or pirated from) Davide Toma and Luca De Gregio, Milano, Italy.

133. An instructor at the Carnegie Mellon College of Fine Arts confirmed that the image was not digitally manipulated or "doctored."

134. *See supra* note 21 and accompanying text.

C. DIGITAL CULTURAL ARTIFACTS

The descriptions lists and their corresponding images offer a rich field of study in psychology, sexuality, and culture. Indeed, the capturing of these lists alone represents a significant resource,[135] for they are fascinating cultural artifacts. In ten or twenty years, researchers will be able to use these descriptives to compare changes in sexual tastes and pornographic repertoires. Yet this remarkable compendium of information will likely disappear in the next few years, as other technologies such as thumbnail images,[136] CD-ROM, and interactive multimedia replace the current short verbal descriptions. Consumers can purchase about 4000 paraphilic or hard-core images on CD-ROM, often for less than $15. Once pornography consumers buy these CD-ROMs, researchers will have no way of determining which types of images they prefer. No doubt there will be "all oral" or "all anal" CD-ROMs, but due to legal concerns among pornographers, it is doubtful that an "all bestiality" or "all coprophilia" CD-ROM could be successfully marketed on a national scale. Moreover, lawmakers are grappling with the enormously complex issues which surround digitized porn, and they may decide to regulate tightly portions of the Usenet, World Wide Web, and "adult" BBS.[137]

---

135. *See supra* note 9.

136. These are very tiny images that customers can use to quickly preview larger images while online.

137. There are many technical problems associated with regulating sexually explicit imagery on the Internet and Usenet. *See supra* note 21. Two additional possible solutions are discussed here: content flags and authentication procedures. Content flags could identify the content of computer files transferred or posted on the Usenet and could have an internationally agreed upon standard definition, to which all Internet member countries assent. Computer users would be permitted to send whatever files/traffic they liked within their community or country, but transfers between communities or countries could be filtered based on local pornography laws.

Each government and, indeed, each site can regulate what sort of traffic they will receive. For example, a computer network run by a religious organization may elect not to carry any sexually explicit material, while major service providers may choose to carry everything permitted by law. Parents who do not want their children to see pornographic images could establish a filter from their homes. If successfully implemented, content flags might allow the government to regulate obscenity without unduly restricting access to other sexually explicit material which is protected by the First Amendment. The obvious difficulty will likely be enforcing a content flag requirement, both on a national and international basis.

To identify the senders of child pornography, or those sending obscene materials without the correct content information, some form of authentication is required. Simply pointing back to a hostname is not viable, because hostnames might be forged. Similarly, pointing back to an IP address, although more reliable, only identifies the site responsible for that particular block of IP addresses. This may work well for entities such as CompuServe, or Carnegie Mellon University, where complying with the law is generally expected, but many other sites exist on the Internet which may not feel obligated to comply with the law as scrupulously.

Without the help of computer system administrators, law enforcement agencies would have to expend an enormous amount of resources tracing a site, which may be connected to another site which is connected to a third site, etc. For authentication to be practical, sites might have to be connected according to a hierarchy, with responsibility defined at each level.

The collapse in the past few years of several of the largest and most active boards in the country, such as the Windy City Freedom Fortress BBS (hebephilic, all paraphilias), The Atlantis BBS (bestiality), and Taste BBS (fisting), appears to have had no measurable effect on current market conditions. The images from Windy City and other defunct BBS are widely distributed via CD-ROM and the Usenet. Thus, it appears unlikely that the conviction of the Amateur Action BBS operator will do more than temporarily encourage other BBS operators to remove their paraphilic and pedophilic repertoires from public display.[138]

D. "FREE" PORNOGRAPHY

Pornographers often recognize before anyone else those applications of a new technology which will make a fast, almost guaranteed profit. After Gutenberg used his printing press to print the first Bible, pornographers were quick to use the new medium to more prurient ends.[139] More recently, they contributed considerably to making VCRs a lucrative and mainstream technology.[140] Pornography has served as a powerful incentive

---

Furthermore, the implementation of content flags and authentication procedures may raise constitutional concerns. With content flags, the government would essentially be requiring computer users to identify the nature of their speech. One question is whether this constitutes "compelled speech," which the Supreme Court has viewed with some suspicion. *See, e.g.,* Wooley v. Maynard, 430 U.S. 705, 713 (1977) (striking down state statute requiring all license plates to display state motto); West Virginia State Bd. of Educ. v. Barnette, 319 U.S. 624, 642 (1943) (striking down state resolution requiring all public school children to salute the American flag and recite Pledge of Allegiance). *But see* Red Lion Broadcasting Co. v. FCC, 395 U.S. 367, 375 (1969) (upholding FCC order requiring broadcasters to air replies to political editorials).

Moreover, in the case of authentication procedures, the government may be requiring computer users, arguably engaged in expressive conduct, to identify themselves. Generally, the First Amendment protects the anonymity of those transmitting speech. The Supreme Court has invalidated a requirement that prohibited the distribution of leaflets which did not identify the author of the leaflet. Talley v. California, 362 U.S. 60, 64-65 (1960). While trading digitized images on computer networks is vastly more complex than leafletting, the question of anonymity continues to be important. Thus, the Supreme Court's anonymity cases may apply to Cyberspace. Because the apprehension of child pornography producers, distributors, and consumers is a particularly compelling government interest, *see* New York v. Ferber, 458 U.S. 747, 761 (1982), carefully drawn authentication procedures may pass constitutional muster.

Even if content flag and authentication requirements are implemented, other forms of electronic communication, such as ftp and World Wide Web sites, pose even more serious challenges to law enforcement. Child pornographers will inevitably develop more effective means of circumventing the law. Currently, they set up anonymous mail bouncers to redirect traffic elsewhere, with a new authenticated identification.

138. Indeed, several BBS contacted by the research team, when asked if they had "any good beasty pics," offered to sell them privately on diskette.

139. *See, e.g.,* John Tierney, *Porn, The Low-Slung Engine of Progress,* N.Y. TIMES, Jan. 9, 1994, at B1.

140. *Id.* In 1978 and 1979, when fewer than 1% of American homes owned VCRs, more than 75% of the videocassettes sold were pornographic. *Id.*

to tens of thousands of Usenet aficionados, already computer literate, to learn enough UNIX to encode, decode, and reconstruct files from the Usenet alt.binaries.pictures.erotica newsgroups.

Yet there is one notable difference between the manner in which pornographers capitalized upon emerging technologies to make a profit in the past, such as the printing press or the VCR, and the Information Superhighway of the 1990s. Pornographers are using the Usenet primarily as a vehicle to advertise their products to a large audience at no cost. Indeed, the concept of hard-core and paraphilic pornography which is widely distributed, yet "free" to the general public, is a novel one. Pornographers are keenly aware that their products remain "free" only to the extent that consumers opt not to subscribe to their BBS. A number of "adult" BBS have reported that their subscriptions "skyrocketed" after posting a few images on the Usenet.

In fact, the Usenet is ideally suited for market niching. A soft-core BBS may choose to advertise on alt.binaries.pictures, erotica.female, alt.binaries. pictures.erotica.blondes, or occasionally, alt.binaries.pictures.erotica. A hard-core BBS might advertise its images on alt.binaries.pictures.erotica. A B&D/S&M BBS may advertise on alt.sex.bondage or alt.binaries.pictures.erotica.bondage. A BBS specializing in any of the paraphilias may advertise on alt.sex.fetish.watersports, alt.sex.bestiality, alt.binaries.pictures.bestiality, or alt.binaries.pictures.tasteless. A gay BBS may advertise on alt.pictures.binaries.erotica.male. An Asian-focused BBS may advertise on alt.binaries.pictures.erotica.orientals.

Many network analysts expect, however, that the Usenet may collapse under its own weight. As more Americans utilize the Internet and Usenet, the proportion of new messages posted each day may be too large for individual sites to carry, or subscribers to read. The trend appears to be moving toward moderated newsgroups, which would exclude most of the alt hierarchy, including the sexually explicit newsgroups. However, mainstream pornography distributors, such as VCA Platinum Pictures, Vivid Video, the Odyssey group, and Leisure Time Entertainment, have begun to promote their products on the World Wide Web.[141] Subscribers are offered "tantalizing QuickTime movie previews of the hottest new releases" and can "browse through our adult video show rooms which feature everything from sizzling new XXX-rated titles, to exotic European releases, to sexy amateur home videos."[142] The companies boast that "shopping for adult videos and novelties has never been easier, more fun, more convenient or more private! And we have an electronic ordering

---

141. *See Entertainment Adult: Web Access to XXX-Rated Movies and Novelties*, Feb. 16, 1995, *posted to* alt.sex.erotica.marketplace.
    142. *Id.*

system that makes shopping for adult products as simple, convenient and easy as clicking a button from the privacy of your own computer screen!"[143]

E. PRIVACY, PORNOGRAPHY AND COMPUTERS

Sophisticated sysops can collect, catalog, and utilize highly personal information acquired when subscribers access pornographic imagery. Consumers may find this an uncomfortable prospect. As author Anne Branscomb has noted:

> A great deal of information we consider to be highly personal, and of interest to ourselves and the town gossip—our names, telephone numbers, marital status, educational accomplishments, job and credit histories, even medical, dental, and psychiatric records—is now being sold on the open market to anyone who believes he or she might be able to use such information to turn a profit. These transactions usually take place without our knowledge or consent.[144]

As noted in this study, computer pornography is still in its infancy, as sysops have failed to capitalize on the detailed information they now possess about each consumer. However, in the coming years, pornography consumption may become an integral part of this information market.

The compilation of these statistics also raises significant privacy issues, which are not limited to pornography. Computer users normally maintain a logfile in their home directory (entitled .newsrc) that keeps track of the Usenet boards they read and their latest access of each board. At the university studied, these logfiles were publicly available to any authorized

---

143. *Id.*

144. ANNE WELLS BRANSCOMB, WHO OWNS INFORMATION? 3-4 (1994).

The collection, retention, and improper use of personal information by businesses is not a phenomenon unique to Cyberspace. In 1972, in California, voters amended the state constitution to include privacy as an inalienable right prohibiting intrusive business practices. *See* CAL. CONST. art. I, § 1; White v. Davis, 13 Cal. 3d 757, 773-75 nn. 8-9 (1975) (discussing the purposes and applications of the state constitutional amendment). Importantly, one of the reasons California voters felt compelled to amend their constitution is that the federally protected penumbral right to privacy operates only against state action. *See* Hill v. NCAA, 7 Cal. 4th 1, 28-29 n.8 (1994) (contrasting California right to privacy with federal privacy right).

In hindsight, California appears to have been prescient. With the aid of computer software applications which can quickly analyze and categorize personal information, businesses can become far more intrusive. It would be erroneous to assume that bulletin board operators who offer extremely explicit, possibly illegal digitized pornography for sale will not collect and use personal information. In fact, the potential for blackmail is readily apparent assuming that few, if any, persons would want their personal pornography consumption habits to be made public. As with California, there may be increasing calls for enacting state and local legislation, which reaches beyond state action, to protect against such abuses of personal information.

user of the campus network.[145] It is possible that any user could obtain another user's logfile and use this information to harass, embarrass, or blackmail unsuspecting users. For instance, if a female student subscribes to talk.abortion and alt.adoption.agency, a user could examine her logfile and infer that this student might be pregnant or have a close friend who is pregnant. Those who subscribe to misc.jobs.offered might not want their employers to know they are looking for another job. With respect to pornography, many users might be embarrassed if their subscriptions to alt.sex.bestiality or alt.sex.fetish.watersports were a matter of public knowledge. Even if other users are blocked from accessing the logfiles of their peers, it is still potentially significant that network administrators have access to these logfiles.[146] Most users appear not to know that these logfiles exist, and were they informed of their existence, might find such monitoring of their accounts objectionable. Unscrupulous network administrators are in a position to compile and sell detailed online information about each of their users to third party vendors.

F. THE MARQUIS DE CYBERSPACE

That many of the most popular images of computer pornographers in the United States—pedo/hebephilia, bestiality, incest, urophilia, coprophilia, enema, fisting, he-she male, and B&D/S&M—are consumed by paying subscribers in at least 2000 cities around the world raises complex and intriguing questions about "community standards" in Cyberspace. Because most of these "adult" BBS are not linked to any public computer network or protocol, such as the Internet, Usenet, or World Wide Web, most customers must pay long distance toll charges, plus the regular subscription fee, to access these images.

Law enforcement efforts have done little to discourage consumers—or indeed the market leader, Robert Thomas—from discussing, trading, and redistributing these images on other computer bulletin boards around the world. As of this writing, Thomas sits in jail and has complained of cockroaches, bad food, filth, and violent prisoners.[147] His wife continues to run Amateur Action BBS, and when she reports to jail, Thomas has indicated that "friends" will run his BBS. His subscriber list still contains citizens from Memphis, Tennessee, where he had been convicted of obscenity charges, and Salt Lake City, Utah, where he faces a federal indictment for distribution of child pornography. Since his trial in July 1994, his

---

145. After seven years of compiling data about its users, the university has since decided to automatically block public access to these logfiles on all new accounts.

146. This is how the worldwide statistics for this study were compiled. However, the statistics reported here do not implicate any individuals, as network administrators apparently did not abuse their access privileges.

147. Usenet newsgroup discussion *posted to* comp.org.eff.news.

subscriptions have increased threefold, to 10,687. His downloads have more than doubled, from 1.6 million to more than 3.7 million. And millions more have likely been downloaded by Usenet aficionados and subscribers to dozens of other commercial "adult" BBS, which have pirated or licensed Amateur Action BBS images.

Thomas is a brilliant marketer, presenting himself as a modern day Marquis de Sade. It is not without irony that he promotes Amateur Action BBS as "the nastiest place on earth." Indeed, the parallels between the lives and "art" of Thomas and Sade would provide fodder for a fascinating study. Both pushed "taboos" and societal mores to the extreme; both flaunted the law and were jailed; both considered themselves renegade artists; and both revolutionized the dissemination of paraphilic pornography—Sade in print, Thomas on computer networks. As historian Lynn Hunt has noted:

> Virtually all of the themes of modern pornography were rehearsed by Sade; indeed, he specialized in the cataloging of pornographic effects. Rape, incest, patricide, sacrilege, sodomy and tribalism, pedophilia and all the most horrible forms of torture and murder were associated with sexual arousal in the writings of Sade. No one has ever been able to top Sade because he had, in effect, explored the ultimate logical possibility of pornography: the very annihilation of the body, the very seat of pleasure in the name of desire.[148]

Men of considerable intelligence have paid homage to Sade, admiring his unrivaled, demented imagination. Yet for all of their efforts, Sade and his disciples pushed pornography only as far as the printed word allowed. Two centuries of technological innovations—the photograph, the digital image, the scanner, computer bulletin boards, computer networks—passed before Robert Thomas would present us with Amateur Action BBS, a hi-tech rendition of *The 120 Days of Sodom*.

The Marquis, it seems, has finally been topped.

V. SUMMARY OF SIGNIFICANT RESULTS OF THE CARNEGIE MELLON STUDY

The findings of this study include:

(1) Computer networks represent a fundamentally new technology for pornography distribution and consumption. Pornographers and their consumers are utilizing it worldwide.

---

148. HUNT, *supra* note 1, at 35.

(2) Due to computer technology, data is now available on a scale several hundred times that of previously established methods. The introduction of an entirely new methodology for the study of pornography assists in the analysis of these massive quantities of data. The following are the three main components of this new methodology: (a) detailed consumption habits can be accurately tabulated; (b) accurate classifications of pornography consumed can be established using a computer program based upon linguistic parsing; (c) year-by-year comparisons of availability of imagery can be studied to identify changing trends in the marketplace. Comparisons can be broken down according to region, state, BBS, or even by category.

(3) Pedophilic and paraphilic pornography are widely available through various computer networks and protocols such as the Usenet, World Wide Web, and commercial "adult" BBS. The Carnegie Mellon research team was able to identify consumers of these types of materials in more than 2000 cities in all fifty states in the United States, most Canadian provinces, and forty foreign countries, provinces, and territories around the world.

(4) 71% of Usenet pornography comes from commercial "adult" bulletin board services (BBS). This suggests that private BBS must be studied in order to understand the explosive growth of pornography on the Usenet.

(5) At the university studied, Usenet newsgroups containing pornography account for thirteen of the top forty groups. These and worldwide statistics suggest that Usenet pornography must be studied according to intensity of activity, because studying the quantity of bulletin boards would result in deceptively low figures.

(6) 83.5% of all images posted on the Usenet are pornographic. This suggests that the next wave of multimedia products, designed to make the Usenet more "interactive," may be fueled largely by pornography.

(7) Paraphilic, hebephilic, and pedophilic imagery accounted for approximately one-half of nearly six million downloads counted on private "adult" BBS. Hard-core and soft-core imagery were in greater availability than demand, whereas the paraphilias and pedophilic imagery were in greater demand than availability. The availability of, and demand for, imagery depicting vaginal intercourse was relatively small. These numbers emphasize a crucial difference between digital and print media pornography.

(8) CD-ROM technology now enables start-up "adult" BBS to acquire large libraries of images (in excess of 50,000) at little cost. Computers have likewise enabled consumers to acquire vast quantities of pornography at a fraction of their comparative print media cost.

(9) A tremendous gap exists between the availability of, and consumer demand for, most classifications of imagery. Computer pornographers have yet to capitalize on the new wealth of information they now maintain about each consumer.

(10) The market leader among "adult" BBS, Amateur Action BBS, relies on three methods to service its clientele: a) power imbalance and disproportionate representation of women in acts which may be considered degrading; b) deceptive marketing; and c) exploitation of children.

(11) Significant privacy issues are raised concerning the sale by pornographers of detailed records of consumption habits.

These and other findings may assist policymakers and others concerned with the future of Cyberspace to make informed decisions, with reliable data, about the evolving Information Superhighway.

[22]

Vindication and Resistance: A Response to the Carnegie Mellon Study of Pornography in Cyberspace*

CATHARINE A. MACKINNON**

Like a trojan horse, each new communication technology—the printing press, the camera, the moving picture, the tape recorder, the telephone, the television, the video recorder, the VCR, cable, and, now, the computer—has brought pornography with it. Pornography has proliferated with each new tool, democratizing what had been a more elite possession and obsession, spreading the sexual abuse required for its making and promoted through its use.[1] Ever more women and children have had to be used ever more abusively in ever more social sites and human relationships to feed the appetite that each development stimulates and profits from filling. More women have had to live out more of their lives in environments pornography has made. As pornography saturates social life, it also becomes more visible and legitimate, hence less visible as pornography. Always the abuse intensifies and deepens, becoming all the time more intrusive, more hidden, less accountable, with fewer islands of respite. In the process, pornography acquires the social and legal status of its latest technological vehicle, appearing not as pornography, but as books, photographs, films, videos, television programs, and images in cyberspace.

Pornography on computer networks is the latest wave in this tide. Pornography in cyberspace is pornography in society—just broader, deeper, worse, and more of it. Pornography is a technologically sophisticated traffic in women; electronically communicated pornography traffics women in a yet more sophisticated form. But as new technologies open new avenues for exploitation, they can also open new avenues for resistance. As pornography comes ever more into the open, crossing new boundaries, opening new markets and pioneering new harms, it also opens itself to new scrutiny.

Carnegie Mellon's landmark study of pornography in cyberspace is also

---

* © 1995 by Catharine A. MacKinnon.

** Professor of Law, The University of Michigan Law School, co-author with Andrea Dworkin of civil rights ordinances recognizing pornography as a sex equality violation.

1. For documentation of the harm of pornography, see generally U.S. DEP'T OF JUSTICE, ATT'Y GEN. COMM'N ON PORNOGRAPHY: FINAL REPORT (1986); Public Hearing on Ordinances to Add Pornography as Discrimination against Women, Minneapolis City Council Government Operations Committee (Dec. 12-13, 1983) (on file with *The Georgetown Law Journal*); Diana E.H. Russell, *Pornography and Rape: A Causal Model*, 9 POL. PSYCHOL. 41 (1988); Mimi H. Silbert & Ayala M. Pines, *Pornography and Sexual Abuse of Women*, 10 SEX ROLES 857 (1984); Evelyn K. Sommers & James V.P. Check, *An Empirical Investigation of the Role of Pornography in the Verbal and Physical Abuse of Women*, 2 VIOLENCE & VICTIMS 189 (1987).

1960 THE GEORGETOWN LAW JOURNAL [Vol. 83:1959

the first massive study of the consumption of pornography in a natural setting. Access to the users using pornography was made possible by the same expanded access to pornography itself that computer networks provide. As pornography invades offices, homes, and schools through upscale computer technology, and the age of the average consumer potentially drops below its already dropping level, Carnegie Mellon's study signals that the possibilities for exposing pornography are keeping pace with its takeover of public and private spaces. The pornographers are clearly betting that they can survive the light. For those who are hoping they cannot, this new technology, like each one before it, merely raises in a new domain the same questions pornography has always raised: what will it take for pornography to be seen for what it is? what will it take to stop it?

At the same time, like each new technology before it, computer networks shift and focus the social and legal issues raised by pornography in specific ways. Like pornography everywhere else, before and after it becomes Carnegie Mellon's "images" in cyberspace, it is women's lives. Women have resisted being made into pornography, being publicly sexually violated for the pleasure and profit of others, long before the materials made using them hit computer screens. And while resistance to pornography from the standpoint of the women in it has centered on visual materials, real women have often posed for the words as well, in the sense that the men who wrote them often did what they wrote about. The Marquis de Sade, seminal pornographer, was jailed for sexual atrocities he committed against women, acts which included the same rape and torture his pornography celebrates.[2] One wonders how far most pornographers' imagination has extended beyond their experience.

Something is done when women are used to make pornography, and then something is done again and again to those same women whenever their violation—their body, face, name, whatever of identity and dignity can be stolen and sold as sex—is sexually enjoyed, in whatever medium. Most pornography, if circulated in a working environment, would be actionable as sexual harassment.[3] If the materials were non-sexual libel, or

---

2. See ANDREA DWORKIN, PORNOGRAPHY: MEN POSSESSING WOMEN 70-100 (1989). Dworkin writes, "[Sade's] life and writing were of a piece, a whole cloth soaked in the blood of women imagined and real." *Id.* at 70. Sade's pornography also celebrates murder.

One new development in computer technology will shed some light on the centrality of the use of real women to pornography's sexual effectiveness. "Interactive" pornography allows customers to customize on screen the desired stimuli, both visual and auditory, without the acts first being performed on a live woman. If this form of pornography works sexually, pornography could end as a slave trade, while its harms to other women throughout society continue. The more active relation of the user to the material, combined with freeing production from the limitation of human flesh, could escalate the harms done through consumption. Taking this a step further, do we want "mirror world" pornography? *See generally* DAVID H. GELERNTER, MIRROR WORLDS, OR, THE DAY SOFTWARE PUTS THE UNIVERSE IN A SHOEBOX (1991).

3. See Robinson v. Jacksonville Shipyards, Inc., 760 F. Supp. 1486, 1526-27 (M.D. Fla.

the persons involved were understood to be persons rather than prostitutes or sex or "some women" who are "like that," the damage done would be clear. For insisting that a woman is violated every time she is sexually trafficked without her permission, by word or celluloid or databyte, for insisting that each act of sexual consumption predicated on the unfree use of a person damages that person, those who oppose pornography's harms have essentially been accused of witchcraft, or at least of a voodoo sensibility. Pornography in the marketplace of life where there are no equality laws—in the world of books, photographs, films, videos, phone sex, and cable television—has fallen into a reality warp. Harmless fantasy, it is called.

Then, in 1995, Michigan undergraduate Jake Baker sent verbal snuff pornography using a woman undergraduate's name and physical description over the Internet.[4] Verbal pornographers have always had the tools visual pornographers are only beginning to develop that allow them to make pornography, including women presented being killed, *without* actually doing it to real women. Still they use real women, presumably for sexual reasons. Jake Baker did not first commit the rape, torture, and murder he wrote sexually about doing. Because he "fantasized" time, place, and manner of execution into the ether of e-mail, he was arrested and jailed before he could try. He did use the identity of a woman he had seen to make pornography of those acts, and then pimped her on the bulletin board alt.sex.stories, if experience is any guide, for men to masturbate over. With its estimated 270,000 consumers, he had, for a pornographer manqué, unprecedented access to spreading his harm. And the FBI had unprecedented access to him.

Federal authorities investigated and prosecuted Jake Baker for interstate transmission of a threat. He was not prosecuted for fantasizing. He was prosecuted for *doing* something, an act which embodied a clear notion of what else he was *going to do*. A threat is an act in itself, the nature of which is a promise of further action. Clearly, a man's threat is more credible than a woman's complaint. What he said he was going to do was

---

1991) (pornography at work actionable as sexual harassment). *Robinson* was settled after appeal was argued before the Eleventh Circuit. *But cf.* Rabidue v. Osceola Refining Co., 805 F.2d 611, 622 (6th Cir. 1986), *cert. denied*, 481 U.S. 1041 (1987) (pornography at work not actionable as sexual harassment because "[t]he sexually oriented poster displays had a de minimis effect on the plaintiff's work environment when considered in the context of a society that condones and publicly features and commercially exploits open displays . . . ." of such materials).

4. Indictment and Superseding Indictment, Criminal No. 95-80106, United States District Court, Eastern District of Michigan, Southern Division, Feb. 14, 1995 and March 15, 1995. *See also* Kaethe Hoffer, *Jake Baker's Pornography is a real threat to real women*, DET. FREE PRESS, Mar. 20, 1995, at A11. As we go to press, the indictment against Jake Baker was dismissed because the facts were not considered to pose a true threat by legal standards. United States v. Baker, No. 95-80106, slip. op. (E.D. Mich. June 21, 1995) (opinion of Cohn, J.). Appeal is contemplated.

more credible than everything all the women who have ever said they *were* used in pornography against their will have said that men *did* do to them. Jake Baker's trial, if it comes to that, will be based on what "he said;" no "she said" is involved. And even though names are only words, making pornography of a name was seen as part of doing real harm to a real person.[5] We still live in a textual world in which suddenly, if perhaps only momentarily, this injury became visible, real. The point is: it took putting pornography in cyberspace to produce this.

What makes VR (virtual reality) more real than RL (real life)? Why is sexual violation in cyberspace taken more seriously, seen as real, when the same pornography elsewhere in social life has been widely passed off as harmless?[6] Why did it take the Internet to make the harm of coerced pornography real enough to produce an indictment for an *act* against a woman for the first time? What is—and will be—the legal and social relation between telecommunicated pornography on computer networks— the Internet, Usenet, World Wide Web, commercial and personal bulletin boards—and the rest of social life? The Carnegie Mellon study provides a rich context of data and analysis in which to consider these questions. The study also raises new possibilities for resistance by documenting, with unprecedented scientific precision and definitiveness, who is using whom, where, when, and how.

That pornography on computers is part of real life, not apart from it, is made indelibly clear by the Carnegie Mellon study. The content, consumers, and patterns documented in this study are the same as those long observed in the pornography industry and in its tracks through the rest of society.[7] The research team documents beyond question the simplest and most obvious, if some of the most contested, facts. Overwhelmingly, it is men who use pornography—98.9% of these consumers, to be exact.[8] Even

---

5. It may be that it was more possible to see this woman as harmed because she was *not* physically sexually violated. Women lose human status when sexually assaulted, hence tend to be seen not as harmed, but as treated appropriately to their less-than-human condition. On this analysis, this woman's name, having been made into pornography, lost its human status.

6. One episode illustrates this. A digital rapist took over a woman's online identity, raped and otherwise tortured her, and made her behave as though she enjoyed it. This was widely termed "a rape in cyberspace," not a fantasy of a rape, or a story of a rape, or a discussion of a rape in cyberspace. Julian Dibbell, *A Rape in Cyberspace*, VILLAGE VOICE, Dec. 21, 1993, at 36. Netniks have suggested to me that verbal rape is taken seriously when it occurs in cyberspace because the community itself is constructed of words. I am not sure what they think other human communities are constructed of. They have also suggested that, in a virtual community, all are witnesses to rape. But consumers of visual pornography are also witnesses to rape and only enjoy it. Why virtual rape is more real than actual rape remains the question.

7. *See generally* DWORKIN, *supra* note 2; CATHARINE A. MACKINNON, ONLY WORDS (1993).

8. *See* Marty Rimm, *Marketing Pornography on the Information Superhighway*, 83 GEO. L.J. 1849, 1904-05 (1995) [hereinafter *CMU Study*].

many of the women who use it, Carnegie Mellon found, are paid by pornographers to be there, in order to give men the impression, while online, that women enjoy women being violated.[9] Women are disproportionately used in violating ways in pornography. More than ninety-nine percent of all the bestiality pictures studied on the "Amateur Action" bulletin board, for instance, present women having sex with animals,[10] in spite of the fact that nearly fifty percent of the pornography studied has men in it.[11] The more violating the act, the more women have it committed against them.

Moreover, the more violating the material, the more it is wanted, out of proportion to supply. Sex with children is 6.9% by supply, 15.6% by demand.[12] The demand to see vaginal sex (not to be assumed harmless) approaches the vanishing point (6.9% by supply, 4.6% by demand),[13] while the demand for women vaginally penetrated by animals on the "Amateur Action" bulletin board approaches fifty percent of all visual bestiality material.[14] When a woman is marketed being intensively physically harmed, consumer demand doubles; fellatio gets a lukewarm response, but downloads double for "choking."[15] Amateur Action BBS, which distributes the most materials in which physical harm is shown being inflicted on women, is the market leader.[16] The Carnegie Mellon study disproves allegations that those who oppose the pornography industry have distorted its largely benign reality through "the use of highly selected examples."[17] By focusing on pornography *as used*, the Carnegie Mellon results also counter the view that "most commercial pornography . . . is not violent."[18]

Pornography is a huge amount of the activity on the Internet, which aspires to be a universal network to unite the world. When men make new

---

9. *Id.* at 1857 n.17.

10. *Id.* at 1900; *see also id.* Figure 10.

11. *Id.* at 1901.

12. *See id.* at 1891 Table 5; *see also id.* at 1891 Figure 7.

13. *Id.* at 1892.

14. *Id.* at 1900 Figure 10.

15. *Id.* at 1899.

16. Hopefully, future studies of the same database will pursue the longitudinal dimension of user patterns, likely confirming what experiments have found and predicted: men enter the market at the "soft" end and quickly escalate sexually to using the "harder" or more intrusive and violating materials. *See* Dolf Zillman, *Effects of Prolonged Consumption of Pornography, in* PORNOGRAPHY 127, 144-45 (Dolf Zillman & Jennings Bryant eds., 1989) (two weeks into pornography study, participants who had been watching "common" pornography, largely defined as not showing sexual aggression, regularly chose to watch "less common" and more violent forms). *See also* WILLIAM O'DONAHUE & JAMES GEER, HANDBOOK OF SEXUAL DYSFUNCTIONS 67-68, 81 (1993). The Carnegie Mellon study also poses the potential, with all its dangers to privacy, that the prior pornography consumption of a campus rapist might be able to be studied after the fact of the rape. *See CMU Study, supra* note 8, at 1911-12.

17. Nan D. Hunter & Sylvia A. Law, *Brief Amici Curiae of Feminist Anti-Censorship Taskforce, et al. in* American Booksellers Association v. Hudnut, 21 U. MICH. J.L. REF. 69, 100 n.2 (1987).

18. *Id.*

communities,[19] they bring their pornography with them. More than that, they bond through it. Computer networks are not only metaphors for society, they track it and happen within it. Pornography takes up much of the Internet's collective brain. Over eighty percent of all pictures available on the Usenet are pornography.[20] Three-quarters of the total space occupied by the visual boards, the lion's share of multimedia activity, is pornography.[21] The pornography bulletin boards, although a small percentage of the BBS overall, are disproportionately accessed. Use of the most violent and dehumanizing materials is not only the most frequent,[22] it is also geographically widespread. The research team documents consumption of such materials by men in at least 2000 cities in all 50 states of the U.S., most Canadian provinces, where it is more clearly illegal, and thirty-nine foreign countries and territories.[23]

Why it was necessary to log on to see what has been just down the street all along is an interesting question. The greatest achievement of the Carnegie Mellon study lies in simply noticing what is there. Apparently the shift in frame from books and videos to cyberspace has had the effect of revealing to simple empirical documentation that what is done to women in pornography is not a fact of nature or an act of liberation or a private peccadillo to be respectfully skirted but an on-going social atrocity. The significance of this recognition, implicit in the entire study, cannot be overstated. Simply treating the content of pornography as a serious database for detailed empirical measurement is almost unprecedented. The refusal to back off from the findings represented by the study's use of at least some concrete descriptive categories and many illustrative quotations is equally remarkable. The political epistemology of this moment is that cyberspace seems to have made possible a clarity of perspective, a reframing of this form of violence against women, a getting out of society in order to get into it, that no mental trip to Mars and back has previously accomplished.

Computer networks do not, as the research team suggests, market unusually abusive materials and thus "redefin[e] the pornographic land-

---

19. *See generally* HOWARD RHEINGOLD, THE VIRTUAL COMMUNITY: HOMESTEADING ON THE ELECTRONIC FRONTIER (1993) (describing the social aggregate of relationships that forms out of webs of exchanges in cyberspace).

20. *CMU Study, supra* note 8, at 1867, 1914.

21. *Id.* at 1874. It is unfortunately typical of legal discussions to manage to overlook such huge proportions of reality when that reality is pornography. *See, e.g.*, Symposium, *Emerging Media Technology and the First Amendment*, 104 YALE L.J. 1613 (1995) (discussing computer networks extensively and pornography on them virtually not at all, the closest being a passing reference at 1695 n.43).

22. This is deducible from the data in Table 5, although the categories used make this less than conclusive.

23. *CMU Study, supra* note 8, at 1854, 1895.

scape."[24] They reveal it. The study expresses occasional skepticism about the fit between pornography in cyberspace and pornography in the rest of the world. For instance, it states that the most abusive pornography (e.g., bestiality and torture) and child pornography are much easier to get online than otherwise.[25] This confuses what is acknowledged as being acceptable with what is actually accepted in the sense of being widely used. Abusive pornography using adult women is readily available, and anyone who wants child pornography can get it with a little effort. Computer networks *are* contributing significantly to abuse of women and children by facilitating access to such pornography, expanding its reach. However, the fact that these materials become more readily available, while they remain illegal, even highly illegal, does not mean that they are not, in fact, otherwise already available. Again, electronic communication makes more visible to scrutiny a reality that was already pervasive.

Some viewers may also be skeptical that the individuals presented as children in computer pornography are really children. More likely, pornographers are using children when they say they are not. This will become much more common after the U.S. Supreme Court's recent ruling in *X-Citement Video*, which held that, if pornographers do not know that the children they use are children, the pornography made using them is legal.[26] This accomplishes an effective drop in the age of consent for use in child pornography to age of physical maturation—for some girls, 10 or 11 years old—a change that pornographers, including those on computer networks, can be predicted to exploit fully. In fact, the research team documents extensive use of children for sex in this forum.[27]

One feature of computer network pornography that appears to distinguish it from the rest of the pornography market is the fact that it is distributed free of charge. Actually, much child pornography is traded as well as sold.[28] A primary form of the profit in pornography is sexual, pure

---

24. *Id.* at 1906; *see also id.* nn.130-131.

25. *See id.* at 1857, 1892, 1906.

26. United States v. X-Citement Video, 115 S. Ct. 464, 471-72 (1994).

27. *See CMU Study, supra* note 8, at 1902-03; *see also id.* Figures 7, 8, 9, 11.

28. *See Exploited and Missing Children: Hearing Before the Subcomm. on Juvenile Justice of the Senate Comm. on the Judiciary*, 97th Cong., 2nd Sess. 39 (1982) (statement of Dana E. Caro, Inspector-Deputy Asst. Dir., Criminal Investigative Div., F.B.I.) ("It has been determined that the largest percentage of child pornography available in the United States today was originally produced for the self-gratification of the members of this culture and was not necessarily produced for any commercial purpose. Pedophiles maintain correspondence and exchange sexual [sic] explicit photographs with other members of this subculture."); Albert H. Belanger et al., *Typology of Sex Rings Exploiting Children, in* CHILD PORNOGRAPHY AND SEX RINGS 79 (Ann W. Burgess & Marieanne L. Clark eds., 1984) (32 of 38 child pornography rings studied were either strictly or partially producing materials for personal use); Gregory Loken, *The Federal Battle Against Child Sexual Exploitation: Proposals for Reform*, 9 HARV. WOMEN'S L.J. 105, 112 (1986).

and simple. Meantime, with computer networks now being used for trafficking, community standards in yet another rapidly expanding elite are created that are toxic to women's humanity and potentiating to male dominance, which has to be good for business. The pornographers of organized crime are at work, with some of the best technical minds money can buy, figuring out how to make money pimping women in cyberspace.[29]

Each new technology raises anew the question of the adequacy of legal approaches. Cyberspace makes vivid, if it was not already, the inefficacy of current obscenity law, which coexists with this exploding market in human abuse, as it has with every other means of sexual trafficking. Just as the harms pornography does are no different online than anywhere else, the legal approach taken to them need be no different. It need only be effective. Computer networks present a newly democratic, yet newly elite, mass form of pornography becoming less elite by the minute, just as pornography always has. In whatever form pornography exists, its harms remain harms to the equality of women, so it is through addressing these harms that pornography can be confronted. Civil rights legislation designed to remedy pornography's harms at their point of impact is well suited to this task.[30]

Computer technology does pose newly complex issues of anonymity and privacy. Unidentified speech has always presented dangers of harassment and reputational destruction but never before on this scale.[31] Privacy has always been fragile, but never before has it been possible to find out what a person is reading while they are reading it. Technical problems of proving liability and measuring damages also exist, although now that the pornographers are figuring out how to get paid for pornography in cyberspace, many of these problems will be solved, as the transactions will leave a trace. Once a legal approach through actual harms is taken, accountability for pornography on computer networks poses no new conceptual prob-

---

29. *See South Pointe, The Adult Entertainment Company Adds Software Development Team with Acquisition*, PR NEWSWIRE, Nov. 3, 1994 (chronicling South Pointe's purchase of Innovative Data Concepts, a high tech software developer); John R. Wilke, *Porn Broker: A Publicly Held Firm Turns X-Rated Videos Into a Hot Business*, WALL ST. J., July 11, 1994, at A1 (describing Kenneth Guarino, South Pointe's largest shareholder (and until July 28, 1994, its chairman, CEO and director) and long-time pornographer with government-alleged links to Gambino crime family).

30. *See* ANDREA DWORKIN & CATHARINE A. MACKINNON, PORNOGRAPHY AND CIVIL RIGHTS: A NEW DAY FOR WOMEN'S EQUALITY (1988) for a detailed discussion of this approach and examples of civil laws that could be used against injuries proven to be produced by pornography, however trafficked.

31. *See* McIntyre v. Ohio Election Comm'n, 115 S. Ct. 1511 (1995) (speech value of anonymity); Comment, *Who are You? Identity and Anonymity in Cyberspace*, 55 U. PITT. L. REV. 1177, 1185-94 (1994) (discussing the historical protection of anonymity in law and the difficulties of continuing that protection in cyberspace); Lindsay Van Gelder, *The Strange Case of the Electronic Lover*, MS. MAG., Oct. 1985, at 94 (deception through anonymity). Anonymous remailers raise special difficulties.

lems, only practical problems of delivery.[32] The legal problem is, women hurt by pornography have no rights against it anywhere. If circulating pornography in this new, still legitimate, forum reframes the same old abuse to alter that impunity, this new technology will be the first to be revolutionary.

The Carnegie Mellon research team has had the vision to see, the technical acumen to capture, and the courage to expose what is there. Beyond further information to be analyzed and organizing opportunities to be pursued, the question the study poses for pornography in cyberspace is the same as pornography poses everywhere else: whether anything will be done about it.

---

32. This seems implicit in Eugene Volokh's observation that while "the advent of electronic communications may change how child pornography is distributed, . . . I don't see how it would change the rules relating to child pornography." Eugene Volokh, *Cheap Speech and What It Will Do,* 104 Yale L.J. 1805, 1844 (1995) (footnote omitted). This is because existing child pornography laws, like the sex equality approach, address the *harm* done by the materials, making how they are trafficked incidental. Volokh does not discuss pornography of adult women.

[23]

A Detailed Analysis of the Conceptual, Logical, and Methodological Flaws in the Article: "Marketing Pornography on the Information Superhighway

July 2, 1995 (version 1.01)
Donna L. Hoffman & Thomas P. Novak
Associate Professors of Management
Co-Directors, Project 2000
Owen Graduate School of Management
Vanderbilt University

In this critique, we provide a detailed analysis of the recent article "Marketing Pornography on the Information Superhighway..." (Rimm 1995, *Georgetown Law Journal*, Volume 83, June, pp. 1849-1934) that was also the subject of a recent *Time* cover story (Elmer-DeWitt, July 3, 1995). For a detailed critique of the *Time* article, see Hoffman & Novak (July 1, 1995, version 1.01).

First, we offer general comments about the study. We criticize thestudy on conceptual, logical, and process grounds, including: 1) misrepresentation, 2) manipulation, 3) lack of objectivity, and 4) methodological flaws. Second, we provide a series of detailed examples that support our general conclusions of these four major difficulties. For ease of exposition, these specific comments follow the order of the article.

Our objective with this note is to begin a constructive and open critique process. Thus, our note is not meant to be an exhaustive cataloging of the lapses, discrepancies, inconsistencies, and errors in this article, only a summary of those we consider to be among the most severe.

We do not debate the existence of pornography in "cyberspace." Indeed, pornography exists and is transmitted through many media, including cable television, books and magazines, video tapes, private "adult" bulletin boards, the postal mail, computer networks, interactive multimedia like CDROM, fax, and telephone, to name a few. What we dispute are the findings presented in this study concerning its extent and consumption on what Rimm calls the "information superhighway." The critically important national debate over first amendment rights and restrictions on the Internet and other emerging media requires facts and informed opinion, not hysteria.

The critique is also important because the *Time* cover story as given the Rimm study a credibility it does not deserve. If it is difficult for a professional journalist to evaluate the validity of such research, it is reasonable to assume that many others will have difficulties, as well.

The general and specific comments that follow represent our professional opinion of the critical flaws and errors in the Rimm study. Our critique has benefitted from the impassioned discussions in the WELL Media conference (topic 1029), of this study and the larger debates of media responsibility and first amendment rights.

1

GENERAL COMMENTS

Misrepresentation

The study is positioned as "marketing pornography on the information superhighway." Yet, it deals neither with marketing nor the information superhighway, and displays a considerable lack of understanding of both areas.

Out of 148 footnotes in Rimm's manuscript, only one (footnote 22) cites a reference to a marketing journal. For a study purporting to deal with "marketing pornography on the information superhighway," this demonstrates a blatant disregard and ignorance of the marketing literature. As "marketing" appears as the first word in the title of this manuscript, and the word "marketing" appears frequently throughout the manuscript, it is particularly disturbing that Rimm does not support any of his "marketing" insights with references to the marketing literature.

This is a study of descriptions of pornographic images on selected adult BBS in the United States. The author finds, not surprisingly, that adult BBSs contain pornography. While the author attempts to generalize beyond this domain to the "Information Superhighway," no generalization is possible, and the results of this study should not be used for this purpose. Unfortunately, the juxtaposition of unrelated analyses of adult BBSs and Usenet newsgroups may create in the casual reader's mind the impression that what is stated about adult BBSs is also true of the "Information Highway" as a whole. We caution, in the strongest possible terms, against such mis-interpretation on the part of the casual reader.

Rimm concludes his study by saying (p.1915) "These and other findings may assist policymakers and others concerned with the future of Cyberspace to make informed decisions, with reliable data, about the evolving Information Superhighway." Unfortunately, this paper provides no actionable insights for policy-makers about the future of Cyberspace, as the results, at the maximum, can only be generalized to all adult BBSs in the United States.

The study is positioned as the product of a "research team" at Carnegie Mellon University. It is described throughout as the "Carnegie Mellon study" and it is frequently mentioned that the "research team" estimated this percentage or counted that set of items. Yet, nowhere is it mentioned that Rimm was an undergraduate electrical engineering student at CMU at the time the study was performed. Instead, Rimm is listed as a "Researcher" and "Principal Investigator." (Note that the four funding sources are identified only as coming from Carnegie, but the type and kind of grants these are is not revealed.) This positioning capitalizes upon the reputation of Carnegie Mellon University, lends an air of authority and credibility to the paper, and increases Rimm's own authority by association.

The article is sole-authored. Not a single member of the extensive research team shared in the credit for the authorship of this paper. Given established standards of authorship as ownership of intellectual property in the academic and scientific community, we can only infer from this that no one on the "research team" felt their contributions merited the significance of shared authorship.

2

Manipulation

The study was not subjected to peer-review. The manuscript was deliberately "embargoed" for at least six months prior to publication, and was not made available to interested researchers. This is highly unusual. The paper was submitted to a law journal which is not peer-reviewed, despite the fact that it probably would be more appropriate in a behavioral science or public policy journal (most of which are peer-reviewed). Since law journals have no one on the board to evaluate the merits of the methodology and likely not even the distinctions among BBSs, Usenet news groups, the Web, and the Internet, we offer the following hypothesis: did Rimm place his article somewhere where it would appear credible and go unchallenged?

At some point, an agreement was negotiated in which *Time Magazine* obtained an advance copy of the manuscript in exchange for an "exclusive." This was used in preparation of the July 3, 1995 *Time* cover story written by Philip Elmer-DeWitt. Given the vast array of conceptual, logical, and methodological flaws in this study, documented thoroughly below, *Time* magazine behaved irresponsibly in accepting the statements made by Rimm in his manuscript at face value. *Time* had a responsibility to its readers to do its own peer reviewing, despite the embargo. Indeed, *Time* reporters were made aware that the study appeared to have serious conceptual, logical, and methodological flaws that *Time* needed to investigate prior to reporting its story. If *Time* was not able to evaluate the manuscript on its own, *Time* should have held the story until the manuscript was publicly available, so that expert opinion could have been solicited, or sought its own panel of objective experts for a "private" peer review. In this way, *Time* would likely have recognized the study for what it was and not what it purported to be and prepared a balanced, critical report on the subject of digital pornography. Instead, *Time* presented, around lurid and sensationalistic art, an uncritical and unquestioning report on "cyberporn" based on Rimm's flawed study. This has had the extremely unfortunate effect of giving the study an instant credibility that is not warranted nor deserved and fueling the growing movement toward first amendment restrictions and censorship.

The study appears to be driven by an underlying political agenda. It is difficult to read the paper in its entirety and not come away with the conclusion that it is written in a manner which provides policymakers with the ammunition they need to obtain support for legislation that would censor certain types of information on the Internet and other emerging media.

Lack of Objectivity

Rimm makes numerous unsubstantiated causal statements. These causal statements are not supported by the data. In many cases, the causal statements are inflammatory and outrageous. Sometimes they are ridiculous. Additionally, data are often interpreted in a biased and selective manner.

Methodological Flaws

The article is rife with methodological flaws, several of them extremely serious. The origins of

3

many numbers presented in the article are difficult, if not impossible,to determine. Much greater attention is paid to sensationalistic and inflammatory descriptions of image files, for example, than accurate descriptions of survey methodology. In fact, in many cases important aspects of the methodology are simply not described at all. Methodological details are either omitted entirely or presented in such sparse detail that it is impossible for other researchers to 1) determine what Rimm actually did and 2) replicate the results.

The study contains numerous discrepancies that cannot be resolved and raises a series of fundamental procedural, analytic, and implementation questions that can only be addressed outside of the article itself.

Operational definitions of "pornography" are ad-hoc, inconsistent, and misleading.

Much of the data presented is consistently misinterpreted, particularly the Usenet data.

The paper describes the results in a confusing manner which makes it very difficult to determine what Rimm actually did. The manuscript is way too long and rambles. It is organized in such a manner as to obscure the methodological issues. This makes it difficult for the casual reader to draw his or her own conclusions about the merits of particular results from the study. For example, discussions of Usenet readership at a single university are interwoven with worldwide Usenet readership statistics. This is confusing and makes it easier to misinterpret his results, thinking that he might be talking about Usenet in general when in fact he is only talking about readership at a single university. Definitions of online media are similarly presented in such a way that the reader is likely to draw the conclusion that BBSs, Usenet news groups, the World Wide Web, and the Information Superhighway are all one and the same, and what applies in one domain, is relevant to all.

Rimm makes numerous unsubstantiated leaps of faith in his logical arguments.

The research methodology is not up to the rigorous standards of a peer-reviewed journal.

The study procedure raises a number of troubling ethical questions.

SPECIFIC COMMENTS

Title and acknowledgement (p. 1849)

The article's title states it concerns the marketing of pornography on the so-called "information superhighway," yet it appears in a law journal that is, by custom, not rigorously peer-reviewed. The acknowledgement indicates that organizations and experts in pornography were consulted (but not listed), but no organizations or experts conversant in marketing research, survey methodology, and marketing on the Internet and related online markets appear to have been consulted.

4

I. Overview (pp. 1849-1864)

Rimm: "The ... study adopts the "definition" utilized in current everyday practice by computer pornographers. Accordingly, "pornography" is defined here to include the depiction of actual sexual contact [hereinafter "hard-core"] and depiction of mere nudity or lascivious exhibition [hereinafter "soft-core"]...Accordingly, data was (sic) collected for this article only from bulletin board systems (BBS) which clearly marketed their image portfolios as "adult" rather than "artistic." Any BBS or World Wide Web site which made even a modest attempt to promote itself as "artistic" or "informational" was excluded." (fn. 1)

Rimm's definition of pornography is central to his study. It is therefore reasonable to expect a detailed analysis of what pornography is, along with arguments for how it may be defined and measured. Such discussion would include the advantages and disadvantages of each measurement approach and lead to a reasoned position of the operational definition employed in the study.

Because the results of his study depend on his definition and measurement scheme, it is surprising that the definition he proposes is so weakly supported, and fluid besides. For example, in analysis to follow, Usenet newsgroups appear to be classified as "pornographic" if they contain the word "sex" in the title (except for alt.safe.sex), or if he judges them to be so. Further, the footnote is misleading, because it implies that Rimm studied the Web with the same energy that he applied to adult BBSs, when in fact, he only searched the Web in order to locate and provide a simple count of sites judged to be "sex-related." (Appendix C, p. 1923 ff).

Rimm: It is essential to note that Usenet and the World Wide Web are merely different protocols." (p. 1869)

This statement is erroneous and suggests a disturbing misunderstanding of the nature of online media, particularly as they relate to consumers and providers. For definitions and discussion, see Hoffman and Novak's paper on Marketing in Computer-Mediated Environments (http:/www2000. ogsm. vanderbilt. educme.conceptual.foundations.html)

Rimm: "...this article discusses only the content and consumption patterns of sexual imagery currently available on the Internet and "adult" BBS..." (fn. 2)

This statement is misleading because, in fact, the article discusses the content analysis of descriptive listings of images obtained from adult BBSs and the readership data from selected Usenet newsgroups. Usenet readership data can only tell that a Usenet group was accessed, but does not tell if any text files were read or any images were downloaded.

Rimm: "Every time consumers log on, their transactions assist pornographers in compiling databases of information about their buying habits and sexual tastes. The more sophisticated computer pornographers are using these databases to develop mathematical models to determine which images they should try to market aggressively."(pp. 1850-51)

Every time consumers log on to what? In the final analysis the article provides very little evidence, other than anecdotal or case study, to support the idea that pornographers are engaging in such activities.

Rimm: "Computer pornographers are also moving from a market saturation policy to a market segmentation, or even individualized, marketing phase." (p. 1851)

The statement is misleading because it implies that pornographers have a strategic policy which is now shifting. However, the article supplies no evidence of the original policy, let alone the shift to a market segmentation strategy.

Rimm: "It is clear that pornography is being vigorously marketed in increasingly sophisticated ways and has now found a receptive audience in a wide variety of computer environments." (p. 1852)

The article supplies no evidence that pornography is being "vigorously marketed," nor does it define marketing. The study does not investigate audience receptivity in a "wide variety of computer environments." Instead, it studies download records from selected be supported from the research presented in this paper.

Rimm: "Information Superhighway' and 'Cyberspace' are used to refer to any of the following: Internet, Usenet, World Wide Web, BBS, other multimedia telephone, computer, and cable networks." (fn. 7)

These two definitions are misleading and do not conform to commonly understood meanings of the terms by researchers and experts in the field.

Rimm: In the top paragraph on page 1853, Rimm argues that his study is the first to systematically examine "pornography on the Information Superhighway," and that it is now possible to obtain "vast amounts of information about the distribution and consumption" of pornography on a much larger scale than previously possible.

Are there any previous studies of pornography on the "Information Superhighway," even if unsystematic? In what ways does this study have to do with the "Information Superhighway?" A framework should be developed for adult BBSs - the focus of this study - in the context of the "information superhighway." For example, what percent of traffic do adult BBSs represent of the total "highway?" What percent of users of the "highway" use adult BBSs? What do the distributions look like nationally and internationally? And so on.

Rimm: "...it maybe be difficult for researchers to repeat this study, as much valuable data is no longer publicly available." (fn. 9)

This is an astonishing and intellectually suspect statement, almost transparent in its effort to set up a case that this study cannot be falsified. If subsequent research shows disagreement with the results of this study, Rimm can discount such results by saying that it could not be repeated anyway. Instead, good scientific practice demands Rimm work to show how the study can be replicated by subsequent researchers. However, as analysis below argues, even the analyses here cannot be replicated because Rimm provides no details of methodology which would enable that to happen.

Rimm: The first full paragraph on page 1853 discusses the 917,410 "pornographic" items downloaded 8.5 million times that form the bulk of the study.

Subsequent sections of the paper show that this paragraph is misleading in the extreme, as is the article title. The title of the article suggests the research will concern a "survey of 917,410 images, descriptions, short stories and animations downloaded 8.5 million times." (Note that Rimm does not perform "survey research" in this study, as no one is surveyed.)

On page 1853, the 917,410 items are broken down as:
*   450,620 items downloaded 6.4 million times from 68 adult BBSs
*   75,000 items with an unspecified number of downloads from 6 adult BBSs
*   391,790 items with no download information from 7 adult BBSs

These items include images, animations, and text files. Rimm says that 10,000 "actual images" were "randomly downloaded" from adult BBSs, the Usenet or CD-ROM and used to verify the accuracy of the descriptive listings. Rimm does not, however, 1) report the methodology used to randomly select the images, 2) provide frequency distributions of the images across the media they were obtained from, 3) specify the exact media used to obtain the listings (e.g. which CDROMS?), nor 4) indicate how the accuracy verification procedure was performed.

In footnote 10 on page 1853, Rimm says the original number of downloads was counted at 6.4 million and that "a total of 5.5 million downloads are analyzed here." (emphasis ours). He explains that the other "0.9 million concern animations, text, and other miscellaneous files" which he presumably excluded from analysis. He continues that "an additional 2.1 million downloads was later obtained from...Amateur Action BBS. In this way, the total number of downloads tabulated is 8.5 million."

We note that this tabulation of 8.5 million downloads is misleading for two reasons: 1) Rimm did not specify the period of time in which the 8.5 million downloads accumulated. Was it one month? One year? Five years? Ten years? 2) Rimm did not actually analyze 8.5 million unique downloads, as at least some were apparently excluded from analysis.

7

While 8.5 million exposures to pornographic images may sound like a large number, let us put it into perspective. Suppose a pornographic newsstand magazine had a circulation of 500,000, including subscriptions, newsstand sales and pass-along readership. If there were 10

pornographic photographs in a single issue of this magazine, there would be 5 million "exposures" in this single issue alone. Thus, 8.5 million must be set in a context which specifies the time period, and the equivalent exposures in "competing" media during this time period.

Rimm: "A total of 292,114 image descriptions remained and are discussed here. At least 36% of the images studied were identified as having been distributed by two or more "adult" BBS." (p. 1854)

Apparently, Rimm analyzed 292,114 descriptive listings of images only, presumably representing 5.5 million downloads. No indication is given of how duplicates were identified as such, nor distributed across the listings, either by individual adult BBS or by, for example, geographic region.

In footnote 11 on page 1854, Rimm suggests that whatever method was used to identify duplicates had its validity confirmed by randomly sampling 100 "suspected duplicates," and presumably examining them. Yet, he does not indicate how he "suspected" them in the first place, how they were sampled, and how the validity was "confirmed," as no details or statistics are provided to support the statements.

Rimm: Part II of this article addresses three issues concerning pornography on the Usenet: (1) the percentage of all images available on Usenet that are pornographic; (2) the popularity of pornographic boards in comparison to non-pornographic boards, at both a university studied and worldwide; and (3) the origins of pornographic imagery on the Usenet. (p. 1854)

Our critique of Part II will show that due to serious methodological flaws, the study does not, in fact, provide accurate data on these issues.

Rimm: All BBS data was (sic) collected in May and June 1994, unless otherwise noted. (p. 1855). In footnote 15 on page 1856, Rimm states that the study "tracks image repertoires over a fourteen-year period." No clarification is provided here or subsequently to reconcile the discrepancy between the two-month data collection period and the 14 years or to illuminate on how the study follows "image repertoires" longitudinally.

Rimm: "...this study focuses entirely upon what people actually consume, not what they say they consume; it thus provides a more accurate measure of actual consumption." (p. 1855)

Rimm analyzes aggregate download counts of descriptive listings of images available on adult

BBSs. Although download patterns would be expected to correlate with actual consumption (i.e. viewing), we do not know the extent to which individuals actually looked at the images (or, indeed, whether they looked at all). These limitations are not addressed in the study and no thoughtful discussion of the consumption experience is ever provided. Further, absolutely no download behavior on Usenet news groups was ever examined by Rimm.

Rimm: Because the data is (sic) in many respects exhaustive, statistical techniques and assumptions that are commonly invoked to impute general consumer behavior are not necessary for this dataset. Thus the research team considers the inferences drawn highly robust." (p. 1856)

Are the data really exhaustive of adult BBS? Rimm does not provide evidence that the listings obtained from the BBSs represent a census. Further, the statement that statistics are not necessary for these data is astonishing. No evidence, statistical or otherwise, is ever provided in the article that the inferences drawn from these data are, indeed, "robust."

Rimm: "The ... study examine 917,410 images, image descriptions, short stories, and short films..." (fn. 15)

Yet earlier on page 1854 and footnote 10 on page 1853, Rimm suggests he deleted all but the images from the database under consideration and retained 292,114 for "discussion." Thus, how many items did the study actually examine?

Rimm: "The study results suggest a tremendous rift between the sexual activities in which Americans claim to engage, as reported most recently by the study Sex in America, and the sexually explicit activities presented in images that many Americans consume." (p. 1857)

This statement is misleading, because Rimm did not study individuals, but aggregate download counts of descriptive listings of images available on adult BBSs. The Sex in America study surveyed the general population, and did not examine individuals' consumption behavior as measured in downloads on adult BBSs in the United States. In other words, the two studies examine two completely different populations. Thus, there is no basis for the conclusion that a "tremendous rift" exists and the statement represents an "apples and oranges" comparison.

Rimm: "Among the ultimate findings of this study are that digitized pornographic images are widely circulated in all areas of the country and that due to market forces, digitized pornographic images treat themes...which are not otherwise widely available." (p. 1857)

The conclusion is not supported by the data because Rimm examined only downloads of pornography on adult BBSs and readership statistics of selected Usenet newsgroups. He did not examine the distribution or consumption of pornography, by category or otherwise, in other media, nor does he provide evidence from others' examination. Thus, there is no basis for the comparison.

9

Rimm: "One of the more intriguing questions raised by this study is whether the general population will demand the same types of imagery currently in high demand among computer users." (p. 1857)

This statement is misleading. All computer users? Some computer users? How many are "demanding" it now? What types? Indeed, why would the general population be expected to exhibit the same types of preferences as subscribers to adult BBSs, which is the only group of "computer users" for which Rimm studied imagery?

Rimm: "The widespread availability of pornography on computer networks may have a profound effect on those who wish to utilize the emerging National Information Infrastructure for non-pornographic purposes." (p. 1858)
This statement is blatantly biased. Rimm did not examine the extent of pornography on "computer networks" such as the Internet or online services, and provides no discussion, nor references to balanced discussion of these issues.

Rimm: "While it may not be possible in the next decade for such technology to automatically classify images with the same precision as the Carnegie Mellon linguistic parsing software..." (fn. 21)

The precision of the noted software is never established, let alone described in any detail.

Rimm: "More than two dozen faculty, staff, graduate and undergraduate students at Carnegie Mellon University contributed in some manner to this study." (p. 1861)

Yet in fact, the article is a sole-authored study, performed when the author was an undergraduate student in Electrical Engineering, that was not subjected to the usual rigors of peer-review and revision that are commonfor this type of research. No one, other than Rimm, has accepted responsibility for the intellectual property in this study. Further, the individuals listed on page 1849 represent an acknowledgement by Rimm, rather than an endorsement by all of them of the manuscript.

Rimm: "After a year of exploring the Internet, Usenet, World Wide Web, and computer Bulletin Board Systems (BBS), the research team discovered that one of the largest (if not the largest) recreational applications of users of computer networks was the distribution and consumption of sexually explicit imagery." (p. 1861)

As we continue to note, Rimm's study concerns download patterns on selected adult BBSs and readership statisticson selected Usenet newsgroups. Rimm may have explored these systems, but provides no evidence for the conclusion stated above. Further, Rimm's statement is misleading, as it implies that the largest recreational application is not just in downloads (i.e. "consumption"), but also in uploads (i.e. "distribution"). Rimm's study does not examine uploads.

10

Rimm: An unusual amount of data was (sic) freely available from commercial "adult" BBS primarily as a consequence of the evolution of the online industry. Large commercial BBS such as American Online, Compuserve, and Prodigy do not carry hard-core pornographic imagery, either for legal or policy reasons. As a consequence, several thousand comparatively small "adult" BBS have sprung up across the country." (p. 1861)

The statements are misleading because no evidence is provided to support the conclusion of a causal link between activities on commercial online services and adult BBSs.

Rimm: "In many instances, the research team was able to persuade the owners of these BBS to provide information about subscriber consumption habits." (p. 1862)

This is a troubling statement. How was Rimm able to obtain such consent? Was it "informed consent?" Did Rimm provide full disclosure to these operators about the nature and objectives of his study? Did Rimm "debrief" them afterwards? Did he get the permission of the subscribers of these BBSs to examine information about their consumption habits? Did Rimm submit a proposal of his methodology for such "persuasion" to the University Human Subjects Committee? Did they approve the research and the methodology?

II. Usenet (pp. 1865-1876)

Rimm: "This article will first discuss the methodology and results of the study of Usenet images and will then explain the methodology and results of the study of BBS images." (p. 1865)

Footnote 28 (p. 1865) appended to this sentence refers the reader to footnotes 25-27 "for discussion of the distinction between the Usenet and commercial BBS." Such distinctions are critical for correct interpretation of Rimm's results and do not belong in footnotes. Nevertheless, examination of the footnotes reveals the following: footnote 25 "assumes that the reader has a basic understanding of Usenet and BBS." (p. 1862), and refers to reader to several books and a magazine; footnote 26 cites a 20-year old FCC document on "MTS and Wats," (p. 1863) and footnote 27 cites a brochure "on file with the Georgetown Law Journal" (p. 1864).

Pornographic vs nonpornographic imagery in the alt.binaries groups

Rimm: Rimm states that he examined "[a]ll of the Usenet newsgroups with the prefix 'alt.binaries'" from September 21-September 27, 1994 and goes on to say that "[t]he number of new images posted each day was tabulated for both pornographic and non-pornographic newsgroups." (p. 1865)

No rationale for excluding audio and text is provided other than they were "not the subject of this study." Does it make sense to look at all types of pornography on the Usenet and compare that to all other types of information? Rimm does not indicate how he determined which alt.binaries groups were pornographic and which were not.

In what manner did Rimm control for duplicates, resent, or non-pornographic images? Did Rimm counts posts or a complete image? (Note that a single image could have up to 10 more files to make it complete.) In effect, what was the unit of analysis: a post or an image? On Saturday, 7/1/95, a colleague counted the number of posts on alt.binaries.pictures.erotica and found 1650 posts. One image was 41 posts long and represented 2.5% of the message volume alone. The article is moot on these important methodological details.

Popularity of Pornographic vs NonPornographic Usenet Newsgroups

Rimm: "The research team was also able to examine the online habits of 4227 users at a mid-
       sized, private university in the northeast." (p. 1865)

This raises troubling issues. How was Rimm able to conduct such examination? Did he obtain "informed consent" from each student? Did Rimm provide full disclosure to these students about the nature and objectives of his study? Did Rimm "debrief" them afterwards? Did the University Human Subjects Committee approve this examination? It is curious that Rimm argues in numerous places about the possible public policy implications of his work, but does not raise the ethical implications of conducting such research (only the implications of reporting it). See, for example, footnote 40 on page 1869, where he discusses his decision not to report "detailed demographics of the university population of computer pornography consumers" but makes no mention of whether it is appropriate to gather the data in the first place.

Rimm: In footnote 30 on page 1865, Rimm argues that the 11% of computer users at the
       privateuniversity "block" site statisticians from monitoring in order to "avoid detection"
       of their online activities. After discussing a behavioral analysis of child molesters, he
       proposes that "it is possible that some Internet users who block their accounts prefer
       sexual images of children and wish to avoid detection."

This argument is one of the more outrageous in the paper and represents an invalid causal link. In the first place, there is no evidence that the 11% who "block" their activities are child molesters, and in the second place, there is no evidence that the 11% are representative of the broader population of Internet users. Thus, there is no basis for the proposal that Internet users who do not wish their activities monitored prefer to look at "sexual images of children."

Percent of pornographic imagery in Usenet binaries groups

Rimm: "Among the pornographic newsgroups, 4206 image posts were counted, or 83.5% of
       the total posts." (p. 1867)

The interpretation is incorrect and the number is grossly inflated. It is based upon 17 alt.binaries groups that Rimm considered "pornographic" and 15 alt.binaries group that Rimm considered "non-pornographic." However, Rimm does not provide a listing of the names of these groups, no distributions of posts in these groups, and no methodological discussion of how he counted and determined posts were either pornographic or not, so there is no objective evidence of whether these groups are, in fact, "pornographic."

Also, no information is provided on the degree to which these 32 groups comprise the complete universe of Usenet imagery. Further, as the methodology for counting the number of images is not specified, it is likely that even given Rimm's definitions and selection of 32 groups, the percentage is inflated due to the inclusion of non-pornographic next comments and multi-part images in the counts. What are the distributions of posts, by type of post (imagery, text, audio) in each of these newsgroups? What were the total numbers of posts to each group and to each set of groups and to Usenet overall during the period? How did Rimm determine that the 4206 image posts to the 17 supposed pornographic alt.binaries groups are, in fact, pornographic?

A more accurate interpretation is that of 83.5% of the images posted to 32 alt.binaries newsgroups came from 17 groups that Rimm determined were pornographic.
To make matters worse, Rimm grossly overgeneralizes his results in footnote 36 (p. 1868) and his summary (p. 1914): "83.5% of all images posted on the Usenet are pornographic." This is a particularly misleading misinterpretation of his narrow result.

Misleading interpretation of "popularity" of types of Usenet newsgroups

Rimm: (p. 1849) "'Pornography' is defined here to include the depiction of actual sexual contact...and depiction of mere nudity or lascivious exhibition."

Rimm uses bold text to identify "newsgroups identified as having pornographic content" in Table 1 and Table 2. Included among pornographic newsgroups are "alt.sex" and "alt.binaries.pictures.supermodels." This is not consistent with Rimm's stated definition of pornography, as there is little of what would be considered pornographic content in these groups. It is a biased and inflammatory characterization of these Usenet groups.

The column headings in Table 1 are not explained. Is the user base 4227 from page 1865 or some other number? This particular site receives only 3600 (p. 1870) of the 14,000 Usenet newsgroups (p. 1862) or only 25.7% of all groups. This seems like a small percentage of total groups. Is it? What do the percentages at other institutions look like? Without knowing this, it is difficult to generalize beyond this site to the entire Usenet domain. What would happen if we included data from the other 10,000+ sites?

It is truly astonishing that there are no .comp or .news groups in the Top 40 Usenet news group at the university studied. Indeed, if the university is Carnegie Mellon, this is simply unbelievable. By this chart, only 99 readers are required in order to put it at number 40.

13

Additionally, the Top 40 newsgroups in Table 1 differ dramatically from the Top 40 overall, according to the arbitron statistics.

Rimm: In footnote 30 on page 1865, Rimm argues that "there is no reason to believe consumption at the university study differs from that of other universities from which pornographic Usenet newsgroups can be accessed."

But, in fact, there are reasons to believe otherwise. A study conducted at Vanderbilt University (Varki 1995) as part of the requirements for a doctoral seminar on "Marketing in Computer-Mediated Environments" showed that the top Usenet news groups in terms of number of postings differs markedly and in important ways from the Top 40 list presented in Table 2 (p. 1872). Since this is a worldwide listing, intuition alone would suggest the likely presence of regional differences, at the least. In any event, no evidence is presented to support his reasoning in footnote 30.

All of these problems suggest that the university in question may actually be fairly atypical in its use of Usenet newsgroups, which limits its generalizability.

Rimm: "In broad terms, the research indicated that pornographic newsgroups are accessed more frequently during the school year than during summer recess. This suggests that, in comparison to teachers, faculty, and staff, a disproportionately large number of students access Usenet pornography." (pp. 1969-1870)

In fact, the conclusion does not follow since Rimm does not present evidence (e.g. counts, frequencies, and proportions) indicating how many students access pornography relative to the other groups. Rimm does not provide a version of Table 1 for the academic year, so that readers may draw their own conclusions.

Rimm: "The   fact   that   alt.sex.stories   is   currently   more   popular   than alt.sex.pictures.binaries.erotica has been often misinterpreted as an indication that stories are more popular than images." (p.1871)

In fact, Rimm presents no evidence that such "misinterpretation" exists, although we can assume the interpretation exists. His alternative explanation is interesting, but no data are offered on how many users are discouraged by the level of technical sophistication required to access these groups. Indeed, a rival hypothesis is that these groups are accessed by a singularly technically sophisticated user, not the reverse.

Percentage of sites containing "pornographic" Usenet newsgroups

Rimm: (p. 1871) "The worldwide statistics suggest that Usenet hosts appear less willing to offer their readers access to pornographic newsgroups than other types of newsgroups. 81.2% of the sites offer access to non-pornographic newsgroups, whereas only 55.8% of the sites offered their readers access to the pornographic newsgroups."

14

In our opinion, Rimm has clearly misinterpreted the data. An examination of Tables 2 and 3 will immediately reveal that the important distinction is not between "pornographic" and "non-pornographic" groups, but between "alt" and "non-alt" hierarchies. All Rimm's "pornographic" groups are from the "alt" hierarchy. No alt group in Tables 2 and 3 is carried by more than 66% of sites. While alt.binaries.pictures.erotic (one of Rimm's "pornographic" groups) is carried by 53% of sites, alt.binaries.pictures (a "non-pornographic" group) is carried by only 49%, and alt.binaries.sounds.tv is carried by only 34% of sites.

Misleading portrayal of newsgroup readership

Rimm: (p. 1873) "The newsgroups are ranked in Table 2 by the estimated total number of readers worldwide."

Rimm identifies Brian Reid's "arbitron" script as the source of the data in Table 2. However, Rimm does not provide Reid's caveat on exactly what "readership" really means. Reid (Usenet Readership Summary Report for May 95) is careful to note that:

> "To 'read' a newsgroup means to have been presented with the opportunity to look at least one message in it." ... "Assuming that 'reading a group' is roughly the same as 'thumbing through a magazine', in that you don't necessarily have to read anything, but you have to browse through it and see what is there."

This is a critical point. There is absolutely no information from Table 2 on how many of the 260,000 "readers" of alt.binaries.pictures.erotica actually downloaded and uudecoded a binary image file. The arbitron data is not tracking downloads. In fact, it would be completely consistent with Reid's definition of readership if none of the "readers" of alt.binaries.pictures.erotica ever saw a pornographic image.

Thus, the results shown in Table 2 simply cannot be used to establish the exposure of "readers" to pornographic imagery. A reasonable hypothesis is that "readers" are simply curious about what is in these groups, and browse the titles to get some idea. As Rimm notes, decoding Usenet binaries requires a non-trivial degree of technical skill.

We should further note that if one takes the estimate of individuals with Internet access as 20 million, then at most we are speaking of about .1% of Internet users accessing the alt.binaries.pictures.erotica newsgroup, and almost surely, the percentage actually downloading and uudecoding pornographic images is much lower than even this very low percentage.

Rimm: In footnote 31 on page 1866, Rimm suggests that the (presumably total) number of readers of alt.binaries.pictures.erotica on Usenet is 260,000 per month.

Rimm provides no discussion of the methodological details necessary to understand this estimate. How is this number estimated? How are multi-part image files counted? How are

15

robot extractions handled? Are these 260,000 people unique? Or, could they possibly represent, for example, the same 9000 individuals per day for 30 days? How does the "arbitron" script keep track of individual users? In other words, are reach and frequency confounded? Does Rimm know?

Amount of pornography in Usenet groups

Rimm: "Of this 11.5%, approximately 3% [of messages on the Usenet] is associated with Usenet newsgroups containing pornographic imagery." (p. 1869)

Rimm fails to take these traffic percentages to their logical conclusion, which is that less than 1/2 of 1% (3% of 11.5%) of the messages on the Internet are associated with newsgroups that contain pornographic imagery. Further, of this half percent, an unknown but even smaller percentage of messages in newsgroups that are "associated with pornographic imagery" actually contain pornographic material. Much of the material that is in these newsgroups is simply text files containing comments by Usenet readers.

Rimm: (p 1873) "Moreover, 20,644 of the 101,211 monthly Usenet posts in the top forty newsgroups, or 20.4%, are pornographic.

This figure is inflated and incorrect. Rimm is assuming that 100% of the content of the so-called "pornographic" newsgroups in Table 2 is pornography. But, this is obviously incorrect. A large number, if not the majority, of messages in these groups are simply text representing discussion and comments - not pornographic. In addition, large images are typically broken into multiple parts, so that one large .gif file might actually consist of ten or more physical files. Further, even single file images often have a separate descriptive leader (which should be considered non-pornographic). While it is impossible to determine from the results Rimm has presented what proportion of monthly Usenet posts are "pornographic," we can safely conclude that the percentage is far below what Rimm states.

Origins of pornographic imagery on the Usenet

Rimm: (p 1874) "71%, or 1671 of the 2534 pornographic images downloaded from the five Usenet newsgroups studied over a four month period, originated from "adult" BBS."

This is a critical percentage, yet we question its validity. Virtually no support is given for this percentage other than Rimm's in the text statement that 1671 images originated from adult BBSs. We cannot determine how Rimm arrived at this number from our reading of the manuscript. Is it an estimate? A count? How was it estimated or counted?
Rimm lists the five Usenet newsgroups on which he says "[t]he largest selection of sexual imagery was discovered" at the northeastern university (p. 1866) and notes in footnote 32 (p. 1867) that these sites were the largest available at the "research site." He further says that between "April and July of 1994,...all available images (3254) [were downloaded] from these five newsgroups." (p. 1867)

There must be a typographical error, because earlier Rimm stated that the alt.binaries groups were not examined until September of that year, so it cannot be possible that months earlier he was able to determine the groups with the largest selection of sexual imagery. The appearance of alt.sex.fetish.watersports is also confusing since it is not an alt.binaries group. It is possible that it all makes sense, but it is very difficult to sort out from the confusing exposition. We also wonder if group size and availability are confounded with amount of imagery.

The main issue is that convincing evidence has not been presented that these five groups contain the largest selection of sexual imagery. Where did this list come from? These groups are at a single university site. Was a systematic analysis of all Usenet groups performed to generate this list?

Did Rimm control for duplicates, resent, or non- pornographic images? Did Rimm counts posts or a complete image? What was the unit of analysis: a post or an image?

Rimm states that the images from the five Usenet groups were classified into three categories (p. 1867): 1) images originating from adult BBSs ("the name, logo, and telephone number of the BBS appeared next to or within the image."; 2) pornographic images which did not originate from BBSs; 3) "PG/R" images ("no sexual contact or lascivious exhibition.").

Curiously, there is no category for images were are not pornographic! Was every single image on these groups pornographic? Rimm does not indicate whether these categories are mutually exclusive; for example, how were "PG/R" images with a BBS logo counted?

In any event, Rimm states (on page 1867) that there were "a total of 2830 images for analysis," but does not report the frequency of images in each of the three categories. (He states that 13% of the images could not be downloaded, which makes us wonder whether other figures presented need to be similarly adjusted to account for technical difficulties which must ultimately lower consumption rates.) However, seven pages later, the total number of pornographic images downloaded from the five groups shrinks to 2354 images, with no explanation! If we accept the 1671 as indicative of the number of images in those five groups that Rimm determined came from adult BBSs, then the percent of images originating is 59% (1671/2830) if we use his first number and 71% (1671/2354), if we use his second.

III. Pornographic "Adult" Commercial BBS (pp. 1876-1905)

Number of adult BBSs examined

Rimm: "...[T]he team either subscribed to, or logged on as a new user or guest, to a number of representative pornographic BBS and collected descriptive lists of the files offered by each." (p. 1876)

Rimm reports that Boardwatch estimates that 5% of BBSs in the country are "adult," (fn. 35, p.

1867) but does not report a figure on the total number of BBSs, only that 5000 BBSs of any type were identified (p. 1877) and that 500 "active" adult boards were located for further study. Since this represents 10% of his list, we can assume that Rimm's list of BBSs was not complete. Rimm indicates that "most" of these 500 adult boards were "chat" boards, and still others were "transient." He gives no figures on how many comprised each category.

Rimm: "To the best of the research team's knowledge, the BBS included in this study comprise most of the medium- and large-sized "adult" BBS in the country that existed at the time of the research." (p. 1877)

Rimm does not indicate how many boards this represents, how they were sampled to be "representative" (p. 1876), whether the list of adult BBSs Rimm sampled from was exhaustive, or whether Rimm used his "judgment" in selecting BBSs or in generating the list of BBSs to sample from.

Number of descriptive lists examined

Rimm: "This portion of the study analyzes a total of 450,620 files that are classified..." (p.1876)

Previously, Rimm indicated that 292,114 descriptivelistings were retained for analysis. How many listings were actually collected? How many pornographic images dothese listings represent? How many were movies? How many were text files? How many images were selected from the BBSs and how were they selected?

Rimm indicates that both "descriptive lists" of pornographic images as well as a "representative sampling of the images themselves" were collected from the BBSs (p. 1877). Rimm does not say how many images were sampled, how they were sampled to be "representative," or what they were supposed to be representative of.

Ethical lapse?

Rimm: "Members of the research team did not, as a rule, identify themselves as researchers." (p.1878)

As before, this is troubling. Why didn't Rimm identify himself and his research objectives to the operators? Did Rimm obtain permission to "collect" the information from the BBSs? Did Rimm provide full disclosure to these operators about the nature and objectives of his study? Did Rimm "debrief" them afterwards? Did he get the permission of the subscribers of these BBSs to examine information about their consumption habits and report the cities they lived in (see Appendix D: pages 1926-1934)? Did Rimm submit a proposal of his methodology for such to the University Human Subjects Committee? Did they approve the research and the methodology? Does CarnegieMellon approve of publishing the cities that consumers of adult BBSs live in? How did Rimm obtain the demographic information on adult BBS subscribers? (as noted on p.1895)

Results of the linguistic classification scheme

Despite twelve pages of largely anecdotal discussion of the content analysis of the descriptive listings, the methodology is never once described formally, either in terms of the algorithm, or the software used to implement the algorithm. In the scholarly literature it is not only customary to offer the software to those who wish to replicate your results, for some journals it is mandatory (as is making the data available). Nowhere does Rimm indicate that the data or the software that categorized the listings are "available from the author."

Validity and reliability are not established. This despite the fact that standard statistical procedures are available for determining reliability and validity. The few numbers that are presented in this section are either poorly defined or not defined at all. Other quantities are mentioned as being "high," but not reported (e.g. see footnote 70 in which Rimm asserts that "[t]he presentation of kappa values...was considered unnecessary because of the high level of reliability." Yet this "high level" is never reported). Elsewhere, Rimm suggests that "validity was high," (p. 1888), but it too is not reported statistically; or, Rimm states that he performed "a statistical analysis" on the data (p. 1894), but the type of analysis nor its results are not reported. Such examples, which render the statements they are intended to support, meaningless, are too numerous to catalog here.

Relatedly, numbers or data are not reported that would help the reader understand the analysis, and numbers that are reported are pursued for additional insights.

This section is ad hoc and weak; no reliable and valid conclusions can be drawn from the analysis as presented.
Moreover, this is a standard content analysis problem. Content analysis has a large and rich literature, yet there is not a single citation to the either that vast literature or the related areas of AI software, and classification and categorization. As Rimm presents it, it is not possible to replicate the categorization he performed, let alone determine how he performed it. Thus, the methodology and this entire section, are impossible to evaluate.

Numerous questions must be raised: What time period or periods are represented in the listings? Did Rimm control for time in his analyses? Were the data adjusted to account for differing lengths of time of each listing? For example, adjusting for date first posted on the BBS?

Rimm's procedure implicitly assumes that all downloads are a function of consumer demand and no other variables. What about availability of certain kinds of images? The cost of the images? Their size? Consumer demographics?

Rimm states that "[m]any BBS either hide [the listing] information from their customers or do not provide it." (pp. 1879-1880). But on page 1878, Rimm states that listings have a typical record structure which he diagrams in Figure 3. If the information is hidden by "many" operators

19

(how many hid it in his study?), or many do not provide it (how many did not provide it in his study?), how did Rimm get it? Rimm suggests that operators were "persuaded" to provide the information "privately." (p. 1881) What does this mean? How were they persuaded? What is meant by "privately?"

How valid are the sixty-three basic categories? Were the categories validated by judges? Did human beings ever look at any descriptions to validate the classification scheme? If so, how many?

What exactly was the procedure the judges went through as part of the classification process? Rimm notes that "judges...were not avid consumers of pornography and thus did not recognize names of particular pornographic 'stars." (p. 1886) Did this lack of experience on the part of the judges affect or bias the classification procedure? Typically, judged are chosen for their expertise.

How was the "final precedence scheme" in Figure 6 arrived at?

Given that Appendix A describes dozens of categories, why are percentages not reported for individual categories within the major groupings. These percentages are important to know because some of the individual categories may be considered less extreme than others. Without knowing the distribution of categories of images within each broad group, it is difficult to know what the group actually represents.

Rimm: Thus, analyzing the data in these four classes presents a highly reliable means of exploring the explosive growth of pornography on the Information Superhighway." (p. 1886)

Rimm never shows that his method of analysis is "highly reliable" and Rimm never shows that the growth in pornography is "explosive," on the "information superhighway" or anywhere else.

Page 1889 adds nothing to the reader's understanding of the methodology. What is the point of including this discussion?

On page 1890, Rimm notes that there were 35 adult BBSs. How is this figure reconciled with the 68, 6 and 27 adult BBSs discussed on page 1853?

What is the point of including the Amateur Action BBS Case Study (pp. 1896-1905)?

In general, the conclusions Rimm makes are not supported by his analysis. Because the content analysis and classification scheme are "black boxes," because no reliability and validity results are presented, because no statistical testing of the differences both within and among categories for different types of listings has not been performed, and because not a single hypothesis has

20

been tested, formally or otherwise, no conclusions should be drawn until the issues raised in this critique are resolved.

IV. Conclusions

Rimm: "[A]ttempts at regulation may be ineffective; "the net interprets censorship as damage and routes around it" is a well known expression among Usenet enthusiasts. The current structure of the Usenet requires that individual sites choose between an "All things not expressly permitted are prohibited policy," or conversely, an "All things not expressly prohibited are permitted." A middle ground does not appear viable.

Curiously, Rimm does not consider the alternative of user-imposed, rather than state-imposed controls.

[24]

Crime on the Internet: Its Presentation and Representation

JON SPENCER

Lecturer in Criminal Justice, Department of Social Policy and Social Work,
University of Manchester

Abstract: The internet is a rapidly expanding communication medium. It has generated considerable anxiety in relation to what is perceived as the easy availability of pornography and other sexually explicit material. There is a considerable amount of police-based internet activity which constructs crime in particular ways. This article explores the way in which crime is constructed on the internet through police pages and goes on to highlight some of the questions which this raises for criminology.

The relationship between the reproduction of the images of crime and the media is one of sociological interest and has been extensively explored (see, for example, Chibnall 1977; Hall *et al.* 1978; Sparks 1993; Young 1996). Sparks (1995) has argued the importance of this form of analysis if the ideological approaches to crime and law and order in contemporary western societies are to be understood. However, the recent growth in internet usage and its emergence as a popular medium has not appeared to stimulate academic criminological interest.

Concern in relation to internet content clusters around common themes: children, violence, sex, pornography and extremist political activity (see, for example, 'Anger of Net "Porn" Magazine', *The Guardian*, 8 April 1977 and 'Porn-addict parents jailed', *The Independent*, 11 April 1997). It is the articulation of this concern which is one of the dominant strands of the discourse in relation to the internet. The broader criminological issues in relation to crime, law and order and internet content and structure have yet to be explored. This article is a consideration of those broader issues, how law and order, crime and offenders are represented on the internet, in particular the World Wide Web (WWW or the web) and contribute to its ideological and political structure.

During the 1990s there has been a substantial growth in the usage of the internet and a realisation of its potential as a form of mass communication. The potential of the web as an essential element of contemporary and future communication technology is evident by the collaboration between News International and British Telecom in launching the *Line One* Internet Access Provider Service which gives the customer on-line web access to News International dialy papers, *The Times*, *The Sunday Times*, *News of the World* and *The Sun* and uses BT internet services. It has been argued that the next computer battleground is not for the operating system, which has effectively been won by Microsoft. But in the provision of web access, the battle lines are being drawn between the two significant corporate players, Bill Gates, the founder and chief of The Microsoft Corporation, the largest manufacturer and developer of software, and Rupert Murdoch, the media magnate who owns a large section of the British press (*The Times, The Sun, News of the World, Sunday Times* and interests in *Sky Television* as well as *Twentieth Century Fox Film Company* ('Can cyberspace slam the gates', *The Guardian*, 22 May 1997).

The web is concerned with the development of new forms of markets in commodities and services as well as the provision of information and opinion. The advent of the web, which is graphically more sophisticated than the previous text-based system, has resulted in there being an increasing number of users, now estimated at over 40 million world wide (Barrett 1996). This proliferation leads to there being a wide variety of uses of the internet from academic to recreational usage and the development of commercial interests. However, what distinguishes the internet from other forms of communication and media is its open access and lack of legal regulation. In economic terms the internet is a product of late 20th century capitalism; it is an unregulated market place where only those who can afford access can enter[1] (see Currie 1997). This economic context is an important factor in understanding the structure of the internet.

The internet is structured, at one level, around the economics and politics of consumption, at another level around the politics of individuality and at another around communitarian concerns. The structuring of the internet around consumption is evidenced by the increasing number of on-line shopping malls and the provision of other on-line services which range from travel to sex. It is at the level of consumption that attempts to control the internet are located. The attempts at control are economically driven with the key concern being the maximisation and generation of profit, even if this is viewed as a long-term objective. The anxieties concerning the social consequences of the processes of defining the internet within this economic framework are one consequence of the development of an unregulated market place and, more broadly, of the economic and social relations of late 20th century capitalism. The economic relationships of capitalism in the late 20th century have, as Currie (1997) has argued, been concerned with allowing unfettered markets to operate and that this has a relationship to crime. The contradiction between the unregulated market place and the need for capital to shape and manipulate the internet for favourable market conditions becomes evident through a range of concerns which can be defined as 'moral concerns'; these concerns are used to justify censorship.

Sanitising the Internet: the Censorship Debate

The internet is exceedingly difficult to normalise and regulate. It is the perceived failure of the normalising and regulating social processes which are at the root of the current anxiety in relation to the internet. Governments are unable to regulate content thus providing the potential for a variety of oppositional discourses to appear on the net, untouched by official censorship, which exploit the freedom to subvert and side-step governmental attempts at control.

The alt.fan.karla~homolka newsgroup site[2] is a good example of such processes. Karla Homolka, a Canadian, was convicted of manslaughter for sexual killings. The judge in the case banned the publication of material associated with Karla Homolka's trial due to the proceedings which still had to take place in relation to her husband, Paul Teale, who was also accused of the killings (see Regan Shade 1996). However, a Bulletin Board[3] was established to bring the 'facts' of the case and publish the daily proceedings of the trial. Universities in Canada prohibited staff and students access to these boards on the basis that they contravened the ban imposed by the trial judge:

Despite the shutting down of the alt.fan.karla~homolka at many Canadian universities, there were still many ways for people to access the newsgroup and other information available on the trial. . . . a diligent citizen could amass a plethora of stories, facts and rumours surrounding the case. As university sites discontinued the newsgroup, it became a fabulous Internet hunt to locate sites where banned material could be found. (Regan Shade 1996, p. 21)

Finally universities lifted the prohibition because of the problems of enforcement. It was also impossible for the Canadian state to prevent internet publication as once the ban was imposed the alt.fan.karla~homolka site was moved to a server[4] situated across the Canadian border in the USA.

The alt.fan.karla~homolka example provides evidence that attempts to prohibit the publication of certain facts and procedures using censorship are spectacularly unsuccessful when it comes to the internet[5] due to its global structure which easily circumvents nationally imposed prohibitions[6]. The publication of alternative views to those what are officially accepted can take place because the current forms of access to the internet are through small service providers who have little or no interest in what is published, as it is not the content which leads to their profits but the provision of service. Currently access to the internet is not concentrated through a small number of access points or gateways and permission to publish is not determined by editorial decision making, as a recent American District Court judgment noted:

No single entity – academic, corporate, governmental, or non-profit – administers the internet. It exists and functions as a result of the fact that hundreds of thousands of separate computers and computer networks independently decided to use common transfer protocols to exchange communications and information with other computers. . . . There is no centralised storage location, control point, or communications channel for the internet, and it would not be technically feasible for a single entity to control all of the information conveyed on the internet. (*ACLU* v. *Reno*, ACLU 1996, para. 11)

It is the problem of controlling internet content which highlights, for national governments, the difficulties of regulation in the global sphere. So, the anxiety in relation to being powerless becomes focused upon particular forms of material which, within the global setting, fail to be influenced by the normalisation processes within the traditional frameworks of news and media communication. This heightens a range of anxieties for governments which they consider demand a legislative response in order to impose control frameworks. In countries where democratic sensibilities render censorship as potentially problematic there is a need to present censorship as the only viable option in relation to controlling and regulating internet content. Consequently the main elements of justification in relation to censorship focus on content orientated arguments and a discourse of protecting and shielding the young.

In considering the processes of censorship on the internet it is helpful to examine policy initiatives of different countries. What is apparent from the outlined British legislation and that in the USA (see ACLU 1996) and proposed legislation in New South Wales (Australia) (Electronic Frontiers 1996) is that it is the *global* nature of internet communication which causes the most problems. It is the lack of ability to be able to legislate for national conditions which creates anxiety and the slow realisation that legislation is futile. Consequently governments develop, or limit, access in an attempt to control access to what they consider inappropriate material[7]. Such policy initiatives have far-reaching implications for the democratic process[8]. The ability to be able to publish in *national* based media is often determined by economic advantage, editorial policy and political influence. Whereas the ability to publish on the internet relies on none of these but on the possession of the computer hardware (which is easily accessible and relatively inexpensive), some programming knowledge (easily acquired) and server access (easily available). There is then no guarantee that those publishing on the internet will abide by the protocols of publishing.

One significant element in the development of the internet as a market place has been the availability of sexual material. This market in sexual material may be the forerunner of more traditional markets; as Regan Shade (1996) notes the process of locating new technology within mainstream culture usually has a relationship with its popularity and purchase by significant numbers of people and households. There appears to be a relationship with, initially, ease of access to sexual material and the consumption of such technology by increasing numbers of people which results in its integration into the domestic sphere (Regan Shade 1996). It is this 'privatising' potential of technology, especially in relation to sexual matters, which establishes technology within the private domain. These processes can be seen working in relation to the introduction of satellite and cable television in the UK as well as the home based computer with CD ROM. These processes of embedding technology within the domestic domain can be witnessed with regard to the internet. The focus of concern and the need for censorship becomes concentrated on what is defined as the need to control 'freely' available sexual material[9].

Once a market has been established, tested, and operationalised primarily in relation to sexual material it has in the past been restructured to incorporate more mainstream and culturally 'acceptable' material. This process of restructuring has also incorporated the introduction of controls over what is defined as 'adult' material. The market becomes structured around

State and commercial 'interests' along with those of the 'moral entrepreneurs' (Hall *et al.* 1978), which combine to create a set of loose alliances. This restructuring process reinforces a particular *market* perspective, supported by censorship strategies which may be used to link issues concerning 'crime, law enforcement, and moral regulation' (Sparks 1995, p. 57). So, crime is presented as a matter of individual responsibility rather than taking account of the wider issues of the relationship between the market and social causation (Currie 1997).

The problem of internet censorship, for national governments, is the global nature of the internet and that the imposition of censorship restrictions across national boundaries are just not possible[10]. One censorship strategy has been to try and regulate server content. This has been the main subject of voluntary agreements and service provider codes of practice. For example America On Line (AOL), one of the largest Internet Service providers (ISP) in the USA, has a set of vulgarity guidelines to assist staff in making decisions about file content, for example:

Hot, wet. These are borderline words. Use your judgment, and consider it vulgar if they're talking about 'hot' as in sex, or 'wet' as in feminine moisture. Hot men/women/cars/videos/etc. are fine, as 'hot' could be referring to 'good looking' or some other non-sexual thing. Nudity. Discussion of nudity is fine; nude room names are a judgment call. Sex. This is a judgment call. 'Sexy' is fine, as an adjective. The word should never appear in room names or screen names as a noun (ILikeSex). In other situations, use the content to determine whether the member was committing a TOS (Terms of Service) violation. For instance, 'Hey babe, anyone here wanna have sex' would be a violation. 'I didn't let my child see the movie because of the sex in it' would not be a violation. (AOL Sucks 1996)

Perhaps the most recent example of this was the ban imposed by Compuserve in Germany on sexual material[11]. Many governments have intimated that they may well attempt to hold service providers responsible for the contents of their servers, however, this is fraught with legal difficulties and complexities (see Electronic Frontiers 1996).

Crime and the Internet

The internet provides an environment for numerous topics to be discussed, for example the very large range of newsgroup sites. Crime is not absent from the range of internet discussion lists, for example there are active discussion lists managed by academic institutions (mailbase Newcastle University, City University New York [CUNY], Sydney University to name but a few). There are graphic representations of crime, offenders and victims on the internet which are located on the various crime orientated web pages, some of which are put on the net by commercial television (see COPS 1997; Unsolved Mysteries 1997) and a vast number of police sites (for example Nashville Police Department 1997; Vancouver Police Department 1996; Metropolitan Police London 1996). There are also a number of link sites to crime pages, the most comprehensive of these being the Cecil Greek Page (1997) and the Police Officers' Internet Directory (1997).

The internet, as in the case of television, not only becomes a method of structuring the problem of crime, law and order and moral regulation but also as a contributory factor to the problem itself (Sparks 1995). Indeed in an attempt to control and regulate the internet it is necessary to make the internet culpable in the provision of inappropriate material and in need of being brought under control through regulatory processes. To date there has been little or no criminology discussion of the relevance of internet activity in relation to crime. For example Kidd-Hewitt and Osborne's (1995) edited collection entitled *Crime and The Media: The Post-Modern Spectacle* does not mention or reference the internet as a means of reproducing images, stereotypes and dominant discourses about crime, criminality and offenders. This is indicative of criminology's failure to explore the development of crime related matters on the internet especially as there is no lack of internet traffic which is interested in crime and criminality.

There is a range of internet sites concerned with crime; however, the sites differ in their approach. There is a range of sites which can be defined as 'official': these sites are put up and maintained by official agencies, usually police departments. These police sites provide access to a range of police-based information, for example, crime prevention with a focus on women's protection from rape and domestic violence (see Nashville Police Department 1997), recruitment, and a range of other areas. One exception to this formula in relation to police sites is that of the Chicago Police Department which uses the internet at a local rather than a global level. The Chicago Police have developed a web site for the majority of their police districts, these sites not only provide policing information but also locally-based information with many of the sites being devised and written by locally-based serving police officers (Chicago Police Department 1997). However, the Chicago Police site is one of a few exceptions to other police devised sites in the USA, although they may well be setting a trend to move away from the technological sophistication to devising locally-based forms of communication.

Police sites are similar in structure and content; many, although not all, police department sites have a 'Most Wanted' site. These local 'Most Wanted' sites may be linked to a national 'Most Wanted' page or to the FBI 'Most Wanted' site; these sites also run links to the real crime television programmes. For example, the Vancouver Police Department (1996) have a web site which is requesting help in solving the murder of David John Malloy; he was the victim of a brutal murder being stabbed 23 times and left in a back alley in North Vancouver on 17 March 1996. This page is directly linked to the 'Unsolved Mysteries Page' of the real crime television programme. It is constructed in the traditional manner of these 'reality crime' programmes. Florida's Department of Law Enforcement organises its appeal for help in these high-profile cases by issuing *Florida's Most Wanted Fugitives*, a newsletter format which is placed on the web, the newsletter lists those who are being sought by Florida State Police. The newsletter gave successful accounts of apprehension so:

Leroy Tillie was captured on 3–31–95 in California.
Arlix Tellez Fuentes was shot and killed in Dade County during a confrontation with the police. (Florida Department of Law Enforcement 1995)

These brief accounts simply but effectively create images of policing and criminals, especially the use of Fuentes full name underlining his possible immigrant status so that he is constructed as an 'outsider' and a potential threat to social cohesion. The utilisation of words such as 'captured' and 'confrontation' successfully conjure the world of popular crime thus linking subtly with the well-worn stereotypes of police and criminal relying as much on popular crime fiction as they do on real police practice.

Police web sites can also be viewed as contributing to the maintenance of the fear of crime. The Bellingham Police Department Crimeline web site (Bellingham Police Department 1996) lists those most wanted in Bellingham. One of those listed is Ronald Eugene Applegate who is wanted for an offence of child rape in the second degree. It is possible to access more details of the offence and also a picture of Ronald Applegate. However, the element of *private trouble* is removed and the case is presented as a *public ill* and thus constructed as being more than just a local event. The placing of such crimes on the web suggests that Ronald Applegate, or someone like him, could possibly be your next door neighbour. It also suggests that we are all *potential* victims of the predatory criminal such as Applegate, but at the same time we are all *possible* predators. We do not know who and where the criminals are located and this contributes to feelings of lack of safety and insecurity. In relation to women there are a number of women offenders 'posted' on the internet but women are predominantly portrayed in the category of victim. Whilst the representation of crime on the internet is exaggerated and simplifies the problem of crime it nonetheless has a resonance with the dominant discourse in western countries concerning crime and offenders.

The internet can be constructed as part of a process which defines *and* excludes offenders from the mainstream of society. This is the exclusionary aspect of the web in relation to offenders and crime as it presents *both* crime and offenders as being outside of 'normal' day-to-day experience yet at the same time ubiquitous. This contradiction is apparent in that untypical crimes become to appear ordinary and everyday rather than uncommon and remarkable; thus reinforcing the exclusionary aspect of crime and offenders. This tendency to render such uncommon crimes as a common and everyday event has, as Garland (1996) argues, a very particular influence on the construction of crime and penality:

For most people, crime is no longer an aberration or an unexpected, abnormal event. Instead, the threat of crime has become a routine part of modern consciousness, an everyday risk to be assessed and managed. . . . High crime rates have gradually become a standard, background feature of our lives – a taken for granted element of late modernity. (p. 446)

This background and all pervasiveness of crime is evidenced by the focus of a number of police pages in relation to missing or abducted children (see for example Lawton Police Department [New Jersey] 1997]. In some cases the children concerned have been abducted by one or other parent, presumably in the aftermath of separation or divorce proceedings.

This discussion of police-based material on the web suggests three things;

247

first, the police utilise the web to indicate their level of activity and their success in combating crime. Second, through the use of traditional images of offenders and crime the police are constructed as maintaining the line between order and chaos, between decency and degradation. This construction has some congruence with the mainstream American detective fiction, as Kinsey Milhone, the private detective in Sue Grafton's alphabet novels, says:

Just for the record, I like cops, . . . anyone who stands between me and anarchy. (Grafton 1993, p. 2)

Finally, offenders are presented within their traditional criminal stereotypical images, men as brutal and animalistic, fathers as potentially dangerous and irresponsible and an array of people who are arrested for street-related crime as being proved guilty by virtue of arrest. Victims on the contrary are constructed as helpless, especially women and children.

Conclusion

Issues of crime, offenders and victims have an ideological significance and are used to define the concerns around which the anxieties of late modernity can be focused and a consensus in relation to social values formulated and reproduced. In many western societies during the 1990s this consensus has been forged around offenders requiring punishment, surveillance and regulation. Thus the focus on crime-based issues within the traditional media and the popularity of crime fiction across the range of media means that the focus of crime as an area of interest on the internet is not unexpected. Issues of crime and victimisation are used by many as a barometer of the wellbeing or otherwise of a society. They are also used to indicate the effectiveness of government interventions into an area of public life which has become over-politicised (Downes and Morgan 1994). The use of crime and crime related stories by the conventional media to sell their publication, whether it be newspapers, television or film is subject to a series of formal and informal controls. The relationship between newspapers, government and the State is complex but agreements over *what* is published and *how* are part of the wider dynamics of the relationship. The issue of crime is part of this agreement and its presentation conforms to a range of agreed and well-used constructions.

The internet signals the possibility of moving away from these alliances between government and media. It could result in the fracturing of the relationship between media interests, government and the State and a possible reshaping of those interests. First, those media interests, such as the global conglomerates, News International being probably the largest, have internet interests but they do not have *control* over the medium as they do in relation to newspapers. Therefore the ideological definitions put on certain events to ensure profit maximisation is not such a powerful defining force in relation to the internet. The easy availability of equipment, the easy acquisition of programming knowledge and the easy availability of server access, are illustrated by the numerous individual home pages on the web; this makes control over the ideological content increasingly problematic[12]. This is partly the consequence of the different arrangements concerning internet access which requires only disk space on a server. For example there are service providers who may have only one server and provide internet access where there are no agreements or regulations concerning content in contrast to the more rigid conditions imposed by the larger ISPs such as AOL or Compuserve. It is of course possible for an individual to provide their own server or if they wish to put up 'offensive' material to do so with a service provider in another country. All of this begins to illustrate the problems of defining acceptable and unacceptable material and prohibiting certain forms of material on a global scale.

Second, crime, offenders and victims are situated on the web in such a manner as to reproduce familiar and known stereotypes. However, the internet, by allowing a greater degree of interactivity than television, can present actual crimes, especially the more unpleasant, as a form of 'real-life' crime fiction. Thus internet crimes have a resonance with 'real-life' crime programmes both in the USA and the UK. The possibilities of blurring the boundaries between real events and fictional accounts is apparent (see Crime Evidence File 1996), and a theme in American crime fiction (Ellroy 1993, Gair 1997). This process of the 'fictionalisation' of real events places an emotional *and* intellectual distance between the *tragedy* of the event and the individual accessing the internet.

This distance increases the process of social exclusion of many who are at greater risk of being victims, the poor, ethnic minorities and women and the structuring of crime on the internet appears to reproduce those processes of exclusion. The internet manages also to conceal the masculinity of internet communication and structure. This masculinity of the internet is influential in the process of what is regarded as valid content on internet crime pages.

Content is the third issue in relation to crime and the internet. Only particular forms of crime are evident. Those crimes which are considered more newsworthy, murder and the more sensational and notorious crimes are evident. An example of this is the full coverage given the trials of O.J. Simpson, Susan Smith in South Carolina and the Dunblane Massacre in Scotland, all of which were exceptional crimes. Other types of 'crime', which are more common, are concealed. Many of the internet crime pages are constructed within a popular culture framework which minimises the personal tragedy of victimisation but yet manages to maintain a level of fear of crime which does not reflect the complexity of victimisation.

Finally, the approach of criminology to considering how crime is represented on the internet reproduces previous flaws in criminology's academic and analytic structure. The failure to critique internet representations and to highlight the masking of disadvantage, ethnicity and gender within those representations is to reproduce the previous failure of criminology to consider the influence of those issues on the definitions and understanding of crime. The importance of the internet is that crime finds a global representation of its most reductive and simplistic form. This is associated with the need to develop economically viable markets. In so doing crime is trivialised and untypical crimes are rendered an everyday occurrence.[13]

Notes

1 This has a general application on a macro level to other countries and on a micro level to individuals (see Dyrkton 1996).

2 A newsgroup is a topic-based discussion and information exchange which is solely text based. There are a vast number of newsgroups. Those which begin their address with alt. are alternative newsgroups and are more concerned with things other than the usual.

3 A Bulletin Board is either free access or charged access where messages of a similar interest are posted. These are now less common with the development of the web.

4 A server is a computer storage system where web sites are located and accessed via a URL (Universal Resource Locator).

5 This was apparent in the publication of opinion polls on the internet in relation to the 1997 French Election in the week proceeding polling, the publication of such polls is banned under French electoral law.

6 Similarly in the case of Michael Portillo who complained to British Telecom that a camera posted outside his house was transmitting pictures to the internet. BT withdrew server access, the client relocated on a server in the USA outside of UK court jurisdiction (the web 1996).

7 However, technologically regulating access is problematic and deciding upon what is appropriate and inappropriate material is also highly problematic.

8 There are particular issues in relation to the development of the internet and democracy. It is not yet clear whether the internet will enhance democratic processes and ideals or will result in more people finding themselves excluded from such processes due to their lack of economic and material wealth (see Kinney 1996).

9 It is perhaps worth noting that the availability of sexual material is part of an entrepreneurial activity undertaken in order to make a profit, it is therefore unlikely that internet-based sexually explicit material will be 'freely' available.

10 The case of satellite television is not comparable, whilst it might be global censorship is not technically difficult to achieve, the 'offending signal is jammed or scrambled'. In relation to the internet the 'offending' signal cannot be jammed in the same way and if one server is jammed another can be found to continue to provide a service.

11 The recent prosecution of a Compuserve Director in Germany for publishing obscene material is yet another example of a national government attempting to censor material through putting pressure on 'service providers'.

12 Many IAPs offer a certain amount of server space, usually in the region of 5mb for personal use.

13 *Acknowledgements*: I owe a debt to Ken Pease for his comments on this paper and to Bill Hebenton who has provided helpful criticism; however, as usual I am solely responsible for the content of this final version.

References

ACLU (1996) *ACLU in the Courts*, hhtp://www.aclu.org/court/cdadec.html

AOL Sucks (1996) 'Censorship on America Online', http: //www.aolsucks.org/ aol/ aol~cens/cens~main.htrml

Barrett, N. (1996) *The State of The Cybernation: Cultural, Political and Economic Implications of the Internet*, London: Kogan Page.

Bellingham Police Department (1996) http: //www.city~govt.ci.bellingham.wa.us

Cecil Greek Page (1997) http://www.fsu.edu/~crimno

Chibnall, S. (1977) *Law and Order News*, London: Tavistock.

Chicago Police Department (1997) http://www.ci.chi.il.us/Community Policing/

COPS (1997) http://www.foxnetwork.com/copsindex.html

Crime Evidence File (1996) http://www.quest.net/crime/crime.htm

Currie, E. (1997) 'Market, crime and community: toward a mid-range theory of post-industrial violence', *Theoretical Criminology*, 1 (2), 147–72.

Downes, D. and Morgan, R. (1994) 'Hostages to fortune'? The politics of law and order in post-war Britain,' in: M. Maguire, R. Morgan and R. Reiner (Eds.), *The Oxford Handbook of Criminology*, Oxford: Oxford University Press.

Dyrkton, J. (1996) 'Cool runnings: "The coming of cyberality in Jamaica" ', in: R. Shields (Ed.), *Cultures of Internet Virtual Spaces, Real Histories, Living Bodies*, London: Sage.

Electronic Frontiers (1996) 'Draft legislation . . . leaked copy', http/wwwcs.newcastle.edu.au/CSS/legislation.html

Ellroy, J. (1993) *The Black Dahlia*, London: Arrow Books.

Florida Department of Law Enforcement (1995) http://www.fdle.fl.us

Gair, C. (1997) 'Policing the margins: Barbara Wilson's *Gaudi Afternoon* and *Troubles in Transylvania*, in: P. Messent (Ed.), *Criminal Proceedings: The Contemporary American Crime Novel*, London: Pluto Press.

Garland, D. (1996) 'The limits of the Sovereign State: strategies of crime control in contemporary society', *British Journal of Criminology*, 36, 443–71.

Hall, S., Clarke, J., Critcher, C., Jefferson, T. and Roberts, B. (1978) *Policing the Crisis, Mugging, the State and Law and Order*, London: Macmillan.

Kidd-Hewitt, D. and Osborne, R. (1995) *Crime and The Media: The Post-Modern Spectacle*, London: Pluto Press.

Kinney, J. (1996) 'Is there a new political paradigm lurking in cyberspace?' in: Z. Sardar and J.J. Ravetz (Eds.), *Cyberfutures Culture and Politics on the Information Superhighway*, London: Pluto Press.

Lawton Police Department (1997) http://www.sirinet.net/~lawtonpd

Metropolitan Police London (1996) http://www.open.gov

Nashville Police Department (1997) http://www.nashville.net/~pence

Police Officers' Internet Directory (1997) http://www.officer.com

Regan Shade, L. (1996) 'Is there free speech on the Internet? Censorship in the global information infrastructure', in: R. Shields (Ed.), *Cultures of Internet Virtual Spaces, Real Histories, Living Bodies*, London: Sage.

Sparks, R. (1993) 'Inspector Morse', in: G. Brandt (Ed.), *British Television Drama in the 1980s*, Cambridge: Cambridge University Press.

Sparks, R. (1995) 'Entertaining the crisis: television and moral enterprise', in: D. Kidd-Hewitt and R. Osborne (Eds.), *Crime and The Media: The Post-Modern Spectacle*, London: Pluto Press.

the web (1996) 'Portillo pictures removed by BT', *the web, September/October*, No. 8.

Unsolved Mysteries (1997) http://www.unsolved.com

Vancouver Police Department (1996) http://vanbc.wimsey.com/~upd

Young, A. (1996) *Imagining Crime: Textual Outlaws and Criminal Conversations*, London: Sage.

Date submitted: July 97
Date accepted: November 97

Part III
Criminal Justice Processes

[25]

WHY THE POLICE DON'T CARE ABOUT COMPUTER CRIME

*Marc D. Goodman**

TABLE OF CONTENTS

---

*   M.P.A., John F. Kennedy School of Government, Harvard University, Class of
1997. Mr. Goodman is a Senior Sergeant/Investigator for the Los Angeles Police
Department.

466   *Harvard Journal of Law & Technology*   [Vol. 10

I. WHY THE POLICE SHOULD CARE

The world isn't run by weapons anymore, or energy, or money. It's run by ones and zeros — little bits of data. It's all electrons . . . . There's a war out there, a world war. It's not about who has the most bullets. It's about who controls the information — what we see and hear, how we work, what we think. It's all about information.[1]

A. Nightmare Scenario

A hacker breaks into the computer systems at Brigham & Women's Hospital at four o'clock on a Monday morning. Before most of the doctors arrive to treat their patients for the day, the malicious computer intruder changes a number of patient files on the hospital's central database system: surgeries slated to be performed on the right leg are now switched to the left leg; recorded blood types are altered from AB-negative to O-positive; warnings for known allergies to medicines such as penicillin are electronically erased from patients' charts; and laboratory records on HIV blood test results are insidiously switched from negative to positive just before patients are to receive their results. The computer intruder effectively covers up all electronic evidence of the crime, and though lives will be lost, the police are powerless to act.

This scenario is a real possibility with current technology. Police forces, however, are not prepared to investigate it. In the first section of this paper, I will discuss why police departments need to work to combat computer crimes. In the second section, I will lay out why this has not happened yet. Finally, I will propose some approaches for preparing departments to police the digital world.

B. Atoms, Bits, and Bytes

The world has been accustomed to dealing with atom-based objects. Things made of atoms are those that we can see, touch, and feel, such as a collection of Shakespeare's plays or an Elvis Presley recording. In the middle of the twentieth century, however, something changed. With the advent of computer technology, electronic bits were born. As Nicholas Negroponte tells us, "[a] bit has no color, size, or weight, and it can travel at the speed of light. It is the smallest atomic element in the DNA of information."[2] Despite these physical properties, bits can be made to represent atom-based objects or analog forms of information. Speech,

---

1. As stated by Cosmos, the villain in the movie *Sneakers*. SNEAKERS (MCA/Universal 1992).

2. NICHOLAS NEGROPONTE, BEING DIGITAL 14 (1995).

text, music, photographs, and video can all be represented in a digital format.

As technology has improved over time, the amount of digital information that can be stored on a single chip has increased exponentially.[3] "Moore's Law" tells us that computer processing power doubles every eighteen months.[4] At the same time, costs of home computers have plummeted since they were introduced twenty years ago. The decreased costs to consumers and increased computational speed have encouraged more and more individuals to own powerful computer processors.[5]

Another trend that has pushed forward the digital revolution is the networking of home and business computers through the Internet. This interconnectivity ties computer users around the globe together in real time so that information retrieval is no more difficult in Johannesburg than in Jacksonville.[6] Those who doubt the success of the Internet need only look at the thirty-seven million-plus Americans who in 1995 had access to it, either directly or indirectly through a friend, co-worker, or commercial online service such as America Online.[7] "Metcalfe's Law" explains that the value of a network increases geometrically with the number of nodes or computers attached.[8] Given this and the clear trend toward more Internet use, it is likely that the number of computer systems connected to the Internet will continue to increase sharply in the years to come.[9]

Computers, like most other tools, can be used for either legitimate or criminal purposes. As the number of computers expands globally, there will be a concomitant rise in both the good and bad purposes for which they are put to use. Greater numbers of cheap, networked computers available to the general public also means greater numbers of cheap, networked computers available to the criminal elements in society.

Communities, individuals, governments, and businesses are legitimately availing themselves of the increasing sophistication and utility of information technology. Networked together, these computers

---

3. *See* Philip E. Ross, *Moore's Second Law*, FORBES MAG., Mar. 25, 1996, at 116.

4. *See* Christopher Anderson, *The Accidental Superhighway*, THE ECONOMIST, July 1, 1995, at S3, S4.

5. *See* THE WORLD ALMANAC & BOOK OF FACTS 1997 212 (Robert Famighetti ed., 1996).

6. *See generally* CLIFFORD STOLL, THE CUCKOO'S EGG: TRACKING A SPY THROUGH THE MAZE OF COMPUTER ESPIONAGE (1989).

7. *See* Peter H. Lewis, *Another Survey of Internet Users is Out and This One Has Statistical Credibility*, N.Y. TIMES, Oct. 30, 1995, at D5.

8. *See* Anderson, *supra* note 4, at S4, S8.

9. *See id.* at S3, S8.

have created a digital infrastructure upon which society has come to depend heavily. This is important for law enforcement officers because computer networks used for legitimate purposes are subject to attack and disruption at the hands of computer-savvy criminals.

Publicly-switched telephone systems, air traffic control networks, police and fire dispatch centers, and utility companies all rely upon computers and information networks to provide their vital services to the public.[10] This National Information Infrastructure ("NII"), as it has come to be called,[11] is now fundamental to our way of life; both the government and the private sector have become increasingly dependent upon it.[12] As our national computer systems become more intertwined with other networks around the world, we will see the NII connect to the Global Information Infrastructure.[13] Since more and more critical information, such as military data, trade secrets, and hospital patient records, will be put into computer networks,[14] their protection will become more vital, yet at the same time more difficult. This increased difficulty will arise because the linking of computer systems means they can be attacked from anywhere in the world via a telephone line.

C. Definition of Computer Crime

There is disagreement nationally and globally as to what exactly constitutes a computer crime.[15] The term "computer crime" covers such a wide range of offenses that unanimity has been an elusive goal. For example, if a commercial burglary takes place and a computer is stolen, does this constitute a computer crime, or is it merely another burglary? Does copying a friend's Microsoft Excel disks constitute a computer crime? What about sending obscene pictures over the Internet? The answers to each of these questions may depend entirely upon the jurisdiction in which one finds oneself.[16]

Computer crimes can be divided into three general categories: crimes where a computer is the target, crimes where a computer is a tool

---

10. *See* ROGER C. MOLANDER ET AL., STRATEGIC INFORMATION WARFARE: A NEW FACE OF WAR, xiii (1996), available at (visited Apr. 15, 1997) <http://www.rand.org/publications/MR/MR661/MR661.pdf>.

11. *See* Al Gore, *Bringing Information to the World: The Global Information Infrastructure*, 9 HARV. J.L. & TECH. 1, 1 (1996).

12. *See* Exec. Order No. 13010, 61 Fed. Reg. 37,345 (1996).

13. *See* Gore, *supra* note 11.

14. *See* MOLANDER ET AL., *supra* note 10.

15. *See* P.A. Collier & B.J. Spaul, *Problems in Policing Computer Crime*, 2 POLICING & SOC'Y 307 (1992).

16. *See* Jodi Mardesich, *Laws Across the Country Become Relevant in Connected World; Jurisdiction at Issue in Net Legal Cases*, SAN JOSE MERCURY NEWS, Oct. 8, 1996, at 1E.

of the crime, and crimes where a computer is incidental.[17] When a computer is the target of a crime, an innocent party's computer system is attacked by a criminal computer intruder. Some examples include trespass, vandalism, sabotage, theft of intellectual property, extortion based on threats to release information stolen from a target's computer system, and terrorist activities threatening parts of the NII for political purposes. If a computer is a tool of the crime, the computer is used to commit an old crime in a high-tech way. Examples of this include creation of counterfeit currency or official documents using computer scanners and graphics programs, embezzlement using a computer to skim very small sums of money from a large number of accounts, distribution of child pornography on the Internet, and theft of digital property. Other crimes can also be committed on the Internet: fraud, hate crimes, stalking, gambling, and money laundering. A computer is incidental to the crime if the computer itself is not required for the crime, but is used in some way connected to the criminal activity. Examples include a threatening letter that was written and stored on a computer, financial records on a drug dealer's machine, and an inculpatory bomb recipe discovered on a computer hard drive after an explosion in the neighboring town.

D. Computer Criminals

For computer crime, as with most crimes, it is valuable for law enforcement to have a "profile" of the average offender in order to investigate and solve a given offense. Since most police officers have yet to encounter a computer crime case, their sense of a high-tech criminal's profile has come not from the police training academy, but from the media. Many police executives still believe the prevalent myth of the neighborhood hacker[18] envisioned in the 1983 film *War Games*.[19] In the movie, actor Matthew Broderick innocently breaks into the computer systems of the United States Strategic Air Command and accidentally launches a countdown to nuclear war. Though the aforementioned stereotype of a hacker as an innocent, maladjusted,

---

17. *See* David Carter, *Computer Crime Categories: How Techno-Criminals Operate,* 64 FBI L. ENFORCEMENT BULL., July 1995, at 21; Scott Charney, *Computer Crime: Law Enforcement's Shift From a Corporeal Environment to the Intangible, Electronic World of Cyberspace,* 41 FED. B. NEWS & J. 489, 489 (1994).
18. *See generally* BRUCE STERLING, THE HACKER CRACKDOWN: LAW AND DISORDER ON THE ELECTRONIC FRONTIER (1992).
19. WAR GAMES (Metro-Goldwyn-Mayer 1983).

teenage nerd might have been true in the early- and mid-1980s, such is not the case today.[20]

Although there are some relatively innocent hackers left, many of the computer intruders today are malicious and often motivated by greed.[21] Skilled computer hackers today are in great demand, often finding employment with organizations such as the Italian Mafia, Colombian drug cartels, Chinese Triads, or Russian organized crime.[22] Their motives range from greed to intellectual challenge, and the profile of each must be considered when investigating high-tech violations.[23] Of course the greatest threat from computer crime will continue to come from the "insider."[24] Law enforcement officers familiar with the problem of retail theft know that most losses occur from employees, not from shoplifters or robbers.[25] Armed with inside knowledge and access to their employers' computer networks, employees may pose new security risks for all types of organizations.

E. Why the Police Should Be Concerned About Computer Crime

According to Kenneth Rosenblatt, Deputy District Attorney for Santa Clara County, California, "our society is about to feel the impact of the first generation of children who have grown up using computers. The increasing sophistication of hackers suggests that computer crime will soar as members of this new generation are tempted to commit more serious offenses."[26] Furthermore, ever-increasing numbers of people today have the ability to learn computer skills and thus have the opportunity to use them for nefarious purposes. Colleges, universities, and technical schools graduate large numbers of computer experts each year, many of whom have the ability to exploit their knowledge for illegal purposes.[27] One expert at the United States Department of Justice has gone so far as to suggest that by the year 2000, nearly 90% of

---

20. *See* Wade Roush, *Hackers: Taking a Bite Out of Computer Crime*, TECH. REV., Apr. 1995, at 32, 34; *see generally* STERLING, *supra* note 18.

21. *See* Roush, *supra* note 20, at 36.

22. *See* Joshua Cooper Ramo, *Crime Online: Mobsters Around the World are Wiring for the Future*, TIME DIGITAL, Sept. 23, 1996, at 32.

23. *See* STERLING, *supra* note 18, at 58-59, 177-78, 185-86.

24. *See* Rory J. O'Connor, *Computers Vulnerable to Insiders*, SAN JOSE MERCURY NEWS, Mar. 6, 1997, at 3C.

25. *See* Mary Guthrie, *Firms Target Employee Thefts*, L.A. TIMES, Jan. 7, 1993, at D7.

26. Larry E. Coutorie, *The Future of High-Technology Crime: A Parallel Delphi Study*, 23 J. OF CRIM. JUST. 13, 14 (1995).

27. *See generally* STAFF OF SENATE COMM. ON GOV'T AFFAIRS, PERMANENT SUBCOMM. ON INVESTIGATIONS, 104TH CONG., SECURITY IN CYBERSPACE (Comm. Print 1996) [hereinafter SECURITY IN CYBERSPACE].

criminals might be computer-literate.[28] Even if that number seems inflated, it should certainly cause some alarm in the world of law enforcement.

In addition, traditional barriers to crime faced by former generations of thieves, thugs, and convicts are being obliterated by digital technologies. In a digital world, there are no state or international borders; customs agents do not exist. Bits of information (contraband and otherwise) flow effortlessly around the globe, rendering the traditional concept of distance meaningless. In the past, the culprit had to be physically present to commit a crime. Now, however, thanks to the digital revolution, a thief can steal millions of dollars from anywhere on the planet simply by moving bits of electronic ones and zeros into his own bank account.[29] Cybercrimes can be committed from anywhere in the world as bits are transmitted over wires, by radio waves, or via satellite. Today, a theft in Los Angeles could just as easily be committed by a criminal in Minsk as one in Malibu.

Information stored in computers may also be more vulnerable to attack than data stored in paper format. Traditionally, companies protected their secrets and bank funds in locked file cabinets and vaults.[30] These locked boxes were located in offices, which themselves were locked in buildings surrounded by electronic fences and armed guards.[31] In the digital world, all of a company's proprietary information may be located on one computer server that is connected to dozens, hundreds or even thousands of other computer systems around the world.[32] Any one of these networks or even a phone line into a company's main computer is a transnational invitation to crime. The person on the other end of the remote computer login session could be a legitimate student user, a business person, or a computer enthusiast. But, she could also be a member of an organized crime group, a saboteur, or even a foreign intelligence agent.

Crime in the digital world has another advantage for crooks over "atom-based" crime: electrons and bits have no effective mass or weight. If one were to rob a bank or an armored car of two million dollars in cash, transportation and storage of the stolen goods would pose a problem. A thousand pounds of U.S. currency is hard to carry away from the bank and even more difficult to hide under one's mattress. In

28. *See* Richard S. Groover, *Overcoming Obstacles: Preparing for Computer-Related Crime*, FBI L. ENFORCEMENT BULL.., Aug. 1996, at 8.

29. *See* Saul Hansell, *Citibank Fraud Case Raises Computer Security Questions*, N.Y. TIMES, Aug. 19, 1995, at 31.

30. *See* SECURITY IN CYBERSPACE, *supra* note 27, at 14-15.

31. *See id.*

32. *See id.*

the digital world, however, money has no weight.[33] The theft, transportation, and storage of electron-based money, or other digital goods for that matter, is greatly facilitated by the fact that they are without mass. A billion dollars of electrons weighs no more than, and is just as easy to transport as, ten dollars of electrons. Thus, the potential to steal large amounts of cash and other goods without detection is enormous.

F. Computer Crime Is on the Rise

Given the advantages of digital crime over its analog counterparts and the growing number of computer-literate thieves, it is undoubtedly in the interest of police agencies to learn as much as possible about computer crime now, while there still remains a possibility of catching up with these criminals.[34] The trends in digital crime grow more alarming each year. According to a 1995 study by Ernst & Young, at least twenty companies responding to an annual security survey had suffered losses exceeding $1 million as a result of computer break-ins.[35] The Business Software Alliance estimates the lost revenue resulting from software piracy alone amounts to $2.8 billion per year.[36] Cellular phone companies lost an estimated $650 million last year to fraud committed by crooks who altered the software in wireless phones to make free calls.[37] A recently-closed "electro-bookie" gambling operation run by the mob in New York City was found to be processing thousands of "marks" each day, netting members of the Gambino, Genovese, and Colombo crime families nearly $65 million per year.[38] Over $2 trillion in international wire transfers happen every day.[39] As Citibank recently found out when its computer network was compromised by a crime group in Russia, even the paltry sum of $10 million can be quite enticing.[40]

---

33. *See infra* notes 41-45 and accompanying text.
34. *See* David L. Carter & Andra J. Katz, *Computer Crime: An Emerging Trend for Law Enforcement*, FBI L. ENFORCEMENT BULL., Dec. 1996, at 1.
35. *See* Peter H. Lewis, *Losses From Computer Breaches Are on the Rise, a Study Finds*, N.Y. TIMES, Nov. 20, 1995, at D2.
36. *See* Elizabeth Corcoran, *In Hot Pursuit of Software Pirates: Industry Sends Out Private Investigators to Fight $15 Billion Trade in Illicit Copying*, WASH. POST, Aug. 23, 1995, at F1.
37. *See* Ruth Larson, *Secret Service Nabs 259 on Cellular-Phone Fraud: "Cloned" Phones Seized*, WASH. TIMES, June 18, 1996, at A4.
38. *See* Ramo, *supra* note 22.
39. *See* SECURITY IN CYBERSPACE, *supra* note 27, at 34.
40. *See* Hansell, *supra* note 29.

G. Other Trends of Concern to Law Enforcement

A number of recent technological developments will significantly frustrate police in their search for cybercriminals. The introduction of budding technologies such as digital cash and sophisticated encryption programs may render it impossible to track future generations of digital wrongdoers. Digital cash technology has existed for several years. For example, DigiCash is a plastic card with a small microprocessor chip that can be used instead of atom-based cash.[41] The introduction of digital cash may eventually mean the decline of real currency as legal tender.[42] These cards have cash values encoded on them but contain no information linking the DigiCash card to its user.[43] Any transaction paid for by DigiCash will be completely anonymous.[44] While possibly a boon to Internet commerce and to those who wish to keep their names and personal shopping habits hidden from credit card companies, electronic payment systems like DigiCash will make it possible for criminals to transfer large sums of money for illegal purposes in a manner that is completely undetectable by law enforcement.[45] Indeed, DigiCash may make today's problems with money laundering seem like child's play.

As if the difficulties in policing a world with digital cash were not daunting enough, the introduction of widely available, highly sophisticated, computer-based encryption programs may mean the demise of incriminating evidence in many cases.[46] Encryption uses mathematical algorithms to convert digital information into a different format so it cannot be decoded without a password.[47]

Of course, there are legitimate uses for encryption. Sent over the Internet, e-mail and other computer files often pass through dozens of computers between sender and recipient. The contents can be copied and viewed anywhere along their path. Encryption prevents unautho-

---

41. *See DigiCash — Numbers That Are Money* (visited Mar. 16, 1997) <http://www.digicash.com/publish/digibro.html>.

42. *See* Kelley Holland & Amy Cortese, *The Future of Money*, BUS. WK., June 12, 1995, at 66; *see generally* Joshua B. Konvisser, Note, *Coins, Notes, and Bits: The Case for Legal Tender on the Internet*, 10 HARV. J.L. & TECH. 321 (1997).

43. *See Digicash — Numbers That Are Money, supra* note 41.

44. *See* A. Michael Froomkin, *Flood Control on the Information Ocean: Living with Anonymity, Digital Cash, and Distributed Databases*, 15 J.L. & COM. 395, 462 (1996).

45. *See Money in CyberSpace* (last modified Feb. 3, 1997) <http://www.ustreas.gov/treasury/bureaus/fincen/cybpage.html>; Vanessa Houlder, *Cash Versus Cashless — Electronic Money Is Becoming a Reality but Questions Remain Over Privacy and Fraud*, FIN. TIMES, Feb. 20, 1996, at 11.

46. *See* Julian Dibbell, *Keys to the Kingdom: Cryptography, the Black Art of Spies and Diplomats*, TIME DIGITAL, Nov. 11, 1996, at 38.

47. *See* A. Michael Froomkin, *The Metaphor is the Key: Cryptography, the Clipper Chip, and the Constitution*, 143 U. PA. L. REV. 709, 714 (1995).

rized reading of the files. The military, government, banking institutions, and other businesses and individuals all have legitimate reasons for wanting to use encryption. But, just as bad guys today wear gloves to cover up their fingerprints, the techno-criminals of the future will use encryption to cover up their electronic tracks.[48] Police agencies must come to grips with these changes taking place in the world of evidence collection and preservation. Officers must be trained to follow the digital equivalent of a "blood trail" if they wish to be able to investigate and prosecute the growing number of criminal offenders in the digital world.

H. Technology-Based Attacks Against Law Enforcement Will Increase

Not only is technology being used by criminals to further their illegal enterprises, but computers, cellular phones, and other sophisticated electronic devices are being used to gather counterintelligence on police operations.[49] When agents of the United States Drug Enforcement Administration recently conducted a raid at the Cali drug cartel head-quarters in Colombia, they discovered two large IBM mainframe computers.[50] The computers were hooked into the national telephone service of Colombia and stored the phone records of millions of Cali residents.[51] These phone records were routinely cross-checked against calls made to the United States Embassy in Colombia and the Colombian Ministry of Defense in an effort to identify Colombians who were cooperating with government drug enforcement efforts.[52]

Federal, state, and local law enforcement agencies and officers can expect to come under increasing attack as digital criminals increase in sophistication. When notorious hacker Kevin Mitnick was targeted by specific law enforcement officers, he would routinely change the police agent's voice-mail greeting at work, cancel or re-route an officer's home telephone service, and even add lines of negative annotations to credit reports of judges and probation officers with whom Mitnick had disagreements.[53] Police agencies may find their 911 systems interrupted, their encoded radio transmissions intercepted, their proprietary databases altered, and intelligence relating to impending drug raids pilfered by

---

48. *See* Vic Sussman, *Policing Cyberspace: Cops Want More Power to Fight Cybercriminals*, U.S. NEWS & WORLD REP., Jan. 23, 1995, at 54.

49. *See* Ramo, *supra* note 22.

50. *See id.*

51. *See id.*

52. *See id.*

53. *See* TSUTOMU SHIMOMURA & JOHN MARKOFF, TAKEDOWN 238 (1996).

cybercriminals who attack at the heart of police command, control, and communications systems.[54] If police agencies cannot appreciate the importance of preparing for technology-based attacks against others, surely they can see the wisdom of self-preservation.

I. Computer Systems Remain Vulnerable

The Computer Emergency Response Team ("CERT") was founded by the Defense Advanced Research Projects Agency ("DARPA") in 1988 to coordinate responses to computer crises and emergencies such as those described earlier.[55] Although police agencies might prefer to leave the investigation of computer crime to specialists such as CERT, they cannot. CERT provides advice and serves as a repository of information for victims of computer crime, but it has no power to conduct any type of criminal investigations. This means that police agencies will be called upon to handle the escalating number of computer crimes.

A study recently completed by the Defense Information Systems Agency ("DISA") demonstrates how vulnerable even "secure" information systems are to attack.[56] DISA has been performing proactive computer hacking on behalf of the government for the past three years.[57] These computer specialists attempt to break into Department of Defense ("DOD") computer systems using only those tools commonly available on the Internet to all other hackers.[58] Based upon an estimated 30,000 attempted electronic penetrations performed as of May 1996, DISA has been able to break into 65% of the systems in under one week.[59] DISA estimated that given more time, it could break into 95-98% of the DOD's unclassified computer systems.[60] The DOD computer network managers affected by the penetrations only detected these intrusions 4% of the time and only reported 27% of those to the appropriate security or law enforcement personnel. Thus, the intrusions by DISA were not reported 98.92% of the time! If there is a 98.92% failure rate in detection and reporting on the military's computer systems, what is the corresponding rate in the civilian world?

---

54. *See* SECURITY IN CYBERSPACE, *supra* note 27, at 153-55.
55. *See* Carnegie Mellon University, *CERT Coordination Center* (visited Mar. 14, 1997) <http://www.cert.org/>.
56. *See* SECURITY IN CYBERSPACE, *supra* note 27, at 37.
57. *See id.*
58. *See id.*
59. *See id.*
60. *See id.*

J. Cyberspace Laws Are Expanding

Whether or not criminal justice agencies want to deal with computer crime may become a moot point in the very near future. Legislators around the nation are passing a flurry of new laws relating to cyberspace.[61] Currently, every state except Vermont has enacted some form of computer-crime statute.[62] At both the federal and local levels, police organizations are being tasked by legislative bodies to assume the responsibility of digital crime enforcement.[63] Thus, law enforcement agencies are being required to update their tactics and techniques for the twenty-first century. Those police departments that earnestly rise to the occasion may be able to make the case for increased funding and training to meet the demands imposed by these new laws. In contrast, those police chiefs who fail to prepare for these new responsibilities may find themselves in conflict with the mayors and city councils who have appointed them.

K. The Most Important Reason Why Police Departments Should Be Concerned About Computer Crime

Law enforcement officers should be concerned about high-technology crime because society has placed the burden upon them to do so. The people have entrusted the police to protect them and their property. The prevention of crime and the apprehension of offenders are duties that the law places on the police. The fact that the nature of crime may change over time and make their role more difficult does not relieve law enforcement agencies of their fundamental responsibility to protect all citizens from crime. The Law Enforcement Code of Ethics reminds all police officers:

> As a Law Enforcement Officer, my fundamental duty is to serve mankind; to safeguard lives and property; to protect the innocent against deception, the weak against oppression or intimidation and the peaceful against violence or disorder; and to respect the Constitutional rights of all men to liberty, equality and

---

61. *See* Xan Raskin & Jeannie Schaldach-Paiva, *Eleventh Survey of White Collar Crime: Computer Crimes*, 33 AM. CRIM. L. REV. 541, 562 (1996).

62. *See id.* at 563.

63. *See, e.g.,* 18 U.S.C. § 1029 (1996) (high-tech fraud and counterfeiting); Communications Decency Act, Pub. L. No. 104-104, 110 Stat. 56 (1996) (codified in scattered sections of 42 U.S.C.); ARK. CODE ANN. § 5-41-103 (Michie 1993) (computer fraud); CAL. PENAL CODE § 502 (Deering 1996) (computer trespass).

> justice . . . . I recognize the badge of my office as a
> symbol of public faith, and I accept it as a public trust
> to be held so long as I am true to the ethics of the
> police service. I will constantly strive to achieve these
> objectives and ideals, dedicating myself before God to
> my chosen profession . . . law enforcement.[64]

Although the concept of "digital crime" may be difficult for many police executives to accept and understand, they must ensure that their departments are ready and able to handle such offenses when they occur. Law enforcement practices and policies have changed in response to changes in society before. Although high-technology crime may be more difficult to comprehend than other events demanding change, the police have a moral obligation to prepare well for the future digital crime wave.

Given the previously enumerated, significant trends in computer crime, one might expect that police departments would be scrambling to improve their ability to investigate high-technology crime. Unfortunately, this is not the case. For a variety of fiscal, cultural, and political reasons, computer crime is not a high priority for the vast majority of law enforcement agencies. The impediments to changing this situation are described in the next section of this Article.

II. WHY THE POLICE DON'T CARE

"I think it is going to take a lot of people dying, unfortunately, before anything will be done about computer crime."[65]

Simply stated, computer crime is not a priority for police departments around the world. In a time when greater and greater emphasis is being placed on issues like violent crime reduction and community-based policing,[66] the detection and investigation of computer-related offenses remains an elusive goal. When asked about the lack of serious progress in the fight against computer crime, police executives almost unanimously cite "money, money, money" as the principal impediment.[67] However, the true reasons for law enforcement's lackadaisical approach to handling digital crime are much more complex and enigmatic.

---

64. SANTA CLARA POLICE DEPARTMENT CODE OF ETHICS (1960).

65. Glenn D. Baker, *Trespassers Will be Prosecuted: Computer Crime in the 1990s,* 12 COMPUTER L.J. 61, 63 (quoting Kenneth Rosenblatt, Deputy District Attorney for Santa Clara, California).

66. *See generally, e.g.,* Barbara A. Webster & J. Thomas McEwen, *Assessing Criminal Justice Needs,* NAT'L INST. OF JUST. RES. IN BRIEF, Aug. 1992.

67. *See* Groover, *supra* note 28.

Computer crime has been recognized as an enforcement dilemma for at least two decades,[68] yet the majority of police agencies seem unconcerned with its presence or effects. Although some strides to investigate and prosecute such crimes have been made recently,[69] the challenges facing the police in their struggle to catch up with the hackers, crackers, and crypto-anarchists of the digital world remain formidable. Despite the recent increase of technology-related crime, 72% of police departments and 88% of sheriff's departments do not have units that specialize in the area.[70] In this section of the paper, I will examine why law enforcement agencies have been slow to recognize and deal with these acts of criminal misconduct, despite the increasing threat they pose to society.

Before the public, the business world, and policymakers can begin to change the current state of affairs, they must first understand why the police do not seem to care about digital crime. Some of the reasons include: police culture itself, the invisibility of digital crime, the difficulty in investigating high-tech crime, an abundance of "real crime," a lack of public outcry on the subject, and the high cost of computer training and specialized units.

A. *That's Not Why I Became a Cop!*

When rookie police officers are asked why they chose a career in law enforcement, most cite reasons such as "I wanted to help people" or "I wanted to arrest bad guys." Many officers developed their sense of job description well before they joined the police force. Television shows such as *Dragnet, Adam-12, Starsky & Hutch, S.W.A.T., Hawaii Five-0, Hill Street Blues, Cagney & Lacey*, and *T.J. Hooker* influenced generations of young men and women to consider a career in law enforcement. However, the newest members of the police service find out quickly that they do not get into blazing gun battles every day of the week. There are no daily vehicle pursuits and not all crimes are solved in sixty-minute episodes.

Yet many officers still long to be heroes. The culture of law enforcement is one in which machismo and physical bravery are greatly rewarded. Indeed, the highest honor most police departments bestow upon their own is the "medal of valor," an award given only to a select few crime-fighters who risk their lives in order to save others. Rescuing people from burning buildings, arresting gang members who are armed

---

68. *See* Bill D. Colvin, *Computer Crime Investigators: A New Training Field*, FBI L. ENFORCEMENT BULL., July 1979, at 9.

69. *See* Webster & McEwen, *supra* note 66, at 4.

70. *See id.* at 4-5.

with AK-47s, and pursuing neighborhood rapists in long foot chases over backyard fences are the types of activities that garner officers the accolades of their peers and promotions from the police brass. Uniformed patrol officers and personnel assigned to high-risk duties such as the Special Weapons and Tactics ("SWAT") team see themselves as the "thin blue line" between anarchy and a peaceful society. These officers are perceived to be the *real* cops.

Of course, there are other cops — police officers who work mostly inside as detectives, desk officers, and administrative officers. The functions assigned to this group of individuals are not accorded the same level of respect given to *real* cops. There is an omnipresent undercurrent of social stigma against those who fulfill less dangerous duties in law enforcement, and derisive names are commonplace: "desk jockey," "station queen," "house mouse," "pogue," and "squint" are among those most frequently heard. When investigating computer crime, life-and-death emergencies are rare; thus far, no medals of valor have been awarded for "cybersleuths." Since the internal culture of police departments places a lower value on catching non-violent offenders,[71] it should come as no surprise that officers are not clamoring to investigate computer crimes.

At a time when most police departments cannot keep up with the hectic pace of constant 911 emergency calls,[72] the thought of dedicating scarce resources to the "fuzzy" concept of computer crime is very hard to sell to most police chiefs. Rapes, murders, drive-by shootings, auto theft, and drugs are all higher on the priority list than computer crime.[73] While many people call the precinct captain to complain about drug dealers in their neighborhood, few, if any, call to complain about "those darn hackers!" Indeed, as I will discuss later, the invisibility of digital crime is one of the major reasons why most police executives can afford not to care about the problem, *for now.*

Other reasons why police departments have been very slow to respond to digital crime issues include lack of computer savvy and the fear of technology, or "technophobia."[74] Technophobia is a serious problem for both police officers and the public at large. According to a recent survey by the Dell Computer Corporation, 55% of the population

---

71. *See* Collier & Spaul, *supra* note 15, at 311.

72. *See* MALCOLM K. SPARROW ET AL., BEYOND 911: A NEW ERA FOR POLICING 105 (1990); Gordon Witkin & Monika Guttman, *This is 911 . . . Please Hold*, U.S. NEWS & WORLD REP., June 17, 1996, at 30, 31.

73. *See Reno Attacks House Budget Plan to Cut Crime Funds*, Reuters World Service, Mar. 17, 1995, *available in* LEXIS, News Library, Wires File.

74. *Cf.* Raoul Vincent, *Police Hope to Nab Criminals in Their Own World Wide Web*, CHI. TRIB., May 19, 1996 (Evening Update), at 2; STERLING, *supra* note 18, at 194.

suffers from some fear of or hesitation about technology.[75] Compounding the problem is the insufficient training law enforcement personnel receive on either computer usage or computer crime. Very few, if any, departments train recruits on high-technology issues. Any computer training that does occur is generally only on how to use proprietary law enforcement and criminal database systems for the purposes of checking for warrants and stolen vehicles. At best, these are rudimentary skills that do not prepare police officers to combat computer-related crime.[76] According to a 1995 University of California study, 40% of police professionals receive no formal training on computers.[77] An additional 20% of police professionals receive no more than two hours of computer instruction.[78] This by no means suggests that police officers as a whole are incapable of learning these skills; rather, it illustrates how far they have to go before they will be prepared to tackle sophisticated computer crime. Since police officers, like other human beings, do not like doing things they are not good at or do not understand, they will continue to ignore high-technology crime until it becomes impossible to do so any longer.

Rank-and-file officers are not alone in their lack of understanding of high-technology issues. The problem also affects higher ranking officers. The majority of senior law enforcement officials have been neither formally nor informally trained in the use of computers.[79] When today's police managers first joined the force in the 1960s, computers were almost unheard of. All a good beat cop needed then was a baton, the ability to fight well, and a "nose" for finding criminals. Police work today, however, is more complicated. New tools are required to meet the challenges posed to law enforcement officers in the twenty-first century. Unfortunately, however, many police chiefs think they can "get by" without having to dedicate additional resources to the issue of high-technology crime because that is what has been done in the past.

Thus, many agencies have tried to "fake it" or "make do" when it comes to handling computer crime. A police chief might designate the most proficient WordPerfect user as the department's "computer expert." To the uninformed, it might make sense that the same officer who is capable of creating the precinct newsletter might be capable of conducting a forensic examination of a UNIX mainframe computer. Nevertheless, this is certainly not the case. Police departments that look internally

---

75. *See* Kevin Hogan, *Technophobia*, FORBES MAG., Feb. 28, 1994, at 116.
76. *Cf.* Alana Northrop et al., *Police Use of Computers*, 23 J. CRIM. JUST. 259, 262 (1995).
77. *See id.* at 270.
78. *See id.*
79. *See id.*

to their own computer hobbyists to solve sophisticated computer crime cases may find they have made a grave error in judgment. After all, who would expect their department's most avid reader of Agatha Christie to be their best homicide investigator?[80] Failure to recognize this critical difference is undoubtedly a pivotal factor in law enforcement's inattention to digital crime.

Any attempt to understand why police are behind in the fight against computer crime must consider the larger historical context of law enforcement's relationship with technology. The police have always been slow to adopt technology; the same cannot be said for criminals.[81] Indeed, criminal organizations have been quick to draw on new technologies which might aid in furthering their illegal enterprises. For example, in the 1930s, members of Chicago's brutal organized crime syndicates had more sophisticated weapons technology than most police officers. Similarly, in the 1980s, well before pagers were common in society, drug dealers availed themselves of these digital communications tools in an effort to avoid detection and wire-tapping by law enforce ment.[82] As soon as the technology advanced, organized criminals turned to fax machines and cellular phones to conduct their criminal enterprises.[83]

What makes law enforcement's slow technological progress with regard to computer crime particularly troublesome is the fact that modern stand-alone and networked computer systems are vastly more complicated than machine guns, pagers, or cellular phones, and they are becoming more so all the time. Therefore, the longer police agencies wait to begin their study of computers and computer-related crime, the more difficult the process will be.

Learning about the issues involved in policing computer crime is as difficult as learning about the technology itself. Commonly-held ideas of crime and criminality must be substantially updated as digital technology continues to reshape the world in which we live. Basic crimes like theft have always meant that one person took something belonging to another without permission; the result was that the first party no longer had possession of the property which was taken. Economic value has always been placed on tangible, visible, and atom-based assets. Yet in an electron-based universe, it is quite possible for

---

80. *See* Coutorie, *supra* note 26, at 27.

81. *See* Michael R. Zimmerman, *Drug Dealers Find Haven in Online Services*, PC WK, Mar. 4, 1991, at 43.

82. *See* Jonathan M. Moses, *Message Is Out on Beepers: Police, Industry Fight Use by Drug Dealers*, WASH. POST, July 11, 1988, at A1.

83. *See* Terry E. Johnson, *Crime: Dialing For Dollars*, NEWSWK., Sept. 14, 1987, at 42.

482   *Harvard Journal of Law & Technology*   [Vol. 10

one person to have taken something that belongs to another without permission and make a perfect copy of the item.[84] The result is that the original owner still has the property even though the thief has taken a version as well. Can a theft truly occur when the victim of the crime has not been deprived of the original copy of the property? The answer is generally yes. Changes like this are difficult for traditionalists in the criminal justice system to comprehend because they represent a fundamental shift in the way law is constructed and enforced.

Not only are criminal laws being reconstructed, but so are traditional concepts of evidence and forensics.[85] As Dan Duncan, senior instructor at the Federal Law Enforcement Training Center, recently stated, "This is a new world for law enforcement [because] cops have always followed a paper trail, and now there may not be one."[86] A shift from an environment where items are stored in tangible forms to an electronic environment means that computer crimes and the methods used to investigate them are no longer restricted by many traditional rules and constraints.[87] Generations of police officers accustomed to following evidentiary "paper trails" may find chasing electronic "data trails" very difficult. Electronic crime investigations require special expertise and training. Since most officers lack this training, they are reluctant or unable to pursue computer criminals. A future that lacks printed or atom-based evidence will continue to thwart most police agencies for some time to come, thereby increasing their reluctance and inability to investigate these crimes.

B. It is Difficult to Police the Internet

Because of the distributed essence of the Internet, many legal difficulties confront law enforcement professionals who attempt to police cyberspace. The Internet was originally created as a project of the DoD's Advanced Research Project Agency ("ARPA")[88] in 1968.[89] The Defense Department's goal was to establish an open and accommodating

---

84. *See* Todd H. Flaming, *The National Stolen Property Act and Computer Files: A New Form of Property, A New Form of Theft*, 1993 U. CHI. L. SCH. ROUNDTABLE 255, 255 (1993).

85. *See* Sussman, *supra* note 48.

86. *Id.* at 59.

87. *See* Charney, *supra* note 17, at 940.

88. ARPA was the original name for the agency currently known as DARPA. The name was changed in 1972. *See* Scott Ruthfield, *The Internet's History and Development: From Wartime Tool to the Fish-Cam*, CROSSROADS, Sept. 1995, at ¶ 4 <http://info.acm.org/crossroads/xrds2-1/inet-history.html>.

89. *See generally Public Broadcasting Service, Life on the Internet: Net History* (visited Apr. 3, 1997) <http://www.pbs.org/Internet/history>.

global communications network of trusted hosts, including military installations, university researchers, and defense contractors.[90] The Internet was designed to survive a nuclear war and provided innumerable pathways for messages to be sent; if one route had been destroyed, the message had to be able to "react" and find a new path to its intended destination.[91] Although this network architecture is well-suited for military command and control operations, it presents a major headache for those who would attempt to limit the access and activities of computer criminals.

Hackers on the Internet often cover their tracks by "looping and weaving" in and out of dozens of computer systems around the world, masquerading as legitimate users on the co-opted system.[92] This can raise serious law enforcement jurisdictional issues for police personnel who attempt to follow the digital evidence trail to the true location of the computer criminal. Under current law, the only way to trace the individual may be with a court-ordered wiretap for each system on which the criminal has traveled.[93] Since hackers often take a different path each time, obtaining the wiretap order in advance poses unique challenges to police.[94] These challenges are further complicated by the fact that wiretap orders may be necessary for different cities, states, and nations — each with its own concept of computer crime.

Complicating any effort to police computer crime is the difficulty in obtaining digital evidence. Not only can incriminating clues be hidden, encrypted, and virus-laden, but they can be strewn anywhere around the world. The current laws regarding the search and seizure of digital evidence are ambiguous at best, and most of these laws remain to be tested. Furthermore, privacy rights asserted by various parties make the search and seizure of computer evidence very difficult.[95] The level of privacy and other rights accorded to an item or place to be searched depends on its actual and intended use. For example, is the computer to be seized acting as a simple storage and communications device or is it also fulfilling some type of publishing function? Legally, a personal computer used by a single individual is easier to search than a thousand-user bulletin board system ("BBS").[96] By seizing the BBS, the police may stop the illegal distribution of contraband, but they may also interfere with the publication of the BBS's newsletter and distribution of

---

90. *See id.*

91. *See id.*

92. *See* SECURITY IN CYBERSPACE, *supra* note 27, at 13.

93. *See id.* at 167.

94. *See id.* at 13.

95. *See* Raphael Winick, *Searches and Seizures of Computers and Computer Data,* 8 HARV. J.L. & TECH. 75, 81-89.

96. *See* SECURITY IN CYBERSPACE, *supra* note 27, at 102-09, 114-25.

e-mail to persons who have no connection to the illegal activity.[97] Because computer crime presents so many unique obstacles to investigation and prosecution, most police agencies would rather avoid the matter altogether. Thus, officers pursue the "low-hanging fruit" — those criminals such as street corner prostitutes and drug dealers — who require fewer resources and less complicated investigations in order to sustain an arrest and conviction.

C. The Lack of Resources

Compared to violent street crime, white collar crime in general, and computer crime in particular, is vastly underreported.[98] Underreporting is significant because law enforcement resources are allocated based upon the number of *reported* crimes.[99] If a particular precinct has a 50% increase in the number of 911 emergency calls for service in a six-month period, it is likely to see additional patrol officers allocated to deal with that problem. Similarly, if a precinct commander notices a 75% increase in commercial burglaries, he or she is likely to ask for more burglary detectives to help abate the problem. Since police agencies receive few complaints about computer crime, there appears to be no problem. In fact, many senior law enforcement administrators state that computer crime simply has not become a problem in their particular jurisdiction.[100] As a result, police chiefs allocate few resources to the problem.[101] A wiser police manager, however, would not confuse invisibility with non-existence.

Law enforcement executives attuned to the issue of computer crime still face financial challenges. Training police officers to investigate digital crime is an expensive proposition. In these times of public fiscal constraint, police chiefs are loath to spend their limited resources on anything that will not provide a sure and noticeable return. A properly trained computer crime investigator may require extensive ongoing professional education to maintain up-to-date skills.[102] Because computer companies introduce many new hardware and software products each year, staying ahead of the educational curve can be a monumental task. Furthermore, no single investigator can know how to

---

97. *See* Charney, *supra* note 17, at 941-42.

98. *See* SECURITY IN CYBERSPACE, *supra* note 27, at 243-45; Michael G. Noblett, *The Computer: High-Tech Instrument of Crime*, FBI L.ENFORCEMENT BULL., June 1993, at 7, 7-9.

99. *See* Collier & Spaul, *supra* note 15, at 308.

100. *See id.* at 307.

101. *See id.*

102. *See* Groover, *supra* note 28.

operate every system.[103] A number of officers must be trained to specialize in a variety of platforms.

As if training costs were not enough to discourage the average police chief from investigating digital crime, there is always the cost of equipment to be considered as well.[104] The specialized hardware and software required for the forensic examination of computers can easily run to tens of thousands of dollars.[105] Digital evidence storage rooms, spaces without magnetic interference, must be established to prevent the break down and destruction of digital evidence.[106] A police department serious about the investigation of high-tech crime must prepare for any eventuality: thousands of dollars could be spent on forensic IBM PC software only to discover the system that must be examined is an Apple Macintosh. In such a case, none of the PC cables or disks would work with the Macintosh, requiring additional funding in order to adequately equip digital crime investigators with the tools they need.

Training and equipment are not the only financial impediments to conducting high-technology crime investigations: the physical distance between perpetrator and victim also poses special problems for those investigating computer crimes. A New York City police detective working on a traditional burglary in lower Manhattan might have to drive to Brooklyn to interview suspects, execute a search warrant, and seize physical evidence, but rarely will her cases take her very far. In the world of digital crime, however, the Manhattan detective is much more likely to be confronted with a suspect who lives outside of the New York City area, in Los Angeles for example. Not only might this necessitate a trip to California, but it would also require significant coordination between the New York City Police Department and the Los Angeles Police Department. This coordination takes not just precious time, but also lots of money. Needless to say, this scenario is more complicated when the suspect and evidence are located outside of the United States.

A suspect who dials into the Oxford University computer system in England and illegally uses that system to break into the University of San Marcos in Peru for the purpose of illegally accessing a NASA computer at Cape Canaveral may commit a crime in three countries. At the very least, the evidence will have traveled, and therefore will need to be traced, through all three countries. Since computer hackers often erase any digital evidence of their illegal presence, monitoring access must be done in real-time at multiple sites in different countries, involving

---

103. *See id.*
104. *See id.*
105. *See generally* Michael Noblett, *Computer Analysis and Response Team (CART): The Microcomputer as Evidence*, 19 CRIME LABORATORY DIG. 11 (1992).
106. *See generally* CLARK & DILBERTO, INVESTIGATING COMPUTER CRIME (1996).

federal, state, and local governments, twenty-four hours a day. Not only does coordination in the above scenario prove to be a nightmare, but the costs involved in such work are often prohibitive. When international cases are pursued, the mechanics of cooperation, such as the execution of mutual legal assistance treaties or the involvement of the State Department, can add substantial delays and expense to an already burdensome and difficult operation. Because computer crime is underreported and relatively expensive to prepare for, many police agencies prefer to ignore the situation and spend their limited resources in other areas, such as purchasing newer police cars, police officer overtime pay, and community policing programs.

The lack of tangible, conspicuous evidence is another factor in the underreporting of computer crime. When a homicide occurs, a body almost always appears and is reported to the authorities. Crimes like homicide are easily defined and quantified and, by law, must be reported to the Federal Bureau of Investigation ("FBI") and the Federal Bureau of Justice Statistics.[107] As mentioned earlier, the definition of a computer crime remains ambiguous.[108] The lack of a standard definition makes it harder for the police to understand and track such crimes. The overwhelming majority of law enforcement organizations do not keep statistics on computer crime.[109]

Each year when the FBI's *Uniform Crime Reports* comes out, the public pays considerable attention to a given community's homicide and auto theft rates. Nowhere in the *Uniform Crime Reports*, however, is there any mention of computer crime statistics.[110] Because the Department of Justice does not mandate their collection, police agencies do not feel compelled to count the number of these crimes.[111] Since computer crime statistics remain invisible to the police department, the police feel no particular compunction to dedicate limited resources to high-tech crimes that nobody bothers to count.

Complicating the invisibility problem, most victims of computer crime and intrusions fail to report their victimization.[112] Individuals often do not know that the violation committed against them actually constitutes a criminal offense. Businesses have different reasons not to report computer crime incidents: mistrust of the police, the fear of

---

107. *See generally* FEDERAL BUREAU OF INVESTIGATION, UNIFORM CRIME REPORTS FOR THE UNITED STATES 1995 (1996) [hereinafter UNIFORM CRIME REPORTS]; U.S. DEPARTMENT OF JUSTICE, SOURCEBOOK OF CRIMINAL JUSTICE STATISTICS — 1995 (Kathleen Maguire & Ann L. Pastore eds., 1996).

108. *See supra* text accompanying notes 15-17.

109. *See* Collier & Spaul, *supra* note 15, at 308.

110. *See generally* UNIFORM CRIME REPORTS, *supra* note 107.

111. *Cf.* SECURITY IN CYBERSPACE, *supra* note 27, at 242-43.

112. *See id.* at 242-45.

negative publicity, and potential loss of future revenues. It is for these reasons that the private security industry attracts billions of dollars each year.[113] Last year alone, corporate America alone spent $6 billion for private computer security services.[114]

The business community clearly believes that police officers cannot handle computer-related crimes and security problems because they think cops will not understand the issues.[115] Corporate managers "believe that police agencies are at best ineffective, and at worst, that their use is counter-productive in prosecuting or restricting computer crime."[116] Perhaps the greatest obstacle to businesses reporting computer crime is the deeply-held fear of losing customer and shareholder confidence.[117] 65% of those who participated in a survey by the San Francisco-based Computer Security Institute ("CSI") cited a fear of negative publicity resulting from disclosure of a break-in.[118] In CSI's survey, 83% of the respondents stated they did not advise the police when they had been victimized by computer crime.[119]

Even the smallest business owner knows that customer confidence is an essential element for financial viability; corporations who lose the confidence of the public can face bankruptcy. For example, a hospital whose patient records system was hacked by computer intruders, as in the nightmare scenario with which I began this Article, would surely lose customers. A major airline that had its flight maintenance database destroyed would rightly be concerned about passengers choosing another carrier. Perhaps no organizations are as susceptible to public perceptions of safety as financial institutions. In 1995, when Citibank lost $10 million to a group of hackers operating out of St. Petersburg, Russia, its top twenty customers were immediately targeted by six of Citibank's competitors who argued that their banks were more secure.[120]

Another problem that contributes to underreporting is that law enforcement agencies and corporations have different goals in mind vis-à-vis computer crime: the police want to prove a crime has occurred and bring the culprits to justice;[121] a corporation is more interested in stopping the intrusion, minimizing losses, and avoiding publicity at all

---

113. *See* Andrew Leckey, *Investing for the 21st Century*, THE FUTURIST, July-Aug. 1995, at 31, 34 (estimating the figure at $65 billion per year).

114. *See* Richard Behar, *Who's Reading Your E-Mail*, FORTUNE, Feb. 3, 1997, at 57, 58.

115. *See* Collier & Spaul, *supra* note 15, at 310.

116. *Id.*

117. *See* SECURITY IN CYBERSPACE, *supra* note 27, at 27.

118. *See id.*

119. *See id.*

120. *See id.* at 51.

121. *See id.*

costs.[122] To this end, many computer crime investigations are conducted through the corporation's general counsel's office so as to provide a veil of secrecy that flows from the attorney-client privilege.[123] According to the FBI, as little as 11% of computer crime is actually reported to law enforcement officials.[124] A few security firm executives recently admitted that their goal is to catch and notify the hacker to stop his attack against the security company's client.[125] Once that particular assault has stopped, businesses do not mind throwing the hacker back into the marketplace, hopefully to attack their competition down the street.[126] Since the goal of the average company is to stop its own financial losses due to computer malfeasance, there is little consideration of the greater public good of getting the computer criminal behind bars.

As long as private computer security firms continue to handle most high-tech crime investigations, businesses will continue to believe that the police are incapable of protecting their corporate and economic interests. This situation can rapidly become a vicious cycle, with businesses balking at future tax increases for police given the little value they derive from such public services. More importantly, however, businesses are integral parts of most communities. Police agencies that neglect their criminal enforcement and investigative obligations to members of the community fail in their publicly chartered mission.

D. The Police Cannot Do It Alone

Even if police agencies properly understood the importance of digital crime, law enforcement does not operate in a vacuum. Mayors, district attorneys, city council members, and judges are among some of the most important participants in the battle against high-technology crime. These public officials must be convinced of the need to expand into the poorly understood arena of digital law enforcement, a difficult sell with many competing political interests at stake. In a time when most police departments are "getting back to the basics" of patrol and community-based policing, creating another specialized unit seems anathema to larger organizational goals.[127]

---

122. *See id.*
123. *See id.* at 52.
124. *See* Noblett, *supra* note 98.
125. *See* SECURITY IN CYBERSPACE, *supra* note 27, at 51.
126. *See id.*
127. *See generally* David Kocieniewske, *Safir Shifts 500 Detectives to Aid Precincts,* N.Y. TIMES, Feb. 2, 1997, at 34 (reporting the reassignment of police investigators from specialized central units to non-specialized precinct units); *The Police Reform That Must Not Die; Community Policing Push Affirms City Hall Commitment,* L.A. TIMES, Jan. 9, 1994, at M4.

Those police departments that choose to pursue computer criminals must therefore include prosecutors and elected officials as an integral part of their overall anti-crime strategy. What is the point of detecting and investigating computer crime if the district attorney's office lacks the expertise or refuses to prosecute these matters? In addition, penalties for conviction in digital crime cases vary enormously, often yielding no more than a mere "slap on the wrist" for the offender.[128] Why expend limited resources on cases that have questionable results? Despite the best efforts of the police department, political authorizers may still not see the value in policing high-technology crime, instead pushing officers to concentrate on crimes which people "care about."[129]

E. Lack of Public Outcry

Most police chiefs have yet to hear any significant complaint about computer crime. Since neither the business community nor citizen groups seem to be upset about these crimes, law enforcement executives are free to put all their resources into something people *are* upset about, violent crime.[130] The public outcry against violence pushes municipal and law enforcement leaders to find a few extra dollars in the budget. There has not yet been such an outcry against cybercrime.

Complicating the lack of general public concern about computer crime is a strong reaction from some against law enforcement entering the world of "digital policing." Policing the Internet will unquestionably put pressures on American notions of privacy, property, and free speech.[131] A number of organizations have legitimate concerns regarding law enforcement's intrusion into cyberspace. Groups such as the American Civil Liberties Union,[132] the Electronic Frontier Foundation,[133] and the Electronic Privacy Information Center[134] are willing to wage

---

128. *See* Collier & Spaul, *supra* note 15.

129. *See supra* text accompanying notes 72-73.

130. *See id.*

131. *See* Sussman, *supra* note 48, at 55.

132. The American Civil Liberties Union ("ACLU") is a public interest organization created in 1920 to protect individual rights through litigation, legislation, and education. *See American Civil Liberties Union* (last updated Mar. 25, 1997) <http://www.aclu.org/>.

133. The Electronic Frontier Foundation ("EFF") is a non-profit, public interest, civil liberties organization working to protect privacy, free expression, and access to public resources and information online, as well as to promote responsibility in new media. *See Electronic Frontier Foundation* (visited Mar. 25, 1997) <http://www.eff.org/>.

134. The Electronic Privacy Information Center ("EPIC") is a public interest research center in Washington, D.C. It was established in 1994 to focus public attention on emerging civil liberties issues and to protect privacy, the First Amendment, and constitutional values. *See Electronic Privacy Information Center* (visited Mar. 25, 1997) <http://www.epic.org/>.

490   *Harvard Journal of Law & Technology*   [Vol. 10

long, drawn-out battles in court when they perceive that police officers have overstepped their constitutional boundaries in enforcing cybercrime.

Thus, the sluggishness with which police agencies are pursuing digital criminals can be attributed to a lack of public outcry combined with significant political pressure warning politicians and police executives to proceed with great caution into this new arena of criminal law. Moreover, mayors have not yet found it necessary to push their police chiefs into doing anything about high-technology crime. In the ever-changing world of law enforcement, it is hard to plan for next week, let alone for ten years from now. Events like high-profile homicides, civil unrest, publicized incidents of police misconduct, and officers killed in the line of duty lead police chiefs to manage from one crisis to the next. Thus, at least for the present time, police departments are willing to turn a blind eye to those crimes taking place in cyberspace.

As we have seen, there are many reasons why police do not yet care about high-technology crime. These impediments include police culture, limited police resources, the invisibility of digital crime, and other high priority concerns like violent crime. Yet, like it or not, law enforcement agencies around the globe have to confront a rapidly changing world in which ever-evolving technologies will fundamentally change society as we know it. The digital revolution has begun. The longer police departments wait to patrol the information superhighway, the more daunting their task will eventually be.

III. How Do We Get To Where We Need to Be?

While computer crime is on the rise, significant cultural, financial, and educational challenges may stymie police agencies who wish to combat high-tech offenses. Yet, something must be done by law enforcement officers to combat computer crime. The race is on and the bad guys have a significant head-start. To turn around police departments will require a paradigm shift in the way policing is done.

Although the information revolution is upon us and changing the way in which criminal activity is taking place, very little attention has been given to the information and computer literacy skills of police professionals. If police agencies are to be considered competent, there must be greater resources dedicated to training officers to understand and investigate computer crime. Many police departments might like to ignore problems of high-technology crime and leave the work to federal agencies. This tactic, however, would be ill-advised.

Police managers who assume they can just call in their federal law enforcement counterparts any time a local high-tech crime takes place are making a serious error. Although organizations like the FBI will likely become involved in any case of computer crime that threatens national security, they do not have the resources to assist with the investigation of local gamblers, child pornographers, or even murderers who had inculpatory evidence stored on their hard drives. The resources simply do not exist for federal law enforcement agencies to handle the bulk of high-technology crimes at the local and municipal levels.

Local and state police agencies will thus have to build mechanisms to deal with these types of crimes. The approach must be two-pronged: both long- and short-term responses are needed. In the short run, most agencies will have to "play catch-up." That is, there will be a need for some rapid growth in the amount of equipment and personnel dedicated to the problem of computer crime. Some officers will have to be trained elsewhere, perhaps by organizations in the private sector that offer basic computer classes. Of course, a small percentage of officers will need advanced training, particularly in computer forensics. On the equipment front, it may make sense for police agencies with limited budgets, particularly those in suburban and rural areas, to form regional task forces to deal with the rising workload in computer crime. Several police agencies could pool their resources and each could purchase smaller amounts of equipment to share among the members of the group.

For the long-term, police executives have to think strategically about computer crime and must be prepared to allocate the appropriate resources for the recruitment, education, and training of personnel capable of investigating these crimes. Departments that have not yet computerized their operations should do so. Not only will this lead to increases in overall efficiency, it will begin to familiarize officers with computing. Employees should be encouraged to think about how technology might help them improve department operations. Furthermore, serious consideration should be given to encouraging young, college-educated computer science majors to join the police force.

Departments also need to find funding for these endeavors. Many agencies, especially smaller police departments, do not have the resources to train personnel for the effective investigation of computer crime. Although some of the necessary equipment can be acquired through donations, police departments should not be put in the position of holding bake sales to pay for necessary and justifiable training. Given the numerous interests competing for each tax dollar, most local and state law enforcement organizations will encounter resistance from their political authorizers as they attempt to expnad their use and understanding of computers. A major funding source for these endeavors must be identified.

In 1968, President Johnson signed the Omnibus Crime Control and Safe Streets Act.[135] Among the Act's provisions was the creation of the Law Enforcement Assistance Administration ("LEAA"),[136] to provide technical assistance to local government law enforcement agencies. Funding for LEAA was withdrawn in 1982, but in the fourteen years of its existence, LEAA provided local agencies with nearly $50 million in funds for police officer training and technology assistance to local criminal justice organizations.[137] It is time to bring back a version of LEAA to help police departments gear up to fight computer crime.

The police officers of today and tomorrow will require certain attitudes, training, and education to effectively control crime in a digital world. Current theories in criminal justice administration have been critical of law enforcement's traditionally reactive responses to crime. Community members and police executives have been calling for a more proactive approach to all facets of law enforcement. This clamor for proactive policing must extend into the world of digital crime.

A. Building a Computer-Competent Police Force

For the bulk of the police force, the levels of computer literacy necessary to function are relatively low. It is certainly not necessary for every police officer to have a Ph.D. in computer science in order to be effective in the twenty-first century. However, a basic level of computer literacy must be mandated so that officers can ask the basic questions about the crimes they will be investigating.

Patrol officers must be trained to recognize a high-technology crime when it occurs. Furthermore, these "first responders" must understand the importance of calling in an expert to deal with such situations. A lack of attention or willingness to call in a computer crime specialist can have negative consequences for police departments attempting to preserve evidence, arrest a perpetrator, or successfully pursue a prosecution in court. If a computer examination is not conducted properly, valuable evidence may be lost, and the police department involved may be liable for any damage caused to the computer.

These days, criminals can install degaussing loops around the door jambs of their apartments. The magnetic field created will erase any magnetic media carried through the door. Specialists responding to handle the investigation would be attuned to the potential presence of such a device and could respond appropriately. An inexperienced

---

135. Pub. L. No. 90-351, 82 Stat. 197 (1968).
136. *See* SUE T. REID, CRIMINAL JUSTICE PROCEDURES AND ISSUES 130 (1987); *see generally* ENCYCLOPEDIA OF POLICE SCIENCE 409 (William G. Bailey ed., 2d ed. 1995)
137. *See* REID, *supra* note 136.

officer, however, might carry the computer out of the house unaware that the magnetic field was destroying all the recordings on the disk. A computer criminal could also alter his computer so that any police officer who turned on the machine without using the appropriate bypass switch would unknowingly cause the hard drive to format itself, thereby destroying any possible evidence contained in the machine. To avoid such catastrophes, the basic rule of thumb for patrol officers and detectives when a computer is found at a crime scene should be: "Don't touch it!"

Although not all police officers need to become computer specialists, all first responders do need basic training to handle crimes and crime scenes involving computers. Even common police calls can take on different dimensions in the world of high-technology. For example, police officers already have an understanding of what it means to stalk somebody, but, the idea of stalking by computer may be a new concept for most officers. Nevertheless, it does not take a specialist to ask a victim to print out copies of the harassing e-mail so they can be attached to a police report and forwarded to the district attorney for prosecution. If an officer has no idea what e-mail is, or even that electronic records of e-mail are kept and can be found, then the chances for a successful prosecution will be severely limited. In this scenario, an officer only needs a minimal amount of computer savvy. Basic guidelines and procedures for handling the preliminary investigation of computer crime should be established. These procedures should include a method for determining when a computer crime expert should be summoned.

Thus, although all officers will require basic literacy in information technology, some police personnel will require in-depth training in order to effectively police the digital world. Seizing electronic material is highly specialized work. Just as every police department in the country has a bomb squad or a SWAT unit, or contracts for such services, they must do the same for computer crime. Delicate protocols have to be followed in order to preserve critical and perishable evidence. Having this work done by those who lack expertise could hurt the agency's reputation, be harmful to the victim, embolden criminals for future acts, and jeopardize prosecutions. If there is any doubt about the competency of an agency to handle more a particular crime, the case should be referred to an expert.

B. Training Officers for Computer Literacy

One of the roles of the specialist division should be to provide training to other members of the police department. Patrol officers need to know how to handle computers found during investigations. Detectives need to include electronic media in the standard repertoire of

494 *Harvard Journal of Law & Technology* [Vol. 10

items included in their search warrants. All officers need to receive more training and more exposure to computers. Such a focus on training could begin by requiring basic computing skills of all academy recruits. Students in the academy need to be trained in the advantages to law enforcement of using information technology as well as the threats posed by computer crime.

Officers who are already on the force need to be encouraged to learn about computers. Departments should offer general computer training to familiarize officers with how word processing, spreadsheets for crime statistics, and databases can be useful in their daily work. They should also be introduced to the Internet. Many departments may not have the resources for in-house training, but they can hire outside consultants to do such training. More advanced training should be provided when possible. This could include comprehensive reimbursement programs for officers who wish to take computer classes at local schools and universities.

IV. CONCLUSION

Society has placed the burden of investigating computer crimes on police departments. Unfortunately, many institutional factors have led police departments to shy away from pursuing these crimes. Programs to address the problem of computer crime need to address the social, cultural, and political factors that are currently stopping police departments from developing teams to combat these crimes. Unless police departments start planning and training now, it may be impossible to keep up with the criminal elements of society as they plan their future misdeeds. In order to protect society from these new cybercrimes, it is necessary for law enforcement agencies not merely to meet the expertise of their criminal counterparts, but rather to exceed their knowledge and skills. Training and equipment must be acquired soon. If not, the U.S. criminal justice system will fall perpetually behind in its efforts to enforce and prosecute a whole new class of criminal activities.

[26]

Policing and the Regulation of the Internet[1]

By David S. Wall

Cyberlaw Research Unit, Centre for Criminal Justice Studies, Department of Law, University of Leeds

Summary: *This paper maps out those contours of the Internet which require policing and then it illustrates the implications for policing. The first part establishes why the cyberspace, created by the Internet, needs to be policed by exploring what we currently understand as a "cybercrime". The second part goes on to look at who is actually policing cyberspace and how they are going about it. The final part considers some of the organisational and constitutional implications for the policing agencies that tread the cyberbeat.*

As we come to terms with the Internet a rather paradoxical situation is emerging. On the one hand, it is now quite clear that the Internet really does have the capacity to transcend economic, political, geographical, social and even racial and gendered boundaries, much as the early commentators had predicted.[2] On the other hand, although the mass media would have us believe otherwise, the anarchy that was predicted by those who favoured early regulation[3] has not materialised. Cyberspace[4] is remarkably ordered considering the large numbers of individuals involved and the breadth of their involvement in it.[5] So, we have either a case of exaggerated claims, or there is some mechanism that is already operating to police or regulate cyberspace. In fact it will be suggested later in this paper that the answer is a bit of

---

[1] My thanks go to my colleagues at the University of Leeds, especially Clive Walker and Yaman Akdeniz.

[2] See for example, J. P. Barlow, "Selling Wine Without Bottles: The Economy of Mind on the Global Net", http://www.eff.org/pub/Publications/John_Perry_Barlow/HTML/idea_economy_ article.html; H. Rheingold, *The Virtual Community: Homesteading the electronic frontier* (New York: Harper Perennial, 1994); Z. Saradar and J. R. Ravetz (eds), *Cyberfutures: Culture and Politics on the Information Superhighway* (London: Pluto Press, 1996), p. 1.

[3] See especially the U.S. Communications Decency Act 1996, later struck down in part in *ACLU v. Reno*, 117 S.Ct. 2329 (1997).

[4] Conceptually, cyberspace is a privately controlled (owned) public space, very similar in concept to more physical spaces such as private shopping malls; see C. Shearing and P. Stenning (eds), *Private Policing* (Newbury Park, Sage, 1987); L. Johnson, *The Rebirth of Private Policing* (London, Routledge, 1992); T. Jones and T. Newburn, *Private Security and Public Policing* (Oxford, Clarendon Press, 1998).

[5] See S. Davies, "Make it safe, but keep it free", *The Independent*, September 4, 1996.

multi-tiered policing

both, but it is with this paradox in mind that this paper will explore the policing[6] of cyberspace. Clearly the policing of the Internet is about more than just simply enforcing the law, rather it is about regulating the behaviour of Internet users. And by engaging the issue at the point where the debate over policing the Internet shifts from legal regulation to the broader issue of governance, the paper will also seek to establish exactly who is regulating the behaviour of whom within the powerplay that is currently taking place to control cyberspace. Futhermore, it will be suggested that a fairly effective system of multi-tiered policing has already developed within cyberspace and that this model will best provide the basis for any future developments in the policing of the medium. Of particular importance is the view that any such developments should include a framework of accountability that would incorporate a series of checks and balances to protect civil liberties against the expression of various political, moral and commercial power interests that are currently vying for control over cyberspace.

So, this paper is essentially a topographical exercise that is designed to map out the contours of policing the Internet. The first part will look briefly at why the cyberspace needs to be policed, especially at what we currently understand as a "cybercrime", who are the victims and who are the offenders. The second part will look at who is actually policing cyberspace, and the third part will offer some conclusions.

The problem: what and who needs policing?

The Internet has impacted upon human activities[7] in two main ways. First, it has acted as a vehicle for the further facilitation of existing activities.[8] Secondly, it has created an environment, a cyberspace, which has facilitated the creation of entirely new types of activities[9] which are largely free of traditional and terrestrial constraints.[10] It is along these same lines that the Internet has also facilitated the development of undesirable behaviours or harms. With regard to the former we find that the Internet has, for example, enabled the execution of fraudulent activity or has enabled paedophiles to conduct their undesirable practices. With regard to the latter, we see the development of new types of harmful activities which are novel in so far as they lie outside our existing experiences and demand new forms of

---

[6] There are various definitions of the term "policing". It is used here in a broad sense to mean the management of behaviour within a space by a definable group according to a particular set of definable values. It is from common support for these values that the policing group draws its mandate. For a useful overview, see R. Reiner, *The Politics of the Police* (Hemel Hempstead, Harvester Wheatsheaf, 1992).

[7] See A. Escobar, "Welcome to Cyberia: Notes on the anthropology of cyberculture", in Z. Saradar and J. R. Ravetz (eds), *op. cit.*; B. Loader (ed.), *The Governance of Cyberspace* (London, Routledge, 1996); H. Reingold, *op. cit.*; J. P. Barlow, *op. cit.*; D. S. Wall, "Policing the Virtual Community: The Internet, cyber-crimes and the policing of cyberspace," in P. Francis, P. Davies and V. Jupp, *Policing Futures* (London, Macmillan, 1997).

[8] E-mail, for example, whilst being revolutionary because of its speed and interactive nature, is simply a communication method that is one step beyond the development of the fax.

[9] An example of such activity is the creation of software or design of imagery which never actually achieves physical expression.

[10] Especially the acceleration of the disembedding of time and space that Antony Giddens mentioned in his book, *The Consequences of Modernity* (London, Polity Press, 1990), p.6. The debates over the development of cyberspace are causing a reformulation of the debates over modernity, see A. Escobar, *op. cit.*, 1996, p.113.

understanding and also legal responses. To give a few examples, we see the creation of new forms of obscenity through computer-generated images (pseudo-photographs); the developments of new forms of appropriation such as the theft of visual imagery that possesses a high intellectual property value; the waging of information warfare via the illegal invasion of computer space and the destruction of materials within it.

A more systematic categorisation suggests that there are four main groups of behaviour relating to the Internet that are currently causing concern. They are obscenity, trespass, theft and violence, and each group illustrates a range of activities rather than actual offences.[11]

- *Cyberobscenity* refers to the trade of obscene materials within cyberspace. The cyberobscenity debate is very complex. Its newsworthiness has not only driven the debate over the regulation of cyberspace, but its resolution is also marred by both normative perceptions and definitional variations across legal jurisdictions. In Britain, for example, individuals regularly consume images that might be classed as obscene in many Middle-Eastern countries. And yet, what individuals class as obscene in the United Kingdom is often acceptable to the citizens of more permissive countries, such as in Scandinavia.[12]

Cybertrespass (unauthorised access to data) relates to the crossing of established boundaries into spaces over which control has already been established. In its mildest form, cybertrespass can be little more than an irritating intellectual challenge resulting in a harmless trespass, but at its worst, it is full blown information warfare between social groups or even nation states. Somewhere between these positions falls the cybervandal, spy and terrorist.

Cybertheft relates to a range of different types of acquisitive harm that can take place within cyberspace. At one level are the more traditional patterns of theft, such as the fraudulent use of credit cards and (cyber)cash. Of particular concern is the increasing potential for the raiding of on-line bank accounts. There have already been incidents of this activity.[13] At another level are those acts which will cause us to reconsider our understanding of property and therefore the act of theft, such as cyberpiracy (the appropriation of intellectual properties).

Cyberviolence describes the violent impact of the cyberactivities of another upon an individual or social grouping. Whilst such activities do not have to have a direct physical manifestation, the victim nevertheless feels the violence of the act and can bear long-term psychological scars as a consequence. The activities referred to here range from cyberstalking[14] to hate speech and bomb-talk.

---

[11] See further D. S. Wall, "Cybercrimes: New wine, no bottles?", in P. Davies, P. Francis and V. Jupp (eds), *Hidden Crimes, Victimisation and Regulation* (London, MacMillan, 1999).

[12] *ibid*. For a more full discussion of obscenity and the Internet see Y. Akdeniz, "Governance of Pornography and Child Pornography on the Global Internet: A Multi-Layered Approach", in L. Edwards and C. Wealde (eds), *Law and the Internet: Regulating Cyberspace* (Oxford, Hart Publishing, 1997).

[13] In one incident, some German students invited people to register to win an $50k prize. The students then used a program they had developed to search for on-line banking programs. If one was found, the student's program, or "cookie" as it is called, would automatically mail an invoice for $20. The students collected a total of $640k. See L. A. Lorek, "Outwitting Cybercrime" (Sun-Sentinel of South Florida, 1997), http://www.sunsentinel.com/money/09130018.htm.

[14] See L. Ellison and Y. Akdeniz, "Cyberstalking: the Regulation of Harassment on the Internet", above p.29.

These four categories demonstrate the range of cyberactivities that are causing concern and are leading to demands for the greater regulation of cyberspace. Their resolution is not simply a matter of engaging specific bodies of criminal law. The issue is rather more complex as the harms are defined by a complex combination of normative, political and legal values. The issue is further complicated by the following four factors.

First, many definitions of offence and offender are being forged by the fight, or "intellectual land grab",[15] that is taking place for control over cyberspace. Of particular importance here is the increasing level of intolerance that is being demonstrated by "the powerful" towards certain "risk groups" which they perceive as a threat to their interests. Such intolerance tends to mould broader definitions of deviance. But the definitions of deviance are not so simply one-sided, as Melossi has argued that definitions of crime and deviance arise, not only from the social activity of élite or power groups, but also from that of "common members" of society and offenders themselves: "the struggle around the definition of crime and deviance is located within the field of action that is constituted by plural and even conflicting efforts at producing control".[16] Secondly, there is often some confusion as to whether or not the harms fall under civil or criminal laws, and to complicate matters further, some harms will be classed as criminal in some jurisdictions and civil in others. Thirdly, there is a degree of confusion over who the victims are and how they are being victimised. Not only can victims vary from individuals to social groupings, but the (cyber)harms done to them can range from the actual to the perceived. In cases such as cyberstalking or the theft of cybercash, the victimisation is very much directed towards the individual. However, in other cases the victimisation is more indirect, such as with cases of cyberpiracy or cyberspying/terrorism. Furthermore, as has been found to be the case with the reporting of white-collar crimes, it is likely that many victims of cybercrimes, be they primary or secondary victims, may be unwilling to acknowledge that they have been a victim, or it may take them some time to realise it. Alternatively, where the victimisation has been imputed by a third party upon the basis of an ideological, political, moral, or commercial assessment of risk, the victim or victim group may simply be unaware that they have been victimised or may even believe that they have not, such is the case with some forms of pornography. Fourthly, the cyberoffenders are fairly non-typical in terms of traditional criminological expectations, which problematises the identification of the offender. Although itself contested, the debate over the policing of traditional crimes has tended to be located within the analysis of working class sub-cultures or the underclass. Offenders in cyberspace are more likely to be middle class, without criminal records, often expert and skilled and motivated by a variety of financial and non-financial goals.

So, what this brief analysis suggests is that the demands for the regulation of the Internet vary considerably. Some behaviours and harms are clearly covered by agencies related to existing criminal and civil law, others however, are more complicated and can only be dealt with by other bodies and means. In both cases, some form of check or test is required in order to establish that the harms are real

---

[15] J. Boyle, *Shamans, Software and Spleens: Law and the Construction of the Information Society* (Harvard University Press, Cambridge, Mass, 1996), p.125.

[16] D. Melossi, "Normal Crimes, elites and social control", in D. Nelken (ed.), *The Futures of Criminology* (London, Sage, 1994), p.205.

and not hypothetical, whether it be in the enforcement of law or during the formulation of policy. The following section will look at how, and by whom, the Internet is currently being policed.

Who is currently policing cyberspace?

When exploring the policing of the Internet, it is important to distinguish between bodies which seek to promote or protect norms and values, and those bodies which seek to enforce them. The former group include policy-making groups and legislators[17] at both a national level and at an international level in the case of the United Nations and the European Union.[18] The mandate of both is derived, directly or indirectly, from the formal democratic process. This group also includes the various pressure groups which represent specific interests and who lobby in order to further their cause or protect the interests of their members. In contrast with the legislators, their mandate is drawn from their support of a range of specific moral or political issues. Such pressure groups range from Cyber-Rights and Cyber-Liberties,[19] to groups of Internet Service Providers, such as the Internet Service Providers Association, which seeks to "promote the interests of Internet Service Providers in the UK . . . ".[20] Finally, there are the various organisations which are actively involved in the policing of cyberspace and which exist to enforce the norms of the former groups through various management strategies that effect a policing function. In practice it is often hard to disaggregate the two, but the following discussion will focus upon the latter group.

~ Currently, there are four main levels at which policing activity takes place within cyberspace: the Internet users themselves; the Internet Service Providers; state-funded non-public police organisations: and state-funded public police organisations. At each level the organisations or groups involved will also tend to find an expression in transnational forms[21] because of the global nature of the Internet. This reflects the "organisational bifurcation"[22] or "spatial polarisation"[23] that is also taking place within the sphere of terrestrial policing.

The *Internet Users* are the largest group of individuals to be inducted into policing the Internet. Within the user groups are a number of sub-groups which have formed around specific issues in order to police websites that offend them. Largely transnational in terms of their membership and operation, these groups tend to be self-appointed and possess neither a broad public mandate nor a statutory basis,

---

[17] In the U.K. these organisations would include the DTI, the Home Office, and the Houses of Parliament.

[18] See C. Walker and Y. Akdeniz, "The governance of the Internet in Europe with Special Reference to Illegal and Harmful Content", above, p.5.

[19] Cyber-Rights and Cyber-Liberties (http://www.cyber-rights.org), along with many others, have recently found an international expression under the umbrella of the Global Internet Liberty Campaign, http://www.gilc.org.

[20] http://www.ispa.org.uk/frame.htm.

[21] See J. Sheptycki, "Policing, Postmodernism and Transnationalism" (1998) 38 *British Journal of Criminology* 485, and "Reflections on the Transnationalisation of Policing: the Case of the RCMP and Serial Killers" (1998) 26 *International Journal of the Sociology of Law* 17.

[22] R. Reiner, "Policing a Postmodern Society" (1992) 55 *Modern Law Review* 761.

[23] L. Johnston, "Privatisation and Protection: Spatial and Sectoral Ideologies in British Policing and Crime Prevention" (1993) 56 *Modern Law Review* 771; T. Jones and T. Newburn, *op. cit.*, p.260.

consequently they lack any formal accountability for their actions which themselves may be intrusive or even illegal. However, they would seem to possess a fairly potent force, and a number of visible examples of virtual community policing have already occurred. In addition to the various complaint "hotlines" and the development of software to screen out undesirable communications,[24] there are a few recorded examples of netizen groups which have attempted to organise Internet users. The Internet Rapid Response Team (IRRT), for example, came to prominence when an e-mail message advertising a collection of child pornography, that carried a New York address, was received by thousands of Internet users all over the world.[25] Its response was to "spam" the New York police with calls for an immediate investigation. The IRRT is a voluntary group which polices the Internet to remove offensive material. The philosophy of the IRRT is that "it is up to Internet users as much as anyone else to react quickly when something like this happens".[26]

Another netizen group which actively police cyberspace are the CyberAngels,[27] a 1,000-strong organisation of net users who are also based, as their name suggests, along the Guardian Angel model. Divided into "Internet Safetly Patrols", they operate in the four main areas of the Internet: Internet Relay Chat (IRC), Usenet, World Wide Web (WWW), and the net services provided by the largest United States ISP, America Online (AOL).[28] Their function is to actively promote, preserve and protect netiquette which "is the collection of common rules of polite conduct that govern our use of the Internet".[29] Importantly, they claim the right to question what they encounter, and they argue that they have a civil, legal and human right to bring it to the attention of the proper authorities.[30] Their mission statement says that they are dedicated to fighting crime on the Internet "where there are clear victims and/or at-risk users", they seek to protect children from on-line criminal abuse, they give support to on-line victims and advise them upon how to seek a remedy, seek out materials that will cause harm, fear, distress, inconvenience, offence or concern, "regardless of whether it is criminal or not".[31]

Groups like the IRRT and CyberAngels perform a broadly ranging function, but other groups of netizens dedicate themselves to specific types of cyberharm, the most common being child pornography. Phreakers & Hackers (UK) Against Child Porn (PH(UK)ACP),[32] for example, claim not to be vigilantes, but aim to track down offensive sites and interfere with their operation. A similar group are Ethical Hackers Against Porn (EHAP)[33] who like, PH(UK)ACP, "want to stop child exploitation" and claim to work in loose co-operation with government and local officials, even though they admit to "using unconventional means to take down the

---

[24] R. Uhlig, "Hunt is on for Internet dealer in child porn" (1996) 518 *Electronic Telegraph*, October 23.

[25] *ibid.* N.B. little evidence is currently available to demonstrate the impact of this, or subsequently named, organisations.

[26] *ibid.*

[27] http://www.cyberangels.org/ and also at http://www.jex.com/cyberangels/.

[28] http://www.aol.com/.

[29] http://www.jex.com/cyberangels/mission.htm.

[30] http://www.jex.com/cyberangels/.

[31] http://www.jex.com/cyberangels/conduct.htm.

[32] http://freespace.virgin.net/pure.kaos/PH(UK)ACP/index.htm.

[33] http://www.hackers.com/ehap/mission.htm.

worst, most unscrupulous criminals known".[34] One of the most interesting paradoxes that currently exists with regard to the issue of child pornography on the Internet is the large amount of support given to efforts to counter it by the "mainstream" pornographers who wish to distance themselves from the issue, but also seek to legitimise their own activities.[35]

The Internet Service Providers: The ISPs have a rather fluid status which arises from the fact that although they are physically located in a particular jurisdiction, they tend to function in a transnational way. The moral panic[36] surrounding the Internet during the mid-1990s over the perceived threat of widespread pornography,[37] and the subsequent threats of legal action,[38] has forced Internet Service Providers to consider the possibility of controlling some of the activities that are taking place on their servers: especially the news discussion groups. In August 1996, the former Science and Technology Minister, warned that "in the absence of self-regulation, the police will inevitably move to act against service providers as well as the originators of illegal material".[39] This statement was quickly followed by a letter sent to Internet Service Providers by the Metropolitan Police Clubs and Vice Unit, warning that they could be liable for any illegal materials that were found to have been disseminated on their servers.[40] Their response in September 1996 was to promote "SafetyNet", a mix of "self-ratings", classification, user control and public reporting plus law enforcement action.[41] SafetyNet was jointly endorsed by the Metropolitan Police, Department of Trade and Industry (DTI), Home Office and the associations of the Internet Service Providers; the Internet Service Providers Association and the London Internet Exchange.[42] In December 1996, SafetyNet became the Internet Watch Foundation (IWF).[43] Since its formation, the standing of the Internet Watch Foundation has increased and it has become the quasi-public face of Internet regulation in the United Kingdom. One of its functions is to overview the use of the Internet and bring to the attention of ISPs any illegal materials that are reported to its hotline. Between December 1996 and November 1997 the IWF received 781 reports, mostly by e-mail, which covered 4,324 items (mostly on newsgroups). Action was taken with regard to 248 reports, and the greater majority, 85 per cent, related to child pornography, the eradication of which is one of the objectives of the Foundation.[44]

---

[34] Of course it is impossible to know whether or not these claims are actually fulfilled.

[35] See the website of ASACP (Adult Sites Against Child Pornography) (http://www. asacp.org/) who claim to have over 700 members and represent over 300 adult websites.

[36] S. Cohen, *Folk Devils and Moral Panics* (Paladin, London, 1972); also see A. Chandler, "The changing definition and image of hackers in popular discourse" (1996) 25 *International Journal of the Sociology of Law* 229.

[37] D. S. Wall (1997), *loc. cit.*

[38] R. Uhlig, "Minister's warning over Internet porn" (1996) *Electronic Telegraph*, August 16.

[39] *ibid.*

[40] See http://www.leeds.ac.uk/law/pgs/yaman/newsban.htm.

[41] W. Grossman, "A grip on the new" (1996) 496 *Electronic Telegraph*, C. Arthur, October 1, "New Crackdown on child porn on the Internet", *The Independent*, September 23, 1996.

[42] R. Uhlig, " 'Safety Net' on Internet will catch child porn" (1996) 488 *Electronic Telegraph*, September 23.

[43] S. Tendler, "Public to help police curb Internet porn", *The Times*, December 2, 1996. Intenret Watch can be found at http://www.Internetwatch.org.uk/.

[44] http://www.Internetwatch.org.uk/stats/stats.html.

The Internet Watch Foundation has a mandate from both the ISPs and also the United Kingdom Government, but Akdeniz argues that the IWF does not command a defined body of public support, especially for its Internet rating system, which has had very little public discussion.[45] However, it is probably the case that were the IWF to canvass public opinion over the issues such as child pornography, then such public support would be considerable. Of considerable further concern is the fact that the Internet Watch Foundation retains the status of being a private organisation with a very public function and as such lacks the structures of accountability that are normally associated with organisations that have a public function.

Although the legal status of ISPs as a publisher is now quite widely acknowledged, their liabilities vary under various bodies of law and have yet to be fully established.[46] Consequently, ISPs tend to tread fairly carefully and be responsive to requests for co-operation. Not only are they very wary of their potential legal liabilities, but also it is probably fair to say that they are fearful of any negative publicity which might arise from their not being seen to act responsibly. Interestingly, the police themselves also appear to be fairly uncertain about their general position with regard to the prosecution of ISPs. Whilst they have continued to warn the ISPs about possible prosecutions since 1996, none of the promised prosecutions has been brought against Internet Service Providers in the United Kingdom. The general rule of thumb that appears to be adopted across many jurisdictions is that liability tends to arise when the ISP fails to remove offensive material, whether it be obscene or defamatory, provided it has been brought to their attention following a complaint.[47]

There is a degree to which the ISPs are organised at a transnational level, for example, the Commercial Internet eXchange,[48] the Pan-European Internet Service Providers' Association (EuroISPA)[49] and Internet Service Providers' Consortium (mainly USA).[50] However these organisations tend to be more involved with technical and commercial issues that are gemane to ISPs than specifically with the self-policing of ISPs.

State-Funded Non-Public Police Organisations: The next level of policing involves state agencies, but these are bodies not normally perceived as "police" nor are they given the title "police".[51] For example, some governments, such as Singapore,

---

[45] For a more detailed discussion of the status of the Internet Watch Foundation see Y. Akdeniz, "Who Watches the Watchmen: Part II: Accountability and Effective Self-Regulation in the Information Age" (1998)_ http://www.cyber-rights.org/watchmen-ii.htm.

[46] See L. Edwards and C. Wealde (eds), *Law and the Internet: Regulating Cyberspace* (Oxford, Hart Publishing, 1997); I. J. Lloyd, *Information Technology Law* (London, Butterworths, 1997); D. Rowland and E. Macdonald, *Information Technology Law* (London, Cavendish, 1997). But see Defamation Act 1996, s.1.

[47] See the case of Felix Somm in Germany, as discussed in G. Leong, "Computer Child Pornography—the Liability of Distributors?" above, p.19; Center for Democracy and Technology, "Regardless of Frontiers: Protecting the Human Right to Freedom of Expression on The Global Internet" (Washington, Global Internet Liberty Campaign, 1998), p.3, footnote 1.

[48] http://www.cix.org/.

[49] http://www.euroispa.org/.

[50] http://www.ispc.org/.

[51] This implies that the core "police" have a mandate to preserve the peace and enforce the criminal law.

China, Korea and Vietnam,[52] have actively sought to control their citizen's use of the Internet, either by forcing users to register with governmental monitoring organisations or by directly controlling Internet traffic coming into their countries through government-controlled Internet Service Providers.[53]

Within Europe, Germany has set up a regulatory agency, the Internet Content Task Force, and has passed new telecommunications laws requiring Internet Service Providers to provide a back door so that security forces can read user's electronic mail if necessary.[54] The Internet Content Task Force also has powers to force German Internet Service Providers to block access to certain materials, such as the Dutch site "xs4all".[55] A similar organisation is currently being set up by the French Government, which has also passed legislation to set up a central regulatory agency.[56]

In the United States, a number of state-funded non-public police organisations have become involved in policing the Internet. In part, this is inevitable because the trans-jurisdictional nature of Internet traffic involves federal rather than provincial state agencies, however such a development does fit in with the United States strategy towards the Internet. The United States Postal Service, for example, was instrumental in investigating the case of *United States of America v. Robert A. Thomas and Carleen Thomas*, after a computer hacker from Tennessee be filed a complaint about the contents of a bulletin board containing obscene materials.[57] The case was subsequently investigated by a United States postal inspector. In another incident the United States Securities and Exchange Commission, which was "anxious about the spread of cyberfraud", brought a case against a publicly-traded company for allegedly conducting fraud through the Internet. The Commission noted that it anticipated that it "will be addressing this kind of conduct on the Internet more frequently" in the coming millennium.[58]

In addition to involving state-funded non-public police organisations, the United States Government have tried, with varying degrees of success, to introduce legal measures and develop technological devices to regulate cyberspace in order to "protect the interests of US industry".[59] For example, the "Clipper Chip" which is an "escrowed encryption system" that provides the government with codes to

---

[52] A useful list of the various states and types of censorship by country can be found at http://www.unikonstanz.de/~dierk/censorship/countries.html.

[53] See the Center for Democracy and Technology, *op. cit.*; "Silencing the New: The Threat to Freedom of Expression On-Line" (1996), gopher://gopher.igc.apc.org:5000/00/int/hrw/expression/7; M. L. Caden and S. E. Lucas, "Accidents on the Information Superhighway: on-line liability and regulation" (1996) 2 *Richmond Journal of Law & Technology*; T. Standage, "Web access in a tangle as censors have their say" (1996) 475 *Electronic Telegraph*, W. Grossman, September 10, "A grip on the new" (1996) 496 *Electronic Telegraph*, October 1.

[54] Grossman, *loc. cit.* See now Teleservices Act 1997.

[55] http://www.xs4all.nl/.

[56] Grossman, *loc. cit.*

[57] W. S. Byassee, "Jurisdiction of Cyberspace: applying real world precedent to the virtual community" (1997) 30 *Wake Forest Law Review* 205.

[58] C. Pretzlik, "Firm accused of fraud on the Internet", *Daily Telegraph*, November 9, 1996.

[59] Hon. J. Reno, "Law enforcement in cyberspace" address to the Commonwealth Club of California, San Francisco Hilton Hotel, June 14, 1996, http://pwp.usa.pipeline.com/~jya/addres.txt.

unscramble encrypted files.[60] Since the impact of many of these measures is also to curb individual freedom of communication, it is therefore not surprising that much of the debate over Internet regulation has revolved around the First Amendment of the United States Constitution, especially during the legal challenge[61] to the Communications Decency Act 1996.

An interesting example of a hybrid state-funded non-public police organisation in the United States is the Computer Emergency Response Team (CERT), based at Carnegie Mellon University in Pittsburgh, United States.[62] Unlike the United Kingdom's IWF, CERT is based within a public institution, however, it appears to be funded by mainly private sources, but like the IWF, it has a public function. CERT exists to combat unauthorised access to the Internet, and 15 programmers log reported break-ins and carry out the initial investigations. Where security breaches are found to be too complicated to deal with in-house, they are farmed out to an unofficial "brain trust".[63]

State Funded Public Police Organisations[64]: The final group of organisations which are involved in policing the Internet are the state-funded public police organisations whose formal status allows them to draw upon the democratic mandate of government. They tend to be organised either locally or nationally, depending upon the jurisdiction. However, whilst they tend to be located within the nation state, they are nevertheless joined by a tier of transnational policing organisations, such as Interpol and EUROPOL, whose membership requires such formal status.[65]

In the United Kingdom, the public police are organised locally, but there also exist national police organisations that deal with the collection of intelligence and the investigation of national organised crime. Within the local bodies, several specialist individual or groups of police officers monitor the Internet.[66] For example, a computer crime unit was established by the Metropolitan Police and a smaller, but similar, unit was set up by the Greater Manchester Police. Elsewhere, officers in the West Midlands Police and the Metropolitan Police Clubs and Vice Unit have used the Internet to collect intelligence about offences relating to the types of crime under their particular responsibility. At a national level, the National Criminal Intelligence Service (NCIS)[67] has taken on the responsibility for providing intelligence on serious offences such as child pornography which cross both force and also international boundaries. From April 1998, the investigation of such

[60] See Y. Akdeniz, "Computer pornography: a comparative study of US and UK obscenity laws and child pornography laws in relation to the Internet" (1996) 10 *International Review of Law, Computers and Technology* 235–261; D. Post, "Encryption vs. The Alligator Clip: The Feds Worry That Encoded Messages Are Immune to Wiretaps" (1995) *New Jersey Law Journal*, January 23, p.8; B. Sterling, *The Hacker Crackdown* (London, Penguin Books, 1994), V. Sussman, "Policing Cyberspace" (1995) 38 *U.S. News*, January 23, p.54.

[61] *ACLU v. Reno*, 117 S.Ct. 2329 (1997). The Act is codified as (47 USC s.223).

[62] http://www.cert.org/.

[63] J. A. Adams, "Controlling Cyberspace: Applying the Computer Fraud and Abuse Act to the Internet" (1996) 12 *Santa Clara Computer and High Technology Law Journal* 416. Also see http://www.cert.org/.

[64] The roles of the various security services are not included here.

[65] Europol brings together national police forces from within the E.U. See Convention based on Article K.3 of the Treaty on European Union, on the Establishment of a European Police Office (Europol Convention) with Declarations. (Cm. 3050, 1995).

[66] See further D. J. Davis, "Criminal Law and the Internet: The Investigator's Perspective", above, p.48.

[67] NCIS and the NCS are respectively defined by the Police Act 1997, Pts I and II.

offences came under the auspices of the National Crime Squad, a role that was previously held by the various regional crime squads. However, there does not yet appear to be a British equivalent to the United States Federal Bureau of Investigation's National Computer Crime Squad.[68]

The emphasis to date upon the creation of specialist police units, whether local or national, raises the question as to the extent to which the public police as a whole should integrate the policing of cyberspace within their "normal" functions.[69] Clearly, it is almost certain that the incidence of cybercrimes will rise considerably as the population of cyberspace increases and there is an expansion of the range of activities carried out within it. But whilst there is an argument that the state-funded public forces operate within existing (albeit contested) structures of accountability, it is highly likely that the public police will not become involved in the "patrolling" of cyberspace, or for that matter in the actual investigation of most cybercrimes. This is because of the largely private nature of the domain, because of the deeply entrenched and traditional nature of police work, and because of the sheer cost to the public purse that would be involved. Yet it is still likely to be the case that the public police will still perform an important gatekeeping function by being the first point of contact for members of the public against whom many of the cybercrimes have been committed. As such the public police will nevertheless have a role to play in the policing of the Internet. This highlights the need for the public police to undergo some training in order to be aware of the various issues so that, on the one hand, they understand when, or indeed when not, to become involved, but also which body has responsibility for addressing the various types of harm.

Conclusions

These are early days in the life and times of cyberspace—too early to start predicting its full impact upon society with any degree of certainty, especially as the initial power-play for control over it is still taking place. It is quite clear that the benefits of the Internet have to be protected from the harms that the could occur, but achieving this task is going to be very difficult because attempts by one group to curb the specific behaviours of another are not going to be well received, and the success of the operation will depend upon which group has the stronger mandate. It is also quite clear from the preceding discussion that a multi-tiered system of policing is already developing which is largely based upon self-regulation by its netizens and the Internet Service Providers. Such a system is not only a far more workable proposition than external regulation, which would be unpopular and very impractical, but it would also be much less costly. This approach was largely endorsed by a recent European Commission report on legal aspects of computer-related crime,[70] thought it went on to argue that for it to be effective there also needed to be in place an infrastructure of international agreements over the boundaries of acceptable and non-acceptable activities which take due account of fundamental civil liberties.

[68] See http://www.fbi.gov/congress/compcrm/compcrm.htm.
[69] For further discussion of this issue see D. S. Wall, *loc. cit.* (1997), pp.223–229.
[70] See U. Seiber, "Legal Aspects of Computer Related Crime in the Information Society, Legal Advisory Board for the Information Market" (1998), http://www2.echo.lu/legal/en/comcrime/sieber.html; C. Walker and Y. Akdeniz, "The Governance of the Internet in Europe with Special Reference to Illegal and Harmful Content", above, p.5.

This latter point raises one of the main concerns with the self-policing model. Not only does it presently tend to operate upon a self-appointed mandate, but it currently lacks formal mechanisms of accountability. So, the principle of self-policing is inherently limited in scope and has a fairly low ceiling of efficacy, after which the various higher levels of policing have to be invoked in order to resolve the situations which self-regulation fails to resolve, does not apply to, or is not applied.[71] Inevitably, the policing functions will be split between all of the levels of policing delineated in this paper.[72] The pluralistic model of policing the Internet that is described here combines elements of both public and private models of policing. It also reflects the increasing plurality of policing in high modernity at both a national and transnational level.[73]

In the final analysis, it is important to keep the issue of cybercrimes in perspective as there currently exist a number of processes which have led to the problem being overstated, especially with regard to pornography. These claims raise a number of important issues.

First, if these estimates are accurate, then we must ask why then are there not more cybercrimes, why are they not more serious and why, for the most part, does the system clearly seem to police itself to the degree that it does? We must assume that these estimates and concerns largely relate to the potential harms that can be inflicted by cybercrimes and which do not necessarily translate into actual harms. Similar, say, to the advent of the motor car, just as not all drivers turned out to be drunks or road-ragers, so not all netizens are pornographers or paedophiles.

Secondly, there is some evidence to suggest that much of the rhetoric regarding the extent of cybercrimes has been deliberately overblown in order to draw funding for security and policing organisations. Duncan Campbell believes that the case of the hackers, Bevan and Pryce (a schoolboy), revealed that "oversold threats" regarding the implications of breaches of security into major United States defence computers won funding from Congress.[74] Bevan, for example, was accused by United States military sources as being "a greater threat to world peace than Adolf Hitler".[75] The truth was subsequently found to be much less dramatic. However, the new funding led to the development of new military and intelligence "infowar" units, which have subsequently sold their security services to private corporations.

Finally, a great danger arising from overstatement is that the (cyber)behaviours which have become labelled as deviant then become the subject of formal regulation without a complete analysis of their impact, implications or extent. A graphic example of this process emerged following the moral panic over obscenity during the mid-1990s. A solution, in the form of the now-compromised (United States)

---

[71] C. P. Walker, "Cyber-contempt: Fair trials and the Internet" (1997) 3 *Year Book of Media and Entertainment Law* (Oxford, Clarendon Press), p.28; D. S. Wall, *loc. cit.* (1997), p.222.

[72] D. S. Wall, *loc. cit.* (1997), p.224.

[73] See J. Sheptycki, *loc. cit.* (1998).

[74] D. Campbell, "More Naked Gun than Top Gun" (1997) *The Guardian* (OnLine), November 27, p.2.

[75] E. Gunner, "Rogue hacker turned legit code-cracker" (1998) *Computer Weekly*, May 7, p.5.

Communications Decency Act 1996, was sought before the problem had been properly identified.[76]

In the not too distant future it is highly likely that many of the undesirable behaviours that were described earlier will simply be worked out of the system, in that the victims and victim groups will find a way of regulating the behaviour. Alternatively, the behaviour may simply cease to be popular any more—a passing fad which ceases to be exciting or is replaced by more exciting, legitimate Internet usage. Moreover, it may also be the case that developments in technology will simply eradicate the problem, either by deliberate design, for example, through more secure communications, encryption and firewalling, or as a by-product or knock-on effect.[77] Nevertheless, at the end of the day we shall be left with a series of new types of "criminal" behaviour, which will continue to challenge our traditional understandings of crimes, deviancy and the anti-social and the way that we police them. Our experience to date strongly suggests that we do not need many new forms of regulation or policing, but rather we need to adapt, develop and build upon those which exist already.

[76] J. Wallace and M. Mangan, *Sex, Laws and Cyberspace* (New York, Henry Holt, 1996), p.174; Y. Akdeniz, "The battle for the Communications Decency Act 1996 is over" (1997) 147 *New Law Journal* 1003.

[77] In much the same way that in our terrestrial world the introduction of steering column locks drastically reduced car crime, crash helmets reduced motorbike theft, and the change-over from coal gas to North-Sea gas reduced the incidence of suicide, see A. Crawford, *Crime Prevention and Community Safety* (Longmans, Harlow, 1998), pp.85–87.

[27]

Technology's ways:
Information technology, crime analysis and the rationalizing of policing

P.K. MANNING
Michigan State University, USA

Abstract _____

The rationalization of policing, linking ends and means, and evaluating the consequences of policies and actions, is progressing in policing. It can be seen in budgeting, career planning, crime audits and performance indicators and goals. One of most powerful tools with capacity, if applied 'on the ground,' to prevent, reduce and control crime and disorder is crime analysis. This case study of crime mapping and crime analysis in one American department, done with interviews and observations in 1999, shows that in spite of progress in knowledge about levels and kinds of social disorganization, repeat offenders, clusters of problems and incidents, crime mapping has no operational effects. The lack of infrastructure of support and interpretation; the distribution of the information, isolated and unintegrated databases, and lack of on-line access by patrol officers, renders the extant software and analytic capacity ineffectual. Some suggestions are made that might link the capacity with practice.

Key Words _____

• crime mapping • case studies • information technology
• rationalization

Introduction

The rationalization of policing, by which I mean explicit connections
between resources, means and objectives, or goals with evaluated outcome,
has proceeded slowly and perhaps rightly so. There is a long and hopeful
history, stretching back to the invention of the telegraph, fire alarm systems
and early police watch stations, that contains the assumption that rapid
and efficient flow of information (by technological means) would in itself
empower policing. This assumption, a technological fallacy, is a seductive
one. While many innovations in scientific technology have been adopted in
policing in this century, the greatest expenditures for technology are for
weapons and transport. The well-promoted computer-assisted dispatching
(CAD) decreases pass-through time and make possible the accumulation of
vast unanalyzed data. New developments in forensic science, setting aside
the emerging use of DNA testing, give evidence apparent credibility leaving
the process of detection, evidence gathering, and investigation hidden. The
canopy of science obscures the primitive analytic tools that persist. These
technological advances, even those enhancing information processing—
information technology (IT)—have little altered police effectiveness.

Rationalization moves slowly and unevenly across the police terrain and
is driven by external developments in social science, and uneven innovation
in large departments. Police are entertaining problem solving and crime
analysis; but as yet, they show more promise than yield. Several kinds of
rationalities, or faces of rationality, are appearing within policing. To
theorize policing, we must address the extent to which one facet of
rationalizing, information-led policing, is now in place and what its
strengths and weaknesses are.

Here I present a case study of crime mapping, one face of rationalizing
policing. Police work remains embedded in the present and animated by the
craft of policing. On the other hand, the analytic potential of crime analysis
and crime mapping is great and could reorient policing to anticipatory and
preventative actions, rather than to response to calls for service. In that
sense problem solving, when combined with crime analysis, unlike unit
beat policing, community policing, and the immodest professionalism of
the past, could re-engineer policing.

Technology

There are many rationalities contesting in policing, and it has many faces.
The heart of rationalization is the use of information to guide budgeting,
management, personnel allocation, and career guidance as well as serving
the public in an explicitly calculative fashion. Information technology (IT)
encompasses the means by which data (raw facts as recorded) are transformed into information (data now placed in some context with a purpose), stored, analyzed, and retrieved. As an aspect of organizational policy

it may become, at best, wisdom.[1] Information technology is a multi-sided mirror. It ingests data, shapes and stores it, transforms it in myriad ways, and then produces the texts, screens, files, images, and sounds used to interpret its work and the nature of the 'outside world.' Although it is easy to mistake imagery and reality, information technology at best is a way of envisioning the external world and shaping it. Technology takes on meaning through practice. Within an organization, technology is framed or understood within a particular attitude of mind or perspective, which Heidegger identified in 'The Question Concerning Technology' (1977). Here, Heidegger argues against decontextualizing and 'enframing' technology because enframing strips it of social consequences and rich meanings, and isolates it, seeing only the core of instrumental activities. Heidegger writes, somewhat mysteriously, '. . . the essence of technology is nothing technological' (1977: 35), and argues for 'questioning' of technology. By questioning, he means examining the producing of the form and the content as artful activities. At the end of his rather opaque essay he suggests we read technology as art—with some awe and mystery, appreciating its depths and contradictions.

Policing's present search for a mandate continues to constrain the present efforts to adopt and adapt to new information technologies. The Anglo-American police have accepted its capacity, and framed many processes as instrumental, rather than exploring their problematic features. When IT is used rationally to enhance police work, it is brought to bear on the work as a result of a stimulus, and is occasioned. In this sense, it represents a kind of situation rationality, rather than long-term rationality directed to defined transcendental objectives.

Policing the present

Background

American police reformers, August Vollmer, O.W. Wilson, Bruce Smith, Harry E. Fosdick, and V.O. Leonard, assembled the key elements of scientific policing, cases brought to court based on valid evidence, mobile and well-trained officers, and an organization administered rationally on the basis of management philosophy that was drawn from the current theories of public administration. This move to rationalize policing became known as 'professional policing' in America because it combined emulation of the ideology of the 'higher professions,' (altruism, service, ideals, and abstract knowledge), with claims for a scientifically based crime control mandate. In time, this mandate, its validation by the public not withstanding, was means-focused rather than on impact on the environment or outcomes produced (Goldstein, 1990), and it centered in time on job control and enhanced status rather than on service.

The evolved strategies of policing—random patrol, investigative work, and response to calls for service—now amplify the strengths and weaknesses of the professional model by focusing on the theme of responsiveness and actively promoting it with the public.

From an information-gathering perspective, the professional model creates an ecology of information gathering. The sources of primary information are a network of officers in vehicles, at desks, and on the street, who serve as conduits of information. They are independent, rarely closely supervised *in situ*, and constitute a diverse and divergent set of source-points. Officers are expected to scan the environment for the problematic, intervene when they judge it necessary, and stand ready to respond to calls for service. The dispersal of officers when combined with elicited demand means that policing is demand-led, and that considerable effort is devoted to screening, diverting, managing, and reducing citizen demand.

This strategy has been well accepted in Anglo-American societies. It now generates sufficient response from the public to create periods of information overload in many large departments. This is a function both of increased tendencies to call, and the massive proliferation of telephones and other personal communication devices (95 million mobile phones are in use in the United States). In many respects, as I review below, demand-management technologies have been 'add ons' introduced on top of the unchanged platform of current strategies and tactics, and seen by officers as not only faddish, but as potentially worrying, representing more and different work obligations.

Current practice

Although departmental policy on dispatching varies, most police work is the response to calls for service, or matters processed by operators and dispatchers, turned into assignments for officers which become jobs on the ground. Thus, calls, those dispatched or assigned, are segmentalized units within a communications flow. Some incidents entail interaction and become encounters. The process of communication, translation and transformation of information, and attending the event (in fact or via another form of communication), is recursive in the sense that some correction of initial definitions and classifications takes place.[2] The organizational structure, resting on information technology, converts raw data into police work.

This evolved structure has important practical implications that shape Anglo-American policing. Because the work is largely reactive, and driven by calls for service, a processing or means-orientation to the job arises. The focal aspect of policing is the incident. The phenomenology of police patrol is based on the incident, a hub of activity responded to, defined, and managed by patrol officers. The devotion to calls might be called a mini-ideology, or set of beliefs that tend to be resistant to fact. Among patrol officers. The incident focus narrows policing to the here and now and absorbs in theory the time available. The logic of incident-driven policing is a misleading and only partially accurate picture of social dynamics. In the following paragraph, I sketch out police beliefs about the character and association of incidents because they are an impediment to change.

Incidents, especially those of most public importance, are randomly distributed in time and space, are semi-autonomous and bounded, and have little if any connection. The future alone can tell whether some level of crime or disorder will arise and have to be dealt with, but without some action, things will get worse (Bittner, 1971). Life is odd; 'things happen.' The patrol culture and cops' stories, a vague set of resources, are ill-fitted to guide response to a given incident confronting an officer. Since the incident orders work, ratiocination, reflection, and paperwork are secondary to real police work on the ground. They may in fact impede accomplishing this work. The core incident defines the needed information: that which is accessible and useful in the incident at hand, and arrives 'just in time' for active use by an officer. Information search is guided by interpersonal trust. Inquiries tend to be restricted to referring to or querying a handful of trusted external data sources: vehicle registration and driving licenses, outstanding warrants and/or criminal records, and field stops. Officers emphasize: 'keeping up the numbers,' 'output,' or 'the counters,' processing calls, moving on quickly to the next, making the odd traffic stop and citation, and showing one is part of the team and working. Thus, all police technologies are contingently relevant (Meehan, 1998). They are used not for the intrinsic merits ascribed by computer scientists, sociologists, or other experts; they are occasioned and used as and when, by the needs of the moment, interpersonal trust, and a subtle assessment of the audiences to which the information might be presented. The audience to which the presentation is directed shapes the face of rationality that is adopted.

The focus on doing something shapes interactions with the public, and is based on a distrust of the public. Police are often lied to, misled, and subject to provocative dramas. They learn to keep some distance from what is said. Public fears, insecurities, and concerns are generally inconsistent with police interpretations of these problems. The 'Dragnet' line, 'just the facts, Ma'am,' is a poignant rendering of this perspective. However, the ideology of the present and the incident is not restricted to the patrol segment. It is revealed in the focus of detective work on the case and its clearance, and the ideology of crisis management at the command level. In general, management, if it takes place at all in policing, is management by crisis; rapid response to the current problem, often taking the size and weight of a refrigerator, which in turn prevents dealing with the day's routine work, and virtually destroys any contemplative approach to planning beyond tomorrow. This urgency perhaps drives all organizations, but it is ideologically supported in policing.[3]

To summarize, the inspectorial nature of policing, i.e. its structure, theme, and origins, provides resources that stand ready to respond to a vast range of contingencies. Policing is therefore ill-prepared to anticipate most problems except mass disorder or disaster at a given time or place.[4] In general, the police stand ready to act in the event, as anticipatory and premonitory agents, rather than as preventive or even ameliorative agents. While they employ a variety of control modes ranging from educational to penal, their focus is the here and now. The importance of this organizational feature is that it reduces the value of information as a basis for action, and shifts fundamental deciding to the 'ground level' in order to reduce the emergent consequence of detected acts.

Some recent market-driven trends

Changes in policing, as in other pubic sector agencies, is in part stimulated by market-driven ideas about public service. Although what police do in theory is endlessly elastic, they are expected not only to be more sensitive to 'the customer' but also more efficient. The apparent successes of private security (and their lower costs) became more salient as attention turned to crime prevention rather than crime control or crime fighting. Historically, private security, including corporate security, guarding and watchmen functions, had emphasized loss prevention since their origins were in transporting money and gold, and later in strike-breaking and industrial asset protection The vocabulary, at least, has penetrated public policing. Here, I include 'customer service' and 'value for money,' auditing for efficient use of resources, 'smart technologies,' and 'information services' (as well as ideas long abandoned in business such as TQM and Quality Circles). New forms of third-party policing were recognized and the overlap in functions noted (Bayley and Shearing, 1996), even as the movement to privatize more of the public functions gained momentum (Jones and Newburn, 1998). These trends pushed policing toward prevention.

Policing is also affected by the transition into newer forms of control, including video surveillance, simulation and anticipation, and these imply increasing concern about the power of information technologies to scan, gather, and digest information about tastes, choices, life style and other matters seen traditionally as 'private.' This means surveillance without the permission or knowledge of the persons or groups watched; increasing use of simulations as a basis for social control; abstract models or profiles that reify the complexity of human choice such as expert systems; 'smart profiles' and 'smart personnel systems' for early warning of incompetence and profiling of all types. Representative of these trends are the various screens by which communication is mediated—monitors, video cameras, webcams, and mobile cameras linked to satellite systems (Crawford, 1998). While government shrinks and increasingly includes a network of semi-private arrangements, policing as a function, both public and private, is growing (see Bogard, 1996; Staples, 1992; Lyon, 1994; Ericson and Haggerty, 1997). The extent to which it has been transformed remains an empirical question.

These developments in social control increase demand, as does public acceptance of the dominant police rhetoric, that of community policing. Community policing highlights notions of citizen responsibility, co-production of order, third-party surrogates for community such as place managers, neighborhood watch committees, citizens' advisory boards, and ad hoc groups usually created and supported by public funds (and the police themselves).

While they suggest quite different directions in social control, these developments should be seen in the context of the incident-based ideology of policing and the demand-led or responsiveness theme in the professional model. These all increase demand and are challenges to the present structure of function of police.

Policing aims to protect lives and property, yet loss of these, as well as complex disorders of urban freedom, are inevitable consequences of the division of labor. These broad aims have been operationalized as providing random patrol for the untoward event and service and responding to calls for service. Proactive crime control, in the form of investigation, intelligence gathering and application—and to a lesser extent vice, have been underfunded relative to the other functions and are poorly developed and resourced. 'Responsiveness' now incorporates the idea that citizens have a direct obligation, like the police, to react to and perhaps even anticipate the dynamics of crime and disorder in their neighborhoods. But the fondest hope has been placed in technology, especially information technology, to solve this paradox. In fact, the dominant technologies are mere record-keeping systems, rather than analytic systems (Ackroyd et al., 1992; Nogala, 1995).[5]

New tools

Research shows that the social nature of crime and disorder can be explicated and understood. What are now called 'incidents' even if defined as 'calls for service,' cluster in time and space and by type of crime and disorder, and can be dramatically displayed via figures, maps, or text. These representational documents display obvious and rather trite ideas that clusters arise and can be attended to, but more importantly they are signs pointing to something else that is more abiding. Moving one step further in the classification schemes, discovered or reported crime is correlated with social disorganization, tolerance of deviance, and general levels of disadvantage in urban neighborhoods. This relationship is patterned and consistent (Sampson and Bartusch, 1998). Thus, calls for service are not randomly distributed in time or space, nor are the crimes subsequently detected or cleared. Known crimes are not a random sample of victims or offenders; repeat offending, co-offending, and repeat victimization are common. These inferences mean that a single slice through data showing one day at a time, or a shift, or even a short-term 'trend' are misleading if one wants to see the long-term picture.

Social factors also link the 'crime side' of the equation, or what is shown about offending and offenses. The relationships between offenders and third parties; repeat victims and repeat offenders, as well as their residences, types of crimes committed, modus operandi, and the incident's location, have well-established correlates. Abstract models of offending (Bottoms and Wiles, 1997) suggest that attention to choices of offenders, places and persons chosen (Felsen, 1998), have potential for active intervention to reduce risks or revictimization (Pease, 1997). It is possible to plan modes of situational crime prevention that modify place and time of activities to reduce risk, as well as to pattern environments to reduce risks (Felsen, 1998). Active third parties, guardians, place managers, or other civil servants active in an area, can be directed using crime maps and can reduce fear of crime and crime incidents differentially depending on the social context of the place.

Most importantly, current interest in information technologies (IT) has elevated enthusiasm for crime mapping and crime intelligence in large urban police departments many of whom already have geo-coded dispatching records. Crime mapping is a technique based on software (usually ERSI, ArcView, or MapInfo) that converts geo-coded addresses or locations (one set of files) so that maps, tables, and figures can be created and printed.[6] They display signs on maps (tables, graphs, or other figures) of a city or political area. In theory, a wide range of information can be included such as fire risks, demographic characteristics, indices of disorder and quality of life offenses, and more conventional police-generated data concerning juveniles, adult crime, and traffic. A range of other sorts of data has been added by some departments such as addresses where restraining orders are to be enforced, addresses of sex offenders, or gang members, as well as demographics of social areas in the city. Variations in density by location, types of crimes, or days of the week can be mapped, as can offenders' residences, and patterns of co-offending (Bottoms and Wiles, 1997). Anything that can be plotted spatially can be represented.

The research taken together suggests that substantive direct impact on disorder and crime can be made via data analysis combining police-gathered and non-police-gathered data, and this data as information can be used to direct and systematize enforcement. Formal, third-party interventions can anticipate the general where and when of crime and disorder. This is not prediction in the usual statistical sense of a given event or case or incident, which has been the police working notion of their job, but in the sense of routine, regular, systematic rates of crime in given places and at given times of day, week, month, and over years. The difference between sensitivity to neighborhood context, and awareness of the general social conditions of a neighborhood, might allow one to respond to an incident differently, or manage it better, but it would not lead in this 'common-sense' police wisdom form to an ability to alter prevent, reduce, or manage crime, victims, offenders, or places. Cops' wisdom, and incident-driven inferences, or oral lore, are inadequate to the task of reshaping policing.

Case materials

I use this case study to highlight some generic problems in implementation of crime mapping as a tool in the rationalizing process. It illustrates the potential and the limits of present practice. The system has been in place barely a year, is still developing, and is rather marginal to the day-to-day police work in the Western City Police Department. The interface between the system of analysis and the craft is undeveloped, but my interests are in the generic issues of developing and using crime analysis, given the present type of Anglo-American policing, rather than the specific issues of implementation.[7]

The Western City Police Department

Western (a pseudonym) is a city of some 127,000 in a metropolitan area of nearly 400,000. It now (July 2000) employs some 263 officers (about 25 percent minority; 19 percent female), about half of whom were hired in the last five years. The other large segment is officers who were hired some 20 to 25 years ago. It has a budget for 1999–2000 of 25 million. The WPD hired 90 new officers in the last 18 months and expects a 20–25 percent attrition rate in the next five. The Chief at the time of the study (fall 1999), Chief B, was concerned with crime control and tightening administration, and is not publicly linked with 'community policing,' as was B's predecessor, Chief A, who staged two massive reorganization efforts in his eight years in office. Patrol officers, numbering some 115, patrol 20 districts on an overlapping four-shift plan of 4/10 (four 10-hour days on and three off). They are divided into two precincts, the East and the West, each headed by a captain. The precincts are 'mini headquarters,' and the former head-quarters (and essentially the west precinct) in City Hall now houses administrative officers, the jail, the communications center, and human resources.

The city has a minority population of slightly over 25 percent (about 18 percent are African-American), a large industrial and union base, and is the home of a large university, and a very large two-year community college. It has a long history of automobile production, UAW strength, and democratic politics. The present Mayor has held office for two plus terms and governs with an area-based elected city council. The crime rate dropped modestly in 1996 (4 percent) and has dropped slightly each year since. It experienced a range of 9–16 homicides in the previous six years and averages about 12 a year.

The Western police maintain a regional 911 center which is connected to one (of the four adjoining and nearby counties) county Sheriff's force, five local police and fire departments, four regional fire departments, and Western City's fire department. The city lies in three counties, each headed by an elected Sheriff. Two of the three refuse to be a part of the regional 911 system and maintain separate, non-linked databases and dispatch centers. The regional 911 system is fragmented and has been a continued source of political conflict for over 20 years. Some 13 separate 'emergency numbers' are listed in Western City telephone book. Emergency medical care is available through the Western 911 system since fire departments serve the emergency medical needs. Those fire departments served by the Western 911 also coordinate emergency medical services (EMS). Occasionally, a state agency or the State Police use the WPD 911 system. Western City funds the police communications center and controls the police budget.

The crime-mapping project is coordinated by a captain and funded by two partnership COPS grants (12 and 130K) given in 1996 and one grant from the US Department of Commerce (400K) in 1998. The aim was to produce a crime-mapping and statistics capacity and to fund the creation of a website with information on police and crime and other social services. The staff of the crime-mapping program (two 'civilians') in Research and Planning are directed by a lieutenant. The server for the crime-mapping process hums in the office of one staff member while the other staff member, a 'crime analyst,' sits in an adjoining room. He enters warrants served and arrests made and puts them on e-mail. Two PhD students, located in a precinct, are on a short-term contract to undertake some trend analyses, and add to the databases (possibly from the 1990 US census). The members of the planning unit are isolated physically and geographically from detectives and patrol officers who work from the two precincts.

It is a decentralized system with some 18 terminals and printers in the headquarters and two precinct buildings. The aim was to make it accessible and 'cop-proof.' Data and maps can be displayed and printed easily. The chief, deputy chief, and other administrative offices have nine terminals; nine others are in offices (two captains', two lieutenants', two sergeants', and three in the two precinct-based detective bureaux). Each week, data are downloaded from LEMs (Law Enforcement Management System) which is a dedicated Western database—offenses, CAD, information on sex offenders, parolees, accidents, contact cards—to a Dataflex program. Information on suspected drug houses are to be entered by investigators. These data are then exported by .txt files to ArcView (geo-coded onto SHAPE files). The ArcView files are then copied to the planning unit's NT server and then can be used to create maps (accessed by the C:\drives of the 18 terminals or mapping stations). Three databases (arrests, offenses, and calls for service) are merged weekly. They are processed four times before being available. The ArcView software can create tables and graphs with a database that now includes roughly the last year of information. The maps show suppressible crimes (breaking and entering, residential and business; alcohol; obstructing; traffic offenses; juvenile crime; and multi-crime locations). The planning unit aims to put selected crimes and information on social services on a website in late 2000.

The command personnel of the department are divided on the value of the system. One captain, now retired (in late 1999) but former precinct head, refused to use computers (he had been head of the laptop project a few years previously). Another captain (who became Chief in June 2000), attended a crime-mapping seminar at Harvard's Kennedy School and actively uses maps to guide and query officers. He prints out crime maps showing recent clusters of crime and urges officers to investigate, problem-solve, and 'do something' about the crime. He prepared a detailed memo (written in summer 1999) comparing drug arrests by team and precinct and arguing for a change in targeting by the drug squad. Chief B, when interviewed, doubted the value of the current system because the various databases are not linked (pawn shops licenses, property room holdings, stolen cars found and where), and because none of the information is on-line (it is approximately one week old). The maps are not used by command staff for strategic planning, aligning resources in either investigation or patrol, evaluation, or tactical movements of resources, although they have been discussed in command staff meetings.

There is little infrastructure in place to encourage use of crime mapping, and minimal training was done. Officers were given a handout and a day's lecture (not hands-on) on crime mapping. The crime analyst's duties (see above) do not include preparing 'packages,' analyzing crime patterns or trends, or receiving feedback on operations other than arrests. Although addresses of 'suspected crack houses' are supposed to be entered routinely into the database, they are not, nor does the system store data on sex offenders, parolees, or those on electronic tethers. The system is unused by investigators (detectives, and the task force on drug enforcement). The crime-mapping network is not part of the laptop database—which permits car-to-car communications, and access to LEMS (the local police database) on-line.

Crime mapping and the craft

In this section of the article, I should like to extract three problematic areas revealed in my work: the need for an infrastructure; easy distribution of information; and integrated databases. While the apparent issue is the effects of technology, the more vexing issue lies in the use and interpretation of the materials produced rather than the means. I key each section with a question or two.

Infrastructure

What infrastructure (social, electrical, support staff) exists to transform the mapping data so that it is useful to investigators, supervisors, and patrol officers? In Western, there was isolation of patrol from investigation and the reactive nature of patrol work puts them 'on the road.' The lack of supervision and evaluation of 'problem solving' means officers have little interest in mapping. Ethnographic research demonstrates further sources of police resistance and/or acceptance of IT—it is based on time and manner of introduction of the IT, officers' rank, specialized function, the level of information to which the officer has access and must use, and local policing practices and traditions. The perceived utility of a given 'tool,' e.g. cellular phones, mobile digital terminals (MDT), computerized databases crime mapping, and other analytic software, interacts with these variables. However, immediate responses to inquiries, accessible databases, and rapid processing of data in pre-formatted records are welcomed. The technical support staff in police departments is typically overworked and inadequate to maintaining complex electronic infrastructure. In very large departments, such as the Washington, DC department, the aging computers, lack of modern wiring (fiber-optic cables that increase band width and communications speed) are major impediments to change. Elaborate technology-based systems, such as expert systems for detectives, are not supported and abandoned when federal funding vanishes (Ratledge and Jacoby, 1989—The Baltimore County Police's expert system).

Distribution

What physical and spatial problems are associated with use and distribution of crime-mapping knowledge? Is the information and terminal centralized, or decentralized? Who has training and access? Is the information 'on-line' or lagged by days or weeks? Recall in Western that the crime-mapping function is isolated physically in headquarters in the planning unit, and the staff has irregular face-to-face contact with detectives or patrol officers. The links to external organizations are being created consistent with developing a community-accessible webpage.

While crime trends, mappings, and distributions of crime by time, area, and even *modus operandi*, can be produced in Western centrally and at each precinct for about a year, the maps are used (when they are used) merely as tactical representations of distributions, incidents that can be suppressed through crime attack tactics. Investigative officers do not use the system, nor do they routinely enter data into the database. Since detectives work on a case-based activity, they have no reference to trends or patterns unless they appear presently, e.g. a series of unsolved house breakings in a particular neighborhood over the last few days or weeks.

How and where is access to the data and output (maps, tables, figures, graphs)? By design, the Western system is decentralized. The various components that constitute the criminal intelligence complex are isolated from each other physically and functionally. The Research and Planning unit has no contact with patrol officers. I asked one of the staff 'What counts [what is seen as a basis for good performance] from a patrol officers' perspective?' and 'What are they expected to produce?' He answered 'I have no clue.'

Patrol officers do not have access to the mapping system on-line in their vehicles, nor do they use the terminals. This is consistent with their view of needed knowledge, their job, and the aesthetics of control on the streets. The Research and Planning division took a decision to decentralize and not to make the mapping data available on-line because they did not see it as contributing to the patrol function. One captain interviewed reported that perhaps 1 percent (of the patrol officers) use it. Sergeants do not use the information to evaluate their officers. The absence of training in the use of the terminals and mapping is doubtless a factor. Moreover, maps are rarely produced and even less commonly used. Since the crime information that is distributed is after the fact, warrants served and arrests made, it has marginal utility for patrol officers, and cannot guide or alter their activities. Maps are not distributed to neighborhood groups, used to register and monitor officers' behavior, nor evaluate their performance except by the one captain.

Databases

What databases exist? Are they connected? How are they connected? How are they accessed? The present databases maintained in Western are disconnected. As in most police departments there are a very large number of independent or quasi-independent databases that cannot be interfaced or have not been. In Western, mapping data cover only the past year, making any sort of trend analysis dubious. The several databases of calls to the police, fire, and EMS as well as criminal records and jail populations in surrounding political entities (townships, unincorporated areas, counties, and small towns), which are interwoven within the city's boundaries in a peculiar fashion, are inaccessible from Western's Center. The data maintained in Western are entered laboriously, are not on-line, and are reprocessed by three sets of software. This system is obviously vulnerable to crashes and data loss in the transformation process. The data have not yet been systematically disaggregated in any useful way, e.g. by producing crime packages, or clusters of crimes for broader attention within the force. Aside from adjusting crime-attack approaches as aspects of 'problem solving,' Western has not linked problem solving, prevention, community policing, and any aspect of crime mapping.

These material and ecological limitations are necessary, but not sufficient for use and application of crime maps.

Interpretive processes

Clearly, crime maps are multi-referential. Many things are symbolized by the signs found on the maps. Signs are not just read, or seen, but are read off, or interpreted. No sign 'speaks for itself,' it has to speak, metaphorically, to someone. Maps, charts, graphs, and figures display four types of signs (an expression and content linked in context to produce meaning):

1 symbols, with an arbitrary link between the expression and content (signified and signifier);
2 indexes—smoke = fire; a finger or hand print = a person's presence is a fairly proximal and direct trace of a thing or person;
3 marks—a mark is simply an arbitrary placing of something to which one wants to return, e.g. a book mark, a marginal check mark at the edge of a page;
4 icons, signs that are miniature representations of the thing itself.

Even at best, maps cry out for interpretation because they are crude and must be seen from some social perspective. There are also technical problems concerning the meaning of 'blocks,' 'block faces,' clusters of addresses that are incorrectly recorded or spelled; the notional location of many kinds of disorder, the fact that high-rise apartments may have multiple calls and complaints all at the same street address. The scale of the map affects the size of a cluster, making it easy to inflate a handful of incidents into a 'hot spot,' or to make a large number of incidents appear rather small or unimportant. The database itself is important, and some departments are using calls for service, while others use reported crime, or crimes known to the police, to map matters of concern. These two databases, taken as examples, represent quite distinctive samples of activities.

Crime maps can include any or all of the types of signs noted above, even on the same map: marks (street locations), indices (the location of gangs, drug dealing or crack houses), and symbols (large blurs, the size of which connotes several crimes in an approximate location, called 'hot spots'). Various icons can represent social processes or locations. Each of the expressions has to be linked to a content or reference in the physical world—the street address; the representation of the activity; and set of crimes. But some of the connections are abstract and analytic while others are merely descriptive. What do the indexes showing traffic accidents represent? Are they signs of drinking drivers? Poor road conditions and bad weather? Children crossing at unexpected times? Speeding? Poor road design and repair? Or are they merely artifactual; mere statistical variation, consistent with the range over the past year? What about expressions showing gang activity? Do they refer to people, crimes, meeting places, graffiti, residences, and to what does each one point?

The range of meaning is restricted and relatively concrete for indexes and marks, but symbols reach out beyond their narrow denotations to touch off other associations (connotations). Symbolic representations, such as tables, figures, graphs, or models (with arrows and directions) require interpretation with reference to the content they stand for.

What is the relationship between three kinds of signs found on maps? The meaning of the quite different character of things mapped is not provided by software. Marks and indexes can be read with some common-sense understanding of an area, e.g. gang territories, stolen cars, traffic stops. Descriptions, such as the number of gangs in a city, or areas of intense dealing, can be produced by officers who know an area. Symbols, such as 'hot spots,' have a variety of causes, possible points of intervention (primary, secondary, or tertiary prevention), offenders, and social consequences. What place, process, group, or crime is to be controlled? Why? How would one know if the intervention 'worked'? The symbols do not have equal promise, and they suggest different points of intervention—in police tactics, in place management, or in use of city codes against buildings or landlords.

When used in Western for crime-focused work (even with citizen access to social services on the department's webpage), it should be noted that the broader questions of the interconnection of crime, disorder, and disarray have not been noted or taken on board.

What has been tried in Western is severely limited, a range of interventions from on-the-spot negotiation to arrests. As used by one captain in Western, crime mapping identifies current, short-term trends or clusters. It does not make alternative approaches to the apparent problem visible, options such as crime-prevention efforts, problem solving, or co-production with local groups, nor non-interventionist approaches. The level of abstraction required of officers is increasing as a result of the introduction of software such as crime mapping, expert systems for detective work, and administrative devices like the NYPD's Compstat (using crime maps to identify crime problems). To develop a broader use, the maps and data 'behind them' would have to be viewed as more than mere collections of colourful icons, or electronic pin maps. Crime maps (and other analytic models), while often colorful, fascinating, and provocative, have no intrinsic actionable meaning. A picture may need a thousand words to explain it. Maps combine diverse types of information, bearing on many aspects of social organization, often with complex linkages, and use dramatic size, color, and dynamics to command attention.

What causal forces are at work, underneath the dots, arrows, and signs? Western's officers, even those with college degrees, like officers in other police departments to my knowledge, have no generalized conception of the nature of crime, its causes, dynamics, or meaning. When asked, they either provide individualistic motives (greed, money, sex, pleasure); 'ready-to-wear sociology'—broken families, lack of values and moral standards, and the inevitable one, deterioration of social bonds (a general police belief), or anecdotes. None of these 'explanations' has value in acting to prevent or intervene in crime. They are useful shorthand recipes for the crime and disorder police encounter daily.

The world represented on the map is not composed totally of ideas, or conceptions, but has a real material social and physical reality. The constraints and visibility of railroad tracks, parks, vacant lots, and high-rise public housing projects are real and visible, whereas the constraints of gang memberships, co-offending, networks of victims and their 'at risk' status is not so easily comprehended. The tacit connections made by officers between the expressions and the content that constitute the sign are the driving forces behind any form of problem solving.

What is the relationship between that which is represented or seen on the map and what is brought to it, matters unseen? Crime mapping reveals information, but it also conceals many underlying social processes not shown on the maps, e.g. social disorganization (Sampson and Bartusch, 1998), but read off or into them. Maps certainly dramatize selected indices of the selected offenses. Maps have vivid texture, variable size and flex-ibility, and can be easily manipulated in public presentations using Power Point software, allowing the presenter to zoom in, bring up details of a particular crime by clicking on an address, and add layers of information while speaking. Graphics packages produce beautifully printed multi-coloured and coded maps of various sizes and detail, and can easily distract the viewer from considering what underlies the display, animates the changes, and what they indicate and symbolize. The more rare the crime, the more dramatic the presentation, e.g. serial murders or rapes, especially when indicated by red blurs, 'mountains' (created by amplifying each crime in an arbitrarily designated area) rising in the middle of large cities, or in a collapsed time frame (showing 10 years' crimes in one location).

What additional information is needed to act on the information shown? Can it be gathered from relational databases accessible from the depart-ment? Even if the indexes are seen as having linkages somewhere (at some place) to someone or to other crime processes, linking requires a relational database and software (Ratledge and Jacoby, 1989: 109–10). The indexes are merely crime-specific and mark the physical location of an accom-plished crime. Ericson and Haggerty (1997) correctly note that the impact of IT is not restricted to the police organizations—it affects their various external audiences: citizens and organizations, neighborhood associations and business groups, the army and other federal and national agencies, all with complex databases. These influences are likely to increase in the UK, following the enactment of the Crime and Disorder Act of 1998. The question is in part which direction the influence is running, and the extent to which police respond to technological initiatives arising in the networks in which they are implicated.

Police gather far too much data for which they have no identified purpose. It is kept in case, or because it has always been kept. Statements about the number of files, record-keeping forms, or databases in themselves do not indicate useful *information*. Databases are not coordinated in the departments I have studied. There are many standard and some new types of data being gathered in policing, some of which can be combined, but others that are not and cannot be. In addition to CAD data, criminal records, vehicles and registration, current and outstanding warrants, and traffic stops, the present arrested-jailed population, stolen/returned property, other functions are being automated and digitalized such as finger print files, mug shots, and other forensic evidence. Some detectives are using expert systems, and/or computerized files (Harper, 1991). For many years, major incidents in England have been organized using the HOLMES system, which can be used for a major investigation, and the current Viclas system in Canada and the National Crime faculty at Bramshill aim to computerize serious crime nationally to enable further pattern analysis. In some systems, dispatching with mapping capacity associated, crime analysis, geographic profiling, network analysis of offenders and offenses, and object-based programming is added.

Policing is not entirely information-driven, but patrol, the activity that is the core of the organization and absorbs most of the time, energy and wages, is incident and demand-driven. Information is a bit that makes a difference but this must be understood in the context of matters in policing that shape or pattern information. Primary data are gathered by officers. The data are shaped by the readings of the interactional context in which they are gathered. This includes tacit understanding of what is relevant; the formatting effect of the forms used, or the on-line menus supplied; and a variety of social and spatial facts that could be relevant when viewed as an analytic problem-solving exercise. The channel by which the messages are sent is an important shaping matter; face-to-face communication is most trusted in the police work. Once these primary data become processed as information, their use is mediated. In policing, a job of assessing trustworthiness, any mediated communication is suspect, and as a general rule of thumb, the more abstract and distant from the officers' experience, the less it is trusted. The database to which the message is sent and from which it comes is also a matter shaping the nature, amount, and kind of information that will be sought and used. Software contains the categories and classificatory system into which the information will be placed. The linking of this software and database to others is problematic as well.

If the task is to move from mapping to interpretation of maps, i.e. true crime analysis, then some idea of what a unit, or PIM (a term used in the Compstat process in the NYPD), or package is, has to be provided to the crime analyst. The format in which information is gathered and processed must be standardized across subdivisions or districts. Interfaces between civilian analysts and CID officers may be problematic as well as the interface between uniformed officers and detectives (see Bratton and Knobler, 1998; Maple with Mitchell, 1999).

In policing, maps are only relevant when they are seen as valuable in use, needed for something. Metaphorically, databases and their links, the terminals, even computers, are really only 'dumb pipes' through which data flow. They represent capacity, future utility, but they must be implicated in some process to become useful. Lists of strategic uses of crime mapping are academic exercises. Capacity is not the critical matter, but actualization through imagination—the problem to which the data are to be attached must be imagined.

Maps are occasioned in the sense that they only make sense when one has a use in mind. The need for them makes their relevance come clear, or emerge. They come to being as a result of what Schutz (1960) calls an 'in order to motive': an explanation based on the conception of the future that one wanted realized. Demand can arise from many sources; but is typically handled as an incident, an encounter, or a case. A map requires that one imagines and makes an imaginative adjustment forward and backward in time. Maps can also be created as a result of having done something that one now sees as resulting from the map. A 'because motive,' according to Schutz, is an account for decisions, based on known outcomes. If we bear in mind that maps can be drawn from any number of databases that are integrated invisibly, data source shapes the meaning of the maps. Use is thus situated as well. Turning this around, we can imagine that reading a map means making it *transparent*, reading back through how it came to pass and forward to how it might be and has been used. Thus, the practical and the abstract find a common ground.

Comment

Information takes on meaning in a context, and the organization, roles and tasks, strategies and tactics, and ideology shape that meaning. Organizational structure and strategy, responsiveness as a theme, and past practices that arise from the 'professional model,' focus police on the here and now. Resistance to problem solving and crime prevention as well as other ideas that suggest a 'longer horizon' are not easily accommodated with the here-and-now focus. The case study suggested the more proximal limitations of ecology, distribution of information, infrastructure, database dissonance, and lack of skills. In a more proximal sense yet, using maps must be occasioned, brought about by some practical exigency the value of which and solution to is seen, or displayed, and rewarded.

In this context, crime mapping and analytics based on IT has no discernible direct purpose. There is no absence of data or software for mapping. What is needed is useful and actionable information gathered and analyzed with a purpose. The kinds and amount of data that can be entered, given modern fast, high-capacity computers, is almost infinite, but time is not.

It is all too easy to dismiss lack of rationalization within police departments to resistance arising from the 'occupational culture.' The craft notion remains powerful in spite of 30 years of development of complex, interlinked databases, management systems for storing, retrieving and aggregating data, geo-coding (TIGER files), and software (since the 1990s) for analyzing crime patterns by space, time, victim, offender, and offense, etc., and reconceptualizing policing (Goldstein, 1990). But more significant matters patterning the use of new IT are structural and historical. The appearance of new technologies brings out the play and ways of technologies, how they fit in, slide around, and are adapted to context and organization.

This study suggests at least that the ways of technology are many, and the argument for an information-based policing, focusing on risk management, and enhancing security is both premature and flawed. The potential of crime analysis and crime mapping as means, combining a technology and a technique, is greater than any other innovation in policing in recent times, arguably, because they raise questions about the basic contradictions in the mandate—that policing can control crime, reduce the fear of crime, and yet be an almost entirely responsive, demand-driven, situational force dispensing just in time and just enough, order maintenance.

Notes

I am grateful to Amanda Robinson for her careful comments on an earlier draft.

1 The title, 'Technology's ways' suggests that technology is artful (Heidegger, 1977), and finds its path through an organization variously. It does not have linear, universal, and straightforward effects, but is rather meandering, uncertain, somewhat opaque, and often concealed in its workings. Technology has no meaning independent of context, but a set of core associations of the word do exist. Technology is a physical matter, or means of accomplishing work; it also affects social roles and tasks, work routines, and shapes ideology. Although modern technology is a form of magic, it also requires imagination if it is to be used effectively. Meaning, or the subjective associations elicited by a phenomenon, arise in interaction. From the immediate physical object, e.g. a computer, outward in increasing levels of abstraction, one finds that the principal constraints and increments in meaning are symbols and rest on context and interpretation. Technologies, especially information technologies, in context, symbolize power, status, and control, and generate fears, dread and loathing. These symbolic matters are patterned by the history and structure of the organization, its practices, ecology, roles, and tasks. It also reflects the power and status of those who use or do not use it (Manning, 1992). Technology is a form of magic in the sense that it is embedded in an ideology or belief system within the organization about the mandate and its audiences, traditional practices surrounding the key technologies in use, and why and how they work the way they do. While technology changes and shapes organizations, it also is shaped by organizations and their politics (Thomas, 1992), as well as practical matters (addressed in the case study format below). In the following discussion, in this light, I set aside the very real problems of lack of training in use of maps and related IT equipment, inability to touch type and use keyboards, and fear and resentment of new IT, because they are so general as not to require explanation. They are also more amenable to training and recruitment strategies then are the issues discussed below.

2 Nesbary (1998) has very carefully shown how reclassification of calls once officers have attended them, is affected by workload, time of day, neighborhood composition, and the particular crime (in the case of crime) used to initially label the event in the world.

3 Policing, like many kinds of work, runs on a crisis mentality from top to bottom, and does virtually no long-distance planning except for disaster and major accidents and incidents such as riots.

4 Disorders are more easily handled because the police act in these instances like a controlling, commanded army in enemy territory.

5 Another distinction within information technologies is between 'high' and 'low' tech (Nogala, 1995). In common-sense terms, these apply to the degree of analytic power, or 'amplification power,' in Nogala's words, associated with a given technique. In the high-tech category, Nogala includes: DNA-based fingerprinting, AVI (automatic vehicle locator and tracking systems and transponder chips for tracing cars and assessing tollway fees), and electronic monitors for offenders; satellite-based tracking (GPS); artificial intelligence or expert systems for detective work; electronic borders (borders guarded by radar and satellites rather than human personnel) and machine-readable identity cards ('smart cards').

6 In part the change has to do with the changing conception of 'prevention' in policing—the police engage in primary prevention historically (altering the opportunities for offenses or offenders, using many sanctioning strategies, highlighting or dramatizing the penal sanction of arrest). Secondary prevention, or changing people, has never had any purchase on the police mind or practice; tertiary prevention based on the application of sanctions, is the domain of prisons, probation, and parole (Pease, 1997). Crime prevention is almost impossible to assess because it deals with something absent.

7 My work in this area is part of a larger project on the rationalizing of policing. The crime mapping and intelligence-led aspects of rationalization have been a key interest of mine. I have not until now done extensive and in-depth work in any one site, but work in a number of sites. I have done fieldwork in a large Canadian city over a month in 1999 (assisted by two undergraduates at York University, Amanda Rigby and Jenny Young); two days in a northern constabulary that had just introduced a crime-mapping center; Western City (a month in the fall of 1999); and previously (see Manning, *Theoretical Criminology* forthcoming). I am presently working on crime mapping in a large Southern City, and have spent over two weeks in fieldwork and interviews thus far (as at August 2000).

References

Ackroyd, S. et al. (1992) *New Technology and Practical Police Work*. Milton Keynes: Open University Press.

Bayley, D. and C. Shearing (1996) 'The Future of Policing', *Law and Society Review* 30: 585–606.

Bittner, E. (1971) *The Functions of the Police in Modern Society*. Washington, DC: NIMH.

Bogard, W. (1996) *The Simulation of Surveillance*. Cambridge: CUP.

Bottoms, A. and P. Wiles (1997) 'Environmental Criminology', in M. Maguire, R. Morgan and R. Reiner (eds) *The Oxford Handbook of Criminology*, 2nd edn, pp. 305–59. Oxford: Clarendon Press.

Bratton, W. and P. Knobler (1998) *Turnaround*. New York: Random House.

Crawford, A. (1998) *Crime Prevention and Community Safety*. London: Longman.

Ericson, R. and K. Haggerty (1997) *Policing the Risk Society*. Toronto: University of Toronto Press.

Felsen, M. (1998) *Crime and Everyday Life*, 2nd edn. Thousand Oaks, CA: Pine Forge Press.

Goldstein, H. (1990) *Problem-Solving Policing*. New York: McGraw-Hill.

Harper, R.R. (1991) 'The Computer Game', *British Journal of Criminology* 31: 292–307.

Heidegger, M. (1977) *The Question Concerning Technology and Other Essays*. Trans. with an Introduction by W. Lovitt. New York: Harper Torchbooks.

Jones, T. and T. Newburn (1998) *Private Security and Public Policing*. Oxford: Clarendon Press.

Lyon, D. (1994) *The Electronic Eye*. Minneapolis, MN: University of Minnestota Press.

Manning, P.K. (1992) 'The Police and Information Technology', in N. Morris and M. Tonry (eds) *Crime and Justice*, pp. 349–98. Chicago, IL: University of Chicago Press.

Maple, J. with C. Mitchell (1999) *Crime Fighter*. New York: Doubleday.

Meehan, A.J. (1998) 'The Impact of Mobile Digital Terminals (MDT) Information Technology on Communication and Recordkeeping in Patrol Work', *Qualitative Sociology* 21: 225–54.

Nesbary, D. (1998) 'Handling Emergency Calls for Service: Organizational Production of Crime Statistics', *Policing* 21: 576–99.

Nogala, D. (1995) 'The Future Role of Technology in the Police', in J.P. Brodeur (ed.) *Comparisons in Policing: An International Perspective*, pp. 191–210. Aldershot: Avebury.

Pease, K. (1997) 'Crime Prevention', in M. Maguire, R. Morgan and R. Reiner (eds) *The Oxford Handbook of Criminology*, 2nd edn, pp. 963–95. Oxford: Clarendon Press.

Ratledge, E. and J. Jacoby (1989) *Expert Systems and Artificial Intelligence in Policing*. Greenwich, CT: Greenwood.

Sampson, R. and D.J. Bartusch (1998) 'Legal Cynicism and (Subcultural?) Tolerance of Deviance', *Law and Society Review* 32: 777–804.

Staples, W. (1997) *The Culture of Surveillance*. New York: St Martins Press.

Thomas, R.J. (1992) *What Machines Can't Do*. Berkeley, CA: University of California Press.

PETER MANNING is a Professor in the School of Criminal Justice, Michigan State University, USA.

[28]

The technological game:
How information technology is transforming police practice

JANET B.L. CHAN

University of New South Wales, Australia

Abstract _____

This article draws on an Australian case study to examine the impact of information technology on police practice. It argues that technological change has altered important aspects of the 'field' of policing—technology has redefined the value of communicative and technical resources, institutionalized accountability through built-in formats and procedures of reporting, and restructured the daily routines of operational policing. Although the cultural dominance of law-enforcement policing style and resentment towards the demands of management and external agencies remains, there is evidence that information technology is gradually changing the deeply embedded assumptions of police practice.

Key Words ____ _____

• accountability • information technology • police culture
• policing

New technologies alter the structure of our interests: the things we think *about*. They alter the character of our symbols: the things we think *with*. And they alter the nature of community: the arena in which thoughts develop.

Postman (1992: 18–20)

139

Introduction

Historically, technology has revolutionized police practices. The introduction of the telegraph in the late 19th century, and the use of two-way radios, motor vehicles and computer-assisted dispatching during the 20th century have brought about dramatic changes in the organization of police work (Manning, 1992a). There is, therefore, every reason to expect that the latest round of technological change—the information technology revolution—would have an equally dramatic impact on policing. This article draws on an Australian case study to examine the extent to which information technology has, as the above quotation from Postman (1992) suggests, altered the structural, symbolic and social organization of policing.

The latest round of technological changes in policing is driven by three imperatives: to improve effectiveness and efficiency, to satisfy the demands of external agencies for information and to meet the requirements of new forms of police management and accountability. The first imperative is technology-driven: not only does technology promise to improve police effectiveness and efficiency in controlling crime, it may also enhance their professional status and organizational legitimacy (Manning, 1992a; Ericson and Haggerty, 1997: 390). Given that information is the stock-in-trade of policing, police are investing in information technology to increase their capacity to store and process large volumes of data; improve their intelligence and investigative capabilities; and provide ready access to criminal records and other crime-related information. The need for technology that is compatible with other agencies is also an important driving force.

The second imperative is information-driven: police organizations regularly provide crime and accident data for external bodies such as road traffic authorities and insurance companies for their own management and risk assessment needs. Increasingly, police information is commodified and sold to external commercial institutions and individuals partly as a cost-recovery measure and partly to discourage frivolous requests (Ericson and Haggerty, 1997: 340–5). These external demands for police information are partly responsible for the need to improve information technology capacities within police organizations.

The third imperative is policy-driven. Police organizations' use of information technology to improve performance and management is the result of externally imposed demands for public accountability, in terms of cost-effectiveness, probity and procedural regularity. Since the 1980s, a new conception of public accountability has arisen in a number of western democracies such as Australia and Britain (Leishman et al., 1996; Power, 1997; Davids and Hancock, 1998; Chan, 1999). Traditionally, police practices and procedures are governed by laws and departmental rules, which are enforced by the courts and the police hierarchies respectively. The predominant mode of control is deterrence through legislation and rule making, investigation and enforcement, criminal sanctions and organizational discipline. The 'new accountability', however, adopts the managerial techniques and administrative structures of private for-profit corporations, emphasizing cost control, efficiency, decentralization of management and the cutting back of the public sector, while creating market or quasi-market mechanisms, contracting out, performance indicators, risk assessment and audit procedures (Leishman et al., 1996; Power, 1997; Chan, 1999; Dean, 1999). In policing, the new managerialism has transformed the traditional police force into organizations with 'mission statements', 'business plans', 'marketing strategies' and a new emphasis on 'crime management', 'customer service' and performance measures (Leishman et al., 1996; O'Malley and Palmer, 1996; Chan, 1997). Ackroyd et al. (1992) call it the 'entrepreneurial revolution' in policing. Under this new order, police are being scrutinized *internally* by management systems, surveillance technologies, internal audits and investigations, and *externally* by 'watchdog' agencies, public complaints systems and central auditors. In effect, information technology provides a tool not only for the policing of citizens, but also for policing the police.

The impact of technology

The use of information technology has become part of everyday life in the 21st century for many individuals and the vast majority of organizations. It is therefore not surprising that a national mailed survey of US city police agencies in the mid-1990s found that only about 6 per cent of the respondents did not have an in-house computer system (Mullen, 1996). Australian police forces, being typically much larger than American ones, have all adopted some form of service-wide computerized information system since the mid-1990s. But has the large-scale adoption of information technology made any difference to policing? Technology certainly has the capability to improve efficiency and enhance accountability, but whether this capability is realized in practice is not a foregone conclusion. Although there is now a growing body of research on technology-based organizational change (see Yates and Van Maanen, 1996), there have been very few research studies on the impact of information technology on policing (Manning, 1992a; Mullen, 1996).

Different perspectives have emerged from the available literature on the extent to which information technology has changed police practices. One view suggests that information technologies 'have been constrained by the traditional structure of policing and by the traditional role of the officer' (Manning, 1992a: 350). Drawing on evaluation studies published in the 1970s and 1980s (e.g. Chaiken et al., 1975; Colton, 1978; Rheinier et al., 1979; Hough, 1980), Manning outlines the disappointing results of various technological innovations such as Computer-Aided Dispatch (CAD) systems, attempts to reduce response time, car locator and tracking systems, crime-mapping techniques and management information systems. He concludes that: 'Such research as exists is often inconclusive or suggests that new technologies have less effect on police practices than their proponents predict or prefer' (Manning, 1992a: 382).

In contrast, studies conducted in the 1990s come to rather different conclusions. Harper's (1991) research on the use of a computerized crime-reporting system (CRS) by detectives in a medium-sized British police constabulary suggests that information technology has made a clear difference to detective work. Not only has the computerized information system made it easier and faster to access and retrieve information, it has transformed the 'spatio-temporal context in which detectives operate': detectives no longer need to travel to different places to locate records and they have virtually 24-hour access to files. Although not originally intended by the technology, the crime-reporting system gave detectives an advantage over offenders when negotiating about 'offences to be taken into consideration' (TICed) by 'enhancing a detective's ability to bluff' (Harper, 1991: 300). This advantage is likely to be temporary, however, as suspects would eventually get used to seeing computers on the desk of detectives and no longer be intimidated by them.

Ericson and Haggerty's (1997) study of Canadian police organizations, carried out in the early 1990s, demonstrates that information technology has had a profound impact on the way officers think, act and report on their activities. The introduction of information technology has meant that individual police discretion is severely circumscribed by the rules, formats and technologies of the reporting systems, whereas supervision has been tightened both *prospectively* as details of police activities are embedded in the 'required fields' of information technology systems and *retrospectively* as supervisors take more seriously their scrutiny of filed reports. The capability of information technology is such that it has become an effective tool for the surveillance of police supervisors, the detection of misconduct and all types of audits, monitoring and risk management (Ericson and Haggerty, 1997: 398–9). The researchers argue that:

> Communication technologies . . . radically alter the structure of police organization by levelling hierarchies, blurring traditional divisions of labor, dispersing supervisory capacities and limiting individual discretion. In the process, traditional rank structures of command and control are replaced by system surveillance mechanisms for regulating police conduct.
>
> (Ericson and Haggerty, 1997: 388)

Information technology has also created new cultures of policing and rendered police organizations more transparent (Ericson and Haggerty, 1997: 412).

The impact of information technology is, however, not always as intended. Ericson and Haggerty (1997) concede that police officers did actively resist some aspects of information technology through refusal to participate, aversion to use or other forms of subtle resistance. Resistance was likely where officers perceived that such technology was used as a surveillance mechanism by supervisors or where the systems were technically difficult or cumbersome. There were also unintended consequences such as the proliferation of 'bootleg forms', an increase rather than a decrease in paper files and police work becoming even more office bound in some cases. As Manning (1992a) points out, the mere availability and accessibility of information does not necessarily mean that information is used effectively or appropriately by police officers and managers. In general, the use of computer technology may increase productivity without resulting in any gain in efficiency (see Henman, 1996).

Understanding technological change

Researchers who study the impact of technology on social life have long argued that technology should not be seen as consisting of a physical, material dimension only; rather, technology operates in a social context, and its meaning is perceived differently by people in different social and organizational positions (Ackroyd et al., 1992; Manning, 1992a; Orlikowski and Gash, 1994). While technological changes have the capacity to transform social and organizational life, it is important to recognize that technology is itself shaped by social and organizational conditions. The impact of a specific technology on social life is often determined by factors beyond its technical capacity—factors which may be psychological, social, political or cultural. Hence, technology may be constraining or enabling, but people have the ability to 'adapt, bend, shape, develop, subvert, misuse and otherwise manipulate technological specifications for various purposes' (Ackroyd et al., 1992: 11). Orlikowski and Robey explain this as the underlying 'duality' (see Giddens, 1984) of information technology:

> This duality is expressed in its *constituted* nature—information technology is the social product of subjective human action within specific structural and cultural contexts—and its *constitutive* role—information technology is simultaneously an objective set of rules and resources involved in mediating (facilitating and constraining) human action and hence contributing to the creation, recreation, and transformation of these contexts. Information technology is both an antecedent and a consequence of organizational action.
>
> (Orlikowski and Robey, 1991: 151)

Orlikowski has therefore argued that the impact of technological change on organizational structure, work practices, communication channels and performance cannot be understood in a *deterministic* or rationalist way (Orlikowski, 1996: 64). Instead, the consequences of information technology should be interpreted via an *interpretive* or *emergent* model, i.e. that they result from the 'interplay among computing infrastructures, conflicting objectives and preferences of different social groups, and the operation of chance' and that information technology is open to interpretation during implementation and use (Robey and Sahay, 1996: 95). These models stress the active role of organizational members and the importance of social context and processes that produce the meanings of technology. From this perspective, technology is 'an occasion for, not a determinant of, organisational change' (Barley, 1986).

Broadly speaking, we can distinguish three types of factors that influence the course of technological change and its impact on organizations: (a) *technical factors*, which include the nature of technology itself and how technological change is managed; (b) *cultural factors*, which include the assumptions inherent in the introduced technology and the extent to which these are congruent with those held by users within organizations; and (c) *political factors*, which consist of the interests at stake in technological change and the conflict or bargaining that may result.

Technical factors

Technological change can have a large or small impact on organizations depending on the nature and design of the technology and the way in which technological change is managed. Ericson and Haggerty's (1997) research suggests that information technology has had a substantial impact on policing partly because of the design and implementation of a more coercive technology which is difficult to avoid or bypass: when the basic routines of police work are built into the system, officers are literally not able to work without using the technology (Ericson and Haggerty, 1997: 394). In fact, where systems are less coercive or less effective, technology can be called upon to correct the problem (Ericson and Haggerty, 1997: 414).

Sparrow has long emphasized the importance of managing information systems properly:

> [I]f badly managed, they can frustrate managerial purposes, enshrine old values, focus attention on outdated and inappropriate performance meas-- ures, give power to the wrong people, cast in concrete old ways of doing business, create false or misleading public expectations, destroy partnerships and impose crippling restrictions to new styles of operation—quite apart from their propensity to consume millions and millions of tax dollars.
>
> (Sparrow, 1991: 26)

Examples of technical and implementation problems of information technology in policing include flaws in system design which resulted in data of poor quality and the failure to build and maintain support for technology within police departments (Hough, 1980).

Cultural factors

Technology is not simply an objective, physical given; people have to make sense of it and, in the process, 'develop particular assumptions, expectations and knowledge of the technology, which then serve to shape subsequent actions toward it' (Orlikowski and Gash, 1994: 175). Orlikowski and Gash coin the term 'technological frames' to describe a subset of the cognitive schemas shared by members of social groups (Schein, 1985;

Sackmann, 1991). Technological frames can be both helpful and constraining: they can help 'structure' people's experience and reduce organizational uncertainty, but they can also inhibit creativity and reinforce established assumptions (Orlikowski and Gash, 1994: 176–7). Technological frames generally vary between social groups, according to the 'purpose, context, power, knowledge base, and the [technological] artifact itself' (Orlikowski and Gash, 1994: 179). In their case study, Orlikowski and Gash distinguished between three domains of technological frames: (a) the nature of technology—people's understanding of *what* technology is capable of; (b) technology strategy—their view of *why* technology was introduced in their organization; and (c) technology in use—their understanding of *how* technology is to be routinely used and the consequences of such use (Orlikowski and Gash, 1994: 183–4). The impact of information technology on organizations can then be explained in terms of the existence of *congruence* or *incongruence* in technological frames between social groups. Where incongruent technological frames exist, the introduction of technology is likely to encounter conflicts and difficulties.

The incongruence between the technological frames of information technology designers and those of the police was evident in the mismatch between the models of policing implicit in the technology introduced in the 1970s and the reality of policing:

> Most attempts to apply analytic techniques such as statistical modelling techniques to police administration are underpinned by a set of assumptions . . .: (i) the primary objective of the police is crime control; (ii) police activity is one of the primary determinants of crime levels; (iii) the police are organised as a rational bureaucracy; (iv) police strategies are primarily those of deterrence. . . . That these basic assumptions are too inaccurate to pass muster even as a provisional statement is becoming increasingly clear.
>
> (Hough, 1980: 351–2)

Such incongruence can create tension in the workplace as workers seek to adjust their practices to conform to the system's requirements:

> . . . systems designers and implementers very often underrate, or even discount, the working context, its social organisation, its tacit skills and knowledge, into which the system has to fit as a tool of that work. The result is often that working practices must be changed to accommodate to the system in some way (which may or may not be the intention behind the introduction of the system) and/or an uneasy tension is created between those who do the work and the requirements of the system.
>
> (Ackroyd et al., 1992: 119)

Sparrow (1991) shows the difficulty in trying to make a computer-aided dispatch (CAD) system designed for traditional-style policing serve a community-based, problem-solving style of policing that management in the Houston Police Department wanted to adopt. Problems of 'call stacking' (holding calls for beat officers to deal with), 'checking by' (allowing patrol cars to do proactive work instead of servicing non-urgent calls), 'call histories' (the amount of time call information should be retained on-line) and 'cherry picking' (officers taking the 'good' calls and leaving the unpleasant ones) revealed the fundamental conflict between traditional-style policing where response time was a major concern and problem-solving policing where police were expected to do proactive work, analyse call histories and make mature, responsible decisions about their work. Sparrow even warns managers against leaving the design and implementation of information systems to technologists. This example illustrates the incongruence of technological frames between information technology designers and managers. If this example can be extrapolated, where information technology is designed to change management culture (Ackroyd et al., 1992), accountability procedures (Ericson and Haggerty, 1997) or rank-and-file work practices, clashes in technological frames would exist almost by definition. The result may be various forms of resistance, breakdown in communication, or even suspension of the information technology project itself (Orlikowski and Gash, 1994: 181).

Political factors

Technological changes often 'destabilize the power balance between organizational segments by altering communication patterns, roles relationships, the division of labor, established formats for organizational communication, and taken-for-granted routines' (Manning, 1996: 54). Since information itself is a source of power, information technology can lead to power struggles, adaptations or reactions which may subvert the original intentions of the new technology (Orlikowski and Robey, 1991: 155).

In policing, the introduction of information technology can restrict the discretion and autonomy of 'street-level' police officers, while at the same time enhancing the status of information technology specialists (Ericson and Haggerty, 1997: 406). Such developments alter the balance of power between workers and supervisors and between sworn officers and civilians. When officers feel that their autonomy is threatened by internal surveillance or external interference, they are likely to resort to resistance or sabotage where possible. Ericson and Haggerty gave examples of patrol officers collaborating with dispatchers to avoid being tracked by computer-aided dispatch systems (1997: 414) as well as examples of officers refusing or resisting the mandatory reporting of family violence as an 'externally driven surveillance technology based on an outlook of distrust' (1997: 386).

Dynamics of technological change

The above discussion may have presented an unduly static view of technological impact. The introduction of new technology is merely the beginning of a 'technological drama' (Manning, 1992b, 1996) of normalization, adjustment, reconstitution and reintegration. The resultant reintegration and normalization may be manifested in various changes as well as continuities in organizational life. Orlikowski's (1996) 'situated change' perspective of organizational change is similarly relevant for understanding the dynamic quality of technological impact. Orlikowski offers a view of organizational change which is emergent and continuous rather than rapid and discontinuous: 'through a series of ongoing and situated accommodations, adaptations, and alterations (that draw on previous variations and mediate future ones), sufficient modifications may be enacted over time that fundamental changes are achieved' (Orlikowski, 1996: 66). Her study of the introduction of a call-tracking system of a customer support department in a software company found that the organizational structures and practices of the department had changed considerably over the two years following the implementation of the new technology, but the transformation, 'while enabled by the technology, was not caused by it' (Orlikowski, 1996: 69). Rather, members of the department 'attempted to make sense of and appropriate the new technology and its embedded constraints and enablements' and through their daily actions and interactions in response to the technology, they enacted 'a series of metamorphic changes in their organizing practices and structures' (Orlikowski, 1996: 89).

The technological game

The above review suggests that technology should not be seen as purely technical and physical—it can shape social life but is itself modified by social and organizational conditions. The impact of technology on policing is dependent on how technology interacts with existing cultural values, management styles, work practices and technical capabilities. A useful way to conceptualize technological change is to examine its relationship to the 'field' and 'habitus' of policing (Bourdieu and Wacquant, 1992; see Chan, 1997). For Bourdieu, a field is like a game; it is a social space of conflict and competition, where participants struggle to establish control over specific power and authority. Central to Bourdieu's concept of field is the notion of 'capital'. Various forms of capital operate in different social fields—these include economic capital, cultural or informational capital, social capital and symbolic capital (Bourdieu, 1987: 3–4). Habitus is a 'feel for the game'. It is a system of dispositions which agents acquire either individually, through family and the education system, or as a group, through organizational socialization. Bourdieu's framework suggests that changes in the game (field) would create new necessities that may require the creation of new strategies (habitus) for coping. Technological change, to the extent that it redefines the game of policing, can bring about changes in the field (through various constraints and resources) as well as transform the habitus (e.g. classifications, assumptions and sensibilities).

An Australian case study

The following discussion is based on a recent study of an Australian police force (see Chan et al., 2001). There are only nine police forces in Australia, eight covering each of the States and Territories plus a federal force. The Eastern Police Service (EPS, a pseudonym) has several thousand sworn officers and provides service to several million people over a vast geographical area. Development of an information technology strategy began in the early 1990s following several public inquiries into the police force. The study was conducted in 1998–9. At the time, the EPS was in the middle of implementing an integrated computer system to incorporate several existing systems dealing with crime reporting, processing of offenders and criminal histories. In addition, a variety of computer-based facilities were operating, including electronic mail and bulletin board, computer-aided dispatch, traffic incidents and transport data, intelligence systems, electronic warrants and linkages to nation-wide systems.

The research was designed to examine the extent to which information technology has modified the accountability structure, the occupational culture and policing practices at the street, supervisory and management levels in the EPS. Several research techniques were used to obtain information on the development and implementation of the systems and their impact on policing: 23 interviews[1] with senior police and information technology specialists; 11 focus groups with a total of 106 participants including general duties officers, detectives, intelligence officers, officers in charge and information management personnel; a representative (but non-random) survey of 506 police officers[2]; approximately 30 hours of ride-along observation over eight half-shifts; and analysis of a large number of documents including annual reports, strategic and implementation plans and programme specifications (see Chapter 2 in Chan et al., 2001 for further details).

Impact of information technology on the field of policing

Information technology had become an integral part of police life in the EPS by the late 1990s. Survey respondents[3] reported spending an average of three hours and 37 minutes per eight-hour shift using computers for administrative tasks. The vast majority (72 per cent) of the respondents thought that information technology had made 'a great difference' to police work, while a minority thought it had made 'a little difference' (26 per cent) or 'no difference at all' (2 per cent). This feeling was more prevalent among respondents who have had longer service in the EPS and those in higher ranks. The new technology has fundamentally altered the field of policing through the various resources (Bourdieu's 'capital') it provided and constraints (Bourdieu's 'necessities') it imposed on police work.

Technology as resource

Effectiveness and efficiency

In spite of many complaints in the focus groups about various technical problems with the systems, EPS officers' assessment of the impact of information technology on their own work was generally positive. The majority of respondents indicated that information technology has allowed them to work more effectively (79 per cent agreed versus 3 per cent disagreed[4]), made their work easier (66 versus 7 per cent) and helped them cope with the amount of information police needed to do their work properly (59 versus 10 per cent). The gain in efficiency as a result of information technology was especially salient to police who had experienced the old technology. For example, one participant in a focus group of specialist investigators (FG9) said that five to six years ago, to type a record of interview for a large investigation would take five to six hours; now it could be done in half an hour from a taped record of interview.

Communication

Survey respondents also rated positively the impact of information technology on workplace relations and communication. The majority agreed that information technology has led to improved information sharing between workers (70 per cent) and improved communication between workers (58 per cent). Less than 10 per cent of respondents disagreed with those statements. Similarly, respondents tended to agree that information technology has allowed people to work more co-operatively (47 per cent agreed versus 7 per cent disagreed) and created a more positive work atmosphere (30 versus 13 per cent). Improvement in communication between workers was largely the result of the availability of electronic mail that facilitated teamwork, information gathering and sharing (FG5).

Technical expertise

With the widespread use of technology in the organization, technical expertise became a much-valued form of cultural capital. The majority of survey respondents agreed that information technology has led to increased computer literacy among police (75 per cent versus 5 per cent disagreed) and enhanced the professional status of police (52 versus 9 per cent). As one intelligence officer explained: 'As intel officers we were considered the leaders in IT. We knew nothing, but we knew so much more than the basic [officer] who knew practically nothing. We were gods to them' (FG5). The growth in funding and staffing of IT-related functions within the EPS was a source of much envy and some bitterness among some officers. The ascendancy of officers with IT expertise may also threaten the traditional power structure of an organization where previously leaders were pre-dominantly drawn from the criminal investigation branch (Interview 1).

Technology as constraint

Time use

A fairly substantial proportion of survey respondents thought that, as a result of information technology, they spent more time satisfying account-ability requirements (41 per cent); doing 'paperwork' (36 per cent); planning, organizing or analysing information (30 per cent); supervising or checking the work of staff (26 per cent). In addition, a fair proportion indicated that they spent less time patrolling the streets (39 per cent); inter-acting with members of the community in non-crime or non-emergency situations (30 per cent); informing citizens on the progress of their case (25 per cent); and responding to calls from citizens (20 per cent). Respondents in the higher ranks (senior constable and above) were more likely to be affected. As an officer-in-charge in one of the focus groups explained:

> Eighty per cent of our time is probably consumed in doing all this sort of stuff. . . . There's huge benefits in [information technology], but we haven't got time to use it. . . . There's accountability issues,. . . I could spend six or seven hours a day just doing compliance without even looking at police work. Officers-in-charge of bigger stations probably would need half a dozen staff to do that properly. Nobody does it properly—we're all aware of that. It's very frustrating.
>
> (FG6)

The issue of police spending more time in front of computers and less time on the streets was often raised in the focus groups. For example, a general-duties officer said that: 'Technology has drawn a lot of people off the street and stuck them into offices'—even though there are a lot of police 'on paper', very few are on the road (FG1).

Discretion

Survey respondents were ambivalent about whether information technol-ogy has limited the amount of discretion police have—25 per cent agreed, 17 per cent disagreed and 59 per cent were neutral. General duties officers were more likely to think that information technology has limited their discretion, compared with detectives. Similarly, officers in lower ranks were more likely than those in higher ranks to agree that their discretion was limited by technology. When the issue of discretion was raised in focus groups, one response was that it is a lot harder to write a file off because of insufficient evidence—a reason has to be entered. However, constables can still find ways of cutting corners, for example, in relation to whether a minor incident should be reported (FG5). Other police said that there are no shortcuts—the system was designed in such a way that it cannot be circumvented (FG4). In fact, the system is capable of monitoring short-cuts: 'the shortcuts can now be assessed—if you are taking shortcuts, [it] can be seen that you are taking shortcuts' (FG5).

Routine operations

A substantial proportion of survey respondents thought that information technology has required police to follow unnecessary steps to get things done (43 per cent agreed versus 13 per cent disagreed). This feeling was particularly strong among detectives, with 59 per cent agreeing and only 9 per cent disagreeing. Responses also vary by rank—percentages who agreed went up from 35 and 36 per cent among first-year constables and constables respectively to 51 per cent for senior constables, 53 per cent for sergeants, 47 per cent for senior sergeants and 60 per cent for inspectors. Much of the focus group discussions centred on the additional steps officers had to follow to get their work done. For example, one general duties officer explained that the old way of doing the court brief was to put it in the typewriter and wind it on, but it was quicker because you knew exactly where you wanted to go, there was no need to wait for each screen to come up. Another participant said that on the old system, it would take 10 to 20 minutes to complete a court brief, whereas now it takes two to three hours (FG1). This view was supported by officers from other focus groups:

> When I was at [name of station] years ago we could . . . do a random breath test, pick up a drink driver, take him into town, process him, . . . have him charged, have a [court brief] typed in the prosecutors box, have all the paper work done, be back on the road and the best we ever did it in was 40 minutes. . . . That was on a manual typewriter. Now, . . . by the time everyone does all their compliance with their custody indexes and all their indexes and does everything else, finally gets through to [crime reporting system] to get a number, then they sit down in front of the computer to do the [court brief] on the computer. And the [court brief] on the computer takes a lot longer than the old manual typewriter. So I'm looking at hours. . . . [Comments from the floor estimate that the process has gone from 40 minutes to two hours.]
>
> (FG6)

Accountability

There was a general feeling that with the advent of information technology came additional reporting and accountability requirements. Two-thirds of the survey respondents agreed that information technology has required them to report on their activities more frequently and made them more accountable for their actions. A number of focus group participants pointed out that it was in fact the need for accountability that caused the additional workload, not the information technology systems per se. As one specialist investigator said: 'The amount of time spent on the computer isn't because of information technology, it's because of legislation that we've got to do' (FG9). Others added that: 'If we didn't have the information technology to meet those regulations, we'd be even slower', or 'We'd be stressed out that much that you'd have half the Police Service on stress leave'. To achieve the same level of reporting using the old manual system would have been impossible (FG9).

The majority of survey respondents agreed that information technology has led to a closer scrutiny of their work by their supervisors (55 per cent) and that information technology has made their supervisors more aware of their day-to-day activities and workload (52 per cent). There is no doubt that information technology has given police supervisors a greater capacity to scrutinize the work of their staff, but whether this capacity has been utilized effectively is debatable. An officer in charge in a focus group explained that the new incident management system allows supervisors to check where their cars are, what their officers are doing, how far they have got in their crime report and whether they have done their job properly. However, this officer said that he does not really use the system, because he does not have time to do it (FG2).

Changes and continuities in the habitus

To what extent have these changes in the field made a difference to the habitus of policing, that is, the cultural assumptions about the aims of policing, appropriate ways of seeing and behaving and treasured values and beliefs? From the accounts of officers who took part in the study, it is possible to discern changes as well as continuities in the habitus that can be attributed to the use of information technology.

Policing style and practice

Information technology has had limited impact on the dominant style of policing in the EPS. Only 38 per cent of the survey respondents agreed (52 per cent were neutral, while 10 per cent disagreed) that information technology has led to a more problem-oriented police service. Respondents in rural divisions were more likely (47 per cent) to agree compared with respondents in metropolitan (37 per cent), suburban (33 per cent) and provincial city (35 per cent) divisions. The idea of 'smarter' policing strategies was raised in one of the focus groups. Some officers mentioned the potential of 'intelligence-driven patrols', analysis of 'hot spots' and repeat offenders and proactive crime investigations. Others were more sceptical: 'Who gets time for that?' It was said that it does not happen—'never will', although in theory it could happen. One focus group participant explained the role conflict experienced by intelligence officers:

Most of them are in Region Offices. Most of their time is [spent] putting stats together for bosses. But that's not their role. Their role is to look at the crimes that are going on to target areas or offences. They don't have time to do it because they are collating crime stats for a management meeting. Because intel officers aren't able to do their job, there's a whole bunch of baddies we can't get because they aren't looking at it. You might say we should do it, but where do we get time?

(FG4)

Only 35 per cent agreed that information technology has led to better proactive policing, half were neutral and 18 per cent disagreed. Information technology has given police the potential for crime prevention but, as a participant from a focus group pointed out, there were insufficient resources to realize this potential:

From an intel perspective . . . . We can identify problems, we can predict where we believe where things are going to happen . . . and we can continue to say if we do this, then we should reduce crime. And we'll do it for six weeks, then stop because that's where the resources finish. And we've done that time and time again. So we've created this technology, or technology has helped us look at what's happened in the past and predict what's going to happen in the future crime-wise, but we don't have the resources to go to the next step. . . . We've got police collecting the information but not the time to actually go and act on what's been collected.

(FG5)

One area where information technology has facilitated proactive policing in a dramatic way was the use of stand-alone computers in police cars to check for outstanding traffic offence warrants based on vehicle or boat licence numbers, persons of interest and drivers licences. As an illustration, during a five-hour period one of the researchers spent on the road with two officers, the officers executed the equivalent of approximately $5,500 worth of warrants (Legosz and Brereton, 2001). Focus group participants were enthusiastic about the system; officers said that they did about 1000 checks a week (FG6).

These findings would not have come as a surprise to the architects of the systems. Organizationally, the EPS was totally 'immature' in the early 1990s, not only in relation to information technology, but more significantly, 'there was really no management infrastructure to speak of at all', following the removal of top levels of management as a result of a damaging corruption inquiry (Interview 12). There was a deliberate strategy to secure support for, and ownership of, the system initially among operational police before targeting managers. The idea was to move gradually from an ad hoc, operationally oriented system to an integrated, tactically, strategically and eventually policy-oriented system (Interview 1). However, this was expected to be a longer-term objective, as the organization has yet to move to the next level of maturity and capability. One of the barriers was precisely the 'technological frame' of traditional culture that sees information as useful only if it leads to arrests:

> ... even our intel people, even the high-end users, our power users, generally see information from an offender perspective—in other words, information analysis is all about how we can ... find an offender ... how do you nick someone, and so that limits what becomes useful information.
>
> (Interview 1)

There was not a clear vision of what problem-oriented policing might offer; it was still seen as 'soft' and marginal. Information technology has, in effect, 'made things easier, rather than made things different' (Interview 1).

Reliance on technology

Some officers were not entirely comfortable with the heavy reliance on information technology for information. As an officer-in-charge observed in a focus group discussion, because of the availability of electronic bulletin boards and databases, police no longer carry policing knowledge in their head (FG2). Reliance on information technology also meant the loss of 'local knowledge', as one general duties officer remarked: 'information technology is good for number crunching, but you don't know the face. You can drive around for whole shift and not see the same face twice' (FG1). Another officer-in-charge thought that police are not as directly involved with the public in criminal investigations as they used to be five to 10 years ago. Even though intelligence is extremely good, these officers felt that it will never take the place of basic hands-on traditional intelligence gathering—getting out on the street, talking to people, finding out what is going on (FG2).

Transparency of procedures

Survey respondents were generally positive about the impact of information technology on the quality of police service. Six out of 10 thought that information technology had led to improved police service to the public (62 per cent agreed versus 12 per cent disagreed) and improved police response to crime (59 per cent versus 12 per cent). Several groups mentioned that the crime reporting system has made a difference. With this system, police procedures are more transparent—the complainant can see the officer getting on the phone to file a report: 'Now the public can see that something's really happening' (FG3). The system also allows victims and complainants to get faster feedback on the progress of their case by ringing up with a system number (FG2, FG8). Police can also respond better to customer inquiries as they can access information about the case and identify whom to contact (FG5).

Resentment towards accountability demands

When survey respondents were asked in general terms whether information technology has led to improved police accountability, six out of 10 agreed, although a similar proportion also thought that information technology has led to an *overemphasis* on accountability. Nearly four in 10 also thought that information technology has led to a less trusting or more paranoid organizational atmosphere. Accountability—internal and external—was a burning issue among many focus group participants. A familiar theme is that accountability has gone too far, and at the expense of doing the job:

> These days after [name of corruption inquiry] or what-have-you, the emphasis on accountability has become much higher, and in doing so they introduce 9321 different registers that's got to be filled out to maintain the accountability. But in doing that, you spend that much time becoming accountable and spend less time doing the job you're paid for. I think accountability is a good thing, but at the same time it's got to be weighed up between getting the job done. And trusting people too, you get to the point where you're so busy being accountable you feel that nobody trusts what you do. . . . You've got to be given that trust and it be understood that you will do that job.
>
> (FG2)

Another concern was whether the information in the systems was going to be used for punishment (FG5). For example, with the crime reporting system, if there is a complaint about inaction on a crime report, the tools are there to find the individual officer responsible, and to show what the person did or did not do.

Some officers felt that 'the Department has gone risk-management crazy' with new databases where it was no longer possible to 'cut corners' (FG5). A participant from a group of detectives agreed: 'It's about auditing and checking . . . and it's overdone . . . it's accountability and it's gone too far . . . . It's not being productive' (FG4). Other members of the group pointed out that many of the risk management or accountability exercises are 'futile' and not worth the time. They argued that risk management should be about minimizing risk, but, according to one of the participants, the Police Service's idea of risk management is there should be no risk, no acceptable level of risk—'They haven't grasped the concept'. Another officer agreed:

> The idea of risk management is to identify something everyone's doing wrong, e.g. entering an index wrong—not to check every index they're doing to make sure they're doing it. It's to check problems with the system, not as an accountability exercise, which is what they're using it as.
>
> (FG4)

A recurrent theme among focus group discussions relates to the abuse of technology-generated performance indicators. One example involved officers in a watchhouse who abused the system by putting in a computer entry every time they fed a prisoner, so that they got a new job number each time. Similarly, an officer can arrest someone with 100 warrants and enter the data for each arrest on each warrant to show how busy he has been (FG1). Another bone of contention was clear-up rates. Detectives blamed the crime reporting system data entry operators for not recording all their clear-ups, while others were concerned that monthly fluctuations in clear-up rates might give misleading indicators of performance (FG2).

Officers particularly resented demands for information and account-ability from external organizations. It was said in one focus group (FG1) that a lot of police work is for the [watchdog organization], insurance companies, security companies and other 'vested interests'. For example, the accident form is a very long form that has to be filled out by the police for every accident. Similarly, there were concerns that the [watchdog organization] has imposed a variety of reporting requirements that make officers' work more cumbersome.

Conclusion

These research findings are consistent with Ericson and Haggerty's (1997) conclusion that information technology has altered important aspects of the field of policing. In the case of the EPS, within a relatively short period of time following its introduction, information technology has redefined the value of communicative and technical resources, institutionalized accountability through built-in formats and procedures of reporting, and restructured the daily routines of operational policing. These changes in the field of policing have led to some changes in the habitus. For example, information technology has allowed police procedures to be more trans-parent at the level of 'customer interface', and this transparency has become accepted as an indicator of good police service. Similarly, officers are beginning to appreciate the value of using technology-generated infor-mation for tactical and strategic purposes such as crime prevention, problem solving and resource allocation. Nevertheless, the dominance of traditional policing styles and values remains. Although information tech-nology has given police the capacity to follow a 'smarter' or more problem-oriented style of policing, this capacity has not been fully utilized. Even where technology facilitated proactive police work such as the checking of outstanding warrants, it has been used mainly to support a traditional law-enforcement style of policing focused on clear-up rates. The cultural suspicion and cynicism against management and external watchdogs is still very much alive, but this has been channelled into hostility towards the organization's 'obsession' with risk management and external agencies' demand for data and accountability.

The case study sheds new light on the role of cultural factors in under-standing the impact of technological change. There was undoubtedly a clash in 'technological frames' (Orlikowski and Gash, 1994) between the users and the architects of the systems. Users of the technology, even the more advanced ones, expected it to make their work easier and more efficient, without their having to change existing policing and management styles. Architects of the systems, on the other hand, have intended the organization to move towards a more sophisticated mode of information usage—for resource management, tactical policing, strategic planning and policy decisions. At the same time, governments and other external bodies continually demand new legislative and accountability requirements to be incorporated into the design, so that the capacity and functionality of the systems have to be constantly expanded. Yet the case study has shown that users' technological frames are not immutable. While police resent the additional workload generated by managerial and accountability demands, they have also become willing players in the new technological game. The coercive nature of the technology gave them no other alternatives. Thus, despite constant complaints about various technical problems, police have generally responded positively to the new technology. Ironically, rather than resisting the burden imposed by the technology, they demand more and better technology in the hope of lightening this burden. If Orlikowski (1996) is correct that organizational change is likely to be emergent and continuous rather than rapid and discontinuous, technology-based organizational change, by gradually and continuously altering the field of policing, will eventually have an impact on the deeply embedded assumptions of police practice.

Notes

This article draws on findings of the final report of the research project 'The Impact of Information Technology on Police Organizations' which was jointly funded by the Australian Research Council and the Criminal Justice Commission in Queensland (see Chan et al., 2001). The author would like to thank David Brereton for his significant contribution to the design and management of this project and Richard Ericson for his comments on an earlier draft of this article. The valuable assistance of Margot Legosz and Sally Doran throughout the project is also gratefully acknowledged.

1. Twenty-three people were interviewed in 17 separate sessions.
2. Partly a result of 'survey fatigue', the response rates of random surveys carried out in the EPS during the 12 months prior to this project were around 20 per cent. The research team therefore decided to follow an alternative strategy by targeting officers in selected training programmes and police stations to ensure a high return rate and a representative sample according to rank, duty and location.
3. Results are based on 506 respondents, although the actual number varies according to each item of the questionnaire depending on the number of missing values.

4. Survey participants chose from a five-point likert scale (strongly agree, agree, neutral, disagree, strongly disagree) in response to various statements. Percentages in the text reflect pooled percentages that combined 'strongly agree' and 'agree', 'disagree' and 'strongly disagree'. Percentages with neutral responses were not cited.

References

Ackroyd, S., R. Harper, J.A. Hughes, D. Shapiro and K. Soothill (1992) *New Technology and Practical Police Work*. Buckingham: Open University Press.

Barley, S. (1986) 'Technology as an Occasion for Structuring: Evidence from Observations of CT Scanners and the Social Order of Radiology Departments', *Administrative Science Quarterly* 31: 78–108.

Bourdieu, P. (1987) 'What Makes a Social Class? On the Theoretical and Practical Existence of Groups', *Berkeley Journal of Sociology* 32: 1–18.

Bourdieu, P. and L.J.D. Wacquant (1992) *An Invitation to Reflexive Sociology*. Cambridge: Polity Press.

Chaiken, J., T. Crabill, L. Holliday, D. Jaquett, M. Lawless and E. Quade (1975) *Criminal Justice Models: An Overview*. Santa Monica, CA: RAND.

Chan, J. (1997) *Changing Police Culture: Policing in a Multicultural Society*. Melbourne: Cambridge University Press.

Chan, J. (1999) 'Governing Police Practice: Limits of the New Accountability', *British Journal of Sociology* 50(2): 249–68.

Chan, Janet, David Brereton, Margot Legosz and Sally Doran (2001) *The Impact of Information Technology on Policing: An Australian Case Study*. Brisbane: Criminal Justice Commission, forthcoming.

Colton, K. (ed.) (1978) *Police Computer Technology*. Lexington, MA: D.C. Heath.

Davids, C. and L. Hancock (1998) 'Policing, Accountability, and Citizenship in the Market State', *Australian and New Zealand Journal of Criminology* 31(1): 38–68.

Dean, M. (1999) *Governmentality: Power and Rule in Modern Society*. London: Sage.

Ericson, R.V. and K.D. Haggerty (1997) *Policing the Risk Society*. Toronto and Buffalo: University of Toronto Press.

Giddens, A. (1984) *The Constitution of Society*. Cambridge: Polity Press.

Harper, R.R. (1991) 'The Computer Game: Detectives, Suspects, and Technology', *British Journal of Criminology* 31(3): 292–307.

Henman, P. (1996) 'Constructing Families and Disciplining Bodies: A Socio-technical Study of Computers, Policy and Governance in Australia's Department of Social Security', Ph.D. diss., University of Queensland.

Hough, M. (1980) 'Managing with Less Technology—The Impact of Information Technology on Police Management', *British Journal of Criminology* 20(4): 344–57.

Legosz, M. and D. Brereton (2001) 'On the Road with Maverick: A Case Study of the Impact of Information Technology on Policing', paper given to the Australian and New Zealand Society of Criminology, Melbourne, February.

Leishman, F., B. Loveday and S.P. Savage (eds) (1996) *Core Issues in Policing.* London: Longman.

Manning, P.K. (1992a) 'Information Technologies and the Police', in M. Tonry and N. Morris (eds) *Modern Policing: Crime and Justice, A Review of Research*, vol. 15, pp. 349–98. Chicago, IL: University of Chicago Press.

Manning, P.K. (1992b) 'Technological Dramas and the Police: Statement and Counterstatement in Organizational Analysis', *Criminology* 30(3): 327–46.

Manning, P.K. (1996) 'Information Technology in the Police Context: The "Sailor" Phone', *Information Systems Research* 7(1): 52–62.

Mullen, K.L. (1996) 'The Computerization of Law Enforcement: A Diffusion of Innovation Study', Ph.D. diss., University of Albany, State University of New York.

O'Malley, P. and D. Palmer (1996) 'Post-Keynesian Policing', *Economy and Society* 25(2): 137–55.

Orlikowski, W.J. (1996) 'Improvising Organizational Transformation over Time—A Situated Change Perspective', *Information Systems Research* 7(1): 63–92.

Orlikowski, W.J. and D.C. Gash (1994) 'Technological Frames—Making Sense of Information Technology in Organizations', *ACM Transactions on Information Systems* 12(2): 174–207.

Orlikowski, W. and D. Robey (1991) 'Information Technology and the Structuring of Organizations', *Information Systems Research* 2: 143–69.

Postman, Neil (1992) *Technopoly: The Surrender of Culture to Technology.* New York: Vintage Books.

Power, M. (1997) *The Audit Society: Rituals of Verification.* Oxford: Oxford University Press.

Rheinier, B., M.R. Greeless, M.H. Gibbens and S.P. Marshall (1979) *Crime Analysis in Support of Patrol. Law Enforcement Assistance Administration Report.* Washington, DC: US Government Printing Office.

Robey, D. and S. Sahay (1996) 'Transforming Work through Information Technology: A Comparative Case Study of Geographic Information Systems in County Government', *Information Systems Research* 7(1): 93–110.

Sackmann, S. (1991) *Cultural Knowledge in Organizations.* Newbury Park, CA: Sage.

Schein, E. (1985) *Organizational Culture and Leadership.* San Francisco, CA: Jossey-Bass.

Sparrow, M. (1991) 'Information Systems: A Help or Hindrance in the Evolution of Policing?', *The Police Chief* 58(4): 26–44.

Yates, J. and J. van Maanen (1996) 'Editorial Notes for the Special Issue', *Information Systems Research* 7(1): 1–4.

JANET CHAN, Ph.D., is Associate Professor and Head, School of Social Science and Policy, University of New South Wales. She is the author of *Changing Police Culture* (Cambridge University Press, 1997).

[29]

Digital Footprints: Assessing Computer Evidence

By Peter Sommer

Computer Security Research Centre, London School of Economics and Political Science

Summary: *This paper describes some of the more common of the new forms of computer evidence and the new techniques of evidence acquisition, preservation and analysis. It shows how inferences are being drawn from computer-derived materials that would not usually be viewed by the ordinary computer user. It attempts to indicate some of the practical problems of assessing reliability. As will be seen, even if as widely expected, section 69 disappears, a number of other issues of admissibility will arise. Finally it makes some provisional policy suggestions.*

Computer evidence used to mean one of two things. Its most typical form was regular print-out from a corporate computer. The alternative form was a reading from any single-purpose measuring or counting device which can be regarded as a mute witness free from human intervention, such as an intoximeter, a telephone call meter or a weighing machine. Overwhelmingly journal articles and legal textbooks have concentrated on issues of admissibility. In the case of regular computer print-out, the problems have been of the scope and circumstances of certification of proper working and notions of "document" and "statement"—what may be referred to in short-hand as "section 69 issues".[1] In the case of the simple measuring devices the problem has been the limits of this area of interpretation of "real evidence".

When the Law Commission produced its Consultation Paper "Evidence in Criminal Proceedings: Hearsay and Related Topics"[2] in May 1995 and then its Report published in June 1997[3] significant consideration was given to the problems of computer evidence both as "real evidence"[4] and as statements which required certification.[5] The main relevant recommendations of the Report are as follows:

"3. that, where a representation of any fact is made otherwise than by a person, but depends for its accuracy on information supplied by a person, it should not

---

[1] In reality, as well as s.69, see Criminal Justice Act 1988, ss.23, 24 and the schedules thereto and, for interpretation, Civil Evidence Act 1995, s.13.

[2] Law Commission, Consultation Paper No. 138, *Evidence in Criminal Proceedings: Hearsay and Related Topics*.

[3] Law Commission, Report No. 245, *Evidence in Criminal Proceedings: Hearsay and Related Topics*.

[4] Consultation Paper No. 138, paras 2.14–2.19, 7.42–7.50 and Recommendation 3 of Law Com. No. 245.

[5] Consultation Paper No. 138, Parts XIV, XIII and Recommendation 50 of Law Com. No. 245.

be admissible as evidence of the fact unless it is proved that the information was accurate . . .

16. that statements falling within the business documents exception should be automatically admissible, but that the court should have power to direct that a statement is not admissible as a business document if it is satisfied that the statement's reliability is doubtful . . .

50. the repeal of section 69 of PACE."

But over the last decade the huge changes in the physical forms computers take, the range of applications, patterns of ownership, the ways in which they are used and the extent to which they can be interlinked across businesses and across the world have produced many new forms of computer-derived evidence. Many of the assumptions in the earlier articles and in the precedents to which they refer are no longer true. For example a computer is not necessarily "just like" a filing cabinet and as a result computer "documents" may not be "just like" the paper equivalent. Again, it is not necessarily the case that computer errors are nearly always manifest in that the result is either no read-out or print-out of any kind or gross nonsense.[6] Depending on circumstances, a computer print-out can look plausibly correct but nevertheless be misleading or be misinterpreted. Increasingly too, the courts are being presented with configuration, logging and other system files which would not normally be viewed by the ordinary computer user—indeed such a user may not even know of their existence—but which investigators and prosecutors are tendering as evidence of an accused's activities or intentions.

In both the Consultation Paper and the Report, the Commissioners showed concern about some of the practical problems of assessing the reliability of computers and computer output, though their focus was on section 69 of the Police and Criminal Evidence Act ("PACE"). They gave the following main reasons for regarding that section as unsatisfactory[7]: that it fails to address the major causes of inaccuracy in computer evidence; that advances in computer technology make it increasingly difficult to comply with section 69; that it is becoming "increasingly impractical to examine (and therefore certify) all the intricacies of computer operation"[8]; that the recipient of computer evidence may be in no position to satisfy the court about the operation of the computer; that it is illogical that section 69 applies where the document is tendered in evidence, but not where it is used by an expert in arriving at his conclusions, nor where a witness uses it to refresh his or her memory.[9] In the Consultation Paper the Commissioners quote Kelman and Sizer[10] with approval: "with a large and complex computer system, it is doubtful whether . . .a manager could have sufficient knowledge [to issue a section 69 certificate] . . .the computer malfunction or an act of unauthorised tampering

---

[6] As suggested by Professor Colin Tapper in "Discovery in Modern Times" (1991) 67 *Chicago-Kent Law Review* 217, 248 and in *Computer Law* (4th ed., Longman, London, 1989), Chap. 9, *passim*.

[7] Law Com. No. 245, paras 13.6–13.22.

[8] Citing S. Castell, "Evidence and Authorisation: is EDI [Electronic Data Interchange] 'legally reliable'?" (1990) 6 *Computer Law and Security Report* 2.

[9] *Golizadeh* [1995] Crim.L.R. 232, *Sophocleous v. Ringer* [1988] R.T.R. 52.

[10] Consultation Paper No. 138, para. 14.15 citing A. Kelman and R. Sizer, *The Computer in Court* (Gower Publishing, London, 1982), p.19.

might be almost impossible to detect by all but experts in the field." A little later, the Commissioners go on to remark[11]:

" . . . comments from judges to the effect that determined defence lawyers can and do examine the prosecution's computer expert at great length. The complexity of modern systems makes it relatively easy to establish a reasonable doubt in a juror's mind as to whether the computer was operating properly. We are concerned about smoke-screens being raised by cross-examination . . . "

The Commissioners' conclusion was that it is not possible to legislate protectively with regard to computer evidence and that where there are specific reasons to doubt the reliability of a particular document generated by a computer these doubts should go to weight and not to admissibility.

In effect, the Commissioners are throwing all the burden of assessment on to the trier of fact, which for more serious offences, will be a lay jury. If we agree that it is a mistake to "legislate protectively" given all the potential problems of rigidity in interpretation, are there any broad tests for "reliability" we can offer? Should we consider codes of practice which might guide law enforcement officers and the courts? Would these be enough? Many of the expressed worries about the use of lay juries in trials of complex fraud[12] transfer very easily to situations where there are complex computer systems. Again, many of the problems of assessing novel scientific evidence, most recently considered in connection with DNA evidence[13] reappear with renewed vigour.

The growth of computer forensics

A few brief paragraphs of historical context-setting may be helpful in understanding how and why the techniques came into existence. Three or four key trends have distinguished the history of computing over the last 15 and particularly the last 10 years; the main trends have in turn spawned many lesser ones and all have interacted with, and reinforced, each other. They are: the growth in use and power of personal computers; the move in the design of corporate computer systems away from the centralised monolithic mainframe towards a multiplicity of smaller but powerful machines which inter-work and inter-connect in a form usually called distributed processing; and the growth of networks, both private and, in the form of the Internet, globally public. All of these changes have had an impact not only on what computers can deliver to their owners but also in the types of evidence that may be found within them.

Personal computers

PCs have been used for non-recreational purposes for almost 20 years, and today the sub-£1,000 PC is more powerful than many business mainframes of 20 years ago. Unlike physically larger computers, they can be easily taken away in their

---

[11] Consultation Paper No. 138, para. 14.20.
[12] For example in the Roskill Report, *Fraud Trials Committee Report* (HMSO, 1986), Chap. 8 *passim*; Home Office, *Juries in Serious Fraud Trials* (London, 1998).
[13] B. Steventon, *The Ability to Challenge DNA Evidence* (Royal Commission on Criminal Justice Research Study No. 9, HMSO, 1993); P. Alldrige, "Recognising Novel Scientific Techniques: DNA as a Test Case" [1992] Crim.L.R. 687 at 689–691; M. Redmayne, "The DNA Database" [1998] Crim.L.R. 437.

entirety during the execution of a search warrant. As they are personal to an individual in addition to formal business documents, they are much more likely to hold informal material which could, for example, indicate intentions or hidden activity. As a result of the increasing complexity of PC operating systems and applications, PCs create many non-obvious files which improve system performance and allow recovery in the event of disaster; on examination these can be interpreted to show how the computer has been used recently. PCs are also the primary means through which the Internet is used for sending global e-mail and viewing information on the World Wide Web. The programs that provide these facilities also create substantial logging and other files on the PC's hard-disk which can subsequently be examined.

Distributed processing

Distributed processing is a way of designing systems which, in contrast to the use of a single very powerful central computer which both holds and processes all organizational information, is easier to design, faster, cheaper and more resilient. A number of smaller computers are linked together so that they feed one another with information and resources; some of the smaller computers may be quite specialised in nature—indeed they can include automatic teller machines, warehouse and manufacturing robots, and bar-code readers. Distributed processing has been common in larger organisations for at least 15 years. From an evidential perspective, one consequence is that many computer documents are "assembled" only on demand and from many different sources. PCs are often used within distributed processing systems as the primary way in which executives see how the business is performing. Such PCs hold programs which interrogate the main system for information but display the results on the individual executive's PC in a way that the executive has personally devised. What appears on a screen or a print-out in these circumstances depends on the actions of the individual executive as well as the quality of the central pool of corporate information. The problem then is what someone seeking to rely on such a document must do to seize and produce it—and then be in a position to show it to be reliable for the purposes of "weight". Can one rely on a single print-out produced on one PC or should the entire corporate database be seized? Computer systems using distributed processing generate many intermediate and logging files; in addition, if care has been taken in introducing security measures, there may be yet other audit and logging files. Again a skilled computer analyst may be able to interpret these to provide assurance of consistency to a court or alternatively demonstrate a critical inconsistency.

Networking

In networks, where several computers are linked together, there are similar problems of discovering where a document is held and how much needs to be seized in order to provide sufficient "weight". There are a number of ways of designing networks: the simplest variety simply provides individual PCs with the capacity to communicate with each other and, depending on how the security is set, access part of each others' hard-disks. A more complex design would include one or more servers, larger computers which hold programs and data. The programs might include internal e-mail and the data may include back-ups of key business records. Servers are an important source of computer evidence. Distributed processing systems rely heavily on complex networks. In the largest of organisations, part of the network may be beyond local jurisdiction. Private networks also exist at an industry level and first-generation EDIs (Electronic Data Interchanges) depend on them.

Internet

The Internet is the largest public network. Although its history goes back to the early 1970s, its real growth for commercial companies and private individuals only began in 1994. The combination of the availability of powerful of PCs with large hard-disks, cheap high-speed modems, the development of inventive software, changes in Internet regulation which enabled private investment in Internet infrastructure and other forms of private enterprise have fuelled the Internet's growth. But these same factors have also encouraged new forms of traditional crimes: for example, the exchanging of paedophile material on the Internet has only become substantial because customers for this material have PCs that can hold and display large numbers of such detailed photographs and because data transfer times are now very quick. Combined with cryptography, Internet e-mail provides a secure means of communicating messages for a criminal purpose. At the same time, there are many opportunities for a skilled investigator to track evidence of Internet activity, but the problem is how to give it weight. In many cases investigating officers seek to strengthen the story told by one strand of computer-derived evidence by corroborating it with one or more others from separate independent sources, or indeed by evidence which has nothing to do with computers at all.

As well as these changes in technology, a further reason for the growth of computer forensics has been the introduction of criminal offences the investigation of which necessarily involves law enforcement officers and the courts to consider internal computer processes.[14]

In response, the new techniques in computer forensics have appeared at astonishing speed: whereas the history of DNA profiling goes back to work at Leicester University in 1984 and has since seen a steady refinement in procedures and technique within the disciplines of traditional forensic science,[15] computer forensics involves many different techniques to cope with a variety of computer hardware and software situations, and with many different potential outcomes and levels of reasonable expectation of reliability. Many advances in computer forensics have come through the initiative of individual law enforcement officers and private sector computer technicians, and the involvement of the established forensic science laboratories has tended to trail behind.

In 1992 Paul Collier and Barry Spaul produced a series of arguments in favour of a discipline to be called "Computer Forensics".[16] The courts had been dealing with computer-derived evidence for many years before that, and the term was already in informal use,[17] but this was probably the first article in an academic journal. At the beginning of the 1990s some individuals within the United Kingdom law enforcement agencies—investigators and technical support operatives—the small number

[14] Especially the Computer Misuse Act 1990 where "unauthorised access" and "unauthorised data modification" must be proved.

[15] See n.13 above and also V. Houlder, "Fingerprints of the Future: Technology DNA Testing", *Financial Times*, May 14, 1998, "Proof under Suspicion: Forensic DNA Testing", *Financial Times*, May 26, 1998.

[16] P. A. Collier and B. J. Spaul, "A Forensic Methodology for Countering Computer Crime" (1992) 32 *Journal of Forensic Science* 27.

[17] See, for example P. Sommer, *Computer Forensics: an Introduction in Proceedings of Compsec International, 1992* (Elsevier Advanced Technology, Oxford, 1992), pp.89–96.

of specialists to whom they turned for advice and the even smaller number of computer experts who were available for defence work began to realise that in computer forensics, as in other similar fields, "standard" techniques, protocols and procedures needed to be evolved. The Conferences initially convened by the Serious Fraud Office, Inland Revenue and Customs and Excise took place at the Police Staff College at Bramshill in 1994 and 1995; subsequent meetings had to move to larger premises at Warwick University. An inter-agency working party has been in existence since then. The National Criminal Intelligence Service have carried out research under the heading Project Trawler,[18] and ACPO have established a Computer Crime Committee. Early in 1997, Edward Wilding had a bold, if premature, attempt at the subject in his *Computer Evidence: a Forensic Investigations Handbook*,[19] but the techniques described in detail are almost exclusively limited to standalone DOS-based PCs, making it already obsolete.[20] In 1998, David Davis, a Detective Inspector at West Midlands Police,[21] who had become interested in computer investigations after involvement in a lengthy paedophile case, produced a guide for police officers. It is not generally available to the public and is principally a guide to the Internet rather than to investigations on the Internet.

Common computer forensic techniques

Seizure of computer hardware

This is probably the best established of the techniques, and the one closest to traditional scene of crime activity. The protocols issued to the police describe a variety of investigative procedures, including[22]: carrying out a pre-raid intelligence review to assess what types of hardware may be expected, what sorts of software, identifying what sorts of back-up might be held and how these might relate to potential evidence; defining the scope of warrants—this is not a forensic procedure as such but is essential if there is to be conformity with admissibility rules; photographing the computer(s) *in situ*, particularly any cabling of peripherals and ancillaries; careful identification and labelling of all items, including cables, peripherals, external data storage such as disks and tapes; careful dismantling, to include preventative measures to avoid inadvertent damage or contamination, and bagging; appropriate record-keeping; precautions to prevent the data being destroyed by hostile individuals immediately prior to the raid; the handling of

---

[18] A conference was held by NCIS in London on May 28, 1997.

[19] E. Wilding, *Computer Evidence: a Forensic Investigations Handbook* (Sweet & Maxwell, London, 1997).

[20] Other books include: D. Icove, K. Seger and W. VonStorch, *Computer Crime: a Crimefighter's Handbook* (O'Reilly & Associates, Inc., Sebastopol, Ca, 1995) and F. Clark and K. Diliberto, *Investigating Computer Crime* (CRC Press, Baco Raton Fa, 1996).

[21] D. Davis, *The Internet Detective—An Investigator's Guide* (Police Research Group, Home Office, London, 1998).

[22] For example *The Federal Guidelines for Searching and Seizing Computers*, U.S. Department of Justice, at http://usdoj.gov/criminal/cybercrime/search_docs/ *passim*; Icove *et al. op. cit.*, p. 391 *et seq.* U.K. Customs and Excise have similar though unpublished procedures which use ISO9001 Quality Controls. In March 1998 the Computer Crime Group of ACPO issued its own guidelines, *Good Practice Guide for Computer-based Evidence*, but has not sanctioned general publication. Guidelines from Scotland Yard's Computer Crime Unit are available at http://www.csfi.demon.co.uk/scotlandyard/index.htm. In the absence of anything more specific, non-consensual searches could be conducted under PACE, s.9 and Sched. 1, to which Code of Practice B applies.

computers that are running at the time of the raid; procedures for safe shutting down; the noting of the time on the computer's internal clock—which is used among other things, to provide date and time stamps on computer files; and the making of an exact sector-by-sector copy of every hard-disk.

This last item needs some explanation. A particular problem of evidence from hard-disks attached to computers is that the very process of turning on a computer and/or seeking to copy its contents can alter the contents to such an extent that they become contaminated. In order to avoid this most United Kingdom law enforcement agencies use a process sometimes called "legal imaging"[23] which, with a combination of special hardware and software and appropriate procedures, is intended to overcome the hazards of contamination.[24] The procedure should take place as soon as possible after a computer has been seized; subsequent examination is then carried out on the copies of the hard-disk.[25] The method consists of starting (or "booting") the computer not from the first hard-disk as would be normal but from the floppy or "A" drive. The computer is booted with a minimal operating system as opposed to a complex one like Windows 95. The operating system contains additional features or "drivers" which make the computer recognise an external data storage device such as a removable hard-disk. Still operating from the floppy drive, software is run which will make an "image" of the hard-disk (or hard-disks if there is more than one) onto the external device. The image is an exact copy (sometimes referred to as a "bit copy" or "sector by sector copy" of the original. It includes not only the visible files on the original disk but others which would normally not be seen, the parts of the disk that contain the information from which the directory details are obtained (file names, sizes, date and time stamp) and also certain other forensic fragments from previously deleted files can sometimes be recovered. The "image" file itself cannot easily be viewed, but by reversing the imaging process onto a second computer similar in specification to the original, an exact clone of the original disk, including all the "hidden" information is created. This process is sometimes called "extraction". The procedures used have certain controls in-built: the original computer remains available for inspection; often two image copies are made, one to act as a control in a manner similar to that used where police station interviews are taped. In addition, the images and the "extracted" files are recorded to CD-ROM, which is a Write Once, Read Many medium which cannot be altered. CD-ROMs made in these circumstances are usually disclosed to the defence. A further feature of the procedures as used by some law enforcement agencies is that, where ever possible, there is a separation between technicians who operate on the raw computer evidence and investigating officers involved in analysing the results. Essentially these protocols address the issue of *freezing the scene*. Witness statements and interview records[26] are needed in support and to provide *continuity of evidence*.

[23] The use of the word "image" is a little confusing as people also refer to files containing pictures as images.

[24] Products to achieve this include DIBS—Digital Image Backup System—and Vogon/Authentec FlightServer, both of which are aimed at professional forensic users but the essential facilities are available within PowerQuest's much cheaper utility, DriveImage 2.0.

[25] *R. v. City of London Magistrates' Court and the SFO, ex p. Greene* [1998] Crim.L.R. 54–56 records a dispute over the adequacy of the word "download" used in an injunction to describe what happens in these circumstances.

[26] For example under PACE Code of Practice C.

Followed properly, hard-disk imaging is uncontroversial. From an admissibility perspective, the computer and its hard-disk are "real evidence"; all subsequent images, copies, print-outs, etc., are "documents" and at the moment appear to need section 69 certification. Problems arise from the types of material produced from the hard-disk and the inferences that may be made, for example:

- *Simple data files*—word-processed documents, database and accounts records, pictures,[27] copies of faxes—produced from regular applications present little difficulty. The date-and-time stamp which can be displayed in the computer's directory is of last modification rather than original creation. Some applications generate records of first creation and also list modifications, but most do not. PCs do not normally create formal audit or logging records.
- *E-mail messages and faxes*, sent and received, may have been retained by the computer owner; but the owner may also have selectively deleted some of them.
- Sophisticated *extended use of directory information* can help build up chronologies of events within a computer, but the data available may be incomplete or imperfect and significant amounts of interpretation may be needed. The basic tool is to request a list of all files in all directories on all disks sorted in date/time order. The chronologies may show, among other things: when an operating system was installed, reinstalled or upgraded; when an application was installed, reinstalled or upgraded; when new hardware was installed or reinstalled; sessions during which files were being created or modified; sessions in which files were viewed without necessarily being modified; dates when faxes were sent and received; sessions on-line to the Internet and other external services; times when diagnostic packages were run because of some suspected system fault.
- *Deleted files*, particularly if the deletion is recent, can be recovered using facilities built into modern operating systems to provide resilience against accident. This is possible because initially unwanted files are only marked for deletion so that they do not appear in a disk directory though the content remains until the specific disk space occupied is reused by newer files. This type of undeleting is uncontroversial, but technicians can also sometimes recover fragments direct from disk sectors; here a greater element of interpretation may be needed. Careful examination of certain application files, for example documents created in Microsoft Word, may include fragments which the creator believes has been discarded. The danger here is that a computer technician, in making a reconstruction of a document, becomes influenced by other aspects of the investigation.[28]

---

[27] *Fellows and Arnold* [1997] 1 Cr.App.R. 244, CA.

[28] Deleted files can be recovered from mainframes and pocket computers as well. As long ago as 1986 drug smuggler Paul Dye was convicted on the basis of files, apparently deleted but recovered from a Psion personal organiser: Channel 4 News, November 27, 1986; *DataLink*, December 1, 1986; *The Guardian*, March 7, 1988. A more celebrated example was that of the recovered White House e-mail records of former National Security Adviser, John Poindexter, during the Iran-Contra Affair (*United States v. Poindexter*, Crim. No. 88–0080–1, and later appeals at 698 F. Supp. 300 (1988); 719 F. Supp. 6 (1989); 732 F. Supp. 142 (1990); 859 F.2d 216 (1988); 910 F.2d 843 (1990); 951 F.2d 369 (1991)).

- *Swap files* are temporary files created on hard-disk by operating systems when there is insufficient random access memory (RAM) for a specific activity, for example when several programs run simultaneously, or a large document or picture is being edited. Here again a technician may uncover evidence of recent activities, including alterations and deletions to files, or the transmission of passwords. Here too one technician's interpretation may be challenged by another.

If an individual PC is handled properly at and after seizure and if it was within the sole control of a suspect, a great deal of important evidence about the suspect's activities is potentially available. However some of the conclusions offered by prosecution experts may depend on interpretation rather than uncontestable fact-finding, and the extent of this may not be obvious.

Larger corporate systems

The larger the computer system, the greater the difficulties of transporting it anywhere, particularly if the system is extensively networked and consists of a number of disparate computers, linked together by networks for some purposes and not for others. The larger the computer system, on the whole the greater the potential that its seizure will cause collateral damage to wholly innocent individuals and organisations; once a computer is seized the business that owned it is likely to come to a sharp halt, affecting employees, customers and creditors. In these circumstances there are no clear guidelines.[29] Investigators then have to make a decision to leave the hardware *in situ*, hope to locate an employee of the raided firm who is technically competent but not under suspicion or other person, and supervise that person while copies of operating systems, logs, software and data are made. Section 19(4) of PACE permits a constable to "require any information which is contained in a computer and accessible from the premises [referred to in the warrant] to be produced in a form in which it can be taken away and in which it is visible and legible". The reference to "accessible from" seems to suggest that provided a warrant referred to a single relevant site, the whole of a corporate network, where ever its components were located, would be included. In practice a selection may have to be made on grounds of cost and bulk. Investigators also need to acquire a detailed hardware and software inventory of the computer system, plus any reports prepared by EDP auditors and the like. If the computer system belongs to an international company, there may be different components in different jurisdictions and time zones.

Once the raw evidence has been acquired, the problem is to show that it can be relied on. Again some of the tests developed in the section 69 cases can be extended to other aspects of probative value. Thus, in the appeal in *Cochrane*[30] which concerned print-out from an automated teller machine (ATM) connected to a complex banking/building society system, Waterhouse J. observed: "It is with some surprise that we record that none of the witnesses who gave evidence in the court below knew even the name of the town in which the mainframe computer was located." He concluded:

---

[29] PACE, s.16(8) states "A search under warrant may only be a search to the extent required for the purpose for which the warrant was issued."

[30] [1993] Crim.L.R. 48.

"In the end, however, it is clear that, whether or not the judge's view was that section 69 of the 1984 Act applied or that at least some of the entries in the till rolls relied upon by the prosecution were real evidence in the sense that they were direct evidence of the transactions carried out, it was necessary for evidence to be adduced on behalf of the prosecution to explain how each of the relevant pieces of information on the till roll came into existence. In particular, it was necessary that appropriate authoritative evidence should be called to describe the function and operation of the mainframe computer, including the extent to which it brought to bear information stored within it in order to validate a transaction and to enable an appropriate record to be made on the till roll."

He went on: "It is necessary to add that the problem of proving transactions of this kind must now arise frequently and it should be possible for the Crown Prosecution Service to devise a standard form of evidence to deal with it." While one sympathises with the judge, there are formidable difficulties in envisioning a "standard form of evidence". Indeed since 1989 when the events in *Cochrane* took place, computer systems have become much more complex and now include personal computers. We will return to this matter later.

Evidence from the Internet

There are two principal situations to be considered: where the offence is concentrated on an individual's use of the Internet and where a remote site holds evidence of an offence. Typical examples of the former include the downloading of paedophiliac material and unauthorised access; a great deal of evidence may exist on the accused's own computer. Examples of the latter include: evidence of fraudulent promises to deliver goods,[31] evidence of fraudulent offers to provide services,[32] evidence of fraudulent or non-compliant investment offers,[33] infringed copyright materials offered in the course of a business,[34] holding or offering pornographic files and pictures,[35] and incitements to racial hatred, terrorism and other offences,[36] and conspiracies.[37]

To understand where evidence of Internet-related offences maybe located we need to recall how Internet connections are made and the forms they may take. Typically an individual uses his computer to connect to the Internet via an Internet Service Provider (ISP); home users dial in via a telephone network. There are thus

---

[31] Under Theft Act 1968, ss.15(1) and 16.

[32] Under Theft Act 1978, s.1.

[33] See, for example, J. Drinkhall, "Internet Fraud" (1997) 4 *Journal of Financial Crime* 258.

[34] For example, under Copyright Designs and Patents Act 1988, s.107.

[35] An extensive review of U.S. and English law appears in Y. Akdeniz, "Computer Pornography; a Comparative Study of the US and English Obscenity Laws and Child Pornography Laws in Relation to the Internet" (1996) 10 *International Review of Law, Computers and Technology* 235.

[36] Racial hatred offences include Public Order Act 1986, ss.18, 19, 21 and 23; terorism is defined in the Prevention of Terrorism (Temporary Provisions) Act 1989, s.20. Simple incitement of another to commit an offence is a common law misdemeanor. Blasphemy also remains a common law misdemeanor—*Whitehouse v. Gay News Ltd and Lemon* [1979] A.C. 617.

[37] Criminal Law Act 1977, s.1(1).

four points at which evidence of various sorts may exist: on an individual's own computer, in his telephone bill, at the ISP and on remote sites. For law enforcement there is also the possibility of eavesdropping on Internet traffic in transit using a technique called "sniffing".

Considering, first, material held on a suspect's own computer, in addition to the material already referred to, PCs are likely to hold the following Internet-specific logging files:

- e-mails sent and received are usually saved to hard-disk during routine use; however, most users regularly delete unwanted material to free up disk space;
- newsgroups subscribed to are also usually saved to hard-disk during routine use; however again, most users regularly delete unwanted material to free up disk space;
- Internet Relay Chat (IRC) sessions are real-time discussions rather like CB radio; logging files which record what all participants have said are optional. There are also commercial and improved versions of IRC like Microsoft Netmeeting and other products which provide Internet telephony and viewphones; again logging may exist;
- browser cache files are a specific sort of temporary file which is used to store data that the computer has recently used and may want again in the very near future. Although caching is used throughout computing, one of the most significant uses is within Internet browsers, the software used to visit sites on the World Wide Web. Here the cache stores copies of each web page as it is visited. Users often need to revisit previously seen pages, particularly if they contain an index to other pages. The browser software can swiftly retrieve such a page from its cache rather than going back to the original source site (which would result in greater delay to the user and also add to the overall traffic on the Internet's main connections). In most browsers cache files are kept after individual sessions, often for weeks and months afterwards; some browsers and some specialist software can be used to view cache files and also associated "history" files which retain some date-and-time information. Thus it is possible to determine what the users of a specific computer have been viewing and, to a limited extent and after careful interpretation, when. There has been at least one attempt by prosecutors to assert that material saved in a web-browser cache but not otherwise intentionally retained constitutes "possession" for the purposes of section 160 of the Criminal Justice Act 1988.[38]

It is sometimes possible to recover deleted logging files. However the completeness of any of these files, previously deleted or otherwise, and the extent to which date-and-time stamps are accurate is a matter that a person producing such forms of evidence must expect to be asked to demonstrate.

As regards to telephone logs, private customers of ISPs usually dial in via telephone—so, the logs provided by telephone companies showing numbers called,

---

[38] A. Hamilton, "Caught Looking" (1998) 9 *Computers & Law* 9–10.

time and duration often give powerful corroboration to other types of evidence.[39] Until relatively recently phone companies collected this type of information from specialist external devices attached to a subscriber's line: from an admissibility perspective it is possible to argue that the output of such call loggers or monitors is real evidence. More recently exhibits have been produced direct from the telephone company's regular billing computer. Although there are so far no recorded cases on the point, it could be argued that in these circumstances a proper section 69 PACE certificate is needed as well as support to show that the exhibit is a "business, etc., document" for the purposes of section 24 of the Criminal Justice Act 1988. If law enforcement wish to capture data traffic on a telephone line between an ISP and its customer, the Interception of Communications Act 1985 (IOCA) applies.[40]

The material held by an ISP may also provide evidence. The ISP may be a commercial entity specifically in business for the purpose or may be an existing body such as a university institution. Business customers may have a permanent link, a leased line, to the ISP. In addition to providing the necessary connections to the Internet, ISPs maintain their own computers to log in subscribers and to hold e-mail and USENET messages against the time when subscribers wish to collect material. The computers holding e-mail and USENET messages are known respectively as mail-servers and news servers. Potentially mail servers and news servers can provide evidence of message content. The current law enforcement procedure appears to be as follows[41]: applications to ISPs to disclose the identity of their customers are made on forms under the Data Protection Act, s.28(3). The position of message content held on ISP computers is more complex: ACPO believe they should use the Special Procedure within PACE[42] to obtain warrants. So far there are no test cases to determine whether an ISP's news server and mail server computers are part of a public telecommunications service, in which case IOCA might apply.[43] ISPs can of course volunteer to help the police without insisting on a warrant but then may later face claims from their subscribers under the Data Protection Act or for breach of confidence. Although the police could also be sued for breach of confidence,[44] the main practical penalty they face for failure to use appropriate procedures is that a judge may use his discretion to exclude unfairly acquired material under section 78 of PACE.

Next, there may be material relevant to the investigation held on remote sites. If, for ordinary purposes we wish to record the contents of a web page on a remote computer the simplest way of doing so is to use the appropriate menu command

---

[39] Law enforcement officers obtain this information in respect of phone lines owned by private individuals by supplying the telephone company with a form referring to Data Protection Act 1984, s.28(3). How far that Act extends to business lines will depend on the likelihood that the business is dealing in personal information. In any event, s.28(3) merely authorises a data user to make a disclosure to the police but does not obligate them to do so; it is therefore distinguishable from the duty imposed by a production order or warrant.

[40] In practice, it would seem that the s.28(3) procedure is preferred—the police search the records and data stored on the ISP servers rather than intercept traffic.

[41] Letter from the Chairman of the ACPO Computer Crime Committee to the *Sunday Telegraph*, September 28, 1998 and article in *Computing*, October 29, 1998, pp.34–35.

[42] Defined in ss.9 and 14 and detailed in Schedule 1.

[43] But the search of recorded data on a server is presumably not an "intercept". Part of such a search may be akin to the searches of call logs under Sched. 2 to the IOCA but investigation of the content of stored messages arguably falls outside of the IOCA altogether.

[44] But see *R. v. Chief Constable of North Wales Police, ex p. AB* [1998] 3 W.L.R. 57.

require other forms of evidence such as witness statements, exhibits indicating ownership of or access to the computer and/or data media, or the possibility of inference from the nature of the content of the files. Can the producing witness give a full and believable explanation of the processes by which the file was acquired from the remote computer to the user's machine to show that the result is accurate, free from contamination and complete? How was the evidence frozen and rendered tamper-proof?[46]

A further problem arises if a complainant needs to demonstrate the existence of a computer-mediated contract, possibly fraudulent, to show that an offer was made and accepted and that authority was given for a payment.[47] Current advice to web designers suggests that each stage is marked by some positive act by the purchaser, a "click" or "enter" in an on-screen-form. What evidence does a purchaser/victim acquire in these circumstances?

In effect the only plausible route to acquiring evidence from a remote Internet site is to seize the remote computer itself. That in turn depends on its being within the jurisdiction of the courts to which investigating officers have access.

The final possible source of evidence is eavesdropped Internet traffic. The principles of Internet eavesdropping are well known to technicians: Internet traffic is despatched as a series of "packets", each of which contain information about originator and destination as well as the actual content. Packets are also numbered so that they can be correctly reassembled if they arrive out of order. An eavesdropping computer anywhere between the originator and destination can capture a transmission and reconstruct it. The practical problems are that at certain points along the path there will be vast amounts of regular Internet traffic to be sifted in order to find the material being sought and in any event it is basic to the design of the Internet that, even within the transmission of a simple e-mail message, constituent packets may use radically different routes, thus creating the possibility that not all of the relevant traffic has been captured. The most effective forms of eavesdropping take place very close—in terms of the topography of the network—to an originator or recipient.[48] For law enforcement wishing to rely on such evidence there is a further problem: the defence will seek disclosure of the precise tool used for eavesdropping and its network location, arguing that without such information the reliability and completeness of the evidence cannot be assessed. A judge asked to consider an application for public interest immunity may also simultaneously be asked to exclude the evidence all together for unfairness.

A number of examples of Internet-eavesdropped evidence were produced by USAF officers in the form of keystroke monitoring in *Pryce and Bevan*, where two young men were accused of unauthorised access into large numbers of computers

---

[46] For a more extended discussion, see P. Sommer, "Evidence from Cyberspace: Downloads, Logs and Captures" (1997) 5 *Journal of Financial Crime* 138.

[47] See C. Gringras, *The Laws of the Internet* (Butterworths, London, 1997), Chap. 2 *passim*.

[48] See P. Sommer, "Intrusion Detection Systems as Evidence", Proceedings of RAID98, Louvain-la-Neuve, 1998.

owned, *inter alia*, by the United States Air Force and the defence company Lockheed.[49] The decision of Pryce to plead guilty on reduced charges and the abandonment of charges against Bevan stopped any court-room examination of the evidence.

In practice most Internet and on-line crime appears to be prosecuted on the basis of evidence found close to the suspect—the computer hard-disk, other data, media and artefacts found on premises associated with the accused, as well as telephone logs.[50] Thus, both in *N*,[51] N's defence that a business rival had planted paedophiliac pictures and text on disks found in his possession and in *W*,[52] W's assertion that similar material had been planted on his computer by a lodger, failed to persuade in the face of a detailed analysis of time-stamped logging files on their computers corroborated by telephone logs. On the other hand, in *G*,[53] G was charged with incitement to commit offences under the Computer Misuse Act 1990, on the basis of a file containing very detailed instructions available for download by visitors to a bulletin board system (BBS) he was running. His defence was that the BBS had been set up for legitimate purposes but that he had been persuaded to add libraries of many more files in order to increase the number of visitors, that he had acquired these further files in bulk had not examined them for content and thus lacked the necessary *mens rea* for incitement. An examination of the computer, the BBS software and the file time-stamps provided strong corroboration for this defence as a result of which the CPS dropped the charge. Poor handling of hard-disk evidence by investigators employed by an industry-funded software anti-piracy enforcement body in *Y*,[54] another bulletin board case, this time involving charges under section 107 of the Copyright, Designs and Patents Act 1988, forced prosecutors to abandon this form of evidence in seeking a conviction. Examinations had been carried out on the hard-disk found at the accused's home rather than a copy; the circumventing of security measures and the explorations of various consultants, not all of them properly recorded in witness statements, were clearly visible to the defence expert.

Most successful prosecutions rely on more than one stream of computer-derived evidence. What is needed is a multiplicity of independent streams of evidence, both computer- and non-computer-derived, which corroborate each other. Any single stream may fail either because of intrinsic inadequacy or because the courts find it too difficult to understand.

---

[49] The events took place in 1994, and the monitoring tools were called Stethoscope, Network Security Monitor and Pathfinder. The cases finally came before the U.K. courts in 1997 (Bow Street Magistrates' Court); the author acted as defence expert. The (U.S.) General Accounting Office Report GAO/AIMD-96-84 Defense Information Security and the Testimony of Jim Christy, Air Force Investigator, Senate Governmental Affairs Committee Permanent Investigations Sub-Committee, "Security in Cyberspace", June 5, 1996, provide a description and give an idea of how the U.S. authorities viewed the case.

[50] So far there do not appear to have been any relevant surveys; this commentary is based on case and newspaper reports, the author's own experiences and anecdotes from prosecution and defence experts.

[51] Bristol Crown Court, January 1998.

[52] Bicester Magistrates' Court, July 1998.

[53] Bow Street Magistrates' Court, January 1998.

[54] Watford Crown Court, June 1996.

Are there any general principles for evaluating computer evidence?

Computer-derived evidence is not intrinsically different from other types of evidence produced in criminal proceedings. Rather the problems arise from the fragility and transience of many of the forms of computer evidence, the fact that provenance may be difficult to understand and the speed with which computer technology, and hence the evidence potentially available, changes.

There are few easy solutions. As we have seen, Waterhouse J. hoped for "a standard form of evidence",[55] but English law is hostile to the idea of giving scientific or forensic evidence a juridical quality. In *Doheny*,[56] DNA statistical evidence was produced in a rape and buggery case. The conviction was overturned on appeal on the basis that the expert had overstepped his role, restricting the role of the jury. A move to the United States procedure of expecting judges to act as the gatekeeper for novel scientific evidence, most recently considered in the 1993 United States case of *Daubert v. Merrell Dow*,[57] is not promising either. Even if the English courts accepted the principle, it is doubtful whether some computer forensic evidence currently being tendered would meet the tests of (1) whether the theory or technique can be (and has been) tested; (2) the error rate associated with the method; (3) publication in a peer-reviewed journal; and (4) whether the technique has gained widespread acceptance. The Royal Commission on Criminal Justice chaired by Lord Runciman[58] devoted Chapter 9 to a consideration of forensic science and expert evidence and proposed, *inter alia,* the setting up of a Forensic Science Council,[59] but how well equipped would it be to assess skills in computer forensics? Similar concerns must apply to the notion of court-appointed experts—how would they be selected? Many of these proposals would have the effect of denying the criminal justice system the benefits of the new techniques. And yet nearly all the arguments about incorporating forensic science within the adversarial procedure that arose around Runciman remain.[60]

In effect, faced with new types of evidence the courts have to fall back on general principles of evidence evaluation. The following are Miller's general tests for the reliability of an exhibit.[61] It should be possible to show that evidence is:

- *authentic*—specifically linked to the circumstances and persons alleged—and produced by someone who can answer questions about such links;
- *accurate*—free from any reasonable doubt about the quality of procedures used to collect the material, analyse the material if that is appropriate and

---

[55] Waterhouse J. in *Cochrane* [1993] Crim.L.R. 48.

[56] *Doheny, Adams* [1997] Crim.L.R. 669.

[57] 509 U.S. 579 (1993).

[58] Cm. 2263, HMSO, London.

[59] Chapter 9.33, recommendation 262. See Further Forensic Science Working Group, *Report* (Royal Society of Chemistry, London, 1997), described in C. Walker and R. Stockdale, "Forensic Evidence" in C. Walker and K. Starmer, *Miscarriages of Justice* (Blackstone Press, London, 1998, forthcoming), Chap. 6. See also Z. Erzinçlioglu, "British forensic science in the dock" [1998] *Nature* 392, 859–860.

[60] See P. Roberts, "Forensic Science Evidence after Runciman" [1994] Crim.L.R. 780; M. Redmayne, "The DNA Database" [1998] Crim.L.R. 437; C. Walker and R. Stockdale, "Forensic evidence" in C. Walker and K. Starmer, *Miscarriages of Justice* (Blackstone Press, London, 1998, forthcoming), Chap. 6.

[61] Adapted and developed from C. Miller, "Electronic Evidence—Can You Prove the Transaction Took Place?" (1992) 9 *Computer Lawyer* 21.

necessary and finally to introduce it into court—and produced by someone who can explain what has been done. In the case of exhibits which themselves contain statements—a letter or other document, for example—"accuracy" must also encompass accuracy of content; and that normally requires the document's originator to be make a witness statement and be available for cross-examination;

- *complete*—tells within its own terms a complete story of particular set of circumstances or events.

In relation to more technical types of evidence—forensic evidence—we can expand on the range of attributes:

- there should be a clear *chain of custody* or *continuity of evidence*;
- a forensic method needs to be *transparent*, that is, freely testable by a third party expert. This creates difficulties if law enforcement think disclosure might result in the design of counter-measures which would prevent its future use; again the devisor of a forensic procedure may find it difficult to maintain commercial confidentiality[62];
- in the case of material derived from sources with which most people are not familiar quite extensive *explanations* may be needed;
- in the case of exhibits which themselves contain statements—a letter, database record or other document produced by a computer, for example "accuracy" must encompass the *accuracy of the process* which produced the statement as well as *accuracy of content*; again normally that requires the document's originator to make a witness statement and be available for cross-examination.

In cases of "hacking" and other sophisticated computer crimes there is the additional concern that the criminal *modus operandi* has corrupted the regular operation of a computer.

The more one looks at it, the clearer it becomes that we are not looking at one problem but several. Tempting as it initially might be to seek to draw up a simple list of types of computer evidence and "rate" them,[63] certain problems become apparent quite soon: any such list ends up including "documents" or "statements" within the meanings of the various Civil and Criminal Evidence Acts (or that "common sense" first seems to suggest) but also types of evidence as produced by or recovered from computers. In the first category we are identifying evidence by content and in the second by the form in which it has been held in or produced by a computer. Actually we need to do both. We need to know about the evidential weight of the *content* of a piece of computer-derived evidence, but we also need to know about the weight of the *process* by which it was produced. Process can, depending on the circumstances, contain several meanings as well—the quality of the original source, the quality of the internal computer manipulations, the strength

---

[62] *Munden*, an unreported ATM phantom withdrawal case with hearings at Mildenhall Magistrates' Court between 1994 and 1996, illustrates the problem. See the articles posted at http://www.cl.cam.ac.uk/users/rja14.

[63] This was one of the suggestions by S. Castell in *The Appeal Report* (Eclipse Publications, London, 1990), pp. 43, 52 *et seq.*, 64 in research originally commissioned by the Cabinet Office's the Central Computer and Telecommunications Agency (CCTA) under the title *The Verdict Report*.

of any control or audit mechanism which might reduce error or provide corroboration, the integrity of the way in which the exhibit—what the court actually considers—has been derived, perhaps even the integrity of the way in which the exhibit has been handled by investigators.[64] But these elements interact with each other—*content* is what you see with your eyes, *process* is what produced it.

Public policy issues

What, apart from the obvious requests for more training and more resources throughout the criminal justice system, can one ask Government to do? One route is to produce a new detailed PACE Code of Practice. Section 66 of PACE requires the Secretary of State to issue Codes and section 67 describes how. The current Code of Practice B has but one computer-specific reference: paragraph 6(5) echoes section 19(4) of the main Act in referring to facilities to carry away evidence in a visible and readable form. Certain aspects of the handling of computer evidence have surely now achieved sufficient stability so that a Code of Practice which will last several years can safety be written.

The proposed Code, unlike the current internal documents produced by law enforcement agencies, would be public and have been subjected to Parliamentary scrutiny. Among the advantages that might flow are that it would provide guidance for a relatively new and rapidly developing source of evidence without the inflexibility of primary legislation. It would ensure fair, regular and consistent procedures and a vocabulary to describe them which would be recognised by the courts. It could describe precautions for the safe acquisition and preservation of computers and hard-disks and forms of listing computer-derived materials in search registers. It would provide guidance for those issuing warrants. It would add to the existing framework for the maintenance of adequate safeguards and records. It would provide fair rules and procedures for the rapid post seizure return of computer hardware and data so that the activities and privacy of companies and individuals are not unduly penalised but without the need for constant recourse to the Police (Property) Act 1897. It would give guidance for judges in assessing the process by which a computer-derived exhibit has arrived in court. It would provide greater fairness to the defence, including procedures for delivery of exhibits and access to specialist software necessary to review the validity of prosecution claims. It would lead to fewer "form" protests by the defence in court or for irresponsible questioning of crown experts as feared by the Law Commission in its Consultative Paper in 1995. It would reduce the costs of trials involving computer-related evidence by the avoidance of the delivery of unnecessarily bulky prosecution bundles of print-out and by allowing prosecution and defence experts access to electronic evidence which can then be analysed with computers. It would provide a framework for specific training of law enforcement officers, leading to greater efficiencies and higher chances of success, while ensuring that fewer poor quality cases are presented to the courts. Finally, it would provide the Legal Aid Board with guidance in assessing the requests for funding by defence interests.

---

[64] Law Commission's Consultation Paper No. 138, *Evidence in Criminal Proceedings: Hearsay and Related Topics, loc. cit.*, discusses this at paras 14.14–14.20.

[30]

Fundamental Rights, Fair Trials and the New Audio-Visual Sector

*Clive Walker**

Introduction

The media reporting of court trials, especially those concerning criminal matters, has long been recognised in this country as creating potential conflicts of interest and clashes of rights. On the one hand, there are individual and collective interests in freedom of expression. That there is a free speech interest, especially based on the argument from democracy as articulated by Meiklejohn,[1] in what happens in the courts cannot readily be denied since it arises in at least three ways. First, courts are a fundamental state responsibility as they dispense state laws and justice. Consequently, no matter who is appearing in them, there is state interest and therefore a legitimate demand for democratic accountability and discussion. Next, there may be added public interest in discussion where the state is one of the litigants, as usually it is in regard to criminal prosecutions. Thirdly, even litigation brought between private litigants may air matters of public concern. On the other hand to these pressures towards publication and discussion lie the individual and collective interests in upholding the fairness of trials and respect for the judicial system in general, both of which may be damaged by unregulated speech. Nevertheless, as has been observed by many before today, the clash of values may be more apparent than real. The individual can usually expect to benefit from the 'sunshine'[2] of public proceedings and the public scrutiny of legal proceedings in which the state is inevitably a stakeholder if not a direct party. Equally, the public has a collective interest in fair trials for suspected individual citizens — as was discovered with cases like the *Birmingham 6*,[3] miscarriages of justice are ultimately very damaging to the criminal justice process as a collective enterprise, as well as representing personal tragedies for the defendants involved.[4]

For the greater part of English legal history, these conflicts of interest and clashes of rights were debated and resolved by the English courts themselves.[5]

---

*Director and Professor, Criminal Justice Studies, University of Leeds.
This article was presented in an earlier draft at the Conference on 'Fundamental Rights and New Information Technologies in the Audiovisual Sector,' organised by the European Audiovisual Observatory, Council of Europe, Strasbourg, November 1995. It also builds on research in the USA on visits facilitated by the University of Louisville, Kentucky and George Washington University, Washington DC. My thanks also go to Adam Crawford and Yaman Akdeniz for their comments.

1   See Schauer, *Free Speech* (Cambridge: Cambridge UP, 1982) ch 3.
2   'Sunshine is said to be the best of disinfectants' (Brandeis, *Other People's Money* (New York: FA Stokes, 1932) p 92).
3   *R v McIlkenny and Others* [1992] 2 All ER 417. See Walker and Starmer, *Justice in Error* (London: Blackstone, 1992) p 9.
4   The legitimation crisis was sufficient to provoke the appointment of the Royal Commission on Criminal Justice (Cm 2263, 1993). See McConville and Bridges (eds), *Criminal Justice in Crisis* (Aldershot: Edward Elgar, 1994); Greer, 'Miscarriages of Criminal Justice Reconsidered' (1994) 57 MLR 538; Nobles and Schiff, 'Miscarriages of Justice: A Systems Approach' (1995) 58 MLR 299; Walker, 'Review in Error' (1995) 35 Brit J Criminology 661.
5   For recent trends in Scotland, see Bonnington, 'Press and Prejudice' (1995) 145 NLJ 1623.

© The Modern Law Review Limited 1996 (MLR 59:4, July). Published by Blackwell Publishers, 108 Cowley Road, Oxford OX4 1JF and 238 Main Street, Cambridge, MA 02142, USA.

Reflecting very much the value of freedom of expression, the judicial principle of 'open justice' was pronounced in *Scott* v *Scott* as long ago as 1913.[6] More recent court pronouncements have likewise often emphasised the importance of free speech.[7] At the same time, the courts have regularly been persuaded that free speech, important though it is, must be overridden by concerns for the administration of justice. Some of the more controversial examples of this conclusion include banning orders in relation to the *Sunday Times'* discussion of the Thalidomide victims,[8] television re-enactments of the *Birmingham 6* appeal,[9] and the wish of a public figure to discuss on television the education of her handicapped daughter.[10]

For good or ill, the English courts no longer have the final word on this delicate and controversial balancing act. As first demonstrated in the *Sunday Times* case itself,[11] an external umpire, the European Convention on Human Rights, can later be called upon by disgruntled domestic litigants. Furthermore, the same case illustrates that the Commission and Court may diverge from the domestic courts in balancing, according to their own lights, free expression under Article 10(1) on the one hand and, on the other hand, respect for the authority of the judiciary (Article 10(2)), the fairness of trials (as in Article 6 of the European Convention),[12] and the interests of privacy under Article 8 arising from the encouragement of the rehabilitation of reformable or reformed offenders.[13] Since 1978, the European Court of Human Rights has shown itself to be particularly active in the field of censorship connected with the legal system, and as shall be described, has adopted a rather more interventionist stand than in other areas of censorship, such as in connection with morality and religion.[14]

Yet, just as this international instrument of scrutiny is becoming well-established and active, so radical developments in the new audio-visual sector now create the possibility that this international layer of normative regulation will in turn become inadequate or at least marginal. It is true that the Convention's normative standards have retained vitality and relevance through the increasingly purposive and programmatic interpretative techniques adopted by the relevant enforcement bodies.[15] Nevertheless, the actual mechanisms of international governance which it

---

6   [1913] AC 417. See also Contempt of Court Act 1981, s 4(1).
7   See especially *R* v *Dover JJ, ex p Dover DC* (1991), *The Times,* 21 October; *R* v *Beck, ex p Daily Telegraph* [1993] 2 All ER 177; *R* v *Clerkenwell Metropolitan Stipendiary Magistrates' Court, ex p The Telegraph plc* [1993] 2 WLR 233; *In re W* [1992] 1 WLR 100; *MGN Pension Trustees* v *Bank of America* [1995] 2 All ER 355; *R* v *Westminster CC, ex p Castelli and Garcia* (1995), *The Times,* 14 August.
8   *AG* v *Times Newspapers Ltd* [1974] AC 273.
9   *In re Channel 4 TV Co Ltd* [1988] CLR 237.
10 *Re Z* [1995] 4 All ER 961.
11 See *Evans, Sunday Times and Times Newspapers* v *UK*, App no 6538/74, Ser A, vol 30 (1979–80) 2 EHRR 245, (1981) 3 EHRR 317, 615.
12 For a full exposition of relevant principles, see Ashworth, *The Criminal Process* (Oxford: Clarendon, 1994).
13 See Children and Young Persons Act 1933, ss 39, 47; Rehabilitation of Offenders Act 1974. Privacy has been rejected as a legitimate ground for restriction under the Contempt of Court Act 1981, s 11: *R* v *Felixstowe JJ, ex p Leigh* [1987] 2 WLR 380; *R* v *Dover JJ, ex p Dover DC* (1991), *The Times,* 21 October; *R* v *Westminster CC, ex p Castelli and Garcia* (1995), *The Times,* 14 August. It is also not the rationale behind the Sexual Offences (Amendment) Act 1976, s 4 (as amended); see Brogarth and Walker, 'Court Reporting and Open Justice' (1988) 138 NLJ 909.
14 *Handyside* v *UK*, App no 5493/72, Ser A, no 24 (1979–80) 1 EHRR 737; *Gay News & Lemon* v *UK*, App no 8710/79, DR 28, p 77 (1983) 5 EHRR 123. But see also *Wingrove* v *UK*, App no 17419/90.
15 See Harris, O'Boyle and Warbrick, *Law of the European Convention on Human Rights* (London: Butterworths, 1995) pp 6, 7.

seeks to promote, an abstract declaration of rights followed by remote and slow oversight, seem inadequate in response to the complex growth of media networks and the increasingly immediate nature of their output.

The purpose of this article is, first, to describe briefly the relevant features of the new audio-visual media; and, second, to identify the problematic capacities they have developed in relation to established forms of regulation, both national and international, which seek to balance free speech and fair trials. Thirdly, it will be considered what regulatory or other responses, based on a wider view of 'governance' might appropriately be advanced.

Problems represented by the new technologies

The new audio-visual technologies might be taken to include primarily satellite television and its relay by cable networks,[16] as well as more recently emergent technologies such as the Internet.[17] Of themselves, such developments should be viewed primarily as wonderful opportunities for communication and education, rather than as sinister and dangerous innovations. Indeed, the new technologies can be harnessed for the considerable benefit of criminal justice systems themselves.

Some of the benefits may be practical and specific. For example, the possibility of television closed-circuit links may facilitate the availability and presentation of evidence in fraud and child abuse cases within the jurisdiction,[18] as well as making it available to litigation abroad.[19] The processing, handling, storage, discovery and presentation of evidence may also be more effectively and efficiently effectuated by way of new technologies, such as CD-ROM and computer graphics.[20] Of course, each of these 'advances' raises almost equal concerns about detriments to the fairness of trials. Thus, the intercession of televisual links may dull the impact of oral cross-examination,[21] which is traditionally viewed as an instrument of great effectiveness in the establishment of truth in adversarial process.[22] Equally, the complexities and costs of the new technologies may threaten the equality of arms between prosecution and defence, with the result that the latter may be unable to explore and expose the defects in

---

16 See Bullinger, 'Freedom of Expression and Information' (1985) 6 Human Rights LJ 339; Collins, *Satellite Television in Western Europe* (London: John Libbey, revised ed, 1992); Long, *Telecommunications Law and Practice* (London: Sweet & Maxwell, 2nd ed, 1995) ch 9.

17 See Cavazos and Morin, *Cyberspace and the Law* (Massachusetts: MIT Press, 1994); Nissen, *Legal Issues on the Internet* (London: Harbottle and Lewis, 1994); Rose, *Netlaw* (Berkeley: Osborne McGraw-Hill, 1995).

18 Criminal Justice Act 1988, s 32.

19 Criminal Justice (International Cooperation) Act 1990, s 4. These powers were recently invoked in pursuance of Norwegian criminal proceedings against the alleged thieves of Edvard Munch's 'The Scream,' by allowing for the evidence of undercover Scotland Yard officers to be presented from the Bow Street Magistrates' Courts: (1995) *The Times*, 15 November.

20 See Michell, 'Controlling the Flow of Information' (1995) 8 *The Lawyer*, 24 October.

21 See Marcus, 'Secret Witnesses' [1990] PL 207; Hansson and Zyl Smit, *Towards Justice?* (Oxford: Oxford University Press, 1990) ch 6; *Unterpertinger v Austria*, App no 9120/80, Ser A, vol 110 (1991) 13 EHRR 175; *Kostovski v Netherlands*, App no 11454/85, Ser A, vol 166 (1990) 12 EHRR 439; *Asch v Austria*, App no 12398/86, Ser A, vol 203 (1993) 15 EHRR 597; *Lüdi v Switzerland*, App no 12433/86, Ser A, vol 238 (1992) 15 EHRR 173; *Stanford v UK*, App no 16757/90, Ser A, vol 282 (1994); *Doorson v Netherlands*, App no 20524/92 (1995) EC Press Release 524.

22 McEwan, *Evidence and the Adversarial Process* (Oxford: Basil Blackwell, 1992).

the former's construction of events.[23] Furthermore, the uncoordinated use of technology may confuse the jury and increase costs and delay.[24]

The categorisation as beneficial or detrimental of the potential impact of the televising of court proceedings is deeply controversial at many national levels,[25] including in the USA where it is most prevalent.[26] If televising is to be supported, it must be mainly on educative grounds. Even here, there may be a trans-European aspect. In this way, the presence of the new audio-visual technologies in the courtroom might provide the opportunity for all European citizens to understand and appreciate that diversity in legal proceedings certainly exists, but that there is not exclusive excellence in just one national system. The confrontation of prejudices in this way may assist with the acceptance of other more tangible Council of Europe ventures, such as its conventions on the transfer of prisoners,[27] extradition[28] and mutual judicial assistance.[29] Equally, in so far as shortcomings are exposed by transnational publicity, the result may allow systems to learn from each other. The breakdown in popular barriers in this way may prove in the long run to be a more vital element to practical police and judicial co-operation in Europe than remote governmental and institutional efforts[30] can ever achieve.[31]

Moving on to impacts which might less equivocally be considered to be dangers[32] to the traditional weighing of values in the reporting of court cases, the problems arise both from the new modes of information transfer and from the consequent inability of traditional forms of governance, whether national or international, to respond effectively to them.[33]

---

23 An example might be the analysis of 'heli-tele' pictures in the Casement Park cases: Committee on the Administration of Justice, *Pamphlet No 19: The Casement Trials* (Belfast, 1992). The European Commission on Human Rights concluded that the screening from the defendants of media witnesses did not violate Article 6(1): *X* v *UK*, App no 20657/92, 15 EHRR CD 113. But this verdict was reached in circumstances where the testimony did not directly implicate the applicant (but concerned how film evidence had been created) and where the witnesses were not shielded from the 'Diplock' judge or the lawyers.

24 Trammell, 'Cirque du OJ' (1995) 7(4) *Court Technology Bulletin* (available at http://www.ncsc.dni.us/).

25 In the United Kingdom, see Walker and Brogarth, 'Televising the Courts' (1989) 153 *Justice of the Peace* 637; Henderson, 'Televising the Courts' (1990) 140 NLJ 1310; McConnell, 'Cameras in Court' (1990) 140 NLJ 1622; Hytner, 'Televising the Courts' (1992) 13 J Media Law & Practice 174; Caplan, 'Televising the Courts' (1992) 13 J Media Law & Practice 176; Catliff, 'On Camera not In Camera' (1994) 144 NLJ 1594; Munday, 'Televising the Courts' (1995) 159 *Justice of the Peace* 37, 57.

26 See *Estes* v *Texas* (1965) 381 US 532; *Chandler* v *Florida* (1989) 490 US 1075; *US* v *Hastings* (1983) 695 F 2d 1278; Heflin, 'Fair Trial v Free Press' (1977) 61 *Judicature* 154; Weinstein, 'Let the People Observe Their Courts' (1977) 61 *Judicature* 156; Thaler, *The Watchful Eye* (New York: Praeger, 1994).

27 European Convention on the Transfer of Sentenced Persons (ETS 112, 1983); Repatriation of Prisoners Act 1984.

28 European Convention on Extradition (ETS 24, 1957); Extradition Act 1989, Parts I and II.

29 European Convention on Mutual Assistance (ETS 30, 1959); Criminal Justice (International Cooperation) Act 1990.

30 See, for example, House of Lords Select Committee on the European Communities, Europol (1994–95, HL 51).

31 See Sheptycki, 'Transnational Policing and the Makings of the Postmodern State' (1995) 35 Brit J Crim 613.

32 The source of the dangers is primarily the (private) media outlets, but it is assumed there is at least state responsibility to react to their actions which threaten the rights of others, and it is arguable that fundamental rights such as in the European Convention are in any event directly applicable to relations between individuals: Clapham, *Human Rights in the Private Sphere* (Oxford: Clarendon Press, 1993).

33 See Katch, 'Rights, Camera, Action' (1995) 104 Yale LJ 1681; Sunstein, 'The First Amendment in Cyberspace' (1995) 104 Yale LJ 1757; Volokh, 'Cheap Speech and What It Will Do' (1995) 104 Yale LJ 1805.

It was already evident before these developments that press interest in court proceedings, especially criminal cases, is voracious and, in order to attract audiences, tends to concentrate on the dramatic and emotional, and so is disinclined to offer a representative picture of court transactions as a whole.[34] Furthermore, there may be manipulation by the parties involved in the litigation, including the police and prosecution in criminal cases.[35] These are commonplace dangers, but they are compounded in the case of new audio-visual technologies by reference to their instantaneous and especially their transnational nature. This new factor means that national arrangements which may have been worked out over many years and represent a careful compromise, may be breached, wittingly or unwittingly, by externally-sited media organisations with neither the intimate knowledge of local rules or cultures[36] nor the willingness to abide by them.

Turning to the international level, the European Court of Human Rights is prepared where necessary to allow restrictions which prevent the evasion of national laws consistent with the protection of the rights (such as in copyright) of others. For example, in *Groppera Radio v Switzerland*,[37] restrictions in Switzerland on the cable retransmission of programmes, which originated from a 'pirate' station in Italy and did not comply with international telecommunications laws, were considered proper as maintaining the orderly and the fair allocation of frequencies. But these restrictions must themselves be justifiable within the legitimate demands of democratic societies under Article 10(2), so the disruption of the flow of information across borders may be viewed as an obstacle to a vital aspect of European democracy and pluralism. Hence, it is no longer justifiable to maintain state monopolies in broadcasting[38] and more specific instances of information censorship, such as bans on information about abortion, as in *Open Door Counselling and Dublin Well Woman v Ireland*,[39] can also amount to a violation of Article 10.

These tendencies towards transnational media configurations (both in activities and ownership) and towards the delimitation of the traditional regulatory powers of government are apparently part of a general dialectical decline in the operational structures and concerns of sovereign nation states. The discourse of postmodernism[40] (which might here be linked with economic analysis in terms of post-Fordism or at least after-Fordism[41]) would suggest a trend towards

---

34 See Sparks, *Television and the Drama of Crime* (Buckingham: Open University Press, 1992); Williams and Dickinson, 'Fear of Crime' (1993) 33 Brit J Crim 33.
35 Graber, *Crime News and the Public* (New York: Praeger, 1980); Ericson, Baranek and Chan, *Representing Order* (Buckingham: Open University Press, 1991); Schlesinger and Tumber, *Reporting Crime* (Oxford: Clarendon Press, 1994).
36 For example, the uplink to the ASTRA satellite is routed through Luxembourg, so regulation of the most British-directed satellite broadcasts falls under the Luxembourg Media Law of 27 July 1991 and the Règlement Grand-Ducal of 21 January 1993. See Pichler, 'Private Satellite Television in the EC' (1993) 14 J Media Law & Practice 101.
37 App no 10890/84, Ser A, vol 173 (1990) 12 EHRR 321. See also *X v UK*, App no 8266/78, DR 16, 190. Compare the situation in which no 'disorder' was threatened from passive reception of Soviet signals: *Autronic v Switzerland*, App no 12726/87, Ser A, vol 178 (1990) 12 EHRR 485.
38 See *Informationsverein Lentia v Austria*, App nos 13914/88, 15041/89, 15717/89, 15779/89, 17207/90, Ser A, vol 276 (1994) 17 EHRR 93; (1993) *The Times*, 1 December. See also *Radio X, S, W and A v Switzerland*, App no 10799/84, DR 37, 236.
39 App nos 14234/88, 14235/88, Ser A, vol 246-A (1993) 15 EHRR 244. See also *SPUC v Grogan* [1990] 1 CMLR 689; [1991] 3 CMLR 849.
40 Alternatively, it may represent a new phase in the development of modernity: Giddens, *The Consequences of Modernity* (Cambridge: Polity Press, 1990).
41 See Jessop, 'Post-Fordism and the State' in Amin (ed), *Post-Fordism* (Oxford: Blackwell, 1994). Its implications in regard to the audio-visual media may be translated first in terms of the decline of

within the browser software and print it out; alternatively it can be saved to disk. This would be wholly inadequate for evidential purposes:

- Some of the facilities within the browsers to save WWW pages to disk are imperfect; text may be saved but not associated images; again, with some very complex pages (for example, involving "frames" and "templates"), what is seen on screen and what is saved to disk may be quite different.
- The method used to save a file to disk may not carry any individual labelling which shows where and when it was obtained.
- Such saved files are very easily modified or forged; accidental alteration is also a substantial hazard.
- Because of the browser cache facility there is no immediate, fool-proof way of telling when a specific page was last acquired. Thus if a whole series of cached pages are examined an entirely false picture could be built up—the pages are almost certainly not contemporaneous. Moreover, during a live session, what is produced on screen could be a mixture of pages immediately acquired from the remote computer and others acquired earlier on.
- Caches exist elsewhere. Many Internet Service Providers have facilities known as proxy servers to speed up the delivery of popular pages and limit congestion problems on the network. Thus a customer of such an ISP may not be able to be sure that what he has received on his computer is the latest version from the source computer as opposed to an earlier cached version held by his ISP.
- When the World Wide Web is used as an interface for electronic commerce, further problems appear. The pages of instruction which are converted into the pages the user actually sees have often been created on-the-fly by the remote computer, which itself may be linked to a further conventional "accounts", "catalogue", "sales/invoice" or "retail bank" computer. Thus, no immediate complete record of what the user actually saw may exist at the remote computer either, though presumably for many purposes the owner of that computer would like to be able convincingly to demonstrate to others the terms and facts of a transaction.

But this is only part of the problem faced by prosecutors: How can they show that the remote computer was behaving reliably at the time? This is important for "weight" even if we discard the need for section 69 certification. Again, how can they show that data has been obtained from a specific computer and nowhere else; website forgery is not uncommon.[45] Can prosecutors link the material from the remote computer to the person accused? Given the volatility of computer files, acquisition also usually needs to be linked to a specific day and time. This level of authentication cannot be done within a purely technological/computer context but will

---

[45] For example, the Labour Party webside (http://www.poptel.org.uk/labour-party/) was "spoofed" in 1996: *The Guardian*, December 10, 1996. The weakness that is exploited arises from the fact that most websites are updated remotely: the pages are created on computers other than the one hosting the site and are FTP'd over the Internet. Packet sniffing enables hackers to identify packets carrying FTP requests destined for the website and which carry sequences associated with log-ons and passwords.

fragmentation within the state and the emergence of 'bubbles of governance'[42] at local, regional, international and global levels[43] alongside the 'semi-sovereign' state.[44] However, the view that the fragmentation of monolithic state powers and authority must inevitably and solely be associated with the loss of state powers and authority — the 'hollowing out of the state'[45] — is contestable. The more accurate view is that the fragmentary state can effectively respond to challenges by more imaginative forms of governance dealing with postmodern and post-Fordist changes in ways which reach beyond the traditional mechanisms of the sovereign nation state, and maintain for itself crucial functions in terms of managing the political linkages in governance.[46] In this way, international and other sub-state relationships and norms can achieve the refilling or rethickening of the post-Hobbesian state. So, in the enterprise of media regulation, state boundaries become both an aid and obstacle to the assertion of regulation by the sovereign state. For media activities within the border, there can be effectively sanctioned controls over the media, though international oversight may intercede against some of the more censorious impositions. Equally, international arrangements may provide for regulation of transnational expression, though on this occasion it may be the resentful sovereign state which causes the international lawmakers and judges to hesitate and to fall back on excuses such as the margin of appreciation.[47] Hence, what emerges at national[48] and especially transnational levels assumes the form, appropriately enough in the age of new technologies, of a web of media regulation and pre- and post-broadcast reflection, rather than a narrow reliance on sovereign pre-licensing and pre-censorship which cannot cope with the polycentric and complex nature of modern media commerce.

These possibilities of multi-layered controls will be explored in detail after some of the new-found dangers have been more fully illustrated. The affected jurisdiction under focus is mainly that of England and Wales, whose legal system provides an especially dramatic example, since there has been a traditional reliance upon pre-trial censorship[49] and informal restraint.[50] Nevertheless, further examples will be drawn where appropriate from comparable jurisdictions, such as Canada and the Republic of Ireland. As for impacts further afield, it may be asserted that the analysis put forward in relation to global tendencies towards transnational

---

state monopolistic, and then even public service, broadcasting. For recent examples, see (French) Law of 29 July 1982; (Greek) Law no 1730 of 1987; (Irish) Broadcasting and Wireless Telegraphy Act (no 19) of 1988. It may secondly be illustrated by the localising channels of communication facilitated by the Internet by which each passive user/reader can readily at the same time become an active provider/publisher.

42 Shearing, 'Governing diversity' (1995) SLSA Conference, University of Leeds.
43 Swyngedouw, 'The Mammon Quest' in Dunford and Kafkalas (eds), *Cities and Regions in the New Europe* (London: Belhaven, 1992); Muller and Wright (eds), *The State in Western Europe* (London: Frank Cass, 1994).
44 Streeck and Schmitter, 'From National Corporatism to Transnational Pluralism' (1991) 19 *Politics and Society* 133.
45 Rhodes, 'The Hollowing Out of the State' (1994) 65 Pol Q 137; Jessop, 'The Regulation Approach, Governance and Post-Fordism' (1995) 24(3) *Economy and Society* 307.
46 Jessop, 'Post-Fordism and the State' in Amin (ed), *Post-Fordism* (Oxford: Blackwell, 1994), at p 274.
47 Jones, 'The Devaluation of Human Rights Under the European Convention' [1995] PL 430.
48 Thus, it is notable that the Broadcasting Act 1990 reduced reliance upon pre-censorship and relies more on post-broadcast sanctions and standard-setting by the Broadcasting Standards Council and the Broadcasting Complaints Commission.
49 Goldfarb, *The Contempt Power* (New York: Columbia UP, 1963).
50 Walker, Cram and Brogarth, 'The Reporting of Crown Court Proceedings and the Contempt of Court Act 1981' (1992) 55 MLR 647.

media configurations and the confinement of national regulatory powers has potentially disturbing consequences for almost all jurisdictions in Western Europe[51] and beyond, but their delineation must remain a matter for future study.

Scenarios

The new dangers to individual rights associated with legal proceedings, especially criminal trials, posed by the new technologies can be illustrated by the following four scenarios.

Prejudicial reporting on domestic cases by non-national journalists

The first problem arises whereby an 'outsider,' non-national journalist, shows less restraint than would be required of reporters resident in the jurisdiction. This may be intentional or unknowing, but the impact may be that proper safeguards are breached so as to cause prejudiced trials. This phenomenon has no doubt always happened to some extent, but its incidence may be increasing for two reasons. One is that there is arguably greater interest in internal European affairs as a result of the convergence of states via the European Union. For example, blockades by French farmers against foreign food imports or fraudulent activities by Italian farmers against the Common Agricultural Policy have become of direct relevance to the British public in a way unthinkable to the peoples of our foggy islands in earlier times. No doubt the same happens in reverse and British affairs (even affairs not involving the Prince and Princess of Wales) may be more likely to be reported in other EU Member States.[52] The second reason is that these overseas reports are more likely to find their way back to the United Kingdom. This was already possible with printed material, and the variation of standards in the law of defamation (often more onerous in the United Kingdom) has resulted in actions here, no matter how small the circulation or audience of the offending foreign publication.

A startling example is provided by *Packard v Andricopoulos and Eleftherotypia*.[53] The first defendant wrote a story in a national Greek daily newspaper (the second defendant) that the plaintiff, an ex-British naval intelligence officer, had collaborated with the Fascist dictatorship of the Colonels between 1967 and 1974. The plaintiff sued for libel. What made the litigation extraordinary was that he sued under English law on the basis that 50 copies of the newspaper had been sold in England, even though hundreds of thousands of copies had been sold in Greece and it was really in Greece where his reputation had suffered. In the event, he was awarded damages of £450,000, the first in a series of wholly excessive libel awards which eventually attracted condemnation by the European Court of Human Rights in *Tolstoy Miloslavsky v United Kingdom*,[54] and later by the Court of Appeal in *John v Mirror Group Newspapers*.[55] The award was in fact likely to be unenforceable in Greece and evoked there 'a mixture of incredulity and some mild

---

51 The issue has attracted the attention of the European Parliament: *The Times*, 13 February 1996.
52 *The Times* recently announced that an edition is to be printed in Belgium: 6 November 1995, p 4.
53 See Douzinas, McVeigh and Warrington, 'It's All Greek To Me' (1987) 137 NLJ 609. See also *Bobolas v Economist Newspaper* [1987] 1 WLR 1101; *Shevill v Presse Alliance SA* [1995] 2 WLR 499.
54 App no 18139/91, Ser A, vol 323 (1995) 20 EHRR 442.
55 *The Times*, 14 December 1995.

amusement of yet another example of English eccentricity at work.'[56] Yet one might be far less incredulous if there arises injury, this time to fair trials rather than to personal reputations, from reports on German satellite television heard in Britain (or vice versa) or to American-based reports carried by Cable Network News (CNN) transmitted to the whole of Europe. So, reporting is not only more likely, but a foreign version of events not tailored to the sensitivities of a specific jurisdiction is more likely to be received.

An illustration is provided by the James Bulger case. The police in Bootle charged two local boys with the murder of the two-year-old victim.[57] The media attention on the evidence and at trial was immense and attracted international dimensions. In line with normal English law practices,[58] an order was made that the defendants' identities should not be disclosed pending the outcome of the trial. The relevance of this case involving 'unparalleled evil and barbarity'[59] is the extent to which such an order could or should be observed given the diversity and intensity of media coverage. As for the British media, the observance was excellent, though there were some complaints that the ban was not in the public interest.[60] The boys were not identified until after their conviction in November 1993, when the trial judge expressly lifted the restraint orders and Robert Thompson and Jon Venables were named. The behaviour of the foreign media was more mixed. The media in the neighbouring jurisdiction of the Republic of Ireland were equally meticulous in obedience to the restraint order.[61] Equally, satellite stations with local offices, including Sky News and CNN, were respectful. But the United Kingdom (including the trial venue which was at Preston in Lancashire) was within footprint (possible reception area) of German, French and Italian satellite stations, some of which did breach the ban, as did a French newspaper, copies of which circulated in the area of the trial court.[62]

One might argue that little harm was done. The people of Preston are probably not avid readers of foreign newspapers and viewers of foreign satellite channels, and the English distributors of foreign newspapers could have been subjected to effective restraint by the English courts.[63] Nevertheless, the newer satellite technology demonstrates the danger which now arises: a range of television stations, readily available in the area, were effectively beyond the control of the British courts. Furthermore, one should not imagine that foreign stations have no attractions for British viewers; for example, Deutche Welle, available through Eutelsat II-F1, transmits several hours of programmes in English.

Even greater problems concerning the control of the new audio-visual media were posed in the Canadian cases of *Karla Bernardo* (also known as *Homolka*) and

---

56 Douzinas, McVeigh and Warrington, *op cit* n 53.
57 *The Times*, 23 February 1993.
58 Children and Young Persons Act 1933, ss 39, 47.
59 This description was applied by the trial judge, Mr Justice Morland: *The Guardian*, 25 November 1993.
60 Crook, 'We Are All Guilty in the Bulger Tragedy' (1993) *The Guardian*, 16 November.
61 See *The Irish Times*, 23 February 1993, 25 November 1993.
62 'Satellite Avoids Ban in Bulger Case' (1993) 14 J Media Law & Practice 157.
63 But note that no offence may have been committed: Contempt of Court Act 1981, s 3(2). Computer network service providers may likewise be treated as distributors rather than publishers: see *Cubby Inc v CompuServe Inc* (1991) 776 F Supp 135 (SDNY); *Stratton Oakmont Inc and Porush v Prodigy Service Co* (1995) NYSC, unreported except on LEXIS; Branscomb, 'Anonymity, Autonomy and Accountability' (1995) 104 Yale LJ 1639. This categorisation is also intended for the United Kingdom: Lord Chancellor's Department, Reforming Defamation Law and Procedure (London: 1995); Milmo, 'The Defamation Bill' (1995) 145 NLJ 1340.

her husband *Paul Teale*.[64] Both were charged with the sexual assault and killings of two girls. Bernardo was to be tried first for manslaughter, to be followed by the trial of Teale for murder. The latter wanted the earlier trial to be reported fully, as he feared a plea bargain would lead to him being treated as the principal offender. The lurid details of the case engendered enormous publicity and this extended to two aspects of 'new technology' which caused acute difficulties for the trial court. One was that there was great interest from United States television reporters from just across the border. The Canadian court could do nothing directly to interfere with, or moderate, United States broadcasts.[65] The court was therefore forced to fall back on the strategy of issuing an order excluding non-Canadian press representatives from the court hearings.[66] This recourse may have been unavoidable, but seems deeply unsatisfactory in a Europe striving for openness of borders and common values. Another problem arose from discussions of the case which appeared on bulletin board services carried by the Internet.[67] These were traced to the University of Western Ontario; more than a dozen universities in Canada placed a block on the relevant newsgroups, and one student publisher was visited and searched by the local police. One might speculate that had there been no locally identifiable source, then the relay of the publication (an anonymous distribution was attempted unsuccessfully via a server in Finland[68]) would have been unstoppable.

Prejudicial reporting on non-national cases by domestic journalists

The opposite to the first scenario can happen when European-based reporters may not be sufficiently respectful of the legitimate interests of foreign parties and proceedings. For example, the detailed reporting of the *O.J. Simpson* case in Los Angeles (including especially the televised court proceedings on Sky News which were interspersed by expert, informative and entertaining commentaries about what impact one side or the other was making) could sometimes be said to be disrespectful for the concerns of the administration of justice. However, it is extremely hard to imagine anything said in the European media, racy though it often was,[69] that was not expressed more prejudicially, more repeatedly and more sensationally by the United States media.

Perhaps the case with the most possible ramifications is that of *Nick Leeson*.[70] Leeson was a futures trader for the Singapore branch of Barings Bank, a venerable merchant bank established in London. His dealings ultimately caused such colossal losses (around £860 million) that the Bank was put into the hands of liquidators

---

64 R v *Bernardo* (1993) Ontario CJ, unreported except on LEXIS. See Shade, 'Desperately Seeking Carla' (1994) 22nd Annual Conference of the Canadian Association for Information Science 109; Donham, 'An Unshackled Internet' (Symposium on Free Speech and Privacy in the Information Age, University of Waterloo, 1994).

65 It seems to have been assumed that any conceivable form of publication, including even live reports from outside the Canadian courthouse, would occur in the USA and would therefore escape Canadian law.

66 R v *Bernardo* (1993) Ontario CJ, unreported except on LEXIS, para 137.

67 The main forum was a new Usenet newsgroup, alt.fan.karla.homolka. See the commentaries at http://www.cs.indiana.edu/canad.

68 anon.penet.fi. allowed anonymous postings to every Usenet newsgroup.

69 The arrest was reported under the headline 'Run, run! Nation joins in the OJ murder sensation' (1994) *The Sunday Times*, 19 June. The reports of his acquittal were equally sensationalist: 'Flabbergasted middle class expects call for law reform' (1995) *The Times*, 4 October.

70 Zhang, *Barings' Bankruptcy and Financial Derivatives* (London: World Scientific, 1995); Leeson, *Rogue Trader* (Boston: Little Brown, 1996).

who sold it to the Dutch group, ING. The losses were alleged to have occurred through the falsification of accounts — the forgery of favourable payments-in and the concealment of losses. Leeson was arrested on foot of an international arrest warrant issued in Singapore and circulated through INTERPOL at Frankfurt airport on 2 March 1995, whilst he was en route from the Far East to London.[71] Potential prejudice to his treatment by the judicial system arose at three levels.

First, there was the immediate prospect of extradition proceedings in Germany itself. These did indeed commence in March and were not concluded until October. It is clear that the British press and media (including satellite television) were less restrained in their comments about the case than they would have been if he were residing in a British rather than German prison. Even the British Government joined in the discussion by allowing the issuance of a report on the collapse of the Bank,[72] even though its findings in regard to the supervision by the regulatory authorities and management within the Bank could be material at the eventual trial.[73] At the same time, it must be recognised that extradition proceedings concentrate principally upon technical matters such as documentation and charges (especially double criminality), and do not involve the services of impressionable jurors or lay witnesses. So the risk of substantial prejudice to a professional and experienced judge was perhaps not particularly great in those circumstances.[74]

Next, the point of those extradition proceedings was, of course, a future criminal trial in Singapore. Extradition was formally requested in April 1995 and was finally granted at the end of October.[75] With multiple frauds carrying a possible 14 years' sentence,[76] there was a great deal at stake in terms of liberty of the individual. Of course, Singapore is not in the 'footprint' of European satellite television. Nevertheless, reporting both in the new and old media alleged in prejudicial terms that he was 'expected to plead guilty to some of the 11 charges of forgery and cheating that he faces in Singapore.'[77] One wonders how much of that message reached Singapore, though the Singapore Finance Ministry itself could be said to have possibly compounded the problems of prejudice by the issuance of the report of a further official inquiry.[78] In the event, Leeson was returned to Singapore in November 1995 and, after pleading guilty, received a heavy sentence of six and a half years' imprisonment.[79]

Thirdly, at one stage in the Leeson saga, it seemed that the news would not have to travel so far, since criminal proceedings in London also remained a live possibility during much of this period.[80] Leeson himself campaigned strongly for a trial in London. It would assist with the mechanics of proving his allegations that senior management in the Bank connived at his activities. In addition, he feared the conditions of detention and severity of sentence likely to be meted out in

---

71 *The Times*, 3 March 1995.
72 Report of the Board of Banking Supervision inquiry into the circumstances of the collapse of Barings (1994–95) HC 673.
73 Compare the handling of the Lonrho attempt to bid for Harrods: *In re Lonrho* [1989] 3 WLR 535.
74 This is the test used in the Contempt of Court Act 1981, s 2(2), but it is hard to see how much of the discussion even of the banking system could be 'incidental' within s 5.
75 *The Times*, 28 April, 31 October 1995.
76 Extradition was eventually ordered on 11 out of 12: *The Times*, 5 October 1995.
77 *The Times*, 31 October 1995.
78 See *The Straits Times*, 18 October 1995. The report put rather more blame on the institutional incompetence and even conspiratorial complicity of senior management than the Bank of England's version.
79 *The Times*, 2 December 1995, 4 December 1995.
80 Admittedly, the proceedings were never 'active': Contempt of Court Act 1981, s 2(3).

Singapore. So, from the outset, he made a 'desperate request'[81] to the German judge to be sent to England not Singapore, and followed it up with an extraordinary public relations campaign in the media and Parliament designed to put pressure on the Serious Fraud Office (SFO), including even a television interview.[82] The SFO did eventually appear on the scene and interrogated him, albeit as a reserve position in case the Singaporean proceedings failed.[83] All the while, the comments about the case continued — he was described as 'disgraced'[84] and it was openly discussed how, having admitted his guilt, he was attempting to plea bargain with the SFO.[85] The SFO did in the event hold to its decision to decline to take action and even blocked a private prosecution begun by investors.[86] It rightly viewed Singapore as the most appropriate legal venue. Furthermore, it could not be sure that any statements made by Leeson would not be recanted on his return to Britain, because they would have been obtained in oppressive or involuntary circumstances.[87] In addition, as the ultimate irony, Leeson might have argued that a fair trial in Britain would be impossible because of all the prejudicial comments about him.[88]

Prejudicial comments on non-national cases by domestic state officials

The third problem arises from possible comments by state authorities, such as police or Ministers of Justice. This may breach the presumption of innocence, as transpired in *Allenet de Ribemont* v *France*.[89] In a television interview on the same day as the defendant's arrest, the French Minister of the Interior and later a police superintendent accused the applicant of being guilty of a murder in Corsica. The European Court of Human Rights pointed out that the presumption of innocence under Article 6.2 of the Convention may be infringed not only by the judge or court, but also by other public authorities. The Minister's statements amounted to a prejudgment of his case and was a breach involving state responsibility. The same scenario occurred in the *Winchester 3* case,[90] when comments about the right to silence by, *inter alia*, Tom King, then Secretary of State for Northern Ireland and the intended victim of the defendants' alleged conspiracy to plant explosives, were adjudged to have caused such prejudice to their trial that their convictions could no longer be upheld as safe.

The same prejudicial comments may well arise on a cross-border basis and be reported by transnational audio-visual media, since both originators and reporters of such comments may be less influenced by respect for local courts. Instances have arisen in connection with projected extradition proceedings. For example, the perception has become prevalent in the Irish Republic that, on a number of occasions, comments by British officials (as well as the British media) about suspected Republican terrorists who are the subject of extradition proceedings have been highly prejudicial, with the result that the extradition should not be granted as

---

81 *The Times,* 14 March 1995.
82 *The Times,* 12 September 1995.
83 *The Times,* 31 August 1995.
84 *The Times,* 30 September 1995.
85 *The Times,* 16 July 1995.
86 *The Times,* 30 September 1995.
87 Police and Criminal Evidence Act 1984, s 76.
88 As in *R* v *Shanahan, McCann and Cullen* (1990) *The Times,* 1 May; *R* v *Wood* (1995) *The Times,* 11 July; *R* v *Knights* (1995) *The Times,* 5 October.
89 App no 15175/89, Ser A, vol 308A, 1994 (1995) 20 EHRR 557.
90 *R* v *Shanahan, McCann and Cullen* (1990) *The Times,* 1 May.

it would facilitate the breach of fundamental rights at any British trial. This concern was first reflected in Irish jurisprudence in *Ellis* v *O'Dea (No 2)*[91] following a request from Britain for the extradition of Desmond Ellis to face explosives charges arising out of IRA activities. The argument failed on the facts in that case, but it succeeded in *Magee* v *O'Dea*,[92] Joseph Magee being wanted in Britain for the murder of a soldier in Derby. A review on this basis is now enshrined in the Irish extradition legislation. The Extradition (Amendment) Act 1987[93] requires the Irish Attorney General not to endorse an extradition arrest warrant unless there is a clear intention to prosecute (rather than a speculative demand for extradition in order to interrogate or otherwise gather further evidence) based on sufficient evidence. This statutory review jurisdiction has been exercised on a wider basis, to stop an extradition which would result in an unfair trial. Thus, in the case of *Father Ryan*,[94] the Attorney General complained of prejudicial material in English newspapers and also of remarks made in the House of Commons by the Prime Minister.[95]

It might appear that the development of transnational media coverage does in fact improve the chances of a trial free from the prejudicial comments of a foreign state official. In bygone years, British governmental representatives, with a home audience solely in mind, might have been less circumspect about what they said to British journalists about IRA suspects and might have assumed that there would be no impact in Ireland itself. Yet, it is not so certain, in the light of the *Nick Leeson* case, that the globalisation of the media has of itself given sufficient pause for thought. In any event, the discontinuance of a criminal prosecution of a suspect against whom there is a *prima facie* case of heinous crimes is also an unsatisfactory outcome. In the circumstances of highly prejudicial comment, there may be no alternative to discontinuance for, as the Irish Supreme Court asserted in *Larkin* v *O'Dea*,[96] the defendant's right to a fair trial is superior to the community's right to prosecute. But from the point of view of justice, it might be better still if state officials were educated to be more aware and respectful of foreign process so as to allow it to reach a conclusion.

Transnational 'jigsaw' identification

The fourth scenario relates to what is known in the United Kingdom as 'jigsaw identification,' which was a concern pointed out as long ago as 1990 by the (Calcutt) Report of the Committee on Privacy and Related Matters.[97] The problem arises in situations where the law seeks to afford anonymity in regard to the victims of rape and other sexual assaults (in the interests of encouraging them to give testimony) or in regard to children who are involved in litigation, whether as victim, perpetrator or otherwise (in the interests of ensuring their proper maturation or rehabilitation). However, these intended protections can be undermined by jigsaw identification:[98]

---

91 [1991] 1 IR 251.
92 [1994] 1 ILRM 540.
93 s 44A–D. This form of intervention was upheld as constitutional in *Wheeler* v *Culligan* [1990] 1 IR 344.
94 See *The Irish Times*, 14 December 1988. Similar worries had prevented the extradition of Father Patrick Ryan from Belgium to England.
95 See Forde, *Extradition Law* (Dublin: Round Hall, 2nd ed, 1995).
96 [1995] 2 ILRM 1.
97 Cm 1102, ch 10.
98 *ibid* para 10.17.

The problem arises where different news organisations report different details from criminal proceedings for sexual offences. For example, one report might name a defendant but not specifically the alleged offence; another might refer to an unnamed father charged with abusing his children. Each report may be compiled with proper regard to the law or any court order in force. Nevertheless, when the reports are read together, it is possible to identify the victim.

The Calcutt Committee recommended the standardisation of reporting practices around the identification of the offence, but not the identity of the personalities.[99] This idea has been followed by guidance issued by the Press Complaints Commission.[100] However, the rules remain imperfectly understood,[101] and in any event the Commission's jurisdiction applies only to the United Kingdom, so one can readily see how difficulties might arise again on a trans-European front.

It is inevitable that the proliferation of media outlets, even at a national level, brought about by the new technologies increases the chances of jigsaw identification. However, the transnational aspect of the growth brings added obstacles, since it reduces the moderating influence of local cultures which, in Britain at least, have been strongly influenced by self-restraint and fear of sanctions via contempt of court. That local cultures remain important was recently shown by research on powers to impose formal postponements or bans on reports of court materials pursuant to sections 4 and 11 of the Contempt of Court Act 1981.[102] The research showed that these formal orders were not very common, but that the courts did often rely on journalists to act without such formal warnings. Yet one cannot realistically expect, say, Italian journalists to share the ingrained cultures of British journalists (or vice versa).

The breach of the barriers resurrected to protect and encourage victims in sex attack or sex abuse cases may be more directly affronted than by the somewhat inadvertent process of creeping 'jigsaw' identification. Consider the case of *William Kennedy Smith* in 1991. The defendant, the nephew of Massachusetts senator Edward Kennedy, was charged with rape and battery in Palm Beach, Florida and was eventually acquitted.[103] The ensuing trial was remarkable, even by American standards, for the degree of publicity it engendered. This publicity even extended in several media outlets (including NBC and the *New York Times*) to the naming of the female victim, often in contradiction of their normal policy on identification. The justifications for the normal rule of suppression may remain debatable,[104] but it was in any event notable that in this case European media outlets did not always follow suit (though the televised trial was relayed in full by Sky News). However, ratings considerations are so influential that one might wonder whether such restraint would be repeated in the future, especially as there is no obvious normative requirement to engage in that form of self-abnegation.

---

99 *ibid* para 10.19.
100 Article 14 of the Code of Practice, 1993: 'The press should not identify victims of sexual assault or publish material likely to contribute to such identification unless, by law, they are free to do so.'
101 *Review of Press Self-Regulation* (1993) Cm 2135, para 7.49. The Report called for further consultation between the PCC and the press on this matter. The House of Commons National Heritage Committee in its report, Privacy and Media Intrusion (1992–93) HC 294, para 92, also expressed disquiet. Both Reports called for protection of the identities of all victims of any crime where identification may be damaging to health or security.
102 Walker, Cram and Brogarth, *op cit* n 50.
103 *The Times*, 10 May 1995.
104 Hutt, 'Note: In Praise of Public Access' (1991) Duke LJ 368; Denno, 'Perspectives on Disclosing Rape Victims' Names' (1993) 61 Fordham L Rev 1113.

Regulatory responses

Consistent with earlier observations about the transformations within Western sovereign states in the late twentieth century, it would be futile to expect effective regulatory responses solely within the confines of national borders. In the current stage of modern or postmodern society, one can expect a trend towards 'governance' rather than 'government,' in which the role of the nation state is not exclusive but may need further sustenance by the activation of more varied levers of power at second hand. In the contexts of the new information technologies in the audio-visual sector, these extra levers of governance may arise at two levels, both formal and informal international normative statements. In addition, there is also a need for national reappraisal in the light of the changed circumstances of the contemporary modes of information transfer.

The problems caused by cross-border audio-visual media have indeed been addressed to some extent by one of the levers just mentioned, namely the formal normative structures of international law. These present themselves in the shape of the Council of Europe's European Convention on Transfrontier Television,[105] which overlaps considerably with the European Communities' Council Directive 89/552, 'Television without Frontiers.'[106] It is intended to concentrate here on the Council of Europe's version, since the European Community version arises more out of concerns for free markets (which are reinforced by decisions under the Treaty of Rome itself)[107] and the promotion of indigenous broadcasting industries, than out of concerns for the treatment of individuals. In addition, the European Court of Justice has accepted that any restrictions which are potentially excusable within the economic regime of the Communities must also accord with Article 10 of the European Convention on Human Rights.[108] Nevertheless, it must be acknowledged that the role of the European Communities is growing. The Maastricht Treaty recognises in Article 128(1) the issue of culture as a community concern, which can only encourage involvement in the first element of the triptych of European media policies, namely, programming content as well as the development of programme industries and technologies.[109]

The Convention on Transfrontier Television is as much concerned, perhaps even primarily so, in the words of Article 1, 'to facilitate ... the transfrontier transmission and the retransmission of television programme services' as it is to impose new regulations which deal with novel consequences. However, matters of regulation (which can apply to terrestrial, cable or satellite broadcasting, according

---

105 1989 (1990) Cm 1068. See Addison, 'Television Without Frontiers' (1985) 6 J Media Law & Practice 157; Scwartz, 'Broadcasting Without Frontiers in the EC' (1985) 6 J Media Law & Practice 26; Olsson, 'Council of Europe and Mass Media Law' (1986) 7 J Media Law & Practice 64; 'Television Without Frontiers' (1986) 7 J Media Law & Practice 73; Hondius, 'Regulating Transfrontier Television' (1988) *Yearbook of European Law* 141; Cassesse and Clapham (eds), *Transfrontier Television* (Baden-Baden: NOMOS, 1990); Debbasch, *Droit de L'Audiovisuel* (Paris: Dalloz, 10th ed, 1991) para 864*bis*.

106 See Goldberg and Wallace, *Regulating the Audio-Visual Industry* (London: Butterworths, 1991); Debbasch, *Droit de L'Audiovisuel* (Paris: Dalloz, 10th ed, 1991) para 851; Barendt, *Broadcasting Law* (Oxford: Clarendon Press, 1993) ch 10; Winn, *European Community and International Media Law* (London: Graham & Trotman, 1994) chs 6, 7. The Directive is reviewed in COM(94) 57.

107 See van Loon, 'National Media Policies under EEC Law Taking into Account Fundamental Rights' (1993) 14 J Media Law & Practice 17.

108 *Cinéthèque* v *Fédération Nationale de Cinémas Français* [1985] ECR 2605; *Elliniki Radiophonia Tileorassi Anonimi* v *Dimoktiki Etaria Pliroforissis* [1991–96] ECR 2925.

109 See Collins, *Broadcasting and Audio Visual Policy in the European Single Market* (London: John Libbey, 1994).

to Article 3) are addressed in both jurisdictional and substantive terms. In terms of jurisdiction, Article 5(2) makes clear that the regulating State shall be identified as follows: in the case of terrestrial transmissions, the State in which the initial emission is effected; or, normally in the case of satellite transmission, the State in which the 'up-link' (point of transmission to the satellite) is situated;[110] or in the case of retransmissions from non-Party States, the retransmitting Party State. The duties of the relevant responsible State include the general requirement to ensure that broadcasters comply with the terms of the Convention (Article 5(1)), and this in turn means that there is enforcement of the general duty of broadcasters to 'respect the dignity of the human being and the fundamental rights of others' (Article 7). Yet, aside from a right to reply (in Article 8), these fundamental rights are not specified. Instead, the Convention goes on to outline, first, restrictions concerning indecency, pornography, violence and incitement to hatred, the development of children, and unbiased news information (Article 7(2) and (3)) and, second, the cultural objective of the development of European based broadcasting (Article 10), neither of which can easily be translated into corresponding rights. Accordingly, the corpus of the Convention mainly addresses what one might view as collective concerns and there are also restraints, arising again out of collective concerns for minimal standards on, and for standardisation of, advertising and sponsorship (Articles 11–18).

In principle, a European-based multilateral treaty is an appropriate instrument for the governance of satellite television. Though United States originated materials comprise a large proportion of transmission time and also, being in the English language, may be potential sources of influence upon witnesses and jurors in England and Wales, there is no direct satellite broadcasting from the United States of America. All relevant United States channels are uplifted from European sites and are thereby subjected to European regulation.[111] However, in practice, whilst relevant and innovative in many respects, the Convention does not properly address the concerns raised in this article. Emphasis must here be placed on the failure to specify in any detail the areas of fundamental rights of individuals which must be respected by the broadcasters.[112] Certainly, the fundamental rights of the subjects of broadcasts entailed in the concept of a fair trial are nowhere specified. The emphasis instead is mainly on the rights of broadcasters (and, to a lesser extent, the viewers) and this narrow focus may prove unacceptable to national authorities in the receiving state who are not satisfied with divergent standards applied by the home based authorities in the responsible state. An example might be *R* v *Secretary of State for the National Heritage, ex p Continental Television BVio and Others* (the *'Red Hot Dutch'* case).[113] In this case, pornographic programmes produced by a Dutch company but broadcast by Denmark were not considered a breach of obscenity laws in Denmark, but went well beyond the bounds of United Kingdom obscenity interpretations.[114] Accordingly, action was taken to ban the sale of relevant decoders and advertising by the Secretary of State under section 177 of the Broadcasting Act 1990. By section 177, the Secretary of

---

110 See also Article 5(2)(b)(ii) and (iii).
111 For example, Cable News Network is routed from Atlanta through Luxembourg to the Astra Satellite.
112 But see the right to reply under Article 8.
113 [1993] 2 CMLR 333, Court of Appeal. Foreign Satellite Service Proscription Order 1993, SI 1024. See Coleman and McMurtrie, 'Too Hot to Handle' (1993) 143 NLJ 10; Coulthard, 'Dutch Television — Too Red Hot for UK' (1993) 14 J Media Law & Practice 116; Coleman and McMurtrie, 'Red Hot Television' [1995] 1 EPL 201.
114 See Obscene Publications Acts 1959–94, as amended by the Broadcasting Act 1990, s 162.

State may make a proscription order against a foreign satellite service, the quality
of which has been considered to be unsatisfactory by the Independent Television
Commission, provided he is satisfied that:[115]

> the making of the order —
> (a) is in the public interest; and
> (b) is compatible with any international obligations of the United Kingdom.

The section was passed to allow for some control by national authorities over
externally-sited broadcasters, but any action must be compatible with international
obligations such as the European Convention and Directive. The ban in the *Red
Hot Dutch* case was said by the National Heritage Secretary to be justified under
Article 22 of the EC Directive, which envisages intervention by the receiving state
in the event of a breakdown of controls in the broadcaster's home state. But there
was in reality no collapse in the civil authorities in Denmark — rather, there was,
and remains, a fundamental difference in tastes and interpretations between
Denmark and the United Kingdom which proved so divergent as to be
unacceptable to the latter. A similar legally dubious fate also befell XXXTV
(formerly TV Erotica), a Swedish based station.[116] Likewise, an externally-based
news satellite station, which simply applies its own well-established local
standards as to court reporting, should not fall within the realms of control
allowed by section 177, and it would be even more difficult to assert in its case that
the small proportion of broadcast time devoted to items about British court cases
warranted such drastic action as proscription.

The difficulties arising from the divergent bounds of publication freedom should
not be interpreted as demanding that external journalists must always observe the
letter of the laws of others. After all, one of the most important aspects, perhaps
unique and certainly innovative, of the European Convention on Human Rights
itself is that it operates as an external bill of rights. This externality is a valuable
feature, since it can ensure that received wisdoms or painful facts which would not
be assailable at a national level can be subjected to a more objective and
dispassionate form of scrutiny. This is perhaps of most evident benefit when States
have been challenged in connection with security and anti-terrorist policies. One
cannot pretend that the recent decision in *McCann, Farrell and Savage* v *United
Kingdom*[117] (concerning the fatal shooting by Special Air Service soldiers of three
suspected IRA bombers in Gibraltar) was at all popular. The Deputy Prime
Minister, Michael Heseltine, threatened to defy the judgment, while the British
press was often even more hostile; for example, the tabloid *Sun* newspaper carried
the headline 'Off Eur Rockers.'[118] Nevertheless, it is the very distance from the
conflict which allows perspectives on rights issues which may not be possible
closer to home. Likewise, it may take foreign journalists to investigate and publish
stories which native journalists wish or are forced to avoid. An example from
Britain might be the treatment of Peter Wright's book, *Spycatcher*.[119] The external
verdict that the internal constraints were excessive in the *Spycatcher* case was
eventually confirmed by the European Court of Human Rights in *Observer*,

---

115   s 177(4). The consequences of proscription follow in s 178.
116   *The Times*, 15 November 1995.
117   App no 18984/91, Ser A, vol 324 (1995).
118   28 September 1995.
119   *AG* v *Guardian Newspapers* [1987] 1 WLR 1248; (No 2) [1988] 2 WLR 805; [1988] 3 WLR 776.
      See Michael, 'Spycatcher's End' (1989) 52 MLR 389; Barendt, 'Spycatcher and Freedom of Speech'
      [1989] PL 204.

Guardian etc and Sunday Times (No 2) v *United Kingdom* in 1991.[120] Further, the real cause of the Government's defeat was publication elsewhere, including in the United States of America, Australia, New Zealand and Hong Kong.[121] Similarly, the publication in Ireland of Joan Miller's book, *One Woman's War*, about her experiences in intelligence during the Second World War, likewise was instrumental in the pre-emption of actions against it in Britain.[122]

Two further strategies remain to be addressed: a national reappraisal of domestic regulation and informal international normative structures. Both will be considered in the next section as more novel and radical approaches to the new technologies.

New approaches to the new technologies

National reappraisal

A national reappraisal of domestic audio-visual regulation in the light of new technologies might suggest, for the United Kingdom and for any other jurisdiction sharing its approach, that there may be a case for progress away from pre-trial legal censorship[123] and cultural restraint,[124] neither of which can discipline and punish in the decentred, multinational, multicultural society.[125] This stance has been adopted in the United States of America, though more explicitly because of the ideological priority accorded to the First Amendment right of free speech rather than because of the difficulties of enforcement in a federated and diverse state. Thus, the easing of media restrictions in regard to contempt of court was most marked in 1941 in the Supreme Court judgment in *Bridges* v *California*.[126] The case arose from newspaper editorials concerning a bitter labour dispute in California in which the judges were asked to impose heavy sentences on union leaders charged with assault; in reply, the unions threatened further unrest if there were convictions. The clear and present danger test there pronounced made it almost impossible for prejudice to be shown to the requisite degree. Thereafter, free comment has prevailed both on matters giving rise to litigation and on litigation itself.

Following this precedent, there would seem to be reason for reform of the United Kingdom pre-censorship model in regard to court reporting on two grounds. One is pragmatic. The transnational and instantaneous (and transitory in the case of the Internet) nature of the new modalities of media expression mean that the old cultures and threats will no longer work. Besides, the United States experience teaches above all that pre-censorship is usually crude, unacceptable and avoidable.[127] Consequently, there are good grounds of principle for change, which means that the right to free speech should more clearly prevail, especially if

---

120 App nos 13166/87, 13585/88, Ser A, vols 216, 217 (1992) 14 EHRR 153, 229. See Duffy, 'Spycatcher in Europe' (1991) 141 NLJ 1703.
121 *Att Gen for UK* v *Heinemann Publishers* (1988) 78 ALR 449; *Att Gen for UK* v *Wellington Newspapers* [1988] 1 NZLR 129; *Att Gen* v *South China Morning Post* [1989] 2 FSR 653.
122 *Att Gen for England and Wales* v *Brandon Books Publishers* [1987] ILRM 135.
123 For comparisons between England and the USA, see Goldfarb, *op cit* n 49.
124 See Walker, Cram and Brogarth, *op cit* n 50.
125 The Internet is especially decentred in that there exists a multiplicity of 'publishers' and no central ordering either by enforcement authority or by professionalisation.
126 (1941) 314 US 252.
127 *Brandenburg* v *Ohio* (1969) 395 US 444; *Organisation for a Better Austin* v *Keefe* (1971) 402 US 415.

bolstered by a right to receive information.[128] One might argue that the *Sunday Times* Thalidomide case points in this direction.[129] The court, admittedly by a majority of 11 to 9, decided in favour of striking down the injunction against further publication, while its usual respect for local, national discretion seemed notably, but perhaps gratifyingly, missing in this case. The same 'hard look' was applied in *Observer, Guardian etc and Sunday Times (No 2)* v *United Kingdom*,[130] where again the interests of freedom of expression exercisable through the press were stressed. However, a rather less interventionist stance was taken in *Prager and Oberschlick* v *Austria*.[131] In that case, critical comments about 'Harsh Judges' in the Austrian criminal courts could be the subject of criminal defamation proceedings consistent with Article 10(2), even though the article did not relate to the substance of any particular case. Perhaps one distinction from the earlier cases was that the article did not amount to serious journalism based on adequate research (at least in the opinion of the Strasbourg Court).[132]

In terms of the details of a new national order following a reappraisal, it is suggested that the United States model again has a lot to offer[133] and therefore the following features should be prominent. Overall, there must be trust in the probity of the jury and/or the judge. Trial judges must learn to assume a rather less paternalistic attitude and to accept that, like judges themselves,[134] the jurors can disregard the noise of background publicity just as we expect them to set aside prejudices in terms of class, gender or race. This attitude has been espoused by the United States Supreme Court: 'pretrial publicity — even pervasive adverse publicity — does not invariably lead to an unfair trial.'[135] Less lofty judicial office-holders have also commented that: 'trials ... are newsworthy ... It is unrealistic to expect to completely sanitize a trial and jury ... The issue is whether the publicity influenced the jury or its verdict.'[136] But justice must not only be done, but manifestly be seen to be done,[137] and this nostrum suggests some practical alternative protections against the influence of prejudicial reporting. These protections have been developed and catalogued in United States jurisprudence, most notably in *Nebraska Press Association* v *Stuart*.[138] In response to a 'gagging order' imposed by a trial court in Nebraska, the Supreme Court observed that alternatives to such a prior restraint must first be considered and had not been fully raised in this case. Thus, the effects of pre-trial publicity should where possible be mitigated by the following: careful challenges to potential jurors, sequestration of the jury and instructions[139] to the

---

128 *Gaskin* v *UK*, App no 10454/83, Ser A, vol 160 (1990) 12 EHRR 36.
129 App no 6538/74, Ser A, vol 30 (1979–80) 2 EHRR 245. See also *Atkinson, Crook and The Independent* v *UK*, App no 13366/87 — the right to receive information claimed by journalists in this case was overridden by Article 10(2).
130 App nos 13166/87, 13585/88, Ser A, vols 216, 217 (1992) 14 EHRR 153, 229.
131 App no 15974/90, Ser A, vol 313 (1995) 20 EHRR 329.
132 App no 15974/90, Ser A, vol 313 (1995) 20 EHRR 329, para 37.
133 See generally Friendly and Goldfarb, *Crime and Publicity* (New York: Twentieth Century Fund, 1967); American Bar Association, *Standards for Criminal Justice* (2nd ed, 1986) ch 8.
134 *In re Lonrho* [1989] 3 WLR 535.
135 *Nebraska Press Association* v *Stuart* (1976) 427 US 539, 554, *per* Burger CJ.
136 *Lucas* v *Commonwealth of Kentucky* (1992) 840 SW 2d 212, 215, *per* Stephens J.
137 *R* v *Sussex Justices, ex p McCarthy* [1924] 1 KB 256.
138 (1976) 427 US 539. See Sack, 'Principle and Nebraska Press Association v Stuart' (1977) 29 Stanford L Rev 411; Barnett, 'The Puzzle of Prior Restraint' (1977) 29 Stanford L Rev 539; Goodale, 'The Press Ungagged' (1977) 29 Stanford L Rev 497.
139 See Erickson, 'Fair Trial and Free Press' (1977) 29 Stanford L Rev 485.

jurors by the trial judge; a change of trial venue;[140] and postponement of the trial.[141]

Perhaps these alternatives are more viable in the United States of America, which is a large continental country with a predominantly locally based media.[142] In comparison, Western European states are geographically more compact and, at least in broadcasting and audio-visual publishing, coverage has hitherto tended to be national. It may also be observed that the expedient of a retrial when all the alternative protections have failed is a more feasible outcome in the United States of America. For instance, a notable lapse in normal protections occurred in the case of Dr Sam Sheppherd.[143] Sheppherd was tried for the murder of his wife in a courtroom filled to the brim with journalists, the publicity being considered good for the pending re-election of both the judge and the chief prosecutor. The trial was turned into a media circus, the only remedy for which was to order a retrial, though not until Sheppherd had served several years' imprisonment.

While alternative approaches may turn out to be occasionally expensive and unsuccessful,[144] the increasing failures of the present emphasis upon pre-censorship must also be taken into account. Even within an insular national context, the breakdown of respectful journalistic cultures and state controls is striking, and has caused prosecutions to be dropped in an increasing number of English cases,[145] all as a result of publicity from outlets within the jurisdiction. Seen in this light, the prospects do not seem bright that there will now spontaneously develop on a global scale a journalistic culture of restraint in respect of the treatment of pending court cases in England and Wales, and so more proactive steps are required.

Informal international normative standard setting

Late modern or postmodern societies are associated with shifting patterns of controls and relationships. This new public management[146] pictures government departments as catalytic helmsmen rather than stokers and labourers, with its operative agencies heavily oriented towards management efficiency and consumer satisfaction. One tangible result in the United Kingdom has been an emphasis on the setting of standards and targets, which become the performance indicators by which public services can be judged by others and by themselves. This trend has now been organised around the concept of the Citizen's Charter,[147] by which citizenship itself comes to be defined in consumerist rather than political terms.

---

140   See Note (1967) *Notre Dame Lawyer* 925.
141   See Kramer, 'Pre-trial Publicity, Judicial Remedies and Jury Bias' (1970) 14 *Law and Human Behaviour* 409.
142   See Siebert *et al, Fair Press and Fair Trial* (Georgia: University of Georgia Press, 1970); Simon, 'Does the Court's Decision in Nebraska Press Association v Stuart Fit the Research Evidence on the Impact on Jurors of News Coverage?' (1977) 29 Stanford L Rev 515; Dreschel, 'An Alternative View of Media–Judiciary Relations' (1989) 18 Hofstra L Rev 1.
143   (1951) 341 US 50. See Kane, *Murder, Courts and the Press* (Illinois: South Illinois University Press, 1986). The retrial may be equally problematic; see *Patton v Yount* (1984) 467 US 1205.
144   See Robertson and Nicol, *Media Law* (London: Penguin, 3rd ed, 1992) p 262.
145   *R v Shanahan, McCann and Cullen* (1990) *The Times*, 1 May; *R v Wood* (1995) *The Times*, 11 July; *R v Knights* (1995) *The Times*, 5 October.
146   Osborne and Gaebler, *Reinventing Government* (Massachusetts: Addison-Wesley, 1992); Stewart and Walsh, 'Change in the Management of Public Services' (1992) 70 *Public Administration* 499; Zifcaf, *New Managerialism* (Buckingham: Open University Press, 1994); Greer, *Transforming Central Government: The Next Steps Initiative* (Buckingham: Open University Press, 1994).
147   (1991) Cm 1599.

Whatever the legitimacy of reconfiguring citizenship in this way,[148] the demand for compliance with standards (often set out as codes of practice) which purport to be in the public interest cannot easily be resisted by those claiming to be responsible professionals, such as civil servants. The same idea has also been applied to groups within the criminal justice system, such as the police[149] and the courts.[150] It would be consistent with the analyses put forward earlier as to the developments in media and society, and indeed may become an irresistible discourse in view of the growing impotence of legalistic regulation, to explore such new forms of ethical standard-making in relation to journalists.[151] In this way, there would be an appeal to the better instincts of journalists who could be encouraged to internalise, as matters of desirable professional practices, standards which can no longer be entirely imposed externally by laws or by state officials.

Ethical standard-making and journalism may not be such strange bedfellows as they might first appear. At a national level, the National Union of Journalists has promulgated a Code of Conduct since 1981.[152] Yet the Code may be a less than perfect response to some of the problems outlined in this article for two reasons.[153] One is that its wording is couched in terms of upholding the rights of the press to investigate and publish; there is little concern for the rights of other individuals, save in respect of aspects of privacy and equality. The right to a fair trial free from prejudicial comment is not a matter expressly drawn to the attention of members. Secondly, the Code is published only to members of the NUJ and so cannot hope to influence non-union United Kingdom journalists[154] or foreign journalists. Similar criticism may even be made of the Press Complaints Commission's Code of Practice.[155] Whilst concerns for privacy are more prominently paraded, and whilst observance of the Code seems to have been increasingly internalised by proprietors and, perhaps through them, editors,[156] the Code still inevitably operates at purely a national level and also is wholly silent as to respect for a fair trial. It follows that new levels and more detailed codes of governance are required.

At an international level, this enterprise of professional ethical standard-setting is now one to which the Council of Europe has begun to turn its attention. Hence, the Assembly Recommendation 1003 of 1993 consists of the adoption of a text on the ethics of journalism, which followed the report of the Committee on Culture and Education.[157] This wide-ranging and detailed document is to be applied by journalistic professions throughout Europe. It first underlines the responsibility which the media have for the provision of news and information which is distinct from mere opinion, is truthful and is comprehensive (paragraphs 3 to 6). It is

---

148 Barron and Scott, 'The Citizen's Charter Programme' (1992) 55 MLR 526.
149 See Home Office Circular 114/1983, *Manpower Effectiveness and Efficiency in the Police Service*; Association of Chief Police Officers, *Statement of Common Purposes and Values* (1990).
150 Courts Service, *Courts Charter* (London: HMSO, 1995).
151 See Belsey and Chadwick, *Ethical Issues in Journalism* (London: Routledge, 1992).
152 NUJ Branch Circular no 36 (1980/81).
153 As with all codes of practice, one might also question the effectiveness of enforceability. Though backed by the Union's disciplinary rules (r 18, 19), there have been no expulsions for breach of the Code.
154 The NUJ's Submission to the Calcutt (no 2) Enquiry in 1992 bemoaned the inadequate ethical training of journalists which was seen as too geared to the needs of the particular employer rather than the needs of the profession in general.
155 For the latest version, see PCC, *Annual Report 1995* (London, 1996).
156 The most stark example was the rebuke of Piers Morgan, then Editor of the *News of the World*, by his proprietor Rupert Murdoch for invading the privacy of Countess Spencer in breach of the PCC Code: *The Times*, 12 May 1995.
157 Doc 6854.

emphasised that the media's work is to provide an information service to the citizen — to service the latter's right to information; it follows that neither government nor media management should obstruct this task (paragraphs 7 to 16), though this should not lead the media into transforming itself into a counter-authority (paragraphs 19 to 21). There then follow a number of specific ethical concerns about the treatment of individuals. Many relate to privacy and rights to reply (paragraphs 23 to 27). There is also a requirement to take special care in times of conflict and when dealing with vulnerable minorities (paragraphs 33 to 35). But of greatest relevance for present purposes is paragraph 22:

> In journalism, information and opinions must respect the presumption of innocence, in particular in cases which are still *sub judice* and must refrain from making judgments.

The expectation is that the principles so adumbrated will be implemented via self-regulatory bodies and that reviews will be undertaken of the impact (paragraphs 36 to 38).

In keeping with this development, the Fourth European Ministerial Conference on Mass Media Policy made a Declaration in Prague in 1994[158] which echoes the growing attention given to self-regulation. Accordingly, Principles 6 to 8 of the Declaration call for journalists to act in an ethical and responsible manner, as reflected in professional codes of conduct applicable to them.

National and international self-regulation is developing in connection with the Internet. Recent years have witnessed the establishment of industry groupings, such as the Internet Society (ISOC)[159] and the Platform for Internet Content Selection (PICS),[160] whose interests include content rating and advisory labelling of materials, and content selection software products.[161] There is also a much more localised aspect to ethical governance which may be particularly appropriate to computer networks, including electronic mail and the World Wide Web. In this way, it becomes appropriate for individual servers,[162] list managers or even corporate users (such as universities[163]) to devise their own ethical guides to good conduct. These developments have indeed occurred, but commercial activities and indecent or racist materials have been much more targeted to date than contemptuous comments. For example, despite the *Bernardo* case, UK university computer use regulations contain no warning as to prejudicial discussion of pending court cases.[164] Equally, the meeting convened by the Home Office in January 1996 with Internet service providers and law enforcement officials focused entirely on the regulation of indecent materials on the Internet, though it is notable that the stated preferred official approach remains 'to encourage the industry to develop a system of self-regulation ... rather than considering statutory options.'[165]

Self-regulation in this field has a number of advantages. Rules devised by the

---

158 DH-MM (95)4. See Porter, 'The New European Order for Public Service Broadcasting' (1995) *Yearbook of Media and Entertainment Law* 81.
159 See http://www.isoc.org/.
160 See http://www.w3.org/pub/www/pics/.
161 The technology of the 'v-chip' can also be applied to television and is currently under consideration by the Department of National Heritage (*The Times*, 19 March 1996) following its enforcement in the USA (see Telecommunications Act 1996 (S 652) ss 551, 552).
162 See, for example, the Acceptable Use Policy of Demon Internet Ltd (available from http://http.demon.net/external/Usenet-AUP.html).
163 See JANET, *Acceptable Use Policy* (Version 4.0, HEFCE, 1995).
164 For example, JANET, *ibid* para 9.
165 See http://www.gold.net/users/cdwf.

The Modern Law Review   [Vol. 59

media are more likely to be internalised and accepted. In addition, it may avoid heavy-handed legal intervention which carries with it the spectre of government censorship. A further advantage with this approach is that the issue of respect for the subject of news is here being dealt with at an international level. In this way, there is the genesis of self-regulation at a European level at the very time when the sullied record of self-regulation of the press in the United Kingdom seems to be improving.[166] To recap, the Press Complaints Commission, which was established in 1991 in the wake of the first Calcutt Report,[167] was widely criticised for a number of years as ineffective and even 'a confidence trick.'[168] The second Calcutt Report, which reviewed its work in 1993, considered it to be a failure and asked for a statutory replacement.[169] However, the impact of a new Chairman (Lord Wakeham), new mechanisms (such as the Privacy Commissioner and a hotline to editors) and the difficulties of devising a workable statutory alternative have convinced the Government recently[170] to abandon earlier inclinations[171] towards statutory regulation of the press.

So, the day of self-regulation may have dawned at a national level and perhaps it is self-regulation mechanisms at a trans-European level which are now apt. Such mechanisms might include the accreditation of court reporters on a transnational basis and this may also be linked to training (such as in knowledge of codes of ethics). Even the notion of a European media ombudsman was floated in Assembly Recommendation 1215 of 1993.[172] This is not to say that we can expect standards of professional ethics in journalism wholly to replace legal enforcement.[173] Nor should ethics be used as synonym for censorship. Rather, one should see ethical standards as a way of taking informed and principled decisions rather than imposing new restraints.

Conclusion

The rate of growth of the new media outlets is phenomenal. For example, CNN's first broadcast was in 1980 to 1.7 million households in the United States of America. The audience is now reckoned to be 62 million US households, plus 150 million households elsewhere in the world.[174] Within the United Kingdom alone, BSkyB now draws 5.2 million subscribers.[175] The numbers are just as great in regard to the Internet. One World Wide Web search engine claims to scrutinise almost 19 million potential information sources,[176] and the total of users who are

---

166   Another encouraging precedent is the Independent Committee for the Supervision of Standards of Telephone Information Services (ICSTIS) in connection with premium rate telephone services. See ICSTIS, Code of Practice (London: 7th ed, 1995), Activity Report 1994 (London: 1995).
167   (1990) Cm 1102.
168   Robertson, *Freedom, the Individual and the Law* (London: Pelican, 7th ed, 1993) p 111.
169   (1993) Cm 2135.
170   Government Response to the House of Commons National Heritage Select Committee, *Privacy and Media Intrusion* (1995) Cm 2918.
171   Lord Chancellor's Department, *Infringement of Privacy* (London: HMSO, 1993).
172   See Doc 6854 from the Committee on Culture and Education.
173   Feldman, *Civil Liberties and Human Rights in England and Wales* (Oxford: Clarendon Press, 1994) p 781.
174   See http://www.cnn.com/.
175   *The Times*, 7 February 1996.
176   See http://www.lycos.com/sow/TrueCounting.html. This total is given for available Uniform Resource Locators; there are an additional 13 million distinctly searchable documents and binary objects.

not also publishers in this way is many times greater. Faced with the vast potential for comment on court cases which these new media outlets now provide, it has been argued that the old mechanisms of legal pre-censorship and media cultures of restraint have grown increasingly weak. The main response must be to welcome the fuller and freer atmosphere in which the administration of justice can now be considered. However, subsidiary attention must be given to protecting the venerable value of the fairness of trials against thoughtless or malicious prejudicial comment. In response, any new web of media regulation should encourage pre- and post-broadcast reflection, and should operate at local, national and transnational levels of governance.

Name Index